THE WOMAN'S DAY
COOKBOOK

VOSNE-ROMANÉE
APPELLATION CONTROLÉE

Sélectionné par le
COMITÉ INTER PROFESSIONNEL DE LA COTE D'OR ET DE L'YONNE POUR
LES VINS D'APPELLATION D'ORIGINE CONTROLÉE DE BOURGOGNE

THE WOMAN'S DAY
COOKBOOK

Great Recipes, Bright Ideas, & Healthy Choices for Today's Cook

Kathy Farrell-Kingsley
and the Editors of Woman's Day

A ROUND STONE PRESS BOOK

VIKING

VIKING
Published by the Penguin Group
Penguin Books USA Inc., 375 Hudson St., New York, New York 10014, U.S.A.
Penguin Books Ltd, 27 Wrights Lane, London W8 5TZ, England
Penguin Books Australia Ltd, Ringwood, Victoria, Australia
Penguin Books Canada Ltd, 10 Alcorn Avenue, Toronto, Ontario, Canada M4V 3B2
Penguin Books (N.Z.) Ltd, 182-190 Wairau Road, Auckland 10, New Zealand

Penguin Books Ltd, Registered Offices: Harmondsworth, Middlesex, England

First published in 1995 by Viking Penguin, a division of Penguin Books USA Inc.

10 9 8 7 6 5 4 3 2

Woman's Day ® is a registered trademark of Hachette Filipacchi Magazines, Inc.

WOMAN'S DAY STAFF:
Editor-in-Chief: Jane Chesnutt
Art Director: Brad Pallas
Managing Editor: Jon Rizzi
Senior Editor, Service: Christopher Canatsey
Food Editor: Elizabeth Alston
Deputy Food Editor: Holly J. Sheppard
Associate Food Editor: Ellen R. Greene
Associate Editors: Nancy L. Dell'Aria, Terry Grieco-Kenny
Test Kitchen Assistant: Dionisia Colon

ROUND STONE PRESS STAFF:
Directors: Marsha Melnick, Susan E. Meyer, Paul Fargis
Developmental Editor: Nick Viorst
Design: Wendy Palitz
Production Design: Smythtype
Copyeditor: Dolores Simon
Nutritional Analysis: Hill Nutrition Associates, Inc.

This book would not have been possible without the culinary and editorial contributions
of Sarah L. Bush.

Special thanks to Louise Burbidge, Hope Farrell, Foodsearch Plus, Mary Goodbody,
Tamara Holt, Helen Jones, Susan Nierendorf, and Roberta Rall.

Photograph and recipe credits will be found on page 720 and constitute an extension
of this copyright page.

LIBRARY OF CONGRESS CATALOGING IN PUBLICATION DATA
Farrell-Kingsley, Kathy.
The Woman's Day cookbook : great recipes, bright ideas, and healthy choices for today's cook /
Kathy Farrell-Kingsley and the editors of Woman's Day.
p. cm.
Includes index.
ISBN 0-670-85876-5
1. Cookery. I. Woman's Day (New York, N.Y.) II. Title.
TX714.F373   1995
641.5—DC20   95-18922

This book is printed on acid-free paper. ∞

Printed in the United States of America
Set in Bembo

CONTENTS

A WORD FROM WOMAN'S DAY

WHEN WE AT WOMAN'S DAY SET OUT TO CREATE a cookbook, we made ourselves a promise: This would not be just another big cookbook with the same old recipes folded into the usual soup-to-nuts chapters. Because that approach simply wouldn't have reflected what American women need in a cookbook. Nor would it have done justice to the way WOMAN'S DAY develops the recipes and food stories that have made our food coverage the most-used and best-loved part of our magazine. We wanted a cookbook for how America cooks today.

In many ways, I think I'm a case in point. On weekends I absolutely love to cook. My favorite way to spend a Saturday evening is to make a special meal for me and my husband, often with a new recipe.

During the week, however, cooking is a chore. I want us to eat well and healthfully (a concern I share with millions), but who has the time? I usually get home late; I seldom have time to shop; and I certainly don't want to to spend the evening in the kitchen.

An encyclopedia of new recipes is not what I need in a cookbook, and I don't think our readers do either. What we do need is strategies, and WOMAN'S DAY, I'm proud to say, understands that. For years the magazine has developed innovative, workable ways to get food on the table. We pioneered an idea that we call Investment Cooking, in which a single afternoon of cooking pays off in fifty or so freezable portions of four or five different main dishes. Our Cook Once–Eat Twice stories draw consistent raves, and our One Pot dinners are simplicity itself.

These strategies are part of what makes this book different, but we haven't forgotten the other hallmarks of WOMAN'S DAY. For years we've been known for our marvelous desserts, and there are plenty of recipes here, such as the famous Best-Ever Devil's Food Cake that our readers so adore. And then, of course, there are our Cook's Tips, which I can confidently say WOMAN'S DAY does better than anyone else.

When I became Editor-in-Chief of WOMAN'S DAY, the wife of my husband's former boss sent me a dogeared, slightly tattered recipe that the magazine had published in the fifties. She wrote to say that she had always treasured that recipe, because during the years when she was raising their four children and going to music school, it had been her salvation—a simple dish that her family never got tired of eating.

I can't promise you'll feel the same about every recipe in this book, but I do know that many of them will become part of the fabric of American lives. Long after this book is out of print, when today's children are grown and even old, some of these foods will live on in childhood memories. Cooking is still about love, after all, and that, more than anything, is behind the WOMAN'S DAY philosophy.

Jane Chesnutt, Editor-in-Chief

IN THE WOMAN'S DAY KITCHENS

AT WOMAN'S DAY, WE KNOW HOW IMPORTANT food is to family life. It goes without saying that food must taste good, but it must be good for you too. And, of course, you must be able to prepare the food within the time you have available.

A priority when we were planning this book was to make sure you could quickly find recipes that suited your practical needs. Let's say, for example, you're looking for two chicken dishes, one that can be made a day or two ahead, another that can be quickly made as an entire meal in itself. Turn to pages 46 and 47, the beginning of our chapter about chicken and turkey. There—spread out in an easy-to-read design—you'll find all the chicken recipes listed according to their special attributes. Look under Make Ahead to find the first recipe you need, then check the One Pot grouping for the second.

If you prefer to skip these listings and go straight to the recipes, you'll find a color banner across the top of each one featuring the same information.

Here's what each category means:

EASY: Recipes that call for a limited number of ingredients and very little effort. These are perfect for super-busy nights, as well as for the beginning cook.

30 MINUTES: From chopping through cooking, that's all the time it will take to get these dishes on the table. Just the thing for busy week nights, when there may be homework to help with, or when you need some time to yourself.

60 MINUTES: Same as above, but these recipes are for when you have a bit more time. (Our countdowns begin with all the ingredients placed on the counter—but with no peeling or chopping done—since it may take one person a few seconds to find carrots or broth while another may have to search for ten minutes!)

MICROWAVE: Here you'll find recipes that can be prepared in the microwave from start to finish, including one-pot meals, main courses, desserts, and soups. Many recipes feature both conventional and microwave cooking instructions, because the microwave can save time and reduce cleanup. (Note: All microwave recipes were tested in a 650-watt microwave. If yours has much higher or lower wattage, you might need to adjust cooking times.)

LOW FAT: To qualify, a recipe has to provide no more than the following grams of fat per serving: one-pot meal, 13 grams; main dish entree, 10 grams; side dish, 3 grams; bread, 2 grams. In the Desserts chapter, recipes qualify as "Light" if they provide no more than 7 grams of fat per serving.

MAKE AHEAD: This means that some of the preparation can be done in advance, or even that the entire recipe can be made ahead, requiring only heating before serving. Directions are given.

ONE POT: This category highlights main-course recipes in which the protein, vegetable, and "starch"—a not-so-appealing word for some very appealing foods, including pasta, rice and potatoes—are simmered together in one pot. Cooking is streamlined and cleanup is a breeze.

CLASSIC: These are traditional recipes that have stood the test of time. Some are quick to prepare, while others are better saved for more relaxed weekend cooking.

Most recipes, of course, fall into more than one category—an easy recipe may also be low fat, for example—and will be listed in all the relevant categories.

COMPANY AND HOLIDAY COOKING

Like most of us, you probably enjoy having friends over for brunch or dinner, or celebrating a holiday in festive style. Our Entertaining menus and recipes are designed to give you confidence in planning formal or informal meals in any season. Our Celebrations menus and recipes reflect time-honored traditions but with a big WOMAN'S DAY plus: Each menu includes a Planning Timetable so that you can be sure everything gets to the table on time and you, too, can sit down and share the festivities.

MEAL PLANNING

Readers say that the most stressful time of day is when thoughts turn to "What shall we have for dinner?" At WOMAN'S DAY we have developed some special ways to help alleviate that late-afternoon stress.

Cook Once—Eat Twice means more than cooking an extra-large pot of stew (although that is a fine time-saving strategy, too). It may mean oven-braising two lamb shanks at one time, combining the first with white beans for a hearty stew, then using the other later in the week for a lamb and pasta pie; or it could mean cooking up a pot of fresh vegetables to serve over couscous Monday night, then creating a Mediterranean sandwich for Wednesday's lunch with the chilled vegetable mixture. Our Cook Once—Eat Twice chapter offers a full range of menus for extending today's cooking into tomorrow's meal.

Another (and very popular) time-saving strategy is called Investment Cooking, and it's a WOMAN'S DAY invention. What you invest is time—perhaps 4 hours—and the dividend is what you wind up with: four, five, or even six different meals based on the same or related ingredients. Along the way you save time (you'll have several meals in the refrigerator or freezer); cleanup (you wash the chopping board once, not five times); and money (investment cooking makes it possible to take advantage of food on sale and sold in bulk). This feature is even more valuable because each collection of recipes comes with its own shopping and equipment lists and each is clearly written in an easy, step-by-step sequence.

Our Year of Menus includes fifty-two weeks of simple meals with quick-and-easy recipe ideas.

You may not want to follow our menus to the letter, but we know they'll inspire you and at least help you plan your shopping and cooking.

NUTRITIONAL INFORMATION

For each one of the many hundreds of recipes and variations in this book, we feature a complete nutritional profile, including data on calories, protein, carbohydrates, fat, cholesterol, and sodium content. Please remember that all nutritional data is approximate and based on averages. One piece of beef is not exactly the same as another, nor is one carrot just like another. But the nutritional information can help you appreciate the relative merits of each recipe so that you can decide whether it's appropriate for you and your family. (If you're watching fat intake, remember that it's the total number of grams of fat that you eat over the course of a day or a week that counts, not the percentage of fat in any one dish.)

BEFORE TRYING A NEW RECIPE

• Read the recipe all the way through to make sure you have all the necessary ingredients, tools, and equipment. Make sure you understand the instructions and are comfortable with any special techniques or skills. As you read, make a note of any ingredients you'll need to get. Double-check pantry staples, in case your supplies are low.
• Anticipate the time. Although preparation and

cooking times are included with each recipe, not everyone slices, chops, measures, or stirs at the same pace. And it always takes longer to make a recipe the first time.

• Organize the ingredients before you begin to cook, peel, and chop. Line up the ingredients in the order you'll use them. (Place pieces of waxed paper, small bowls, or measuring cups on a tray or countertop.) Experienced cooks know that organizing in advance is the best way to avoid making mistakes.

• Clean up as you go. Before you begin, clear the counter space. Soak used utensils in a sink of soapy water as you proceed, and use odd moments to wash them or to put clean things away. This is the most efficient way to work, and it's nice to have the kitchen in relatively good shape when you finish cooking.

• Remember that we are here for you. We never leave your side in the kitchen. When you have a question about cooking and don't find the answer in the recipe or in the recipe notes, refer to the index or appendix. You're sure to find the information you need. After all, we've planned the WOMAN'S DAY cookbook with you in mind.

Elizabeth Alston, Food Editor

PASTA

> *"No man is lonely while eating spaghetti."*
> ROBERT MORLEY

The American passion for pasta is sure to be a lasting one. Infinitely varied, economical, nutritious, and quick and simple to prepare—or more extravagant if desired—it could very well be the perfect food.

In this chapter we include recipes for such standbys as vegetable lasagna and tuna-noodle casserole. We invite you to try other pasta dishes as well. Serve chicken Bolognese sauce, ladle-it-on lasagna, and Mexican manicotti for a new twist on an old theme, or Asian noodles for something different. Many of the recipes in this chapter are low in fat, some that will probably surprise you, like macaroni and cheese or stuffed shells Florentine. When it comes to pasta the possibilities are endless.

Macaroni & Cheese, 23
Microwave Stuffed Shells, 37
Microwave Tomato, Shrimp, &
    Broccoli Sauce, 21
Microwave Tomato-Meat Sauce, 16
Pasta with Eggplant Sauce, 25
Pasta with Fresh Tomato-
    Mozzarella Sauce, 19
Pasta with Tomato, Shrimp,
    & Broccoli Sauce, 21
Penne with Escarole, 26
Rigatoni with Zucchini &
    Prosciutto, 28
Sausage-Kale Sauce, 14
Shrimp & Goat Cheese Pasta, 24
Spinach Pesto with Ham &
    Tomatoes, 20
Tomato-Meat Sauce, 16
Tortellini with Vegetables, 32
Tuna Niçoise Sauce, 18

60 MINUTES

Asian Noodles, 43
Capellini with Scallops, 27
Pasta al Forno, 41
Pasta Skillet Pie, 39
Tuna-Noodle Casserole, 40
Vegetable Lasagne, 31
Ziti with Meatballs, 29

MICROWAVE

Stuffed Shells, 37
Tomato, Shrimp, & Broccoli
    Sauce, 21
Tomato-Meat Sauce, 16
Vegetable Lasagne, 31

LOW FAT

Asian Noodles, 43
Broccoli & Chick-Pea Sauce, 17
Chicken Bolognese Sauce, 15
Creamy Pasta Primavera, 25
Creamy Sausage Sauce, 14

Egg Noodles with Vegetables, 42
Ladle-It-On Lasagne, 22
Macaroni & Cheese, 23
Penne with Escarole, 26
Sausage-Kale Sauce, 14
Stuffed Shells Florentine, 37
Tuna-Noodle Casserole, 40

MAKE AHEAD

Chicken Bolognese Sauce, 15
Chili-Meat Sauce, 22
Clam & Spinach Sauce, 18
Creamy Sausage Sauce, 14
Garden Orzo, 44
Ladle-It-On Lasagne, 22
Mexican Manicotti, 38
Microwave Tomato-Meat Sauce, 16
Spinach Pesto with Ham &
    Tomatoes, 20
Stuffed Shells Florentine, 37
Tomato-Meat Sauce, 16
Ziti with Meatballs, 29

ONE POT

Creamy Pasta Primavera, 25
Egg Noodles with Vegetables, 42
Fettuccine & Vegetables Alfredo, 30
Shrimp & Goat Cheese Pasta, 24
Tuna-Noodle Casserole, 40

CLASSIC

Creamy Pasta Primavera, 25
Stuffed Shells Florentine, 37
Tomato-Meat Sauce, 16
Tuna-Noodle Casserole, 40

PASTA TOPPERS

Broccoli & Chick-Pea Sauce, 17
Chicken Bolognese Sauce, 15
Chili-Meat Sauce, 22
Clam & Spinach Sauce, 18

Creamy Sausage Sauce, 14
Microwave Tomato, Shrimp, &
    Broccoli Sauce, 21
Microwave Tomato-Meat Sauce, 16
Pasta with Eggplant Sauce, 25
Pasta with Fresh Tomato-
    Mozzarella Sauce, 19
Sausage-Kale Sauce, 14
Tomato-Meat Sauce, 16
Tuna Niçoise Sauce, 18

VEGETARIAN
MAIN DISHES

Creamy Pasta Primavera, 25
Fettuccine & Vegetables Alfredo, 30
Pasta with Fresh Tomato-
    Mozzarella Sauce, 19
Pasta with Tomato, Shrimp, &
    Broccoli Sauce, 21
Penne with Escarole, 26
Stuffed Shells Florentine, 37
Vegetable Lasagne, 31

PASTA & SEAFOOD

Capellini with Scallops, 27
Clam & Spinach Sauce, 18
Pasta with Tomato, Shrimp, &
    Broccoli Sauce, 21
Shrimp & Goat Cheese Pasta, 24
Tuna Niçoise Sauce, 18

KID'S CHOICE

Chili-Meat Sauce, 22
Egg Noodles with Vegetables, 42
Ladle-It-On Lasagne, 22
Macaroni & Cheese, 23
Microwave Tomato-Meat
    Sauce, 16
Tomato-Meat Sauce, 16
Tortellini with Vegetables, 32
Ziti with Meatballs, 29

CREAMY SAUSAGE SAUCE

Serves 4

Total time: 15 minutes

A slimmed-down version of a well-loved Italian sauce, this is best served over chunky pasta shapes. If you can't find rigatoni, a good substitute could be penne, rotelle (wagon wheels), or fusilli (spirals).

8 ounces sweet Italian-style turkey
    sausages, removed from casings and crumbled
6 ounces small white mushrooms, cleaned and quartered (2 cups)
1 teaspoon Worcestershire sauce
⅔ cup evaporated (not sweetened condensed) skim milk
1 tablespoon dried basil or oregano leaves, crumbled
¼ teaspoon ground black pepper
1 package (10 ounces) frozen green peas, thawed (1⅔ cups)
12 ounces rigatoni pasta (4 generous cups), cooked and drained
¼ cup grated Parmesan cheese

1. In a medium-size skillet, brown the sausage meat over medium heat. Remove with a slotted spoon to a bowl.

2. Add the mushrooms to the drippings in the skillet. Cook, stirring often, for 3 to 4 minutes, or until lightly browned. Sprinkle with the Worcestershire sauce, then stir in the evaporated milk. Bring the mixture to a simmer. Stir in the basil and pepper. Simmer for 3 to 4 minutes, or until slightly thickened. Stir in the peas and sausage. Simmer for 1 to 2 minutes, or until heated through.

3. Toss the sauce with the hot pasta. Sprinkle with Parmesan cheese and serve right away.

Per serving: 536 cal, 30 g pro, 83 g car, 9 g fat, 36 mg chol, 615 mg sod

MAKE AHEAD

Prepare the sauce as directed and let cool. Refrigerate in an airtight container up to 3 days. Reheat on the range top or in the microwave.

COOK'S TIP

Unopened evaporated milk can be stored at room temperature up to 6 months. Once opened, pour the unused portion into an airtight container and refrigerate up to 5 days.

SAUSAGE-KALE SAUCE

Serves 5

Total time: 15 minutes

This sauce's rich taste belies its healthful profile. Kale contributes an assertive flavor and lots of vitamins A and C. Served over rigatoni or penne, it makes a fast and hearty meal.

12 ounces fresh kale

8 ounces sweet Italian-style turkey sausages, removed from casings
and crumbled

1 tablespoon all-purpose flour

1 cup chicken broth

1 can (about 14½ ounces) diced tomatoes in juice

1 can (about 16 ounces) red kidney beans, drained

½ teaspoon crushed hot red pepper flakes

1 pound rotini (twists) pasta, cooked and drained

1. Wash the kale and tear the leaves off the stems and into bite-size pieces (discard the stems).

2. In a large nonstick skillet, cook the sausage over medium heat for about 3 minutes, stirring often, until browned. Remove the sausage with a slotted spoon to a plate.

3. Put the kale in the skillet and toss for about 45 seconds, or until the kale turns bright green. In a small bowl, stir the flour into the broth. Add to the kale and bring to a boil.

4. Add the tomatoes, beans, and crushed red pepper.

5. Simmer for about 6 minutes for the flavors to blend. Stir in the sausage and simmer for 1 minute more or until heated through. Toss the sauce with hot pasta and serve right away.

Per serving: 526 cal, 27 g pro, 88 g car, 8 g fat, 24 mg chol, 768 mg sod

---

EASY • 30 MINUTES • LOW FAT • MAKE AHEAD

CHICKEN BOLOGNESE SAUCE
Serves 5
Total time: 15 minutes

A rich red sauce with the color contrast of yellow squash and the health benefits of ground chicken (rather than fattier ground beef and pork). Also good with ziti, elbows, or shells.

4 small yellow summer squash (about 1 pound), rinsed

12 ounces ground chicken, turkey, or extra-lean ground beef

1 jar (about 26 ounces) low-fat spaghetti sauce

1½ teaspoons dried rosemary leaves, crumbled

4 medium-size scallions

1 pound rigatoni pasta, cooked and drained

For garnish: grated Parmesan cheese (optional)

MAKE AHEAD

Prepare the sauce as directed and let cool. Refrigerate in an airtight container up to 3 days, or freeze up to 2 months. Thaw in the refrigerator.

1. Quarter the squash lengthwise, then cut crosswise into ¼-inch-thick slices.

2. Crumble the ground chicken into a large nonstick skillet. Cook over medium-high heat for 3 minutes, stirring constantly, until no pink remains.

3. Add the spaghetti sauce and rosemary. Bring to a boil, then add the squash. Reduce the heat to medium, cover, and simmer for 6 minutes, stirring twice, until the squash is tender. Remove the skillet from the heat.

4. Slice the scallions thin. Stir into the sauce. Pour the sauce over the hot pasta. Sprinkle with grated Parmesan cheese and serve right away.

Per serving with chicken: 522 cal, 27 g pro, 84 g car, 8 g fat, 56 mg chol, 522 mg sod. With turkey: 514 cal, 27 g pro, 84 g car, 7 g fat, 50 mg chol, 530 mg sod. With beef: 534 cal, 29 g pro, 84 g car, 9 g fat, 42 mg chol, 515 mg sod

---

EASY • 30 MINUTES • MAKE AHEAD • CLASSIC

TOMATO–MEAT SAUCE

Serves 4

Total time: 15 minutes

This full-bodied meat sauce is so quick and easy to prepare that you may never reach for a jar of prepared sauce again. For a leaner version of this delicious sauce, substitute 12 ounces of ground turkey for the beef.

2 tablespoons olive oil
1 medium-size onion, chopped
12 ounces lean ground beef
1 teaspoon salt
1 teaspoon minced fresh garlic
1 teaspoon dried basil leaves, crumbled
¼ teaspoon granulated sugar
1 can (about 35 ounces) whole tomatoes, undrained
3 tablespoons tomato paste
1 pound spaghetti, cooked and drained

1. In a large skillet, heat the oil over medium heat. Add the onion and cook, stirring often, for 3 to 4 minutes, or until softened.

2. Crumble the ground beef into the skillet. Add the salt, garlic, basil, and sugar. Cook for 3 to 4 minutes, breaking up the meat with a fork, until the meat is no longer pink.

3. Cut up the tomatoes in the can with kitchen scissors or a long sharp knife. Stir the tomatoes with their juices and the tomato paste into the meat mixture. Simmer uncovered for 3 to 4 minutes.

MAKE AHEAD

Prepare the sauce as directed and let cool. Refrigerate in an airtight container up to 3 days, or freeze up to 2 months. Thaw in the refrigerator and slowly reheat on the range top. The sauce recipe can be doubled or tripled.

VARIATION

MICROWAVE TOMATO-MEAT SAUCE

• Put the onion and oil in a 3-quart microwave-safe bowl. Cover with a lid or vented plastic wrap. Microwave on High for 2 to 3 minutes, stirring once, until the onion is softened.

• Crumble the ground beef into the bowl. Stir in the salt, garlic, basil, and sugar. Cover and microwave on High for 3 to 4 minutes, stirring once to break up meat, until the meat is no longer pink.

• Cut up the tomatoes as directed. Stir tomatoes with their juices and the tomato paste into the meat mixture. Cover and microwave on High for 4 to 5 minutes, stirring once, until the sauce is hot. Proceed as directed.

Per serving: 785 cal, 33 g pro, 102 g car, 27 g fat, 64 mg chol, 1,120 mg sod

• EASY • 30 MINUTES
• MAKE AHEAD

4. Toss about 1 cup of sauce with hot pasta to coat lightly and prevent the pasta from sticking. Serve the remaining sauce at the table.

Per serving: 785 cal, 33 g pro, 102 g car, 27 g fat, 64 mg chol, 1,120 mg sod

EASY • 30 MINUTES • LOW FAT

BROCCOLI & CHICK–PEA SAUCE

Serves 5

Total time: 15 minutes

A wonderful, brothy sauce full of good-for-you broccoli and chick-peas. It's also great over medium-size shells or wagon-wheel pasta.

1 bunch fresh broccoli (about 1¼ pounds)
1 medium-size red onion
3 large cloves garlic
1 tablespoon olive oil
1 can (about 13¾ ounces) chicken broth (1¾ cups)
1 tablespoon all-purpose flour
1 can (about 16 ounces) chick-peas, drained
⅓ cup grated Romano or Parmesan cheese
1 pound farfalle (bow-tie) pasta, cooked and drained

1. Cut the broccoli into small florets (save the stems for another use).

2. Peel the onion, halve it lengthwise, and cut lengthwise into thin slices. Peel the garlic and slice lengthwise into slivers.

3. In a large skillet, heat the oil over medium-high heat. Add the onion and garlic. Cook, stirring often, for about 3 minutes, or until the onion is softened.

4. Whisk the flour into the skillet until blended. Gradually stir in the broth. Add the broccoli, chick-peas, and cheese. Bring to a boil. Reduce the heat to medium-low. Cover and simmer for 5 minutes, or until the broccoli is crisp-tender and the liquid slightly thickened. Toss with the hot pasta and serve right away.

Per serving: 494 cal, 20 g pro, 86 g car, 8 g fat, 5 mg chol, 495 mg sod

EASY • 30 MINUTES • MAKE AHEAD

CLAM & SPINACH SAUCE

Serves 4

Total time: 15 minutes

This satisfying pasta dish is simplicity itself. Keep the ingredients on hand so it can be assembled quickly during the week or for unexpected guests.

1 package (10 ounces) frozen leaf spinach
3 tablespoons olive oil
2 teaspoons minced fresh garlic
1 teaspoon dried oregano leaves
¼ teaspoon crushed hot red pepper flakes (optional)
2 cans (10 ounces each) whole baby clams, undrained
12 ounces capelli (angel hair) pasta or extra thin spaghetti, cooked, drained, and tossed with 1 tablespoon olive oil

1. Cut the block of spinach in half with a sharp knife and put into a colander. Place under hot running water until thawed. Squeeze dry.

2. In a large skillet, heat the oil over medium-high heat. Add the garlic and cook for 30 seconds, or until fragrant. Stir in the oregano and red pepper flakes. Drain the liquid from the clams into the skillet and stir in the spinach.

3. Bring to a boil. Reduce the heat to low. Cover and simmer for 3 minutes. Add the clams and stir for 1 minute, or just until heated through.

4. Toss with the hot pasta and serve right away.

Per serving: 566 cal, 32 g pro, 71 g car, 17 g fat, 49 mg chol, 141 mg sod

 AKE AHEAD

Prepare the sauce as directed and let cool. Refrigerate in an airtight container up to 3 days. Slowly reheat on the range top.

EASY • 30 MINUTES

TUNA NIÇOISE SAUCE

Serves 5

Total time: 15 minutes

This pasta dish has the flavors of the famous tuna, green bean, potato, and black-olive salad from Nice, in the south of France.

1 large russet potato (10 ounces), scrubbed and cut into ½-inch cubes
8 ounces fresh green beans, rinsed and snapped into 2-inch lengths
1⅓ cups chicken broth
½ teaspoon dried thyme leaves, crumbled

1 can (12 ounces) solid white tuna in oil
8 sprigs Italian (flat-leaf) parsley, chopped coarse
1 can (5¾ ounces) large ripe pitted black olives, drained
¼ cup olive oil
12 ounces rotelle (wagon-wheel) pasta (4 generous cups),
  cooked and drained
1 medium-size lemon
Ground black pepper to taste

1. In a large skillet, bring the potato, green beans, chicken broth, and thyme to a boil. Reduce the heat to medium-low. Cover and simmer for 8 minutes, or until the vegetables are tender.

2. Meanwhile, drain the tuna and flake into a medium-size bowl. Stir in the parsley and olives. Add the vegetable mixture and oil, tossing to mix.

3. Toss the hot pasta with tuna mixture. Cut the lemon in half. Squeeze the juice over the pasta (watch out for pits) and toss again. Season with pepper to taste. Serve right away.

Per serving: 580 cal, 29 g pro, 69 g car, 21 g fat, 20 mg chol, 822 mg sod

EASY • 30 MINUTES

PASTA WITH FRESH TOMATO–MOZZARELLA SAUCE

Serves 5
Total time: 30 minutes

For a creamier sauce, substitute feta cheese for the mozzarella. This recipe calls for pasta shells, but the sauce also goes well with pasta twists or elbows.

1 pound medium-size pasta shells
3 large tomatoes (1½ pounds), cut into ½-inch chunks
1 cup frozen green peas
4 ounces mozzarella cheese, cut into ½-inch chunks
¼ cup olive oil
1¾ teaspoons Italian seasoning mix
½ teaspoon salt
¼ teaspoon crushed hot red pepper flakes
⅓ cup grated Parmesan or Romano cheese

1. Bring a large pot of lightly salted water to a boil. Add the pasta and cook according to the package directions. ▶

2. Meanwhile, put the tomatoes into a medium-size bowl.

3. Put the peas into a small strainer. Thaw under cold running water; drain well. Add to the bowl. Add the mozzarella, oil, Italian seasoning, salt, and red pepper flakes. Stir to blend.

4. Remove the pasta pot from the heat. Ladle out and reserve ¼ cup of cooking liquid from the pot, then drain the pasta in a colander. Add the reserved ¼ cup cooking water from the pasta to the tomato mixture.

5. Toss the sauce with the hot pasta, sprinkle with Parmesan cheese, and serve right away.

Per serving: 573 cal, 21 g pro, 79 g car, 19 g fat, 22 mg chol, 458 mg sod with Parmesan, 424 mg sod with Romano

---

EASY • 30 MINUTES • MAKE AHEAD

SPINACH PESTO WITH HAM & TOMATOES

Serves 5

Total time: 15 minutes

If you've ever made pesto with fresh basil, you already know how easy it is. For a new take, try this one that uses spinach instead.

1 bag (10 ounces) fresh spinach
1 pint (12 ounces) cherry tomatoes
8 ounces sliced boiled ham
3 large cloves garlic
¼ cup olive oil
¼ cup grated Romano or Parmesan cheese
3 tablespoons slivered almonds
½ teaspoon salt
1 pound linguine, cooked and drained
For garnish: Romano or Parmesan cheese, grated or shaved with a
    vegetable peeler (optional)

1. Soak the spinach (leaves and stems) in warm water for 10 minutes, changing the water once.

2. Meanwhile, quarter the cherry tomatoes. Stack the ham slices and cut crosswise into thin strips. Separate the strips. Smash the garlic cloves with the flat side of a knife and remove the papery skins.

3. Drain the spinach. In a food processor, put half the spinach, with the oil, cheese, almonds, garlic, and salt. Process until chopped fine. Add the remaining

---

MAKE AHEAD

Prepare the spinach pesto as directed. Refrigerate in an airtight container up to 3 days. Bring to room temperature before using.

spinach and process to a thick purée. (The pesto can also be made in several batches in a blender.)

4. Toss the hot pasta with the spinach pesto. Gently stir in the tomatoes and ham. Garnish with grated or shaved cheese. Serve right away.

Per serving: 575 cal, 26 g pro, 76 g car, 19 g fat, 28 mg chol, 871 mg sod with Romano, 897 mg sod with Parmesan

EASY • 30 MINUTES

PASTA WITH TOMATO, SHRIMP, & BROCCOLI SAUCE

Serves 4

Total time: 30 minutes

Pasta twists, also known as rotini, rotelle, or fusilli, are a good choice for this tasty and colorful sauce. Serve with warm bread and a mixed green salad for a perfect midweek dinner.

1 bunch (about 1¼ pounds) fresh broccoli
1 pound rotini (twists) pasta
2 tablespoons olive oil
1 can (about 28 ounces) crushed tomatoes
1 teaspoon minced fresh garlic
1 teaspoon salt
12 ounces medium-size uncooked shrimp, shelled and deveined
For garnish: Romano or Parmesan cheese, grated and shaved with a
  vegetable peeler (optional)

1. Cut the broccoli into florets. Peel the stems, cut in half lengthwise, then cut crosswise into ½-inch-thick slices.

2. Bring a large pot of lightly salted water to a boil. Add the pasta and cook according to the package directions. About 5 minutes before the pasta is done, add the broccoli. Continue cooking, stirring twice, until pasta and broccoli are firm-tender.

3. Meanwhile, in a large skillet, heat the oil over medium heat. Add the tomatoes, garlic, and salt. Simmer for 1 to 2 minutes. Add the shrimp, cover, and simmer for 2 minutes, stirring once, until the shrimp are pink and opaque at center. Remove the skillet from the heat.

4. Drain the pasta and broccoli and return to the pot. Add the sauce and toss to mix. Garnish with grated or shaved cheese. Serve right away.

Per serving: 619 cal, 33 g pro, 99 g car, 11 g fat, 105 mg chol, 1,395 mg sod

---

VARIATION

MICROWAVE TOMATO, SHRIMP, AND BROCCOLI SAUCE:

• Cook the pasta and broccoli as directed. Put the oil, tomatoes, garlic, and salt into a 3-quart microwave-safe bowl. Stir, then cover with a lid or vented plastic wrap. Microwave on High for 4 to 5 minutes, or until hot.
• Stir in the shrimp. Cover and microwave on High for 3 to 4 minutes, stirring once, until the shrimp are pink and opaque in center. Proceed as directed.

Per serving: 619 cal, 33 g pro, 99 g car, 11 g fat, 105 mg chol, 1,395 mg sod

• EASY • 30 MINUTES

EASY • 30 MINUTES • MAKE AHEAD

CHILI–MEAT SAUCE

Serves 5

Total time: 15 minutes

A quick and easy meat sauce with a Tex-Mex twist. It goes well with long strands of pasta—linguine, spaghetti, vermicelli, or fettuccine.

1 tablespoon olive oil
1 large onion, chopped
12 ounces lean ground beef
1 jar (15 ounces) spaghetti sauce
1 can (15½ ounces) chili-style chunky tomatoes
1 teaspoon ground cumin
1 cup frozen or canned corn kernels
4 medium-size scallions, sliced thin
1 pound linguine, cooked and drained
⅓ cup grated Parmesan cheese

1. In a large skillet, heat the oil over medium-high heat. Add the onion and cook, stirring often, for 4 minutes, until lightly browned.
2. Crumble the beef into the skillet. Cook for 3 minutes, stirring often until no longer pink.
3. Add the spaghetti sauce, tomatoes, cumin, and corn. Reduce the heat to medium. Cover and simmer for 6 minutes, stirring twice, until the onion is tender. Remove the skillet from the heat.
4. Stir the scallions into the sauce.
5. Toss with the hot pasta and Parmesan cheese. Serve right away.
Per serving: 734 cal, 30 g pro, 98 g car, 24 g fat, 55 mg chol, 1,074 mg sod

MAKE AHEAD

Prepare the sauce as directed and let cool. Refrigerate in an air-tight container up to 3 days, or freeze up to 2 months. Thaw in the refrigerator.

EASY • 30 MINUTES • LOW FAT • MAKE AHEAD

LADLE–IT–ON LASAGNE

Serves 5

Total time: 15 minutes

Call it lasagne, in a clever, delicious disguise. It's lower in fat and takes a fraction of the time to prepare, yet it tastes remarkably like the original. As diners stir up their platefuls, the mozzarella melts and gets stretchy. This is also good with extra-wide egg noodles, ziti, or penne.

MAKE AHEAD

The tomato sauce can
be prepared ahead.
Refrigerate in an air-
tight container up to 1
week. Slowly reheat on
the range top.

1 tablespoon olive oil
1 large onion, chopped
1 can (about 28 ounces) crushed tomatoes in thick purée
2 teaspoons minced fresh garlic
1 teaspoon dried basil leaves, crumbled
1 teaspoon dried oregano leaves, crumbled
2 tablespoons grated Romano or Parmesan cheese
12 ounces mafalde (mini-lasagne) pasta, cooked and drained
1¼ cups nonfat ricotta cheese
½ cup shredded nonfat mozzarella cheese

1. In a large skillet, heat the oil over medium-high heat. Add the onion and cook, stirring often, for 3 to 4 minutes, until softened.

2. Add the tomatoes, garlic, basil, and oregano. Bring to a simmer and cook uncovered for 7 to 8 minutes. Remove the skillet from the heat and stir in the Romano cheese.

3. To assemble, spoon the hot pasta onto serving plates. Top each serving with about ¾ cup tomato sauce, ¼ cup ricotta cheese, and 1½ tablespoons mozzarella cheese. Serve right away.

Per serving: 413 cal, 23 g pro, 68 g car, 5 g fat, 4 mg chol, 449 mg sod with Romano, 462 mg sod with Parmesan

COOK'S TIP

For extra-smooth
cheese sauce, add the
shredded cheese in
batches over the lowest
possible heat setting.
Stir to melt each
addition of cheese
before adding more.

EASY • 30 MINUTES • LOW FAT

MACARONI & CHEESE

Serves 4
Preparation time: 3 minutes
Cooking time: 10 minutes

Every cook needs a macaroni and cheese recipe, especially one that delivers a satisfying bite with less fat.

8 ounces elbow macaroni (2 cups)
2 cups skim milk
2 tablespoons cornstarch
1 teaspoon Dijon mustard
½ teaspoon salt
¼ teaspoon ground black pepper
4 ounces reduced-fat Cheddar cheese, shredded (1 cup)

1. Bring a large saucepan of water to a boil. Add the macaroni and ▶

cook according to the package directions. Drain in a colander.

2. Meanwhile, in a medium-size nonstick saucepan, whisk together the milk and cornstarch until blended. Bring to a boil over medium-high heat, stirring often.

3. Stir in the mustard, salt, and pepper. Reduce the heat to low and simmer for 1 minute, or until thickened.

4. Stir in the cheese until melted. Stir in the macaroni and heat through. Serve right away.

Per serving: 350 cal, 20 g pro, 52 g car, 6 g fat, 22 g chol, 592 mg sod

---

EASY • 30 MINUTES • ONE POT

SHRIMP & GOAT CHEESE PASTA

Serves 4

Preparation time: 15 minutes

Cooking time: 15 minutes

Here is a great one-dish meal for entertaining. It can be served either as a main course with tossed greens, French bread, and maybe a chilled white wine, or in smaller portions as a first course followed by broiled meat or poultry. Other cheeses can be used, try feta for a sharper flavor or Saga Blue for a creamer one.

1 pound fettuccine
12 ounces uncooked large shrimp, peeled and deveined
2 garlic cloves, peeled
2 large ripe tomatoes, seeded and chopped (about 1½ cups)
4 ounces Montrachet (mild goat cheese), cut into small pieces
⅓ cup chopped fresh basil
¼ cup olive oil
2 tablespoons heavy cream
⅓ cup freshly grated Parmesan cheese
Freshly ground black pepper to taste
Crushed hot red pepper flakes to taste

1. Bring a large pot of lightly salted water to a boil. Add the pasta and cook according to the package directions. About 3 minutes before the pasta is done, add the shrimp and garlic. Continue cooking, stirring twice, until the pasta is firm-tender and the shrimp are pink and opaque in the center. Drain.

2. Meanwhile, in a large serving bowl, mix the tomatoes, goat cheese, basil, oil, and cream.

3. Remove the garlic from the pasta. Chop the garlic fine and add to the tomato mixture along with the pasta, shrimp, Parmesan, and black pepper. Toss gently to mix. Sprinkle with crushed red pepper flakes and serve right away.

Per serving: 678 cal, 36 g pro, 68 g car, 29 g fat, 217 mg chol, 395 mg sod

EASY • 30 MINUTES • LOW FAT • ONE POT • CLASSIC

CREAMY PASTA PRIMAVERA

Serves 4
Preparation time: 20 minutes
Cooking time: 10 minutes

Try this dish with a crisp tossed green salad and crunchy breadsticks.

12 ounces tricolor fusilli (spiral) pasta (4 generous cups)
4 medium-size carrots, cut in matchstick-size pieces (about 3 cups)
12 ounces sugar snap peas (3 cups)
1 tub (6.5 ounces) light herb and spice spreadable cheese
½ cup grated Parmesan cheese

1. Bring a large pot of lightly salted water to a boil. Add the pasta and cook according to the package directions. About 4 minutes before the pasta is done, add the carrots. Three minutes later add the sugar snap peas. Continue cooking, stirring twice, until the pasta is firm-tender.

2. Remove the pot from the heat. Reserve ½ cup of cooking water. Drain the cooked pasta and vegetables in a colander.

3. Return the reserved ½ cup water to the pot. Stir in the herb and spice cheese and Parmesan cheese until blended. Add the hot pasta and vegetables and toss to coat. Serve right away.

Per serving: 537 cal, 24 g pro, 85 g car, 12 g fat, 32 mg chol, 552 mg sod

EASY • 30 MINUTES

PASTA WITH EGGPLANT SAUCE

Serves 4
Preparation time: 10 minutes
Cooking time: 15 minutes

The eggplant is cooked, but the tomatoes aren't, in this delicious pasta sauce, which is good served hot, at room temperature, or chilled. ▶

12 ounces penne pasta (4 generous cups)

4 tablespoons olive oil

3 medium-size tomatoes, cut into 1½-inch pieces

12 pitted black olives (preferably oil-cured), halved

½ cup fresh basil leaves, stacked and cut into thin strips

1 teaspoon red wine vinegar

½ teaspoon minced fresh garlic

¼ teaspoon crushed hot red pepper flakes, or to taste (optional)

1 medium-size eggplant (about 1 pound), halved lengthwise
  and cut crosswise into ¼-inch-wide slices

½ teaspoon salt

¼ cup grated Parmesan cheese

1. Bring a large pot of lightly salted water to a boil. Add the pasta and cook according to the package directions. Drain and toss with 2 tablespoons of oil.

2. Meanwhile, in a large bowl, combine the tomatoes, olives, basil, vinegar, garlic, and red pepper. Toss gently to mix.

3. In a large skillet, heat the remaining oil over medium-high heat. Add the eggplant and salt and cook, stirring often, for 8 to 10 minutes, or until soft.

4. Add the eggplant and hot pasta to the tomato mixture. Toss gently to mix. Sprinkle with the Parmesan cheese. Serve right away.

Per serving: 537 cal, 15 g pro, 77 g car, 19 g fat, 4 mg chol, 914 mg sod

> **SERVE IT HOT**
>
> Pasta cools quickly. Heating the serving bowl or plates will help keep it warm. To warm a serving bowl, pour some hot water into it and let stand until ready to use. Then pour out the water and dry the bowl. Warm plates by putting them into a 250°F oven for 10 to 15 minutes just before serving.

EASY • 30 MINUTES • LOW FAT

PENNE WITH ESCAROLE

Serves 6

Preparation time: 10 minutes

Cooking time: 15 minutes

In this robust dish, dark green escarole provides a slightly bitter counterpoint and colorful contrast to the pasta. You may also use broccoli rabe or spinach.

1¼ pounds escarole

1 pound penne pasta

½ cup olive oil

1 cup packaged plain bread crumbs

1 tablespoon minced garlic

1 can (2 ounces) flat anchovy fillets, drained and cut crosswise into thirds

1 teaspoon salt

½ teaspoon crushed hot red pepper flakes

1. Separate the escarole leaves and rinse once or twice. Stack bunches of the leaves and cut crosswise into 1-inch strips. You should end up with about 20 cups.

2. Bring a large pot of lightly salted water to a boil. Add pasta and cook according to package directions.

3. Meanwhile, in a large skillet, heat ¼ cup of oil over medium heat. Add the bread crumbs and cook, stirring often, for 4 to 5 minutes, or until lightly browned. Scrape the mixture into a small bowl and wipe the skillet clean with paper towels.

4. Heat the remaining ¼ cup of oil in the same skillet. Stir in the garlic and cook until its aroma is released, about 30 seconds to 1 minute, stirring once or twice. Add the escarole. Cover and cook for about 4 minutes, stirring and turning the escarole with two spoons two or three times, until the leaves are just wilted. Stir in the anchovies, salt, and crushed hot pepper.

5. Add ¼ cup of pasta cooking water to the skillet. Drain the pasta and return to the pot. Add the escarole mixture and toss to mix. Top with bread crumbs just before serving.

Per serving: 546 cal, 15 g pro, 73 g car, 21 g fat, 4 mg chol, 1,082 mg sod

CAPELLINI WITH SCALLOPS

Serves 5
Preparation time: 15 minutes
Cooking time: 20 minutes

Capellini are long, thin strands of pasta that are slightly thicker than capelli d'angelo (angel hair). Both are delicate and the perfect choice to serve with this succulent sauce of tender scallops and fragrant basil. The tiny bay scallop is sweeter and more tender than the larger sea scallop, but either can be used here. Scallops only need to be cooked briefly, just until they turn opaque.

1 pound capellini or capelli (angel hair) pasta
¼ cup olive oil
2 teaspoons minced garlic
1 pound bay or sea scallops (cut sea scallops in half)
½ teaspoon salt
¼ teaspoon crushed hot red pepper flakes
1 cup coarsely chopped fresh basil
2 tablespoons butter or margarine
For garnish: 3 tablespoons toasted pine nuts (optional)

COOK'S TIP

To toast pine nuts: Spread in a jelly roll pan or small baking pan and bake at 325°F for 10 to 15 minutes, or until light golden. Or toast the nuts in a small heavy skillet over low heat for 3 to 5 minutes, shaking the pan frequently, until the pine nuts have turned light brown.

▶

1. Bring a large pot of lightly salted water to a boil.

2. Meanwhile, in a large skillet, heat the oil over medium heat. Add the garlic and cook over medium-low heat for 2 to 3 minutes, stirring often, until tender.

3. Stir in the scallops, salt, and crushed red pepper. Cook over medium heat for 2 to 4 minutes, stirring occasionally, until the scallops are opaque in the center. Remove the skillet from the heat, stir in the basil, and keep warm.

4. Add the pasta to the boiling water and cook according to the package directions. Ladle ¼ cup of the cooking water into a large serving bowl. Drain the pasta and add to the bowl.

5. Pour the sauce over the pasta. Add the butter and pine nuts. Toss to mix and coat. Serve right away.

Per serving: 564 cal, 28 g pro, 73 g car, 18 g fat, 42 mg chol with butter, 30 mg chol with maragarine, 734 mg sod

---

EASY • 30 MINUTES

RIGATONI WITH ZUCCHINI & PROSCIUTTO

Serves 6
Preparation time: 10 minutes
Cooking time: 15 minutes

Prosciutto, the Italian word for ham, is used to a describe a ham that has been salt-cured and air-dried and is usually sliced very thin. It is available in Italian markets, specialty food shops, and some large supermarkets.

1 pound rigatoni pasta
1 cup chicken broth
6 medium-size zucchini (about 6 ounces each), quartered lengthwise, then cut crosswise into ½-inch pieces
1½ tablespoons all-purpose flour
1 cup milk
5 thin slices prosciutto (2½ ounces), trimmed of fat, cut into thin strips
½ cup plus 2 tablespoons grated Parmesan cheese
¼ cup (½ stick) butter or margarine
½ teaspoon ground black pepper

1. Bring a large pot of lightly salted water to a boil. Add the pasta and cook according to the package directions. Drain and return to the pot.

2. Meanwhile, in a large skillet, bring the chicken broth to a boil over

---

PASTA PERFECT

If you don't smother it with cheese, cream, or meat sauce, pasta is a nutritional winner. Consider that 1 cup of dried, cooked pasta

◆ has surprisingly few (200 to 220) calories.

◆ is rich is complex carbohydrates—something health experts suggest we eat more of.

◆ is cholesterol-free. (The exceptions: egg noodles and fresh pasta, which contain only about 50 to 55 milligrams per 2-ounce serving—one quarter the amount in a single egg.)

◆ has only 1 gram of fat (except egg noodles, which have about 3 grams, and fresh pasta, in which fat makes up about 10 percent of its calories—not enough to sabotage your diet).

medium-high heat. Add the zucchini and cook, stirring often, for 6 to 7 minutes, or until crisp-tender.

3. In a small bowl, whisk the flour into the milk (it's okay if a few tiny lumps remain). Whisk this mixture into the zucchini and chicken broth. Boil the sauce gently for 1 to 2 minutes, whisking constantly, until slightly thickened.

4. Pour the sauce over the hot pasta in the pot. Add the prosciutto, ½ cup of Parmesan cheese, the butter, and pepper. Toss to mix and coat. Spoon into serving bowls. Sprinkle with the remaining 2 tablespoons of Parmesan cheese and serve right away.

Per serving: 475 cal, 20 g pro, 65 g car, 15 g fat, 43 mg chol with butter, 22 mg chol with margarine, 907 mg sod with butter, 918 mg sod with margarine

---

60 MINUTES • MAKE AHEAD

ZITI WITH MEATBALLS

Serves 6

Preparation time: 20 minutes

Cooking time: 30 minutes

ⓜAKE AHEAD

The meatballs and sauce can be prepared ahead. Let cool, then refrigerate in an airtight container up to 3 days. Slowly reheat on the range top.

The tomato sauce for this all-time favorite pasta dish has vegetables added to it for an extra taste dimension. Although ziti is the pasta of choice for this recipe, you can also use rotelle, shells, or bow-ties.

½ cup buttermilk

2 slices whole-grain bread

12 ounces lean ground beef

1 large egg

2 tablespoons grated Parmesan cheese

1 teaspoon dried oregano leaves, crumbled

½ teaspoon garlic powder

½ teaspoon salt

1 can (about 28 ounces) crushed tomatoes

1 bunch broccoli (about 1¼ pounds), stems peeled and diced (¾ cup); florets separated and reserved (about 3 cups)

2 teaspoons dried basil leaves, crumbled

1 teaspoon granulated sugar

1 medium-size zucchini (6 ounces), cut in half lengthwise, then crosswise into ½-inch pieces

1 medium-size yellow summer squash (6 ounces), cut in half lengthwise, then crosswise into ½-inch pieces

12 ounces ziti pasta (about 4 cups)

▶

1. Pour the buttermilk into a medium-size bowl. Crumble in the bread and let soak for 1 to 2 minutes. Add the beef, egg, cheese, oregano, garlic powder, and salt. Mix with your hands or a large spoon until well blended.

2. Shape the mixture by level tablespoonfuls into 24 meatballs.

3. In a large deep nonstick skillet or saucepan (add 1 tablespoon vegetable oil if not using a nonstick skillet) cook the meatballs over medium-high heat for 3 minutes, turning often, until browned on all sides. Discard the pan drippings.

4. Add the tomatoes, broccoli stems, basil, and sugar. Bring to a boil. Reduce the heat to medium-low and simmer uncovered for 10 minutes.

5. Meanwhile, bring a large pot of water to boil. Add the pasta to the boiling water and cook according to package directions.

6. Add the squash to the skillet. Cook the sauce for 8 to 10 minutes more, stirring occasionally, until the vegetables are crisp-tender.

7. Drain the pasta and return to the pot. Add the sauce and toss to mix and coat. Serve right away.

Per serving: 463 cal, 23 g pro, 58 g car, 15 g fat, 80 mg chol, 562 mg sod

---

EASY • 30 MINUTES • ONE POT

FETTUCCINE & VEGETABLES ALFREDO

Serves 4

Total time: 15 minutes

This pasta recipe has only five ingredients and it's downright delicious! To save time, cut up the tomatoes while the pasta cooks.

12 ounces fettuccine
1 package (10 ounces) frozen peas
1 cup reduced-fat sour cream
¾ cup grated Parmesan cheese
1⅓ cups quartered cherry tomatoes

For garnish: chopped fresh parsley (optional)

1. Bring a large pot of lightly salted water to a boil. Add the pasta and cook according to the package directions. About three minutes before the pasta is done, add the peas and cook until the pasta is firm-tender.

2. Remove the pot from the heat. Ladle out and reserve ⅓ cup of cooking liquid from the pot, then drain the pasta and peas in a colander.

3. In a large serving bowl, mix the sour cream, Parmesan cheese, and

COOKING PASTA

◆ Start with at least 1 quart of water for every 4 ounces of pasta (1 gallon of water for 1 pound of pasta). Salting the water is optional and not necessary for proper cooking of pasta. Let the water come to a full boil before gradually adding pasta so that the water keeps boiling. Cook the pasta uncovered and at a fast boil. If the water stops boiling, cover it until it returns. (Take the cover off again as soon as it begins to boil.) Stir the pasta often so it will cook evenly and to prevent sticking.

◆ Check the pasta often for doneness. The cooking time on the package is only a guideline. Begin to test dried pasta after about 4 minutes of cooking

reserved cooking liquid.

4. Add the pasta, peas, and cherry tomatoes. Toss to mix and coat well.

5. Garish with chopped fresh parsley and serve right away.

Per serving: 554 cal, 26 g pro, 76 g car, 16 g fat, 113 mg chol, 670 mg sod

EASY • 60 MINUTES • MICROWAVE

VEGETABLE LASAGNE

Serves 4
Preparation time: 15 minutes
Cooking time: 23 minutes plus 20 minutes to stand

Though the lasagne is very soft after cooking, it will firm up during standing time, making it easy to slice and serve.

VEGETABLE SAUCE
3 tablespoons cornstarch
2½ cups milk
2 small zucchini, halved lengthwise and sliced thin crosswise (2 cups)
1 cup chopped red bell pepper
½ cup sliced scallions
½ cup grated Parmesan cheese
½ teaspoon salt
½ teaspoon ground black pepper

5 no-boil lasagne noodles
1 container (about 15 ounces) ricotta cheese

1. Make the sauce: In a 2-quart microwave-safe bowl, whisk together the cornstarch and milk until blended. Cover with vented plastic wrap and microwave on High for 6 to 8 minutes, whisking twice, until smooth, thickened, and boiling. Stir in the zucchini, bell pepper, scallions, Parmesan, salt, and pepper.

2. Spread ¾ cup of the sauce over the bottom of a 9 x 5-inch microwave-safe loaf pan. Top with 1 lasagne noodle. Spread ¾ cup sauce over the noodle, then spoon ½ cup of ricotta over the sauce. Repeat the layers (noodle, sauce, ricotta) 3 more times. Top with the last noodle and the remaining sauce.

3. Cover loosely with waxed paper. Microwave on High for 13 to 15 minutes, rotating the dish ¼ turn twice, until the noodles are almost tender when pierced with the pointed tip of a knife. Let stand covered for 15 to 20 minutes before cutting.

Per serving: 435 cal, 25 g pro, 34 g car, 22 g fat, 83 mg chol, 630 mg sod

PASTA SHAPES

There are literally hundreds of pasta shapes and sizes available today and the confusion is increased by manufacturers who often use different names for the same shape. The following is a description of the most common pasta shapes.

Agnolotti: Small crescent-shaped stuffed pasta

Anelli (anellini): Small pasta rings

Cannelloni: Large round pasta tubes used for stuffing

Capelli d'angelo: Also called angel hair; delicate, long, and extremely fine pasta strands

Capellini: Long, fine strands slightly thicker than capelli

Cappelletti: Small, hat-shaped stuffed pasta

Cavatelli: Short, narrow, ripple-edged pasta shells

Conchiglie: Shell-shaped pasta

Ditali: Small macaroni about 1/2 inch long; used in soups

Ditalini: Smaller ditali

Elbow macaroni: Small, slightly curved tubes

Farfalle: Bow tie-shaped pasta

Fettuccine: Long, thin, flat ribbons about 1/2 inch wide

Fusilli: Spiral-shaped or twisted pasta that comes either in spaghetti length strands or cut about 1 1/2 inches long

Gnocchi: Small dumplings made from potatoes, flour, or farina, and usually eggs and cheese

Lasagne: Long, broad ribbons with straight or rippled edges

Linguine: Narrow, flat ribbons about 1/8 inch wide

Macaroni: Tube-shaped pasta of various lengths

Malfade: Mini-lasagne noodles

Manicott: Very large pasta tubes used for stuffing

Orecchiette: Small disc-shaped or ear-shaped pasta

Orzo: Rice-shaped pasta

Pappardelle: Ribbons about 1/2-inch-wide with rippled sides

Pastina: Tiny star-shaped or round pasta

Penne: Diagonally cut tubes with smooth or ridged sides

Radiatore: Short, chunky-shaped pasta with rippled edges

Ravioli: Square-shaped stuffed pasta

Rigatoni: Large ridged macaroni about 1 1/2 inches wide

Rotelle: Wagon wheel-shaped pasta

Rotini: Short spiral-shaped pasta about 1 to 2 inches long

Spaghetti: Long, thin round strands in various thicknesses

Spaghettini: Thin strands of spaghetti

Tagliatelle: Long, thin flat ribbons about 1/4 inch wide

Tortellini: Small stuffed pasta in a ring or hat shape

Vermicell: Very thin strands of spaghetti

Ziti: Long, thin straight-cut tubes that range in length from 2 to 12 inches

---

EASY • 30 MINUTES

TORTELLINI WITH VEGETABLES

Serves 4

Preparation time: 5 minutes

Cooking time: 10 minutes

Look for fresh tortellini in your grocer's refrigerated section. You can use cheese tortellini for this recipe too.

1 bag (16 ounces) frozen mixed vegetables
  (carrots, peas, zucchini, pearl onions, red peppers)
2 packages (about 9 ounces each) fresh meat-filled tortellini pasta
1/4 cup olive oil
1 teaspoon minced fresh garlic
1/4 teaspoon crushed hot red pepper flakes
1/4 cup grated Parmesan cheese
2 tablespoons chopped fresh parsley (optional)

▶ *p. 37*

SIMPLICITY
Spinach replaces basil in this easy-to-make Spinach Pesto with Ham & Tomatoes (p.20), tossed with linguine.

Delicious, healthful, homemade pasta sauces that can be made in 15 minutes or less are a real boon for the busy weekday cook.

HEALTHFUL
Broccoli & Chick-Pea Sauce (p.17) over pasta offers a tasty way to add vitamins A and C and calcium to your diet.

1. Bring a large pot of water to boil over high heat.

2. Rinse the vegetables in a colander under warm running water until partially thawed and the pieces can be separated. Add the tortellini and vegetables to the boiling water. Cover and return to a boil. Uncover and boil for 3 minutes, or until the tortellini are tender.

3. Meanwhile, in a small saucepan, heat the oil and garlic over medium-low heat just the until garlic starts to sizzle. Remove the pan from the heat.

4. Drain the tortellini and vegetables and return them to the pot. Toss the pasta with the hot garlic oil, Parmesan cheese, and parsley. Serve right away.

Per serving: 570 cal, 26 g pro, 70 g car, 21 g fat, 79 mg chol, 725 mg sod

LOW FAT • MAKE AHEAD • CLASSIC

STUFFED SHELLS FLORENTINE

Serves 6

Preparation time: 30 minutes

Cooking time: 45 minutes plus 5 minutes to stand

These pasta shells, stuffed with a mixture of spinach, ricotta cheese, Parmesan, and mozzarella, are lower in fat than you might think.

24 jumbo pasta shells
2 cups part-skim ricotta cheese or 2 percent fat cottage cheese
Whites of 2 large eggs, or 1 large whole egg
1 package (10 ounces) frozen chopped spinach, thawed and squeezed dry
½ cup grated Parmesan cheese
½ cup shredded part-skim mozzarella cheese
½ teaspoon dried oregano leaves, crumbled
½ teaspoon dried basil leaves, crumbled
Pinch grated nutmeg (optional)
Ground black pepper to taste
2 cups meatless spaghetti sauce

1. Bring a large pot of lightly salted water to a boil. Add the pasta and cook according to the package directions. Drain in a colander.

2. Meanwhile, in a medium-size bowl, mix the ricotta cheese, egg whites, spinach, Parmesan, ¼ cup of mozzarella cheese, the oregano, basil, nutmeg, and pepper.

3. Heat the oven to 350°F. Spread half the spaghetti sauce in the bottom of a shallow 2-quart baking dish.

4. Fill each shell with a scant 2 tablespoons of the cheese mixture ▶

MAKE AHEAD

The recipe can be prepared through step 4. Cover tightly and refrigerate overnight. Bake at 350°F for 50 minutes, or until bubbly and heated through. Uncover and bake for 5 minutes more. Let stand 5 minutes before serving.

and arrange in a single layer in the baking dish. Pour the remaining sauce over the shells and sprinkle with the remaining mozzarella cheese.

5. Loosely cover the dish with foil and bake for 40 minutes, or until bubbly and heated through to the center. Uncover and bake for 5 minutes more. Let stand for 5 minutes before serving.

Per serving with ricotta: 443 cal, 24 g pro, 53 g car, 15 g fat, 36 mg chol with egg whites, 72 mg chol with whole egg, 736 mg sod. With cottage cheese: 397 cal, 25 g pro, 51 g car, 10 g fat, 17 mg chol with egg whites, 52 mg chol with whole egg, 943 mg sod

`EASY • MAKE AHEAD`

MEXICAN MANICOTTI

Serves 4
Preparation time: 20 minutes
Cooking time: 43 minutes

Serve this spicy manicotti with sliced avocado on lettuce or a green salad.

8 manicotti shells
8 ounces lean ground beef
½ cup chopped onion
2½ teaspoons minced fresh garlic
1½ teaspoons dried oregano leaves, crumbled
1½ teaspoons chili powder
1 cup nonfat or regular refried beans
1 jar (about 8 ounces) picante sauce, mild or medium
⅓ cup low-fat shredded Monterey Jack cheese
⅓ cup thinly sliced scallions
2 tablespoons chopped fresh cilantro (optional)
½ cup nonfat sour cream (optional)

1. Heat the oven to 350°F. Grease a 10 x 6-inch or 9-inch square baking dish.

2. Bring a large pot of lightly salted water to a boil. Add the manicotti shells and cook according to the package directions. Drain well.

3. Meanwhile, in a large skillet, cook the ground beef, onion, and garlic over medium heat for 6 to 7 minutes, stirring often, until the onion is softened. Add the oregano and chili powder and cook, stirring occasionally, for 1 minute more. Stir in the beans. Remove the skillet from the heat.

4. Fill each manicotti shell with ¼ to ⅓ cup of the meat mixture. Arrange the filled manicotti in the prepared dish. Pour the picante sauce over the top and sprinkle with the cheese.

VARIATION

MICROWAVE STUFFED SHELLS

● Prepare the recipe as directed through step 2.
● Spread half the sauce over the bottom of an 11½ x 7¾ -inch microwave-safe baking dish. Fill the shells as directed and arrange in a single layer in the baking dish. Pour the remaining sauce over the shells. Cover with vented plastic wrap and microwave on High for 10 to 12 minutes, rotating the dish ¼ turn 3 times, until bubbly.
● Remove the wrap. Sprinkle with the remaining mozzarella cheese and let stand for 5 minutes for the cheese to melt.

Per serving with ricotta: 443 cal, 24 g pro, 53 g car, 15 g fat, 36 mg chol with egg whites, 72 mg chol with whole egg, 736 mg sod. With cottage cheese: 397 cal, 25 g pro, 51 g car, 10 g fat, 17 mg chol with egg whites, 52 mg chol with whole egg, 943 mg sod

● 30 MINUTES

MAKE AHEAD

The meat filling for the

manicotti can be

prepared ahead. Let

cool, then refrigerate

tightly covered up to 3

days. There's no need

to reheat it before

filling the manicotti;

just increase the

baking time by 5 to

10 minutes.

5. Cover with foil and bake for 35 minutes, or until the sauce is bubbly. Uncover and bake for 8 minutes more. Sprinkle with the scallions and cilantro and serve right away with sour cream.

Per serving with nonfat beans: 365 cal, 20 g pro, 36 g car, 15 g fat, 49 mg chol, 806 mg sod. With regular beans: 382 cal, 21 g pro, 38 g car, 16 g fat 49 mg chol, 873 mg sod

PASTA SKILLET PIE
Serves 6
Preparation time: 15 minutes
Cooking time: 35 minutes

This protein-rich dish is a great way to use leftover cooked pasta. Wrap plastic-handled skillets with a double thickness of heavy foil before putting under the broiler to prevent the plastic from melting.

8 ounces capelli (angel hair) pasta or extra-thin spaghetti
4 tablespoons margarine
1 cup chopped onion
2 teaspoons minced fresh garlic
1 can (8 ounces) tomatoes, drained and coarsely chopped
2 teaspoons dried basil leaves, crumbled
1 teaspoon salt
¼ teaspoon ground black pepper
2 packages (10 ounces each) frozen chopped turnip greens,
    thawed and drained
8 large eggs
¼ cup grated Parmesan cheese
4 ounces mozzarella cheese, cut into 6 slices
1 can (16 ounces) stewed tomatoes, heated

1. Bring a large pot of lightly salted water to a boil. Add the pasta and cook according to package directions. Drain in a colander.

2. Meanwhile, in a medium-size saucepan, melt 2 tablespoons of margarine over medium heat. Add the onion and garlic and cook, stirring often, for 3 minutes, or until softened. Stir in the tomatoes, basil, salt, pepper, and greens. Cook for 5 to 7 minutes, stirring twice, until the greens are tender. Remove the pan from the heat.

3. In a large bowl, beat the eggs and Parmesan with a fork. Add the pasta and toss to coat. ▶

4. In a medium-size nonstick broiler-proof skillet, melt the remaining 2 tablespoons of margarine over medium heat. Spread half the pasta mixture over the bottom of the pan. Arrange the mozzarella slices over the pasta. Cover with the greens mixture, then the remaining pasta mixture.

5. Reduce the heat to medium-low. Cook uncovered for 15 to 18 minutes, or until the eggs are almost set and the underside is browned (gently lift the edge with a spatula to check). Remove the skillet from the heat.

6. Heat the broiler. Broil 4 inches from the heat source for 4 to 6 minutes, or until lightly browned and the eggs are set.

7. Invert the pie onto serving a plate. Cut into wedges and serve with the warm stewed tomatoes.

Makes 6 wedges. Per wedge: 43 cal, 22 g pro, 43 g car, 21 g fat, 301 mg chol, 1,070 mg sod

---

EASY • 60 MINUTES • LOW FAT • ONE POT • CLASSIC

TUNA-NOODLE CASSEROLE

Serves 4
Preparation time: 15 minutes
Cooking time: 35 minutes

Using solid white tuna packed in water, yolk-free noodles, and fat-free soup saves on fat and calories in this classic casserole.

6 ounces yolk-free wide egg noodles (about 3 cups)
1 can (10¾ ounces) reduced-fat cream of mushroom soup
½ cup skim milk
½ teaspoon salt
⅛ teaspoon ground red pepper (cayenne)
1 can (6⅛ ounces) solid white tuna in water, drained and flaked
½ cup frozen green peas
1 jar (2 ounces) diced pimiento, drained (¼ cup)
½ cup crushed baked potato-chip snacks (like Tater Crisps)

1. Bring a large pot of water to a boil. Add the noodles and cook according to the package directions. Drain in a colander.

2. Heat the oven to 400°F. In a deep 1½-quart casserole, mix the soup, milk, salt, and pepper. Gently stir in the noodles, tuna, peas, and pimiento.

3. Cover and bake for 25 minutes, until hot. Uncover and sprinkle with crushed chips. Bake uncovered for 10 minutes more, or until bubbly.

Per serving: 311 cal, 21 g pro, 46 g car, 5 g fat, 24 mg chol, 857 mg sod

HIGH-FIBER PASTA

Whole wheat pasta contains about 4 times the fiber of regular pasta and slightly more protein, vitamins, and minerals. Try mixing whole wheat pasta with regular pasta to acclimatize your family. (Choose matching shapes that will cook in the same time in the same pot.)

EASY • 60 MINUTES

PASTA AL FORNO

Serves 8
Preparation time: 25 minutes
Baking time: 15 minutes

This rustic baked pasta dish combines the flavors of fresh zucchini, yellow squash, plum tomatoes, and arugula (also known as rocket). For a less peppery flavor, use spinach or Swiss chard leaves instead of arugula. Rigatoni and pasta shells will also work here. Serve this hearty dish with an antipasto or tossed salad and garlic bread.

1 pound rotelle (wagon-wheel) pasta
3 tablespoons virgin olive oil (preferably extra-virgin)
1 medium-size zucchini (8 ounces), cut into ½-inch pieces (1½ cups)
1 medium-size yellow summer squash (8 ounces),
    cut into ½-inch pieces (1½ cups)
1½ pounds ripe plum tomatoes, halved, seeded,
    and cut into ¼-inch pieces (1½ cups)
8 ounces mozzarella cheese, cut into ½-inch pieces
½ cup Kalamata or oil-cured (black) olives, pitted and cut into pieces
½ cup grated good-quality Parmesan cheese
    (preferably Parmigiano-Reggiano)
1 small bunch arugula, trimmed, rinsed, drained, and torn into
    bite-size pieces (about 3 loosely packed cups)
½ teaspoon salt
½ teaspoon crushed hot red pepper flakes

1. Bring a large pot of lightly salted water to a boil. Add the pasta and cook according to package directions. Drain the pasta and return to the pot.

2. Meanwhile, heat the oven to 375°F. Lightly grease a 13 x 9 x 2-inch baking dish with 1 tablespoon of the oil.

3. In a large skillet, heat the remaining 2 tablespoons oil over medium heat. Add the zucchini and yellow squash and cook for 5 to 7 minutes, stirring a few times, until crisp-tender.

4. Add the squash to the cooked pasta, then add the tomatoes, mozzarella, olives, Parmesan cheese, arugula, salt, and hot pepper flakes.

5. Transfer to the prepared baking dish. Bake for 12 to 15 minutes, or until the cheese is melted and the pasta starts to brown slightly on the top and around the edges. Serve right away.

Per serving: 408 cal, 16 g pro, 50 g car, 16 g fat, 27 mg chol, 640 mg sod

STORING PASTA

Dried pasta can be stored in an airtight container in a cool, dark place almost indefinitely. However, dried whole wheat pasta should be used within 1 month. Fresh pasta can be wrapped tightly and refrigerated up to 5 days, or double-wrapped and frozen up to 4 months. Frozen pasta does not have to be thawed before cooking.

EGG NOODLES WITH VEGETABLES

Serves 6
Preparation time: 15 minutes
Cooking time: 15 minutes

This deliciously different and quick-to-prepare noodle dish features vitamin-rich beet greens, rutabaga, and carrots.

- 1 bunch (about 12 ounces) fresh beet greens, or tops cut from 1 bunch beets
- 1 tablespoon plus 1 teaspoon salt
- 1 pound rutabaga (yellow turnip), peeled and cut into julienne strips (4 cups)
- 3 medium-size carrots (6 ounces), peeled and cut into julienne strips (1½ cups)
- 12 ounces medium-wide egg noodles (4 cups)
- 3 tablespoons butter or margarine
- 2 tablespoons finely chopped fresh dill
- 1 tablespoon cider vinegar

1. Cut the beet stems into 2-inch lengths and cut the beet leaves into 1-inch-wide strips.

2. Bring a large pot of water and 1 tablespoon of salt to a rapid boil. Stir in the rutabaga and carrots. Return to a boil and cook for 2 minutes.

3. Stir in the noodles and beet stems. Return to a boil and cook for 6 minutes.

4. Stir in the beet leaves. Boil for 2 minutes, or until the vegetables and noodles are firm-tender and the beet leaves are limp. Drain in a colander.

5. Melt the butter in the same pot over medium heat. Stir in the dill, vinegar, and the remaining 1 teaspoon salt. Return the noodles and vegetables to the pot. Toss to mix and coat. Serve right away.

Per serving: 313 cal, 10 g pro, 51 g car, 8 g fat, 69 mg chol with butter, 54 mg chol with margarine, 945 mg sod

PASTA YIELDS

8 ounces dry macaroni (2 cups) = 4 cups cooked (4 to 6 servings)

8 ounces spaghetti = 4 cups cooked (4 to 6 servings)

8 ounces egg noodles (4 to 5 cups) = 4 cups cooked (4 to 6 servings)

EASY • 60 MINUTES • LOW FAT

ASIAN NOODLES

Serves 4

Preparation time: 15 minutes

Cooking time: 10 minutes plus 15 minutes to cool

These sesame-flavored noodles can be served as a main dish, or in smaller portions as an accompaniment to barbecued food or simple broiled chicken or fish.

8 ounces spaghettini (thin spaghetti)

DRESSING

¼ cup thinly sliced scallions

3 tablespoons soy sauce

1 tablespoon vegetable oil

1 tablespoon balsamic vinegar

1 teaspoon granulated sugar

2 teaspoons minced peeled fresh gingerroot

½ teaspoon hot Asian sesame oil, or ½ teaspoon dark Asian
   sesame oil and ¼ teaspoon crushed hot red pepper flakes

1. Bring a large pot of lightly salted water to a boil. Add the spaghettini and cook according to the package directions.

2. Meanwhile, make the dressing: In a large serving bowl, mix the scallions, soy sauce, oil, vinegar, sugar, ginger, and sesame oil.

3. Drain the spaghetti in a colander. Add the hot pasta to the dressing, tossing to mix and coat. Let stand for about 15 minutes to cool, stirring occasionally to allow the spaghetti to absorb the dressing. Serve at room temperature.

Per serving: 260 cal, 8 g pro, 45 g car, 5 g fat, 0 mg chol, 971 mg sod

PRONTO PASTA

Toss 1 pound of cooked pasta with one of the following sauces for a hearty low-fat meal:

◆ Heat 2 cans (14½ ounces each) pasta-ready tomatoes with 1 can (16 ounces) drained chick-peas or white beans.

◆ Heat one 10-ounce package frozen California-style vegetables with sauce and 1 can (about 6 ounces) water-packed chunk light tuna.

◆ Chop 1 medium-size head escarole, 1 medium-size red bell pepper, and 1 clove garlic. Simmer in 1 cup chicken broth.

◆ Purée in a blender or food processor: 1 pound fresh spinach leaves, 1 cup loosely packed fresh basil leaves, 2 teaspoons minced garlic, and 1 cup chicken broth.

GARDEN ORZO

Serves 4 to 6
Preparation time: 20 minutes
Cooking time: 10 minutes

By the time the orzo is cooked, the sautéed fresh vegetables are ready to be added. This recipe calls for diced zucchini, red bell pepper, and onion, but other vegetables such as carrots, peas, and sliced mushrooms can also be used. Serve this dish as a colorful and delicious substitute for rice.

3 cups chicken broth
1¼ cups orzo (rice-shaped) pasta (8 ounces)
1 tablespoon olive oil
1 cup diced zucchini
1 cup diced red bell pepper
⅓ cup diced onion
½ teaspoon minced fresh garlic
¼ cup grated Parmesan cheese
1 tablespoon chopped fresh basil (optional)
⅛ teaspoon ground black pepper
For garnish: fresh basil leaves (optional)

1. In a medium-size saucepan, bring the chicken broth to a boil. Add the orzo and simmer for 8 to 10 minutes, or until tender. Drain if necessary.

2. Meanwhile, in a medium-size skillet, heat the oil over medium heat. Add the zucchini, bell pepper, and onion and cook for 5 minutes, stirring often, until the vegetables are softened. Add the garlic and cook for 1 minute more. Remove the skillet from the heat.

3. In a medium-size serving bowl, mix the orzo, the vegetable mixture, Parmesan cheese, basil, and pepper. Garnish with fresh basil leaves. Serve warm or at room temperature.

Per serving: 242 cal, 9 g pro, 37 g car, 6 g fat, 3 mg chol, 679 mg sod

MAKE AHEAD

This dish can be prepared ahead and refrigerated tightly covered up to 3 days. Bring to room temperature or slowly reheat on the range top before serving.

CHICKEN & TURKEY

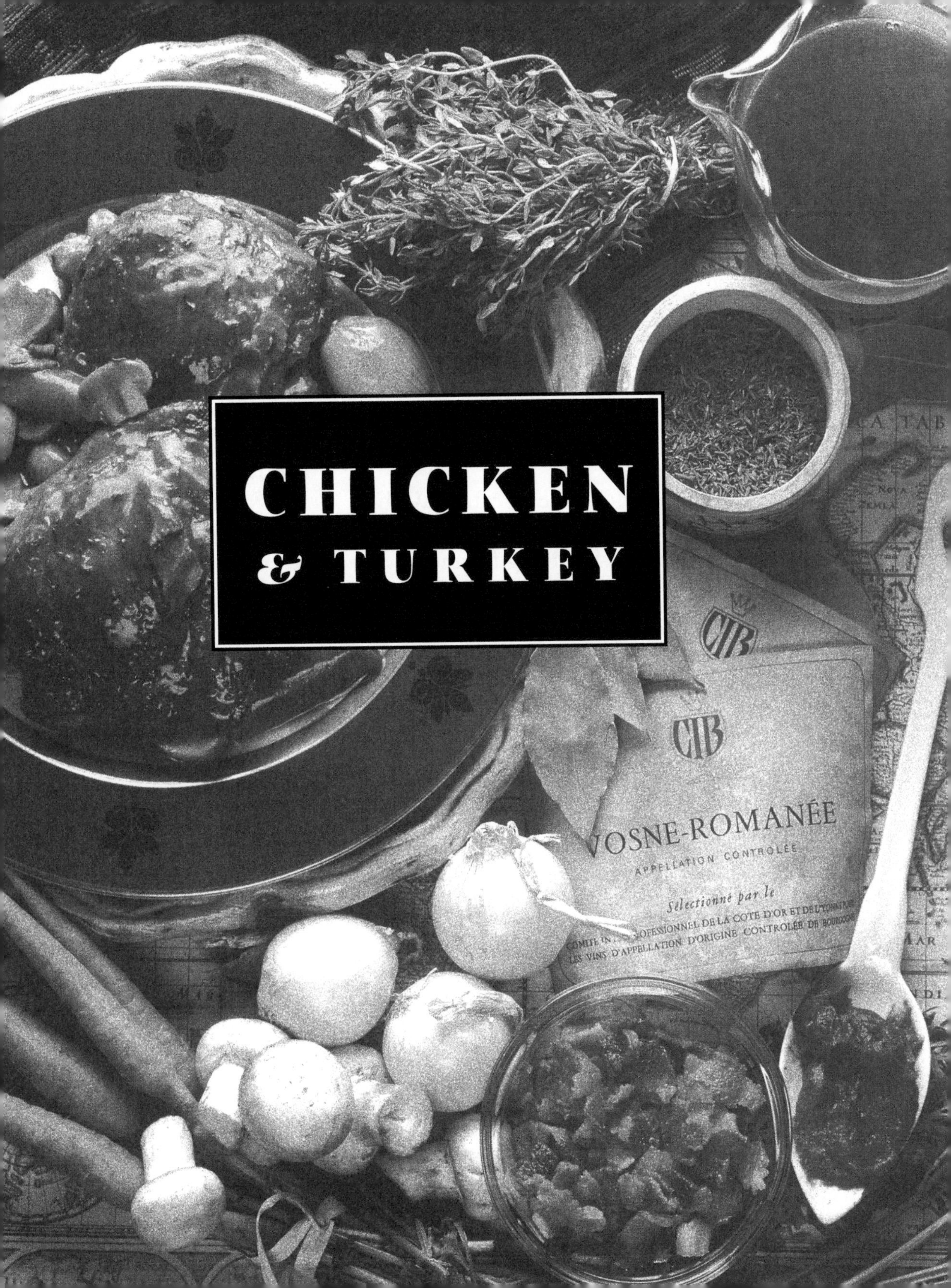

"...Poultry is for the cook what canvas is for the painter."
BRILLAT-SAVARIN

During the Depression, the phrase "a chicken in every pot" was a measure of comfort and prosperity. Today, chicken appears on the table as a weekly or even twice-weekly ritual. With the current emphasis on reducing fat and calories in the diet, chicken is a natural choice with the added bonus of being extremely economical. And its counterpart, turkey, is not just for traditional family feasts anymore. It is finding its way into more weeknight meals for the same reasons as chicken.

With their excellent flavor and versatility, chicken and turkey fit easily into today's menus. This chapter offers a large and varied selection of recipes designed to please just about everyone.

EASY • LOW FAT

CHICKEN BREASTS WITH CITRUS SALSA

Serves 4

Preparation time: 20 minutes plus at least 1 hour to marinate
Cooking time: 16 minutes

A portion of the salsa is used to marinate the chicken and the remainder makes fresh-tasting topping. Serve with rice and a green salad.

3 medium-size oranges, preferably navel
½ cup finely chopped red bell pepper
¼ cup thinly sliced scallions
2 tablespoons fresh lime juice
½ teaspoon salt
¼ teaspoon crushed hot red pepper flakes
4 skinless, boneless chicken breast halves (about 1 pound)

1. Scrub 1 orange well; finely grate 1 teaspoon of the peel into a small bowl. Cut off and discard the peel and white pith from all 3 oranges. Cut off between the membranes to release the orange sections, dropping them into another small bowl. Squeeze the juice from the remaining membrane (with your hand) over the grated peel and stir in the bell pepper, scallions, lime juice, salt, and red pepper flakes.

2. Put the chicken in a 1-gallon zipper-type bag. Add about ⅓ cup of the bell pepper mixture. Close the bag, pressing out the air, and turn to coat. Refrigerate for at least 1 hour and not more than 4 hours. Turn the bag occasionally.

3. Meanwhile, cut the orange sections crosswise in thirds and add to the remaining bell pepper mixture in the bowl. Cover and refrigerate the salsa until ready to serve.

4. Heat the broiler. Coat a broiler-pan rack with vegetable oil cooking spray. Remove the chicken from the marinade and arrange on the rack. Drizzle with the marinade in the bag and lightly spray with vegetable oil cooking spray.

5. Broil the chicken 4 to 5 inches from the heat source for 6 to 8 minutes on each side, or until the chicken is no longer pink in the center. Serve warm or at room temperature with the salsa.

Per serving: 185 cal, 28 g pro, 14 g car, 2 g fat, 66 mg chol, 350 mg sod

LEMONY CHICKEN BREASTS

Serves 2

Preparation time: 10 minutes

Cooking time: 10 minutes

Serve this dish with pasta and sautéed bell pepper strips for a delicious dinner in short order. The recipe can easily be doubled to serve more.

1 tablespoon all-purpose flour
¼ teaspoon salt
¼ teaspoon ground black pepper
2 skinless, boneless chicken breast halves
    (about 4 ounces each), tenderloins removed
2 teaspoons olive oil
⅓ cup chicken broth
2 tablespoons fresh lemon juice
1 tablespoon drained capers (optional)
1 tablespoon chopped fresh parsley

1. On a sheet of waxed paper or in a shallow dish, mix the flour, salt, and pepper. Coat each breast with the mixture, shaking off the excess.

2. In a large skillet, heat the oil over medium-high heat. Add the chicken and cook for about 3 minutes on each side, or until lightly browned and no longer pink in the center. Remove to a serving platter.

3. Add the chicken broth and lemon juice to the skillet. Cook over medium-high heat, stirring to scrape up any browned bits in the pan, for 2 to 3 minutes, or until the sauce is reduced slightly. Stir in the capers and parsley. Pour the sauce over the chicken and serve right away.

Per serving: 314 cal, 53 g pro, 5 g car, 8 g fat, 132 mg chol, 584 mg sod

---

VARIATION

ORANGE-MINT CHICKEN BREASTS

Omit the capers. Use fresh orange juice instead of lemon juice and fresh chopped mint instead of parsley. Proceed with the recipe as directed.

Per serving: 317 cal, 53 g pro, 5 g car, 8 g fat, 132 mg chol, 583 mg sod

• EASY • 30 MINUTES
• LOW FAT

CHICKEN & TURKEY COOKING CHART

Use this chart for cooking-time guidelines, or cook until a meat thermometer registers 180° F when inserted in the inner thigh and the juices run clear when the meat is pierced with a sharp knife.

WHOLE CHICKEN (4 to 7 pounds)	20 minutes per pound plus 20 minutes with stuffing at 350°
WHOLE CHICKEN (3 to 3½ pounds)	13 to 15 minutes per pound plus 20 minutes with stuffing at 350°
STUFFED TURKEY	12 to 15 minutes per pound (16 to 24 pounds) at 325°
CORNISH GAME HENS (1 to 1½ pounds)	45 minutes to 1 hour plus 15 minutes if stuffed at 375°

60 MINUTES • MICROWAVE • LOW FAT • ONE POT

ROSEMARY GARLIC CHICKEN

Serves 4

Preparation time: 15 minutes

Cooking time: 24 minutes

Eight cloves of garlic may seem like a lot for this recipe, but as it cooks the bite is taken out and the flavor is wonderfully mild. Be sure to serve with crusty bread to soak up the delicious sauce.

2 medium-size carrots, cut into thin sticks (1½ cups)

3 tablespoons water

1 quartered 3½-pound broiler-fryer chicken, wings, back, and skin removed

8 small new potatoes (about 12 ounces) or 4 medium-size

8 medium-size cloves garlic, crushed with flat side of knife and peeled

1¼ cups chicken broth

¼ cup dry white wine or chicken broth

2 teaspoons chopped fresh rosemary, or ½ teaspoon dried rosemary leaves, crumbled

¼ teaspoon ground black pepper

2 teaspoons cornstarch

1. In a 1-quart microwave-safe measuring cup, mix the carrots and 1 tablespoon of the water. Cover with vented plastic wrap and microwave on High for 2 to 3 minutes, or until crisp-tender.

2. Meanwhile, cut through the chicken legs and thighs at the joint to separate them and cut the breasts in half. (You will have 8 pieces of chicken.) Cut a ¾-inch-wide strip of skin from around the center of each small potato with a vegetable peeler (or cut medium-size potatoes in half).

3. Arrange the potatoes and garlic in the corners of a 13 x 9-inch microwave-safe baking dish. Arrange the chicken with the meaty portions toward the outer edge. Put the partially cooked carrots in the center. Pour the chicken broth and wine over the top, then sprinkle with rosemary and pepper.

4. Cover with a lid or vented plastic wrap and microwave on High for 9 to 11 minutes, rotating the dish ¼ turn twice. Uncover and turn the chicken over. Stir the potatoes and garlic. Cover and microwave on High for 2 to 4 minutes longer, or until the chicken is barely opaque near bone. Remove the vegetables and chicken with a slotted spoon to a serving dish. Cover with foil and let stand for 6 to 8 minutes, or until the meat near the bone is

---

GARLIC TIPS

◆ Store fresh garlic in an open container in a cool dark place. Unbroken bulbs will keep up to 2 months. Once the bulb is broken, the cloves will keep from 7 to 10 days.

◆ 1 fresh medium-size garlic clove = ½ teaspoon finely chopped garlic = ⅛ teaspoon garlic powder or dried minced garlic.

◆ To quickly peel garlic cloves, smash the clove lightly with the flat side of a broad knife, which helps to loosen the skin.

◆ If the garlic clove shows signs of sprouting, cut it in half and remove the green sprouting core, which can have a strong or harsh flavor.

◆ Be careful when sautéing not to

opaque and the juices run clear when tested with a sharp knife.

5. Meanwhile, make the sauce: In a small bowl, mix the cornstarch and remaining 2 tablespoons of water until blended. Slowly stir into the liquid in the baking dish until smooth. Microwave uncovered on High for 4 to 6 minutes, stirring twice, until slightly thickened and clear. Spoon the sauce over the chicken. Serve right away.

Per serving: 338 cal with wine, 339 cal with broth, 44 g pro, 23 g car, 7 g fat, 133 mg chol, 482 mg sod with wine, 544 mg sod with broth

EASY • 60 MINUTES • LOW FAT • MAKE AHEAD

SESAME CHICKEN CUTLETS

Serves 4

Preparation time: 15 minutes plus 30 minutes to chill

Cooking time: 12 minutes

Sliced chicken breast cutlets vary in size and thickness. Look for ones that are about ¼ inch thick for this recipe. Serve with sautéed mustard greens and rice.

1½ teaspoons dark Asian sesame oil
1½ teaspoons teriyaki sauce
1¼ pounds chicken breast cutlets
⅓ cup packaged plain bread crumbs
2 tablespoons sesame seeds
¼ teaspoon ground ginger
¼ teaspoon garlic powder
1 tablespoon vegetable oil
For garnish: lemon slices and chopped fresh parsley (optional)

1. In a medium-size bowl, mix the sesame oil and teriyaki sauce until well blended. Add the cutlets, tossing to coat.

2. On a sheet of waxed paper or in a shallow dish, mix the bread crumbs, sesame seeds, ginger, and garlic.

3. Coat each cutlet with the bread crumb mixture, patting the meat so the crumbs adhere. Refrigerate for at least 30 minutes.

4. In a large nonstick skillet, heat the oil over medium heat. Add the chicken cutlets and cook for 5 to 6 minutes on each side, or until golden and crisp and no longer pink in the center.

5. Transfer the cutlets to serving plates. Garnish with lemon slices and parsley and serve right away.

Per serving: 265 cal, 35 g pro, 8 g car, 10 g fat, 82 mg chol, 256 mg sod

---

overbrown garlic; it imparts a bitter taste. Finely chopped fresh garlic will usually cook in about 30 seconds over medium-high heat.

Ⓜ AKE AHEAD

Prepare the recipe through step 3 but do not refrigerate (the recipe can also be multiplied). Place the coated chicken cutlets in a single layer on a waxed paper-lined tray or baking sheet. Freeze uncovered for 1 to 2 hours, or until firm. Pack in plastic freezer bags and freeze up to 4 months.

EASY • 30 MINUTES • CLASSIC

CHICKEN CORDON BLEU

Serves 4

Preparation time: 9 minutes

Cooking time: 9 minutes

Topped with slices of baked ham and melted Muenster cheese, this quick and easy chicken cutlet recipe is perfect for a midweek celebration. Serve with steamed asparagus and parsleyed potatoes.

4 skinless, boneless chicken breast halves (about 1 pound)
¼ cup all-purpose flour
2 tablespoons olive oil
4 slices ham (about 1 ounce each) preferably baked, each slice about 3 by 5 inches
4 slices (about 1 ounce each) Muenster, Havarti, Port Salut, or Bel Paese cheese
½ cup reduced-sodium chicken broth
1 scallion, thinly sliced
Freshly ground pepper to taste

1. Sprinkle a little cold water over both sides of each piece of chicken. Place each, smooth side down, between 2 pieces of plastic wrap. With a rolling pin or the bottom of a heavy skillet, pound the chicken until it is about ¼ inch thick.

2. Spread the flour on a sheet of waxed paper. Coat the chicken with the flour, shaking off the excess.

3. In a large nonstick skillet, heat 1 tablespoon of oil over medium–high heat. Add the chicken and cook for 1 to 2 minutes, or until browned. Turn the chicken and cook for 1 minute more, or just until cooked through. Remove to a plate.

4. Add the remaining oil to the skillet. Return the chicken to the skillet (slightly overlapping is okay). Top each with one slice of ham and one slice of cheese. Pour in the broth and sprinkle the scallions and pepper on top. Bring to a boil over high heat. Reduce the heat to low. Cover and simmer for 1 to 2 minutes, or until the cheese melts.

5. Transfer the chicken to serving plates and pour over the pan juices. Serve right away.

Per serving with Muenster: 371 cal, 40 g pro, 7 g car, 19 g fat, 110 mg chol, 748 mg sod

CALORIE GOBBLERS

Chicken and turkey are naturally nutritious, but there are a number of ways to make them even better for you:

◆ Almost half the fat in chicken and turkey is in the skin, so removing it before or after cooking will lower your fat calorie intake.

◆ Trim visible fat before preparation or cooking.

◆ Use herbs, spices, and marinades to add extra flavor instead of heavy sauces and gravies.

◆ Broil, roast, bake, grill, or poach for healthier results. If you pan-fry, use a nonstick skillet and vegetable oil cooking spray.

EASY • 60 MINUTES • LOW FAT • ONE POT

AUTUMN CHICKEN STEW WITH THYME

Serves 4

Preparation time: 15 minutes

Cooking time: 20 minutes

Cracked black pepper balances the sweetness of the squash and apple. Serve this over couscous dotted with raisins and slivered almonds when company comes, or with mashed potatoes for a family-style meal.

1 tablespoon olive oil

1 large red bell pepper, seeded and chopped coarse (1½ cups)

1 large red onion, cut into thin wedges

2 medium-size Granny Smith apples

4 skinless, boneless chicken breast halves (about 1 pound), cut into bite-size pieces

2 small zucchini, sliced into ½-inch rounds

1 tablespoon minced fresh garlic

2½ cups chicken broth

2 tablespoons chopped fresh thyme, or 1 teaspoon dried thyme leaves, crumbled

2 teaspoons coarsely ground black pepper

½ teaspoon salt

1 package (20 ounces) frozen butternut squash chunks

1. In a 4- to 5-quart pot, heat the oil over medium heat. Add the bell pepper and onion and cook, stirring occasionally, for 4 to 5 minutes, or until the onion is softened.

2. Meanwhile, core and coarsely chop the apples (you can leave the skin on, if desired).

3. Add the apples, chicken, zucchini, garlic, chicken broth, thyme, pepper, and salt to the pot. Bring to a boil.

4. Reduce the heat to low, cover, and simmer for 8 to 10 minutes, stirring occasionally, until the zucchini is crisp-tender.

5. Stir in the butternut squash. Return to a boil. Reduce the heat to low. Cover and simmer for 3 to 5 minutes longer, or until the vegetables are tender and the chicken is cooked through. Serve right away.

Per serving: 343 cal, 32 g pro, 42 g car, 7 g fat, 66 mg chol, 985 mg sod

CHICKEN POTPIE

Serves 6
Preparation time: 40 minutes
Baking time: 40 minutes

This homey, old-fashioned meal-in-one is perfect to warm a chilly evening.

2 tablespoons butter or margarine
6 tablespoons all-purpose flour
1½ cups chicken broth
1½ cups milk
4 cups cooked chicken meat, cut into bite-size pieces (about 1½ pounds)
1 package (10 ounces) frozen mixed vegetables (carrots, peas, corn, green beans), thawed and drained
1 tablespoon chopped fresh parsley
½ teaspoon chopped fresh thyme, or ¼ teaspoon dried thyme leaves, crumbled
⅛ teaspoon ground red pepper (cayenne)
1 teaspoon salt
½ teaspoon ground black pepper

POTATO TOPPING
2 pounds all-purpose potatoes
¼ cup milk
2 tablespoons butter or margarine
½ teaspoon salt
¼ teaspoon ground black pepper

1. Heat the oven to 375°F. In a large saucepan, mix the butter, flour, chicken broth, and milk. Bring to a boil over medium heat, whisking constantly. Reduce the heat to low and simmer for 5 minutes.

2. Stir in the chicken, vegetables, parsley, thyme, ground red pepper, salt, and black pepper. Transfer the mixture to a 3-quart ovenproof baking dish. Set aside to cool slightly.

3. Meanwhile, make the topping. Peel and dice the potatoes. Bring a large pot of water to a boil. Add the potatoes, cover and cook over medium heat for 12 to 15 minutes, or until tender. Drain and mash with the milk and butter. Season with salt and pepper.

4. Spread the potatoes over the chicken mixture. Draw a circular pattern over the top of the potatoes with the tines of a fork.

MAKE AHEAD

To speed up preparation time, make the filling up to 2 days ahead and refrigerate in an airtight container. Make the potato topping just before cooking.

5. Bake for 30 to 40 minutes, or until the top is golden and the pie is heated through. Serve right away.

Per serving: 448 cal, 35 g pro, 36 g car, 18 g fat, 115 mg chol with butter, 94 mg chol with margarine, 1,023 mg sod with butter, 1,034 mg sod with margarine

EASY • 60 MINUTES • LOW FAT • ONE POT

DILLED CHICKEN FRICASSEE

Serves 4

Preparation time: 10 minutes

Cooking time: 35 minutes

Here's a good old-fashioned one-pot meal that will never let you down.

⅓ cup all-purpose flour
1 teaspoon salt
½ teaspoon paprika
1 tablespoon vegetable oil
4 bone-in chicken breast halves (about 2 pounds), skin removed
2 cups chicken broth
¼ cup chopped fresh dill
8 small new potatoes (12 ounces), scrubbed
12 ounces fresh asparagus, ends trimmed
1 tablespoon lemon juice

1. In a medium-size bowl, mix the flour, salt, and paprika. Coat the chicken with the flour, shaking off the excess. Reserve the flour mixture.

2. In a large, deep nonstick skillet, heat the oil over medium-high heat. Add the chicken, meaty side down, and cook for 1½ minutes on each side, or until well browned. Remove to a plate with a slotted spoon.

3. Pour the broth into the flour mixture remaining in the bowl and whisk until smooth.

4. Drain the fat from the skillet and wipe it clean with paper towels. Add the chicken broth mixture and 2 tablespoons of the dill. Stir to mix. Add the chicken, meaty side up, and the potatoes. Bring the mixture to a boil over high heat. Reduce the heat to low. Cover and simmer for 10 minutes.

5. Lay the asparagus over the top. Cover and simmer for 15 to 20 minutes more, or until the chicken and vegetables are tender.

6. Remove the pan from the heat. Stir in the lemon juice and the remaining 2 tablespoons of dill.

Per serving: 327 cal, 39 g pro, 26 g car, 7 g fat, 86 mg chol, 1,156 mg sod

HUNGARIAN PAPRIKA CHICKEN

Serves 4

Preparation time: 10 minutes

Cooking time: 50 minutes

Paprika is a brilliant red powder prepared from any of several different varieties of chile peppers. The flesh of ripe chiles is ground for sweet and mild paprika—for spicier versions the seeds are included.

1 tablespoon vegetable oil
1 medium-size onion, cut lengthwise into thin wedges
1 medium-size green bell pepper, seeded and cut in strips
2 teaspoons minced fresh garlic
1½ cups chicken broth
1 can (8 ounces) stewed tomatoes
2 tablespoons paprika (preferably Hungarian paprika)
¼ teaspoon salt
¼ teaspoon ground black pepper
4 whole chicken legs (about 1¾ pounds), skin removed
1 cup nonfat sour cream
2 tablespoons all-purpose flour

1. In a large skillet, heat the oil over medium-high heat. Add the onion, bell pepper, and garlic. Cook, stirring often, for 4 to 5 minutes, or until the onion is soft and the bell pepper is crisp-tender.

2. Stir in the broth, tomatoes, paprika, salt, and pepper. Bring to a gentle boil. Add the chicken legs in a single layer. Reduce the heat to low. Cover and simmer for 35 to 40 minutes, turning the chicken once, until the meat nearest the bone is opaque and the juices run clear when the meat is pierced with a sharp knife.

3. Meanwhile, in a small bowl, whisk the sour cream and flour until smooth. With a slotted spoon, remove the chicken to a serving platter. Increase the heat under the skillet to medium and whisk in the sour cream mixture. Simmer for 2 to 3 minutes, stirring often, until the sauce has thickened slightly. Spoon some of the sauce over the chicken. Serve the remaining sauce at the table.

Per serving: 280 cal, 30 g pro, 18 g car, 9 g fat, 91 mg chol, 795 mg sod

COOK'S TIP

Instead of 4 whole chicken legs, you can use 8 skinless chicken drumsticks, 8 skinless chicken thighs, or 4 skinless chicken breast halves.

SOUTHERN−FRIED DRUMSTICKS

Serves 4
Preparation time: 10 minutes plus at least 2 hours to marinate
Cooking time: 29 minutes

COOK'S TIP

Refrigerating fried chicken can make it soggy. Recrisp it by putting it, uncovered, in a hot oven.

Nothing can replace the simple goodness of old-fashioned homemade fried chicken. However, for the tenderest, most flavorful chicken, soak the pieces in buttermilk for a minimum of two hours and season them with plenty of salt and pepper. For a real southern-style meal, serve fried chicken with potatoes, black-eyed peas, and biscuits.

8 chicken drumsticks (about 1¾ pounds), skin removed
1 cup buttermilk
⅔ cup all-purpose flour
1¼ teaspoons salt
1 teaspoon onion powder
1 teaspoon paprika
¼ teaspoon ground black pepper
½ cup vegetable oil

1. In a large zipper-type food-storage bag, mix the drumsticks and buttermilk. Close the bag, pressing out the air, and turn to coat the chicken. Refrigerate for at least 2 hours or up to 8 hours, turning the bag occasionally.

2. In a large plastic or paper bag, mix the flour, salt, onion powder, paprika, and pepper.

3. Heat the oil over medium heat in a large nonstick skillet until very hot and rippling but not smoking.

4. Remove the drumsticks from the buttermilk, letting the excess drip off, and put into the bag with the seasoned flour. Shake vigorously to coat.

5. With tongs, carefully add the chicken to the hot oil. Cook, turning the drumsticks every 2 minutes, for about 6 minutes, or until golden brown.

6. Reduce the heat to medium-low. Partially cover and cook, turning the drumsticks occasionally, for 18 to 22 minutes, or until the meat is tender and opaque near the bone when tested with a sharp knife.

7. Remove the chicken to paper towels to drain. Serve right away.

Per serving: 337 cal, 28 g pro, 14 g car, 18 g fat, 97 mg chol, 682 mg sod

EASY • 60 MINUTES • LOW FAT • MAKE AHEAD

OVEN–FRIED CHICKEN

Serves 4
Preparation time: 15 minutes
Cooking time: 45 minutes

This is a healthier way to produce fried chicken that's moist inside and crisp outside. There is over 50 percent less fat and 100 fewer calories per serving than in flour-dipped chicken that is fried in vegetable shortening.

⅔ cup packaged plain bread crumbs
½ teaspoon celery salt
½ teaspoon onion powder
½ teaspoon paprika
½ teaspoon dried thyme leaves, crumbled
3 pounds broiler-fryer chicken pieces (thighs, drumsticks, breasts), skin and visible fat removed
3 tablespoons plain low-fat or nonfat yogurt

1. Heat the oven to 400° F. Place a wire rack, large enough to hold the chicken, in a baking dish or pan. (The dish may be lined with foil for easy cleanup.)

2. On a piece of waxed paper or in a shallow dish, mix the bread crumbs, celery salt, onion powder, paprika, and thyme.

3. Use your fingertips to coat the chicken with the yogurt. Press the chicken into the crumb mixture, patting the meat so the crumbs adhere. Place on the rack, leaving spaces between the pieces.

4. Bake for 45 minutes, or until the coating is lightly browned and the juices run clear when the meat is pierced with a sharp knife. Serve right away.

Per serving: 274 cal, 38 g pro, 14 g car, 6 g fat, 115 mg chol, 369 mg sod

MAKE AHEAD

Prepare the chicken through step 3, but place on a waxed paper-lined baking sheet instead of the rack. Freeze uncovered until firm. Pack airtight and freeze up to 3 months. Thaw in the refrigerator overnight.

HANDLING POULTRY

◆ Always wash your hands, knife, and cutting board thoroughly in hot soapy water after preparing raw poultry.

◆ Never use the same utensils and cutting board for other ingredients without thoroughly washing them first.

◆ Always marinate poultry in the refrigerator.

◆ Do not reuse the marinade for basting purposes.

◆ If the marinade is to be used as a basis of a sauce, bring to a boil and boil for 2 minutes.

◆ Do not place cooked poultry on the same plate used to transport the raw poultry.

CHICKEN & BOK CHOY STIR-FRY

Serves 4

Preparation time: 15 minutes

Cooking time: 10 minutes

Bok choy, also called Chinese cabbage, comes in a range of sizes, from small young plants with green stalks to large mature ones with thick white stalks. When stalks are white, halve them lengthwise, then cut in ½-inch-thick slices. Add the leaves after the stems have had a chance to cook a little.

8 ounces chicken tenderloins (tenders), white tendon
    cut out and tenderloins cut in half crosswise
⅓ cup bottled stir-fry sauce
1½ teaspoons minced fresh garlic
¼ teaspoon crushed hot red pepper flakes
1 pound bok choy, preferably small, separated into stalks
    and washed
1 large yellow or red bell pepper
1 bunch large scallions
3 ripe plum tomatoes
1 teaspoon sesame seeds
2 tablespoons vegetable oil

1. In a medium-size bowl, toss the chicken with 1 tablespoon of the stir-fry sauce, the garlic, and red pepper flakes until evenly coated. Let marinate at room temperature while preparing the vegetables.

2. Cut the bok choy crosswise into 1-inch pieces. Halve the bell pepper, remove the seeds and white ribs, then cut lengthwise into ½-inch-thick strips and halve the strips. Cut the scallions into 1-inch lengths. Cut the tomatoes into small chunks.

3. In a wok or large, deep skillet, cook the sesame seeds over medium-high heat, stirring constantly, for 1 to 2 minutes, or until lightly toasted. Remove to a paper towel.

4. In the same wok or skillet, heat the oil over medium-high heat until very hot and rippling but not smoking. Add the chicken and stir-fry for about 1½ minutes, or until lightly browned (insides will still be pink). Remove to a plate with a slotted spoon.

5. Add the bell pepper and stir-fry for 1 minute. Add the bok choy and stir-fry for about 3 minutes, or until the vegetables are crisp-tender. ▶

6. Add the scallions, tomato, remaining stir-fry sauce, and chicken. Stir-fry for about 2 minutes, or until the chicken is just cooked through.

7. Sprinkle with the sesame seeds and serve right away over rice.

Per serving: 193 cal, 17 g pro, 18 g car, 8 g fat, 33 mg chol, 595 mg sod

---

EASY • LOW FAT • ONE POT

BRAISED CHICKEN & CABBAGE

Serves 4

Preparation time: 15 minutes

Cooking time: 1 hour

A real dollar-saver, this homey chicken dish is also simple to prepare. Serve with mashed potatoes for a great week-night supper.

2 slices bacon, cut in small pieces
4 whole chicken legs (about 2¼ pounds), skin removed and separated
    into thighs and drumsticks (see Cook's Tip)
¼ cup water
1 envelope onion-mushroom soup mix (from a 1.8-ounce box of 2)
12 ounces green cabbage, shredded (4 cups)
2 medium-size carrots, chopped coarse
1 teaspoon dried thyme leaves, crumbled
1 can (16 ounces) black-eyed peas, drained and rinsed

1. In a 6-quart pot, cook the bacon over medium heat, stirring often, until crisp. Remove with a slotted spoon to paper towels, leaving the drippings in the skillet.

2. Add the chicken pieces to the pot and cook for 3 to 4 minutes on each side, until lightly browned.

3. Remove the chicken to a plate. Add the water to the pot and stir to scrape up the brown bits on the bottom. Stir in the soup mix, cabbage, carrots, thyme, and bacon.

4. Return the chicken to the pot. Reduce the heat to medium-low. Cover and cook, stirring occasionally, for 35 to 45 minutes, or until the vegetables are tender and the meat near the bone is opaque when tested with the tip of a sharp knife.

5. Stir in the black-eyed peas and cook just until heated through. Serve right away.

Per serving: 383 cal, 38 g pro, 28 g car, 13 g fat, 124 mg chol, 957 mg sod

COOK'S TIP

Buy whole chicken legs and cut the thigh from the drumstick yourself. To separate leg and thigh, wiggle drumstick to feel where it joins the thigh. Grasp the drumstick and use a small sharp paring knife to cut through the ball joint. To remove chicken skin: Grip the chicken meat with a paper towel; then, using another paper towel, pull off skin. Snip off visible fat with kitchen scissors.

60 MINUTES • LOW FAT

ITALIAN TOMATO-HERB CHICKEN

Serves 4
Preparation time: 20 minutes
Cooking time: 25 minutes

Although dried basil is fine for the coating, use fresh basil for the sauce if you can. The flavor is wonderful and gives an authentic touch to the dish.

HERB COATING

2 tablespoons packaged plain bread crumbs
1 teaspoon grated Parmesan cheese
¼ teaspoon dried basil leaves, crumbled
⅛ teaspoon dried oregano leaves, crumbled

4 skinless, boneless chicken breast halves (about 1 pound)
2 tablespoons olive oil
1 medium-size yellow or red bell pepper, seeded and cut into thin strips
¼ cup chopped fresh basil, or ½ teaspoon dried basil leaves, crumbled
1 tablespoon chopped fresh oregano, or ¼ teaspoon dried oregano
    leaves, crumbled
1 teaspoon minced fresh garlic
½ teaspoon salt
1 can (16 ounces) crushed tomatoes
2 tablespoons grated Parmesan cheese

1. On a sheet of waxed paper or in a shallow dish, mix the coating ingredients. Coat each breast half with the mixture, patting the meat so the crumbs adhere.

2. In a large skillet, heat the oil over medium-high heat. Add the chicken and cook for about 3 minutes on each side, or until golden.

3. Remove the chicken to a plate. Add the bell pepper, and the basil and oregano (if using dried), to the skillet. Cook for 2 to 3 minutes, stirring often, or until the pepper is beginning to soften. Stir in the garlic, salt, and tomatoes.

4. Return the chicken to the skillet. Reduce the heat to medium-low. Cover and cook for 10 to 15 minutes, stirring occasionally, or until the chicken is no longer pink in the center.

5. Stir in the basil and oregano (if using fresh), along with the Parmesan cheese. Serve right away.

Per serving: 241 cal, 29 g pro, 9 g car, 10 g fat, 68 mg chol, 616 mg sod

EASY • 30 MINUTES • MICROWAVE • LOW FAT

CHICKEN PARMESAN

Serves 4

Preparation time: 10 minutes

Cooking time: 15 minutes plus 5 minutes to stand

This dish, when made traditionally, requires several steps and really heats up the kitchen. The chicken is pan-fried, then baked, but using a microwave cuts the cooking time to 20 minutes and the kitchen and you stay cool. Serve this dish with pasta, a green salad, and Italian bread.

COATING

⅓ cup cornflake crumbs

3 tablespoons grated Parmesan cheese

1 tablespoon finely chopped fresh parsley

½ teaspoon dried Italian herb seasoning

4 bone-in chicken breast halves (about 1½ pounds), skin removed

1 can (14½ ounces) diced tomatoes in olive oil, garlic and spices, or plain chopped tomatoes

½ cup shredded mozzarella cheese

1. On a sheet of waxed paper or in a shallow dish, mix all the coating ingredients until well blended. Coat each breast with the mixture, patting the meat so the crumbs adhere.

2. In an 11 x 7-inch microwave-safe baking dish, arrange the breasts, meaty side up, in a single layer with the thicker parts toward the outside edges. Cover loosely with waxed paper and microwave on Medium High for 7 minutes, rotating the dish ¼ turn twice, until the outer edges of chicken have started to turn opaque.

3. Keeping the meaty sides up, turn each piece of chicken so the thinner parts are near the outside edges of the dish. Cover loosely and microwave on Medium High for 4 minutes longer.

4. Pour the tomato mixture over and around the chicken. Cover loosely and microwave on High for 3 to 4 minutes, or until the sauce is hot and the chicken is barely opaque near the bone when tested with a sharp knife.

5. Sprinkle with the cheese. Cover and let stand for 5 minutes, or until the meat near the bone is opaque and the cheese has melted. Serve right away.

Per serving with tomatoes in oil: 257 cal, 32 g pro, 15 g car, 7 g fat, 79 mg chol, 764 mg sod.

With plain tomatoes: 238 cal, 32 g pro, 13 g car, 6 g fat, 79 mg chol, 482 mg sod

---

DON'T FORGET STANDING TIME

When you remove food from a microwave oven it's still cooking, and it continues to do so as it sits. That's why standing time—the period after you take the food from the oven—is as important as the in-oven cooking. (If you cook food to perfection, it may be overcooked by the time you eat it.)

EASY • 60 MINUTES • LOW FAT • ONE POT

TUSCAN CHICKEN & WHITE BEANS

Serves 4

Preparation time: 15 minutes

Cooking time: 30 minutes

This is one of those traditional supper dishes that you will cook time and time again. You can substitute different beans such as navy, borlotti, or whatever takes your fancy. And any leftover sauce and beans can be turned into a hearty soup. Serve with Italian bread and a tossed green salad.

2 teaspoons olive oil

1 medium-size onion, sliced thin (1½ cups)

1 tablespoon minced fresh garlic

1 cup chicken broth

8 medium-size carrots (about 1 pound), cut into 1-inch chunks

2 cans (16 ounces each) white kidney beans (cannellini), drained and rinsed

1 teaspoon dried thyme leaves, crumbled

1 teaspoon dried sage leaves, crumbled

1 teaspoon salt

½ teaspoon ground black pepper

4 chicken thighs (about 1⅓ pounds), skin and visible fat removed

1½ cups loosely packed fresh parsley, minced

1. In a large nonstick skillet, heat the oil over medium-high heat. Add the onion and garlic and cook, stirring often, for 3 to 5 minutes or until the onion is soft.

2. Stir in the broth, carrots, beans, thyme, sage, salt, and pepper.

3. Arrange the chicken on top of the bean mixture. Cover and simmer for 10 minutes. Turn the thighs over and simmer uncovered for 10 to 15 minutes, stirring 2 or 3 times, until the chicken is opaque near the bone, the carrots are tender, and some beans have broken up and thickened the stew. Remove the skillet from the heat and stir in the parsley. Serve right away.

Per serving: 377 cal, 32 g pro, 45 g car, 8 g fat, 72 mg chol, 1,209 mg sod.

EASY • 60 MINUTES • LOW FAT • ONE POT

MEXICAN CHICKEN PICANTE

Serves 4

Preparation time: 15 minutes

Cooking time: 32 minutes

This chicken dish is rich with the pungent flavors of cumin and allspice, tangy vinegar, and the earthy flavor of oregano. Serve it hot or cold with warm flour tortillas.

½ cup cider vinegar

⅓ cup water

2 teaspoons minced fresh garlic

1 teaspoon dried oregano leaves, crumbled

½ teaspoon ground allspice

½ teaspoon ground cumin

2 medium-size red onions, sliced thin and separated into rings

⅓ cup all-purpose flour

1 teaspoon salt

½ teaspoon ground red pepper (cayenne)

1 quartered 3-pound broiler-fryer chicken (remove wings for
  another use), skin removed

2 tablespoons olive oil

1 can (4 ounces) chopped green chiles

½ cup loosely packed fresh cilantro leaves, chopped

1. In a large bowl, mix the vinegar, water, garlic, oregano, allspice, and cumin. Add the onion rings, tossing to coat. Let marinate at room temperature while preparing the chicken.

2. Mix the flour, salt, and red pepper in a large plastic food-storage bag. Put the leg quarters into the bag and shake until well coated.

3. In a large, preferably nonstick skillet, heat the oil over medium-low heat. Add the leg quarters. Cook for 7 to 9 minutes, or until well browned on one side. Meanwhile coat the breast sections with the flour mixture.

4. Turn the legs over and add the breasts, skin side down, to the skillet. Cook for 8 minutes longer, or until browned. Turn the breasts and legs over.

5. Drain the fat from the skillet. Pour the vinegar mixture from the onions into the skillet (reserve the onions). Spoon the green chiles around the chicken pieces. Bring the mixture to a boil over medium-high heat. Reduce the heat to low. Cover and simmer for 15 to 20 minutes, or until the chicken is opaque near the bone and the juices run clear when the meat is

pierced with a sharp knife.

6. Remove the chicken to a serving platter with a slotted spoon and cover loosely with foil to keep warm.

7. Add the reserved onions to the sauce. Increase the heat to medium-high. Cook uncovered, stirring often, for 3 to 5 minutes, or until the onions are crisp-tender.

8. Remove the skillet from the heat. Stir in the cilantro, then pour the sauce over the chicken. Serve right away.

Per serving: 344 cal, 38 g pro, 20 g car, 12 g fat, 114 mg chol, 860 mg sod

---

60 MINUTES • MAKE AHEAD

CHICKEN ENCHILADAS

Serves 8

Preparation time: 25 minutes

Cooking time: 20 minutes

This Mexican specialty is made by rolling soft corn tortillas around a sumptuous chicken filling, then topping with cheese and mildly spicy enchilada sauce. Look for canned enchilada sauce in the Mexican section of your market.

16 corn tortillas, stacked and wrapped in foil
1 medium-size onion, chopped (1 cup)
1 tablespoon vegetable oil
1 teaspoon chili powder
1 teaspoon garlic powder
1 teaspoon ground cumin
1 package (8 ounces) light cream cheese
6 cups shredded cooked chicken (see Cook's Tip)
¾ cup bottled salsa
1½ cups Cheddar cheese, shredded (6 ounces)
¼ cup chopped black olives
2 cans (14 ounces each) enchilada sauce

1. Heat the oven to 350°F.

2. Put the wrapped tortillas in the oven and heat for 8 to 10 minutes. Turn the oven off and keep the tortillas in the oven until ready to use.

3. Meanwhile, in a large saucepan, heat the oil over medium-high heat. Add the onion and cook, stirring often, for 5 minutes, or until softened. Stir in the chili powder, garlic powder, and cumin. Add the cream cheese and cook over low heat, breaking up the cheese with a wooden spoon until ▶

COOK'S TIP

To get 6 cups of shredded cooked chicken, cook 6 pounds of cut-up broiler-fryer chicken or 2 large bone-in chicken breasts (about 1 ½ pounds each).

MAKE AHEAD

You can prepare the enchiladas ahead. After they have been filled, cover and refrigerate for up to 3 days. Bake for 30 to 35 minutes.

melted. Add the chicken and salsa. Cook over medium heat, stirring often for 2 to 3 minutes, or until heated through.

4. Remove the pan from the heat. Stir in 1 cup of the Cheddar cheese and the olives.

5. Remove the tortillas from the oven. Spread ¼ cup of enchilada sauce over the bottom of each of two 11 x 7 inch baking dishes.

6. Spoon ⅓ cup of the chicken mixture slightly below the center of each warm tortilla. Roll up from the bottom and arrange seam side down in the prepared dishes.

7. Top with the remaining enchilada sauce and sprinkle with the remaining cheese. Bake for 15 to 20 minutes, or until hot and bubbly. Serve right away.
Makes 16 enchiladas. Per 2 enchiladas: 536 cal, 42 g pro, 39 g car, 23 g fat, 129 mg chol, 1,669 mg sod

MARINADES

Few marinades actually tenderize meat, but they can impart wonderful flavors. When a marinade contains acids (such as citrus juice or vinegar), use only glass, stainless steel, ceramic, or heavy-duty plastic containers to mix and marinate. Also, 1-gallon-size plastic zipper-type bags can be used. Marinate chicken and turkey up to 30 minutes at room temperature, or from 6 to 12 hours in the refrigerator.

HERB-GARLIC MARINADE
Makes about 2 cups
Preparation time: 10 minutes

1 medium-size onion, coarsely
  chopped (1 cup)
⅔ cup red wine vinegar
6 to 8 cloves garlic, chopped
2 tablespoons Italian seasoning
1 teaspoon salt
1 teaspoon ground black pepper
⅔ cup olive oil

1. In a blender or food processor, combine all the ingredients except the olive oil and process until finely chopped. With the motor running, slowly add the oil through the feed tube until well blended.
2. Cover and refrigerate until ready to use.

TERIYAKI MARINADE
Makes about 1¾ cups
Preparation time: 10 minutes

1 cup reduced-sodium soy sauce
½ cup honey
¼ cup unsweetened pineapple
  juice or orange juice
1 tablespoon peeled minced fresh
  gingerroot
2 teaspoons minced fresh garlic

1. In a medium-size bowl, mix all the ingredients until well blended.
2. Cover and refrigerate until ready to use.

SOUTHWESTERN MARINADE
Makes about 1½ cups
Preparation time: 15 minutes

1 cup dark Mexican or other dark
  beer
4 teaspoons fresh lime juice
1 small onion, finely chopped
  (about ½ cup)
1 tablespoon minced fresh garlic
3 tablespoons chopped fresh
  cilantro
1 teaspoon crushed hot red
  pepper flakes
¼ teaspoon salt

1. In a medium-size bowl, mix all ingredients until well blended.
2. Cover and refrigerate until ready to use.

EASY • 60 MINUTES • LOW FAT • ONE POT

CIDER–BRAISED CHICKEN WITH APPLES

Serves 6
Preparation time: 10 minutes
Cooking time: 50 minutes

Sure, apples make for nutritious snacking and fabulous desserts, but there's more to them than that. This sublime dish combines chicken, cider, and apples with a delicious sauce. Serve with buttered egg noodles tossed with broccoli florets.

½ cup all-purpose flour
1 teaspoon salt
¼ teaspoon ground black pepper
6 bone-in chicken breast halves (about 2 pounds)
1½ tablespoons vegetable oil
1 medium-size onion, sliced
1 large carrot, scrubbed and sliced
1 large rib celery, sliced
⅔ cup apple cider or apple juice
½ cup chicken broth
1 teaspoon dried rosemary leaves, crumbled
1½ teaspoons minced fresh garlic
3 Braeburn, Winesap, or Empire apples (about 1¼ pounds)

1. In a large plastic food-storage bag, mix the flour, salt, and pepper. Add the chicken and shake to coat. Remove the chicken and shake off the excess flour. Reserve the flour mixture.

2. In a large, deep skillet, heat the oil over medium heat. Add the chicken, skin side down, and cook for about 3 minutes on each side, or until browned. Remove the chicken to a plate.

3. Add the onion, carrot, and celery to the drippings in the skillet. Cook for 3 to 4 minutes, stirring often. Sprinkle with 2 tablespoons of the reserved flour and cook for 3 minutes longer, stirring often.

4. Stir in the cider, broth, rosemary, and garlic. Return the chicken, skin side up, to the skillet. Bring to a boil over medium-high heat. Reduce the heat to low. Cover and simmer for 25 to 30 minutes, or until the chicken is opaque near the bone when tested with a sharp knife.

5. Meanwhile, quarter and core the apples. Cut into thin wedges.

6. With a slotted spoon, remove the chicken to a serving platter and ▶

cover loosely with foil to keep warm. Skim off and discard the fat from the liquid in the skillet. Put the liquid and vegetables into a blender or food processor and blend or process until smooth.

7. Pour the sauce back into the skillet. Add the apples. Cook over low heat for 5 to 7 minutes, or until the apples are tender.

8. With a slotted spoon, remove the apples to the serving platter. Serve right away; pass the sauce separately.

Per serving: 317 cal, 26 g pro, 29 g car, 10 g fat, 69 mg chol, 523 mg sod

---

EASY • LOW FAT • ONE POT • CLASSIC

CHICKEN & RED WINE STEW

Serves 4

Preparation time: 15 minutes

Cooking time: 1 hour and 15 minutes

Thyme is actually a member of the mint family. It's one of the hardier herbs and holds its flavor well when dried, so it is an excellent choice for recipes that are cooked for a long time. The red wine gives a truly authentic taste to this dish, but chicken broth can be used if preferred. All this dish needs is some French bread to round it out.

1 slice bacon, cut in small pieces
8 small chicken thighs (about 2¼ pounds), skin removed
2 cups dry red wine, preferably Burgundy
24 small white onions (8 ounces), peeled
2 medium-size carrots, cut into sticks
3 tablespoons all-purpose flour
1 cup beef broth
1 tablespoon tomato paste
1 teaspoon salt
1 teaspoon minced fresh garlic
½ teaspoon dried thyme leaves, crumbled
1 bay leaf (1½ inches), broken in half
8 ounces small mushrooms, trimmed and halved (about 2 cups)

1. In a large deep skillet, cook the bacon over medium heat until crisp. Remove with a slotted spoon to paper towels, leaving the drippings in the skillet.

2. Add the chicken and cook 5 to 6 minutes on each side, or until lightly browned. Remove the chicken to a plate.   ▶ *p.73*

COOK'S TIP

To clean mushrooms, use a soft brush or damp cloth to brush the dirt off. If very gritty, rinse under cold running water as quickly as possible so they don't soak up liquid.

THE VERSATILE APPLE
Apples make a great companion for chicken. They lend a sweet-tart flavor to this Cider-Braised Chicken (p.67), here accompanied with noodles.

CHICKEN VARIATIONS Bok Choy Stir-Fry (p.59), left, and Chicken with Barley (p.78), below, make for perfect dinners.

Work grains and vegetables into your chicken recipes to broaden the range of nutrients and stretch your food dollars.

SINGLE-POT SUPPER
With good old-fashioned Dilled Chicken Fricassee (p.55), your whole meal—except the dessert—can be cooked in one pan.

3. Pour ½ cup of the wine into the skillet. Cook for 1 to 2 minutes, scraping up the brown bits on the bottom of the pan.

4. Return the chicken to the skillet along with the onions and carrots. Cover and cook for 8 to 10 minutes, stirring occasionally, or until the vegetables begin to soften.

5. Sprinkle the flour over the chicken and vegetables, stirring until coated. Cover and cook for 3 to 4 minutes, stirring occasionally, to cook the flour.

6. Stir in the remaining wine and the broth. Add the bacon, tomato paste, salt, garlic, thyme, and bay leaf. Bring to a boil over medium-high heat. Reduce the heat to low. Cover and simmer for 25 to 30 minutes, stirring occasionally, until the vegetables are almost tender. Add the mushrooms, cover, and simmer for 5 to 7 minutes longer, or until the vegetables and chicken are tender.

7. Discard the bay leaf and serve warm.

Per serving: 295 cal, 33 g pro, 19 g car, 10 g fat, 124 mg chol, 1,183 mg sod

BASTING SAUCES

Basting sauces are brushed onto the poultry or meat while it is cooking. Here are two favorites:

ORANGE-CHILI BASTING SAUCE

Makes about 3 cups
Preparation time: 15 minutes
Cooking time: 30 minutes

¼ cup vegetable oil
½ cup minced red onion
2 teaspoons minced fresh garlic
2 tablespoons chili powder
1 tablespoon dry mustard
1 teaspoon dried rosemary leaves
1 teaspoon ground dry ginger
1 teaspoon curry powder
½ teaspoon ground black pepper
2 cups tomato ketchup
Grated peel and juice of 1 orange
¼ cup packed dark brown sugar
2 tablespoons Worcestershire sauce
2 tablespoons soy sauce

1. In a medium-size saucepan, heat the oil over low heat. Stir in the onion, garlic, chili powder, mustard,

rosemary, ginger, curry powder, and pepper. Cover and cook for 10 minutes, stirring occasionally.

2. Stir in the remaining ingredients. Cover and cook for 20 minutes, or until thickened slightly. Remove the pan from the heat and use right away or let cool completely and refrigerate in an airtight container up to 2 weeks.

YANKEE BASTING SAUCE

Makes about 1½ cups
Preparation time: 10 minutes
Cooking time: 15 minutes

1 cup tomato sauce
⅓ cup minced onion
¼ cup packed dark brown sugar
¼ cup cider vinegar
⅛ teaspoon ground black pepper
½ teaspoon ground allspice

1. In a small saucepan, mix all the ingredients until well blended.

2. Bring to a boil over medium heat, stirring occasionally. Reduce the heat to low and simmer for 10 minutes, stirring occasionally. Remove the pan from the heat and use right away or let cool completely and refrigerate in an airtight container up to 2 weeks.

COOK'S TIP: If doubling or tripling recipe, simmer for 20 minutes.

STEWED CHICKEN WITH RICE & GREENS

Serves 4

Preparation time: 15 minutes

Cooking time: 1 hour

For this recipe, use whichever greens strike your fancy. Kale, collard, or turnip greens are all tasty and nutritious, and buying them frozen cuts out the washing, trimming, and chopping chore. Basmati or Texmati rice has a sweet, nutty flavor and smell. Look for it alongside regular rice in your market. Serve this Southern-inspired dish with warm buttermilk biscuits for a satisfying one-pot meal.

2 tablespoons olive oil

4 skinless, boneless chicken thighs (about 1¼ pounds),
   visible fat removed, and cut into 1½-inch pieces

1 large onion, chopped coarse (1½ cups)

2 teaspoons minced fresh garlic

1½ cups brown long-grain basmati or Texmati rice

1 teaspoon poultry seasoning (See Cook's Tip)

1 teaspoon salt

½ teaspoon ground red pepper (cayenne)

3 cups chicken broth

1 cup water

2 packages (10 ounces each) frozen chopped greens,
   thawed and drained

4 medium-size carrots, quartered lengthwise then cut crosswise
   into 2-inch pieces

1. In a 5-quart pot, heat the oil over medium-high heat. Add the chicken and cook for 1 to 2 minutes on each side, or until no longer pink on the outside. Remove with a slotted spoon to a plate.

2. Add the onion and garlic to the pot. Cook, stirring often, for 3 to 4 minutes, or until the onion is beginning to soften.

3. Stir in the rice, poultry seasoning, salt, red pepper, broth, and water. Bring to a boil. Reduce the heat to low. Cover and simmer for 35 minutes.

4. Return the chicken to the pot and stir in the mustard greens and carrots. Cover and simmer for 15 minutes longer, or until the rice is tender and the chicken is no longer pink in the center. Serve right away.

Per serving: 594 cal, 40 g pro, 72 g car, 16 g fat, 118 mg chol, 1,495 mg sod

COOK'S TIP

Poultry seasoning is a powdered spice blend that usually includes rosemary, oregano, sage, celery seed, marjoram, thyme, and black pepper. It can be used to season chicken, turkey, veal, pork, stuffings, or biscuits.

EASY • 60 MINUTES • LOW FAT • ONE POT

MOROCCAN CHICKEN STEW

Serves 4
Preparation time: 20 minutes
Cooking time: 35 minutes

COOK'S TIP

If you have leftover tomato paste from a can, scoop it by tablespoonfuls onto a waxed paper-lined baking sheet. Freeze uncovered until firm. Pack in a plastic freezer bag and freeze up to 6 months. You can add frozen tomato paste to soups, stews, or sauces, or thaw quickly in the microwave.

This chicken stew has an exotic, complex flavor. In fact, the sweet and spicy spices that make this dish traditional are probably sitting in your pantry right now. It's best to serve the stew over couscous or rice, or with toasted whole wheat pita bread, to soak up all the juices.

2 cups chicken broth
¼ cup tomato paste
1 teaspoon ground cumin
1 teaspoon salt
¼ teaspoon ground red pepper (cayenne)
⅛ teaspoon ground cinnamon
½ cup dark raisins
1 medium-size onion, sliced thin
1 tablespoon minced fresh garlic
2 pounds butternut squash, peeled, seeded, and cut into 1½-inch
   chunks (5 cups)
2 cups frozen green peas
1 can (16 ounces) chick-peas, drained and rinsed
4 chicken thighs (about 1 ⅓ pounds), skin and visible
   fat removed

1. In a 4- to 5-quart pot, whisk together the chicken broth, tomato paste, cumin, salt, red pepper, and cinnamon until blended.
2. Stir in the raisins, onion, garlic, squash, peas, chick-peas, and chicken. Bring to a gentle boil over medium-high heat.
3. Reduce the heat to low. Cover and simmer for 25 to 30 minutes, or until the squash is tender and the chicken is opaque near the bone and the juices run clear when the meat is pierced with a sharp knife.
Per serving: 426 cal, 30 g pro, 66 g car, 7 g fat, 72 mg chol, 1,472 mg sod

CHICKEN VINDALOO

Serves 4

Preparation time: 15 minutes plus at least 2 hours to marinate
Cooking time: 1 hour

Direct from India and laced with a Portuguese influence comes this very spicy dish. It gets much of its fire from the jalapeños, so if you've got a tenderfoot palate, reduce the amount.

⅓ cup cider vinegar
2 tablespoons light molasses
4 medium-size jalapeño peppers, seeded and minced
2 tablespoons curry powder
1 teaspoon minced fresh garlic
1 (3- to 3½-pound) broiler-fryer chicken, cut in 8 pieces, skin removed
8 small red-skinned new potatoes (about 1 pound), halved
2 tablespoons vegetable oil
2 cups chopped onions
½ teaspoon crushed hot red pepper flakes
2 medium-size ripe tomatoes, peeled and chopped
2 cups frozen green peas

1. In a medium-size shallow baking dish or a 1-gallon-size plastic zipper-type bag, mix the vinegar, molasses, jalapeños, curry powder, and garlic. Add the chicken. Close the bag, pressing out the air, and turn to coat. Refrigerate for at least 2 hours or up to 24 hours, turning once or twice.

2. In a medium-size saucepan, cook the potatoes in boiling water to cover for 12 to 15 minutes, or until tender. Drain.

3. In a large skillet or 4-quart pot, heat the oil over medium heat. Add the onions and red pepper flakes and cook, stirring often, for 5 to 6 minutes until onions are soft.

4. Stir in the tomatoes and cook, stirring often, for 4 to 5 minutes until the tomatoes are very soft.

5. Add the chicken with the marinade. Increase the heat to medium-high. Cook for about 8 minutes, stirring occasionally, until the sauce is as thick as applesauce.

6. Reduce the heat to medium-low. Cover and simmer for about 10 minutes. Stir in the potatoes and peas. Cover and simmer for 5 to 8 minutes, or until the chicken is opaque near the bone when tested with a sharp knife.

Per serving: 526 cal, 49 g pro, 52 g car, 14 g fat, 133 mg chol, 251 mg sod

SOME LIKE IT HOT

Strange as it sounds, spicy foods are commonplace in countries where temperatures soar. As cooks from Mexico to Morocco know, the trick is to balance the heat with other flavors. Try a sprinkling of chopped fresh cilantro over Mexican dishes, especially those that get their oomph from chile peppers or cumin. Or add a squeeze of fresh lemon or lime juice.

For Indian dishes spiced with curry powder, sprinkle on a little chopped fresh mint.

If you do eat something that's just too hot to handle, don't reach for water or beer to cool the fire in your mouth. Neither one dilutes

60 MINUTES • MICROWAVE • LOW FAT

SINGAPORE CHICKEN

Serves 4

Preparation time: 10 minutes

Cooking time: 18 minutes plus 5 minutes to stand

Serve this mildly spiced curry over rice with small bowls of mango chutney, raisins, and almonds as accompaniments.

1 tablespoon olive
4 teaspoons curry powder
1 large onion, sliced (2 cups)
1 pound chicken breast cutlets, trimmed of visible fat and cut into
   3 x 1-inch strips
1 can (8 ounces) pineapple chunks in juice, drained and juice reserved
1 tablespoon cornstarch
1 cup fresh or canned mung bean sprouts, rinsed and drained
2 tablespoons reduced-sodium soy sauce

1. In a deep 3-quart microwave-safe casserole, mix the oil and 3 teaspoons of the curry powder. Microwave on High for 1 minute.

2. Stir in the onion. Cover with a lid or vented plastic wrap and microwave on High for 6 to 9 minutes, stirring twice, until tender.

3. Stir in the chicken. Cover and microwave on High for 3 to 4 minutes, stirring once, until the outside of the chicken is opaque.

4. Meanwhile, in a small bowl, mix the reserved pineapple juice and cornstarch until smooth. Stir into the chicken mixture.

5. Cover and microwave on High for 1 to 1½ minutes, stirring once, until the sauce is slightly thickened.

6. Stir in the pineapple chunks, bean sprouts, soy sauce, and the remaining 1 teaspoon of curry powder. Cover and microwave on High for 2 minutes, stirring once, until heated through.

7. Remove from the microwave and let stand covered for 5 minutes to complete cooking before serving.

Per serving: 246 cal, 29 g pro, 21 g car, 5 g fat, 66 mg chol, 380 mg sod

ROASTED CHICKEN WITH BARLEY

Serves 4
Preparation time: 18 minutes
Cooking time: 1 hour plus 5 minutes to stand

Baking the barley in the oven while the chicken roasts helps keep the grains separate so they become fluffy. Whether or not you eat the chicken skin (where much of the fat is) is up to you.

1 (3-pound) whole broiler-fryer chicken, giblets and excess fat removed
½ teaspoon garlic powder
¼ teaspoon paprika
¼ teaspoon rosemary leaves, crumbled
¼ teaspoon dried sage leaves, crumbled
¼ teaspoon dried thyme leaves, crumbled
¼ teaspoon salt
¼ teaspoon ground red pepper (cayenne)
4 teaspoons olive oil
1 cup medium pearl barley, rinsed
½ cup chopped onion
3 cups chicken broth
2 tablespoons chopped fresh dill
For garnish: cherry tomatoes and fresh dill sprigs (optional)

1. Heat the oven to 400°F. Rinse the chicken and pat dry with paper towels.

2. In a small bowl, mix the garlic powder, paprika, rosemary, sage, thyme, salt, and red pepper. Rub the mixture all over the chicken.

3. Tie the chicken legs together with kitchen string. Tuck the wing tips under the back.

4. Coat the bottom of a large ovenproof skillet or small shallow roasting pan with 1 teaspoon of the oil. Add the chicken, breast side down. Roast for 20 minutes.

5. Meanwhile, in a 1½- to 2-quart Dutch oven, heat the remaining 3 teaspoons oil over medium heat. Stir in the barley and onion. Cook, stirring occasionally, for 5 minutes, or until the barley is lightly browned. Add the broth and dill, bring to a boil, and cover.

6. Insert a long-handled wooden spoon into the body cavity of the chicken and gently turn it breast side up (if the skin sticks, loosen with a metal spatula). Place the pot containing the barley in the oven next to the chicken.

Bake both for 40 minutes, or until the drumsticks move easily, the juices run clear when a thigh is pierced with a sharp knife, and the barley is tender.

7. Transfer the chicken to a serving platter. Let stand for 5 minutes. Fluff the barley with a fork.

8. Spoon the barley around the chicken and garnish with halved cherry tomatoes and dill sprigs. Serve right away.

Per serving with skin: 580 cal, 48 g pro, 41 g car, 26 g fat, 132 mg chol, 1,014 mg sod.
Without skin: 389 cal, 33 g pro, 41 g car, 10 g fat, 85 mg chol, 985 mg sod

---

VARIATION

BEIJING CHICKEN

• Brush the chicken with ⅓ cup hoisin sauce and bake at 425°F in the foil-lined pan for 15 minutes.
• Stack twelve 6-inch flour tortillas and wrap in aluminum foil. Place beside the chicken and bake for 10 minutes.
• Cut the chicken from the bones or pull the meat off with 2 forks. Spoon extra hoisin sauce on the warm tortillas, sprinkle each with about 2 teaspoons finely chopped scallions, and top with shredded chicken. Roll tortilla around filling.

Per serving with skin: 680 cal, 49 g pro, 46 g car, 30 g fat, 136 mg chol, 839 mg sod. Without skin: 529 cal, 46 g pro, 46 g car, 15 g fat, 122 mg chol, 826 mg sod

• EASY •30 MINUTES

EASY • 30 MINUTES

BUFFALO CHICKEN PLATTER

Serves 4
Preparation time: 20 minutes
Baking time: 10 minutes

This easy recipe starts with a fully cooked oven-roasted chicken that you can purchase from your market's meat case or deli counter, or from a take-out store. It's the perfect dish for impromptu gatherings.

1 fully cooked, oven-roasted chicken (about 2½ pounds), cut into 10 pieces (2 drumsticks, thighs, and wings; each breast cut in half)
1 to 2 tablespoons hot-pepper sauce
1 small loaf French bread (12 inches), cut into 16 slices
3 tablespoons bottled blue-cheese dressing
2 large carrots, cut into sticks
3 large ribs celery, cut into sticks

1. Heat the oven to 500°F. Line a broiler-pan rack (or a shallow pan large enough to hold the chicken and bread in a single layer) with foil for easy cleanup.

2. Brush the chicken with hot-pepper sauce and arrange on lined rack. Brush one side of the bread slices with blue-cheese dressing and arrange on the pan.

3. Bake for 7 to 10 minutes, or until the chicken is hot and the bread is golden and crisp.

4. Arrange the chicken, bread, carrots, and celery sticks on a serving platter. Serve right away.

Per serving with skin: 762 cal, 56 g pro, 51 g car, 35 g fat, 153 mg chol, 986 mg sod.
Without skin: 611 cal, 53 g pro, 51 g car, 20 g fat, 139 mg chol, 973 mg sod

MEDITERRANEAN CHICKEN BAKE

Serves 4 to 6 with leftovers
Preparation time: 15 minutes
Cooking time: 1 hour 45 minutes

If the addition of prunes and olives raises your eyebrows, rest assured they taste wonderful when cooked with chicken. The olives add a piquant saltiness and the prunes a sweet, dark richness.

4 teaspoons olive oil
1 tablespoon minced fresh garlic
1 tablespoon dried oregano leaves, crumbled
1 teaspoon salt
½ teaspoon ground black pepper
1 (5- to 5¼-pound) roasting chicken, giblets and excess fat removed
1¼ cups chicken broth
½ cup red wine vinegar
½ cup pimiento-stuffed Spanish olives
⅓ cup packed light brown sugar
1 pound red-skinned potatoes, quartered if large
1 cup pitted prunes (7 ounces)
For garnish: chopped fresh parsley (optional)

1. Heat the oven to 400° F. Grease a deep, lidded roasting pan or an oval 8-quart Dutch oven with 1 teaspoon of oil. Rinse the chicken and pat dry.

2. In a small bowl, mix the garlic, oregano, remaining 3 teaspoons of oil, salt, and pepper. Rub the mixture all over the chicken.

3. Tie the chicken legs together with kitchen string. Tuck the wing tips under the back. Put the chicken into the pan and add the broth, vinegar, and olives. Sprinkle with the brown sugar.

4. Cover and bake for 1 hour, then scatter the potatoes and prunes around the chicken.

5. Cover and bake for 30 to 45 minutes longer, stirring the potatoes once, until the drumsticks move easily, the juices run clear when a thigh is pierced with a sharp knife, and the potatoes are tender.

6. With a slotted spoon or spoons remove the chicken, potatoes, prunes, and olives to a deep serving platter. Pour the liquid left in the pan into a 4-cup measure. Skim off and discard the fat. Serve the juices with the chicken.

Per serving: 854 cal, 61 g pro, 58 g car, 42 g fat, 187 mg chol, 1,207 mg sod

OLIVE PRIMER

The olive is the small pitted fruit of the hardy olive tree, native to the Mediterranean region. There are dozens of varieties ranging in size, shape, and flavor. Whether an olive is green or black depends on whether it was harvested ripe (black) or unripened (green). When first picked, olives have a bitter taste. A curing process removes the bitterness and produces their characteristic flavor and appearance. Unopened jars of olives can be stored in a cool dark place up to 1 year. Once opened, they need to be refrigerated and will keep up to 1 month.

CHICKEN IN THE MICROWAVE

Not only does it cook quickly, but chicken is also juicy and tender when cooked in the microwave. For successsful microwave cooking, follow these tips:

◆ Rearrange the chicken, moving the center pieces to the outside of the dish and the outside pieces to the center, and rotate the dish during cooking to promote even cooking.

◆ Cooking time guidelines for microwaving pieces of chicken:
2 pieces, 4 to 6 minutes on High (100% power), let stand 5 minutes
4 pieces, 6 to 10 minutes on High (100% power), let stand 5 minutes
6 pieces, 8 to 12 minutes on High (100% power), let stand for 5 minutes.

◆ Always check foods for doneness after the minimum cooking time given in a recipe. Some microwave cooked foods look as if they are not done, but remember they will continue to cook while they stand.

MAKE AHEAD • CLASSIC

STUFFED CORNISH GAME HENS

Serves 4

Preparation time: 1 hour

Cooking time: 1 hour plus 5 minutes to stand

Ⓜ AKE AHEAD

The stuffing can be prepared and refrigerated in an airtight container up to 2 days. Stuff the game hens just before roasting.

Try to find small game hens that weigh between 1 and 1¼ pounds each, as they are perfect for one serving. The hens have a delicate flavor which is complemented by the earthy-flavored shiitake mushroom and wild rice stuffing. These mushrooms have meaty brown caps and thin tough stems.

MUSHROOM–SPINACH STUFFING
1 tablespoon olive oil
1 cup chopped onion
1 teaspoon minced fresh garlic
4 ounces shiitake mushrooms, stems removed, sliced (1½ cups)
½ cup chopped Canadian bacon (3 ounces)
¼ cup uncooked brown long-grain rice
¼ cup uncooked wild rice
1 cup chicken broth
2 packages (10 ounces each) frozen chopped spinach, thawed and squeezed dry
2 tablespoons toasted slivered almonds (optional)
¼ teaspoon salt
¼ teaspoon ground black pepper

4 Cornish game hens (1 to 1¼ pounds each) ▶

1. Heat the oven to 400°F.

2. Make the stuffing: In a medium-size saucepan, heat the oil over medium heat. Add the onion and garlic and cook for about 5 minutes, stirring often, until the onion is soft. Add the mushrooms and bacon and cook, stirring often, for 3 to 4 minutes, until the mushrooms are wilted. Add the brown rice and wild rice. Stir to coat with the oil. Add the broth. Bring the mixture to a boil over high heat. Reduce the heat to low. Cover and simmer for 45 minutes, or until the rice is tender.

3. Remove the pan from the heat and stir in the spinach, almonds, salt, and pepper.

4. Rinse the game hens and pat dry with paper towels.

5. Pack each body cavity with about ¾ cup of the stuffing mixture. Place, breast side up, on a rack in a roasting pan.

6. Roast uncovered for 45 to 55 minutes, until the juices run clear when pierced with a sharp knife and the skin is crisp and golden, or a meat thermometer registers 170°F when inserted into the thigh joint. Remove the pan from the oven and let stand for 5 minutes before serving.

Per serving: 864 cal, 87 g pro, 28 g car, 44 g fat, 252 mg chol, 1,019 mg sod

QUICK FIXES FOR CORNISH GAME HENS

Here are seven ways to quickly enhance Cornish game hens (or roast chicken). Start with four hens weighing 1 to 1¼ pounds each and a quick fix of your choice. Roast the hens at 375°F for about 1 hour, or until the juices run clear when a thigh is pierced with a knife and a meat thermometer registers 170°F.

◆ Citrus Glaze—Mix ¼ cup thawed, frozen orange juice concentrate, 2 tablespoons Dijon mustard, and 2 tablespoons honey until well blended. Brush the glaze over the hens during the last 15 to 20 minutes of roasting.

◆ Asian Accent—Mix 2 tablespoons soy sauce, 2 tablespoons chicken broth, and 1 teaspoon sesame oil. Brush the mixture over the hens and pour a little into the cavities before roasting as directed.

◆ Apricot Glaze—In a small bowl, mix ½ cup apricot jam, 2 tablespoons soy sauce, 2 tablespoons Dijon mustard, and 2 tablespoons honey. Roast hens as directed. Brush the apricot glaze over the hens during the last 15 to 20 minutes of roasting.

◆ Mexican Spiced—Rub the outside of the hens with packaged taco seasoning and lightly spray with nonstick vegetable oil cooking spray. Roast as directed.

◆ Lemon-Basil—Rub the outside of the hens with a cut lemon and brush with melted butter. Place one lemon half and sprig of fresh basil into each cavity. Roast as directed.

◆ Mustard-Herb—Coat the outside of each hen with about 1 tablespoon of Dijon mustard. Sprinkle with a mixture of dried tarragon, basil, and thyme. Roast as directed. Deglaze the pan with ¾ cup white wine and serve with the pan juices.

◆ Garlic-Herb—Mix 2 tablespoons minced fresh garlic, 2 teaspoons finely chopped fresh thyme, 2 teaspoons finely chopped fresh rosemary, and 2 teaspoons finely chopped sage. Loosen the breast skin of each hen and rub one quarter of the mixture under the skin of each bird. Roast as directed.

EASY • 60 MINUTES • ONE POT

PROVENÇAL TURKEY PATTIES

Serves 4

Preparation time: 20 minutes

Cooking time: 30 minutes

The vegetable mixture in this recipe is a variation of ratatouille, a popular Mediterranean dish made of tomatoes, bell peppers, onions, and zucchini. You can use ground beef or lamb instead of the turkey.

TURKEY PATTIES

1 pound ground turkey

1 large egg

3 tablespoons packaged seasoned bread crumbs

1 teaspoon salt

¼ teaspoon dried thyme leaves, crumbled

⅛ teaspoon ground red pepper (cayenne)

1 tablespoon olive oil

1 medium-size onion, sliced thin and rings separated

1 can (14½ ounces) tomatoes

8 ounces zucchini, cut into ¼-inch-thick rounds

1 teaspoon minced fresh garlic

¼ teaspoon salt

¼ teaspoon thyme

1 can (about 16 ounces) small whole white potatoes, well drained

1 tablespoon minced fresh parsley (optional)

1. Make the patties: In a large bowl, mix the ground turkey, egg, bread crumbs, salt, thyme, and red pepper with your hands or a wooden spoon until well blended. Shape the mixture into 8 patties, about ¼ inch thick.

2. In a large heavy skillet, heat the oil over medium-high heat. Add the patties and cook for about 3 minutes on each side, or until browned. Remove with a slotted spoon to a plate.

3. Reduce the heat to medium. Add the onion to the pan drippings and cook, stirring occasionally, for 3 minutes, or until softened.

4. Add the tomatoes, zucchini, garlic, salt, and thyme. Stir to mix and break up the tomatoes. Cover and cook for 10 minutes, or until the zucchini is just tender.

5. Stir in the potatoes and parsley. Add the turkey patties and spoon ▶

over some of the vegetable mixture. Cover and simmer for 10 minutes, or until heated through. Serve right away.

Makes 8 patties. Per 2 patties: 323 cal, 25 g pro, 25 g car, 14 g fat, 136 mg chol, 1,127 mg sod

---

EASY • 30 MINUTES • ONE POT

PICADILLO POCKETS

Serves 4

Preparation time: 5 minutes

Cooking time: 22 minutes

This skillet meal is made with ground turkey, vegetables, and seasonings.

1 tablespoon olive oil

1 pound ground turkey

1½ teaspoons ground cumin

2 medium-size onions, halved and sliced thin (3 cups)

1 medium-size green bell pepper, chopped fine (1 cup)

1 teaspoon minced fresh garlic

¾ cup water

¼ cup tomato paste

⅓ cup golden raisins

¼ cup small pimiento-stuffed green olives

½ teaspoon salt

¼ teaspoon ground black pepper

4 (6-inch) pita pockets, plain or whole wheat

1. In a large skillet, heat ½ tablespoon of oil over high heat. Add the turkey and cumin and cook for 5 minutes, stirring often to break up the pieces, until the meat is no longer pink. Remove with a slotted spoon to a bowl.

2. Add the remaining ½ tablespoon of oil and the onions to the skillet. Cook for 4 minutes, stirring often, until the onions are softened. Add the bell pepper and garlic and cook for 3 minutes, stirring often, until crisp-tender.

3. Return the turkey to the skillet. Add the water, tomato paste, raisins, olives, salt, and pepper. Stir until boiling. Reduce the heat to medium-low and simmer uncovered for 8 minutes, or until slightly thickened.

4. Cut the pitas in half. Spoon about ½ cup of the picadillo mixture into each half. Serve right away.

Per serving: 475 cal, 29 g pro, 60 g car, 14 g fat with plain pita, 15 g fat with whole wheat pita, 83 mg chol, 1,042 mg sod with plain pita, 1061 mg sod with whole wheat pita

COOK'S TIP

Serve picadillo over cooked rice, spoon it into flour tortillas, or use the mixture to stuff bell pepper or baked acorn squash. It's also good served with wedges of corn bread.

EASY • 30 MINUTES

TURKEY BURGERS

Serves 4
Preparation time: 15 minutes
Cooking time: 8 minutes

Take a break from traditional burger cookery and use low-calorie ground turkey instead of beef. Top the burgers with ketchup, mustard, chili sauce, and/or pickles, and serve with a pasta salad.

1 large egg
2 teaspoons Worcestershire sauce
½ teaspoon minced fresh garlic
½ teaspoon prepared mustard
1 pound ground turkey
½ cup packaged seasoned bread crumbs
⅓ cup finely chopped onion
4 hamburger buns

1. Heat a gas grill to medium, prepare a charcoal fire, or heat the broiler.
2. In a large bowl, beat the egg, Worcestershire sauce, garlic, and mustard until blended. Mix in the turkey and bread crumbs. Shape the mixture into 4 patties, about ½ inch thick.
3. Place the patties on a lightly oiled grill rack or broiler-pan rack. Grill or broil 4 to 6 inches from the heat source for 3 to 4 minutes on each side, or until no longer pink in the center. Serve right away on hamburger buns.
Makes 4 burgers. Per burger: 366 cal, 27 g pro, 34 g car, 12 g fat, 136 mg chol, 797 mg sod

EASY • 60 MINUTES • MICROWAVE • LOW FAT

TURKEY–STUFFED PEPPERS

Serves 4
Preparation time: 15 minutes
Cooking time: 26 minutes

Here is a heathful rendition of a ground beef favorite, made in the microwave and perfect for the hot, lazy days of summer. Serve with stir-fried vegetables or a crisp salad and extra salsa on the side. ▶

SCANDINAVIAN TURKEY BURGERS

In a large bowl, mix 1 pound ground turkey with 1½ tablespoons prepared horseradish, 1½ tablespoons Dijon mustard, 1½ teaspoons paprika, ¼ teaspoon ground black pepper, and ⅛ teaspoon salt. Cook as directed and serve on toasted rye bread.

Per burger: 338 cal, 25 g pro, 32 g car, 11 g fat, 83 mg chol, 739 mg sod

• EASY •30 MINUTES

ITALIAN TURKEY BURGERS

In a large bowl, mix 1 pound ground turkey with 1 teaspoon minced fresh garlic, ½ teaspoon crumbled dried oregano leaves, ½ teaspoon salt, and ¼ teaspoon ground black pepper. After turning the burgers, top with a slice of mozzarella cheese. Serve on Italian bread with sliced tomato.

Per burger: 329 cal, 28 g pro, 17 g car, 16 g fat, 105 mg chol, 663 mg sod

• EASY •30 MINUTES

4 medium-size bell peppers, stem ends sliced off and seeded
  (trim bottoms so they stand straight)
2 tablespoons water
12 ounces ground turkey
1 cup bottled salsa
1 can (8 ounces) no-salt-added tomato sauce
¾ cup uncooked 10-minute brown rice
2 teaspoons chili powder
½ teaspoon ground cumin
¼ teaspoon minced fresh garlic

1. Stand the peppers evenly spaced in a 9-inch microwave-safe pie dish. Add the water to the dish. Cover with waxed paper. Microwave on High for 6 to 8 minutes, or until crisp-tender.

2. Meanwhile, in a large bowl, mix the turkey, salsa, tomato sauce, rice, chili powder, cumin, and garlic until well blended.

3. Fill the peppers with the turkey mixture. Cover with waxed paper and microwave on High for 16 to 18 minutes, rotating the dish ¼ turn every 4 minutes, until a thermometer inserted in the center of the turkey mixture registers 160°F and the peppers are tender. Remove the peppers from the oven and let stand for 5 minutes to finish cooking. Serve right away.

Per serving: 253 cal, 18 g pro, 30 g car, 8 g fat, 62 mg chol, 755 mg sod

EASY

SPICY GRILLED TURKEY WINGS

Serves 4

Total time: 1 hour 20 minutes

Meaty turkey wings are delicious when basted with this sauce. When the turkey is cooked, the meat just under the skin may appear pink in color. This is not a sign of undercooked meat; it is caused by the smoke from the coals.

4 cups chicken broth
2 large or 4 small turkey wings (2½ to 3 pounds)

SPICY TOMATO SAUCE
½ cup olive oil
1 can (about 16 ounces) whole tomatoes, drained
½ cup chicken broth

GREAT GRILLING

◆ Oiling the grill rack will help to prevent skinless chicken or turkey from sticking.

◆ For chicken parts and similar cuts of turkey, use direct heat grilling. Place the meat on a lightly oiled grill rack directly over hot coals.

◆ For large cuts of turkey and whole chickens, use indirect heat grilling with coals banked up on the sides and a drip pan placed in the center, for slow even cooking.

◆ Useful grilling utensils include: a meat thermometer, long-handled tongs, oven mitts, basting brush, wide spatula for turning, and skewers.

¼ cup white wine vinegar
1 small onion, coarsely chopped (about ½ cup)
2 tablespoons Worcestershire sauce
2 tablespoons light or dark brown sugar
½ teaspoon curry powder
½ teaspoon chili powder
¼ teaspoon salt
Ground black pepper to taste

1. In a large saucepan, bring the 4 cups of chicken broth to a boil over high heat. Add the turkey wings. Reduce the heat to low and cook for 30 to 40 minutes, depending on the size of the wings.

2. Meanwhile, make the sauce. In a blender or food processor, combine the oil, tomatoes, chicken broth, vinegar, onion, Worcestershire sauce, sugar, curry powder, chili powder, salt, and pepper. Blend or process for 1 to 2 minutes, or until smooth.

3. Pour the mixture into a medium-size saucepan. Cook over medium heat, stirring occasionally, for 20 minutes, or until slightly thickened. Remove the pan from the heat.

4. Heat a gas grill to medium-high, prepare a charcoal fire, or heat a broiler. Remove the turkey wings from the broth and reserve the liquid for another use. Place the wings on the grill or broiler-pan rack and brush with the sauce. Grill or broil 4 to 6 inches from the heat source for 30 to 40 minutes, turning often and basting generously with the sauce, until the juices run clear when the meat is pierced with a knife.

5. Transfer the wings to a serving platter and serve right away with any remaining sauce.

Per serving with skin: 624 cal, 42 g pro, 16 g car, 43 g fat, 158 mg chol, 1,634 mg sod.
Without skin: 488 cal, 32 g pro, 16 g car, 33 g fat, 92 mg chol, 1,604 mg sod

EASY

TURKEY THIGHS WITH CRANBERRY COMPOTE

Serves 6 to 8
Preparation time: 10 minutes plus 30 minutes to marinate
Cooking time: 35 minutes

Serve this tasty turkey dish as an alternative to the whole roasted bird at the holidays. You won't have the luxury of the leftovers, but it will take a lot less preparation. The compote combines canned whole-berry cranberry ▶

sauce with fresh oranges, brown sugar, and vinegar. If you plan on serving the cranberry compote cold, increase the vinegar by 1 to 2 teaspoons.

4 large turkey thighs (about 4 pounds)
1 tablespoon olive oil
½ teaspoon salt
¼ teaspoon fresh ground black pepper
½ teaspoon fresh chopped rosemary, or
   ¼ teaspoon dried rosemary leaves, crumbled
For garnish: orange slices and sprigs of fresh rosemary (optional)

CRANBERRY COMPOTE

1 teaspoon olive oil
½ cup chopped onion
1 can (about 16 ounces) whole-berry cranberry sauce
½ teaspoon freshly grated orange peel
1 medium-size orange, peeled, sectioned, and chopped coarse
   (about ½ cup)
1 tablespoon light or dark brown sugar
1 tablespoon balsamic vinegar
½ teaspoon fresh chopped rosemary or ¼ teaspoon dried
   rosemary leaves, crumbled
½ teaspoon salt
¼ teaspoon ground black pepper

1. In a 1-gallon-size plastic zipper-type bag, combine the turkey thighs, olive oil, salt, pepper, and rosemary. Close the bag, pressing out the air, and turn to coat the turkey. Refrigerate for 30 minutes.

2. Meanwhile, make the compote. In a medium-size saucepan, heat the oil over medium heat. Add the onion and cook, stirring often, for 4 to 5 minutes, or until soft. Stir in the remaining ingredients and simmer gently for 10 minutes, stirring occasionally. Spoon the compote into a medium-size bowl and let cool to room temperature.

3. Heat a gas grill to medium-high, prepare a charcoal fire, or heat a broiler. Grill or broil the turkey thighs 4 to 6 inches from the heat source for about 20 minutes, turning 3 or 4 times during cooking, until crispy golden on the outside and cooked through.

4. Transfer the turkey to a serving platter and garnish with fresh orange slices and sprigs of rosemary. Serve with the compote.

Per serving: 447 cal, 37 g pro, 30 g car, 20 g fat, 138 mg chol, 469 mg sod

MARINATING BASICS

Always marinate foods in a plastic food storage bag or a glass, ceramic, or stainless steel container. Most marinades contain acidic ingredients such as lemon juice or vinegar, which can react with metal and impart an off-taste to foods. Also, be sure to turn the food often so it is evenly exposed to the marinade.

BARBEQUE
The flavor of grilled turkey is enhanced when marinated, as in Herbed Turkey Tenderloins (p.105) with fresh tomato relish.

The secret to achieving a truly international flavor when cooking chicken and turkey lies in the seasoning that is used.

CHICKEN GOES GLOBAL
Chicken is very responsive to herbs and spices, as Chicken Vindaloo (p.76), above, and Rosemary Garlic Chicken (p.50), right, so clearly demonstrate.

DOLLAR-SAVER
If you're looking for a nutritious, economical meal for your family, try this down-home Braised Chicken & Cabbage (p.60).

CHICKEN & TURKEY GRILLING CHART

Use this chart as a guideline for grilling times. The times may vary depending on the temperature of coals or the thickness of meat. Cook chicken and turkey until the meat is white throughout and the juices run clear when pierced with a sharp knife, or a meat thermometer registers 170°F for white meat and 180°F for dark meat. Mix and match the chicken and turkey cuts with any of the marinades on page 66 and/or basting sauces on page 73. Any combination will work—let your taste buds guide you.

CUT	GRILLING TIME
Boneless chicken breasts	10 to 15 minutes (direct heat)
Bone-in, cut-up chicken parts	
(breasts, thighs, drumsticks, whole legs)	30 to 40 minutes (direct heat)
Chicken quarters	40 to 45 minutes (direct heat)
Chicken wings	15 to 20 minutes (direct heat)
Turkey wings	50 to 60 minutes (indirect heat)
Turkey thigh	50 minutes to 1¼ hours (indirect heat)
Turkey breast tenderloins	15 to 20 minutes (direct)
Turkey breast steaks (¾ inch thick)	15 to 20 minutes (direct heat)
Boneless turkey roast	1 to 1½ hours (indirect heat)
Bone-in turkey breast half	1 to 1½ hours (indirect heat)
Bone-in whole turkey breast	2 to 2½ hours (indirect heat)

EASY • LOW FAT

GRILLED CURRIED TURKEY

Serves 4

Preparation time: 15 minutes plus at least 3 hours to marinate

Cooking time: 16 minutes

In this recipe, the tenderloins are marinated in a curry-yogurt mixture, which is then cooked and served as a delicately flavored sauce. Serve with rice and a crunchy cucumber and radish salad.

1 cup plain low-fat yogurt
2 teaspoons curry powder
2 tablespoons olive oil
¼ cup chicken broth
½ teaspoon salt
½ teaspoon ground black pepper
2 turkey tenderloins (8 to 10 ounces each), white tendons removed
2 teaspoons cornstarch

1. In a shallow glass baking dish, mix the yogurt, curry powder, oil, ▶

broth, salt, and pepper. Add the turkey, turning to coat. Cover with plastic wrap and refrigerate for at least 3 hours, turning the meat occasionally.

2. Heat a gas grill to medium-high, prepare a charcoal grill fire, or heat a broiler. Grill or broil the tenderloins 5 to 6 inches from the heat source for 9 to 10 minutes, or until lightly browned. Turn the tenderloins and cook for 5 to 6 minutes longer, or until lightly browned and opaque in the thickest part when tested with a sharp knife. Remove the tenderloins to a cutting board.

3. Meanwhile, pour the reserved marinade into a small saucepan. Stir in the cornstarch until well blended and bring to a boil over medium heat, stirring or whisking constantly. Boil for 2 minutes.

4. Thinly slice the tenderloins across the grain and serve with the sauce.
Per serving: 248 cal, 35 g pro, 6 g car, 9 g fat, 82 mg chol, 439 mg sod

EASY • MAKE AHEAD

SOUTHWEST TURKEY LOAF

Serves 6

Preparation time: 20 minutes

Cooking time: 50 minutes plus 5 minutes to stand

Here's a meatloaf that is sophisticated and down-home at the same time. It's also good cold, and can be sliced thin and served on Kaiser, or French bread rolls with chili sauce or salsa.

½ cup chili sauce
½ cup water
2 large eggs
1 tablespoon Worcestershire sauce
1 tablespoon Dijon mustard
1 tablespoon chili powder
1 teaspoon salt
¼ teaspoon ground black pepper
¾ cup quick-cooking oats
2 pounds ground turkey
½ cup finely chopped red bell pepper
¼ cup finely chopped scallions
1 cup frozen corn kernels

1. Heat the oven to 375°F. Lightly grease a roasting pan.

2. In a medium-size bowl, mix ¼ cup chili sauce, the water, eggs, Worcestershire sauce, mustard, chili powder, salt, and pepper until blended.

GRILLING SAFETY TIPS

◆ Do not use grill during high wind conditions.

◆ Position grill in an open area.

◆ Do not leave grill unattended.

◆ Do not add starter fluid to hot coals.

◆ Make sure grill vents are opened and free of ashes.

◆ To extinguish coals, close all vents and cover with lid. Check coals in a charcoal grill several hours later to make sure they are completely extinguished.

Stir in the oats. Let stand for 5 minutes.

3. Add the turkey, bell pepper, scallions, and frozen corn to the oat mixture. Mix lightly but not thoroughly.

4. In the prepared pan, shape the mixture into two 8 x 4 x 1½-inch loaves. Bake for 40 minutes.

5. Spread the remaining chili sauce over the loaves. Bake for 10 minutes longer, or until a meat thermometer inserted into the thickest part registers 165°F. Let stand for 5 minutes before slicing.

Per serving: 346 cal, 32 g pro, 20 g car, 15 g fat, 181 mg chol, 937 mg sod

EASY • 60 MINUTES • MICROWAVE • LOW FAT • ONE POT

BOMBAY TURKEY CASSEROLE

Serves 4

Cooking time: 50 minutes plus 5 minutes to stand

This is an easy microwave casserole seasoned with curry powder and ginger.

4 medium-size baking potatoes, scrubbed
3 tablespoons water
2 medium-size carrots
1 medium-size onion
⅔ cup water
¼ cup Zante currants
2 chicken bouillon cubes, crumbled
1½ teaspoons curry powder
½ teaspoon ground ginger
1 small yellow summer squash
1 pound ground turkey, crumbled
1 tablespoon all-purpose flour
¾ cup nonfat sour cream

1. Slice the potatoes ½ inch thick and put them into a 3-quart microwave-safe casserole with the water. Cover with vented plastic wrap. Microwave on High for 12 to 14 minutes, stirring once, until tender; drain. Transfer to a plate and cover with foil.

2. Meanwhile, chop the carrots and onion and put into the casserole with the water, currants, bouillon, curry, and ginger. Cover and microwave on High for 4 to 6 minutes, stirring once, until crisp-tender.

3. Meanwhile, dice the squash. Add with the turkey to the casserole. ▶

Cover and microwave on Medium for 15 to 18 minutes, stirring 3 times, until turkey is no longer pink.

4. In a small bowl, whisk the flour into the sour cream until well blended. Stir into the casserole. Microwave on Medium for 1 to 2 minutes longer, or until heated through. Serve right away with the potatoes.

Per serving: 392 cal, 29 g pro, 49 g car, 9 g fat, 83 mg chol, 644 mg sod

---

EASY • 30 MINUTES

DIJON TURKEY SCHNITZEL

Serves 4

Preparation time: 15 minutes

Cooking time: 5 minutes

Crisp turkey cutlets that have been prepared and cooked like their veal counterpart are just as delicious and a lot less expensive. Here the cutlets have a crispy, crunchy golden-brown bread crumb coating. They make a simple and tasty meal with steamed green beans and hash brown potatoes.

Whites of 2 large eggs
2 tablespoons water
2 tablespoons Dijon mustard
¼ teaspoon salt
¼ teaspoon ground black pepper
1 cup packaged seasoned bread crumbs
1 pound turkey breast cutlets
3 tablespoons olive oil
For garnish: fresh parsley sprigs and lemon slices (optional)

1. In a shallow dish, beat the egg whites, water, mustard, salt, and pepper with a fork until blended. Place the bread crumbs on a sheet of waxed paper.

2. Dip the turkey slices into the egg-white mixture, then coat with the crumbs, patting the meat so the crumbs adhere.

3. In a large nonstick skillet, heat 1½ tablespoons of the oil over medium-high heat. Add half the turkey slices and cook for 1 minute on each side, or until lightly browned. Remove to a plate. Repeat with the remaining turkey, adding more oil to the skillet as needed.

4. Arrange the turkey cutlets on serving plates and garnish with parsley and lemon to squeeze over each serving. Serve right away.

Per serving: 342 cal, 34 g pro, 21 g car, 12 g fat, 70 mg chol, 1,193 mg sod

VARIATION

MUSHROOM TURKEY SCHNITZEL

• **Prepare the recipe through step 3. Remove the turkey cutlets to a plate and cover with foil to keep warm.**

• **Melt 1 tablespoon of butter or margarine in the skillet over medium heat. Add 1 cup sliced fresh mushrooms, 2 tablespoons finely chopped onion, and 1 teaspoon minced fresh garlic. Cover and cook over low heat for 4 minutes, stirring often. Stir in 1 tablespoon dry vermouth or chicken broth. Spoon the mushrooms over the turkey cutlets, garnish as directed and serve right away.**

Per serving: 379 cal, 34 g pro, 23 g car, 15 g fat, 78 mg chol with butter, 70 mg chol with margarine, 1,225 mg sod

• **EASY •30 MINUTES**

EASY • 30 MINUTES • LOW FAT

SANTA FE TURKEY FAJITAS

Serves 4
Preparation time: 10 minutes
Cooking time: 14 minutes

This version uses lean turkey cutlets instead of strips of grilled skirt steak, but without any loss of flavor. Serve with salsa, sour cream, and avocado. Instead of peeling and mashing the avocado, halve and pit it, then set it out with a spoon for scooping. This recipe will multiply easily, making it perfect to serve to a crowd. Rice and a black bean salad make tasty accompaniments.

8 (6-inch) flour tortillas, stacked and wrapped in foil
2 teaspoons chili powder
½ teaspoon dried oregano
12 ounces turkey breast cutlets
2 teaspoons vegetable oil
2 medium-size bell peppers, preferably 1 red and 1 green
   (1 pound), thinly sliced
8 lettuce leaves, rinsed and patted dry

1. Heat the oven to 350°F. Place the wrapped tortillas in the oven and heat for 8 to 10 minutes. Turn the oven off and keep the tortillas in the oven until ready to use.

2. Meanwhile, on a sheet of waxed paper, mix the chili powder and oregano. Rub the spice mixture into the turkey cutlets.

3. In a large nonstick skillet, heat 1 teaspoon of the oil over medium-high heat. Add the bell peppers and cook for 4 to 6 minutes, stirring often, or until lightly browned and crisp-tender. Remove to a bowl with a slotted spoon.

4. Heat the remaining 1 teaspoon of oil in the same skillet. Add the turkey cutlets and cook for 4 to 6 minutes, turning once, or until browned and no longer pink in the center.

5. Slice the turkey crosswise into narrow strips. Top each warm tortilla with a lettuce leaf and arrange the turkey and bell pepper strips down the middle. Roll the tortillas, arrange on a serving platter, and serve right away.

Makes 8 fajitas. Per 2 fajitas: 356 cal, 31 g pro, 45 g car, 7 g fat, 53 mg chol, 288 mg sod

EASY • 60 MINUTES • LOW FAT • MAKE AHEAD • ONE POT

TURKEY CHILI

Serves 6

Preparation time: 15 minutes

Cooking time: 38 minutes

A really good turkey chili is a must for every cook's repertoire, and this one is a great way to use leftover cooked turkey. But if you don't have any left over, it's worth buying cooked turkey meat for the recipe. Serve with rice or warm tortillas and a salad.

2 tablespoons vegetable oil

1 medium-size onion, chopped coarse (1 cup)

2 teaspoons minced fresh garlic

2 celery stalks, coarsely chopped (1 cup)

2 small carrots, peeled and sliced (about ¾ cup)

1 can (about 28 ounces) crushed tomatoes

1 teaspoon chili powder

1 teaspoon ground cumin

1 can (about 4½ ounces) chopped mild green chiles

1 can (about 15 ounces) kidney beans, drained

2 cups chopped cooked turkey

For garnish: grated cheese and sour cream or
    plain yogurt (optional)

1. In a large saucepan, heat the oil over medium heat. Add the onion and cook for about 4 minutes, stirring occasionally, or until soft. Add the garlic and cook, stirring occasionally, for 1 minute.

2. Add the celery and carrots and cook for 2 to 3 minutes, stirring often, until the celery is slightly tender.

3. Add the tomatoes, chili powder, cumin, and green chiles. Reduce the heat to medium-low. Cover and simmer for 20 to 25 minutes, or until the carrots are tender.

4. Stir in the beans and turkey. Cook for 3 to 5 minutes, stirring occasionally, until the turkey is heated through.

5. Ladle the chili into serving bowls and garnish with grated cheese and sour cream or plain yogurt. Serve right away.

Per serving: 224 cal, 20 g pro, 20 g car, 8 g fat, 36 mg chol, 496 mg sod

MAKE AHEAD

Keep this recipe in mind if you need to feed a crowd. It multiplies easily and will keep tightly covered in the refrigerator up to 3 days, or frozen up to 1 month. Thaw frozen chili in the refrigerator before reheating.

EASY • 60 MINUTES • LOW FAT • ONE POT

TEX–MEX TURKEY CASSEROLE

Serves 6
Preparation time: 5 minutes
Cooking time: 45 minutes

Canned Mexican-style corn comes with red and green bell pepper mixed with the kernels. It adds color to this great pantry recipe, which needs only a crisp salad for a complete meal.

4 cups (about 8 ounces) cornbread stuffing mix
1 can (about 11 ounces) Mexican-style corn, drained
½ cup sliced scallions
1½ cups hot water
1 pound turkey breast cutlets
1 can (about 14½ ounces) chili-style chunky tomatoes
For garnish: sliced scallions (optional)

1. Heat the oven to 375°F. Grease a shallow 2-quart baking dish.
2. In the prepared dish, mix the stuffing mix, corn, and scallions. Add the hot water and stir to mix well. Arrange the turkey cutlets on top. Spread evenly with the chili-style tomatoes.
3. Cover with a lid or foil and bake for 35 to 45 minutes, or until the turkey is no longer pink in the center. Garnish with sliced scalliona and serve right away.

Per serving: 302 cal, 25 g pro, 93 g car, 3 g fat, 47 mg chol, 885 mg sod

EASY • 30 MINUTES • ONE POT

CASHEW & TURKEY STIR–FRY

Serves 4
Preparation time: 20 minutes
Cooking time: 10 minutes

Stir-frying helps keep turkey low-fat because it uses very little oil for cooking. Pieces of uniform size are tossed almost continuously over high heat until opaque and springy. Cook rice as an accompaniment while preparing the ingredients for this stir-fry.

▶

1 tablespoon minced peeled fresh gingerroot

1½ teaspoons minced fresh garlic

5 tablespoons dry sherry

2 turkey tenderloins (8 to 10 ounces each), white tendon removed
  and meat cut into ¼-inch pieces

2 tablespoons cornstarch

3 tablespoons soy sauce

1 tablespoon granulated sugar

½ cup plus 2 tablespoons chicken broth

2 tablespoons vegetable oil

8 ounces fresh broccoli, cut into florets with 1-inch-long stems

1 medium-size carrot, peeled and cut diagonally into thin slices

1¼ cups thinly sliced scallions

½ teaspoon salt

½ cup roasted salted cashews

1. In a medium-size bowl, mix the gingerroot, garlic, and 2 tablespoons of the sherry. Add the turkey, tossing to coat.

2. In a small bowl, mix the cornstarch, soy sauce, sugar, ½ cup chicken broth, and remaining 3 tablespoons sherry until blended.

3. In a wok or large heavy skillet, heat 1 tablespoon of the oil over high heat until very hot and rippling but not smoking. Add the broccoli, carrot, scallions, and salt and stir-fry for 2 minutes. Remove the vegetables to a bowl.

4. In the same skillet, heat the remaining tablespoon of oil. Add the turkey mixture and stir-fry for 2 minutes, then add the remaining 2 tablespoons of chicken broth and stir-fry for 1 to 2 minutes, or until the turkey is opaque.

5. Reduce the heat to medium. Add the cornstarch mixture and stir for about 30 seconds, or until the sauce is thickened.

6. Return the vegetables to the skillet, add the cashews, and stir for about 1 minute, or until blended and heated through. Serve right away.

Per serving: 395 cal, 38 g pro, 21 g car, 16 g fat, 79 mg chol, 1,394 mg sod

TENDERLOIN TECHNIQUE

To remove tendon, place the tenderloin flat on a work surface. With a sharp knife, cut very close to the thin white membrane (the tendon). Repeat the cut along the other side of the tendon, pulling it up as you go.

FRESH GINGERROOT

One of the oldest and most important spices, ginger has been cultivated and used in Asia for over 3,000 years. Fresh ginger is the hard, knobby root (or rhizome) of the ginger plant. It has a lively, fresh aroma and a slightly hot and pungent flavor.

• When choosing fresh gingerroot, select roots with a smooth skin that are firm and heavy without any shriveled ends.

• Store unpeeled gingerroot tightly wrapped in plastic up to 3 weeks. For longer storage, immerse peeled slices of fresh gingerroot in wine, oil, or sherry and refrigerate tightly covered up to 3 months. It can also be frozen, wrapped in plastic then placed in a freezer bag, up to 1 year. Cut or grate off what you need, then return the rest to the freezer.

• Ground ginger tastes much different than fresh ginger and should not be used as a substitute.

60 MINUTES

MUSHROOM TURKEY STROGANOFF

Serves 4

Total time: 45 minutes

This rendition of a classic beef dish uses turkey breast and a combination of dried and fresh mushrooms. If you wish, you can use fresh morel or chanterelle mushrooms in place of some of the white ones. Serve this dish with egg noodles or a rice pilaf.

½ ounce dried porcini mushrooms
¾ cup hot water
1½ pounds skinless, boneless turkey breast, cut into 1-inch chunks
¼ cup all-purpose flour
½ teaspoon salt
½ teaspoon ground black pepper
1 tablespoon butter or margarine
1 tablespoon vegetable oil
1 tablespoon minced fresh garlic
8 ounces white mushrooms, cleaned and sliced (2 cups)
¾ cup low-sodium chicken broth
1 cup reduced-fat sour cream
For garnish: chopped fresh parsley (optional)

1. In a small bowl, combine the dried mushrooms and water and let soak for 30 minutes.

2. Meanwhile, on a sheet of waxed paper, mix the flour, salt, and pepper. Coat the turkey in the flour mixture, shaking off the excess.

3. In a large skillet, heat 1 teaspoon of butter and 1½ teaspoons of oil over medium heat. Cook half the turkey, turning frequently, for about 5 minutes, until browned on at least 2 sides. Remove to a plate with a slotted spoon. Add another teaspoon of butter and the remaining 1½ teaspoons oil to the skillet and brown the remaining turkey. Remove to the plate.

4. Add the remaining 1 teaspoon butter and the white mushrooms to the skillet. Cook, stirring often, for about 5 minutes, or until golden. Remove to a plate with a slotted spoon. Add the garlic to the pan drippings in the skillet. Cover and cook for 1 minute.

5. Strain the dried mushroom soaking liquid and add to the skillet. Bring to a boil and boil for 3 minutes, or until the mixture is reduced by half. Add the chicken broth and porcini mushrooms. Return to a boil. ▶

6. Return the turkey and white mushrooms to the skillet. Simmer uncovered for 4 to 5 minutes, or until the turkey is just cooked through. Remove the skillet from the heat and stir in the sour cream. Garnish with chopped parsley and serve right away.

Per serving: 406 cal, 49 g pro, 16 g car, 16 g fat, 133 mg chol with butter, 126 mg chol with margarine, 412 mg sod with butter, 416 mg sod with margarine

EASY • 30 MINUTES • LOW FAT

TURKEY PICANTE

Serves 4

Preparation time: 10 minutes

Cooking time: 8 minutes

Few turkey recipes are as easy and tasty as this one. Serve with lemon slices and one-pot pasta and vegetables (add a package of frozen mixed vegetables to pasta 5 minutes before cooking time is up).

1 pound turkey breast cutlets
¼ cup all-purpose flour
2 tablespoons olive oil
½ cup dry white wine or chicken broth
2 tablespoons fresh lemon juice
2 tablespoons chopped fresh parsley
2 tablespoons capers, drained
½ teaspoon Worcestershire sauce
½ teaspoon salt
½ teaspoon ground black pepper

1. Lightly coat the turkey cutlets with the flour, shaking off the excess.

2. In a large nonstick skillet, heat 1 tablespoon of the oil over medium-high heat. Add half the turkey and cook for about 1 minute on each side, or until lightly browned. Remove to a plate. Repeat with the remaining turkey, adding more oil to the skillet as needed.

3. Add the remaining ingredients to the skillet and bring to a boil over high heat. Cook for 1 to 2 minutes, stirring to scrape up any browned bits on the bottom of the skillet, until slightly thickened. Return the turkey to the skillet, spoon the sauce over the tops, and cook just until heated through. Serve right away.

Per serving: 238 cal, with wine, 222 cal with broth, 29 g pro, 7 g car, 8 g fat, 70 mg chol, 448 mg sod with wine, 572 mg sod with broth

A WORD ABOUT FREE-RANGE

Free-range chickens and turkeys are farm-raised in a relatively spacious setting that allows room for them to run around. These birds develop more muscle, which makes the meat more flavorful and sometimes a little tougher. Free-range bieds are also raised organically, meaning that their feed is natural and free of antibiotics. They are leaner, with skin that is creamy white as opposed to yellow. Free-range chicken and turkeys are available in specialty food markets and many supermarkets.

TANDOORI TURKEY BREAST

Serves 6

Preparation time: 10 minutes plus 8 hours to marinate
Cooking time: 1 hour 30 minutes plus 15 minutes to stand

This spicy treatment for turkey breast takes its flavor cue from India. It's equally good served hot from the grill or at room temperature, and chilled leftovers are a great addition to a tossed green salad. The cilantro-cucumber sauce is a refreshing accompaniment to this dish but is also an excellent dip served with raw vegetables or crackers.

2 cups nonfat yogurt
2 tablespoons minced peeled fresh gingerroot
1½ tablespoons paprika
1 tablespoon minced fresh garlic
1 tablespoon ground coriander
1 tablespoon ground cumin
2 teaspoons salt
2 teaspoons ground red pepper (cayenne)
¼ teaspoon ground cinnamon
⅛ teaspoon ground cloves
1 whole skinned and boned turkey breast (3 pounds)
For garnish: fresh cilantro leaves (optional)

CILANTRO–CUCUMBER RELISH
1 cup nonfat yogurt
2 cups fresh cilantro, chopped
1 medium-size cucumber, halved, seeded, and diced (1 cup)
¾ teaspoon minced fresh garlic
¼ teaspoon salt

1. In a gallon-size zipper-type food storage bag, mix the 2 cups of yogurt, ginger, paprika, garlic, coriander, cumin, salt, red pepper, cinnamon, and cloves until well blended.

2. With a sharp knife, make several 1-inch-deep slits 1 inch apart in the underside (bone side) of the turkey breast. Put the turkey breast in the plastic bag. Press out the air, seal the bag, and turn to coat the turkey. Refrigerate for at least 8 hours or up to 24 hours, turning once or twice.

3. To make the relish: In a small bowl, mix the yogurt, cilantro, cucumber, garlic, and salt until well blended. Cover the bowl with plastic wrap and ▶

refrigerate for at least 1 hour before serving.

4. To grill: Put a 15½ x 10½ x 3½-inch disposable foil drip pan in the bottom of a barbecue. Arrange briquettes or lava rocks around all sides of the pan. Adjust the grill rack to 4 to 6 inches above the hot coals. If using a gas grill, set to medium-low. Place the turkey breast on the grill over the drip pan. Cover with a grill lid or foil tent. Grill the turkey, turning once, for 1½ hours, or until a meat thermometer inserted in the thickest part registers 170°F to 175°F. Let stand for 15 minutes before serving.

To roast and broil: Heat the oven to 375°F. Line a broiler pan with foil for easy cleanup and lightly oil the broiler-pan rack. Place the turkey breast on the rack and roast for 40 minutes, turning once. Remove from the oven. Turn off the oven and heat the broiler. Broil 4 to 6 inches from the heat source, turning once for 30 to 40 minutes, or until a meat thermometer inserted in the thickest part registers 170°F to 175°F, or the juices run clear when the meat is pierced with the tip of sharp knife. Let stand for 15 minutes before serving.

5. Thinly slice the turkey across the grain and arrange on a platter. Garnish the turkey slices with fresh cilantro leaves. Serve the cilantro-cucumber relish on the side.

Per serving: 335 cal, 63 g pro, 12 g car, 2 g fat, 143 mg chol, 1,026 mg sod

---

EASY • 30 MINUTES • LOW FAT

TURKEY SALTIMBOCCA

Serves 4

Preparation time: 10 minutes

Cooking time: 6 minutes

Where you see saltimbocca (literally "jump-in-the-mouth") in the name of a recipe, you can expect the ingredients to include ham and sage. Serve with cooked rice and crusty breadsticks.

½ teaspoon dried sage leaves, crumbled
½ teaspoon ground black pepper
8 thin turkey breast cutlets (about 2 ounces each)
4 slices boiled ham (1 ounce each), cut in half
1 tablespoon butter or margarine
½ teaspoon minced fresh garlic
1 medium-size head escarole (12 ounces), rinsed, cored, and quartered
1 can (8¼ ounces) peeled tomatoes, drained and chopped
¼ teaspoon salt

COOK'S TIP

This grilling technique is referred to as the Indirect Heat Method. The meat is slowly cooked over a moderate to moderately low fire in a covered grill to trap the hot smoky air. Do not open the grill often as you will release too much of the heat. If using a charcoal grill, you may have to add additional coals to maintain a constant temperature. Do not add instant-light briquettes, which will impart a lighter-fluid taste to the meat.

1. Sprinkle the sage and pepper on one side of each turkey breast cutlet. Top with a piece of ham.

2. In a large skillet, melt the butter over medium-high heat. Add the cutlets, ham side down, and cook for about 1½ minutes, or until browned. Turn with a wide spatula and cook for 1½ minutes more, or until the turkey is just cooked through. Remove to the serving platter and cover with foil to keep warm.

3. Add the garlic, escarole, tomatoes, and salt to the skillet and reduce the heat to medium. Stir for about 2 minutes, or until hot and the escarole has wilted. Remove the skillet from the heat.

4. Serve the cutlets with the escarole, pouring the sauce from the skillet over the meat. Serve right away.

Per serving: 218 cal, 35 g pro, 6 g car, 5 g fat, 93 mg chol, 672 mg sod

EASY • LOW FAT • MAKE AHEAD

HERBED TURKEY TENDERLOINS

Serves 6

Preparation time: 12 minutes plus 30 minutes to marinate
Cooking time: 12 minutes plus 10 minutes to stand

These rosemary scented tenderloins are served with a fresh tomato relish.

½ cup minced fresh parsley
3 tablespoons finely chopped fresh rosemary, or 1 tablespoon dried rosemary leaves, crumbled
2 tablespoons minced shallot or white part of scallion
2 tablespoons olive oil
2 tablespoons fresh lime juice
2 turkey tenderloins (about 12 ounces each), white tendons removed
Ground black pepper to taste

FRESH TOMATO RELISH
1 small onion, sliced thin
2 tablespoons fresh lime juice
1 large ripe yellow or red tomato, diced (1 cup)
1 large ripe red tomato, diced (1 cup)
1 tablespoon minced fresh parsley (optional)
¼ teaspoon salt
¼ teaspoon ground black pepper

Ⓜ AKE AHEAD

The colorful, mild fresh tomato relish can be made up to 1 day ahead and refrigerated in an airtight container.

▶

1. In a small bowl, mix the parsley, rosemary, shallot, oil, and lime juice. Rub the herb mixture all over the tenderloins, then season them with pepper. Marinate at room temperature for 30 minutes.

2. Meanwhile, make the relish. In a medium-size bowl, mix the onion and the lime juice and let stand at room temperature for 15 minutes, or until slightly wilted. Stir in the tomatoes, parsley, salt, and pepper. Let stand at room temperature until ready to serve.

3. Heat a gas grill to medium-high, prepare a charcoal fire, or heat a broiler. Put the tenderloins on a lightly oiled grill or broiler-pan rack. Grill or broil 4 to 6 inches from the heat source, turning several times for 10 to 12 minutes, or until just barely pink in the center.

4. Remove the tenderloins to a cutting board. Cover loosely with foil and let stand for 10 minutes. Thinly slice on an angle and serve with the relish.

Per serving: 174 cal, 29 g pro, 7 g car, 3 g fat, 70 mg chol, 154 mg sod

TURKEY CUTS

It used to be that turkeys were only sold whole, but today many turkey cuts are available both fresh and frozen:

◆ **Whole**—The entire turkey, sold unbasted or self-basting, ranging from 6 to 25 pounds. Self-basting birds have been injected with a solution of broth, fat, and/or flavorings. The younger the turkey, the more tender the meat will be. Select a bird labeled "young turkey." Some are also labeled "young hen" or "young tom," which indicates the sex. A hen usually has more white meat than a tom. Turkeys labeled fryer-roaster are also young.

◆ **Boneless turkey roast**—A tied boneless breast that can be all white meat, all dark meat, or a combination of the two, ranging from 2 to 3½ pounds. They are sold with or without skin.

◆ **Turkey breasts**—Whole or half, bone-in, white-meat breast. Whole breasts range from 4½ to 8 pounds, half breasts range from 2 to 3½ pounds. Boneless turkey breasts are also available.

◆ **Thighs**—All dark-meat pieces with bone that can weigh between ½ and 1½ pounds each.

◆ **Hindquarters**—Turkey pieces consisting of the thigh and drumstick. Hindquarters contain all dark meat and weight between 2 and 5 pounds.

◆ **Drumsticks**—All dark meat with bone, these can weigh between ½ and 1½ pounds each.

◆ **Wings**—All white-meat pieces with bone that can weigh between ¾ and 1¼ pounds each. Sometimes the meaty first joints are sold separately as turkey drumettes.

◆ **Breast steaks** - Crosswise cuts from the breast that are between ½ and 1 inch thick.

◆ **Breast cutlets or slices**—Crosswise cuts from the breast that are between ¼ and ½ inch thick and range in weight from 3 to 5 ounces each.

◆ **Tenderloin**—The whole muscle attached on the inside of the turkey breast. Tenderloins usually come two or three to a 1-pound package.

◆ **Tenderloin steaks**—Lengthwise cuts from the tenderloin that are about ½ inch thick.

◆ **Sausages**—Ground turkey that is processed to give it a traditional sausage flavor. Available in links or loose, fresh or smoked.

◆ **Ground**—A mixture of white and dark turkey meat. The proportion of white to dark meat, and therefore the fat content, depends on the brand. Skin is included in the ground turkey meat because the fat adds needed moisture.

BEEF

"Beef is the soul of cooking."
MARIE-ANTOINE CARÊME

Whether it's a Sunday roast or a backyard barbecue, beef has always been America's favorite meat. And although we are eating less red meat today than we did ten years ago, we still enjoy a juicy steak or meltingly tender pot roast. And why not? Beef is a great source of protein and iron.

The good news for beef lovers is that today's cattle are raised to produce much leaner meat. And at the market, the meat is trimmed more thoroughly and leaner cuts are emphasized.

From quick and easy grilling and stir-fries to roasts and stews you can forget about while they cook, the following pages include many delicious ways to prepare beef.

PERFECT HAMBURGERS

Serves 4

Preparation time: 3 minutes

Cooking time: 16 minutes

There's no sense in trying to build a better burger if you don't start with the right foundation. Remember that hamburgers will continue to cook after they're taken from the skillet, so serve them as soon as possible. Baffled by what kind of beef to buy? Check "Where's the Beef," page 112.

1½ pounds ground beef

⅛ teaspoon salt

4 hamburger buns

1. Gently shape the meat into 4 patties, slightly less than 1 inch thick. Don't overwork the meat or the texture will be tough.

2. Lightly coat the bottom of a large nonstick skillet with vegetable oil cooking spray. Sprinkle the skillet with half the salt. Place over medium heat until the oil is hot but not smoking. Put the patties in the skillet, close together but not touching. Sprinkle the patties with the remaining salt.

3. Cook for 8 to 10 minutes on each side for well done, or until the juices run clear when the patties are pierced and the meat is no longer pink in the center.

To grill: Place the patties 4 to 6 inches above the coals. Cover and grill for 4 to 5 minutes on each side, or grill uncovered for 7 to 8 minutes on each side for well done, or until the juices run clear when the patties are pierced and the meat is no longer pink in the center.

To broil: Place the patties on a broiler-pan rack. Broil 4 to 5 inches from the heat source for 9 to 11 minutes on each side for well done, or until the juices run clear when the patties are pierced and the meat is no longer pink in the center.

4. Serve on the hamburger buns with the topping of your choice.

Makes 4 burgers. Per burger with 21% fat ground beef: 462 cal, 34 g pro, 22 g car, 26 g fat, 103 mg chol, 404 mg sod. With 10% fat ground beef: 416 cal, 38 g pro, 22 g car, 20 g fat, 106 mg chol, 432 mg sod

HAMBURGER HISTORY

In the late 1800s, business was slow for an Athens, Texas, potter named Fletcher Davis. So he opened a lunch counter and started selling his own special sandwich: a ground meat patty served between two slices of homemade bread. In 1904 he took it to the World's Fair in St. Louis, where it gained national fame and its name. Seems the people of Hamburg, Germany, were known for eating a lot of ground beef, and somebody— probably a jokester—called Davis's sandwich a hamburger.

PERFECT HAMBURGER VARIATIONS

EASY • 30 MINUTES

RANGE BURGERS

Heat 1 can (about 20 ounces) vegetarian baked beans with ¼ cup barbecue sauce. Spoon over the hamburgers on buns. Sprinkle with chopped green bell pepper and onion.

Per burger with 21% fat ground beef: 605 cal, 40 g pro, 53 g car, 27 g fat, 103 mg chol, 1,094 mg sod. With 10% fat ground beef: 559 cal, 45 g pro, 53 g car, 20 g fat, 106 mg chol, 1,122 mg sod

EASY • 30 MINUTES

AEGEAN BURGERS

Line 4 whole-wheat pita pockets with shredded lettuce and 2 slices of tomato. Tuck in the hamburgers. Top with a sauce made of ½ cup fat-free bottled ranch dressing, ½ cup diced cucumber, and ¼ teaspoon ground cumin.

Per burger with 21% fat ground beef: 567 cal, 36 g pro, 48 g car, 25 g fat, 103 mg chol, 817 mg sod. With 10% fat ground beef: 521 cal, 41 g pro, 48 g car, 19 g fat, 106 mg chol, 845 mg sod

EASY • 30 MINUTES

CALIFORNIA BURGERS

Arrange ½ cup shredded lettuce on 4 split Kaiser rolls. Top each with a hamburger, then top each hamburger with 2 slices of ripe avocado, 2 tablespoons salsa, and 1 tablespoon sliced scallions.

Per burger with 21% fat ground beef: 600 cal, 37 g pro, 36 g car, 34 g fat, 103 mg chol, 800 mg sod. With 10% fat ground beef: 554 cal, 41 g pro, 36 g car, 27 g fat, 106 mg chol, 828 mg sod

EASY • 30 MINUTES

PROVENÇAL BURGERS

In a medium-size saucepan, cook 1½ cups sliced onion and 1½ cups sliced green bell pepper in 2 teaspoons of vegetable oil over medium-high heat for 8 to 10 minutes, or until softened. Spread the split hamburger buns with 2 tablespoons reduced-fat mustard spread. Add the hamburgers, top each with

½ ounce creamy garlic-and-spices cheese and then some of the vegetables.

Per burger with 21% fat ground beef: 538 cal, 35 g pro, 30 g car, 30 g fat, 110 mg chol, 434 mg sod. With 10% fat ground beef: 491 cal, 40 g pro, 30 g car, 24 g fat, 113 mg chol, 461 mg sod

EASY • 30 MINUTES

REUBEN BURGERS

Place the hamburgers on toasted rye bread. Top each with 1 slice reduced-fat Swiss cheese, ½ cup rinsed, drained, and heated sauerkraut, 1 tablespoon fat-free Thousand Island dressing, and a slice of red onion.

Per burger with 21% fat ground beef: 550 cal, 43 g pro, 25 g car, 30 g fat, 123 mg chol, 842 mg sod. With 10% fat ground beef: 504 cal, 48 g pro, 25 g car, 23 g fat, 126 mg chol, 870 mg sod

EASY • 30 MINUTES

PIZZA BURGERS

Split and quarter a loaf of Italian bread. Fill each wedge with a hamburger, ¼ cup heated no-fat pasta sauce from a jar, ¼ cup reduced-fat shredded mozzarella, and 1 teaspoon grated Parmesan cheese.

Per burger with 21% fat ground beef: 65 cal, 46 g pro, 47 g car, 30 g fat, 114 mg chol, 1,030 mg sod. With 10% fat ground beef: 609 cal, 51 g pro, 47 g car, 24 g fat, 117 mg chol, 1,058 mg sod

EASY • 30 MINUTES

FRIED ONION BURGERS

Melt 1 tablespoon butter or margarine in a nonstick skillet over medium-high heat. Add 3 cups thinly sliced onion and cook for 7 to 8 minutes, stirring occasionally, or until browned and tender. Remove the skillet from the heat and stir in ⅛ teaspoon each salt and pepper. Place the hamburgers on buns and top each with the onions.

Per burger with 21% fat ground beef: 533 cal, 35 g pro, 32 g car, 29 g fat, 111 mg chol, 506 mg sod. With 10% fat ground beef: 487 cal, 40 g pro, 32 g car, 23 g fat, 113 mg chol, 534 sod

WHERE'S THE BEEF?

Thanks to the intricacies of government regulations, deciphering the label on a package of ground beef is a little like reading ancient Greek—backward. In simple terms, the names and numbers break down like this:

GROUND BEEF
No more than 30% fat (or at least 70% lean)
LEAN OR EXTRA-LEAN
No more than 22.5% fat (or at least 77.5% lean)

Take note! The government regulations don't even distinguish between lean and extra-lean. If your store uses these terms, be sure the label spells out exactly what they mean. In the end, the difference between lean and extra-lean may be negligible, but the price probably won't be.

When you have doubts about what you're getting, trust your own two eyes and check the color. The redder the ground beef, the less white fat it has ground into it. Or if your store still sells ground beef by the cut, use this rule of thumb: Ground round is usually leanest; ground sirloin is in the middle (and usually the most expensive); and ground chuck has the most fat.

Frankly, there's no need to buy the most expensive ground beef you can find. Ground chuck makes a beautiful burger, and although it shrinks during cooking, that won't change the flavor much.

EASY • 60 MINUTES

TOPSY-TURVY BEEF PIE

Serves 6
Preparation time: 20 minutes
Cooking time: 35 minutes

This is a simplified version of beef potpie and a great way to use leftover mashed potatoes. We suggest broccoli and cauliflower in this dish, but any frozen vegetables will do.

1 pound lean ground beef
1 large egg
½ cup milk
½ cup packaged seasoned bread crumbs
¼ teaspoon salt
⅛ teaspoon ground black pepper
2 cups mashed potatoes, at room temperature
1 package (about 8 ounces) frozen mixed vegetables (carrots, peas, beans, and corn), thawed and drained (2 cups)
⅓ cup tomato ketchup
1 teaspoon prepared mustard
2 ounces shredded Cheddar cheese (½ cup)

1. Heat the oven to 375° F. Lightly grease a 9-inch pie dish.
2. In a medium-size nonstick skillet, cook the beef over medium-high

 VARIATION

MICROWAVE TOPSY-TURVY BEEF PIE:

• In a deep 1-quart microwave-safe casserole, mix the vegetables with 2 tablespoons of water. Cover with a lid or vented plastic wrap. Microwave on High for 3 to 4 minutes, stirring once, until crisp-tender. Remove the dish from the oven. Stir in the ketchup and mustard.
• In a large bowl, beat the egg with a fork. Add the beef, milk, crumbs,

salt, and pepper. Mix until well blended.

• Press the beef mixture over the bottom and up the sides of a 9-inch microwave-safe pie dish. Cover loosely with waxed paper. Microwave on High for 6 to 8 minutes, turning dish ¼ turn twice, until the meat is no longer pink. Remove the plate from the oven and carefully drain off the fat.

• To assemble the pie, spread the mashed potatoes over the meat crust. Top with the vegetable mixture and sprinkle the cheese over the top. Microwave uncovered on High for 1 to 2 minutes, or until the cheese melts. Cut into wedges and serve right away.

Per serving: 388 cal, 21 g pro, 28 g car, 21 g fat, 100 mg chol, 868 mg sod

• EASY • 30 MINUTES

---

heat until no longer pink, stirring to break up any large chunks. Drain off any fat and cool slightly.

3. Stir in the egg, milk, bread crumbs, salt, and pepper until well blended.

4. Press the beef mixture over the bottom and up the sides of the prepared dish. Spread the mashed potatoes evenly over the meat.

5. In a medium-size bowl, mix the vegetables, ketchup, and mustard. Spread the vegetable mixture over the potatoes and top with the cheese.

6. Bake the casserole for 30 to 35 minutes, or until the cheese melts and the vegetables are tender.

7. Cut into wedges and serve right away.

Per serving: 369 cal, 21 g pro, 28 g car, 19 g fat, 95 mg chol, 869 mg sod

EASY • 30 MINUTES

MEXICO JOES

Serves 6
Preparation time: 10 minutes
Cooking time: 15 minutes

Sometimes it's fun to serve something a little different, and these hot, spicy ground-beef sandwiches topped with salsa and shredded cheese do the trick. Serve with a crisp green salad or coleslaw.

1 pound lean ground beef
⅔ cup chopped onion
⅔ cup chopped green bell pepper
2 teaspoons minced fresh garlic
1 can (8 ounces) tomato sauce
1 teaspoon Worcestershire sauce
2 teaspoons chili powder
¼ teaspoon salt
Dash of hot-pepper sauce
6 hamburger buns, split
For garnish: shredded lettuce, salsa, and shredded
    Cheddar cheese (optional)

1. In a large nonstick skillet, cook the beef, onion, bell pepper, and garlic over medium-high heat, stirring with a fork to break up the chunks of meat, until the beef is no longer pink. Drain off any fat.

2. Stir in the tomato sauce, Worcestershire sauce, chili powder, salt, and hot-pepper sauce. Bring to a boil. Reduce the heat to medium and ▶

simmer uncovered for 3 to 5 minutes, or until thickened, stirring occasionally.

3. Spoon the beef mixture over the bun bottoms. Garnish each serving with 2 teaspoons salsa, 2 tablespoons lettuce, and 1 tablespoon cheese. Replace the tops and serve right away.

Makes 6 sandwiches. Per sandwich: 299 cal, 18 g pro, 28 g car, 13 g fat, 46 mg chol, 622 mg sod

SPINACH & OATS MEAT LOAF

Serves 8

Preparation time: 15 minutes

Cooking time: 1 hour plus 10 minutes to stand

Stretch ground beef with spinach and oats for better nutrition. Spinach is a good source of vitamin A and iron. Oats, though known for their high fiber content, are also full of B vitamins and vitamin E.

Whites of 2 large eggs, or 1 whole egg
¾ cup water
¾ cup uncooked old-fashioned or quick-cooking oats
1½ pounds extra-lean ground beef
1 package (10 ounces) frozen chopped spinach, thawed and squeezed dry
½ cup chopped onion
1 tablespoon Dijon mustard
1 teaspoon dried thyme leaves, crumbled
1 teaspoon salt
½ teaspoon ground black pepper

1. Heat the oven to 350° F.

2. In a large bowl, mix the egg whites, water, and oats. Let stand for 5 minutes.

3. Add the remaining ingredients and mix with your hands or an electric mixer on low speed just until blended.

4. Press the mixture into a 9 x 5-inch loaf pan. Bake for 50 to 60 minutes, or until the juices run clear or a meat thermometer inserted into the center registers 170° F.

5. Remove the pan from the oven, cover loosely with foil, and let stand for 10 minutes. Drain off any juices before slicing and serving.

Per serving: 231 cal, 19 g pro, 8 g car, 13 g fat, 56 mg chol with egg whites, 82 mg chol with whole egg, 405 mg sod

MICROWAVE MEXICO JOES

• Crumble the beef into a 2-quart microwave-safe casserole. Scatter the onion, bell pepper, and garlic on top. Cover with a lid or vented plastic wrap. Microwave on High for 5 to 7 minutes, or until the beef is no longer pink and the vegetables are crisp-tender. Drain.

• Stir in the tomato sauce, Worcestershire, chili powder, salt, and hot sauce. Microwave uncovered on High for 6 to 8 minutes, stirring twice, until the sauce is slightly thickened. Serve as directed.

Per serving: 299 cal, 18 g pro, 28 g car, 13 g fat, 46 mg chol, 622 mg sod

• EASY • 30 MINUTES

 AKE AHEAD

Double the recipe and make 2 meat loaves. Bake one. Wrap the unbaked meat loaf in the pan with plastic, then foil, and freeze up to 1 month. Thaw before baking.

CACTUS–COUNTRY MEAT LOAF

Serves 8
Preparation time: 25 minutes
Cooking time: 1 hour plus 10 minutes to stand

COOK'S TIP

Dried tomato bits are
usually sold packed in
jars and are perfect for
meat loaf, stews, and
many sauces.

Here's a meat loaf recipe that features the flavors of the Southwest with chile peppers, cornmeal, and cilantro. Serve with brown rice and mixed vegetables.

¾ cup dried tomato bits
¼ cup plus 1 tablespoon yellow cornmeal
2½ teaspoons minced fresh garlic
¾ cup boiling water
1½ pounds lean ground beef
2 large eggs
⅔ cup sliced scallions
1 can (4 ounces) chopped mild green chiles
⅓ cup chopped fresh cilantro or parsley
2 medium-size jalapeño peppers (fresh or canned), seeded and chopped
    fine (2 tablespoons)
1 teaspoon salt
¼ teaspoon ground black pepper

1. Heat the oven to 375° F.
2. In a large bowl, mix the tomato bits, ¼ cup of cornmeal, the garlic, and water. Let stand for 10 minutes.
3. Add the remaining ingredients and mix with your hands or a wooden spoon just until blended.
4. In a large roasting pan, form the mixture into 2 loaves, each about 6 inches long and 4 inches wide. Sprinkle with the remaining cornmeal. Bake for 50 to 60 minutes, or until the juices run clear.
5. Remove the pan from the oven, cover loosely with foil, and let stand for 10 minutes before slicing and serving.

Per serving: 268 cal, 19 g pro, 12 g car, 16 g fat, 110 mg chol, 437 mg sod

BEEF TACOS

Serves 4
Total Time: 22 minutes

This Mexican-style sandwich contains a spicy ground beef filling topped with a tangy shredded lettuce mixture plus cheese and onion. Keep a batch of the beef filling in the refrigerator and the other ingredients on hand for a quick lunch or dinner. It's tasty, too, with reduced-fat cheese.

8 packaged taco shells

BEEF FILLING
½ teaspoons whole cumin seeds, or 2 teaspoons ground cumin
1 pound lean ground beef
¼ cup water
1 cup chopped onion
1 tablespoon minced fresh garlic
1 can (about 4 ounces) chopped green chiles
½ teaspoon salt
¼ teaspoon ground black pepper

LETTUCE MIXTURE
2 cups shredded lettuce
2 tablespoons cider vinegar
½ teaspoon finely minced fresh garlic
¼ teaspoon salt

1 cup shredded Cheddar cheese
2 tablespoons chopped scallion
For garnish: salsa or taco sauce (optional)

1. Heat the oven to 350°F. Put the taco shells on a baking sheet. Heat in the oven for 8 to 10 minutes, turn the oven off, and keep the taco shells in the oven until ready to use.

2. Make the filling: If using whole cumin seeds, put in a large skillet over medium-high heat and toast, shaking the pan, for 1 to 2 minutes, or until an aroma is released. Transfer the seeds to a small bowl.

3. Put the ground beef and water in the skillet. Cook over medium heat for 2 minutes, breaking up the meat with a spoon. Add the toasted cumin seeds or ground cumin, onion, garlic, chiles, salt, and pepper. Cook, stirring

CHILI POWDER

The first chili powder was produced in Texas in the late 1800s by William Gebhardt. It contained ground chiles, cumin, black pepper, oregano, and garlic—the same basic ingredients that it does today. This advance facilitated chili making, and soon chili parlors, chili lovers, and distinctive regional styles spread throughout the country.

occasionally, for about 5 minutes, or until the meat is no longer pink.

4. Meanwhile, make the lettuce mixture. In a medium-size bowl, combine the lettuce, vinegar, garlic, and salt, tossing to mix.

5. Remove the taco shells from the oven. Fill each with about ⅓ cup of the meat mixture. Top with the shredded lettuce mixture. Toss the cheese and scallions together, then sprinkle over the lettuce. Garnish with taco sauce or salsa and serve right away.

Makes 8 tacos. Per 2 tacos: 591 cal, 31 g pro, 29 g car, 40 g fat, 115 mg chol, 1,042 mg sod

---

EASY • 60 MINUTES • MAKE AHEAD • CLASSIC

HEARTWARMING CHILI

Serves 8
Preparation time: 15 minutes
Cooking time: 40 minutes

The undying passion for a bowl of chili makes it a dish to serve during any season. It can be prepared ahead of time and in fact should be—allowing chili to mellow for 24 hours will enhance the flavor. Leftovers are never a problem; chili freezes beautifully. Serve with cornbread or warm flour tortillas.

2 tablespoons vegetable oil
3 pounds lean ground beef
3 large onions, chopped (3 cups)
1 large green bell pepper, seeded and chopped (1 cup)
1 tablespoon minced fresh garlic
⅓ cup chili powder
1½ tablespoons ground cumin
1½ tablespoons dried oregano leaves, crumbled
¾ teaspoon crushed hot red pepper flakes
1 can (28 ounces) crushed tomatoes
1 can (14½ ounces) stewed tomatoes
2 cups beef broth
Salt and ground black pepper to taste
For garnish: shredded Monterey Jack or Cheddar cheese, diced onion,
    diced bell pepper, diced avocado, and sour cream (optional)

1. In an 8-quart pot, heat the oil over medium high heat. Add the meat and cook, stirring to break up lumps, until no longer pink. Spoon off any fat.

2. Stir in the remaining ingredients. Bring to a boil. Reduce the heat ▶

 AKE AHEAD

Cool the chili to room temperature, then refrigerate in an airtight container up to 1 week, or freeze up to 2 months. Thaw in the refrigerator.

VARIATION

TURN-UP-THE-HEAT CHILI

Add 1 to 2 finely chopped medium-size jalapeño peppers and an extra ¼ to ½ teaspoon crushed red pepper flakes in step 2 and proceed as directed.

Per serving: 457 cal, 33 g pro, 18 g car, 28 g fat, 103 mg chol, 851 mg sod

• EASY • 60 MINUTES
• MAKE AHEAD

to low and simmer uncovered for 30 minutes. Season with additional salt and pepper if needed.

3. Ladle the chili into serving bowls and garnish with the toppings of your choice.

Per serving: 457 cal, 33 g pro, 18 g car, 28 g fat, 103 mg chol, 851 mg sod

---

EASY • 30 MINUTES • ONE POT

BEEF NOODLE PAPRIKASH

Serves 4

Preparation time: 5 minutes

Cooking time: 21 minutes

Paprika, a favorite Hungarian spice, is what gives this dish its distinctive flavor and color. It is ground from peppers and varies in color and pungency depending on what peppers were used. Most supermarkets carry paprika with a mild, slightly sweet flavor. More pungent varieties are found in specialty food stores or ethnic markets. In this recipe, there's no need to cook the noodles separately; they cook in the same pot as the sauce.

1 pound lean ground beef
1 tablespoon minced fresh garlic
1 cup frozen chopped onion
1 cup frozen chopped green bell pepper
3 tablespoons paprika
½ teaspoon dried thyme leaves, crumbled
3½ cups beef broth
8 ounces (4 cups) medium-size egg noodles
1 package (10 ounces) frozen broccoli cuts
¾ cup nonfat sour cream
1 tablespoon all-purpose flour

1. In a large skillet, cook the beef over medium-high heat until no longer pink, stirring to break up any large chunks.

2. Stir in the garlic, onion, and bell pepper. Cook, stirring occasionally, until thawed. Stir in the paprika and thyme.

3. Add the broth, noodles, and broccoli and bring to a boil. Reduce the heat to low and simmer, stirring twice, for 8 to 10 minutes, or until the noodles are tender.

4. Meanwhile, in a small bowl, whisk the sour cream with the flour until well blended. Stir this mixture into the noodle mixture. Simmer for 2 to 3

MICROWAVE REHEATS

Just because you make a meal in one pot doesn't mean everybody will be there to eat it at one sitting. So after cooking, portion out the main course in individual microwave-safe dishes. Cool, cover, and refrigerate for your off-hour eaters to heat in the microwave. Tips:

◆ Add a little water to rice or noodles before reheating.

◆ Loosely cover any sauced foods before microwaving. Touch the bottom center of the dish to make sure it's warm before serving the food. (Steaming and bubbling around the edges doesn't necessarily mean the food is hot throughout.)

minutes, stirring often, until the sauce is thickened. Remove the skillet from the heat and serve right away.

Per serving: 630 cal, 36 g pro, 57 g car, 27 g fat, 139 mg chol, 1,576 mg sod

EASY • 60 MINUTES • CLASSIC

BEEF STROGANOFF

Serves 4
Preparation time: 20 minutes
Cooking time: 17 minutes

Traditional components of this dish, named after the nineteenth-century Russian diplomat Count Paul Stroganoff, include tender strips of beef and sliced mushrooms in a rich sauce thickened with sour cream. It is wonderful served over egg noodles or accompanied by rice pilaf.

1 pound boneless beef sirloin, thinly sliced across the grain
1 tablespoon vegetable oil
1 medium-size onion, chopped fine (½ cup)
2 teaspoons minced fresh garlic
8 ounces mushrooms, cleaned, trimmed, and sliced (2½ cups)
1 can (about 10¾ ounces) condensed cream of mushroom soup, undiluted
¼ cup water
¼ teaspoon ground black pepper
½ cup nonfat sour cream

1. Cut the meat slices into 1½-inch-long pieces.
2. In a large skillet, heat the oil over medium heat. Add the onion, garlic, and mushrooms. Cook, stirring often, for 3 to 4 minutes, or until softened. Remove the vegetables to a plate with a slotted spoon.
3. Increase the heat to medium-high. Add the meat and cook for about 7 minutes, stirring occasionally, until browned.
4. Reduce the heat to low. Return the vegetables to the skillet. Stir in the soup, water, and pepper. Cover and simmer for 5 minutes.
5. Remove the skillet from the heat. Stir in the sour cream and serve right away.

Per serving: 399 cal, 26 g pro, 13 g car, 26 g fat, 77 mg chol, 700 mg sod

CHICKEN–FRIED STEAKS

Serves 4

Preparation time: 20 minutes

Cooking time: 25 minutes

This popular dish is a staple in the South and Southwest. The name refers to the style of cooking, similar to Southern fried chicken. Pounding the meat into very thin cutlets tenderizes inexpensive beef shoulder steak and reduces the cooking time. Here, the steaks are topped with an oregano-scented tomato sauce. For real comfort food, serve these fried steaks accompanied by mashed potatoes and carrots.

3 tablespoons olive oil

1 large clove garlic, cut in 3 slices

1 can (about 16 ounces) no-salt-added plum tomatoes
   with basil, undrained

4 teaspoons chopped fresh oregano, or 2 teaspoons
   dried oregano leaves, crumbled

¼ teaspoon salt

¼ teaspoon ground black pepper

⅔ cup packaged plain bread crumbs

3 tablespoons grated Parmesan or Romano cheese

1 tablespoon chopped fresh parsley

¼ teaspoon ground red pepper (cayenne)

¼ teaspoon paprika

1 large egg

1 tablespoon water

4 (¼-inch-thick) boneless beef shoulder or round steaks
   (sometimes labeled as braciole), trimmed (about 4 ounces each)

For garnish: fresh oregano sprigs (optional)

1. In a medium-size saucepan, heat 1 tablespoon of oil over high heat. Add the garlic and cook until browned. Discard the garlic.

2. Add the tomatoes and 2 teaspoons of oregano and bring to a boil. Reduce the heat to medium. Cook for about 10 minutes, stirring occasionally, until the liquid has cooked down and the sauce is thick and chunky. Stir in the salt and pepper.

3. Meanwhile, on a sheet of waxed paper, mix the remaining 2 teaspoons oregano, the bread crumbs, cheese, parsley, red pepper, and paprika until blended. In a shallow bowl, beat the egg and water with a fork.

MAKE AHEAD

Cook extra cutlets and make them into sandwiches the next day. Just reheat in the microwave with any leftover tomato sauce and some Parmesan cheese.

4. Pound each steak to ⅛-inch thickness with a mallet or rolling pin (place a heavy-duty plastic bag over the meat and pound from the center out, toward the edges).

5. Dip each cutlet into the beaten egg, then into the crumb mixture, patting the meat to make the crumbs adhere.

6. In a large nonstick skillet, heat 1 tablespoon of oil over medium-high heat until hot and almost smoking. Place 2 cutlets in the skillet and cook for 2 to 3 minutes on each side, or until crisp and golden. Remove to paper towels to drain.

7. Wipe out the skillet and repeat the procedure with the remaining oil and cutlets.

8. Transfer the cutlets to serving plates and spoon over the tomato sauce. Garnish with oregano sprigs and serve right away.

Per serving: 455 cal, 30 g pro, 19 g car, 28 g fat, 128 mg chol, 452 mg sod

---

EASY

LEMON–PEPPER FLANK STEAK

Serves 4

Preparation time: 10 minutes plus at least 2 hours to marinate
Cooking time: 14 minutes plus 5 minutes to stand

Flank steak is an inexpensive cut of meat that benefits from marinating. Try the lemony marinade given here or choose from the variations listed to the left. Serve with skewered grilled potatoes and a tomato salad.

1 (1¼-pound) beef flank steak
½ cup fresh lemon juice
2 tablespoons olive
1 teaspoon chopped fresh garlic
Ground black pepper to taste

1. Score both sides of the steak in a diamond pattern, cutting no deeper than ⅛ inch.

2. In a 1-gallon zipper-type food storage bag, combine the lemon juice, oil, and garlic. Add the steak. Close the bag, pressing out the air, and turn to coat. Marinate in the refrigerator at least 2 hours, or up to 6 hours.

3. Heat a gas grill to medium-high, prepare a charcoal fire until the coals form white ash, or heat a broiler.

4. Remove the steak from the bag and sprinkle generously on both ▶

VARIATION

SESAME-GINGER FLANK STEAK

• In a zipper-type food storage bag, mix ¼ cup reduced-sodium soy sauce, ¼ cup dry sherry or vermouth, 2 tablespoons dark Asian sesame oil, 2 tablespoons finely chopped scallions, 1 tablespoon vegetable oil, 2 teaspoons minced peeled fresh gingerroot, and 2 crushed large cloves garlic.

• Add the steak, marinate, and cook as directed.

Per serving: 298 cal, 28 g pro, 2 g car, 18 g fat, 70 mg chol, 397 mg sod

• EASY

sides with the pepper. Grill or broil 4 to 6 inches from the heat source for 5 to 7 minutes on each side for medium-rare. (Flank steak is best served medium-rare. If cooked too long it will toughen.)

5. Remove the steak to a cutting board and let it stand for 5 minutes before slicing. Cut thin diagonal slices across the grain. For wide slices, hold the knife almost parallel with meat. Serve right away.

Per serving: 270 cal, 27 g pro, 2 g car, 16 g fat, 70 mg chol, 84 mg sod

---

30 MINUTES

SPICY BEEF STIR-FRY

Serves 4

Preparation time: 20 minutes
Cooking time: 10 minutes

When stir-frying, it's best to have everything ready to use before you start because the cooking goes so quickly. Parsleyed rice is good to serve with this dish. If you are watching your family's sodium intake, use reduced-sodium soy sauce or tamari sauce.

1 beef flank steak (about 12 ounces), fat trimmed
2 tablespoons olive
1 large red or green bell pepper, cut into thin strips (1⅓ cups)
8 ounces yellow summer squash or zucchini, cut into thin strips (1¼ cups)
8 medium-size scallions, cut into 1-inch pieces
1 teaspoon minced fresh garlic
1 teaspoon minced peeled fresh gingerroot
2 tablespoons hoisin or tonkatsu sauce
1 tablespoon cider vinegar
1 tablespoon soy sauce
¾ teaspoon dark Asian sesame oil

1. Lay the flank steak flat on a waxed paper-lined baking sheet. Place in the freezer for about 15 minutes for easier slicing.

2. Transfer the steak to a cutting board. Halve lengthwise, then cut each half crosswise on the diagonal into ½-inch-thick slices.

3. In a wok or large heavy skillet, heat 1 tablespoon of oil over medium-high heat until hot but not smoking. Add the flank steak strips and stir-fry for 1 to 2 minutes, or until lightly browned. (The meat will be rare.) Remove the meat to a plate with a slotted spoon.

VARIATION

MOLASSES BARBECUED FLANK STEAK

● In a zipper-type food storage bag, mix ½ cup canned tomato sauce, 2 tablespoons molasses, 2 tablespoons vegetable oil, 1½ tablespoons cider vinegar, and ½ teaspoon dry mustard.

● Add the steak, marinate, and cook as directed.

Per serving: 307 cal, 28 g pro, 7 g car, 18 g fat, 70 mg chol, 225 mg sod

● EASY

COOK'S TIP

Arrange the steak strips (recipe can be multiplied) in a single layer on a waxed paper-lined baking sheet. Freeze uncovered for 1 to 1½ hours, or until firm. Pack into plastic freezer bags or containers and freeze up to 4 months.

4. Heat the remaining 1 tablespoon of oil in the wok over medium-high heat until hot but not smoking. Add the bell pepper and stir-fry for 2 minutes.

5. Add the squash, scallions, garlic, and ginger. Stir-fry for 2 minutes, or until the vegetables are crisp-tender.

6. Stir in the remaining ingredients. Cook, stirring occassionally, for 2 minutes to develop the flavor.

7. Return the steak strips to the wok and stir-fry for 1 minute longer, or just until heated through. Serve right away.

Per serving: 254 cal, 19 g pro, 12 g car, 14 g fat, 43 mg chol, 484 mg sod

EASY • MAKE AHEAD

PEPPERY RIB–EYE STEAKS

Serves 4 to 6
Preparation time: 10 minutes plus at least 1 hour to marinate
Cooking time: 14 minutes

Beef rib-eye steaks are tender and delicious, but this zesty dry marinade can give any beefsteak a lift. Make a large batch of the dry rub and store airtight in a cool dry place. It's also good rubbed on pork, chicken, or turkey.

DRY RUB
1½ teaspoons minced fresh garlic
1½ teaspoons coarsely ground black pepper
1 teaspoon dry mustard
1 teaspoon paprika
1 teaspoon chili powder
½ teaspoon dried thyme leaves, crumbled
½ teaspoon salt
½ teaspoon ground red pepper (cayenne)

1 tablespoon olive oil
2 (1-inch-thick) boneless beef rib-eye steaks (12 ounces each),
    fat trimmed
For garnish: fresh thyme sprigs (optional)

1. Make the dry rub: In a small bowl, mix the garlic, black pepper, mustard, paprika, chili powder, thyme, salt, and red pepper until well blended.

2. Brush the oil on both sides of the steaks and place each steak on a large sheet of plastic wrap. Rub the marinade on both sides of steaks. Wrap tightly and refrigerate at least 1 hour or up to 24 hours.

▶

Ⓜ AKE AHEAD

The dry rub can be prepared and stored airtight up to 3 months.

3. Heat a gas grill to high, prepare a charcoal fire until the coals form white ash, or heat a broiler.

4. Grill or broil the steaks 4 to 6 inches above the heat source for 5 to 7 minutes on each side for rare, 7 to 9 minutes for medium, or 9 to 11 minutes for well done.

5. Remove the steaks to serving plates, garnish with thyme sprigs, and serve right away.

Per serving: 218 cal, 24 g pro, 1 g car, 13 g fat, 66 mg chol, 282 mg sod

ONE POT

BRAISED STUFFED FLANK STEAK

Serves 6
Preparation time: 45 minutes
Cooking time: 1 hour 30 minutes

The stuffing is made in the same pot in which the flank steak is browned and cooked, so make sure the pot is wide enough to hold the meat. Serve with a tossed green salad.

HERB STUFFING
1 tablespoon butter or margarine
1 cup finely chopped onion
1 cup water
3 cups packaged herb bread stuffing mix
¼ teaspoon dried thyme leaves, crumbled

1 (1½-pound) beef flank steak
3 tablespoons butter or margarine
1 pound mushrooms, trimmed and sliced (6 cups)
1 cup beef broth
1 cup dry red wine or additional beef broth
¼ teaspoon dried thyme leaves, crumbled
½ cup cold water
2 tablespoons all-purpose flour

1. Make the stuffing: In a heavy medium-size saucepan, melt the butter over medium heat. Add the chopped onion and cook for 4 to 5 minutes, stirring often, until softened. Add the water and bring to a boil over high heat. Remove the pan from the heat and stir in the stuffing mix ▶ *p. 129*

CARVE ME TENDER

Carving meat across the grain isn't really very difficult, but it may take a few stabs to get it right.

To carve: Hold meat steady with a large fork. (If possible, don't pierce the meat. Just press the fork against it, which helps retain juices.) Starting at one end and using a long, sharp knife, slice into the meat, cutting down at a 45° angle. If you're cutting across the grain, you'll see a kind of cross section of thin bundles, almost like the tips of a bundle of wooden matchsticks. If the cut surface reveals long, stringy fibers—like matchsticks lined up side by side—you're cutting with the grain. Don't worry. Just turn the meat and try again.

MICROWAVE MAIN DISH
Cooking this Roast Beef with Mushroom Gravy (p.138) in the microwave keeps the kitchen cool.

WHOLE
OMATOES

Each tomato individually selected for its size and quality.

DOWN-HOME FLAVOR

Tasty, timeless dishes like Chicken-Fried Steaks (p.120) always inspire feelings of well-being. Here, the cutlets are topped with a tangy tomato sauce and accompanied by carrots and green beans.

Ground, chopped, or sliced beef is featured in scores of favorite American meals, from the beloved burger or meat loaf to the Sunday roast or hearty beef stew.

and the thyme until evenly moistened.

2. Holding the flank steak flat with one hand, cut a horizontal pocket into the meat from the cut edge, leaving a ½-inch edge uncut on the remaining 3 sides. Spoon the stuffing into the pocket, then close the opening with a skewer or toothpicks.

3. Wipe the pan clean. Add 2 tablespoons of butter and melt over medium heat. Add the mushrooms and cook for 5 to 6 minutes, stirring often, until very lightly browned. Remove with a slotted spoon to a bowl.

4. Melt the remaining 1 tablespoon of butter in the pan. Add the flank steak and cook over high heat for about 3 minutes on each side, until browned.

5. Add the broth, wine, and thyme. Bring to a boil over medium-high heat. Reduce the heat to low. Cover and simmer for 1¼ to 1½ hours, turning two or three times, until the meat is tender. Remove to a cutting board.

6. In a small bowl, mix the water and flour until blended. Whisk into the pan juices. Simmer for 2 to 3 minutes, stirring constantly, until the gravy is smooth and slightly thickened. Add the sautéed mushrooms.

7. Remove the skewer and slice the meat across the grain. Arrange the slices on serving plates and spoon over some of the gravy. Serve the remaining gravy at the table.

Per serving: 453 cal, 29 g pro, 36 g car, 21 g fat, 80 mg chol with butter, 59 mg chol with margarine, 944 mg sod with butter and wine, 1,215 mg sod with butter and broth, 955 mg sod with margarine and wine, 1,226 mg sod with margarine and broth

GRILLING STEAK RIGHT

◆ If using a charcoal grill, start the fire 30 to 40 minutes before grilling. The fire's right when coals look ash-covered and you can hold your hand 4 to 5 inches (grill height) over the coals for 4 seconds.

◆ Trim steaks of excess fat.

◆ Lightly brush steaks or grilling surface with oil to prevent sticking.

◆ Grill 1-inch-thick steaks 12 to 14 minutes, turning once, for medium rare; 5 minutes longer for medium. Grill 18 to 20 minutes for 2-inch-thick steaks (5 minutes longer for medium).

◆ Make a small cut in the thickest part of the meat and check the color to tell if it's done. Or touch it. Rare will be soft, medium will give slightly, and well done will be firm. For steaks more than 1½ inches thick, insert a meat thermometer into the thickest part—145° to 150°F is medium rare, 160°F is medium.

◆ Let steaks stand at room temperature for a few minutes after grilling to give the juices a chance to settle and the meat to firm up for easier slicing.

INDOOR GRILLING

The best alternative to outdoor grilling is a cast iron grill pan with raised ridges. The meat should be at room temperature so it doesn't char. Heat the pan over high heat for 4 to 6 minutes before starting, then adjust the heat to medium and cook the steak(s) as you would on an outdoor gas or charcoal grill.

Oven broiling is not the ideal way to cook steaks. The oven just isn't hot enough for proper searing. But if you must oven-broil, use steaks 1 to 2 inches thick and heat your broiler and broiler pan for at least 10 minutes. Then place the steaks as close to the heating unit as you can without flare-ups.

STEAK FAJITAS

Serves 6

Preparation time: 30 minutes plus at least 1 hour to marinate
Cooking time: 10 minutes plus 5 minutes to stand

Fajitas (pronounced fah-HEE-tas), whose name is derived from the Mexican word for skirt steak, were created by Mexican farmhands, who grilled this cut of meat, wrapped it in flour tortillas, and ate them out of hand. This is a fun dish to serve because everyone can make their own using the toppings of their choice. You may grill the steak instead of broiling it, and heat the wrapped tortillas alongside it on the grill. Fajitas are a meal in themselves, but you can serve them with guacamole or a black bean salad.

FAJITA MARINADE
3 tablespoons oil
2 teaspoons fresh lime juice
2 teaspoons minced fresh garlic
1 teaspoon ground cumin
½ teaspoon salt
½ teaspoon ground black pepper

1 (1½-pound) beef flank steak
12 (8-inch) flour tortillas, stacked and wrapped in foil
1½ cups shredded lettuce
3 medium-size ripe tomatoes, sliced
6 scallions, sliced
Sour cream (optional)

1. Make the marinade: In a 1-gallon zipper-type food storage bag, mix the oil, lime juice, garlic, cumin, salt, and pepper. Add the flank steak. Close the bag, pressing out the air, and turn to coat. Refrigerate at least 1 hour or up to 24 hours.

2. Heat the oven to 350° F. Place the wrapped tortillas in the oven to heat for 8 to 10 minutes. Turn the oven off and keep the tortillas in the oven until ready to use.

3. Heat the broiler. Place the steak on a broiler-pan rack and broil 4 to 5 inches from the heat source for about 5 minutes on each side for medium-rare, 7 minutes on each side for medium.

4. Remove the steak to a cutting board, and let it rest for 5 minutes. Thinly slice across the grain.

5. Place a few strips of meat in the center of each tortilla. Top with lettuce, tomato, scallions, and sour cream. Roll up and eat out of hand.
Per serving: 468 cal, 29 g pro, 44 g car, 19 g fat, 57 mg chol, 502 mg sod

EASY • 30 MINUTES

BARBECUED BEEF ON BUNS

Serves 4
Preparation time: 15 minutes
Cooking time: 13 minutes

Bring the taste of Texas to your table in under 30 minutes with these tender beef sandwiches. For a more authentic flavor use hickory or smoked barbecue sauce and serve with potato salad or coleslaw.

1 tablespoon vegetable oil
1 (1-pound) beef flank steak or top round steak, cut in half lengthwise and sliced thin crosswise
1 large green bell pepper, cut into chunks
2 scallions, cut into ½-inch pieces
1 package (10 ounces) frozen whole-kernel corn
1 cup bottled barbecue sauce
1 large tomato, cut into chunks
4 split and toasted hamburger buns

1. In a heavy large skillet, heat the oil over medium-high heat until hot but not smoking. Add the beef and stir-fry for about 3 minutes, or until browned. Remove the meat to a bowl with a slotted spoon.

2. Reduce the heat to medium. Add the bell pepper and scallions to the skillet with the drippings. Cook, stirring once or twice, for 5 minutes, or until softened.

3. Return the meat to the skillet. Stir in the corn, barbecue sauce, and tomato. Cook for 2 to 3 minutes, or until heated through. Put the split buns on serving dishes and spoon over the beef mixture.
Makes 4 sandwiches. Per sandwich: 484 cal, 30 g pro, 48 g car, 19 g fat, 59 mg chol, 838 mg sod

EASY

GRILLED BEEF SHORT RIBS

Serves 8

Preparation time: 20 minutes plus at least 3 hours to marinate

Cooking time: 10 minutes

Flanken beef short ribs are cut crosswise from the sixth, seventh, and eighth rib. Each piece should contain 3 crosscut rib bones. If you don't see them in the meat case, you can usually special-order them from your butcher.

MARINADE

½ cup medium-sweet sherry or pineapple juice

½ cup reduced-sodium soy sauce

¼ cup packed light or dark brown sugar

¼ cup vegetable oil

2 large cloves garlic, peeled and crushed

½ teaspoon ground black pepper

4 pounds well-trimmed flanken beef short ribs, about ½ inch thick

1 cup bottled barbecue sauce

For garnish: fresh chives (optional)

1. Make the marinade: In a medium-size saucepan, bring the sherry and soy sauce to a boil over medium-high heat. Stir in the brown sugar and reduce the heat to low. Cover and simmer for 5 minutes, or until the sugar dissolves.

2. Remove the pan from the heat. Whisk in the oil, garlic, and pepper and let cool completely.

3. In a shallow large bowl, combine the ribs and marinade, turning to coat. Cover with plastic wrap and refrigerate for 3 to 12 hours, turning the ribs occasionally.

4. Heat a gas grill to medium-high, prepare a charcoal fire, or heat a broiler.

5. Drain the ribs and discard the marinade. Grill or broil the ribs 4 to 6 inches from the heat source for 10 minutes for medium-rare, 12 minutes for medium, and 14 minutes for well done, turning and basting with barbecue sauce twice. Remove the ribs to serving plates and serve right away.

Per serving: 263 cal, 20 g pro, 9 g car, 15 g fat, 57 mg chol, 592 mg sod

BUYING AND STORING BEEF

◆ When shopping, make the meat counter your last stop to keep the beef as cold as possible while transporting it home. For flavorful beef, choose cuts that have some marbling. The meat should be red and firm, with any fat creamy white, not yellow. Avoid beef that is mushy or brown.

◆ Refrigerate beef as soon as you get it home. Remove the store wrapping and wrap in waxed paper or butcher paper and place on a dish to catch any drippings. Avoid wrapping meat tightly in plastic wrap, which seals in moisture and allows bacteria to grow. Ground beef or beef

EASY • MAKE AHEAD • ONE POT

PARTY STEW

Serves 8
Preparation time: 15 minutes
Cooking time: 3 hours

Make this stew when you have time to put it in the oven, then serve as is for the family, or fancied up for guests. For party fare, just add 12 ounces of small mushrooms and 2 tablespoons of coarse-grain Dijon mustard before you reheat the stew. Simmer for 10 minutes, then stir in 1 package (10 ounces) of frozen green peas and simmer for 4 minutes longer. For a simple family meal, serve it over buttered noodles or steamed rice or with dinner rolls or garlic bread.

1 can (about 16 ounces) crushed tomatoes
⅔ cup dry red wine or water
½ cup beef broth
¼ cup quick-cooking tapioca
1 tablespoon granulated sugar
2 teaspoons dried fines herbes, Italian herb seasoning, or
 other herb blend
2 small bay leaves
2 teaspoons salt
½ teaspoon ground black pepper
3 pounds well-trimmed lean boneless beef chuck, cut into 1-inch pieces
1 pound carrots, scrubbed and quartered crosswise
4 large ribs celery, trimmed, washed, and cut into 1-inch chunks
3 medium-size onions, peeled and quartered ▶

MAKE-AHEAD STEWING TIPS

◆ Stews will keep in the refrigerator tightly covered up to 4 days. Quickly cool the portion you plan to refrigerate or freeze by putting the pot in a sink full of cold water. Packing cooled food is easier than hot, and getting it put away as fast as possible guarantees fresher flavor.
◆ One reheating is best. Take out only the portion you plan to eat and leave the rest in the refrigerator for another time. Reheat on the range top or in a microwave oven, adding a little water if too thick.

◆ Freeze stew in single or family-size portions. Good freezer containers: zipper-type food storage bags (stack them flat) and plastic containers. Leave about 1/4 inch at the top of the container for expansion and put a piece of plastic wrap directly on the stew to keep air from getting at it. Use freezer tape to double-seal lids, or place the container in a plastic food-storage bag and close tightly. Label with contents, date, and number of servings. Thaw in the refrigerator or microwave before reheating.

1. Heat the oven to 325°F.

2. In a heavy 5- to 6-quart Dutch oven, mix the tomatoes, wine, broth, tapioca, sugar, herbs, bay leaves, salt, and pepper. Stir in the meat. Add the carrots, celery, and onions.

3. Cover and bake for about 3 hours, stirring twice, or until the meat is tender when tested with a fork and the sauce has thickened. Discard the bay leaves before serving or cooling and refrigerating.

Per serving: 347 cal, 35 g pro, 22 g car, 13 g fat, 111 mg chol, 948 mg sod

---

EASY • MAKE AHEAD • ONE POT

HERBED BEEF & VEGETABLE STEW

Serves 8 to 10
Preparation time: 15 minutes
Cooking time: 2 hours 25 minutes

The best thing about stew is its relatively low cost and the fact that it can be cooked slowly with little attention. Serve over egg noodles or mashed potatoes. Basil, rosemary, oregano, and thyme add flavor and aroma to this stew, while carrots, green beans, and mushrooms provide color and texture.

½ cup all-purpose flour
1½ teaspoons salt
4 pounds well-trimmed boneless beef chuck, cut into 1¼-inch pieces
¼ cup olive or vegetable oil
1 can (35 ounces) Italian plum tomatoes in juice, undrained
1⅔ cups beef broth
½ cup dry white wine or additional beef broth
1 tablespoon minced fresh garlic
1 teaspoon dried basil leaves, crumbled
1 teaspoon dried rosemary leaves, crumbled
1 teaspoon dried oregano leaves, crumbled
1 teaspoon dried thyme leaves, crumbled
½ teaspoon ground black pepper
2 bay leaves (1½ inches long)
1 pound carrots, cut into ¼-inch rounds
12 ounces small mushrooms, cleaned, trimmed, and halved
12 ounces fresh green beans, trimmed and cut into 2-inch pieces
4 large ribs celery, chopped
½ cup finely chopped fresh parsley
For garnish: sprigs of fresh herbs (optional)

MAKE AHEAD

This stew will taste best if you make it a day or two ahead. Refrigerate (or freeze up to 3 months) and reheat on the stovetop.

1. Mix the flour and salt on a sheet of waxed paper. Coat the meat with the flour mixture, shaking off the excess.

2. In a 4- to 5-quart pot, heat the oil over medium-high heat. Add half the beef and brown on at least 2 sides. Remove with a slotted spoon to a plate. Repeat with the remaining beef.

3. Return all the meat and its juices to the pot. Stir in the tomatoes, broth, wine, garlic, herbs, pepper, and bay leaves. Bring to a boil. Reduce the heat to medium-low. Cover and simmer for 1½ hours, stirring 3 or 4 times.

4. Add the carrots, mushrooms, green beans, celery, and parsley. Cover and simmer for 45 minutes longer, stirring once or twice, until the meat and vegetables are tender.

5. Ladle the stew into shallow serving bowls and garnish with fresh herbs.

Per serving: 513 cal, 48 g pro, 24 g car, 25 g fat, 148 mg chol, 1,180 mg sod with wine, 1,281 mg sod with broth

EASY • MAKE AHEAD • ONE POT

BEEF BARLEY STEW

Serves 4

Preparation time: 15 minutes

Cooking time: 2 hours 15 minutes

This recipe provides a complete meal and is delicious the next day. It takes only minutes to assemble, and while it simmers on the stove the aroma will whet everyone's appetite.

2 tablespoons vegetable oil
1 pound well-trimmed boneless beef chuck, cut into 1-inch pieces
2 medium-size onions, sliced thin (2 cups)
3 medium-size carrots, sliced thin (1½ cups)
3 ribs celery, halved lengthwise, cut into ½-inch pieces (1½ cups)
2¼ cups beef bouillon (3 bouillon cubes dissolved in 2¼ cups water)
1 can (8 ounces) tomatoes, undrained and chopped coarse
  (see Cook's Tip)
1 teaspoon chili powder
1 teaspoon ground allspice
1 teaspoon salt
¾ cup uncooked barley

1. In a 4- to 5-quart pot, heat the oil over medium-high heat. Add the beef and brown on at least 2 sides. Remove to a plate. ▶

COOK'S TIP

Use scissors to cut up tomatoes right in the can.

2. Add the onions, carrots, and celery to the pot drippings. Cook for 5 minutes, stirring often, until beginning to soften.

3. Add the bouillon, tomatoes with their juice, chili powder, allspice, and salt. Stir to break up the tomatoes and scrape up the browned bits on the bottom of the pot.

4. Bring to a boil. Return the beef and its juices to the pot and reduce the heat to low. Cover and simmer for 1¼ hours, stirring once or twice.

5. Stir in the barley. Cover and simmer for 40 to 45 minutes, stirring once or twice and adding more water as needed (barley swells and absorbs liquid), or until the meat and barley are tender.

Per serving: 426 cal, 29 g pro, 42 g car, 17 g fat, 74 mg chol, 1,445 mg sod

EASY • MAKE AHEAD • CLASSIC

RED WINE COUNTRY
BEEF STEW

Serves 4
Preparation time: 15 minutes
Cooking time: 2 hours 45 minutes

An added bonus to this stew is that it needs no browning. And once you put it together, it requires no attention, not even stirring. Parsleyed egg noodles and steamed kale with carrots complete the meal.

3 tablespoons butter or margarine
2 medium-size onions, sliced thin (1½ cups)
1 pound well-trimmed lean boneless beef chuck, cut into
   1½ inch pieces
1 bay leaf (about 2 inches long)
2 tablespoons currants
5 tablespoons tomato paste
¾ cup dry red wine
2 tablespoons red wine vinegar
1 tablespoon packed light or dark brown sugar
2 teaspoons minced fresh garlic
1 teaspoon ground cumin
½ teaspoon salt
¼ teaspoon ground black pepper
¼ teaspoon ground cinnamon
Pinch of ground cloves
For garnish: walnut halves (optional)

1. In a medium-size saucepan, melt the butter over medium heat. Add the onions and cook, stirring often, for 8 to 10 minutes, or until softened and golden.

2. Add the beef. Stir to coat well with the onion mixture. Cook for 5 minutes, or until the outside of the meat loses its pink color. Add the bay leaf and currants.

3. In a small bowl, mix the remaining ingredients except the walnuts. Stir this mixture into the saucepan. Bring to a boil over medium-high heat. Reduce the heat to low. Cover and simmer without stirring for about 2½ hours, or until the meat is very tender when tested with a fork.

4. Ladle the stew into a shallow serving bowl and garnish with walnuts.

Per serving: 321 cal, 24 g pro, 18 g car, 17 g fat, 97 mg chol with butter, 74 mg chol with margarine, 617 mg sod with butter, 630 mg sod with margarine

EASY • ONE POT • CLASSIC

RIB–EYE ROAST WITH MADEIRA SAUCE

Serves 8
Preparation time: 15 minutes
Cooking time: 1 hour 40 minutes

Madeira wine adds a distinctive slightly sweet flavor to the sauce in this easy roast recipe. Serve with roasted potatoes and carrots and peas. The wine takes its name from the Portuguese island of Madeira, where it is made, and makes an excellent cooking wine. The rib-eye roast is one of the most tender cuts of beef you can buy. Serve with roasted or steamed potatoes and steamed mixed vegetables.

1 tablespoon minced fresh garlic
1 teaspoon salt
1 teaspoon cracked or coarsely ground
    black pepper
1 teaspoon dried thyme leaves, crumbled
½ teaspoon dried tarragon leaves
1 boneless beef rib-eye roast (about 5 pounds)
¼ cup finely chopped shallots or white part of scallions
1 cup beef broth
½ cup Madeira wine
1 tablespoon tomato paste
For garnish: fresh herbs (optional)

1. Heat the oven to 350°F.

2. In a small bowl, sprinkle the garlic with the salt and mash to a paste with the blade of a knife or the bottom of a glass. Add the pepper, thyme, and tarragon. Mash until blended. Rub the mixture evenly over the entire roast.

3. Place the roast, fat side up, on a rack in a roasting pan. Insert a meat thermometer so the bulb is in the thickest part, not touching the fat.

4. Roast uncovered for 18 to 20 minutes per pound for rare, 20 to 22 minutes per pound for medium. Remove the meat from the oven when the meat thermometer registers 145°F for medium-rare or 160°F for medium.

5. Transfer the roast to carving board and cover loosely with foil. Let stand for 15 to 20 minutes in a warm place before carving. (The temperature of the roast will continue to rise about 5° to 140°F for rare and 160°F for medium.)

6. Meanwhile, remove the rack from the roasting pan. Drain off the fat. Add the shallots to the pan drippings. Position the pan over one or two burners on the stovetop. Stir over medium heat for 2 to 3 minutes, or until the shallots are softened. Add the broth and Madeira and stir until dried meat juices sticking to the pan dissolve. Stir in the tomato paste until blended. Increase the heat to medium-high and cook at a gentle boil for 4 to 5 minutes, or until the sauce is reduced to about ¾ cup and is thick enough to coat a metal spoon.

7. Slice the roast and serve with the sauce.

Per serving : 443 cal, 49 g pro, 4 g car, 23 g fat, 140 mg chol, 618 mg sod

---

MICROWAVE

ROAST BEEF WITH MUSHROOM GRAVY

Serves 6

Preparation time: 15 minutes

Cooking time: 50 minutes plus 15 minutes to stand

Be sure the roast is trimmed of surface fat, since it attracts microwaves and can cause the meat beneath it to overcook. Serve with garlicky mashed potatoes to spoon the gravy over.

2 teaspoons dried thyme leaves, crumbled
1 teaspoon ground black pepper
¼ teaspoon garlic powder
1 (3-pound) boneless beef bottom round roast, trimmed of surface fat and tied
¼ teaspoon salt

C OOK'S TIP

◆ If you plan to use a disposable aluminum roasting pan, nest 2 pans together. (One won't be sturdy enough for a heavy roast.) Make the sauce or gravy by pouring 1 or 2 tablespoons of fat drippings into a saucepan and cooking the shallots or onions as directed. Discard the rest of the fat. Add a little broth to the juices in the roasting pan and scrape to dissolve them. Add the dissolved juices, along with any remaining broth, and the sauce ingredients to the saucepan and cook as directed.

COOK'S TIPS

◆ Let roasted or grilled meat or poultry stand after cooking to give the juices a chance to settle and the meat to firm up for easier carving.

◆ If possible, carve a roast on a wooden board with grooves to help hold the meat and a well to catch juices. Carving on a platter is difficult and it dulls the knife.

MUSHROOM GRAVY

1½ cups beef broth

4 ounces small mushrooms, trimmed and sliced thin (1½ cups)

2 tablespoons all-purpose flour

Pan juices from roast

⅛ teaspoon salt

⅛ teaspoon ground black pepper

⅛ teaspoon dried thyme leaves, crumbled

For garnish: thyme sprigs (optional)

1. In a small bowl, mix the thyme, pepper, and garlic powder. Rub all over the roast. Place the roast on a microwave-safe roasting rack with sides or a microwave-safe rack set in a shallow 11 x 7-inch microwave-safe baking dish.

2. Microwave uncovered on Medium Low for 30 minutes, rotating the dish ¼ turn twice. Turn the roast over. (If you have a microwave-safe meat thermometer or your microwave has a meat probe, now is the time to insert it into the center of the roast.) Microwave for 7 to 10 minutes longer, or until a microwave or conventional meat thermometer inserted into the center of the roast registers 135°F. Sprinkle the roast with the salt and transfer to a serving platter. Save the pan juices for the gravy.

3. Cover the meat loosely with foil and let stand for 15 minutes (the temperature will rise to 145°F and the meat will be cooked to medium-rare).

4. Meanwhile, make the gravy: Put ¼ cup of broth and the mushrooms in a 1-quart microwave-safe measuring cup or bowl. Cover with vented plastic wrap and microwave on High for 2 to 3 minutes, or until the mushrooms are cooked.

5. Meanwhile, in a medium-size bowl, whisk ¼ cup of broth with the flour until smooth. Whisk in the remaining 1 cup broth, the pan juices, salt, pepper, and thyme. Stir into the mushrooms. Microwave uncovered on High for 5 to 7 minutes, stirring twice, until thickened.

6. Garnish the platter with sprigs of fresh thyme. Thinly slice the meat and serve with the gravy.

Per serving: 274 cal, 34 g pro, 3 g car, 13 g fat, 92 mg chol, 622 mg sod

FAST AND EASY MINUTE STEAKS

◆ Pan-fry minute steaks and serve on hoagie rolls along with bowls of heated au jus gravy from a can or jar for dipping. Serve with prepared three-bean salad and a sensible number of crunchy potato chips.

◆ Sauté thinly sliced onion and red and green bell pepper sprinkled with soy sauce in oil or butter. Remove from the skillet, then pan-fry minute steaks and serve topped with the bell pepper mixture.

EASY • ONE POT • CLASSIC

POT ROAST
OF YOUR CHOICE

Serves 8

Preparation time: 15 minutes

Cooking time: 3 hours 10 minutes plus 10 minutes to stand

Now you can make any around-the-world pot roast you like. Here's how it works: Start with a basic pot roast recipe, then choose a country and chart a flavor course for a delicious dinner entree with a foreign accent. The roast should be at room temperature before it is cooked. Using a sharp knife, cut off as much of the fat as possible. If necessary, tie the roast with kitchen string to form a compact mass. Just before cooking, quickly rinse the meat under cold running water and pat dry with paper towels.

2 tablespoons vegetable oil
1 (3 to 4 pound) boneless beef chuck roast, trimmed of visible fat
Flavoring vegetables (see Around-the-World Pot Roasts chart, page 142)
Liquids (see chart, page 142)
Seasonings (see chart, page 142)

1. Heat the oven to 325°F.

2. In a 4- to 5-quart Dutch oven, heat the oil over medium heat. Pat the meat dry with paper towels. Add the meat to the hot oil along with flavoring vegetables. Brown the meat on all sides. Stir vegetables occasionally.

3. Add the liquids and seasonings. Cover and bake for 2½ to 3 hours, or until the meat is fork-tender.

4. Transfer the meat to a cutting board. Cover loosely with foil and let stand for 10 to 15 minutes.

5. Discard any bay leaves and/or citrus peel and skim the fat from the sauce. If you like, thicken the sauce by stirring in 3 tablespoons flour mixed with ¼ cup water (unless otherwise noted on chart).

6. Slice the meat across the grain and serve with the sauce.

VARIATION

MICROWAVE POT ROAST OF YOUR CHOICE

• Omit the oil. Put 1 tablespoon of all-purpose flour into a 20 x 14-inch oven cooking bag. Shake to coat the bag, then put the bag into a 13 x 9-inch microwave-safe baking dish. Add the roast. (If the roast has a high point, shield it with a small piece of foil.) Surround with the flavoring vegetable(s).

• Mix the liquid ingredients until well blended. Pour over the roast. Sprinkle with the seasonings. Close the bag with a nylon tie.

• Make six ½-inch slits in the top of the bag. Microwave on Medium for 1½ to 2 hours, rotating the dish twice, until the meat is almost tender when pierced with a fork through the slit in the bag. Let stand in the bag for 15 minutes, or until the meat is fork-tender.

• Carefully cut open the top of the bag. Transfer the roast to a cutting board and let rest for 10 minutes before slicing.

• Discard any bay leaves and/or citrus peel. Pour or strain the sauce into a 4-cup microwave-safe measure. Skim off the fat. To thicken, whisk the thickening ingredients into the sauce. Microwave on High for 3 to 4 minutes, whisking once, until thickened. (For Mexican pot roast, simply whisk the chocolate into the liquid until melted.)

• EASY • ONE POT

EASY • ONE POT • CLASSIC

BRISKET WITH ONION GRAVY

Serves 6
Preparation time: 15 minutes
Cooking time: 3 hours 30 minutes

This recipe couldn't be easier—it produces tender, juicy meat and a savory gravy at the same time. Serve with lots of warm crusty bread to mop up the extra gravy.

2 cups water
1 envelope (from a 2.3-ounce box) beef-flavor mushroom soup mix
4 cups sliced onions
1 (3-pound) beef brisket (thin cut), top fat trimmed to ¼ inch
2 pounds small red potatoes (about 12), scrubbed and cut in half
1 pound carrots, cut into 2-inch pieces

1. Heat the oven to 350°F.
2. In a 4- to 5-quart Dutch oven, mix the water and soup mix. Bring to a boil over high heat. Remove the pan from the heat.
3. Scatter half the onions over the soup mixture. Add the meat, fat side up. Scatter the remaining onions over the meat. Cover and bake for 1½ hours.
4. Scatter the potatoes and carrots around the meat. Cover and bake for 1 ½ to 2 hours longer, or until the meat and vegetables are tender.
5. Transfer the meat to a cutting board and slice across the grain in thin slices. Serve with the vegetables and pan gravy.

Per serving: 920 cal, 44 g pro, 47 g car, 61 g fat, 166 mg chol, 593 mg sod

BEEF ROASTING CHART

Use this chart as a guide for roasting times. A meat thermometer will register 145°F to 150°F for medium-rare, 160° F for medium. Allow the roast to sit for 15 minutes before carving and remember that the internal temperature will continue to rise 5 to 10°F

CUT:	COOKING TIME:
Eye round, 2 to 3 pounds	20 to 22 minutes per pound at 325°F
Rib eye, boneless 4 to 5 pounds	18 to 22 minutes per pound at 350°F
Rib, bone in, 4 to 6 pounds	25 to 30 minutes per pound at 325°F
Top round 4 to 6 pounds	30 to 35 minutes at 325°F
Tenderloin 2 to 3 pounds	35 to 45 minutes total at 425°F
4 to 6 pounds	45 to 1 hour total at 425°F

AROUND-THE-WORLD POT ROASTS

FRENCH
VEGETABLES: 1½ cups thinly sliced leeks, ¾ cup each chopped carrots and celery (with leaves), 1 tsp minced garlic

LIQUIDS: 1 cup dry red wine or ¾ cup beef broth and 2 Tbsp red-wine vinegar

SEASONINGS: 1 tsp salt, ½ tsp each pepper and dried thyme leaves, 2 small bay leaves

Per serving: 281 cal, 30 g pro, 5 g car, 15 g fat, 100 mg chol, 412 mg sod with wine, 289 mg sod with broth.
Microwave: 254 cal, 30 g pro, 6 g car, 11 g fat, 100 mg chol, 412 mg sod with wine, 289 mg sod with broth

ITALIAN
VEGETABLES: 1 cup finely chopped onion, 1 tsp minced garlic

LIQUIDS: 1 can (14 oz) Italian plum tomatoes, broken up; ½ cup dry Marsala wine or beef broth

SEASONINGS: ½ tsp salt (only with Marsala), ½ tsp each dried basil and thyme leaves, 2 small bay leaves

Per serving: 285 cal with wine, 279 cal with broth, 30 g pro, 5 g car, 15 g fat, 100 mg chol, 338 mg sod with wine, 302 mg sod with broth.
Microwave: 255 cal, 30 g pro, 7 g car with wine, 5 g car with broth, 12 g fat, 100 mg chol, 338 mg sod with wine, 302 mg sod with broth

WEST AFRICAN
VEGETABLES: 1 cup thinly sliced onion

LIQUIDS: 1 cup water mixed with ½ cup peanut butter, ⅓ cup lemon juice and ¼ cup tomato paste

SEASONINGS: ½ tsp each dried thyme leaves and ground red pepper

Per serving: 371 cal, 35 g pro, 7 g car, 23 g fat, 100 mg chol, 261 mg sod.
Microwave: 344 cal, 35 g pro, 7 g car, 20 g fat, 100 mg chol, 261 mg sod

EASTERN MEDITERRANEAN
VEGETABLES: 1 cup chopped onion, 1 Tbsp minced garlic

LIQUIDS: 1 cup dry red wine or beef broth mixed with 2 Tbsp tomato paste

SEASONINGS: 1 tsp ground cumin, 1 tsp salt (only with wine), ½ tsp pepper, ¼ tsp ground cinnamon, 2 small bay leaves, peel of 1 lemon (removed with vegetable peeler), ½ cup each dried apricots and pitted prunes

Per serving: 318 cal, 31 g pro, 14 g car, 15 g fat, 100 mg chol, 398 mg sod with wine, 358 mg sod with broth.
Microwave: 291 cal, 31 g pro, 15 g car, 12 g fat, 100 mg chol, 397 mg sod with wine, 358 mg sod with broth

SCANDINAVIAN
VEGETABLES: 1 cup thinly sliced onion

LIQUIDS: 12 oz beer or 1¼ cups beef broth and 2 Tbsp cider vinegar

SEASONINGS: 2 Tbsp packed brown sugar, 2 Tbsp snipped fresh dill or 1 tsp dried dillweed, 1 tsp salt (only with beer), 1 tsp pepper, ½ tsp ground allspice, 2 small bay leaves

Per serving: 286 cal, 30 g pro, 7 g car with beer, 6 g car with broth, 15 g fat, 100 mg chol, 398 mg sod with beer, 377 mg sod with broth.

Microwave: 260 cal, 30 g pro, 7 g car, 11 g fat, 100 mg chol, 398 mg sod with beer, 377 mg sod with broth

Note: To thicken, stir in ½ cup sour cream or plain low-fat yogurt mixed with 3 Tbsp all-purpose flour.

MEXICAN
VEGETABLES: ½ cup chopped green onions, 1 Tbsp minced garlic

LIQUIDS: 1 cup beef broth mixed with 2 Tbsp tomato paste

SEASONINGS: ¼ cup chili powder, ¼ cup raisins, ½ tsp each ground red pepper and cinnamon, ⅛ tsp ground cloves

Per serving: 294 cal, 31 g pro, 7 g car, 15 g fat, 100 mg chol, 395 mg sod.
Microwave: 268 cal, 31 g pro, 8 g car, 12 g fat, 100 mg chol, 395 mg sod

Note: To thicken, stir in 1 square (1 ounce) unsweetened chocolate.

CHINESE
VEGETABLES: White part only of 4 medium-size green onions, 2 Tbsp chopped fresh gingerroot, 1 Tbsp minced garlic

LIQUIDS: 1 cup water, 3 Tbsp soy sauce, 2 Tbsp dry sherry wine or ¼ cup orange juice

SEASONINGS: Peel of 1 orange (removed with vegetable peeler), ½ tsp Szechuan peppercorns (optional)

Per serving: 270 cal, 30 g pro, 3 g car, 15 g fat, 100 mg chol, 506 mg sod.
Microwave: 244 cal, 30 g pro, 3 g car, 11 g fat, 100 mg chol, 506 mg sod

Note: To thicken, stir in 2 Tbsp cornstarch mixed with ½ cup water.

FISH
& SEAFOOD

"Food is meant to tempt as well as nourish, and everything that lives in the water is seductive."
JEAN-PAUL ARON

Fish is gaining in popularity, and for good reason: it's nutritious, light on fat and calories, and its versatility and easy preparation fit perfectly into our fast-paced lifestyle. And there's the added bonus of the Omega-3 oils, which recent studies show are particularly beneficial in the prevention of heart disease. A wider selection of fish and shellfish is available to us than ever before, mostly due to improved methods of transportation. So even people who don't live near water can enjoy fresh fish whenever they want. With all these advantages, it's hard to think of a reason not to eat fish.

> **EASY • 60 MINUTES • LOW FAT • ONE POT**

FISH STEW

Serves 4
Preparation time: 10 minutes
Cooking time: 30 minutes

This economical dish is made with cod, one of the most popular saltwater fish available. Its delicate sweet flavor and firm texture lend themselves to many flavor combinations. Here cod is combined with corn, pimientos, and rice for a wonderfully fragrant and easy casserole. Serve it with a crisp green salad and whole-grain bread.

1 tablespoon olive oil
1 tablespoon butter
2 large onions, cut into ¼-inch-thick slices (2 cups)
1 teaspoon minced fresh garlic
1 cup uncooked white long grain rice
4 cups water
3 tablespoons minced parsley
1 teaspoon chopped fresh tarragon (optional)
1 teaspoon salt
½ teaspoon ground black pepper
2 cups frozen corn kernels
1 jar (5 ounces) pimientos, drained and chopped (about ½ cup)
1 pound firm-textured white fish fillets, such as cod, ocean perch,
   or flounder

1. In a heavy 5-quart pot, heat the oil and butter over medium heat. Add the onions and garlic and cook for about 6 minutes, stirring often, until the onion is softened. Stir in the rice, water, 2 tablespoons of parsley, the tarragon, ¾ teaspoon of salt, and ¼ teaspoon of pepper.

2. Bring the mixture to a boil over medium-high heat. Reduce the heat to low. Cover and simmer for 8 to 10 minutes, or until the rice is almost tender.

3. Stir in the corn and pimiento. Arrange the fish fillets over the top and sprinkle with the remaining parsley, salt, and pepper. Cover and simmer for 10 to 15 minutes longer, or until the fish is opaque at it thickest part when tested with a fork.

4. Remove the pan from the heat and serve right away.

Per serving: 431 cal, 27 g pro, 63 g car, 8 g fat, 57 mg chol, 654 mg sod

CRISP FISH STICKS

Serves 4

Preparation time: 10 minutes

Cooking time: 18 minutes (6 minutes per batch)

OOK'S TIP

You can substitute a mixture of ⅓ cup all-purpose flour, 3 tablespoons cornmeal, ¾ teaspoon baking powder, and ¼ teaspoon salt for the self-rising cornmeal mix.

AKE AHEAD

Prepare the recipe through step 2 (recipe can also be multiplied). Place the coated fish in a single layer on a waxed paper–lined baking sheet or tray. Freeze for 1 to 2 hours, or until firm. Pack in plastic freezer bags and freeze up to 2 months.

Some supermarkets carry lemon-pepper- or Cajun-seasoned marinated fish fillets, which can be used for this recipe. Just cut the fillets into strips and toss in the cornmeal mixture as directed.

1½ pounds firm-textured fish fillets, cut crosswise into 1-inch-wide strips
1 teaspoon olive oil
1 tablespoon fresh lemon juice
¼ teaspoon coarsely ground black pepper
½ cup self-rising white or yellow cornmeal mix (see Cook's Tip)
2 to 3 tablespoons vegetable oil

1. In a large bowl, combine the fish, olive oil, lemon juice, and pepper, tossing to coat.
2. Put the cornmeal in a small bowl. Add a few strips of fish at a time, tossing to coat. Remove to a plate and repeat with the remaining fish.
3. In a large skillet, heat 2 tablespoons of vegetable oil over medium-high heat. Cook the fish in batches for 4 to 6 minutes, turning 2 or 3 times, until golden and crisp.
4. Remove to paper towels to drain. Cook the remaining fish as directed, adding more oil to the skillet if necessary. Serve warm.

Per serving: 288 cal, 32 g pro, 14 g car, 11 g fat, 74 mg chol, 319 mg sod

FISH & CHIPS DINNER

Serves 4

Total time: 45 minutes

Look for bags of coleslaw mix (shredded cabbage and carrots) in the produce section of your supermarket. Serve lemon wedges and/or cocktail sauce, tartar sauce, or malt vinegar with the fish.

▶

½ cup bottled low-fat ranch dressing

4 cups coleslaw mix (from an 8-ounce or larger bag)

4 cups frozen shoestring-style French-fried potatoes
  (from a 12-ounce or larger package)

½ teaspoon chili powder

2 packages (7.6 ounces each) frozen breaded fish fillets (8 fillets)

1. Heat the oven to 450°F. Line a 15½ x 10½-inch jelly roll pan with foil for easy cleanup.

2. In a medium-size bowl, mix the dressing and coleslaw until blended. Cover with plastic wrap and refrigerate for about 30 minutes, or until well chilled.

3. Meanwhile, sprinkle the frozen French fries with the chili powder in the prepared pan. Toss to coat evenly. Arrange the fries and fish fillets in a single layer in the pan.

4. Bake for 25 to 30 minutes, or until the fillets and fries are golden and crisp. Serve right away with the coleslaw.

Per serving: 451 cal, 16 g pro, 47 g car, 23 g fat, 0 mg chol, 851 mg sod

EASY • 30 MINUTES

CATFISH DINNER

Serves 4

Preparation time: 5 minutes

Cooking time: 10 minutes

This light summer dinner is a breeze to prepare. While the fish and tomatoes broil, simmer shucked ears of corn in a large covered skillet for about 4 minutes. (Or microwave unshucked corn on High for about 2 minutes per ear. Wear oven mitts to shuck.) Serve with a lettuce salad tossed with more of the same dressing used to season the fish. The perfect dessert? A juicy peach eaten out of hand.

4 catfish fillets or other firm-textured fish fillets (about 6 ounces each),
  thawed if frozen

2 large ripe tomatoes, halved

⅛ teaspoon salt

⅛ teaspoon ground black pepper

4 tablespoons bottled low-fat ranch dressing

¼ cup grated Parmesan cheese

2 teaspoons olive oil

1. Heat the broiler. Line a broiler pan with foil for easy cleanup.

2. Arrange the fish and the tomatoes cut-side up on the broiler-pan rack. Sprinkle with the salt and pepper. Spread 1 tablespoon of ranch dressing on each fillet. Sprinkle the fish and tomatoes with the Parmesan cheese. Drizzle the oil on the cut sides of the tomatoes.

3. Broil about 5 inches from the heat source for 8 to 10 minutes, or just until the top is nicely browned and the fish is opaque at its thickest part when tested with a fork.

4. Transfer the fish and tomatoes to serving plates and serve right away.

Per serving: 296 cal, 28 g pro, 6 g car, 17 g fat, 60 mg chol, 385 mg sod

---

EASY • 30 MINUTES • MAKE AHEAD

SALMON CROQUETTES

Serves 4
Preparation time: 20 minutes
Cooking time: 10 minutes

In this recipe one can of salmon is stretched into four servings by combining it with mashed potatoes. The cucumber-dill sauce is easy to prepare and can be made up to one day ahead.

CUCUMBER-DILL SAUCE
1 small cucumber, peeled, seeded, and sliced thin (1 cup)
1 cup plain low-fat or nonfat yogurt
2 tablespoons chopped fresh dill, or ¾ teaspoon dried dillweed
½ teaspoon minced fresh garlic

1 can (about 14¾ ounces) pink salmon, drained
1½ cups mashed cooked potatoes
1 small onion, grated
1 large egg
½ teaspoon ground black pepper
¼ cup packaged plain bread crumbs
3 tablespoons vegetable oil
For garnish: dill sprigs (optional)

1. Make the sauce: In a small bowl, mix the cucumber, yogurt, dill, and garlic until well blended. Cover with plastic wrap and refrigerate until ready to use.

2. In a medium-size bowl, mix the salmon, potatoes, onion, egg, and pepper until blended. Form into 8 patties, each about ¾ inch thick. ▶

VARIATION

OVEN-FRIED SALMON CROQUETTES

• Heat the oven to 400°F. Coat a baking sheet with vegetable oil cooking spray.

• Prepare the salmon croquettes as directed and place on the prepared baking sheet. Bake for 10 to 12 minutes, turning once, until golden on both sides.

Per serving: 279 cal, 26 g pro, 25 g car, 8 g fat, 90 mg chol, 543 mg sod

• EASY • 30 MINUTES
• LOW FAT
• MAKE AHEAD

3. Spread the bread crumbs onto a sheet of waxed paper. Gently press the patties in the crumbs to coat evenly.

4. In a large nonstick skillet, heat the oil over medium heat. Cook the patties, in batches if necessary, for about 4 minutes on each side, or until heated through, golden, and crisp. Remove to a plate lined with paper towels to drain.

5. Transfer the patties to serving plates. Garnish with dill sprigs and serve right away with the sauce.

Makes 8 patties. Per 2 patties: 360 cal, 26 g pro, 25 g car, 18 g fat with low-fat yogurt, 17 g fat with nonfat yogurt, 89 mg chol, 544 mg sod

---

60 MINUTES • MAKE AHEAD • CLASSIC

MARYLAND CRAB CAKES

Serves 4

Preparation time: 15 minutes plus 30 minutes to chill

Cooking time: 10 minutes

These crab cakes are sure to be a crowd pleaser, as appropriate for a weekday meal as they are for weekend entertaining.

1 pound fresh or canned crabmeat, picked over well
½ cup packaged plain bread crumbs
1 large egg
3 tablespoons mayonnaise
1 tablespoon Dijon mustard
2 tablespoons minced fresh parsley
¼ teaspoon salt
¼ teaspoon ground black pepper

TARTAR SAUCE
½ cup mayonnaise or salad dressing
¼ cup sweet-pickle relish
2 teaspoons prepared mustard
2 to 3 tablespoons vegetable oil
For garnish: lemon wedges (optional)

1. In a medium-size bowl, gently mix the crabmeat, bread crumbs, egg, mayonnaise, mustard, parsley, salt, and pepper. Form the mixture into 8 patties, about 3 inches in diameter. Put the crab cakes on a plate, cover with plastic wrap, and chill for 30 minutes.

2. Meanwhile, make the tartar sauce. In a small bowl, mix the mayonnaise,

MAKE AHEAD

Prepare the recipe through step 3. Wrap the uncooked croquettes in plastic wrap, then in foil, and freeze up to 2 months. Thaw in the refrigerator and cook as directed.

MAKE AHEAD

Prepare the recipe through step 1. Wrap the uncooked crab cakes in plastic wrap, then in foil, and freeze up to 2 months. Thaw in the refrigerator and cook as directed.

relish, and mustard until well blended. Cover with plastic wrap and refrigerate until ready to use.

3. In a heavy large skillet, heat the oil over medium heat. Add the crab cakes and cook for 3 to 4 minutes on each side, or until golden and crisp. Remove to paper towels to drain.

4. Transfer the crab cakes to a serving platter and garnish with lemon wedges. Serve right away with the tartar sauce.

Makes 8 cakes. Per 2 cakes with 2 tablespoons tartar sauce: 491 cal, 27 g pro, 15 g car, 36 g fat, 184 mg chol, 935 mg sod

60 MINUTES • MAKE AHEAD

COD CAKES WITH PAPAYA SALSA

Serves 4

Preparation time: 30 minutes

Cooking time: 16 minutes (4 minutes per batch)

In Cuba, this would probably be made with dried, salted fish. Fresh cod or scrod fillets work beautifully, though, and you can even substitute any plain cooked fish. If using instant mashed potatoes, make the mixture stiff.

PAPAYA SALSA

1 medium-size ripe papaya (about 14 ounces)

2 tablespoons minced scallions

1 tablespoon fresh lime or lemon juice

⅛ teaspoon ground cumin

⅛ teaspoon ground black pepper

12 ounces cod or scrod fillets

2 cups stiff mashed potatoes

½ cup lightly packed fresh cilantro leaves, chopped fine

⅓ cup minced scallions

2 medium-size jalapeño peppers, seeded and minced

1½ teaspoons minced fresh garlic

1 teaspoon salt

1 large egg

¼ cup vegetable oil

1. Make the salsa: Peel, halve, seed, and finely chop the papaya. In a small bowl, mix the papaya with the scallions, lime juice, cumin, and black pepper. Set aside until ready to use. ▶

Ⓜ AKE AHEAD

Prepare the recipe through step 3. Wrap the uncooked cod cakes in plastic wrap, then in foil, and freeze up to 2 months. Thaw in the refrigerator and cook as directed. Store the salsa in an airtight container in the refrigerator up to 3 days.

2. Fill a large skillet with ½ inch of water. Add the fillets and bring to a boil over high heat. Reduce the heat to low. Cover and simmer for about 10 minutes, or just until the fish is opaque at its thickest part when tested with a fork. Drain off the water and cool the fish. Carefully flake the fish, discarding any bones (you should have 2 cups of fish).

3. In a medium-size bowl, mix the potatoes, cilantro, scallions, jalapeños, garlic, salt, and egg until blended. Stir in the flaked fish. Form the mixture into 16 patties, about ½ inch thick.

4. In a large skillet, heat the oil over medium-high heat. Cook the patties in batches for about 2 minutes on each side, or until golden brown. Remove to a plate lined with paper towels to drain.

5. Transfer the cod cakes to serving plates and serve right away with the salsa.
Makes 16 cakes. Per 4 cakes: 356 cal, 20 g pro, 27 g car, 20 g fat, 92 mg chol, 927 mg sod

---

EASY • 30 MINUTES

LEMON–SAGE RED SNAPPER

Serves 4
Preparation time: 10 minutes
Cooking time: 12 minutes

Eat the lemon slices with the fish if you wish, but the lemon is really there to flavor the juices. Serve with buttered cooked green beans and sliced carrots.

4 (½-inch-thick) red snapper fillets (6 ounces each), or cod,
    sea bass, lingcod, or scrod
½ teaspoon salt
¼ teaspoon ground black pepper
8 very thin lemon slices with peel, seeded and cut in half
.2 teaspoons minced scallion (white part only)
8 to 12 fresh sage leaves, or 1 teaspoon dried sage leaves, crumbled
3 tablespoons butter or margarine
½ cup chicken broth

1. Heat the oven to 350°F. Lightly grease a shallow baking dish large enough to hold the fish in a single layer.

2. Season the fish on both sides with the salt and pepper. Place in the prepared dish. Arrange the lemon slices over the fillets, sprinkle with scallion, then top with sage leaves (or sprinkle with dried sage). Dot with the butter. Pour the broth into the dish.

3. Bake the fish, basting occasionally with the pan juices, for 10 to 12

minutes, or just until opaque at its thickest part when tested with a fork.

4. Transfer the fish to serving plates, spoon some of the pan juices over the fish, and serve right away.

Per serving: 265 cal, 35 g pro, 2 g car, 12 g fat, 86 mg chol with butter, 63 mg chol with margarine, 596 mg sod with butter, 608 mg sod with margarine

MOROCCAN–STYLE MAHI MAHI

Serves 4
Preparation time: 20 minutes
Cooking time: 22 minutes

Mahi mahi is the Hawaiian name for the dolphin fish, not to be confused with the mammal. Its mild flavor and firm texture account for its universal appeal. You may use swordfish, shark, or grouper instead.

3 tablespoons butter or margarine, cut into small pieces
1½ teaspoons minced fresh garlic
¾ teaspoon ground cumin
¾ teaspoon salt
¾ teaspoon ground turmeric
½ teaspoon ground cinnamon
¼ teaspoon ground black pepper
3 small onions, halved and sliced thin (2 cups)
¼ cup Zante currants
2 tablespoons pine nuts (optional)
2 tablespoons water
4 (1-inch-thick) mahi mahi fillets (about 8 ounces each)
3 medium-size plum tomatoes (9 ounces), quartered lengthwise, seeded, and cut lengthwise into ½-inch-wide strips
2 bay leaves (2 inches long)

1. Heat the oven to 425°F. Have ready a 13 x 9-inch baking dish.

2. In a large, preferably nonstick skillet, mix the butter, garlic, cumin, salt, turmeric, cinnamon, and pepper. Cook over medium heat, stirring occasionally, until the butter is melted.

3. Reduce the heat to medium-low and add the onions. Cover and cook for 10 minutes, stirring occasionally, until the onions are beginning to soften.

4. Stir in the currants, pine nuts, and water. Cover and cook for 4 to ▶

5 minutes longer, until the onions are tender.

5. Scatter half the onion mixture in the baking dish. Top with the fish fillets, then top the fillets with the remaining onion mixture. Scatter the tomato slices over the top and add the bay leaves.

6. Cover the dish tightly with foil. Bake for 20 to 22 minutes, or just until the fish is opaque at its thickest part when tested with a fork. Serve right away.

Per serving: 344 cal, 44 g pro, 18 g car, 11 g fat, 189 mg chol with butter, 166 mg chol with margarine, 709 mg sod with butter, 721 mg sod with margarine

---

30 MINUTES • MICROWAVE

SALMON–STUFFED SOLE

Serves 4
Preparation time: 15 minutes
Cooking time: 15 minutes

Here is an easy and elegant dish. The salmon stuffing and cream sauce dress up the fish enough to make it special but not fussy.

SALMON STUFFING
¼ cup chopped onion
¼ cup chopped celery
2 tablespoons butter or margarine
1 can (about 7¾ ounces) salmon, drained
3 tablespoons packaged plain bread crumbs
1 teaspoon freshly grated lemon peel (optional)
⅛ teaspoon salt
⅛ teaspoon ground black pepper

2 sole or flounder fillets (about 8 ounces each)
⅛ teaspoon paprika

CREAM SAUCE
2 tablespoons butter or margarine
1 tablespoon all-purpose flour
½ teaspoon salt
⅛ teaspoon ground black pepper
⅛ teaspoon paprika
¾ cup half-and-half
¼ cup dry white wine or
   1 tablespoon fresh lemon juice

VARIATION

CRAB-STUFFED SOLE

Substitute 8 ounces of fresh or canned crabmeat for the salmon and proceed with the recipe as directed from step 1.

Per serving: 366 cal with wine, 359 cal with lemon juice, 35 g pro, 9 g car, 20 g fat, 159 mg chol with butter, 128 mg chol with margarine, 780 mg sod with butter, 799 mg sod with margarine

• 30 MINUTE
• MICROWAVE

1. Make the stuffing: In a medium-size microwave-safe bowl, mix the onion, celery, and butter. Microwave uncovered on High for 3 to 4 minutes, stirring once, until the vegetables are tender. Add the salmon, then stir in the bread crumbs, lemon peel, salt, and pepper until blended.

2. Lightly coat a 9-inch microwave-safe pie dish with vegetable oil cooking spray. Put 1 fillet into the dish, spread the stuffing on top, and cover with the remaining fillet. Sprinkle with the paprika. Cover loosely with waxed paper. Microwave on High for 4 to 6 minutes, rotating the plate ½ turn once, just until the fish is barely opaque at its thickest part when tested with a fork.

3. Remove the plate from the microwave and let stand covered on a heatproof surface for 5 minutes to complete cooking.

4. Meanwhile, make the sauce. Put the butter in a microwave-safe 2-cup measure or medium-size bowl and microwave on High for 30 seconds, or until melted. Stir in the flour, salt, pepper, and paprika until smooth, then the half-and-half and wine. Microwave uncovered on High for 4 to 5 minutes, stirring 3 or 4 times, until the sauce is thick and bubbly.

5. Transfer the fish to a serving plate and spoon some of the sauce over the fish. Serve right away, with the remaining sauce served separately.

Per serving: 372 cal with wine, 365 cal with lemon juice, 34 g pro, 9 g car, 21 g fat, 119 mg chol with butter, 89 mg chol with margarine, 844 mg sod with butter, 861 mg sod with margarine

FISH BUYING, COOKING, AND STORING TIPS

◆ Freshness makes all the difference in the way fish tastes. Look for firm-textured, moist, glossy flesh with no sign of dryness. Odor, if any, should be mild and fresh, never strong and fishy.

◆ Fillets are the meaty sides of the fish cut off the bone. Steaks are the crosswise slices. Large fish, such as halibut, salmon, and swordfish, are commonly sold as steaks. If very large, they can be cut in two and the bone removed before cooking.

◆ Buy fish pieces of roughly equal thickness and weight for even cooking.

◆ Immediately refrigerate fresh fish tightly wrapped in plastic wrap and use within 1 to 2 days. The colder the storage temperature the less rapidly the fish will spoil. Never store ungutted fish, which spoils quite rapidly. To freeze, tightly wrap the fish, first with plastic wrap and the with aluminum foil, and freeze up to 6 months. Thaw in the refrigerator. To speed up thawing, place the wrapped package of fish under cold running water. Never refreeze fish once it has been unfrozen.

◆ Test fish for doneness by cutting a slit in the thickest part near the end of cooking time. Remove the fish from the cooking source when the flesh in the center looks just slightly opaque. Remember that fish will continue to cook in the time it takes to serve it.

◆ Lean fish, such as cod, sole, or snapper is particularly well suited to moist-heat cooking methods like sautéeing, steaming, and poaching. Oily fish, such as swordfish, salmon, and tuna are better suited to grilling, broiling, and baking. As long as they are basted frequently during cooking, lean fish can also be grilled, broiled, or baked.

ROASTED MONKFISH

Serves 6
Preparation time: 10 minutes
Cooking time: 18 minutes

This low fat, firm textured fish is also known as angler, lotte, goosefish, and sea devil. It has a mild, sweet flavor that is often compared with that of lobster (shellfish is an important part of the monkfish diet). Steamed spinach and roasted new potatoes would make nice accompaniments to this dish.

2 pounds monkfish fillets
2 large eggs
2 tablespoons milk
2¼ cups fresh bread crumbs, made from crusty Italian or
    sourdough bread
1 teaspoon chopped fresh rosemary, or ¼ teaspoon dried rosemary
    leaves, crumbled
¼ teaspoon freshly grated lemon peel
½ teaspoon salt
¼ teaspoon ground black pepper
2 large cloves garlic, peeled and crushed
⅓ cup olive oil
⅓ cup yellow cornmeal
For garnish: lemon wedges and sprigs of fresh rosemary
    (optional)

1. Heat the oven to 400°F.
2. Rinse the fillets and trim off any dark purple membrane.
3. In a shallow medium-size bowl, beat the eggs and milk with a fork. In another shallow medium-size bowl, mix the bread crumbs, rosemary, lemon peel, salt, and pepper.
4. In a large roasting pan, mix the garlic and oil. Place the pan in the oven for about 5 minutes, or until the oil is hot.
5. Meanwhile, sprinkle the cornmeal onto a sheet of waxed paper. Coat each fillet with the cornmeal, shaking off the excess. Dip each fillet into the egg mixture, then into the bread crumbs to coat evenly.
6. Remove the pan from the oven and add the fillets. Roast uncovered for 8 minutes. With 2 spatulas, carefully turn the fillets and roast for 8 to 10 minutes longer, or until the crumbs are crisp and golden and the fish is opaque at its thickest part when tested with a fork.

QUICK FILLET IDEAS

Use mild-flavored, firm-textured fish fillets such as flounder, cod, haddock, halibut, skate, or catfish for these quick ideas.

◆ Dip skinless fillets in skim milk, then in a mixture of bread crumbs, grated Parmesan cheese, black pepper, paprika, oregano, and basil. Drizzle with melted margarine and bake.

◆ Grill or broil fish fillets and serve with salsa.

◆ Flake broiled fish fillets on top of tomato-rice salad seasoned with soy sauce, olive oil, and lime, or onto mixed greens with fresh vegetables.

◆ Broil or bake seasoned nuggets of fish fillets and dip into sweet-and-sour sauce.

♦ Mixed flaked poached fish fillets with low-fat cream cheese and mayonnaise, chopped onion, Worcestershire sauce, fresh lemon juice, and garlic salt for a dip.

♦ Lightly brush fish fillets with tomato sauce and sprinkle with Creole seasonings before broiling or grilling.

7. Transfer the fish to a serving platter and garnish with lemon wedges and sprigs of fresh rosemary. Serve right away.

Per serving: 325 cal, 26 g pro, 15 g car, 17 g fat, 110 mg chol, 317 mg sod

EASY • 30 MINUTES • MICROWAVE • LOW FAT

COD CANCÚN

Serves 4

Total time: 22 minutes

A deliciously spicy fish recipe that's made from start to finish in the microwave. When seeding and chopping jalapeños or other hot peppers, remember not to rub your eyes or mouth.

2 tablespoons fresh lime juice
3 teaspoons vegetable oil
¼ teaspoon salt
¼ teaspoon ground black pepper
4 cod or other firm-textured white fish fillets (about 6 ounces each)
1 teaspoon minced fresh garlic
1 teaspoon minced seeded pickled jalapeño pepper, or to taste
½ teaspoon ground cumin
½ cup chopped onion
½ cup chopped yellow or red bell pepper
¼ cup chopped fresh cilantro or parsley

1. In a microwave-safe 9-inch pie dish or 11 x 7-inch baking dish, mix the lime juice, 1 teaspoon of oil, the salt, and pepper. Add the fish, turning to coat, then arrange in the dish so the thickest parts are toward the outside edge. Cover and let stand for 15 minutes to marinate.

2. Meanwhile, in a medium-size microwave-safe bowl, mix the remaining 2 teaspoons oil, the garlic, jalapeño, and cumin. Cover loosely with waxed paper and microwave on High for 1 minute. Stir in the onion and bell pepper. Cover and microwave on High for 2 minutes, or until the onion and pepper are crisp-tender, stirring once.

3. Spoon the mixture over the fish. Cover with vented plastic wrap and microwave on High for 4 to 6 minutes, rotating the dish ¼ turn once, or until the fish is barely opaque at its thickest part when tested with a fork. Remove the dish from the microwave and let stand for 1 minute. Sprinkle with the cilantro and serve right away.

Per serving: 186 cal, 31 g pro, 4 g car, 5 g fat, 73 mg chol, 239 mg sod

BAKED CODFISH WITH POTATOES

Serves 4
Preparation time: 8 minutes
Cooking time: 22 minutes

This traditional dish could not be easier or tastier and will please just about everyone—especially kids. If cod is unavailable, you can use other lean white fish fillets such as scrod, bass, or flounder.

3 tablespoons olive oil
1 pound thin-skinned potatoes, sliced thin (about 3 cups)
1 medium-size onion, sliced thin
1 jar (2 ounces) chopped pimientos, drained
½ teaspoon dried rosemary leaves, crumbled
½ teaspoon salt
1 pound codfish fillet, about ¾ inch thick, cut into 4 pieces
1 tablespoon packaged seasoned bread crumbs
1 tablespoon grated Parmesan cheese

1. Place the oven rack in the lowest position. Heat the oven to 450°F.

2. In a large ovenproof skillet or range-top-to-oven baking dish, heat the oil over medium heat. Add the potatoes and onion, stirring to coat. Reduce the heat to medium-low and cook, stirring occasionally, for about 10 minutes, or until the potatoes and onions start to brown and are barely tender. Stir in the pimientos, rosemary, and salt. Arrange the fish over the potatoes.

3. In a small bowl, mix the bread crumbs and cheese. Sprinkle the mixture over the top.

4. Bake for 10 to 12 minutes, or until the fish is opaque at its thickest part when tested with a fork. Serve right away.

Per serving: 307 cal, 24 g pro, 26 g car, 12 g fat, 50 mg chol, 420 mg sod

SARDINES

Believe it or not, sardines aren't hatched right in the can. But because they're rarely found fresh in the United States, that's how we're accustomed to seeing them. Look for sardines packed in oil, tomato, mustard sauce, or even spring water—but don't be surprised if some die-hard purist tells you oil is the only way to go. Once you peel open that can, whatever the packing medium, you'll be on your way to great flavor and good nutrition. Indeed, good nutrition is packed into sardines like— you guessed it— sardines in a can. A 2½-ounce serving of sardines has: Protein—As much as 20 percent of your recommended

30 MINUTES • MICROWAVE

ORANGE ROUGHY WITH LEMON SAUCE

Serves 6

Total time: 15 minutes

This lean, tender New Zealand fish, so named because of its bright orange skin, is fast becoming popular in the United States. However, if it is unavailable, this dish is also good made with scrod or tilefish. Serve with steamed mixed vegetables and a wild rice pilaf.

6 orange roughy fillets (about 4 ounces each)
⅛ teaspoon salt
⅛ teaspoon ground black pepper

LEMON SAUCE
1 tablespoon butter or margarine
2 teaspoons all-purpose flour
¼ teaspoon salt
⅔ cup half-and-half or light cream
1 tablespoon fresh lemon juice
1 teaspoon snipped fresh chives or thinly sliced scallion

1. Arrange the fish in a microwave-safe 9-inch pie dish or 11 x 7-inch baking dish with the thickest parts toward the outside of the dish. Sprinkle the fish with the salt and the pepper. Cover with vented plastic wrap.

2. Microwave on High for 4 to 6 minutes, rotating the dish ¼ turn once, until the fish is still slightly translucent at its thickest part when tested with a fork. Remove the dish from the microwave and let stand covered on a heat-proof surface for about 5 minutes to complete cooking.

3. Meanwhile, make the sauce: Put the butter in a 2-cup microwave-safe measure and microwave on High until melted. Stir in the flour and salt until smooth. Stir in the half-and-half and microwave uncovered on High for 3 to 4 minutes, or until the sauce is thick and bubbly, stirring 2 or 3 times. Stir in the lemon juice and chives.

4. Transfer the fish to serving plates, spoon the sauce over the fish, and serve right away.

Per serving: 199 cal with half-and-half, 216 cal with cream, 2 g car, 13 g fat with half-and-half, 15 g fat with cream, 38 mg chol with half-and-half and butter, 33 mg chol with half-and-half and margarine, 46 mg chol with cream and butter, 41 mg chol with cream and margarime, 240 mg sod

A SARDINE SAMPLER

SARDINES CARIBE Toss 2 cups chopped tomatoes with 1/4 cup chopped scallions and 1/4 cup chopped cilantro. Divide between 2 plates. Top each with 1 (2 1/2 ounce) can of drained sardines. Serve with lemon wedges, salt, and hot-pepper sauce.

SARDINE AND SPUD SALAD Boil 2 pounds all-purpose potatoes (about 6 medium) for 15 to 20 minutes, or until tender when tested with a fork. Drain and cool slightly, then slice. Add 1 cup chopped red onion, 1/4 cup chopped fresh dill, and 1/4 cup rinsed and chopped dill pickle. Drain and break up the sardines from 2 (2 1/2 ounce) cans and add, along with 1 cup nonfat yogurt.

SARDINE PUFFS Drain 1 (2 1/2 ounce) can sardines and mash with 2 tablespoons light mayonnaise mixed with 2 tablespoons minced scallions or chives and 1 teaspoon Dijon mustard. Spread thinly on thin slices French bread. Dust with grated Parmesan cheese. Toast under broiler.

MACARONI SALAD Boil 8 ounces macaroni, adding 3 cups fresh broccoli florets to the pot about 3 minutes before the pasta is done. Drain and cool under cold running water. Transfer to a large bowl, add 1 pint halved cherry tomatoes, 2 (2 1/2 ounce) cans drained sardines, 1/3 cup chopped red onion, and 1/2 cup low-fat or nonfat Italian dressing. Toss gently to mix and coat.

EASY • 30 MINUTES

SPICY SALMON

Serves 4

Preparation time: 10 minutes

Cooking time: 11 minutes

The spicy coating comes from cracked black peppercorns and fresh ginger. To crack the peppercorns, put them whole into a plastic food bag and pound with a mallet or hammer, or use a mortar and pestle. (Purchased "cracked" pepper is too fine.) Good accompaniments for this dish include broccoli and buttered orzo (rice-shaped pasta) with sliced scallions.

4 (3/4- to 1-inch-thick) salmon fillets (5 ounces each)
1/2 teaspoon salt
2 1/2 tablespoons minced peeled fresh gingerroot
1 tablespoon coarsely cracked black peppercorns
2 tablespoons butter or margarine, melted

1. Heat the oven to 450°F. Lightly grease a shallow baking dish large enough to hold the fish in a single layer.

2. Season the fish on both sides with the salt. On a plate or sheet of waxed paper, mix the ginger and pepper. Dip only 1 side of each fillet into the mixture, patting gently so it adheres. Arrange the fish, topping side up, in the prepared dish and drizzle with the butter. ▶ *p. 165*

BEAT THE CLOCK
The traditional Spanish meal Paella (p.173) can be ready in no more than 20 minutes, thanks to the microwave oven.

Fish and shellfish are the key ingredients in a variety of meals, including soups, salads, stews, and casseroles. This versatility makes fish and seafood very popular today.

EASY FINE DINING
Sole is prized for its fine texture, and mahi mahi for its superior flavor. Salmon-Stuffed Sole (p.154), above, and Moroccan-Style Mahi Mahi (p.153), right, are both simple, elegant meals.

FABULOUS FISH DISHES
Most fish dishes can be made from start to finish within 30 minutes. Ever-popular Crisp Fish Sticks (p.147), above, and elegant Orange-Basil Halibut (p.170), left, are two of many examples.

**SALMON WITH
PARSLEY SAUCE**

• Omit the ginger and
cracked pepper and
prepare the fish as
directed.

• While the fish is bak-
ing, place 2 cups fresh
parsley leaves, 1/3 cup
plain low-fat yogurt, 1/3
cup chopped scallions,
2 teaspoons Dijon mus-
tard, and 2 teaspoons
water in a blender or
food processor and
process until blended
and smooth.

• Transfer the salmon
to serving plates and
spoon the sauce over
each serving.

Per serving: 289 cal,
30 g pro, 4 g car, 16 g
fat, 95 mg chol with
butter, 79 mg chol with
margarine, 485 mg sod

• EASY • 30 MINUTES

3. Bake the fish, basting once with pan juices, for 9 to 11 minutes, or just until opaque at its thickest part when tested with a fork.

4. Transfer the fish to serving plates, spoon the pan juices over the fish, and serve right away.

Per serving: 269 cal, 28 g pro, 2 g car, 16 g fat, 93 mg chol with butter, 78 mg chol with margarine, 400 mg sod

EASY • 30 MINUTES • LOW FAT • CLASSIC

BLACKENED CATFISH

Serves 4
Preparation time: 7 minutes
Cooking time: 10 minutes

This version of a Cajun favorite goes as light on fat as possible without sacrificing any flavor. Serve with herbed rice and a refreshing cucumber salad.

1 teaspoon paprika
1/2 teaspoon dried sage leaves, crumbled
1/2 teaspoon ground cumin
1/2 teaspoon garlic powder
1/2 teaspoon granulated sugar
1/2 teaspoon salt
1/4 teaspoon ground red pepper (cayenne)
1/4 teaspoon onion powder
4 catfish fillets (about 4 to 5 ounces each)
1 teaspoon olive oil
For garnish: lemon wedges (optional)

1. In a 1-gallon food-storage plastic bag, mix the paprika, sage, cumin, garlic powder, sugar, salt, red pepper, and onion powder. Seal the bag and shake until well blended.

2. Put 1 fillet into the bag at a time and shake until lightly coated.

3. Lightly coat a large nonstick skillet with vegetable oil cooking spray. Add the olive oil and heat over medium heat until hot.

4. Add the fillets to the skillet, skinned side up, and cook for 4 to 5 minutes, or until the underside is lightly blackened. With a spatula, carefully turn the fillets and cook for 4 to 5 minutes longer, or until the fish feels firm and is just opaque at its thickest part when tested with a fork.

5. Transfer the fillets to serving plates and garnish with lemon wedges.

Per serving: 180 cal, 19 g pro, 1 g car, 10 g fat, 42 mg chol, 316 mg sod

TARRAGON SALMON STEAKS

Serves 4

Preparation time: 15 minutes

Cooking time: 12 minutes plus 3 minutes to stand

Salmon is a good source of B vitamins and Omega-3 oils, shown to play a protective role against cardiovascular disease. In this recipe, salmon steaks are topped with a tarragon-flavored butter that melts over the fish like a sauce. Cooked with corn and asparagus, all this dish needs is rice to complete it.

3 tablespoons butter or margarine

1 tablespoon chopped fresh tarragon, or 1 teaspoon dried tarragon leaves, crumbled

4 (1-inch-thick) salmon steaks (about 6 ounces each)

2 tablespoons fresh lemon juice

2 tablespoons snipped fresh chives, or finely chopped scallion tops

Ground black pepper to taste

2 medium-size ears of fresh corn, husked and halved

8 ounces fresh thin asparagus spears, trimmed to 5-inch lengths

1. Put the butter in a small microwave-safe cup or bowl. Microwave on Medium Low for 15 seconds, or until soft but not melted. Stir in the tarragon. Cover with plastic wrap and leave the tarragon butter at room temperature until ready to serve.

2. Place the salmon steaks spoke-fashion on a 12-inch round microwave-safe plate, with the thickest parts toward the outside edge. Brush with the lemon juice. Sprinkle with the chives and black pepper.

3. Place the corn around the outside edge, then add the asparagus with the tips toward the center.

4. Cover the plate with vented plastic wrap. Microwave on High for 10 to 12 minutes, rotating the dish ¼ turn twice, just until the fish is barely opaque at its thickest part when tested with a fork and the vegetables are almost tender.

5. Remove the plate from the microwave and let stand on a heatproof surface for 3 minutes, or until the fish is opaque all the way through and the vegetables are tender.

6. Drain off the juices through the vent opening before uncovering the platter. Serve the salmon with the tarragon butter.

Per serving: 342 cal, 33 g pro, 11 g car, 19 g fat, 106 mg chol with butter, 82 mg chol with margarine, 162 mg sod with butter, 174 mg sod with margarine

---

OMEGA-3 MYSTERY

Fish oils, particularly the Omega-3 fatty acids found in fish oil, seem to reduce the chances of a heart attack and nobody is exactly sure why. Recent studies show that these unsaturated oils are beneficial to preventing heart disease because they thin blood (therefore reducing the chance of blood clots) and reduce cholesterol. One thing we are sure of is that researchers will continue to unfold the mystery. In the meantime, some of the best sources of these oils include sardines, mackerel, herring, bluefish, tuna, and salmon.

EASY • 60 MINUTES

SWORDFISH WITH CILANTRO DRESSING

Serves 6

Preparation time: 10 minutes plus 20 minutes to marinate

Cooking time: 10 minutes

The mild-flavored, moderately fat flesh of the swordfish is dense and meat-like, making it one of the most popular fish consumed in America. In this dish, the swordfish is drenched in a delicate cilantro dressing while still hot. For those who are not fond of cilantro's musky flavor, you can substitute finely chopped scallion greens.

SOY–SESAME MARINADE

¼ cup rice wine or sake

2 tablespoons soy sauce

1 tablespoon minced peeled fresh gingerroot

1 teaspoon dark Asian sesame oil

6 (1-inch-thick) swordfish steaks (6 to 8 ounces each), or tuna, halibut, or salmon

CILANTRO DRESSING

3 tablespoons chicken broth or water

3 tablespoons soy sauce

1 tablespoon granulated sugar

2 tablespoons dark Asian sesame oil

1½ tablespoons rice wine or sake, or 2 teaspoons rice wine vinegar

⅔ cup loosely packed cilantro leaves, chopped (3½ tablespoons)

1. Make the marinade: In a small bowl, mix the rice wine, soy sauce, ginger, and sesame oil until well blended. Place the fish steaks in a shallow glass or ceramic dish. Pour the marinade over the fish, turning to coat. Marinate for 20 minutes at room temperature, turning the fish several times.

2. Heat a gas grill to medium-high, prepare a charcoal fire, or heat a broiler.

3. Meanwhile, make the dressing. In a small bowl, mix the chicken broth, soy sauce, sugar, sesame oil, rice wine, and cilantro until well blended. Set aside at room temperature until ready to use.

4. Place the fish on a lightly oiled grill rack or broiler-pan rack. Grill or broil the fish 3 to 4 inches from the heat source for 4 to 5 minutes on each side, or just until opaque at its thickest part when tested with a fork. ▶

5. Transfer the fish steaks to serving plates, spoon the dressing over the fish, and serve right away.

Per serving: 315 cal, 41 g pro, 4 g car, 13 g fat, 78 mg chol, 900 mg sod with broth, 869 mg sod with water

EASY • 30 MINUTES

GREMOLATA SWORDFISH

Serves 4
Preparation time: 15 minutes
Cooking time: 15 minutes

Gremolata, an Italian seasoning made with fresh parsley, lemon peel, and garlic, complements fish, such as swordfish, that have a rich, full flavor. For a quick and easy meal accompany this dish with rice and mixed steamed vegetables. This recipe works nicely with either fish steaks or fillets. A steak is created when a fish is cut crosswise, and a fillet is the boneless strip of flesh produced when a fish is cut lengthwise along the bone.

4 (1-inch-thick) swordfish steaks or fillets (4 to 5 ounces
   each), or tuna, mahi mahi, sturgeon, or shark
½ teaspoon salt
½ teaspoon ground black pepper
2 tablespoons olive oil

GREMOLATA
¼ cup finely chopped parsley
2 tablespoons freshly grated lemon peel
1 teaspoon minced fresh garlic

1. Heat the oven to 350°F. Lightly grease a shallow baking dish large enough to hold the fish in a single layer.

2. Season the fish on both sides with the salt and pepper. Arrange in the prepared dish. Drizzle the oil evenly over the fish.

3. Bake the fish, basting occasionally with pan juices, for 12 to 15 minutes, or just until the fish is opaque at its thickest part when tested with a fork.

4. Meanwhile, make the gremolata. In a small bowl, mix the parsley, lemon peel, and garlic until blended.

5. Transfer the fish to serving plates, spoon the pan juices over the fish, then sprinkle with the gremolata. Serve right away.

Per serving: 212 cal, 23 g pro, 1 g car, 12 g fat, 44 mg chol, 378 mg sod

EASY • 60 MINUTES

GRILLED SHARK STEAKS

Serves 4

Preparation time: 10 minutes plus 20 minutes to marinate

Cooking time: 8 minutes

Shark is similar to swordfish but often less expensive. Here, the fish is marinated for 20 minutes in a piquant sauce. If you want to marinate the fish ahead of time, cover and refrigerate it for up to 2 hours, but no longer or the acid in the marinade will begin to "cook" the fish. Serve the shark steaks with a rice salad and steamed snow peas.

MARINADE

¼ cup fresh orange juice

2 tablespoons reduced-sodium soy sauce

2 tablespoons vegetable oil

2 tablespoons chopped fresh parsley

1 tablespoon chopped fresh basil

1 tablespoon fresh lemon juice

2 teaspoons minced fresh garlic

½ teaspoon ground black pepper

4 (½-inch-thick) mako shark steaks (6 to 8 ounces each)

For garnish: orange slices and sprigs of fresh parsley (optional)

1. Make the marinade: In a large glass or ceramic shallow dish, mix the orange juice, soy sauce, oil, parsley, basil, lemon juice, garlic, and pepper until well blended. Add the shark steaks, turning to coat. Marinate at room temperature for 20 minutes, turning the fish occasionally.

2. Meanwhile, heat a gas grill to medium-high, prepare a charcoal fire, or heat a broiler.

3. Remove the fish from the marinade and place on a lightly oiled grill rack or a broiler-pan rack. Grill or broil 4 to 6 inches from the heat source, brushing often with the marinade, for 3 to 4 minutes on each side, or just until the fish is opaque at its thickest part when tested with a fork.

4. With a spatula, remove the shark steaks to individual serving plates. Garnish with orange slices and parsley sprigs and serve right away.

Per serving: 288 cal, 38 g pro, 3 g car, 13 g fat, 90 mg chol, 366 mg sod

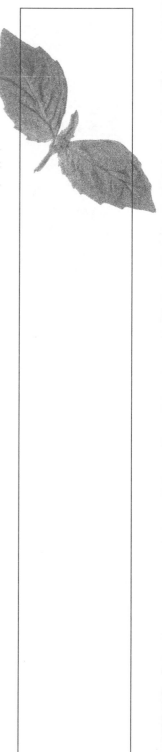

ORANGE–BASIL HALIBUT

Serves 4

Preparation time: 5 minutes

Cooking time: 15 minutes

Be more generous with the seasoning if you are using a fuller-flavored fish such as bass or cod instead of mild halibut. Take care not to overcook halibut because it tends to dry out. Serve this dish with roasted or sautéed cubed new potatoes and steamed zucchini.

4 (½-inch-thick) halibut steaks or fillets (about 6 ounces each),
  or sea bass, red snapper, cod, or scrod
½ teaspoon salt
½ teaspoon ground black pepper
4 teaspoons freshly grated orange peel
1 teaspoon dried basil leaves, crumbled
¼ cup (½ stick) butter or margarine

1. Heat the oven to 350°F. Lightly grease a shallow baking dish large enough to hold the fish in a single layer.

2. Season the fish on both sides with the salt and pepper. Arrange in a single layer in the prepared dish. Sprinkle with orange peel and basil, then dot with the butter.

3. Bake the fish, basting occasionally with the pan juices, for 12 to 15 minutes, or just until opaque at its thickest part when tested with a fork.

4. Transfer the fish to serving plates, spoon the pan juices over the fish, and serve right away.

Per serving: 267 cal, 29 g pro, 1 g car, 16 g fat, 75 mg chol with butter, 44 mg chol with margarine, 465 mg sod with butter, 482 mg sod with margarine

GREEK TUNA STEAKS

Serves 5

Preparation time: 5 minutes

Cooking time: 10 minutes

This recipe also works well with other fish steaks, such as halibut, shark, and tilefish. Buy fish steaks that are the same thickness so they will cook evenly.

5 (½-inch-thick) tuna steaks (about 8 ounces each)

2½ tablespoons fresh lemon juice

1 teaspoon salt

2½ teaspoons chopped fresh oregano leaves, or ¾ teaspoon dried oregano leaves, crumbled

¼ teaspoon ground black pepper

¼ cup extra-virgin olive oil

COOK'S TIP

To squeeze more juice from a lemon or lime, first roll it between the countertop and your palm.

1. Heat a gas grill to medium-high, prepare a charcoal fire, or heat a broiler.

2. Place the tuna steaks on a lightly oiled grill rack or broiler-pan rack. Grill or broil 4 to 6 inches from the heat source for 4 to 5 minutes on each side, or just until the fish is opaque at its thickest part when tested with a fork.

3. Meanwhile, in a small bowl, beat the lemon juice and salt with a fork until the salt dissolves. Stir in the oregano and pepper. Slowly drizzle in the olive oil, whisking until blended, thick, and creamy.

4. Transfer the steaks to a large warm serving platter. Prick each steak with a fork in several places to let the lemon mixture seep in.

5. Using a fork, beat and at the same time pour the oil and lemon-juice mixture evenly over the fish.

6. Spoon some of the remaining sauce from the platter over each fish portion and serve right away.

Per serving: 389 cal, 47 g pro, 1 g car, 21 g fat, 77 mg chol, 519 mg sod

HOT TIPS FOR GRILLING FISH AND SEAFOOD

◆ For extra flavor when grilling fish or seafood on a covered grill, add a handful or wood chips such as apple, cherry, peach, or mesquite to the fire. Be sure to soak the chips in water for 1 hour and drain thoroughly before adding them. The damp wood chips will also keep the fire burning slowly and increase smoke.

◆ For more fragrance and flavor, add dampened fresh herb branches and sprigs such as rosemary, oregano, or tarragon to the hot coals toward the end of grilling.

◆ Allow the grill to heat thoroughly before adding food.

◆ To keep fish from sticking, keep the grill rack clean and oiled. After each use, scrub the still-warm grill with a stiff wire brush and rub with vegetable oil. The next time you grill, apply more oil or vegetable oil cooking spray after the grate has warmed.

◆ Fish steaks and fillets should be basted with oil, marinade, or butter while grilling to keep them moist. Position thinner sections of fillets toward the cooler outside of the grill for even cooking.

◆ Whole fish are best cooked on a covered grill, so the distribution of heat will help to cook the fish evenly without burning. Whole fish weighing over 3 pounds should be cooked using this indirect heat method.

◆ Small food such as shrimp, scallops, and small pieces of fish are more manageable on a grill when threaded onto skewers about ¼ inch apart.

EASY • 30 MINUTES • LOW FAT

TUNA WITH FRESH PINEAPPLE SALSA

Serves 4

Preparation time: 20 minutes

Cooking time: 10 minutes

The easy-to-make salsa in this dish mixes the bright color and tropical flavor of fresh pineapple with cilantro and chile peppers. Here it lends a south-of-the-boarder flair to simple hoisin-glazed tuna steaks and yields a delicious and attractive entree with a minimum of preparation. Hoisin sauce is a popular sweet and spicy Chinese cooking sauce available in the Asian section of most supermarkets.

PINEAPPLE SALSA

1 cup finely chopped fresh or drained canned juice-packed pineapple

1 tablespoon chopped fresh cilantro

1 tablespoon finely chopped red onion

1½ teaspoons cider vinegar

1 teaspoon minced jalapeño pepper (optional)

HOISIN GLAZE

2 tablespoons hoisin sauce

1 tablespoon ketchup

1½ teaspoons cider vinegar

4 (1-inch-thick) tuna steaks (about 6 ounces each)

1½ teaspoons olive oil

1. Heat a gas grill to medium-high, prepare a charcoal fire, or heat a broiler. If using a broiler, line the pan with foil for easy cleanup.

2. Make the salsa: In a small bowl, mix the pineapple, cilantro, onion, vinegar, and jalalpeño until blended.

3. Make the glaze: In a small bowl, mix the hoisin sauce, ketchup, and vinegar until well blended.

4. Brush the fish on both sides with the oil. Grill or broil the fish 4 to 6 inches from the heat source for 8 to 10 minutes, turning once and brushing each side with the glaze during the last 2 minutes of cooking. Cook just until the fish is opaque at its thickest part when tested with a fork. Serve right away with the salsa.

Per serving: 280 cal, 36 g pro, 11 g car, 9 g fat, 58 mg chol, 262 mg sod

SELECTING AND STORING SHELLFISH

◆ When selecting shrimp, look for meat that is firm and shells that are shiny and firm. Black spots are a sign of aging. Cooked shrimp should be firm and bright white with a very mild odor.

◆ Scallops should be firm and moist with a creamy white color and fresh scent. Those that are not fresh have an unmistakable sulfurous odor.

◆ Shucked mussels and clams should be fresh-smelling, plump, and surrounded by a clear, slightly opalescent liquid. If purchasing them in their shells, choose closed shells that are not broken or chipped.

◆ Refrigerate live shellfish in a dry bowl covered by damp paper towels up to 2 days. Do not store on ice, in water, or in plastic.

◆ Freeze shucked clams, mussels, or oysters in their liquid in an airtight container up to 2 months. Freeze other cooked or uncooked shellfish such as shrimp or scallops, in an airtight container up to 2 months. Thaw slowly in the refrigerator.

COOK'S TIP

To devein shrimp: Remove the shells from the shrimp. Using a small sharp knife, cut a shallow slit down the center of the outside curve. Remove the dark vein, then rinse the shrimp under cold water.

EASY • 60 MINUTES • MICROWAVE • LOW FAT • ONE POT

PAELLA

Serves 4

Total time: 35 minutes plus 5 minutes to stand

Paella is a Spanish dish that combines saffron-flavored rice with shellfish and meats. This easy and economical version uses shrimp, ham, and turmeric instead of saffron. The best part about this recipe is that it's a meal- in-one.

1 large onion, chopped (1 cup)
1 tablespoon olive oil
1 teaspoon minced fresh garlic
1½ cups chicken broth
½ teaspoon ground turmeric
¼ teaspoon dried thyme leaves, crumbled
1 cup uncooked white long-grain rice
8 ounces uncooked medium-size shrimp
4 ounces lean ham, cut into small chunks (¾ cup)
1 cup frozen green peas
1 jar (4 ounces) pimientos, drained and cut into strips

1. In a deep 3-quart microwave-safe casserole, mix the onion, oil, and garlic. Cover with a lid or vented plastic wrap. Microwave on High for 3 to 5 minutes, or until the onion is beginning to soften.

2. Stir in the broth, turmeric, thyme, and rice. Cover and microwave on High for 14 to 16 minutes, stirring twice, until the rice is almost tender.

3. Meanwhile, shell and devein the shrimp. ▶

4. Add the ham, peas, pimientos, and shrimp to the rice. Cover and microwave on High for 2 to 4 minutes longer, or until the rice is tender and the shrimp are almost cooked through but still look slightly raw.

5. Remove the dish from the microwave and let stand on a heatproof surface for 5 minutes, or until the shrimp are opaque all the way through. Serve right away.

Per serving: 348 cal, 22 g pro, 48 g car, 7 g fat, 83 mg chol, 896 mg sod

---

60 MINUTES • LOW FAT • ONE POT • CLASSIC

SHRIMP CREOLE

Serves 6
Preparation time: 20 minutes
Cooking time: 40 minutes

Don't be daunted by the number of ingredients in this recipe. They're not exotic and take little time to prepare. Serve this heart-healthy dish over rice.

2 tablespoons olive oil
1½ cups coarsely chopped green bell pepper
1 cup chopped onion
½ cup sliced celery
3 cups sliced white mushrooms (about 8 ounces)
1 tablespoon minced fresh garlic
1 can (28 ounces) crushed tomatoes in purée
1 bay leaf (2 inches long)
1 tablespoon chopped fresh thyme, or 1 teaspoon dried thyme leaves, crumbled
½ teaspoon salt
¼ teaspoon ground black pepper
½ to 1 teaspoon hot-pepper sauce
1½ pounds medium-size shrimp, shelled and deveined
3 tablespoons chopped fresh parsley
For garnish: chopped fresh parsley (optional)
Cooked white long-grain rice (optional)

1. In a large skillet, heat the oil over medium heat. Add the bell pepper, onion, and celery. Cook for 5 minutes, stirring often, or until softened. Add the mushrooms and garlic; cook for 5 minutes, or until just beginning to soften.

2. Stir in the tomatoes, bay leaf, thyme, salt, pepper, and hot-pepper sauce. Bring the mixture to a boil over medium-high heat. Reduce the heat to low

COOK'S TIP

Don't discard shrimp shells. Instead, place them in a saucepan with water to cover. Bring to a boil, then cover and simmer for 30 minutes. Let the shells cool in the liquid, then strain the mixture through a fine sieve set over a medium-size bowl and discard the shells. Use the shrimp-flavored stock in soups or sauces. Store in an airtight container in the refrigerator up to 1 week, or freeze up to 3 months.

and simmer uncovered for 20 minutes to allow the flavors to blend.

3. Add the shrimp. Cover and simmer for 5 to 7 minutes, or until the shrimp are opaque.

4. Remove the skillet from the heat. Garnish with chopped parsley and spoon over rice.

Per serving: 205 cal, 21 g pro, 16 g car, 6 g fat, 140 mg chol, 558 mg sod

60 MINUTES

SHRIMP FOO YUNG

Serves 4

Preparation time: 20 minutes

Cooking time: 30 minutes (4 minutes per batch)

These flavorful egg pancakes are a wonderful way to use up fresh or leftover cooked vegetables. Serve them on their own for lunch or with rice for dinner.

SHRIMP PANCAKES

6 large eggs
8 ounces Napa cabbage leaves, quartered lengthwise, then finely
   shredded (1¾ cups)
1 cup fresh or canned bean sprouts, rinsed and drained
8 ounces shrimp, cooked, peeled, and chopped (¾ cup)
½ cup thinly sliced scallions
1 teaspoon minced peeled fresh gingerroot, or ½ teaspoon ground ginger
¼ teaspoon salt
¼ teaspoon ground black pepper
¼ cup vegetable oil

SAUCE

2 teaspoons cornstarch
1 tablespoon cold water
1 cup chicken broth
2 tablespoons reduced-sodium soy sauce
1 teaspoon dark Asian sesame oil

1. Make the pancakes: In a large bowl, mix the eggs, cabbage, bean sprouts, shrimp, scallions, ginger, salt, and pepper until well blended.

2. In a large nonstick skillet, heat 1 tablespoon of the oil over medium-high heat. For each pancake, drop ⅓ cup of the egg mixture into the hot skillet without crowding. Cook for 1½ to 2 minutes on each side, or ▶

VARIATION

MICROWAVE SHRIMP CREOLE

• Omit the oil. In a deep 3-quart microwave-safe casserole, combine 2 tablespoons margarine, the onion, garlic, bell pepper, and celery. Cover with a lid or vented plastic wrap. Microwave on High for 7 to 9 minutes, stirring twice, until the vegetables are soft.

• Stir in the tomatoes, bay leaf, thyme, salt, pepper, and hot-pepper sauce. Cover and microwave on High for 5 to 7 minutes, stirring once, until the sauce has thickened.

• Stir in the mushrooms. Cover and microwave on High for 2 to 3 minutes, or until softened. Add the shrimp. Cover and microwave on High for 3 to 5 minutes, or until the shrimp are almost cooked through but still look slightly raw.

• Remove the dish from the oven and let stand for 5 minutes, or until the shrimp are opaque throughout.

Per serving: 200 cal, 21 g pro, 16 g car, 6 g fat, 140 mg chol, 602 mg sod

• 30 MINUTES
• LOW FAT • ONE POT

until browned, adding more oil to the skillet as needed.

3. Transfer the pancakes to a warm serving platter and cover with foil to keep warm.

4. Make the sauce: In a small bowl, mix the cornstarch and water until the cornstarch is dissolved.

5. Wipe the skillet clean. Pour in the broth and soy sauce and bring to a boil over medium-high heat. Stir in the cornstarch mixture and sesame oil. Boil the mixture, stirring constantly, for 1 to 2 minutes, or until thickened and clear. Remove the skillet from the heat.

6. Pour the sauce over the pancakes and serve right away.

Makes 16 pancakes. Per 4 pancakes: 330 cal, 21 g pro, 8 g car, 24 g fat, 389 mg chol, 856 mg sod

BRAZILIAN SHRIMP

Serves 6

Preparation time: 30 minutes plus 20 minutes to stand

Cooking time 13 minutes

In Brazil, this creamy, spicy dish would be made with palm oil, which tints it a pale yellow. If palm oil isn't one of your pantry staples, you may color the sauce with a pinch of turmeric. Serve with rice.

2 pounds medium-size shrimp, peeled and deveined
1 teaspoon minced fresh garlic
1¼ cups canned coconut milk (not cream of coconut)
2 medium-size ripe tomatoes, peeled, seeded, and chopped coarse (see Cook's Tip)
2 medium-size onions, halved lengthwise and sliced thin crosswise
4 medium-size jalapeño or serrano chile peppers, seeded and minced
¼ cup loosely packed cilantro leaves, chopped
¼ cup lemon juice
1 teaspoon salt
Pinch of turmeric (optional)

1. In a medium-size bowl, mix the shrimp and garlic. Let stand for 15 to 20 minutes for the flavors to develop.

2. In a large skillet, mix ¼ cup of coconut milk, the tomatoes, onions, jalapeños, cilantro, lemon juice, salt, and turmeric. Bring to a simmer and cook, uncovered, over medium-low heat for 5 minutes, stirring occasionally,

COOK'S TIP

To peel tomatoes, submerge them in boiling water for 15 to 20 seconds, then slip off the skins. To seed, cut the tomatoes in half crosswise and squeeze out seeds.

until the onions are softened.

3. Stir in the shrimp and garlic. Cook for 5 to 7 minutes, stirring 3 or 4 times, until the shrimp are opaque in the center. Stir in the remaining coconut milk and heat for about 1 minute. Remove the skillet from the heat and serve right away.

Per serving: 260 cal, 27 g pro, 11 g car, 12 g fat, 186 mg chol, 563 mg sod

---

EASY • 30 MINUTES • LOW FAT

SZECHUAN SCALLOPS

Serves 4

Preparation time: 15 minutes

Cooking time: 10 minutes

Spicy Szechuan chili sauce can be found in the Asian foods section of most supermarkets. If it is unavailable, substitute ½ to 1 teaspoon of minced garlic and ⅓ to ¼ teaspoon of crushed red pepper flakes. Serve this dish over rice.

SZECHUAN SAUCE

½ cup water

2 teaspoons soy sauce

1 to 2 teaspoons Szechuan chili sauce

2 teaspoons cornstarch

2 teaspoons vegetable oil

1 small red bell pepper, seeded and chopped coarse (1 cup)

4 ounces snow peas, trimmed and cut in half if large (1 cup)

3 medium-size scallions, cut in half lengthwise, then cut crosswise into
    1½-inch pieces (¾ cup)

1 pound sea scallops, rinsed and patted dry

⅓ cup chopped fresh cilantro

1. In a measuring cup, mix the water, soy sauce, chili sauce, and cornstarch until blended.

2. In a wok or heavy large skillet, heat the oil over high heat until very hot and rippling but not smoking. Add the bell pepper, snow peas, and scallions. Stir-fry for 3 to 5 minutes, or until crisp-tender.

3. Add the scallops and stir-fry for 1 to 2 minutes, or just until they start to turn opaque.

4. Stir the sauce and pour it into the skillet. Bring to a boil, stirring often. Cover and cook over medium-high heat for 1 to 2 minutes, stirring ▶

SHRIMP COUNT

The amount of shrimp you get per pound depends on their size.

On the average:

Small—36 to 45 shrimp per pound

Medium—31 to 35 shrimp per pound

Large—21 to 30 shrimp per pound

Extra Large—16 to 20 shrimp per pound

Jumbo—11 to 15 shrimp per pound.

VARIATION

SZECHUAN SHRIMP

Substitute 1 pound of large peeled and deveined shrimp for the scallops and proceed as directed from step 1.

Per serving: 173 cal, 25 g pro, 8 g car, 4 g fat, 173 mg chol, 345 mg sod

• EASY • 30 MINUTES
• LOW FAT

once. The scallops should be just opaque in the center. Stir in the cilantro and serve right away.

Per serving: 153 cal, 21 g pro, 10 g car, 3 g fat, 37 mg chol, 360 mg sod

EASY • LOW FAT

INDIAN–STYLE SEAFOOD KEBABS

Serves 6

Preparation time: 10 minutes plus at least 2 hours to marinate

Cooking time: 6 minutes

Yellow rice, sugar snap peas, and a fresh fruit salsa made with pineapple would make tasty accompaniments for these skewers.

MARINADE

⅓ cup olive oil

¼ cup chopped fresh cilantro

1 tablespoon minced fresh garlic

2½ teaspoons ground cumin

¼ teaspoon ground ginger

¼ teaspoon ground turmeric

¼ teaspoon salt

¼ teaspoon ground red pepper (cayenne)

1 pound medium-size shrimp, peeled (with tails left on) and deveined

1 pound large sea scallops, rinsed and patted dry

Six (10- to 12-inch) skewers (if bamboo, soak in water for 1 hour or more)

1. Make the marinade: In a large bowl, whisk together the oil, cilantro, garlic, cumin, ginger, turmeric, salt, and red pepper until well blended. Add the shrimp and scallops, tossing gently to coat. Cover and refrigerate for 2 to 3 hours for the seafood to absorb the flavors.

2. Heat a gas grill to medium-high, prepare a charcoal fire, or heat a broiler.

3. Remove the seafood from the marinade and place on a lightly oiled grill rack or broiler-pan rack. Grill or broil 4 to 6 inches from the heat source for about 6 minutes, turning occasionally, until the seafood is lightly browned and just barely opaque in the center when tested with a fork. Serve right away.

Per serving: 189 cal, 25 g pro, 3 g car, 8 g fat, 118 mg chol, 260 mg sod

VARIATION

CAJUN-STYLE SEAFOOD KEBABS

• In a large bowl, whisk together ½ cup vegetable oil, ¼ cup red wine, ¼ cup soy sauce, 1 teaspoon grated lemon peel, ¼ cup fresh lemon juice, ¼ cup minced fresh parsley, 2 tablespoons Worcestershire sauce, 2 tablespoons red-wine vinegar, 1 tablespoon dry mustard, 1½ teaspoons paprika, 1½ teaspoons minced fresh garlic, and ¼ teaspoon ground red pepper. Add the shrimp and scallops and marinate at room temperature for 30 minutes.

• Thread on skewers and grill the seafood as directed. Boil the leftover marinade for 3 to 5 minutes and serve it as a dipping sauce for shrimp and scallops.

Per serving: 227 cal, 26 g pro, 4 g car, 11 g fat, 118 mg chol, 598 mg sod

• **EASY**

60 MINUTES

CHILI–GARLIC SOFT SHELL CRABS

Serves 4

Preparation time: 20 minutes

Cooking time: 16 minutes (4 minutes per batch)

A soft shell crab is not a species, but rather a condition of blue crabs. The blue crab sheds its hard outer shell up to 18 times during its 3-year life span. Each time it sheds a hard shell, it becomes a soft shell crab for a few hours. You can purchase the crabs already cleaned; or ask your fishmonger to clean them for you.

CHILI–GARLIC SAUCE

1 tablespoon cornstarch
3 tablespoons soy sauce
3 tablespoons cooking sherry
2 teaspoons vegetable oil
¼ cup finely chopped onion
2 fresh red chiles or jalapeño peppers, seeded and chopped fine
  (about 2½ tablespoons)
2 teaspoons minced fresh garlic
2 tablespoons minced peeled fresh gingerroot
1 cup chicken broth
1 cup sliced scallions, including green tops

8 large soft shell crabs, cleaned (2 to 4 ounces each)
½ cup all-purpose flour
¼ teaspoon ground red pepper (cayenne)
2 tablespoons vegetable oil
½ cup fresh cilantro leaves

1. Make the sauce: In a small bowl, mix the cornstarch, soy sauce, and sherry.

2. In a medium-size skillet, heat the oil over medium heat. Add the onion and cook for 1 minute, stirring often. Add the chiles, garlic, and ginger and cook for 1 minute, stirring often. Add the chicken broth and scallions. Bring the mixture to a boil over high heat. Reduce the heat to medium-low and simmer for 2 minutes.

3. Whisk the cornstarch mixture into the sauce and bring to a boil. Cook for 2 minutes, stirring constantly, until the sauce has thickened.

4. Remove the pan from the heat, stir in the cilantro, and keep warm. ▶

VARIATION

SOFT SHELL CRABS DIJON

• Brush the undersides of 8 soft shell crabs with 1 teaspoon Dijon mustard each and refrigerate for 30 minutes.

• Coat the crabs in flour, shaking off the excess. In a large skillet, heat 2 tablespoons of butter and 2 tablespoons of vegetable oil over medium-high heat until hot. Add 2 peeled and crushed cloves garlic and cook, stirring often, for 1 minute. Discard the garlic. Cook the crabs in batches for 3 to 4 minutes on each side, until lightly browned. Serve right away.

Per serving: 327 cal, 33 g pro, 10 g car, 15 g fat, 174 mg chol, 743 mg sod

• 60 MINUTES

5. Rinse the crabs under cold water and pat dry.

6. In a shallow bowl, mix the flour and red pepper. Coat the crabs with the flour, shaking off any excess.

7. In a large nonstick skillet, heat the oil over medium-high heat. Cook the crabs in batches for 3 to 4 minutes on each side, or until golden. With a slotted spoon or spatula, remove the crabs to a serving platter and keep warm.

8. Transfer the crabs to individual serving plates and spoon the sauce over them. Serve right away.

Per serving: 331 cal, 35 g pro, 18 g car, 12 g fat, 159 mg chol, 1,540 mg sod

EASY • 60 MINUTES • LOW FAT

MUSSELS PROVENÇAL

Serves 4

Preparation time: 35 minutes plus 15 minutes to stand
Cooking time: 10 minutes

This easily prepared and economical recipe makes a delicious first course or light supper. Serve it with crusty French bread for dipping into the broth.

4 pounds mussels
2 tablespoons olive oil
1 medium-size yellow onion, chopped fine (1 cup)
2 tablespoons minced fresh garlic
1 can (about 14½ ounces) whole tomatoes, drained and chopped
1 cup fish broth or bottled clam juice
2 tablespoons chopped fresh parsley

1. To clean the mussels: Drop them into lightly salted water to cover and let stand for 15 minutes to rid them of sand. Scrub the mussels thoroughly with a stiff brush and remove the fuzzy beards. Discard any mussels with broken or open shells.

2. In a 6-quart pot, melt the oil over medium heat. Add the onion and garlic and cook, stirring often, for 5 minutes, or until softened.

3. Add the tomatoes, broth, and parsley and bring to a boil over high heat. Reduce the heat to low. Add the mussels. Cover and cook for 3 to 5 minutes, or just until the shells open. Gently stir once or twice to ensure even cooking.

4. With a slotted spoon, transfer the mussels to individual bowls, discarding any mussels that haven't opened. Ladle some of the broth into each bowl and serve right away.

Per serving: 218 cal, 18 g pro, 15 g car, 10 g fat, 37 mg chol, 676 mg sod

PORK,
HAM, & SAUSAGE

*"But I will place this carefully fed pig
Within the cracklin oven; and, I pray
What nicer dish can e'er be given to a man?"*
AESCHYLUS

Americans have recently renewed their love affair with pork. In part this is because today's fresh pork is lower in fat, calories, and cholesterol and higher in protein than that consumed twenty years ago; and the varied selection of cuts is economical and suitable for many preparations.

Pork sells in the marketplace as either fresh, including chops, cutlets, and loin, or smoked and cured like ham and bacon. A tempting mixture of both these is offered here. Most of the recipes are quick and easy, but also included are slow-cooking meals that you can set a timer for and then forget about once they are in the oven.

ORANGE–ROSEMARY PORK

Serves 4
Preparation time: 5 minutes
Cooking time: 10 minutes

This recipe is one that all cooks should have at their fingertips. It's perfect for family or for guests and can be prepared in next to no time. If you can't find pork cutlets in your supermarket you can use thin boneless pork chops instead. Serve the cutlets with steamed rice and broccoli or green beans.

2 tablespoons all-purpose flour
¼ teaspoon salt
¼ teaspoon ground black pepper
1 pound pork cutlets (6 to 8)
2 teaspoons vegetable oil
1 cup orange juice
¼ cup chicken broth
1 teaspoon dried rosemary leaves, crumbled

1. Mix the flour, salt, and pepper on a sheet of waxed paper. Coat the pork in the flour mixture, shaking off the excess.

2. In a large nonstick skillet, heat the oil over medium-high heat. Add the pork and cook for 2 to 3 minutes on each side, or until golden brown and no longer pink in the middle when tested with a sharp knife. Remove to a serving platter and cover loosely with foil to keep warm.

3. Add the orange juice, chicken broth, and rosemary to the skillet. Stir and bring to a boil over high heat. Boil for 3 to 4 minutes, or until slightly thickened. Pour the sauce over the pork and serve right away.
Per serving: 220 cal, 24 g pro, 10 g car, 9 g fat, 77 mg chol, 261 mg sod

DEVILED PORK CUTLETS

Serves 4
Preparation time: 8 minutes
Cooking time: 10 minutes

In this recipe, pork cutlets are coated with mustard and bread crumbs and quickly pan-fried for a simple but tasty dinner. If your family likes spicy

OUT OF BREAD CRUMBS?

Not to worry. If you want to make breaded meat or fish, assemble a meat loaf, or top a casserole, you can substitute packaged bread stuffing, crackers, unsweetened crisp cereal, or croutons. Just process in a blender or food processor, or put in a plastic food storage bag and crush with a rolling pin, tin can, or heavy skillet.

food, mix either ½ teaspoon of hot-pepper sauce with the mustard or ¼ teaspoon of ground pepper with the bread crumbs before coating. Serve with buttered orzo and stewed zucchini.

⅓ cup packaged seasoned bread crumbs
1 pound pork cutlets (6 to 8)
3 tablespoons Dijon mustard
3 tablespoons vegetable oil
For garnish: lemon wedges (optional)

1. Spread the bread crumbs on a sheet of waxed paper. Brush the pork cutlets on both sides with the mustard, then coat with the bread crumbs.

2. In a large nonstick skillet, heat 1 tablespoon of oil over medium-high heat. Cook the cutlets, in batches if necessary, for 2 minutes on each side, or until golden brown and no longer pink in the center when tested with a knife. Add more oil to the skillet as needed. Serve with lemon wedges.
Per serving: 292 cal, 25 g pro, 7 g car, 17 g fat, 77 mg chol, 595 mg sod

EASY • 30 MINUTES • LOW FAT

NEWFANGLED PORK & BEANS

Serves 6
Preparation time: 6 minutes
Cooking time: 12 minutes

Few pork dishes are as easy and tasty as this low-fat version of a New England classic. The recipe calls for lean and tender pork cutlets, but it's also a good way to use the last morsels of a pork roast or baked ham.

1 tablespoon vegetable oil
1 cup finely chopped green bell pepper
1 cup finely chopped onion
1 teaspoon minced fresh garlic
1 pound pork cutlets (6 to 8), cut into ½-inch-square pieces
1 can (about 28 ounces) reduced-fat baked beans
2½ teaspoons Dijon mustard
6 hamburger buns
1 cup shredded lettuce

1. In a large skillet, heat the oil over medium heat. Add the bell pepper, onion, and garlic and cook for 5 to 7 minutes, stirring often.

LEAN PORK POINTER

Today's leaner pork cooks quickly. Overcooking will keep pork from being tender, juicy and flavorful. Cook just until the pork is no longer pink in the center but still moist and gives a little when pressed.

2. Increase the heat to high. Add the pork and stir-fry for 1 to 2 minutes, or until no longer pink.

3. Stir in the beans and mustard and cook for 3 minutes, or until the pork is cooked through.

4. Remove the skillet from the heat. Spoon about ⅓ cup of the pork mixture over each bun and top with the lettuce. Serve right away.

Per serving: 428 cal, 28 g pro, 57 g car, 10 g fat, 51 mg chol, 559 mg sod

---

EASY • 60 MINUTES • MAKE AHEAD

PEPPERY BREADED PORK CHOPS

Serves 6
Preparation time: 15 minutes
Cooking time: 35 minutes

The breading blends with the meat juices to make a moist coating.

⅓ cup (5⅓ tablespoons) butter or margarine
1 teaspoon minced fresh garlic
1 cup packaged plain bread crumbs
1 tablespoon minced fresh parsley
1 teaspoon salt
½ teaspoon ground red pepper (cayenne)
¼ teaspoon ground black pepper
¼ teaspoon onion powder
6 (¾-inch-thick) center-cut pork chops (about 2½ pounds),
  trimmed of visible fat

1. Heat the oven to 425°F. Lightly grease a 13 x 9-inch baking pan.

2. In a small saucepan, melt the butter with the garlic.

3. In a shallow dish, mix the bread crumbs, parsley, salt, red and black pepper, and onion powder until blended.

4. Dip the chops into the garlic butter, then into the crumb mixture to coat them. Arrange the chops in a single layer in the prepared pan. Drizzle with any remaining garlic butter and sprinkle with any remaining crumb mixture.

5. Bake uncovered for about 35 minutes, or until golden brown and the meat nearest the bone is no longer pink when tested with a sharp knife. Serve right away.

Per serving: 342 cal, 30 g pro, 13 g car, 18 g fat, 105 mg chol with butter, 78 mg chol with margarine, 707 mg sod with butter, 721 mg sod with margarine

---

Ⓜ AKE AHEAD

Coat the pork chops with the garlic butter and crumb mixture as directed. (The recipe can also be easily multiplied.) Place on a waxed paper–lined baking sheet and freeze uncovered until hard, about 2 hours. Pack in plastic freezer bags and store up to 2 months. Thaw overnight in the refrigerator.

VARIATION

MICROWAVE PEPPERY PORK CHOPS

• Put the butter and garlic in a microwave-safe pie plate and microwave on High for 1½ to 2 minutes, or until the butter melts and sizzles.

• Meanwhile, mix the breading ingredients. Dip the chops in the garlic butter, then the breading mixture to coat. Place in a single layer in a 13 x 9-inch microwave-safe baking dish with meaty sides toward the edges. Sprinkle with the remaining breading mixture and drizzle with the remaining butter.

• Cover the dish with waxed paper and microwave on Medium High for 22 to 25 minutes, rotating the dish and rearranging the chops twice, until the meat nearest the bone is no longer pink.

Per serving: 335 cal, 30 g pro, 13 g car, 17 g fat, 105 mg chol with butter, 78 mg chol with margarine, 707 mg sod with butter, 721 mg sod with margarine

• EASY • 30 MINUTES
• MAKE AHEAD

`30 MINUTES • MICROWAVE`

TEX–MEX PORK CHOPS

Serves 4

Preparation time: 10 minutes

Cooking time: 10 minutes plus 5 minutes to stand

With a little planning, this dish can be ready to cook even when you're not. Arrange the pork chops and stuffed peppers on the microwave-safe dish early in the day, cover with plastic wrap, stick on a note with the cooking time, and refrigerate. Then whoever is home first can get dinner cooking right away. Serve with slices of avocado.

4 (1-inch-thick) boneless loin pork chops (4 to 5 ounces each), trimmed of visible fat
1 tablespoon fresh lime juice
1 tablespoon chopped fresh cilantro, or 1½ teaspoons dried cilantro leaves, crumbled
2 large red bell peppers (8 ounces each), halved crosswise, stems and seeds removed
1 package (10 ounces) frozen corn kernels (2 cups)
½ cup sliced scallions
1 tablespoon butter or margarine
⅛ teaspoon dried oregano leaves, crumbled
¼ teaspoon ground black pepper
¼ teaspoon ground cumin
½ teaspoon salt (optional)
For garnish: lime wedges (optional)

1. Brush the pork chops with the lime juice and sprinkle with the cilantro. Arrange spoke-fashion on a 12-inch round microwave-safe dish.

2. Fill the bell pepper halves with the corn. Scatter the scallions over the top, dot with butter and sprinkle with the oregano, pepper, cumin, and salt. Place the stuffed peppers between the chops.

3. Cover the dish with vented plastic wrap. Microwave on High for 8 to 10 minutes, rotating the dish ¼ turn twice, until the chops are slightly pink in center when tested with a sharp knife.

4. Remove the dish from the microwave and let stand covered on a heatproof surface for 5 minutes, or until the pork is no longer pink. Garnish with lime wedges and serve right away.

Per serving: 322 cal, 31 g pro, 22 g car, 13 g fat, 86 mg chol with butter, 79 mg chol with margarine, 88 mg sod

60 MINUTES

PORK CHOPS WITH PLUM SALSA

Serves 4

Preparation time: 15 minutes plus 30 minutes to marinate

Cooking time: 10 minutes

Pork chops are perfect for grilling, but don't despair if you do not have a grill. They taste mighty good broiled, too. Here, the chops are topped with a fresh plum salsa that accentuates the pork's natural sweetness. The salsa can be made up to 2 days ahead and stored airtight in the refrigerator.

PLUM SALSA

4 medium-size red or black plums, pitted and cut into ½-inch chunks (about 1½ cups)

1 medium-size mango, peeled and cut into ½-inch chunks (about 1½ cups)

1 small red onion, chopped fine (about ¼ cup)

1 to 2 medium-size jalapeño peppers, seeded and chopped fine

¼ cup chopped fresh cilantro

1 tablespoon fresh lime juice

½ teaspoon ground coriander

¼ teaspoon salt

2 teaspoons ground coriander

¼ teaspoon paprika

1 teaspoon salt

¼ teaspoon ground black pepper

4 (1-inch-thick) boneless pork chops (about 6 ounces each), trimmed of visible fat

1. Make the salsa: In a medium-size bowl, mix the plums, mango, onion, jalapeños, cilantro, lime juice, coriander, and salt until well blended. Refrigerate until ready to use.

2. In a small bowl, mix the coriander, paprika, salt, and pepper until blended. Rub the mixture over the pork chops. Wrap airtight and refrigerate for at least 30 minutes.

3. Heat a gas grill to medium-high, prepare a charcoal fire, or heat a broiler.

4. Place the chops on a lightly oiled grill rack or broiler-pan rack. Grill or broil 4 to 6 inches from the heat source for about 10 minutes, turning once, until browned on both sides.

VARIATION

APRICOT GRILLED PORK CHOPS

● In a small saucepan, mix ½ cup apricot preserves, ⅓ cup Dijon mustard, 2 teaspoons crumbled dried sage leaves, and 2 teaspoons minced onion. Cook over low heat, stirring, until the preserves are melted and the ingredients are well blended.

● Grill the chops as directed, turning 3 or 4 times and brushing with the apricot sauce each time.

Per serving: 387 cal, 37 g pro, 26 g car, 13 g fat, 101 mg chol, 1,124 mg sod

● 60 MINUTES

5. Transfer the pork chops to serving plates and serve right away with the plum salsa alongside.

Per serving: 351 cal, 38 g pro, 21 g car, 13 g fat, 101 mg chol, 770 mg sod

60 MINUTES • MICROWAVE • ONE POT

SMOKED PORK CHOP CASSEROLE

Serves 6
Preparation time: 15 minutes
Cooking time: 42 minutes

Here's a simple and filling one-dish meal that requires nothing more than rolls or rye bread as an accompaniment. It is also great reheated the next day.

2¼ pounds all-purpose potatoes, well scrubbed and cut into 1-inch chunks (8 cups)
1 bag (16 ounces) sauerkraut, rinsed and drained
1 cup chopped onion
¾ cup chopped carrots
½ cup chicken broth
¼ cup dry white wine or chicken broth
2 teaspoons dried parsley flakes
1 bay leaf (1½ inches long)
¼ teaspoon ground black pepper
Pinch ground cloves
6 (¾-inch-thick) fully cooked smoked pork chops (about 2½ pounds), trimmed of visible fat

1. In a 13 x 9-inch microwave-safe baking dish, mix the potatoes, sauerkraut, onion, carrots, chicken broth, wine, parsley, bay leaf, pepper, and cloves. Cover with vented plastic wrap and microwave on High for 25 to 30 minutes, stirring 4 times, until the potatoes, onion, and carrots are tender.

2. Place the pork chops on top of the vegetables in a single layer, with the meatier portions toward the edges of the dish. Cover and microwave on Medium High for 10 to 12 minutes, rotating the dish ¼ turn twice, until the meat is heated through.

3. Remove the dish from the microwave, discard the bay leaf, and serve right away.

Per serving: 383 cal, 28 g pro, 38 g car, 14 g fat, 75 mg chol, 2,725 mg sod with wine, 2,767 mg sod with broth

`EASY • 60 MINUTES • LOW FAT`

CHINESE PORK TENDERLOIN

Serves 8

Preparation time: 5 minutes

Cooking time: 30 minutes plus 5 minutes to stand

In Chinese restaurants, savory-sweet hoisin sauce is served with Peking duck or moo shu pork. Look for hoisin sauce near soy sauce in the Asian-food section of your supermarket. This dish is delicious hot, but also equally good served at room temperature or shredded and stirred into Chinese fried rice.

½ cup hoisin sauce

⅓ cup minced scallions

1 tablespoon minced peeled fresh gingerroot

1½ teaspoons minced fresh garlic

2 pork tenderloins (about 12 ounces each)

1. Heat the oven to 500°F. Line a jelly roll pan with foil and lightly grease a wire rack, or line a broiler pan with foil and grease the broiler-pan rack.

2. In a large shallow dish, mix the hoisin, scallions, ginger, and garlic. Add the tenderloins, turning to coat. Place the pork on the rack in the pan.

3. Bake for 25 to 30 minutes (no need to turn meat), or until the meat is barely pink in center (a meat thermometer should register 160°F when inserted into the center). Remove from the oven and let stand for 5 minutes.

4. Cut the pork into thin slices and serve with extra hoisin sauce on the side.

Per serving: 158 cal, 18 g pro, 10 g car, 4 g fat, 50 mg chol, 351 mg sod

CURRIED TENDERLOIN

Spread ⅓ cup of packaged plain bread crumbs on a sheet of waxed paper. In a shallow dish, mix 1 tablespoon curry powder, 1 tablespoon Dijon mustard, and ¼ cup plain low-fat or nonfat yogurt. Coat the tenderloins with the yogurt mixture, then with the bread crumbs. Bake the tenderloins as directed.

Per serving: 137 cal, 19 g pro, 4 g car, 4 g fat, 51 mg chol, 124 mg sod

• EASY • 60 MINUTES
• LOW FAT

BUYING AND STORING PORK

◆ Select fresh pork with a pale pink or pink color and white fat that is firm to the touch. It should have a fresh smell, with no off-odors.

◆ Prepackaged meat can be stored in its original wrapper. Pork wrapped in butcher paper should be rewrapped in plastic wrap or foil.

◆ Store fresh pork in the coldest part of the refrigerator for up to 3 days with the exception of ground pork, which should be used within 2 days.

◆ Freeze fresh pork immediately after purchase. Wrap it in plastic wrap, then with foil, and freeze chops or ground pork up to 3 months and larger cuts up to 6 months.

◆ Leftover cooked pork can be stored airtight in the refrigerator up to 5 days.

◆ Select unsmoked bacon with pale pink meat and white fat; smoked bacon with rosy red meat and yellowish fat.

◆ Bacon can be stored airtight in the refrigerator up to 2 weeks and frozen up to 2 months. Canadian bacon can be stored airtight in the refrigerator up to 4 days and frozen up to 1 month.

◆ Canned or packaged hams should be refrigerated even before opening. After opening, use within 1 week.

EASY • 30 MINUTES

SAUCY PORK MEDALLIONS

Serves 4
Preparation time: 10 minutes
Cooking time: 15 minutes

When a recipe refers to medallions of meat, it means that a boneless cut, such as tenderloin, has been sliced into round or oval pieces. Here, the medallions are served with a sage-scented sauce, making the dish stylish enough for entertaining but also quick and easy for a weekday meal. Serve with buttered noodles or orzo and steamed leafy green vegetables.

¼ cup all-purpose flour
2 tablespoons grated Parmesan cheese
½ teaspoon salt
¼ teaspoon ground black pepper
1 pound pork tenderloin, sliced diagonally into 8 pieces
   (medallions)
2 tablespoons olive oil
⅔ cup dry white wine or apple juice
2 large shallots, sliced thin, or ¼ cup sliced white part of scallions
1 cup chicken broth
3 tablespoons chopped fresh sage, or 1 tablespoon dried
1 tablespoon butter (optional)

1. Mix the flour, cheese, salt, and pepper on a sheet of waxed paper. Add the pork to the flour mixture, tossing to coat.

2. In a large nonstick skillet, heat the oil over medium heat. Add the pork and cook for about 3 minutes on each side, or just until barely pink in the center. Remove the pork to serving platter.

3. Wipe out the skillet. Add the wine and shallots and bring to a boil over high heat. Boil until the wine is reduced to about 2 tablespoons.

4. Add the chicken broth, bring to a boil, and boil for 2 to 3 minutes, or until reduced to about ½ cup.

5. Remove the skillet from the heat. Add the sage and butter. Swirl the skillet slightly until the butter has melted and blended with the sauce. Pour the sauce over the pork and serve right away.

Per serving: 260 cal, 26 g pro, 8 g car with wine, 12 g car with apple juice,
11 g fat, 77 mg chol, 628 mg sod

PORK & BLACK BEAN BURRITOS

Serves 4

Total time: 35 minutes

A salad of sliced avocado, orange, red onion, and lettuce with vinaigrette dressing complements these meat-packed burritos.

  1 pork tenderloin (about 8 ounces), quartered lengthwise and cut
    crosswise into ½-inch-wide pieces
  3 tablespoons fresh lemon or lime juice
  2 teaspoons chili powder
  ½ teaspoon ground cumin
  ½ teaspoon ground coriander
  8 (7-inch) flour tortillas, stacked and wrapped in foil
  2 cans (about 16 ounces each) black beans, drained and rinsed
  1½ cups chicken broth
  2 teaspoons minced fresh garlic
  1 tablespoon olive oil
  1 cup chopped onion
  1 can (14½ to 16 ounces) tomatoes, drained, seeded, and chopped coarse
  1 can (4 ounces) chopped green chiles
  ½ cup low-fat or nonfat sour cream
  For garnish: cherry tomatoes, quartered (optional)

1. Heat the oven to 250°F. Put the pork into a large bowl. Add the lemon juice, chili powder, cumin, and coriander, tossing to coat

2. Place the wrapped tortillas in the oven for 8 to 10 minutes. Turn the oven off and keep the tortillas in the oven until ready to use.

3. Meanwhile, in a medium-size saucepan, combine the beans, chicken broth, and garlic. Bring the mixture to a boil over medium-high heat. Reduce the heat to medium and boil gently for 7 minutes, or until about half the broth is left. Remove the pan from the heat. With a potato masher or slotted spoon, mash to a thick paste. (You'll have about 2 cups.)

4. In a large skillet, heat the oil over medium-high heat. Add the onion and cook, stirring frequently, for 7 minutes, or until lightly browned and almost tender.

5. Add the pork and stir-fry for 2 to 3 minutes, or until lightly browned on the outside and barely pink in the center. Add the tomatoes and all but 1 tablespoon of the chopped green chiles. Cook, stirring occasionally, for 2

MAKE AHEAD

Prepare the pork as directed in step 1. Place on a waxed paper-lined baking sheet and freeze uncovered until hard, about 2 hours. Pack in plastic freezer bags and store up to 2 months.

minutes, or until the pork is cooked through. Remove the skillet from the heat.

6. In a small bowl, mix the reserved 1 tablespoon of chilies and the sour cream. Remove the tortillas from the oven.

7. To assemble, spoon ¼ cup of the bean mixture slightly below the center of each tortilla. Top with a scant ⅓ cup of the pork mixture. Fold the bottom of the tortilla to cover the filling. Fold the sides toward the center, then roll up from the bottom. Serve with the sour cream mixture to spoon over the tops.

Makes 8 burritos. Per 2 burritos : 505 cal, 29 g pro, 65 g car, 15 g fat with low-fat sour cream, 13 g fat with nonfat sour cream, 38 mg chol, 1,419 mg sod

EASY • 30 MINUTES • LOW FAT • ONE POT

PORK TENDERLOIN DINNER

Serves 4

Preparation time: 5 minutes

Cooking time: 14 minutes

Lean pork tenderloin is usually sold in packages of 2, each weighing between 8 and 16 ounces. Here, it's broiled with potatoes and zucchini for an easy and tempting dinner.

  1 pork tenderloin (about 12 ounces)
  ¼ cup bottled barbecue sauce
  12 ounces frozen French fries (½ a 24-ounce bag)
  1 teaspoon chili powder
  2 small zucchini, cut in half lengthwise
  2 teaspoons vegetable oil

1. Heat the broiler. Line a broiler pan with foil for easy cleanup and grease the broiler-pan rack.

2. Place the pork on the rack. Brush with 2 tablespoons of the barbecue sauce. In a large bowl, toss the frozen French fries with the chili powder to coat. Spread the fries on the rack, leaving enough space for the zucchini. Add the zucchini cut side up and brush with the oil.

3. Broil 4 to 6 inches from the heat source for 8 minutes. Turn the pork and brush with the remaining barbecue sauce.

4. Broil for 4 to 6 minutes longer, or until the meat is barely pink in the center (a meat thermometer should register 160°F when inserted into the center), the fries are crisp, and the zucchini is tender and golden.

5. Cut the pork into thin slices. Serve with the potatoes and zucchini.

Per serving: 297 cal, 21 g pro, 25 g car, 13 g fat, 56 mg chol, 197 mg sod

PORK & VEGETABLE STIR-FRY

Serves 4
Preparation time: 5 minutes
Cooking time: 20 minutes

This simple, healthy stir-fry dish goes together quickly.

1 tablespoon vegetable oil
1½ teaspoons minced peeled fresh gingerroot
12 ounces pork tenderloin, trimmed of visible fat and sliced thin
1 package (about 8 ounces) frozen sugar snap peas
1 package (about 16 ounces) frozen vegetables (broccoli, mushrooms, red
  bell pepper, and onions)
¼ cup water
¼ cup bottled stir-fry sauce
For garnish: mung bean sprouts (optional)

1. In a wok or heavy large nonstick skillet, heat the oil over medium-high heat. Add the pork and ginger and stir-fry for about 10 minutes, or until the pork is no longer pink.

2. Stir the vegetables, water, and stir-fry sauce into the skillet. Bring to a boil. Cover and simmer for 6 to 8 minutes, or until the vegetables are heated through. Garnish with sprouts and serve right away.

Per serving: 210 cal, 23 g pro, 19 g car, 6 g fat, 55 mg chol, 485 sod

COOK'S TIP

Partially freezing the uncooked pork tenderloin for about 40 minutes will make slicing it easier.

JUNIOR CHEFS AND THE MICROWAVE

More kids are cooking with microwave ovens than ever before, making hot snacks, breakfasts, and lunches. Show kids (7 years old and up) how to use the microwave and have them practice while you watch. Review the following safety tips with them:

◆ Never turn on an empty microwave oven.

◆ Use only microwave-safe cookware. (To make it easier for kids, keep the dishes and utensils that are to be used for the microwave in a specific spot or write MW on the bottom in indelible marker.)

◆ Always use pot holders to remove dishes from the microwave oven. Hot food can heat up its container. And remember, even if the dish is cool, the contents may be very hot. Let the heated item stay in the microwave about 1 minute before removing (This will help avoid eruptive boiling and also cool the food slightly so mouths won't get burned.)

◆ Open lids and remove the plastic wrap away from the face and hands to avoid steam burns.

◆ Post cooking times and instructions for favorite foods near the microwave or tape directly to containers of leftovers.

◆ In case of sparks or a fire: Do not open the door of the oven. This will make the fire worse. Get out of the room at once. Inform an adult or call the fire department.

BAVARIAN PORK

Serves 4

Preparation time: 10 minutes

Cooking time: 2 hours 30 minutes

The meat in this rich and satisfying dish doesn't require browning. Flavored with paprika, sauerkraut, and caraway seeds, it needs only some rye bread, crisp cucumber spears, and a mug of dark beer to round out the meal.

1 tablespoon bacon fat

2 medium-size onions, sliced thin (2 cups)

2 tablespoons paprika

1 pound lean boneless pork shoulder (Boston Butt), trimmed
    and cut into 1-inch chunks

½ teaspoon salt

½ teaspoon sugar

¼ teaspoon ground black pepper

½ cup water

1 can (about 16 ounces) sauerkraut, rinsed and drained (2¾ cups)

1 tablespoon caraway seeds

½ teaspoon minced fresh garlic

½ teaspoon dried marjoram leaves, crumbled

¼ cup light sour cream

For garnish: chopped fresh parsley

1. In a medium-size saucepan, heat the bacon fat over low heat. Add the onions and cook for 15 to 20 minutes, or until golden, stirring occasionally.

2. Add the paprika, stirring to coat the onions. Stir in the pork, salt, sugar, and pepper. Increase the heat to medium and cook uncovered for 5 to 7 minutes, stirring occasionally.

3. Stir in the water, sauerkraut, caraway seeds, garlic, and marjoram. Reduce the heat to low.

4. Cover and simmer for 2 hours, or until the pork is tender, stirring occasionally and adding more water as needed to prevent sticking.

5. Stir in the sour cream. Remove the pan from the heat. Sprinkle with the parsley.

Per serving: 283 cal, 25 g pro, 14 g car, 14 g fat, 83 mg chol, 634 mg sod

ONE POT

RAGOUT OF PORK & SQUASH

Serves 6
Preparation time: 20 minutes
Cooking time: 2 hours

Boneless pork shoulder can be tough, but when braised and simmered, as in this ragout, it becomes tender and succulent. Some markets sell it already cubed for stewing. Or ask the butcher to cut it for you while you shop.

2 tablespoons vegetable oil
2 pounds boneless pork shoulder (Boston butt), trimmed of fat
   and cut into 1½-inch chunks
2 large onions, chopped coarse
1 tablespoon minced fresh garlic
1 tablespoon curry powder
1 teaspoon ground cumin
2 cups chicken bouillon (3 bouillon cubes dissolved
   in 2 cups water)
3 tablespoons tomato paste
2 teaspoons salt
½ teaspoon ground black pepper
1 butternut squash (2 pounds), peeled (see Cook's Tip), seeded,
   and cut into 1-inch chunks (4 cups)
3 large potatoes (1½ pounds), scrubbed and diced (4 cups)
1 cup frozen green peas

1. In a 4- to 5-quart Dutch oven, heat the oil over medium-high heat. Cook half the pork until brown on all sides. Remove with a slotted spoon to a plate. Repeat with the remaining pork.

2. Reduce the heat to medium-low. Add the onions, garlic, curry powder, and cumin to the drippings. Cook for 1 minute, stirring often, until the onions are coated with the spices.

3. Add the bouillon, tomato paste, salt, and pepper. Stir to scrape up the browned bits on the bottom. Bring the mixture to a boil over high heat.

4. Return the meat to the pan and reduce the heat to low. Cover and simmer for 1 hour 10 minutes, stirring occasionally.

5. Stir in the squash and potatoes. Cover and simmer for 35 minutes, stirring twice. Add the peas and simmer 5 minutes longer, or until the meat and vegetables are very tender and the sauce is slightly thickened.

Per serving: 479 cal, 36 g pro, 47 g car, 17 g fat, 101 mg chol, 1,437 mg sod

OOK'S TIP

To peel the butternut squash, cut off the top and bottom ends, then halve lengthwise. Use a large spoon to scrape out the seeds and fibers. Place cut side down and carefully cut off the outer skin with a sharp knife.

FAST SKILLET MEAL

From start to finish, Knockwurst Casserole (p.213) is cooked in the skillet, making it the solution for preparing a one-pot dinner after a busy day.

SUPPER IN A SNAP

Pork sausage is extremely tasty and comes sweet or spicy. This entree of Sausage & Peppers (p.210) is simple to prepare, tastes terrific, and is really easy to clean up.

Beat the clock with meals you can make in a single pan. What could be more convenient for nights when you're short on time and have hungry stomachs to fill?

FIRE UP THE GRILL
For Spicy Dry-Rubbed Pork Loin (p.208), a savory blend of herbs and spices are worked into the meat. Here it's served with grill-roasted sweet potatoes.

SPICED PORK PATTIES

Serves 6
Preparation time: 10 minutes
Cooking time: 16 minutes

These spiced patties will remind you of sausage but with a lot less fat. They're perfect to make ahead and freeze, then just reheat and serve with a frittata or omelet for a quick and hearty meal. For extra crisp patties, lightly coat with flour before cooking.

1½ pounds lean ground pork
1 teaspoon salt
1 teaspoon ground black pepper
1 teaspoon ground sage
½ teaspoon ground coriander
¼ teaspoon dried marjoram leaves, crumbled
Applesauce (optional)

1. In a medium-size bowl, mix the pork, salt, pepper, sage, coriander, and marjoram until well blended. Form the mixture into 12 patties, about 2 inches in diameter.

2. Heat a large nonstick skillet (no need to add fat) over medium-high heat. Add half the patties and cook for about 4 minutes on each side, or until brown and crisp. Remove to a plate lined with paper towels to drain. Keep warm. Repeat with the remaining patties. Serve right away with applesauce.

Makes 12 patties. Per 2 patties: 233 cal, 20 g pro, 0 g car, 16 g fat, 73 mg chol, 424 mg sod

PORK LO MEIN

Serves 4
Preparation time: 10 minutes
Cooking time: 15 minutes

Believe it or not, this colorful Chinese-style dinner starts with inexpensive packaged noodle-soup mix. It's so easy to make, but the best part is that it's a complete meal in one. And if you thought lettuce was only for salads, be prepared to change your mind. Try it with ground turkey or chicken, too. ▶

8 ounces ground pork

1 cup chopped onion

1 cup thinly sliced carrots

1 teaspoon minced fresh garlic

2 packages (3 ounces each) mushroom-flavor Oriental noodle-soup
  mix (with seasoning packets)

1½ cups water

1 cup frozen green peas

6 cups coarsely shredded romaine lettuce (6 ounces)

1. In a large skillet, cook the pork, onion, carrots, and garlic over medium-high heat for 5 to 6 minutes, stirring often, until the pork is lightly browned.

2. Break the noodles into the skillet. Stir in the seasoning packets, water, and peas. Bring to a boil over high heat. Reduce the heat to medium-low. Cover and cook for 3 to 5 minutes, or until the noodles and vegetables are almost crisp-tender.

3. Stir in the lettuce. Cook uncovered for 3 to 4 minutes, stirring almost constantly, until the lettuce is wilted, the noodles are soft, and the carrots are crisp-tender. Remove the skillet from the heat and serve right away.
Per serving: 412 cal, 17 g pro, 39 g car, 20 g fat, 41 mg chol, 1,276 mg sod

EASY • ONE POT

COUNTRY-STYLE RIBS
& KRAUT

Serves 4
Preparation time: 15 minutes
Cooking time: 1 hour

Make this hearty dish with meaty country-style ribs—also sold as country-style spareribs or blade-end spareribs. This recipe calls for 1 pound of sauerkraut, but it can be increased to 2 pounds if you prefer.

2 tablespoons vegetable oil

2 pounds country-style pork ribs, trimmed of visible fat

2 cups chicken broth or water

1 pound sauerkraut, rinsed and drained

1 teaspoon garlic powder

½ teaspoon ground black pepper

2 bay leaves (about 1 inch long)

1 pound all-purpose potatoes, scrubbed and cut into 1½-inch chunks

ABOUT KRAUT

◆ Precooked sauerkraut is available in jars or cans. Fresh sauerkraut is sold in bags in the refrigerated section of the supermarket. Fresh sauerkraut generally has a milder flavor than precooked.

◆ To cook fresh sauerkraut, simmer, covered, in a liquid (water, broth, wine, or beer) for about 30 minutes. Pre-cooked sauerkraut only needs to be reheated for 5 to 10 minutes.

◆ Canned or jarred sauerkraut will keep unopened up to 6 months. Keep fresh sauerkraut refrigerated and use with in 1 week.

VARIATION

**MICROWAVE
COUNTRY-STYLE
RIBS AND KRAUT**

• Prepare the recipe
as directed through
step 2.

• In a 13 x 9-inch
microwave-safe baking
dish, mix the broth,
garlic powder, pepper,
and bay leaves. Add
the browned ribs.
Cover with a lid or
vented plastic wrap.
Microwave on Medium
for 30 minutes,
rotating the dish 1/2
turn once.

• Stir in the sauerkraut
and potatoes. Cover
and microwave on
Medium for 25 to 30
minutes, stirring once,
until the meat and
potatoes are fork-tender.

• Remove from the
microwave and let
stand covered on a
heatproof surface for
10 minutes. Discard
the bay leaves.

Per serving: 374 cal,
29 g pro, 22 g car, 19 g
fat, 81 mg chol, 848 mg
sod

• EASY

1. Heat the oven to 350° F.

2. In a 5- to 6-quart Dutch oven, heat the oil over medium-high heat. Add the ribs and cook, turning often, until well browned. Remove with slotted spoon to a plate. Drain off the fat in the pan.

3. Add the broth, sauerkraut, garlic powder, pepper, and bay leaves. Stir in the potatoes. Return the ribs to the pan, covering them with the sauerkraut.

4. Bring the mixture to a gentle boil on top of the stove, then cover and transfer to the oven. Bake for 40 minutes, or until the ribs and potatoes are tender, stirring once.

5. Discard the bay leaves and serve right away.

Per serving: 374 cal, 29 g pro, 22 g car, 19 g fat, 81 mg chol, 848 mg sod

EASY • CLASSIC

BARBECUED BABY BACK RIBS

Serves 4

Preparation time: 10 minutes plus at least 1 hour to marinate

Cooking time: 40 minutes

Baby back ribs, cut from the loin, are smaller and meatier than spareribs, which are cut from the side, and either can be used here. This is the easiest and most foolproof way to cook ribs, and the recipe can be multiplied to feed a crowd. Be sure to serve with lots of crusty bread to mop up the extra homemade sauce.

2 pounds baby back pork ribs

¼ cup honey

¼ cup ketchup

¼ cup red wine vinegar

¼ cup fresh orange juice

3 tablespoons soy sauce

2 teaspoons minced fresh garlic

½ teaspoon dry mustard

¼ teaspoon hot-pepper sauce, or to taste

¼ teaspoon paprika

For garnish: orange slices and watercress (optional)

1. Put the ribs and all the remaining ingredients into a large zipper-type food storage bag. Close the bag, pressing out the air, and turn to coat. Refrigerate for at least 1 hour and no more than 6 hours. ▶

2. Transfer the ribs to a large plate. Pour the marinade into a medium-size saucepan. Remove ¼ cup of the marinade to a small bowl and set aside. Bring the remaining marinade to a boil over medium heat, stirring constantly. Reduce the heat to low and simmer, stirring occasionally, for 20 minutes, or until the sauce is thick and syrupy

3. Meanwhile, heat a gas grill to medium-high, prepare a charcoal fire, or heat a broiler.

4. Grill or broil the ribs 4 to 6 inches from the heat source for 15 to 20 minutes, turning once and brushing with the reserved ¼ cup marinade, until crisp on the outside and cooked through.

5. Transfer the ribs to a serving platter and pour the sauce over the ribs. Garnish with orange slices and sprigs of watercress and serve right away.

Per serving: 499 cal, 24 g pro, 25 g car, 33 g fat, 114 mg chol, 1,066 sod

EASY • ONE POT • CLASSIC

NEW ENGLAND BOILED DINNER

Serves 8
Preparation time: 15 minutes
Cooking time: 1 hour 50 minutes

Many countries have boiled meals. In France it's called pot-au-feu, in Italy bollito misto, and the New England boiled dinner is based on the English version. Serve this hearty meal with strong mustard or bottled creamy horse radish sauce. Any leftover meat is good served hot or cold.

1 smoked pork shoulder butt (about 2½ pounds), removed from netting
   as directed on wrapper
2 bay leaves (1 inch long)
2 large cloves garlic
4 quarts water
8 medium-size red-skinned potatoes
1 large rutabaga (yellow turnip), about 2 pounds, peeled and cut into
   1½-inch chunks
8 small white onions (about 1 pound), peeled
1 head green cabbage (about 2½ pounds), cut into 8 wedges
6 large carrots, cut into chunks
4 large parsnips, peeled and cut into chunks

1. In an 8-quart pot, combine the pork, bay leaves, garlic, and water. Bring

COOK'S TIP

Marinades can make delicious sauces. Just be sure to boil for at least 3 minutes to destroy any harmful bacteria that may have been transferred from the raw meat.

to a boil over high heat. Reduce the heat to medium-low. Partially cover and simmer for 1 hour.

2. Add the potatoes, rutabaga, and onions. Cover and simmer for 30 minutes, or until the meat and vegetables are tender.

3. Remove the meat to a cutting board and the vegetables to a large serving platter. Cover both tightly with foil to keep warm.

4. Add the cabbage, carrots, and parsnips to the pot. Cover and simmer for 20 minutes, or until tender.

5. Add the vegetables to the platter. Discard the bay leaves. Slice the pork and serve on the platter with the vegetables.

Per serving: 718 cal, 33 g pro, 69 g car, 35 g fat, 88 mg chol, 1,345 mg sod

EASY • CLASSIC

ITALIAN BRAISED PORK

Serves 8
Preparation time: 10 minutes
Cooking time: 3 hours 10 minutes

Braising pork shoulder in milk, a classic Italian treatment, renders the meat extra tender and juicy, and the milk cooks down to a rich and creamy sauce. Serve this memorable dish with sautéed broccoli rabe and bow-tie pasta.

4 teaspoons dried sage leaves, crumbled
1½ teaspoons dried rosemary leaves, crumbled
1 teaspoon salt
½ teaspoon ground black pepper
1 boneless pork shoulder roast (about 2½ pounds), trimmed and tied
2 tablespoons minced fresh garlic
2½ cups milk
For garnish: fresh sage leaves (optional)

1. Heat the oven to 350°F.

2. In a small bowl, mix the sage, rosemary, salt, and pepper. Rub the mixture over the pork and put into a well-greased 4-quart Dutch oven. Cover and bake for about 2 hours, or until browned.

3. Remove the pan from the oven. Skim off and discard the fat from the pan juices. Add the garlic and 1 cup of milk, agitating the pan so the milk blends with the pan juices.

4. Cover the pan and bake for 45 minutes to 1 hour longer, or until the meat is tender.

▶

5. Transfer the meat to a serving platter. Skim off and discard the fat from the pan juices. Add the remaining 1½ cups milk and bring to a boil over high heat. Boil for 5 to 7 minutes, stirring constantly, until slightly thickened and only about 1½ cups remain.

6. Slice the pork, arrange on a serving platter, and pour some of the sauce over the top. Garnish with sage leaves. Serve right away with the remaining sauce separately.

Per serving: 212 cal, 23 g pro, 5 g car, 11 g fat, 80 mg chol, 392 mg sod

---

CLASSIC

ROAST PORK LOIN WITH APPLES & ONIONS

Serves 6 to 8

Preparation time: 20 minutes

Cooking time: 1 hour 30 minutes

The flavors of garlic and sage infuse this elegant bone-in pork loin, while cider, mustard, and sage enhance the gravy. Serve with roasted or mashed potatoes and glazed carrots.

1 (4-pound) bone-in pork loin roast
2 large cloves garlic, cut into slivers
1 tablespoon chopped fresh sage, or 1½ teaspoons dried
2 tablespoons all-purpose flour
1 teaspoon coarsely ground pepper
½ teaspoon salt
12 small yellow onions (about 1½ pounds), peeled
½ cup water
3 large Cortland, Golden Delicious, or Granny Smith apples, peeled, halved, and cored

GRAVY

2 tablespoons all-purpose flour
1¼ cups chicken broth
½ cup apple cider or apple juice
1 teaspoon Dijon mustard
1 teaspoon chopped fresh sage, or ½ teaspoon dried sage leaves, crumbled

For garnish: fresh sage leaves (optional)

COOK'S TIP

To add color to a pale gravy, stir in a few drops of bottled gravy browner, which can be found in the spice section of most supermarkets.

1. Heat the oven to 450°F. With a small knife, poke slits in the meat and push a garlic sliver into each. Press the sage between the chops.

2. In a small bowl, mix the flour, pepper, and salt. Rub the roast with the flour mixture.

3. Place the roast, fat side up, in a large roasting pan. Arrange the onions around the roast and pour the water into the pan.

4. Roast for 20 minutes. Stir the onions to coat with the pan juices. Reduce the oven temperature to 375°F. Roast for 50 minutes. Add the apple halves and roast for 25 to 30 minutes longer, turning the apples over once to coat with pan juices, or until the onions and apples are tender and a meat thermometer inserted into the thickest part of the meat, not touching bone, registers 160°F.

5. Remove the meat, onions, and apples to a serving platter. Cover loosely with foil and let stand for 10 minutes.

6. Meanwhile, make the gravy. Pour off all but 2 tablespoons of drippings from the pan. Stir in the flour and cook over medium-low heat until golden, scraping up brown bits from the bottom of the pan. Remove the pan from the heat and slowly stir in the broth and cider until blended. Bring to a boil over high heat. Reduce the heat to medium-low and simmer for 5 minutes, stirring constantly until thickened. Stir in the mustard and sage.

7. Cut the pork into chops. Garnish with sage leaves and serve the gravy separately.

Per serving: 598 cal, 44 g pro, 23 g car, 36 g fat, 139 mg chol 438 mg sod

ROASTING CHART FOR PORK AND HAM

Use this chart as a guide for roasting pork or ham, or cook pork until a meat thermometer registers 160° to 170°F. Always use an accurate meat thermometer, inserting it each time into a different spot in the meat. Allow meat to stand for 10 to 15 minutes before serving. Remember that during this time the temperature will continue to rise 5 to 10 degrees.

CUT:	ROASTING TIME:
Pork loin, boneless, bone-in, or crown roast, stuffed or unstuffed	20 minutes per pound at 350°F
Tenderloin, 8 ounces to 11/2 pounds	20 to 30 minutes at 425°F
Leg, bone-in 31/2 pounds	40 minutes per pound at 350°F
Boston butt, 3 to 6 pounds	45 minutes per pound at 350°F
Ham, bone-in and fully cooked 12 to 14 pounds	10 to 12 minutes per pound at 350°F
	(internal temperature 130 to 140°F)

SPICY DRY-RUBBED PORK LOIN

Serves 12

Preparation time: 15 minutes plus at least 24 hours to marinate

Cooking time: 2 hours plus 15 minutes to stand

This pork is so juicy and flavorful it doesn't need a sauce. Serve it with baked sweet potatoes and a green vegetable. Make up a large batch of the spice rub and keep it on hand for chops and steaks as well. It will keep in an airtight container in a cool, dry place up to 3 months.

1 (5- to 5½-pound) boned and tied pork loin, with a thin layer of fat

2 teaspoons salt

2 teaspoons ground black pepper

2 teaspoons garlic powder

1½ teaspoons onion powder

1½ teaspoons dry mustard

1½ teaspoons paprika

1 teaspoon dried sage leaves, crumbled

¼ to ½ teaspoon ground red pepper (cayenne)

3 tablespoons olive oil

For garnish: fresh sage leaves (optional)

1. Pat the pork loin dry with paper towels. Place the meat on a large sheet of heavy-duty foil.

2. In a small bowl, mix the salt, black pepper, garlic powder, onion powder, dry mustard, paprika, sage, and red pepper. Rub the mixture all over the pork, turning to coat the sides and ends. Wrap the pork in foil or plastic wrap, twist the ends to secure, and marinate for 1 to 2 days in the refrigerator.

3. Heat the oven to 400°F. Unwrap the pork, drizzle with the olive oil, and turn to coat all sides. Put the pork on a rack in a large roasting pan. Roast uncovered for 1 hour 30 minutes to 2 hours, or until a meat thermometer inserted in the thickest part registers 160°F.

4. Remove the pork to a cutting board and let it stand for 15 minutes. Remove the strings and slice the meat thin. Arrange on a serving platter and garnish with sage leaves. Serve right away.

Per serving: 506 cal, 34 g pro, 1 g car, 40 g fat, 133 mg chol 461 mg sod

---

GRILLED SPICY DRY-RUBBED PORK

• Put a 15½ x 10½ x 3½-inch disposable drip pan in the bottom of a barbecue grill. Arrange briquettes or lava rocks around all sides of the pan. Pour 1-inch of water into the pan. Adjust grill 4 to 6 inches above the coals. If using a gas grill, set to medium-low.

• Unwrap pork, drizzle with the olive oil, and turn to coat on all sides. When coals are hot, place the pork over the drip pan. Cover with a lid or foil tent.

• Grill pork for 30 minutes, until it begins to brown on the underside. Turn and grill for 1 hour and 15 minutes (replenish water in drip pan if necessary) to 2 hours and 30 minutes, turning every 30 minutes after first turn, or until a meat thermometer inserted into the thickest part registers 160°F.

Per serving: 506 cal, 34 g pro, 1 g car, 40 g fat, 133 mg chol, 461 mg sod

• EASY • MAKE-AHEAD

HARVEST HAM DINNER

Serves 4
Preparation time: 5 minutes
Cooking time: 15 minutes

COOK'S TIP

To keep the ham steak from curling while cooking, cut a few slashes through the fat edges at about 2-inch intervals.

Ham steak is enlivened with pears and sweet potatoes in this quick and easy skillet meal. Accompany with warm buttermilk biscuits.

    2 tablespoons butter or margarine
    2 medium-size ripe pears or apples, sliced thin
    1 fully-cooked center-cut ham steak (about 1 pound)
    1 to 2 cans (about 16 ounces each) sweet potatoes, drained
    ⅓ cup maple syrup
    2 tablespoons Dijon mustard

1. In a large skillet, melt the butter over medium heat. Add the pears and cook for about 5 minutes, stirring often, until slightly softened.

2. Push the pears to one side of the pan. Add the ham steak and cook over medium-high heat for about 3 minutes on each side, or until browned and heated through. Remove the ham steak to a serving platter and cover with foil to keep warm.

3. Add the sweet potatoes to the skillet. Cover and cook over medium heat for about 5 minutes, or until heated through.

4. In a small bowl, mix the syrup and mustard, then add it to the skillet. Bring to a boil, stirring gently to coat the pears and potatoes. Remove the skillet from the heat. Spoon the pears, potatoes, and sauce around the ham. Serve right away.

Per serving: 459 cal, 24 g pro, 65 g car, 11 g fat, 64 mg chol with butter, 49 mg chol with margarine, 1,699 mg sod

HAM & BISCUIT SKILLET

Serves 4
Preparation time: 5 minutes
Cooking time: 20 minutes

Crowned with golden buttermilk biscuits, this skillet dinner is a quick and delicious way to stretch a small portion of ham.

▶

1 tablespoon vegetable oil

1 medium-size onion, cut into thin wedges

1 can (about 14½ ounces) no-salt-added stewed tomatoes

1 package (10 ounces) frozen kale or other greens

2 cans (about 16 ounces each) butter beans, drained and rinsed

8 ounces ham, in 1 piece

¼ cup ketchup

1 can (about 10 ounces) refrigerator buttermilk biscuits

1. Heat the oven to 400° F.

2. In a large skillet, heat the oil over medium-high heat. Add the onion and cook, stirring often, for 2 to 3 minutes, or just until beginning to soften.

3. Add the tomatoes and frozen greens. Cover and cook for 2 to 3 minutes, or until the greens are thawed.

4. Cut the ham into bite size pieces. Stir in the beans, ham, and ketchup. Bring the mixture to a boil.

5. Arrange the biscuits in a circle around the edge of the skillet. Bake for 10 to 12 minutes, or until the biscuits are golden on top and fully cooked on the bottom (lift one to check). Serve right away.

Per serving: 562 cal, 27 g pro, 78 g car, 20 g fat, 32 mg chol, 2,071 mg sod

---

EASY • 30 MINUTES • MAKE AHEAD

SAUSAGE & PEPPERS

Serves 4

Preparation time: 12 minutes

Cooking time: 16 minutes

Most supermarkets carry sweet and/or hot Italian sausages. Both are pork sausages seasoned with fennel and garlic, but the hot version has red pepper too. Serve this robust dish with a mixed green salad and hero rolls.

1 pound sweet or hot Italian sausages (or a combination of the two), cut into bite-size pieces

½ cup water

2 medium-size green bell peppers, seeded and cut into bite-size pieces

1 medium-size onion, cut into bite-size pieces

1 tablespoon minced fresh garlic

1 can (28 ounces) crushed tomatoes

1 teaspoon Italian seasoning

½ teaspoon salt

MAKE AHEAD

Store the cooked, cooled sausage-and-pepper mixture in an airtight container in the refrigerator up to 1 week, or freeze up to 3 months.

1. In a large skillet, bring the sausages and water to a boil over high heat. Reduce the heat to low. Cover and simmer for 4 to 5 minutes, or until the sausages are no longer pink. Remove the skillet from the heat. Drain off the water and sausage fat.

2. Add the bell peppers, onion, garlic, tomatoes, seasoning, and salt to the skillet and bring to a boil over medium-high heat. Reduce the heat to low. Cover and simmer for 8 to 9 minutes, stirring occasionally, until the vegetables are tender. Serve right away.

Per serving: 339 cal, 19 g pro, 17 g car, 22 g fat, 65 mg chol, 1,370 mg sod

EASY • 30 MINUTES • ONE POT

SMOKY SAUSAGE & BLACK-EYED PEAS

Serves 4
Preparation time: 5 minutes
Cooking time: 15 minutes

You can replace the black-eyed peas with canned white kidney beans and the collard greens with frozen chopped kale, turnip greens, or spinach. To quick-thaw the frozen greens, put in a colander and run warm water over them. Serve this hearty one-pot meal with pumpernickel or rye bread.

8 ounces kielbasa (smoked Polish sausage), sliced ½ inch thick
1 can (about 16 ounces) black-eyed peas, drained and rinsed
1 can (about 14½ ounces) diced tomatoes in olive oil, garlic, and spices
1 package (10 ounces) frozen chopped collard greens, thawed and drained
¾ cup chicken broth
2 teaspoons cornstarch
½ teaspoon dried thyme leaves, crumbled

1. In a large deep skillet (no need to add fat), cook the kielbasa over medium-high heat for 3 to 4 minutes, stirring occasionally, or until browned on both sides.

2. Stir in the black-eyed peas, tomatoes, and greens. Bring to a boil. Reduce the heat to medium-low and simmer uncovered for 5 to 6 minutes, stirring occasionally.

3. Meanwhile, in a small bowl, mix the broth, cornstarch, and thyme. Stir this mixture into the skillet and cook for 2 to 3 minutes, or until slightly thickened. Remove the skillet from the heat and serve right away.

Per serving: 348 cal, 18 g pro, 31 g car, 18 g fat, 38 mg chol, 1,286 mg sod

EASY • 30 MINUTES

BRATWURST ON GARLICKY BUNS

Serves 4
Preparation time: 10 minutes
Cooking time: 12 minutes

Bratwurst is a German pork sausage that is sold either fresh or fully cooked. If fresh, it must be boiled first for about 5 minutes before grilling. The mustard sauce is also delicious on grilled knockwurst, kielbasa, or frankfurters.

MUSTARD SAUCE
1 tablespoon butter or margarine
¼ cup packed light brown sugar
1 tablespoon fresh lemon juice
1 tablespoon dry mustard

4 links bratwurst (about 12 ounces)

GARLICKY FRENCH BUNS
4 teaspoons butter or margarine, softened
½ teaspoon minced fresh garlic
4 French or club rolls (each about 5 inches long), split horizontally

1. Heat a gas grill to medium-high, prepare a charcoal fire, or heat a broiler.
2. Meanwhile, make the sauce: In a small saucepan, melt the butter over medium heat. Stir in the sugar, lemon juice, and mustard until well blended. Keep warm.
3. Cut 3 diagonal slits in each bratwurst.
4. Grill or broil the bratwurst, slit sides down, 4 to 6 inches from the heat source for 4 to 6 minutes, or until the sausages open up along the slits. Turn the sausages and grill or broil for 3 to 4 minutes longer, or until the bratwurst are evenly browned on the bottom.
5. Meanwhile, prepare the rolls. In a small bowl, mix the butter and garlic. Spread on the cut sides of the rolls.
6. To grill, place the buns, buttered side down, around the outside edge (coolest part) of the grill. Grill for 2 to 3 minutes, or until golden. To broil, place the buns, buttered side up, on a broiler-pan rack. Broil for 1 to 2 minutes, or until golden.
7. Serve the bratwurst on the rolls with the mustard sauce.

Makes 4 sandwiches. Per sandwich: 512 cal, 17 g pro, 42 g car, 31 g fat, 69 mg chol with butter, 51 mg chol with margarine, 852 mg sod with butter, 862 mg sod with margarine

EASY • 60 MINUTES • LOW FAT • ONE POT

KNOCKWURST CASSEROLE

Serves 4

Preparation time: 15 minutes

Cooking time: 25 minutes

This easy casserole is a surefire way to please anyone with a penchant for German fare. The apple and cabbage give the dish a decidedly sweet and sour flavor. Any fully cooked sausage, such as knockwurst, or smoked sausage, such as kielbasa, can be used here. Serve with rye bread and mustard for a complete dinner.

1 can (about 13¾ ounces) chicken broth

1 tablespoon prepared mustard

1 teaspoon mustard seeds (optional)

1 pound sweet potatoes, peeled, quartered, and cut into ½-inch chunks

⅔ cup coarsely chopped onion

1¼ pounds green cabbage, shredded coarse (6 packed cups)

1 pound fully cooked reduced-fat sausage, such as knockwurst,
    diagonally cut into ½-inch-thick slices

1 large Golden Delicious or firm apple, quartered, cored, and cut into
    ½-inch pieces

1. In a large, deep skillet, mix the chicken broth and mustard until blended. Stir in the mustard seeds.

2. Bring the mixture to a boil over high heat. Add the sweet potatoes and onion. Reduce the heat to medium. Cover and cook for about 5 minutes, shaking the pan occasionally, until the potatoes are almost tender.   ▶

EASY KIELBASA DINNERS

◆ **HOT POTATO SALAD**

Sauté frozen O'Brien potatoes in oil until hot and browned. Stir in sliced kielbasa and heat through. Serve on shredded lettuce with bottled Dijon vinaigrette.

◆ **OVEN DINNER**

Cut green or red bell peppers and chunks of kielbasa in half lengthwise.

Core the peppers. Arrange cut sides up on a broiler-pan rack with frozen potato wedges. Brush the kielbasa and bell peppers with honey-mustard. Bake at 450°F until hot and browned.

◆ **PIEROGI AND KIELBASA DINNER**

Cook store-bought frozen or fresh pierogi (filled dumplings, sometimes called piroshki) according to package directions.

Serve with sautéed sliced onions and grilled kielbasa.

3. Add the cabbage and sausage. Cover and cook for about 15 minutes, stirring occasionally, until the potatoes are tender and the cabbage is crisp-tender.

4. Stir in the apple. Cover and simmer for 3 minutes, or until the apple is crisp-tender. Remove the skillet from the heat and serve right away.

Per serving: 309 cal, 20 g pro, 45 g car, 4 g fat, 50 mg chol, 1,642 mg sod

THE LOWDOWN ON HAM

Ham is meat from the hind leg of a hog, usually sold cured. Turning it from fresh meat into cured, though, may involve a number of different steps.

BRINE-CURING: Meat is injected with a solution of water, salt, sodium nitrate and nitrites, plus sugar or honey, before cooking.

DRY-CURING: Salt, sugar, sodium nitrate and nitrites, and sometimes ingredients such as smoke flavoring, are mixed together and rubbed on the meat's surface. This process, which is used for most speciality hams, draws out the moisture and deepens the flavor and color.

SMOKING: After curing, some hams are hung in a smokehouse over smoldering fires. Smoking imparts a distinctive flavor, which can vary according to the type of wood used, and continues the aging and drying process.

HEATING IT UP

If a fully cooked ham has no heating instructions on the label, you can follow these general rules.

BAKING: Heat the oven to 325°F. Place the ham, fat side up, in a foil-lined pan and bake for 15 to 20 minutes per pound, or until a meat thermometer registers 130° to 140°F. (Cook-before-eating hams must be cooked to an internal temperature of 160°F, about 18 to 22 minutes per pound.)

BROILING is fine for slices or chunks (for kebabs) of fully cooked or cook-before-eating ham. Arrange the ham on a broiler-pan rack (over foil-lined pan for easy cleanup). Broil 3 to 5 inches from the heat source for 8 to 10 minutes, turning once, for 1 inch thickness. Don't overcook or meat will toughen.

PAN-BROILING is great for heating up steaks and slices. Cut several slashes in the fat around the edges to prevent curling. Heat a small amount of butter or oil in a skillet over medium heat. Add the ham and, depending on the thickness, cook for 2 to 5 minutes, or until lightly browned, turning once.

MICROWAVING is ideal for fully cooked hams. Hams weighing up to 3 pounds can be microwaved whole. Cut a larger ham in half and microwave each half separately. Place the ham on a rack in a microwave-safe baking dish. (To prevent overcooking, place a strip of foil along the cut edges and cover with plastic wrap.) Cook on Medium for 6 to 8 minutes per pound for canned ham, 10 to 15 minutes per pound for boneless ham, or until a meat thermometer registers 130°F. Remove the foil and/or plastic wrap and brush on any glaze for the last 2 to 3 minutes of cooking. Remove from the oven, cover with a foil tent, and let stand for 10 to 15 minutes before serving. Place ham steaks in a microwave-safe baking dish and cover loosely with waxed paper to prevent splattering. Cook on Medium for 3 to 4 minutes, turn the ham, and cook for 6 to 8 minutes more, depending on thickness. Let stand covered for 3 minutes before serving.

STORAGE TIPS

Fully cooked, brine-cured hams, either smoked or nonsmoked, may be stored in their original packaging up to 7 days in the coldest part of the refrigerator. Leftovers may be refrigerated, tightly wrapped in plastic, for 7 to 10 days. If you must freeze ham, do it in large chunks, tightly wrapped in plastic and foil, for up to 2 months. Thaw before using.

CANNED HAMS: Refrigerate in can until ready to use. Check label, but most can be stored up to 6 months. Tightly wrap leftovers and refrigerate up to 1 week.

THINKLY SLICED HAMS: Best used within 3 to 4 days of purchase. Wrap tightly in plastic and store in the coldest part of the regrigerator to prevent the meat from drying out.

LAMB
& VEAL

Lamb and veal, prized by European cooks for centuries, are coming into their own in American kitchens. Perhaps one of the reasons is that these meats are not only tender and flavorful, but also extremely adaptable. As majestic as a rib or loin roast, as simple as a juicy chop, or as modest as a succulent stew, lamb and veal are equally at home served as a casual meal to the family as they are offered to guests for an elegant dinner party.

In this chapter, we present a wide array of recipes designed to please just about everyone. There are quick and simple weeknight preparations like veal scallops with herbs and lamb steaks with plum sauce. For heartier weekend fare, try osso buco Milanese or harvest lamb stew. Parmesan rack of lamb and roasted veal loin and shallots are sure bets for entertaining. Or for something exotic, consider the lamb curry or moussaka stir-fry. However you prepare lamb or veal for dinner, you won't be disappointed.

MUSTARD SEED LAMB

Serves 4

Preparation time: 25 minutes

Cooking time: 1 hour 35 minutes

You can do the covered cooking at a slow simmer on top of the range or in the oven. Oven simmering lends the stew a rich color, glow, and flavor.

1⅓ pounds boneless lamb shoulder, well trimmed
   and cut into 1-inch chunks

¼ teaspoon salt

¼ teaspoon ground black pepper

¼ cup all-purpose flour

2½ tablespoons olive oil

1¼ cups dry red wine

1 cup chicken broth

2 teaspoons minced fresh garlic

1 bay leaf (1 inch)

¼ teaspoon dried thyme leaves, crumbled

¼ teaspoon dried rosemary leaves, crumbled

2 teaspoons whole mustard seeds

2 tablespoons chopped fresh parsley

1. Season the meat chunks with the salt and pepper, then coat with the flour and shake off the excess.

2. In a deep medium-size ovenproof skillet or 4-quart Dutch oven, heat 1 tablespoon of oil over medium heat. Add the meat in 2 or 3 batches, browning each piece well on two sides. As the pieces brown, remove them to a bowl with a slotted spoon. Add more oil to the skillet between batches if necessary.

3. Heat the oven to 350°F. When all the meat is browned, drain the fat from the skillet. Pour in ½ cup of wine. Increase the heat to high. Boil, stirring to scrape up the browned bits on the bottom, until ¼ cup is left.

4. Return the browned meat and any accumulated juices to the skillet. Stir in ½ cup chicken broth, the garlic, bay leaf, thyme, and rosemary. Reduce the heat to medium-high. When the stew is simmering, cover the skillet with a lid or foil and place in the oven. Bake for about 1½ hours, or until the lamb is very tender, turning the meat over three or four times and adding more wine or broth as needed. (There should be enough liquid to cover the meat halfway.)

5. With a slotted spoon, remove the meat to a bowl. Discard the bay leaf. Add any remaining wine and broth to the pan juices in the skillet. Boil over

MAKE AHEAD

The stew can be prepared through step 4 up to two days ahead. Cool completely and refrigerate in an airtight container. Proceed as directed with step 5 when ready to serve.

BUYING AND STORING LAMB

◆ Choose meat that is pinkish-red and has a velvety texture. Since lamb is from young animals that have little time to store fat, there is little marbling and only a thin layer of fat around the outside of the meat. The bones should be porous and reddish.

◆ Place the lamb as soon as possible in the coldest part

medium-high heat for 4 to 5 minutes, stirring constantly, until ¾ cup of liquid is left. Return the lamb to the skillet and heat through. Sprinkle with the parsley and mustard seeds just before serving.

Per serving: 338 cal, 31 g pro, 7 g car, 16 g fat, 100 mg chol, 496 mg sod

MOUSSAKA STIR-FRY

Serves 4

Preparation time: 10 minutes

Cooking time: 11 minutes

Use regular or colorful Japanese eggplant for this quick and easy dish.

1 pound lean ground lamb or beef
1 teaspoon garlic powder
1 teaspoon dried oregano, crumbled
¼ teaspoon ground black pepper
½ cup beef or chicken broth
¼ cup tomato paste
¼ cup sour cream
3 tablespoons olive oil
1 small eggplant (about 8 ounces), cut into
    ¼-inch-thick rounds (3 cups)
1 medium-size yellow or green bell pepper,
    seeded and cut into
    1-inch pieces
1 cup frozen chopped onion
1 cup frozen green peas
2 ounces feta cheese, crumbled fine (½ cup)

1. In a large bowl, mix the lamb, garlic powder, oregano, and pepper.

2. In a medium-size bowl, mix the broth, tomato paste, and sour cream.

3. In a wok or large, deep skillet, heat 1 tablespoon of oil over high heat until hot but not smoking. Add the meat mixture and stir-fry, breaking up the meat with a large spoon, until no longer pink. Remove to a large bowl.

4. Heat the remaining 2 tablespoons oil in the wok. Add the eggplant and stir-fry for 2 to 3 minutes, or until slightly softened. Add the bell pepper and stir-fry for about 1 minute, or until the pepper is crisp-tender and the eggplant is tender. Add to the lamb.

5. Put the chopped onion and frozen green peas in the skillet. Stir-fry ▶

for 1 minute, or until thawed. Add the broth mixture, bring to a boil, and boil for 30 seconds, or until thickened slightly.

6. Return the lamb and vegetables to the wok. Stir for 1 minute, or until the lamb and vegetables are evenly coated with the sauce. Sprinkle with the cheese. Serve right away.

Per serving with lamb: 561 cal, 25 g pro, 18 g car, 43 g fat, 102 mg chol, 612 mg sod with beef broth, 523 mg sod with chicken broth. With beef: 541 cal, 27 g pro, 18 g car, 40 g fat, 104 mg chol, 623 mg sod with beef broth, 543 mg sod with chicken broth

EASY • 30 MINUTES

LAMB BURGERS WITH RAITA

Serves 4

Preparation time: 20 minutes

Cooking time: 8 minutes

Raita, a yogurt sauce often served with spicy Indian food, offers a refreshing contrast to the lamb. If you want, serve the burgers in pita pockets.

RAITA

¾ cup plain low-fat yogurt
¼ cup chopped fresh mint leaves
½ teaspoon ground cumin
¼ teaspoon salt
¼ teaspoon ground black pepper
1 small cucumber, seeded and diced (1 cup)

LAMB BURGERS

1 pound ground lamb
2 tablespoons chopped fresh oregano
1 teaspoon minced fresh garlic
1 teaspoon ground black pepper

1. Make the raita: In a small bowl, mix the yogurt, mint, cumin, salt, and pepper. Stir in the cucumber. Let stand while preparing burgers.

2. Make the burgers: In a large bowl, mix the lamb, oregano, garlic, and pepper until blended. Shape the mixture into four ¾-inch-thick patties.

3. Heat a gas grill to medium, prepare a charcoal fire, or heat a broiler. Grill or broil the patties 4 to 6 inches from the heat source for 3 to 4 minutes on each side for medium meat. Serve topped with the raita.

Makes 4 burgers. Per burger: 258 cal, 22 g pro, 5 g car, 16 g fat, 79 mg chol, 230 mg sod

ABOUT LAMB

Today's lamb is the result of sophisticated crossbreeding. Most lamb sold in the U.S. is Certified American Lamb, which indicates that the meat is tender and mild because the lamb was butchered at an early age, less than one year old. This lamb must also have ¼ inch or less fat trim. Lamb that is butchered between 12 to 24 months is sold as yearling lamb, and lamb two years or older as mutton. These meats will have a richer, stronger flavor than younger lamb, although they are rarely sold here. The term spring lamb no longer has any significant meaning. In the past, ewes gave birth in September or October, and the

EASY • 30 MINUTES • LOW FAT

LAMB & VEGETABLE COUSCOUS

Serves 4

Total time: 30 minutes

This dish is equally delicious made with ground beef in place of the lamb.

8 ounces lean ground lamb
1 small eggplant (about 12 ounces), cut into 1-inch cubes (4 cups)
1 medium-size zucchini (about 6 ounces), cut into
    ½-inch slices (1¼ cups)
⅔ cup water
1 teaspoon minced fresh garlic
1 teaspoon curry powder
½ teaspoon salt
¼ teaspoon crushed hot red pepper flakes

COUSCOUS
2¼ cups water
¼ cup shredded carrot
½ teaspoon salt
1½ cups couscous

1. Crumble the lamb into a large nonstick skillet. Cook for 3 to 4 minutes over medium heat, breaking up any large chunks of meat. Remove to a bowl with a slotted spoon. Pour off and discard all but 1 teaspoon of the drippings.

2. Add the eggplant, zucchini, water, garlic, curry powder, salt, and red pepper flakes to the skillet. Stir to mix. Bring to a boil over medium-high heat. Reduce the heat to medium, cover, and cook for 5 to 7 minutes, stirring occasionally, until the vegetables are tender.

3. Meanwhile, prepare the couscous. In a medium-size saucepan, bring the water, carrot, and salt to a boil over high heat. Remove the pan from the heat. Stir in the couscous, then cover and let stand for 4 to 5 minutes, or until the water is absorbed.

4. Return the lamb to the skillet with the vegetable mixture. Stir over medium-low heat for 1 minute until heated through.

5. Fluff the couscous with a fork to separate the grains. Spoon the couscous onto serving plates. Spoon the lamb and vegetable mixture on top.

Per serving: 412 cal with lamb, 420 cal with beef, 20 g pro, 61 g car, 10 g fat, 39 mg chol, 593 mg sod

COOK'S TIP

Couscous, made from ground semolina, can be found in most supermarkets, specialty food shops, or Middle Eastern markets.

EASY • MAKE AHEAD • ONE POT • CLASSIC

WINE-BRAISED LAMB SHANKS

Serves 4

Preparation time: 15 minutes

Cooking time: 2 hours 35 minutes

The initial oven-browning removes the excess fat. Serve with canned cannellini beans, heated and seasoned with lemon juice, olive oil, parsley, salt, and pepper, and cherry tomatoes heated quickly in a little butter. Wine suggestion: a sturdy Cabernet Sauvignon sets this meal off beautifully.

4 lamb shanks (12 ounces to 1 pound each)

1 teaspoon salt

½ teaspoon ground black pepper

3 tablespoons all-purpose flour

1½ cups dry red wine or beef broth

2 tablespoons chopped fresh parsley

2 tablespoons chopped onion

2 tablespoons minced fresh garlic

2 teaspoons grated lemon peel

1 tablespoon fresh lemon juice

½ teaspoon dried thyme leaves, crumbled

½ teaspoon dried rosemary leaves, crumbled

For garnish: chopped fresh parsley (optional)

1. Heat the oven to 350°F.

2. Season the lamb with the salt and pepper. Coat with the flour and shake off excess. Arrange the lamb shanks in a single layer in a well-greased 4- to 5-quart Dutch oven.

3. Cover and bake for about 2 hours, or until tender and browned. Remove the pot from the oven. Skim off and discard the fat from the pan juices.

4. In a medium-size bowl, mix the remaining ingredients except the garnish and pour over the shanks. Cover and bake for 35 minutes, or until very tender.

5. Remove the lamb shanks to a serving platter. Whisk the pan juices to blend. Pour over the shanks. Sprinkle with the parsley.

Per serving: 680 cal, 60 g pro, 8 g car, 43 g fat, 213 mg chol, 738 mg sod with wine, 1,348 mg sod with broth

Ⓜ AKE AHEAD

This dish can be prepared ahead through step 4. Let cool, then refrigerate tightly covered up to 3 days. Slowly reheat on the range top and proceed as directed.

EASY • MAKE AHEAD • ONE POT

HARVEST LAMB STEW

Serves 6
Preparation time: 25 minutes
Cooking time: 2 hours 15 minutes

MAKE AHEAD

This stew will keep tightly covered in the refrigerator up to 3 days. Reheat on the range top or in the microwave, adding a little water if too thick.

We love this recipe for its hearty flavor and incredibly easy preparation. What's more, you can use boneless beef chuck or round stew meat instead of lamb.

2 tablespoons olive oil
3 pounds boneless lean lamb stew meat, cut into
    2-inch chunks
2 cups sliced onions
¾ cup dry vermouth or white wine (optional)
1 can (16 ounces) tomatoes, drained
1 can (about 13¾ ounces) beef broth
2 tablespoons tomato paste
2 tablespoons all-purpose flour
8 medium-size cloves garlic, peeled and halved
1 tablespoon fresh thyme, or 1½ teaspoons dried
    thyme leaves, crumbled
¼ teaspoon ground black pepper
4 medium-size carrots, peeled, halved lengthwise,
    and cut into 4-inch pieces
4 medium-size parsnips, peeled, halved lengthwise,
    and cut into 4-inch pieces
For garnish: fresh thyme sprigs (optional)

1. In a 5- or 6-quart Dutch oven, heat the oil over medium-high heat. Add the meat in two batches, browning each piece well on two sides. Remove to a bowl with a slotted spoon. Add more oil to the skillet between batches if necessary.

2. Add the onions to the pot and cook for 5 minutes, stirring occasionally, until softened. Return the lamb to the pot and add the vermouth. Cook for 3 minutes, or until the liquid is reduced by half.

3. Add the tomatoes, beef broth, tomato paste, flour, garlic, thyme, and pepper, stirring to break up the tomatoes and dissolve the paste and flour. Bring to a boil over medium-high heat. Reduce the heat to medium-low, cover, and simmer for 1½ hours.

4. Stir in the carrots and parsnips. Cover and simmer for 45 minutes more, or until the meat and vegetables are tender. Garnish with thyme sprigs.

Per serving: 506 cal, 49 g pro, 31 g car, 21 g fat, 150 mg chol, 678 mg sod

GREEK LAMB KEBABS

Serves 6

Preparation time: 15 minutes plus at least 4 hours to marinate
Cooking time: 10 minutes

Lamb kebabs, marinated in olive oil, lemon juice, oregano, and garlic, are grilled, then served in pita bread pockets topped with a sauce made of yogurt, tomatoes, and mint. One taste of this savory combination and you'll know why it's a Greek favorite. Serve with buttered orzo and a tossed salad containing feta cheese and Greek olives.

MARINADE

⅓ cup olive oil

¼ cup fresh lemon juice

1 tablespoon chopped fresh oregano, or 1 teaspoon
   dried oregano, crumbled

1 teaspoon minced fresh garlic

¼ teaspoon salt

2 pounds boneless leg of lamb, trimmed of fat and cut into
   1-to 1 ½-inch cubes (about 36 pieces)

TOMATO RAITA

½ cup reduced-fat mayonnaise

½ cup nonfat plain yogurt

1 medium-size ripe tomato, cored, peeled, and diced

3 tablespoons chopped fresh mint

½ teaspoon ground cumin

½ teaspoon minced fresh garlic

12 (12-inch-long) skewers (if bamboo, soak in water for 1 hour)
Accompaniments: grilled regular-size pita breads,
   shredded romaine lettuce (optional)

1. Make the marinade: In a 1-quart zipper-type food-storage bag, combine the oil, lemon juice, oregano, garlic, and salt. Add the lamb. Press out the air, seal, and turn to coat. Refrigerate for at least 4 hours, but not more than 8 hours, turning the bag occasionally.

2. Meanwhile, make the raita: In a small bowl, mix the mayonnaise and yogurt until well blended. Stir in the tomato, mint, cumin, and garlic. Cover

and refrigerate at least 1 hour.

3. Heat a gas grill to medium-high, prepare a charcoal fire, or heat a broiler. Thread the lamb onto the skewers (4 pieces per skewer), leaving a little space between each piece. Grill or broil 4 to 6 inches from the heat source for 4 to 5 minutes on each side, turning once.

4. Remove the lamb from the skewers. Fill pita bread halves with shredded lettuce and lamb, then spoon on the raita.

Per serving: 343 cal, 33 g pro, 7 g car, 19 g fat, 101 mg chol, 300 mg sod

LAMB ROASTING CHART

Use the chart below as a guide for roasting times. A meat thermometer will register 140°F for rare, 160°F for medium meat, and 170°F for well done. Allow the roast to stand for 15 minutes before serving. Remember that during this time the temperature will continue to rise 5 to 10° degrees.

CUT	COOKING TIME AT 325°F
Lamb leg, 5 to 7 pounds	20 to 25 minutes per pound for rare
	25 to 30 minutes per pound for medium
	30 to 35 minutes per pound for well done
Lamb leg, 7 to 9 pounds	15 to 20 minutes per pound for rare
	20 to 25 minutes per pound for medium
	25 to 30 minutes per pound for well done
Lamb leg, shank half, 3 to 4 pounds	30 to 35 minutes per pound for rare
	40 to 45 minutes per pound for medium
	45 to 50 minutes per pound for well done
Lamb leg, sirloin half, 3 to 4 pounds	25 to 30 minutes per pound for rare
	35 to 40 minutes per pound for medium
	40 to 45 minutes per pound for well done
Lamb shoulder, boneless, 3½ to 5 pounds	30 to 35 minutes per pound for rare
	35 to 40 minutes per pound for medium
	40 to 45 minutes per pound for well done
	COOKING TIME AT 375°F
Lamb rib roast (rack), 1½ to 2 pounds	30 to 35 minutes per pound for rare
	35 to 40 minutes per pound for medium
	40 to 45 minutes per pound for well done
Lamb rib roast (rack), 2 to 3 pounds	25 to 30 minutes per pound for rare
	35 to 40 minutes per pound for medium
	40 to 45 minutes per pound for well done

EASY • 60 MINUTES

LAMB STEAKS WITH PLUM SAUCE

Serves 4

Preparation time: 10 minutes plus at least 30 minutes to marinate

Cooking time: 9 minutes

Lean and tender lamb steaks, cut either from the center of the leg or from the sirloin just above, are becoming increasingly popular and more widely available. However, if you cannot find the steaks, use blade or shoulder chops instead. Accompany this savory dish with fried rice and steamed green beans.

MARINADE

⅓ cup orange juice

½ cup plus 2 tablespoons sliced scallions

2 tablespoons soy sauce

1 teaspoon minced fresh garlic

2 (½-inch thick) lamb steaks, about 8 to 9 ounces each

1 tablespoon vegetable oil

⅓ cup Chinese plum sauce (from a jar)

For garnish: orange slices (optional)

1. Make the marinade: In a medium-size, nonaluminum bowl, combine the orange juice, ½ cup of scallions, the soy sauce, and garlic. Add the lamb steaks, turning to coat. Cover and refrigerate for at least 30 minutes, or up to 8 hours, turning the steaks occasionally.

2. Remove the lamb steaks from the marinade, and reserve the marinade. Cut each steak in half. In a large nonstick skillet, heat the oil over medium-high heat. Add the lamb steaks and cook for 2 to 3 minutes on each side, or until no longer pink. Remove the lamb steaks to a serving platter, cover with foil, and keep warm.

3. Add the reserved marinade and plum sauce to the skillet. Cook over medium-high heat for 2 to 3 minutes, or until the sauce has thickened and will coat the back of a metal spoon.

4. Spoon the sauce over the lamb steaks. Sprinkle with the remaining 2 tablespoons of scallions and garnish with orange slices.

Per serving: 388 cal, 21 g pro, 11 g car, 29 g fat, 83 mg chol, 684 mg sod

COOK'S TIP

Chinese plum sauce is also called duck sauce and is made from plums, apricots, sugar, and seasonings. It has a sweet and sour flavor and can be found in most supermarkets in the Asian foods section.

MAKE AHEAD • ONE POT • CLASSIC

LAMB CURRY

Serves 6
Preparation time: 20 minutes
Cooking time: 1 hour

Ⓜ AKE AHEAD

The lamb curry can be prepared ahead. Let cool, then refrigerate tightly covered up to 3 days. Slowly reheat on the range top, adding a little water if the sauce is too thick. Serve as directed.

Lamb curry, which originated in the royal kitchens of the Moghuls, remains one of the most popular dishes in Indian households. The main flavoring ingredient is curry powder—a blend of several spices including cumin, coriander, turmeric, ginger, and chiles. It can vary from mild to hot.

⅓ cup flour
½ teaspoon salt
⅛ to ¼ teaspoon ground red pepper (cayenne)
2½ pounds boneless leg of lamb, well trimmed and
    cut into 1½-inch cubes
1½ tablespoons butter
1½ tablespoons vegetable oil
1 large onion, chopped (about 1¼ cups)
1 large green bell pepper, chopped (about 1¼ cups)
1 teaspoon minced fresh garlic
1 tablespoon curry powder
1 can (about 14¼ ounces) diced tomatoes
1 cup chicken broth
Accompaniments: mango chutney, shredded coconut,
    chopped dry-roasted peanuts, golden raisins (optional)

1. On a sheet of waxed paper, mix the flour, salt, and red pepper. Coat the lamb in the flour mixture and shake off the excess.

2. In a large saucepan, heat ½ tablespoon of butter and ½ tablespoon of oil over high heat. Brown the meat in 2 or 3 batches, browning each piece well on 2 sides. Remove to a bowl with a slotted spoon. Add more oil to the skillet between batches if necessary.

3. Add any remaining butter and oil to the pan and cook the onion, bell pepper, garlic, and curry powder for about 5 minutes, stirring often, until the vegetables are beginning to soften.

4. Return the lamb with any accumulated juices to the pan and add the tomatoes and chicken broth. Bring to a boil over medium-high heat. Reduce the heat to low. Cover and simmer for 1 hour, or until the lamb is tender.

5. Put the accompaniments into small bowls and serve with the curry.

Per serving: 315 cal, 34 g pro, 13 g car, 14 g fat, 105 mg chol, 584 mg sod

EASY • MAKE AHEAD

MAPLE-GLAZED LAMB RIBLETS

Serves 6 to 8
Preparation time: 10 minutes
Cooking time: 1 hour 55 minutes

These succulent meaty riblets offer a delicious change from pork or beef ribs. Parboiling the riblets breaks down the connective tissue to ensure tenderness and the glaze coats them with a sweet and sour lacquer. If lamb riblets are unavailable, buy 4 pounds breast of lamb, cut into 4-rib sections and cracked between each rib. Parboil as directed, then cut the breast into individual riblets.

4 pounds lamb riblets (see Cook's Tip)
2 tablespoons cider vinegar

MAPLE GLAZE
½ cup maple syrup
½ cup coarse-grained mustard
1 tablespoon cider vinegar
½ teaspoon salt
½ teaspoon ground black pepper

For garnish: fresh parsley sprigs (optional)

1. Place the riblets in a large pot and add enough cold water to cover by 2 inches. Stir in the vinegar. Bring to a boil over high heat. Reduce the heat to low and simmer, partially covered, for 1 hour. Drain.

2. Meanwhile, make the glaze: In a small bowl, mix the maple syrup, mustard, vinegar, salt, and pepper.

3. Heat the oven to 400°F. Arrange the riblets in a single layer in a large shallow baking dish.

4. Bake for 40 minutes, or until crisp and brown. Drain off fat.

5. Spoon half the glaze over the riblets and bake for 8 minutes. Spoon on the remaining glaze and bake for 5 to 7 minutes more, or until very brown.

6. Remove the riblets to a serving platter. Garnish the platter with sprigs of fresh parsley and serve right away.

Per serving: 527 cal, 28 g pro, 17 g car, 38 g fat, 121 mg chol, 421 mg sod

 MAKE AHEAD

The riblets can be parboiled, drained, cooled, and refrigerated tightly wrapped up to 1 day. The glaze can be prepared and refrigerated in an airtight container up to 1 week.

EASY • MAKE AHEAD

GRILLED BUTTERFLIED LEG OF LAMB

Serves 12

Preparation time: 15 minutes plus at least 24 hours to marinate

Cooking time: 40 minutes plus 15 minutes to stand

You will need to start this recipe up to 2 days ahead so the meat will have time to marinate. Ask your butcher to bone and butterfly the lamb and remove as much fat as possible to save time.

MARINADE

½ cup olive oil

6 tablespoons red wine vinegar

8 cloves garlic, peeled

4 teaspoons dried oregano

1 tablespoon dried thyme

1 tablespoon dried rosemary

1 tablespoon ground black pepper

1 (5- to 5½-pound) boned leg of lamb, butterflied and
    trimmed of visible fat

4 bay leaves (2 inches long)

½ teaspoon salt

For garnish: fresh rosemary, thyme, and oregano (optional)

1. Make the marinade: In a food processor or blender, combine the oil, vinegar, garlic, oregano, thyme, rosemary, and pepper and process until well blended. Put the lamb in a large baking dish or bowl. Pour the marinade over the meat, rubbing it in and turning the meat to coat. Place the bay leaves over the lamb. Cover and refrigerate for 1 to 2 days, turning once or twice.

2. Heat a gas grill to medium, prepare a charcoal fire, or heat a broiler. Remove and discard the bay leaves from the lamb. Reserve the marinade. Lay the lamb flat on the oiled grill rack or broiler pan rack. If grilling, cover with a grill lid or foil tent. Grill or broil 4 to 5 inches from the heat source for 30 to 40 minutes, turning and basting with the marinade every 10 to 15 minutes, until a meat thermometer inserted into the thickest part registers 150°F for medium-rare.

3. Remove the lamb to a cutting board. Sprinkle with the salt. Let stand for 15 minutes. Thinly slice the meat and arrange on a serving platter. Garnish with fresh herbs.

Per serving: 374 cal, 42 g pro, 2 g car, 21 g fat, 133 mg chol, 194 mg sod

ⓒOOK'S TIP

To butterfly a boneless leg of lamb, split the meat down the center, cutting almost but not all the way through. Spread the meat flat.

EASY • 60 MINUTES

PARMESAN RACK OF LAMB

Serves 4

Preparation time: 5 minutes

Cooking time: 40 minutes plus 10 minutes to stand

Tender rack of lamb makes a stunning presentation for any occasion.

¼ cup packaged dry bread crumbs
¼ cup chopped fresh parsley
¼ cup grated Parmesan cheese
1 tablespoon olive oil
2 teaspoons Dijon mustard
1 teaspoon minced fresh garlic
½ teaspoon ground black pepper
¼ teaspoon salt
1 rack of lamb (8 chops, about 2 pounds)

1. Heat the oven to 425°F. In a small bowl, mix the bread crumbs, parsley, Parmesan, oil, mustard, garlic, pepper, and salt. Spread the mixture over the lamb.

2. Place the rack, fat side up, in a shallow roasting pan. Roast for 40 minutes, or until a meat thermometer registers 150°F, for end chops that are medium-well and center chops that are medium-rare. Let stand for 10 minutes, before carving into chops.

Per serving: 541 cal, 30 g pro, 6 g car, 43 g fat, 127 mg chol, 441 mg sod

COOK'S TIP

For easier carving, ask the butcher to cut through the backbone between the ribs. After roasting, the rack can be neatly carved into chops.

LAMB BROILING CHART

Use the chart below as a guide for broiling times for lamb chops. A meat thermometer will register 140°F for rare, 160°F for medium, and 170°F for well done. The chop should be 3 to 4 inches from the heat source.

CUT	TOTAL COOKING TIME
Lamb shoulder chop, 1 inch thick	7 to 11 minutes
Lamb rib chop, 1 inch thick	7 to 11 minutes
1½ inches thick	15 to 19 minutes
Lamb loin chop, 1 inch thick	7 to 11 minutes
1½ inches thick	15 to 19 minutes
Lamb sirloin chop 1 inch thick	12 to 15 minutes
Ground lamb patties, ½ inch thick	5 to 8 minutes

OSSO BUCO MILANESE (BRAISED VEAL SHANKS)

Serves 4

Preparation time: 20 minutes

Cooking time: 2 hours

This specialty, which originated in Milan, uses a crosscut of the center foreshank of veal. An ideal accompaniment to this dish is the fragrant mixture of lemon peel, garlic, and parsley called gremolata.

4 meaty 2- to 3-inch-thick pieces veal shank (12 to 14 ounces each),
   or 4 whole lamb shanks (12 ounces each)
¼ cup all-purpose flour
2 tablespoons butter or margarine
2 tablespoons olive oil
1 cup finely chopped onion
2 teaspoons minced fresh garlic
1 cup dry red wine, white wine, or chicken broth
½ teaspoon salt (reduce to ¼ teaspoon if using chicken broth)
¼ teaspoon ground black pepper
¼ teaspoon dried thyme
¼ teaspoon dried rosemary leaves

GREMOLATA
2 tablespoons minced fresh parsley
1 tablespoon freshly grated lemon peel
1 teaspoon minced fresh garlic

For garnish: fresh rosemary sprigs (optional)

1. Heat the oven to 325°F.
2. If it has not already been done by the butcher, tie a single strand of kitchen twine around each piece of meat to hold it to the bone during cooking. Coat the shanks with the flour and tap off the excess.
3. In a lidded stovetop-to-oven casserole large enough to hold meat in one layer, heat the butter and oil over medium heat. Brown the shanks on tops and bottoms for 3 to 4 minutes on each side. Remove to a plate.
4. Put the onion and garlic in the casserole and cook for 4 to 5 minutes, stirring often, or until the onion is softened. Add the wine, salt, pepper, thyme, and rosemary. Bring the mixture to a gentle boil and scrape up any ▶

MAKE AHEAD

These veal shanks can be prepared ahead through step 5. Let cool, then refrigerate tightly covered up to 3 days. Slowly reheat on the range top, adding a little water if the sauce is too thick, and proceed as directed.

browned bits on the bottom of the casserole.

5. Remove from the heat and arrange the meat in a single layer, cut side up, in the casserole. Spoon a little of the liquid over the top of the meat. Cover (if the lid does not cover tightly, cover first with foil, then with the lid) and bake for 2 hours, or until the meat is very tender.

6. Carefully lift the shanks from the cooking liquid to a serving platter. Skim and discard the fat from the liquid, then spoon the cooking liquid around the shanks.

7. Make the gremolata: In a small bowl, mix the parsley, lemon peel, and garlic. Sprinkle the mixture over the shanks. Insert rosemary sprigs in the marrow of each shank.

Per serving with veal: 509 cal, 63 g pro, 11 g car, 22 g fat, 245 mg chol with butter, 230 mg chol with margarine, 526 mg sod with wine, 500 mg chol with broth. With lamb: 757 cal, 57 g pro, 11 g car, 53 g fat, 213 mg chol with butter, 198 mg chol with margarine, 509 mg sod with wine, 482 mg sod with broth

---

EASY • 30 MINUTES • MAKE AHEAD

VEAL CUTLETS WITH ITALIAN SALSA

Serves 4
Preparation time: 15 minutes
Cooking time: 6 minutes

For an even easier entree you can omit the salsa and serve the cutlets with lemon wedges. Arugula, also called rocket, is a peppery salad green.

ITALIAN SALSA
1 tablespoon olive oil
1½ teaspoons red wine vinegar
⅛ teaspoon salt
⅛ teaspoon ground black pepper
1 large tomato (about 8 ounces), cored and cut into bite-size pieces
  (about 1 ¼ cups)
1 small bunch arugula, rinsed, drained, and chopped coarse (about 3 cups)

½ cup packaged seasoned bread crumbs
1 large egg
12 ounces veal cutlets
1 large egg
3 tablespoons olive oil

MAKE AHEAD

The salsa can be prepared up to 1 day ahead, but add the arugula just before serving. Store tightly covered in the refrigerator and bring to room temperature just before serving.

▶ *p. 237*

CAREFREE OVEN-COOKING
For Osso Buco Milanese (p.231), just season the meat, then put it in the oven and forget about this entree until it's ready to eat.

NO FUSS LAMB
Both Harvest
Lamb Stew
(p.223), left, and
Wine-Braised
Lamb Shanks
(p.222), above
are easy one-pot
meals that can be
made ahead.

Stewing and braising—two easy methods of slow-cooking lamb—yield meat that is tender and succulent. Spices and herbs enhance the flavor.

HERBS
Oregano and mint add a fragrant and flavorful touch to Lamb Burgers with Raita (p.220).

1. Make the salsa: In a medium-size bowl, mix the oil, vinegar, salt, and pepper. Add the tomato and arugula. Toss to mix and coat. Let stand at room temperature while preparing the cutlets.

2. Spread the bread crumbs on a sheet of waxed paper. In a shallow dish, beat the egg with a fork. Dip the cutlets into the egg, letting the excess drip off, then dip into crumbs to coat.

3. In a large, preferably nonstick skillet, heat 1½ tablespoons of oil until hot but not smoking. Cook the cutlets in 2 batches for 1 to 1½ minutes on each side, or until golden brown and no longer pink in the center. Add more oil to the skillet as needed. Remove the cutlets to a serving platter and top with salsa.

Per serving: 317 cal, 24 g pro, 14 g car, 18 g fat, 173 mg chol, 568 mg sod

LOW FAT • MAKE AHEAD • ONE POT

VEAL STEW WITH LEMON & ARTICHOKES

Serves 8
Preparation time: 30 minutes
Cooking time: 1 hour 10 minutes

This delicate stew, flavored with lemon and artichoke hearts, is a recipe that all cooks should have at their fingertips. It's a wonderful one-pot meal for a family celebration or to serve to company, and the best part is that it can be prepared in advance. Serve this dish over egg noodles or rice.

2 tablespoons olive oil
3 pounds boneless veal stew meat, cut into 2-inch cubes
2 tablespoons all-purpose flour
2 medium-size onions, sliced thin
1¾ cups chicken broth
1 teaspoon dried oregano, crumbled
2 strips lemon rind, removed with a vegetable peeler
1 teaspoon salt
½ teaspoon ground black pepper
2 packages (10 ounces each) frozen artichoke hearts, thawed
3 tablespoons fresh lemon juice
2 tablespoons chopped fresh parsley

1. In a large deep skillet, heat the oil over medium-high heat. Cook the meat in batches until lightly browned on two sides, about 8 minutes. Remove to a bowl with slotted spoon. Add more oil to the skillet between batches ▶

MAKE AHEAD

The stew can be prepared through step 3. Let cool, then refrigerate tightly covered up to 3 days. Slowly reheat on the range top, add the lemon juice, parsley, and artichoke hearts, and proceed as directed.

if necessary. Sprinkle the veal with the flour and toss until well coated.

2. Reduce the heat to medium. Put the onions in the skillet and cook, stirring often, for about 6 minutes, or until softened. Return the veal to the pan and add the chicken broth, oregano, lemon rind, salt, and pepper.

3. Bring to a boil over medium-high heat. Reduce the heat to a low. Cover and simmer for 1 hour, or until the meat is tender.

4. Meanwhile, cut the artichokes in half lengthwise and pat dry with paper towels. Add the lemon juice, parsley, and artichoke hearts to the pan. Simmer uncovered for 10 minutes more, or until heated through. Remove and discard the lemon peel. Serve hot over egg noodles or rice.

Per serving: 311 cal, 36 g pro, 11 g car, 13 g fat, 148 mg chol, 684 mg sod

VEAL ROASTING CHART

Use the chart below as a guide for roasting times. A meat thermometer will register 160°F for medium meat and 170°F for well done. Allow the roast to stand for 15 minutes before serving. Remember that during this time the temperature will continue to rise 5 to 10 degrees.

CUT	COOKING TIME AT 300° TO 325°F.
Veal loin roast, 3 to 4 pounds	34 to 36 minutes per pound for medium
	38 to 40 minutes per pound for well done
Veal loin roast, boneless, 2 to 3 pounds	18 to 20 minutes per pound for medium
	22 to 24 minutes per pound for well done
Veal rib roast, 4 to 5 pounds	25 to 27 minutes per pound for medium
	29 to 31 minutes per pound for well done
Veal crown roast (12 to 14 ribs), 7½ to 9½ pounds	19 to 21 minutes per pound for medium
	21 to 23 minutes for well done
Veal rib eye roast, 2 to 3 pounds	26 to 28 minutes per pound for medium
	30 to 33 minutes for well done
Veal rump roast, boneless, 2 to 3 pounds	33 to 35 minutes per pound for medium
	37 to 40 minutes per pound for well done
Veal shoulder roast, boneless 2½ to 3 pounds	31 to 34 minutes per pound for medium
	34 to 37 minutes per pound for well done

60 MINUTES

VEAL MEATBALLS

Serves 4 to 6
Preparation time: 25 minutes
Cooking time: 35 minutes

Simmered in a tomato-vegetable sauce, these meatballs are good served over pasta and sprinkled with Parmesan cheese.

MEATBALLS
1 pound lean ground veal
½ cup finely chopped onion
2 tablespoons packaged seasoned bread crumbs
½ teaspoon salt
1 large egg, beaten
1 tablespoon vegetable oil

TOMATO–VEGETABLE SAUCE
1 tablespoon vegetable oil
1 medium-size yellow squash or zucchini, diced
2 cups thinly sliced white mushrooms
1 small red bell pepper, seeded and diced
1 medium-size onion, finely chopped
2 teaspoons minced fresh garlic
1 can (about 28 ounces) Italian plum tomatoes, undrained
1 teaspoon granulated sugar
½ teaspoon Italian seasoning
½ teaspoon salt

1. Make the meatballs: In a large bowl, mix the ground veal, onion, bread crumbs, and salt. Stir in the egg and mix until well blended. Shape the mixture into 16 meatballs, about 1½ inches in diameter.

2. In a large nonstick skillet, heat the oil over medium–high heat. Working in batches if necessary, add the meatballs and cook for 6 to 7 minutes, turning occasionally, until no longer pink. Remove the meatballs to a plate with a slotted spoon.

3. Make the sauce: In the same skillet, heat the oil over medium heat. Add the squash, mushrooms, bell pepper, onion, and garlic. Cook for about 5 minutes, stirring often, until the vegetables are beginning to soften.

4. Add the tomatoes, sugar, Italian seasoning, and salt. Cook for about 5 minutes, stirring occasionally. Return the meatballs to the skillet and ▶

bring to a gentle boil over medium-high heat. Reduce the heat to medium-low and simmer for 13 to 15 minutes, or until the sauce has thickened slightly and the vegetables are tender. Serve over pasta.

Per serving: 278 cal, 22 g pro, 18 g car, 13 g fat, 117 mg chol, 868 mg sod

---

EASY • 60 MINUTES

VEAL CHOPS WITH CARAMELIZED ONIONS

Serves 4

Preparation time: 10 minutes

Cooking time: 25 minutes

An assortment of steamed fresh vegetables and cooked egg noodles or mashed potatoes will complement this dish nicely.

2 tablespoons butter or margarine

3 large onions, sliced thin (about 4 cups)

2 teaspoons sugar

4 (½-inch-thick) veal loin chops, about 4 to 5 ounces each

½ teaspoon salt

¼ teaspoon ground black pepper

¼ cup chicken broth or water

1 tablespoon balsamic or red wine vinegar

1 tablespoon chopped fresh sage, or 1 teaspoon dried sage leaves, crumbled

For garnish: fresh sage leaves (optional)

1. In a large nonstick skillet, heat the butter over medium heat. Add the onions and sugar and cook for 12 to 15 minutes, stirring occasionally, until golden brown. Remove the onions to a serving platter with a slotted spoon and keep warm.

2. Sprinkle the veal chops with the salt and pepper. Place the chops in the same skillet and cook over medium-high heat for about 3 minutes on each side, or until no longer pink. Remove the chops to a serving platter.

3. Add the chicken broth and vinegar to the pan juices in the skillet. Cook for about 1 minute, stirring constantly, until the sauce has reduced slightly. Stir in the sage.

4. Pour the pan juices over the veal chops and onions. Garnish with fresh sage leaves.

Per serving: 255 cal, 17 g pro, 16 g car, 14 g fat, 80 mg chol with butter, 64 mg chol with margarine, 473 mg sod with broth, 410 mg sod with water

---

BUYING AND STORING VEAL

◆ Look for veal with a fine grain and creamy pink color; any fat covering it should be milky white.

◆ Packages should be securely wrapped without any tears or punctures. The packages should also be cold to the touch. Check the sell-by date.

◆ Store veal in the coldest part of the refrigerator as soon as you get home.

◆ Unopened packages of veal can be refrigerated up to 2 days after purchase.

◆ Veal can be frozen in its original wrapping up to 2 weeks. For longer freezer storage (up to 9 months) rewrap or overwrap the package in foil or plastic wrap, or place in a freezer bag and squeeze out the air before sealing.

◆ Thaw frozen veal

EASY • 60 MINUTES • LOW FAT

ROASTED VEAL LOIN & SHALLOTS

Serves 6

Preparation time: 10 minutes

Cooking time: 45 minutes

Roasted shallots, which taste like a cross between garlic and onion but milder than both, are the ideal accompaniment to this tender, delicate veal roast scented with fresh rosemary.

1 (2-pound) boneless veal loin, well trimmed and tied
2 tablespoons chopped fresh rosemary
2 medium-size garlic cloves, crushed and peeled
2 teaspoons olive oil
½ teaspoon salt
½ teaspoon ground black pepper
12 shallots (9 ounces), peeled
¼ cup dry white wine
1 cup chicken broth

1. Heat the oven to 425°F. Rub the veal with the rosemary, garlic, and oil and sprinkle with the salt and pepper.

2. Place the roast on a rack in a roasting pan. Scatter the shallots around the meat. Roast for 20 minutes. Reduce the oven temperature to 325°F. Roast for about 25 minutes more, or until a meat thermometer registers 150°F to 155°F. Remove to a cutting board and let stand for 10 minutes. (The internal temperature will continue to rise about 5 to 10 degrees as the meat stands.) Remove the shallots to a bowl and cover with foil to keep warm.

3. Add the wine to the pan and place over medium heat, stirring to ▶

VEAL BROILING CHART

Use the chart below as a guide for broiling times. A meat thermometer will register 160°F for medium, 170°F for well done.

CUT	TOTAL COOKING TIME (4 to 5 inches from the heat source)
Loin or rib chop,1 to 1½ inches thick	14 minutes for medium
Arm or blade chop, ¾ inch thick	14 minutes for medium
Ground veal patties, ½ inch thick	8 minutes for medium

scrape up bits from the bottom of the pan. Simmer for about 2 minutes. Add the broth and simmer for about 4 minutes, or until reduced to about ⅓ cup.

4. Cut the roast into ¼-inch-thick slices. Arrange slices of veal on serving plates, drizzle with the pan juices, and serve with the shallots.

Per serving: 250 cal, 32 g pro, 7 g car, 9 g fat, 121 mg chol, 492 mg sod

EASY • 30 MINUTES • LOW FAT • CLASSIC

VEAL SCALLOPS WITH HERBS

Serves 4

Preparation time: 15 minutes

Cooking time: 10 minutes

This simple and light veal entree is perfect to serve any time of year. Veal scallops are very thin, boneless slices of meat cut from the round. If veal scallops are unavailable, veal, chicken, or turkey cutlets will also work nicely.

¼ cup all-purpose flour

¾ teaspoon ground black pepper

¾ teaspoon salt

1 pound veal scallops

4 teaspoons vegetable oil

1 cup reduced-sodium chicken broth

¾ cup thinly sliced shallots

1 tablespoon fresh lemon juice

1 teaspoon chopped fresh thyme, sage, or rosemary

1 tablespoon chopped fresh parsley

1. On a sheet of waxed paper, mix the flour, ½ teaspoon pepper, and ½ teaspoon salt. Coat the veal scallops in the flour mixture, shaking off the excess.

2. In a large nonstick skillet, heat the oil over medium-high heat. Brown the veal scallops in batches for 1 minute on each side. Remove to a serving platter, and cover with foil to keep warm.

3. Add the chicken broth, shallots, lemon juice, herbs, and the remaining pepper and salt to the skillet, stirring to scrape any brown bits from the bottom of the pan. Cook over medium-high heat until slightly syrupy. Drizzle the sauce over the veal scallops, sprinkle with the parsley, and serve right away.

Per serving: 219 cal, 26 g pro, 12 g car, 7 g fat, 89 mg chol, 629 mg sod

EGGS & CHEESE

Eggs and cheese are two of the most useful and nutritious foods available to the cook. They are a delicious food in their own right, showing up in every meal of the day, and are a natural to pair together.

Both these foods are a powerhouse of protein, vitamins, and minerals, but can also be high in fat and cholesterol. The egg yolk, however, does not contain as much cholesterol as once thought, and eating three to four eggs a week is within the recommended guidelines set by the American Heart Association for a healthy adult. There are also a number of low-fat cheeses available to select from. Some are naturally low in fat and others are made with part-skim milk. To learn more about cheese, turn to the Cheese Primer on page 684.

On the following pages are recipes for scrambled and baked eggs, omelets, savory pies, and other dishes that are all easy to prepare. So keep a supply of fresh eggs and cheeses on hand and you will never be at a loss for a quick and tasty meal.

EGGS IN TOMATO BROTH

Serves 4
Preparation time: 10 minutes
Cooking time: 16 minutes

One might describe this dish as eggs Italian-style. Simmered in a tomato-herb sauce, these eggs make a splendid country-style supper or brunch dish accompanied with warm Italian or French bread and sausage patties. You can prepare the sauce ahead and reheat it to simplify meal preparation. The eggs are cooked when the whites are set and a thin transparent film covers the yolks.

1 tablespoon olive oil
1 large clove garlic, quartered
1 can (about 16 ounces) crushed tomatoes
½ cup water
1½ teaspoons chopped fresh basil, or ½ teaspoon dried
    basil leaves, crumbled
1½ teaspoons chopped fresh thyme, or ½ teaspoon dried
    thyme leaves, crumbled
¼ teaspoon granulated sugar
¼ teaspoon salt
4 large eggs

1. In a large nonstick skillet, heat the oil over medium-low heat. Add the garlic and cook, shaking the pan often, for 2 to 3 minutes, or until lightly golden. Discard the garlic.

2. Stir in remaining ingredients except the eggs. Bring the mixture to a gentle boil. Reduce the heat to low and simmer, uncovered, for 7 minutes, stirring occasionally.

3. Break the eggs one at a time into a cup, then slide each gently into the sauce. Cover and simmer for 5 to 6 minutes, or until the eggs are set. Serve right away.

Per servings: 130 cal, 7 g pro, 6 g car, 9 g fat, 213 mg chol, 383 mg sod

---

EGG BASICS

Proper handling of eggs is necessary to prevent the growth of potentially harmful bacteria such as salmonella.

◆ Select clean eggs from a refrigerated case. Don't buy any that are dirty, cracked, or leaking, because they may have become contaminated with harmful bacteria. Slightly move each egg in the carton to make sure it isn't stuck to the bottom because of a crack that you cannot see.

◆ Refrigerate eggs in their carton (not the slot in the door) as soon you get home. Storing eggs in the carton keeps them

```
EASY • 30 MINUTES • ONE POT
```

CHEESY GRITS & EGG PIE

Serves 4

Total time: 25 minutes

Many Northerners are not familiar with the delicious down-home taste of grits, a Southern staple. It has long been enjoyed as breakfast fare. Here, the grits are formed into a pie and cooked with eggs.

2 cups water
¾ cup quick-cooking grits
½ teaspoon salt
¾ cup shredded Cheddar cheese
4 large eggs
Ground black pepper to taste
For garnish: chopped fresh cilantro or parsley (optional)
1 cup bottled salsa

1. In a large nonstick skillet, bring the water to a boil over high heat. Slowly stir in the grits and salt. Stir until boiling, then reduce the heat to low and cook, stirring often, for 6 minutes, or until thickened. Remove from the heat.

2. Stir the cheese into the grits. Spread the mixture in an even layer over the bottom of the skillet. Grease the back of a serving spoon and press it into the grits to make 4 indentations, each large enough to contain an egg.

3. Break an egg into each indentation. Cover and cook over medium heat for 12 minutes, or until the eggs have set.

4. Sprinkle with pepper and chopped cilantro. Cut into 4 wedges with an egg in each. Serve right away with salsa.

Makes 4 wedges. Per wedge: 278 cal, 14 g pro, 27 g car, 12 g fat, 235 mg chol, 1,108 mg sod

```
EASY • 30 MINUTES
```

HERB–PARMESAN SCRAMBLED EGGS

Serves 4

Preparation time: 10 minutes

Cooking time: 7 minutes

Turn ordinary scrambled eggs into a special dish by adding chopped fresh herbs and Parmesan cheese. Serve with Canadian bacon and toasted ▶

English muffins. To assure that the eggs will be moist and tender, cook over medium to low heat. Cooked too fast over high heat, they will become tough.

8 large eggs
3 tablespoons milk
¼ teaspoon salt
¼ teaspoon ground black pepper
2 tablespoons chopped fresh parsley
1 tablespoon chopped fresh chives
1 teaspoon chopped fresh tarragon or thyme
1 tablespoon butter or margarine
¼ cup grated Parmesan cheese

1. In a medium-size bowl, beat the eggs with the milk, salt, and pepper. Stir in the herbs.

2. In a large nonstick skillet, melt the butter over medium heat. Pour the egg mixture into the skillet. Cook, stirring gently, for about 5 minutes, or until the eggs are creamy and softly set. Gently stir in the cheese. Serve right away.

Per serving: 206 cal, 15 g pro, 2 g car, 15 g fat, 433 mg chol, 392 mg sod

MEXICAN ROLL-UPS

Scramble eggs your favorite way, spoon onto warm flour tortillas, and top with sour cream and salsa. Roll up and serve with a quick-to-make salad of drained, canned black beans and sliced scallions dressed with bottled vinaigrette.

EASY • 30 MINUTES • CLASSIC

PIPERADE

Serves 4
Preparation time: 12 minutes
Cooking time: 16 minutes

You can always count on this recipe for an enjoyable, quick, and nourishing meal. Also called a Basque omelet, it's full of bell peppers, onions, and tomatoes.

2 teaspoons olive oil
1 medium-size onion, sliced thin (1 cup)
2 medium-size green bell peppers, seeded and cut into thin strips
 (1½ cups)
3 to 4 ripe plum tomatoes, chopped (1½ cups)
2 teaspoons minced fresh garlic
6 large eggs
3 tablespoons water
2 tablespoons finely chopped scallion
¼ teaspoon salt
¼ teaspoon ground black pepper

VARIATION

HAM PIPERADE

Add 1 cup of lean chopped ham to the skillet with the toma-toes and proceed as directed.

Per serving: 221 cal, 18 g pro, 11 g car, 12 g fat, 335 mg chol, 745 mg sod

• EASY • 30 MINUTES

1. In a large nonstick broiler-proof skillet, heat the oil over medium-high heat. Add the onion and bell peppers and cook, stirring often, for 6 to 8 minutes, or until softened. Add the garlic and tomatoes. Increase the heat to medium-high and cook, stirring often, for about 2 to 3 minutes, or until the liquid has evaporated.

2. Heat the broiler. In a small bowl, beat the eggs with the water, scallion, salt, and pepper. Pour the egg mixture over the vegetables and cook for 1 minute. Stir the mixture gently for 1 to 2 minutes more, or until the eggs are set but still shiny and moist. Place the skillet under the broiler for 1 to 2 minutes, or until lightly browned. Remove the piperade to a serving platter and serve right away.

Per serving: 175 cal, 11 g pro, 11 g car, 10 g fat, 319 mg chol, 238 mg sod

---

EASY • 30 MINUTES • MICROWAVE • MAKE AHEAD

BREAKFAST BURRITOS

Serves 4

Total time: 20 minutes

 MAKE AHEAD

These burritos can be made up to one day ahead. Cool completely, cover, and refrigerate. Unwrap and reheat before serving.

Here is a no-fuss fast-food egg dish borrowed from a popular Mexican concept—you just pick it up in both hands and eat it as a sandwich.

6 large eggs
1 can (about 4 ounces) chopped green chiles
2 tablespoons taco sauce or salsa
½ teaspoon salt
4 (6-inch) flour tortillas
¾ cup shredded Cheddar or Monterey Jack cheese
¼ cup thinly sliced scallions

1. Coat a 2-quart microwave-safe bowl with vegetable oil cooking spray.

2. Add the eggs, chiles, taco sauce, and salt. Beat with a fork until well blended.

3. Cover with vented plastic wrap. Microwave on Medium High for 5 to 6 minutes, stirring twice, until the egg mixture is almost set.

4. Remove the bowl from the microwave and let stand on a heatproof surface for 2 minutes, or until set and no moist spots remain.

5. Meanwhile, stack the tortillas between paper towels. Microwave on High for 15 to 30 seconds, or until softened.

6. Spoon some of the egg mixture on each tortilla, slightly below center. Sprinkle with cheese and scallions. Fold the bottom up to cover the ▶

filling. Fold the sides toward the center, then roll up from bottom.

7. Place, seam side down, in a spoke pattern on a microwave-safe plate. Microwave on High for 25 seconds, or until the cheese is melted.

Per serving: 273 cal, 17 g pro, 15 g car, 16 g fat, 341 mg chol, 841 mg sod with salsa, 816 mg sod with taco sauce

EASY • 60 MINUTES • LOW FAT • ONE POT

DUTCH OMELET

Serves 4 to 6
Preparation time: 20 minutes
Cooking time: 17 minutes

Here is a simple way to make an omelet without having to fold it. Filled with sausage, bell pepper, and potatoes, it makes hearty breakfast fare—or try it for lunch or supper.

> 6 ounces turkey breakfast sausage links, casings removed and sausage crumbled
> ¾ cup chopped onion
> ½ cup diced green bell pepper
> 3 medium-size all-purpose potatoes, peeled and shredded (2 cups)
> ½ teaspoon salt
> 4 large eggs
> 3 tablespoons milk

1. In a large nonstick broiler-proof skillet, cook the sausage, onion, and pepper over medium heat, stirring often, until the vegetables are softened.

2. Add the potatoes and salt to the skillet. Cover and cook for 5 minutes, stirring occasionally.

3. Heat the broiler. In a small bowl, beat the eggs with a fork. Add the eggs to the skillet and stir. Cook uncovered over medium-low heat, without stirring, for 10 minutes, or until almost set.

4. Place the skillet under the broiler for 1 to 2 minutes, or until the top is cooked. Serve right away.

Per servings: 154 cal, 11 g pro, 12 g car, 7 g fat, 161 mg chol, 385 mg sod

---

AN EGG OF ANY COLOR

The color of an egg's shell—white or brown—or the color of the yolk—pale or deep yellow —is determined by the breed and diet of the hen and has nothing to do with taste, nutritional value, or cooking performance.

 OOK'S TIP

You can use leftover boiled potatoes. Just heat through.

EASIEST–EVER EGG SALAD

Serves 4

Preparation time: 8 minutes

Cooking time: 5 minutes

With this method you'll never have to face hard-to-peel eggs again. Serve on rolls or tucked into pita pockets with lettuce and tomato.

8 large eggs

4 scallions

⅓ cup light mayonnaise or salad dressing

1 teaspoon dry mustard

½ teaspoon salt

1. Break the eggs into a microwave-safe pie plate. Stir with a fork just until the yolks start to run into the egg whites. Microwave, uncovered, on High without stirring for 2 minutes, or until the edges begin to set. Gently push the edges into the center with a rubber spatula. Microwave for 3 to 3½ minutes more, or just until the eggs look dry and have set.

2. Meanwhile, trim the scallions and slice thin.

3. Chop the eggs in the pie plate with a pastry blender or fork. Gently stir in the scallions, mayonnaise, mustard, and salt. Serve right away or cover and refrigerate until ready to serve.

Makes 2 cups. Per 1/2 serving with mayonnaise: 209 cal, 13 g pro, 4 g car, 16 g fat, 432 mg chol, 509 mg sod. With salad dressing: 232 cal, 13 g pro, 7 g car, 17 g fat, 430 mg chol 540 mg sod

MAKING THE GRADE

The majority of eggs on the market are sold by grade and size. Standards for grade and size are established by the U.S. Department of Agriculture. The grades, in descending order, are Grade AA, Grade A, and Grade B. Grade AA eggs spread less and have a slightly firmer and higher yolk and white than Grade A eggs. Eggs that are Grade B will spread more than the other two grades and have a flattened yolk. Almost no grade B's find their way to the retail supermarket. Some go to institutional egg users such as bakeries or food service operators, or to egg breakers for use in egg products.

Egg are also sold by size —Jumbo, Extra Large, Large, Medium, Small, and Peewee. They are sized according to the minimum weight per dozen; Jumbo (30 ounces), Extra large (27 ounces), Large (24 ounces), Medium (21 ounces), Small (18 ounces), and Peewee (15 ounces). The price differences are based largely on egg size, with larger eggs costing more per dozen than smaller ones. The egg sizes most often available are Extra Large, Large, and Medium.

APPLE–CHEDDAR OMELET

Serves 2

Preparation time: 15 minutes

Cooking time: 15 minutes

One of the nicest things about omelets is that they can be filled with virtually anything you have in the refrigerator. We used a spicy apple filling here, which would taste good any time of day. Serve it with tea and toasted bagels.

APPLE FILLING

1 tablespoon butter or margarine

1 medium-size tart apple such as Granny Smith, peeled, cored, and sliced thin (1¼ cups)

1 tablespoon light or dark brown sugar

¼ teaspoon ground cinnamon

Pinch of grated nutmeg

¼ cup shredded Cheddar cheese

OMELET

3 large eggs

2 teaspoons water

¼ teaspoon salt

¼ teaspoon ground black pepper

1 tablespoon butter or margarine

1. Make the filling: In a medium-size nonstick skillet, melt the butter over medium heat. Add the apple and cook, stirring often, for 5 minutes, or until tender. Stir in the sugar, cinnamon, and nutmeg until well blended. Remove the skillet from the heat.

2. Make the omelet: In a small bowl, beat the eggs with the water, salt, and pepper.

3. Heat an 8- to 10-inch nonstick omelet pan or skillet over medium-high heat. Pour in the beaten eggs. Swirl the pan by the handle to distribute the eggs evenly over the surface. Cook, without stirring, for 10 seconds, or until the bottom and edges begin to set.

4. As the bottom begins to set, lift the cooked portion of the omelet with a thin spatula to let the uncooked egg mixture flow under it. Repeat until most of the omelet is set but the center is still moist and creamy.

5. Spoon the apple filling over one half of the omelet and sprinkle with the Cheddar cheese. Using a spatula, fold the remaining half over the filling and

VARIATION

MUSHROOM OMELET

• In a medium-size skillet, melt the butter over medium heat. Add ½ cup thinly sliced onion and cook, stirring often, for 2 minutes, or until softened. Add 1½ cups sliced white mushrooms (4 ounces). Cook for 5 minutes, stirring often, until softened and the liquid has evaporated. Add 1 tablespoon chopped fresh parsley, and ½ teaspoon chopped fresh thyme (optional). Remove the skillet from the heat.

• Make and fill the omelet as directed, using ¼ cup shredded part-skim mozzarella instead of the Cheddar cheese. Serve right away.

Per serving: 229 cal, 15 g pro, 8 g car, 16 g fat, 342 mg chol with butter, 327 mg chol with margarine, 499 mg sod

• EASY • 30 MINUTES

cook until the filling is heated through and the cheese has melted. Slide the omelet onto a plate and serve right away.

Per serving: 337 cal, 13 g pro, 19 g car, 24 g fat, 365 mg chol with butter, 334 mg chol with margarine, 573 mg sod with butter, 590 mg sod with margarine

---

60 MINUTES • CLASSIC

ASPARAGUS–SMOKED HAM ROULADE

Serves 6
Preparation time: 15 minutes
Baking time: 18 minutes

This roulade is a delicate soufflé-like egg mixture, baked in a jelly roll pan, then rolled around a filling and sliced. For an elegant brunch, accompany the roulade with a fresh fruit salad and mini muffins.

4 large eggs
1 cup 1 percent fat milk
½ cup all-purpose flour
3 tablespoons finely chopped scallions
1 teaspoon dried dillweed
⅛ teaspoon ground black pepper
¼ teaspoon salt
¾ cup finely chopped smoked ham (3½ ounces)
1 package (10 ounces) frozen cut asparagus spears
1 cup shredded Gruyère cheese

1. Heat the oven to 350°F. Line a 15 x 10½ x 1-inch jelly roll pan with foil. Lightly coat the foil with vegetable oil cooking spray.

2. In a medium-size bowl, beat the eggs, milk, flour, scallions, dill, pepper, and salt until well blended. Pour the mixture into the prepared pan. Sprinkle with the ham. Bake for 8 minutes, or until the eggs are beginning to set.

3. Meanwhile, cook the asparagus according to the package directions. Drain well and gently blot dry with paper towels. Arrange the spears over the egg mixture, horizontal with the short edge of the pan. Bake for 7 to 10 minutes more, or until the egg mixture is firm when gently pressed.

4. Remove the pan from the oven. Sprinkle with the cheese, then the pepper. Starting with a narrow end, roll up the roulade, using the foil to lift and roll. Transfer the roulade to a serving platter. Cut into slices and serve right away.

Per serving: 218 cal, 17 g pro, 13 g car, 11 g fat, 172 mg chol, 457 mg sod

SPINACH QUICHE

Serves 8

Preparation time: 25 minutes plus 1 hour to chill

Baking time: 1 hour 10 minutes

Enjoy this savory custard pie with a mixed green salad as a supper or luncheon main course. It also makes a favorite party dish because it can be served at room temperature.

DOUGH

1½ cups all-purpose flour

¼ teaspoon salt

½ cup (1 stick) margarine, chilled and cut into small pieces

¼ cup cold water

SPINACH FILLING

2 cups (16 ounces) egg substitute

⅓ cup all-purpose flour

1 teaspoon baking powder

¼ teaspoon ground red pepper (cayenne)

¼ teaspoon salt

2 cups (16 ounces) 1 percent fat cottage cheese

1 (10-ounce) package frozen chopped spinach, thawed
   and squeezed dry

¼ cup thinly sliced scallions

1. To make the dough in a food processor: Process the flour, salt, and margarine with on/off turns until coarse crumbs form. With the motor running, add the water through the feed tube. Process just until the dough leaves the side of the bowl. To make the dough by hand: In a medium-size bowl, mix the flour and salt. Cut in the butter with 2 knives until the mixture resembles coarse crumbs. Sprinkle the crumbs with the water, stirring with a fork until the mixture clumps together to form a dough.

2. Press the dough into a 1-inch-thick round. Wrap in waxed paper and chill for at least 1 hour.

3. Heat the oven to 400°F. Remove the dough from the refrigerator and allow to stand at room temperature for a few minutes.

4. On a lightly floured surface with a lightly floured rolling pin, roll the dough into a 13-inch circle. Line a 10-inch quiche dish or deep-dish pie pan with the dough; turn under and flute or crimp the edge. Prick the bottom

ⓂAKE AHEAD

The quiche can be made up to two days ahead. Cool completely, wrap with plastic, and refrigerate. To reheat, remove the plastic, cover with foil, and place in a 300°F oven until just heated through.

and sides of the dough all over with a fork.

5. Bake for 12 to 14 minutes, or until the crust just begins to take on some color. Set the pan on a wire rack to cool slightly.

6. Meanwhile, make the filling. In a large bowl, whisk together the eggs and a mixture of the flour, baking powder, peppers, and salt. Stir in the cottage cheese, spinach, and scallions. Pour the filling into the crust.

7. Bake for 15 minutes. Reduce the oven temperature to 350°F and bake for 35 to 40 minutes more, or until the filling is set and a toothpick inserted near the center comes out clean. Set the pan on a wire rack to cool for 10 minutes before serving, or serve at room temperature.

Per serving: 292 cal, 17 g pro, 27 g car, 12 g fat, 2 mg chol, 687 mg sod

VARIATION

BROCCOLI PIE
Instead of the cauliflower, use 1 package (10 ounces) frozen chopped broccoli, thawed and squeezed dry.

Per serving: 194 cal, 11 g pro, 15 g car, 10 g fat, 159 mg chol, 586 mg sod

• EASY • 60 MINUTES
• LOW FAT

EASY • 60 MINUTES • LOW FAT

CAULIFLOWER PIE

Serves 6
Preparation time: 2 minutes
Baking time: 35 minutes

A vegetarian favorite, this quichelike, no-crust pie can be served for breakfast, lunch, or dinner. Accompany with a tossed green or Caesar salad.

⅔ cup reduced-fat buttermilk baking mix
⅔ cup milk
4 large eggs
¼ teaspoon salt
1 package (10 ounces) frozen cauliflower, thawed and drained
4 ounces process cheese spread, cut in cubes (1 cup)
½ cup sliced scallions

1. Heat the oven to 350°F. Lightly grease a 9-inch pie pan.

2. In a large bowl, whisk the buttermilk baking mix, milk, eggs, and salt until blended. Stir in the remaining ingredients. Pour the mixture into the prepared pie pan.

3. Bake for 30 to 35 minutes, or until puffed and golden. Cut into wedges and serve right away.

Per serving: 193 cal, 11 g pro, 15 g car, 10 g fat, 159 mg chol, 586 mg sod

EASY • 30 MINUTES

FRENCH–TOASTED CHEESE SANDWICH

Serves 4

Preparation time: 5 minutes

Cooking time: 9 minutes per batch

This recipe is a cross between French toast and a grilled cheese sandwich. Filled with mild fontina cheese and fresh tomato slices, it makes a simple and satisfying light meal when served with a tossed green salad. Other ingredients can be substituted or added to these sandwiches, such as thin slices of baked ham or roasted turkey.

8 slices white, whole-wheat, or sourdough bread
4 teaspoons prepared mustard
4 thin slices fontina, Muenster, or Monterey Jack cheese
1 medium-size ripe tomato, sliced thin
3 large eggs
1 tablespoon milk
Pinch of grated nutmeg

1. Spread 4 bread slices lightly with the mustard. Cover each with a slice of cheese, trimming to fit the bread if necessary. Top each with some of the tomato. Cover with the remaining bread slices to complete the sandwiches.

2. In a shallow dish, beat the eggs with the milk and nutmeg.

3. Heat a large nonstick skillet over medium heat. Lightly coat the skillet with vegetable oil cooking spray.

4. Dip the sandwiches into the egg mixture to coat well on both sides. Cook the sandwiches, in batches if necessary, over medium-low heat for 3 to 4 minutes on each side, turning and pressing lightly with a spatula, until golden brown.

5. Remove the sandwiches to serving plates. Cut in half and serve right away.

Makes 4 sandwiches. Per sandwich with fontina cheese: 323 cal, 17 g pro with white or sourdough breads, 18 g pro with whole-wheat bread, 28 g car, 16 g fat, 193 mg chol, 613 mg sod with white bread, 845 mg sod with whole-wheat or sourdough breads

60 MINUTES • CLASSIC

CHEESE SOUFFLÉ

Serves 4

Preparation time: 16 minutes

Baking time: 35 minutes

This puffed soufflé is such a hit to serve that it's well worth mastering these straightforward steps to create one. It's easier than you might think.

3 tablespoons plus 2 teaspoons butter or margarine
2 tablespoons packaged plain bread crumbs
3 tablespoons butter or margarine
3 tablespoons all-purpose flour
1 cup milk
5 large eggs, whites and yolks separated
1 cup shredded Cheddar cheese (4 ounces)
½ teaspoon salt
¼ teaspoon ground red pepper (cayenne)
⅛ teaspoon cream of tartar or vinegar

1. Heat the oven to 375°F. Coat the inside of a 2-quart, straight-sided soufflé dish or other deep 2-quart baking dish with 2 teaspoons of butter. Add the bread crumbs and tilt the dish to coat. Shake out the loose crumbs.

2. In a small saucepan, melt the remaining butter over low heat. Add the flour and cook, whisking constantly, for 2 to 3 minutes, or until frothy and very pale gold. Remove the pan from the heat. Gradually whisk in the milk.

3. Put the pan over medium heat and whisk constantly until the sauce is smooth, thickened, and boiling. Reduce the heat to low and simmer for 5 minutes, whisking often.

4. Remove the pan from the heat. Keep whisking while dropping in the yolks, one at a time. Stir in the cheese, salt, and red pepper.

5. Cook over low heat for about 1 minute, whisking constantly, or just until the cheese has melted and the sauce is smooth. Do not simmer or boil.

6. Put the egg whites into a dry, deep medium-size bowl. Add the cream of tartar and beat with an electric mixer set at high speed. (Move hand-held beater around the bowl. With stand mixer, frequently push whites from edges toward beaters.) Beat just until stiff, shiny peaks form when beaters are lifted.

7. With a rubber spatula, gently stir about ⅓ of the whites into the yolk mixture until blended. Add the yolk mixture to the whites remaining in bowl and gently stir (fold) together. (Don't overmix; some egg white may remain.)

8. Scrape the mixture into the prepared soufflé dish and smooth the top with a spatula. To give the soufflé a classic "top-hat" look, use a knife to ▶

COOK'S TIP

Separate eggs when cold, but allow whites to come to room temperature before beating. They'll whip up lighter and fluffier. Beat whites until tripled. The surface will be shiny and stiff peaks will form when the beaters are lifted. Don't overbeat. Overbeaten whites look dry and bumpy and the soufflé won't rise properly.

draw a ½-inch-deep circle 1 inch in from the edge.

9. Bake for 30 to 35 minutes without opening the oven door for first 25 minutes. To test, shake the soufflé gently. It's done when the center is no longer wobbly. Remove from the oven and serve right away.

Per servings: 449 cal, 18 g pro, 11 g car, 37 g fat, 356 mg chol with butter, 304 mg chol with margarine, 782 mg sod with butter, 810 mg sod with margarine

---

EASY • 60 MINUTES • MAKE AHEAD • ONE POT

HAM & CHEESE STRATA

Serves 4
Preparation time: 15 minutes
Baking time: 45 minutes

Try this recipe for a simple brunch dish. It can be doubled and baked in a 3-quart baking dish. Serve it with ripe melon slices or other fresh fruit.

8-inch-long piece of French or Italian bread, cut into ½-inch-thick slices
2 tablespoons mustard, preferably whole-grain Dijon
4 slices baked ham, such as Virginia, Black Forest, or honey baked (4 ounces)
1 medium-size ripe tomato, sliced thin
2 ounces cheese such as fontina, Swiss, or Cheddar, cut into thin strips
    or shredded (½ cup)
2 medium-size scallions, sliced thin (½ cup)
2 large eggs
1 cup low-fat milk
⅛ teaspoon ground black pepper

1. Heat the oven to 350°F. Lightly grease a shallow 1½-quart baking dish.

2. Spread one side of the bread slices with the mustard. Arrange half the slices, mustard-side up, over the bottom of the prepared baking dish, slightly overlapping if necessary. Cut or tear the ham into strips and distribute evenly over the bread. Top with the tomato slices, cheese, scallions, and remaining bread, mustard-side down. Press down gently.

3. In a small bowl, beat the eggs, milk, and pepper until blended. Pour the mixture evenly over the bread.

4. Bake for 40 to 45 minutes, or until the custard is set and the edges of the bread are golden brown. Set the pan on a wire rack and let cool for 10 minutes before serving.

Per serving with fontina cheese: 259 cal, 18 g pro, 17 g car, 12 g fat, 144 mg chol, 915 mg sod

Ⓜ AKE AHEAD

The casserole can be assembled, covered, and refrigerated overnight. Uncover and bake as directed.

GRAINS
& BEANS

> *"They touched earth*
> *and grain grew."*
>
> MARGARET ABIGAIL WALKER

Long a primary staple and source of protein for many countries, grains and beans have finally moved into a position of importance in the American diet—and it's easy to see why. Both are low in fat, high in complex-carbohydrates, and rich in vitamins and minerals. Together, grains and beans provide us with a complete protein and offer a healthy alternative to meat dishes.

One of the exciting things they offer to meal planning is a wide variety of tastes and textures. Don't think of them as only side dishes. Serving these nutritious-packed foods as a main course makes healthful as well as economic sense.

LOW FAT • CLASSIC

RED BEANS & RICE

Serves 4

Preparation time: 10 minutes plus soaking time for beans

Cooking time: 1 hour 55 minutes

The words budget and beans go together. Keep your pantry stocked with dried and canned beans. They will keep almost forever and provide more protein for your dollar than any other food—and without fat or cholesterol.

RED BEANS

8 ounces (1 cup plus 1½ tablespoons) dried small red beans,
   rinsed and picked over

8 cups water

1 smoked ham hock (about 8 ounces)

1 cup coarsely chopped onion

1½ teaspoons minced fresh garlic

1 teaspoon salt

1 teaspoon ground cumin

1 cup coarsely chopped green bell pepper

1 cup coarsely chopped ripe tomato

For garnish: ¼ cup chopped red onion (optional)

RICE

2 cups water

1 teaspoon salt

1 cup uncooked long-grain white rice

1. Make the beans: In a large saucepan, combine the beans and 4 cups of water and let soak overnight. Or use the quick-cooking method: boil for 2 minutes, then remove the pan from the heat, cover, and let stand 1 hour.

2. Drain the beans and add the remaining 4 cups water, the ham hock, onion, garlic, salt, and cumin. Bring to a boil over high heat. Reduce the heat to medium-low and simmer uncovered for about 1 hour and 15 minutes, stirring occasionally, until the beans are almost tender.

3. Add the bell pepper and tomato and simmer for 20 to 30 minutes more, stirring occasionally, until the beans are very tender and the liquid has cooked down to a rich sauce.

4. Meanwhile, make the rice. Bring the 2 cups water and the salt to a boil in a medium-size saucepan. Add the rice, cover, and simmer over medium-low heat for 15 to 20 minutes, or until tender and the liquid is absorbed.

PERFECT RICE EVERY TIME

The Rice Council of America suggests this method for cooking rice: In a medium-size saucepan, combine 1 cup uncooked, regular milled white rice with 2 cups liquid, and 1 tablespoon butter or margarine (optional). Bring to a boil, stir once with a fork, reduce to a simmer, cover and simmer over medium-low heat for 15 minutes. If the rice is not quite tender or the liquid is not fully absorbed, cover and cook for 3 to 5 minutes more. Fluff the rice with a fork.

5. Remove the ham hock from the beans and cut the meat into bite-size pieces. Stir into the beans. Spoon the beans over the rice and sprinkle with the chopped onion.

Per serving: 434 cal, 21 g pro, 80 g car, 3 g fat, 12 mg chol, 1,396 mg sod

EASY • 30 MINUTES

TORTILLA PIZZAS

Serves 4
Preparation time: 15 minutes
Cooking time: 4 minutes

Tortilla pizzas are easy and quick to make, and they provide a tasty and nutritious lunch or snack.

4 (7- or 8-inch) flour tortillas
1 can (about 15 ounces) black beans, rinsed and drained
1¼ cups shredded Monterey Jack cheese with jalapeño peppers
1 pound ripe tomatoes (3 medium-size), sliced thin
For garnish: fresh cilantro sprigs (optional)

1. Lay the tortillas flat on a work surface. Spoon ½ cup of beans onto each tortilla, mashing the beans lightly with the back of a spoon.
2. Sprinkle ¼ cup cheese over each tortilla. Top with tomatoes, then with the remaining cheese.
3. Grill the tortillas 4 to 6 inches above hot coals for 3 to 4 minutes, or until the cheese melts. Or heat in a medium-size skillet over medium heat for 4 to 5 minutes. Garnish with cilantro.

Makes 4 pizzas. Per serving: 334 cal, 17 g pro, 36 g car, 15 g fat, 37 mg chol, 587 mg sod

EASY • 60 MINUTES • MICROWAVE • LOW FAT

NEW MEXICAN MEATLESS CHILI

Serves 6
Preparation time: 15 minutes
Cooking time: 35 minutes plus 10 minutes to stand

The subtle, spicy flavor of this meatless main dish simply can't be beat. The texture of the bulgur wheat is surprisingly like that of ground beef. Top ▶

each serving with a dollop of low-fat yogurt, shredded cheese, and chopped onion and bell pepper, and serve with corn bread.

1 cup chopped onion
1 cup chopped green bell pepper
1 tablespoon vegetable oil
1 teaspoon minced fresh garlic
2 cans (16 ounces each) pinto or red kidney beans, drained and rinsed
2 cans (14½ ounces each) stewed tomatoes, undrained,
    tomatoes broken up
1 can (8 ounces) tomato sauce
1 can (6 ounces) tomato paste
⅔ cup bulgur
½ cup water
1 can (4 ounces) chopped green chilies
1½ tablespoons chili powder
1 teaspoon ground cumin
¼ teaspoon crushed hot red pepper flakes
Toppings: chopped onions and bell pepper, shredded Jack cheese,
    sour cream, or plain low-fat yogurt (optional)

1. In a 3-quart microwave-safe casserole, combine the onion, green pepper, oil, and garlic Stir to mix. Cover with a lid or vented plastic wrap. Microwave on High for 4 to 5 minutes, or until the vegetables are crisp-tender.

2. Stir in the remaining ingredients, except the toppings. Cover and microwave on High for 25 to 30 minutes, stirring once, until the bulgur is tender and the chili is bubbly.

3. Remove the casserole from the microwave. Stir again, cover, and let stand on a heatproof surface for 10 minutes. Serve the toppings alongside.

Per serving with pinto beans: 256 cal, 11 g pro, 48 g car, 4 g fat, 0 mg chol, 1,184 mg sod. With kidney beans: 279 cal, 13 g pro, 52 g car, 4 g fat, 0 mg chol, 1,127 mg sod

MEDITERRANEAN WHITE BEAN STEW

Serves 4
Preparation time: 15 minutes plus soaking time for beans
Cooking time: 1 hour 25 minutes

MAKE AHEAD

The stew can be refrigerated in an airtight container up to 1 week. Reheat on the rangetop or in the microwave.

COOK'S TIP

Always cook dried beans at a simmer. Boiling will cause the cooking liquid to overflow and the beans to break apart.

Offer a fine olive oil in a small cruet to drizzle over and stir into the stew to taste. This is good with steamed Swiss chard seasoned with olive oil, salt, and black pepper. For dessert, serve thinly sliced peeled navel oranges flavored with a little sugar and fresh lemon juice.

1 cup dried Great Northern white beans, picked over and rinsed
2 tablespoons olive oil
2 large onions, chopped fine (2 cups)
2 medium-size yellow or red bell peppers, seeded and cut into
  ½-inch squares (2 cups)
1 can (14½ ounces) whole tomatoes
2 cups chicken broth
1 tablespoon plus 2 teaspoons minced fresh garlic
1½ teaspoons dried sage leaves, crumbled
½ teaspoon salt
¼ teaspoon ground black pepper
¼ teaspoon granulated sugar
1 teaspoon balsamic vinegar, or 2 teaspoons red wine vinegar

1. In a large saucepan, combine the beans with cold water to cover and let soak overnight. Or boil for 2 minutes, then remove the pan from the heat and let stand, covered, 1 hour.

2. Drain the water from the beans and add enough fresh cold water to cover the beans by 2 inches. Bring to a boil over high heat. Reduce the heat to medium-low, cover, and simmer for 30 to 40 minutes, or until the beans are almost tender. Drain in a colander.

3. Heat the oil in the same saucepan over medium heat. Stir in the onions and bell peppers. Cover and cook over medium-low heat for about 10 minutes, stirring occasionally, until the vegetables are tender but not browned. Add the beans and the remaining ingredients except the vinegar, stirring to break up the tomatoes. Bring to a boil over medium-high heat. Reduce the heat to medium low. Cover and simmer 30 to 35 minutes, stirring occasionally, or until the beans are tender. Stir in the vinegar.

Per serving: 303 cal, 14 g pro, 45 g car, 9 g fat, 0 mg chol, 952 mg sod

EASY • 30 MINUTES

PIZZA BEANBURGERS

Serves 4
Preparation time: 7 minutes
Cooking time: 10 minutes

Here is a speedy canned bean supper. Serve with a crunchy salad and extra warmed marinara sauce on the side. To give the burgers a Tex-Mex flavor, substitute chili powder for the Italian seasoning and serve on toaster corn muffins with shredded lettuce and salsa.

2 cans (about 15 ounces each) red kidney beans, rinsed and drained
1 large egg
¼ cup packaged seasoned bread crumbs
1½ teaspoons dried Italian seasoning
1½ tablespoons vegetable oil
½ cup marinara sauce
½ cup shredded mozzarella cheese

1. In a large bowl, mix the beans, egg, bread crumbs, and seasoning. Mash with a potato masher until most of the beans are crushed. (Or process in a food processor using on/off turns.) With wet hands, shape the mixture into four ½-inch-thick patties.

2. In a large nonstick skillet, heat the oil over medium-high heat. Add the patties and cook for 3 to 4 minutes on each side, or until heated through and crusty.

3. Reduce the heat to low. Top each patty with the sauce, then the cheese. Cover and cook for 1 to 2 minutes, or until cheese melts. Serve right away.

Makes 4 burgers. Per burger: 305 cal, 17 g pro, 33 g car, 12 g fat, 64 mg chol, 735 mg sod

EASY • 30 MINUTES • LOW FAT • ONE POT

BRAISED ROMAINE
& WHITE BEANS

Serves 4
Preparation time: 10 minutes
Cooking time: 13 minutes

This is a variation on an Italian favorite. Braising the lettuce reduces its volume so you actually eat more of this fiber-rich green.

FREEZING BEANS

To have beans on hand when needed, they may be cooked, drained, cooled, and frozen in small airtight containers. Thaw at room temperature for about 1 hour.

½ cup chicken broth

3 medium-size cloves garlic, sliced thin

1 pound romaine lettuce leaves, stacked and sliced crosswise
   into ½-inch-wide strips (10 cups)

¼ teaspoon salt

¼ teaspoon ground black pepper

1 can (16 ounces) white kidney beans, rinsed and drained

1½ cups coarsely chopped tomato

1 tablespoon olive oil, preferably extra-virgin

1. In a large skillet, bring the broth and garlic to a boil over high heat. Reduce the heat to low. Cover and simmer for 4 to 5 minutes, or until the garlic is tender.

2. Add the lettuce, salt, and pepper. Cover and cook over medium-high heat, stirring often, for 4 to 6 minutes, or until the lettuce is wilted and tender.

3. Add the beans and tomato. Stir for 1 to 2 minutes, or until heated through. Remove the pan from the heat. Stir in the olive oil and serve immediately.

Per serving: 150 cal, 9 g pro, 19 g car, 5 g fat, 0 mg chol, 417 mg sod

SOY POWER

Let's face it—even the names tofu, tempeh, and miso sound a little strange. But the virtues of soybean-based foods such as these are nothing to snicker about. They're versatile, easy to prepare, and, according to research, may be real allies in the prevention of breast and colon cancer. Here's a brief guide to the soybean products available and how to use them:

◆ Tofu- A cheeselike product made from curdled soy milk, tofu may also be called "bean curd." Firm tofu can be cut into chunks and used instead of meat in many recipes; soft tofu can be blended into many creamy dishes. Nearly tasteless, it calls for plenty of spicing up. Look for tofu in the produce section, either as thick rectangular cakes in a tub of water, or sealed in plastic packages.

◆ Tempeh- A tender soybean cake with a nutty, slightly smoky flavor. It makes a good stand-in for pork and other meats. Look for it in the frozen foods case.

◆ Miso- A salty, earthy-tasting paste made from boiled soybeans that are crushed and fermented. There are several varieties of miso, made by adding another grain to the soybeans. Yellow miso is made from soybeans and rice and is slightly sweet. Red miso is made from barley and soybeans and is heartier and used in soups. A very dark thick miso also available is made almost entirely from soybeans. Miso is sold packed in tubs, jars, tubes, and plastic bags and is usually stored in the refrigerated section.

◆ Soy milk- A creamy, dairy-free beverage that tastes fairly close to whole milk with half the fat (and roughly twice the fat of skim milk). Substitute it for milk in cooking and baking, and pour over cereal.

◆ Soybean oil - It is often the main ingredient in bottles labeled vegetable oil because it heats to a high frying temperature and has a bland taste. You can also find pure soybean oil in health food stores and large supermarkets.

BRAISED LIMA BEANS

Serves 4
Preparation time: 5 minutes
Cooking time: 20 minutes

This recipe is simple, colorful, and delicious, and is a very good accompaniment to chicken or pork. Lima beans are also called butter beans, and are a good source of protein, calcium, and iron.

1 tablespoon butter
1 cup chopped onion
1 teaspoon minced fresh garlic
½ cup diced red bell pepper
1 package (10 ounces) frozen baby lima beans
1 cup water
1 teaspoon chopped fresh thyme
¼ teaspoon salt
¼ teaspoon ground black pepper
2 tablespoons chopped fresh Italian (flat-leaf) parsley

1. In a medium-size nonstick skillet, melt the butter over medium heat. Add the onion and garlic and cook, stirring occasionally, for 4 to 5 minutes, or until the onion is softened. Add the bell pepper and cook, stirring often, for 1 minute.

2. Add the lima beans, water, thyme, salt, and pepper. Cover and simmer over medium-low heat for 15 minutes, or until the beans and bell pepper are tender. Stir in the parsley and serve right away.

Per serving: 140 cal, 6 g pro, 23 g car, 3 g fat, 8 mg chol, 204 mg sod

HOPPING JOHN

Serves 4
Preparation time: 15 minutes
Cooking time: 1 hour 5 minutes

Comprised of black-eyed peas, okra, pork, and brown rice, this dish is a Southern specialty said to bring luck to those who eat it. We've made it even luckier by substituting lean ham for the more traditional hog jowls or bacon. Serve with biscuits and offer hot-pepper sauce on the side. ▶ *p. 273*

LENTIL LOWDOWN

Lentils are one of the oldest cultivated crops, and references to them date back as far back as 2400 B.C. Although they are not beans, they have most of the same properties as beans and are used in similar ways. Lentils are high in protein and provide an excellent substitute for meat when combined with grains or nuts. Their big advantage is that they do not have to be presoaked and they cook faster than dried beans. Most lentils are green or greenish-brown, but there are also yellow and pink lentils which are pretty, but lose much of their color when cooked. Store lentils in an airtight container in a cool, dry place up to 1 year.

MAIN-DISH GRAINS
Topped with black beans, tomatoes, and cheese, Tortilla Pizzas (p.263) are tasty, nutritious, and very inexpensive.

FUEL FOODS
Polenta with
Sausage Sauce
(p.274), left, and
New Mexican
Meatless Chili
(p.263), above,
are equally
nourishing.

A nutritional bonanza, beans and grains are also

some of the best sources for dietary fiber, which

is so critical to good health.

TROPICAL TASTE
Mango salsa lends an exotic punch to these Caribbean Black Beans (p.284), perfect as a low-fat side dish or entree.

4 cups water

2 chicken bouillon cubes, or 2 teaspoons instant bouillon granules

1 cup coarsely chopped onion

1 bay leaf (1½ inches)

1 teaspoon dried thyme leaves, crumbled

1½ cups uncooked brown rice

1 can (16 ounces) black-eyed peas, rinsed and drained

1 package (10 ounces) frozen sliced okra, thawed

6 ounces cooked ham, cut into ½-inch cubes

1. In a large saucepan, bring the water, bouillon, onion, bay leaf, and thyme to a boil over high heat.

2. Stir in the rice. When the liquid boils again, reduce the heat to low. Cover and simmer for 35 to 40 minutes, until the rice is almost tender.

3. Stir in the black-eyed peas, okra, and ham. Cover and simmer for 8 to 10 minutes, or until the rice and okra are tender.

Per serving: 463 cal, 23 g pro, 78 g car, 7 g fat, 25 mg chol, 1,538 mg sod

EASY • LOW FAT • MAKE AHEAD • ONE POT

CURRIED LENTILS, CHICKEN, & BARLEY

Serves 4

Preparation time: 15 minutes

Cooking time: 1 hour 10 minutes

By combining the chicken with a tasty medley of vegetables and grains, you stretch it into a main dish. The bell pepper, carrots, and kale add lots of vitamins A and C, and the lentils and barley boost B vitamins and fiber.

1 teaspoon olive oil

1 cup chopped onion

1¼ cups chopped red bell pepper

2 cups chicken broth

2 cups water

¾ cup uncooked pearl barley

½ cup sliced carrots

1½ teaspoons curry powder

¾ cup dried lentils, rinsed and picked over

1 package (10 ounces) frozen chopped kale, thawed

8 ounces skinned and boned chicken breasts, cut into bite-size pieces ▶

Ⓜ AKE AHEAD

The recipe can be prepared ahead and refrigerated airtight up to 1 week. Reheat on the range top or in the microwave.

Ⓜ AKE AHEAD

This dish can be made ahead and refrigerated airtight up to 3 days. Reheat slowly on the range top.

1. In a large saucepan, heat the oil over medium heat. Add the onion and cook for 3 to 4 minutes, stirring occasionally, until lightly browned.

2. Add the bell pepper, broth, water, barley, carrots, and curry powder. Bring to a boil over medium-high heat. Reduce the heat to low. Cover and simmer for 10 to 15 minutes.

3. Stir in the lentils. Cover and simmer for 30 to 35 minutes, stirring once or twice, or until the barley and lentils are tender.

4. Stir in the remaining ingredients. Cover and cook over medium heat for 4 to 6 minutes, stirring occasionally, until the chicken is no longer pink in center.

Per serving: 393 cal, 31 g pro, 60 g car, 4 g fat, 33 mg chol, 561 mg sod

POLENTA WITH SAUSAGE SAUCE

Serves 4
Preparation time: 10 minutes
Cooking time: 50 minutes

Polenta is a silky mush made from yellow cornmeal. It is an age-old staple of northern Italy, where it is enjoyed numerous ways. Here the polenta is topped with a sausage and eggplant sauce for a hearty main-dish meal. It has all the elements of a nutritious meal, yet is inexpensive to prepare. Serve it with a salad of mixed greens.

SAUSAGE SAUCE

2 teaspoons vegetable oil
12 ounces sweet or hot Italian sausages, cut into ½-inch pieces
1 small eggplant (about 1 pound), quartered lengthwise and sliced ¼ inch thick
1 can (28 ounces) crushed tomatoes
1 teaspoon minced fresh garlic
½ teaspoon dried rosemary leaves, crumbled
½ teaspoon salt

POLENTA

3 cups water
1½ teaspoons salt
1 cup yellow cornmeal

1. Make the sauce: In a large deep skillet, heat the oil over medium-high heat. Add the sausages and cook for 8 to 10 minutes, stirring often, until

MAKE AHEAD

The sausage sauce can be prepared ahead and refrigerated in an airtight container up to 3 days. Reheat the sauce on the range top and prepare the polenta just before serving.

browned on all sides. Drain off the fat from the skillet.

2. Add the eggplant, tomatoes, garlic, rosemary, and salt to the skillet and bring to a boil over medium-high heat. Reduce the heat to medium-low. Cover and simmer for 35 to 40 minutes, stirring occasionally, until the eggplant is tender and the sauce thickened.

3. Meanwhile, make the polenta: In a medium-size saucepan, bring the water and salt to a boil over high heat. Reduce the heat to medium. Gradually sprinkle in the cornmeal, whisking constantly to prevent lumps from forming. Gently boil for 15 to 20 minutes, stirring often, until very thick.

4. Spoon the polenta onto serving plates. Ladle the sausage sauce over the polenta. Serve right away.

Per serving: 418 cal, 18 pro, 44 g car, 19 g fat, 48 mg chol, 1,999 mg sod

EASY • 30 MINUTES • LOW FAT

SOUTH–OF–THE–BORDER GRITS

Serves 4
Preparation time: 5 minutes
Cooking time: 20 minutes plus 5 minutes to stand

Hominy grits—finely ground, dried hulled corn kernels—are not only great breakfast fare but a delicious side dish as well. Serve this Southwestern-inspired version flavored with tomatoes, cumin, and sliced scallions as an accompaniment to baked ham slices, pork chops, or grilled steaks.

4½ cups water
1 teaspoon salt
1 cup regular hominy grits (not instant)
1 can (about 14½ ounces) tomatoes, drained and chopped
1 teaspoon ground cumin
¼ cup sliced scallions

1. In a heavy medium-size saucepan, bring the water and salt to a boil over high heat.

2. Gradually stir in the grits, then stir in the tomatoes and cumin.

3. When the mixture returns to a boil, reduce the heat to medium-low. Cover and simmer for 15 to 20 minutes, stirring occasionally, until smooth and thick.

4. Remove the pan from the heat. Let stand covered for 5 minutes. Stir in the scallions.

Per serving: 169 cal, 5 g pro, 36 g car, 1 g fat, 0 mg chol, 720 mg sod

COOK'S TIP

If it seems that you cannot make polenta without lumps forming, try whisking the cornmeal into cold water, then heat and cook.

VARIATION

MICROWAVE SOUTH-OF-THE-BORDER GRITS

• In a 2-quart microwave-safe bowl, mix all the ingredients except the scallions. Cover with a lid or vented plastic wrap.
• Microwave on High for 15 to 18 minutes, stirring once, until smooth and thick. Let stand, covered, on a heatproof surface for 5 minutes. Stir in the scallions.

Per serving: 169 cal, 5 g pro, 36 g car, 1 g fat, 0 mg chol, 720 mg sod

• EASY • 30 MINUTES • LOW FAT

THE MAIN GRAIN: RICE

There is hardly a culture in the world that doesn't enjoy rice, and Americans are consuming more of it than ever before. From the creamy risottos of Italy to the fried-rice dishes of Asia, rice is the culinary king of all grains.

Rice is not only high in complex carbohydrates—the fuel nutritionists tell us we should be eating more of—but also has a trace of fat and sodium. Rice is also a fair source of B vitamins and minerals and contains all 8 essential amino acids. A ½-cup serving of cooked white rice has 103 calories. The same amount of brown rice has 106 calories.

Regular white rice has been milled to remove the hull, germ, and most of the bran, and it comes short-, medium- and long-grained. The shorter the grain the more starch it contains. That means that short-grain rice tends to stick together when cooked, while long-grain rice separates when cooked. Long-grain is the most common all-purpose rice.

There are many aromatic rices available. This is a catch-all term for varieties that have a nutty flavor and an aroma which is often compared to popcorn. Texmati, Jasmine, and Basmati are all aromatic rices.

Brown rice is not a separate variety, but any type of rice that has the bran layer intact left. The bran layer gives it a slightly chewy texture.

Converted or parboiled rice has undergone a steam-pressure process which forces all the nutrients from the bran layer into the grain. It makes fluffy, separated grains.

Wild rice isn't rice at all, but rather the seed of a tall aquatic grass that grows native in the Midwest. It is also cultivated in Minnesota and California.

---

60 MINUTES • MAKE AHEAD

BARLEY–STUFFED PEPPERS

Serves 4
Preparation time: 20 minutes
Cooking time: 40 minutes

Chewy, delicious barley is teamed with sausage to make a lighter, healthier stuffing for green peppers. All you need is a tomato salad to round out the meal.

4 medium-size green bell peppers
    (1½ pounds) stem ends, seeds, and membrane removed

FILLING
8 ounces hot or sweet Italian sausage, casings removed
1 cup coarsely chopped onion
1 teaspoon minced fresh garlic
¼ teaspoon dried thyme leaves, crumbled
3 cups cooked pearl barley (yield from 1 cup raw)
1 can (8 ounces) tomato sauce

1. Heat the oven to 350°F. Bring a large pot of water to a boil. Add the bell peppers and boil for 2 to 3 minutes, or until crisp-tender. Drain.

M AKE AHEAD

The peppers can be stuffed (and not baked) up to one day ahead; cover tightly and refrigerate. Remove from the refrigerator about 30 minutes before baking.

2. Meanwhile, prepare the filling: In a large skillet, combine the sausage, onion, garlic, and thyme. Cook over medium heat for 7 to 8 minutes, stirring often and breaking up the meat with a spoon until the sausage is browned and the onions are tender.

3. Stir in the barley and tomato sauce. Remove the skillet from the heat.

4. Spoon the mixture into the peppers. Put the peppers into an 8-inch square baking dish. Cover with foil and bake for 25 to 30 minutes, or until the peppers are tender.

Per serving: 444 cal, 16 g pro, 56 g car, 19 g fat, 43 mg chol, 766 mg sod

---

EASY • 60 MINUTES • LOW FAT

RICE WITH GREENS

Serves 6
Preparation time: 10 minutes
Cooking time: 45 minutes

This colorful dish is simple to prepare and a good way to include vitamin and fiber-rich greens in your meal. And the microwave variation is a bonus in the summer months when you don't want to heat up the kitchen.

1 slice bacon, cut into ½-inch pieces
1 cup chopped onion
2½ cups chicken broth
1 box (10 ounces) frozen collard, kale, turnip, or mustard greens
1¼ cups uncooked long-grain white rice

1. In a medium-size saucepan, cook the bacon over medium-high heat until crisp.

2. Stir in the onions. Cook for 5 to 6 minutes, stirring often, until the onions are softened and golden. Pour in the broth.

3. Bring to a boil, add the frozen greens, and cook for 3 to 4 minutes, stirring occasionally, or until thawed and separated.

4. Add the rice and return the liquid to a boil. Reduce the heat to medium-low. Cover and simmer for 20 to 25 minutes, or until the rice is firm but tender and the liquid is absorbed.

Per serving: 200 cal, 6 g pro, 36 g car, 3 g fat, 3 mg chol, 468 mg sod

VARIATION

MICROWAVE RICE WITH GREENS

• In a 2-quart microwave-safe bowl, put the bacon and onions. Microwave uncovered on High for 3 to 4 minutes, stirring once, until the bacon is crisp and the onion softened.
• Pour in the broth and add the greens. Cover with a lid or vented plastic wrap. Microwave on High for 4 to 5 minutes, or until the greens are easily broken up.
• Stir in the rice. Cover and microwave on High for 20 to 22 minutes, stirring once, until the rice is tender and all the liquid is absorbed.

Per serving: 200 cal, 6 g pro, 36 g car, 3 g fat, 3 mg chol, 468 mg sod

• EASY • 30 MINUTES
• LOW FAT

MIDDLE EASTERN RICE & LENTILS

Serves 4
Preparation time: 20 minutes
Cooking time: 28 minutes plus 5 minutes to stand

This protein-rich dish will add a flavorful accent to broiled or grilled lamb chops or steaks. A combination of cinnamon, cumin, and cloves gives the dish a spicy Middle Eastern taste and aroma. Toss any cold leftovers with a mustard vinaigrette for an easy luncheon salad.

¾ cup coarsely chopped onion
1 tablespoon vegetable oil
3½ cups chicken broth, or 3½ cups water plus 1 teaspoon salt
¾ cup uncooked converted white rice
½ cup dried lentils, rinsed and picked over
1 cup diced peeled baking potato
¾ cup diced peeled carrot
½ cup raisins
¾ teaspoon ground black pepper
½ teaspoon ground cinnamon
½ teaspoon ground cumin
⅛ teaspoon ground cloves
1 cup diced red bell pepper
¾ cup frozen green peas

1. In a 3-quart microwave-safe casserole, combine the onion and oil. Microwave uncovered on High for 2 to 3 minutes, stirring once, until crisp-tender.

2. Add the broth, rice, lentils, potato, carrot, raisins, and seasonings. Cover with a lid or vented plastic wrap. Microwave on High for 18 to 20 minutes, stirring 3 times, until the rice and lentils are almost tender.

3. Stir in the bell pepper and peas. Cover and microwave for 3 to 5 minutes more, or until the liquid is absorbed and the rice and lentils are tender. Let stand on a heatproof surface for 5 minutes before serving.

Per serving: 401 cal with broth, 375 cal with water, 14 g pro, 74 g car, 5 g fat, 0 mg chol, 923 mg sod with broth, 598 mg sod with water

RICE YIELDS

1 cup white rice = 3 cups cooked

1 cup converted white rice = 3½ to 4 cups cooked

1 cup precooked (instant) white rice = 2 cups cooked

1 cup brown rice = 4 cups cooked

1 cup wild rice = 3 cups cooked

NO PEEKING

Lifting the lid while cooking rice will allow valuable steam to escape, which will slow the cooking process.

EASY • 30 MINUTES • LOW FAT

COUSCOUS & SQUASH

Serves 6
Preparation time: 10 minutes
Cooking time: 15 minutes plus 5 minutes to stand

Couscous is made from ground wheat kernels (called semolina flour) and water, rubbed into small pellets. In supermarkets look for boxes of couscous near the rice. Natural-food stores and Middle Eastern shops sell it too.

    1 tablespoon olive oil
    1 medium-size zucchini, shredded coarse (2 cups)
    1 medium-size yellow summer squash, shredded coarse (2 cups)
    2 cups chicken broth
    1½ cups couscous
    ⅓ cup minced fresh parsley
    1 to 2 tablespoons lemon juice
    ½ teaspoon ground black pepper

1. In a large skillet, heat the oil over medium-high heat. Add the zucchini and summer squash and cook for 8 to 9 minutes, stirring often, until the liquid released from the squash evaporates.

2. Pour in the broth and bring to a boil over high heat. Stir in the couscous. Remove the skillet from the heat, cover, and let stand for 5 minutes, or until the broth is absorbed.

3. Stir in the parsley, lemon juice, and pepper. Fluff the mixture with a fork and spoon onto serving plates.

Per serving: 219 cal, 8 g pro, 39 g car, 3 g fat, 0 mg chol, 342 mg sod

60 MINUTES • CLASSIC

RISOTTO WITH ASPARAGUS

Serves 4
Preparation time: 15 minutes
Cooking time: 30 minutes

Risotto is rice which is first sautéed with butter or margarine then cooked in broth until it has a creamy consistency. Italians often serve risotto as a separate course, but you may want to try it as an accompaniment to roast meat. But bear in mind: Once you start cooking a risotto it demands almost ▶

constant attention—and it needs to be served immediately. Limit the rest of the menu to simple dishes that don't have to cook at the last minute.

4 cups chicken broth

1 cup water

2 tablespoons butter or margarine

1 tablespoon olive oil

½ cup finely chopped onion

2 teaspoons minced fresh garlic

1½ cups arborio rice or converted long-grain white rice

½ cup dry white wine or water

¼ teaspoon saffron threads, crushed (optional)

1 pound thin asparagus, tough lower part of stalks snapped off, remaining stalks with tips cut into 1½-inch-long pieces

⅓ cup grated Parmesan cheese

1. In a 2-quart saucepan, bring the broth and water just to a simmer over medium-low heat.

2. While the broth is heating, heat the butter and olive oil in a large, deep, preferably nonstick skillet or a medium-size heavy saucepan. Stir in the onion and garlic and cook for 4 to 5 minutes over medium heat, stirring often, until the onion is softened.

3. Stir in the rice and stir constantly for about 1 minute to completely coat the rice grains. Add the wine and stir until almost completely absorbed, for about 2 minutes.

4. While the rice is absorbing the wine, ladle about ½ cup of hot broth into a small cup or bowl. Add the saffron threads and stir until the broth is bright yellow. Stir into the rice, then stir in the asparagus.

5. Cook, stirring gently, until the rice absorbs the liquid and comes away easily from the sides of the pan. Add ½ cup hot broth. Cook and stir until the liquid is almost completely absorbed.

6. Continue adding broth ½ cup at a time, making sure that most of the liquid is absorbed before adding more. Remove the pan of broth from the heat when only about ¼ cup remains. Start checking doneness by biting into a grain of rice—it should be firm but tender. The asparagus should be tender and the risotto creamy. Remove the pan from heat. (Timing from first to last addition of broth is 20 to 25 minutes.)

7. Stir in the Parmesan cheese and the reserved ¼ cup broth until well blended. Serve right away.

Per serving: 453 cal, with arborio rice and wine, 433 cal with arborio rice and water, 442 cal with long grain rice and wine, 422 cal with long grain rice and water, 12 g pro, 63 g car, 14 g fat, 21 mg chol with butter, 5 mg chol with margarine, 1,192 mg sod

ABOUT RISOTTO

Risotto is a rich, creamy rice dish that's cooked just until the individual grains are tender, yet still slightly firm. Generally, a risotto should be creamy enough to run slightly when spooned onto a plate, but never so thick that a spoon stands up in it. Traditional risotto requires nearly constant stirring and the gradual addition of much more liquid than you'd normally use to cook rice. But that's what makes a risotto what it is, and there's no question that it's worth the effort. The best rice to use is a short-grain variety called arborio, available in gourmet sections of many supermarkets. A much less expensive choice is converted white rice. The taste will be wonderful, but

RISOTTO VARIATIONS

MICROWAVE • 30 MINUTES

MICROWAVE RISOTTO WITH ASPARAGUS

◆ Reduce chicken broth to 3¼ cups and water to ¾ cup. In a 13 x 9-inch microwave-safe baking dish, microwave the onion, garlic, butter, and oil, uncovered, on High for 3 to 4 minutes, stirring once until onion is softened.

◆ Stir in the rice to mix and coat. Microwave uncovered on High for 2 to 3 minutes, stirring once. Add the wine, 3¾ cups unheated broth mixture, and ¼ teaspoon saffron threads, crushed. Microwave uncovered on High for 13 to 14 minutes more, stirring 2 or 3 times, until the rice grains are firm but tender, the asparagus is tender, and risotto is very creamy.

◆ Cover and let stand for 5 minutes. Stir in the remaining ¼ cup broth and the ⅓ cup Parmesan.

Per serving: 448 cal with arboroio rice and wine, 427 cal with arborio rice and water, 436 cal with long grain rice and wine, 416 cal with long grain rice and water, 11 g pro, 63 g car, 13 g fat, 21 mg chol with butter, 5 mg chol with margarine, 1,003 mg sod

60 MINUTES

SHRIMP RISOTTO

Omit the asparagus and Parmesan cheese. After cooking the rice about 12 minutes, or when a little more than half the broth is used, stir in 1 pound medium-size shelled and deveined raw shrimp. Continue to cook the risotto as directed. The shrimp should be opaque at the center when done.

Per serving: 530 cal with arboric rice and wine, 510 cal with arborio rice and water, 520 cal with long grain rice and wine, 500 cal with long grain rice and water, 30 g pro, 61 g car, 14 g fat, 188 mg chol with butter, 173 mg chol with margarine, 1,235 mg sod

---

the texture will be quite different. In Italy, risotto is almost always served as a separate first course, but we've included a shrimp risotto here, which can be served as a fine main dish.

60 MINUTES • MAKE AHEAD

BAKED POLENTA WITH BASIL BUTTER

Serves 4

Total time: 1 hour

This is a satisfying side dish, especially with roasted meats or spicy sausages.

POLENTA

4 cups water

1½ teaspoons salt

1 cup yellow cornmeal

¼ cup (½ stick) butter or margarine

¼ cup grated Parmesan cheese

BASIL BUTTER

¼ cup (½ stick) butter or margarine, melted

3 tablespoons finely chopped fresh basil, or 1½ teaspoons dried basil, crumbled

½ teaspoon minced fresh garlic

2 tablespoons grated Parmesan cheese

▶

1. In a large heavy saucepan, bring the water and salt to a boil. Reduce the heat to medium-low. Gradually sprinkle in the cornmeal, whisking constantly to prevent lumps from forming. Boil gently for 20 to 25 minutes, stirring often with a wooden spoon, until very thick but still pourable.

2. Remove the pan from the heat and stir in the butter and cheese.

3. Rinse a 15½ x 10½-inch jelly roll pan with cold water. Do not dry pan. Spread the hot polenta evenly in the pan with a rubber spatula. Refrigerate for at least 30 minutes, or until firm.

4. Heat the oven to 350°F. Lightly grease a 13 x 9-inch baking dish or other shallow 3-quart baking dish.

5. Make the basil butter: In a small bowl, mix the melted butter, basil, and garlic until blended.

6. Make 3 lengthwise and 5 crosswise cuts in the polenta to yield 15 squares. Arrange the polenta squares, slightly overlapping, in the baking dish. Drizzle the basil butter over the polenta. Sprinkle with the cheese.

7. Bake for 30 to 35 minutes, until the edges are very lightly browned. Serve right away.

Per serving: 375 cal, 6 g pro, 28 g car, 27 g fat, 68 mg chol with butter, 6 mg chol with margarine, 375 mg sod with butter, 408 mg sod with margarine

---

EASY • MAKE AHEAD

CANNELLINI BEANS WITH ANCHOVIES

Serves 9

Preparation time: 10 minutes plus soaking time for beans
Cooking time: 1 hour 40 minutes

These beans are equally delicious served cold the next day.

1 pound dried cannellini beans (white kidney beans)
1 medium-size onion, peeled and halved
1 bay leaf (3 inches long)
3 large cloves garlic, peeled
¼ cup Italian (flat-leaf) parsley
¼ cup olive oil, preferably extra-virgin
5 anchovy fillets
3 tablespoons red wine vinegar
Ground black pepper to taste

1. In a large saucepan, combine the beans with cold water to cover and let

---

MAKE AHEAD

The polenta can be prepared through step 3 and refrigerated up to one day ahead.

MAKE AHEAD

The beans can be prepared ahead and refrigerated in an airtight container up to 1 week. Reheat on the range top or in the microwave.

soak overnight. Or boil for 2 minutes, then remove the pan from the heat and let stand, covered, 1 hour.

2. Drain the water from the beans and add enough cold water to cover the beans by 2 inches. Add the onion, bay leaf, and 1 clove of garlic. Bring to a boil, reduce the heat to low, and simmer for 1½ hours, or until the beans are tender but still hold their shape.

3. Meanwhile, mince the remaining garlic and chop the parsley fine.

4. Drain the beans in a colander. Discard the onion and bay leaf.

5. In the same pan, heat the oil over medium heat. Cook the minced garlic until light golden. Stir in the anchovies, vinegar, and half the parsley. Cook and stir 2 to 3 minutes, until the anchovies dissolve. Add the beans, stir gently to coat, and cook for about 3 minutes, or just until heated through.

6. Remove the pan from the heat. Stir in the remaining parsley and season to taste with pepper.

Per serving: 233 cal, 13 g pro, 32 g car, 7 g fat, 1 mg chol, 95 mg sod

EASY • 60 MINUTES

BULGUR PILAF

Serves 6
Preparation time: 20 minutes
Cooking time: 20 minutes

In this dish, bulgur is combined with carrots, celery, Swiss chard, and Asian sesame oil for a tasty main-dish or as an accompaniment to roast lamb.

3 tablespoons olive oil
12 medium-size scallions, sliced thin (1½ cups)
2 medium-size ribs celery, sliced thin (1¼ cups)
2 medium-size carrots, peeled, cut in half
   lengthwise, and sliced thin (1 cup)
1½ teaspoons minced fresh garlic
8 ounces Swiss chard, tough ends trimmed, leaves and stalks
   cut into small pieces (3¾ cups)
2 cups water
1 cup bulgur (cracked wheat)
1 teaspoon salt
½ teaspoon ground black pepper
2 tablespoons chopped fresh parsley
1½ tablespoons dark Asian sesame oil
2 teaspoons dry white wine (optional)

▶

UTTERLY BULGUR

People have been gobbling down bulgur for something like 3,000 years, and once you've sampled it, you'll know why. It's easy to prepare, quite versatile, and tastes—well, like nothing else. Delicate and little bit nutty. What's more, bulgur is practically a whole grain (just wheat kernels that have been steamed, dried, and then cracked), so its nutritional profile is hard to beat. In addition to protein, complex carbohydrates, and a wealth of vitamins, bulgur boasts iron, calcium, and niacin. Best of all, you get all that goodness, plus lots of fiber, with almost no fat.

1. In a large saucepan, heat the oil over medium-high heat. Cook the scallions, celery, carrots, and garlic for 5 minutes, stirring often, until crisp-tender.

2. Add the chard, water, bulgur, salt, and pepper to the vegetables. Stir to mix. Bring to a boil. Reduce the heat to low. Cover and simmer for 12 to 15 minutes, or until all the liquid is absorbed and the bulgur is tender.

3. Stir in the remaining ingredients. Serve warm or at room temperature.

Per serving: 196 cal, 4 g pro, 24 g car, 11 g fat, 0 mg chol, 478 mg sod

---

30 MINUTES • LOW FAT

CARIBBEAN BLACK BEANS WITH MANGO SALSA

Serves 4

Preparation time: 15 minutes

Cooking time: 15 minutes

Mango gives this dish quite a flavor boost. For a complete meal, spoon the beans and salsa over hot rice.

1 teaspoon vegetable oil

1 cup chopped onion

¼ cup water

1½ teaspoons minced fresh garlic

1½ teaspoons minced peeled fresh gingerroot

2 cans (about 19 ounces each) black beans (drain only 1 can)

¼ cup orange juice

¼ teaspoon salt

¼ teaspoon crushed hot red pepper flakes

2 tablespoons chopped fresh cilantro

MANGO SALSA

1 large mango (about 14 ounces), peeled and chopped coarse

2 tablespoons chopped fresh cilantro

2 teaspoons orange juice

1 teaspoon cider vinegar

1. In a large nonstick skillet, heat the oil over medium heat. Add the onion. Cover and cook for 3 to 5 minutes, stirring occasionally, until almost tender and very lightly browned.

2. Stir in the water, garlic, and ginger. Cover and cook for 5 minutes more,

> **DRIED BEANS YIELD**
>
> 1 cup dried beans = 3 cups cooked beans
>
> 1 pound dried beans (2½ cups beans) = 5½ to 6 cups cooked beans

stirring occasionally, or until the onion is tender.

3. Add the beans, orange juice, salt, and hot pepper flakes. Bring to a boil over medium-high heat. Reduce the heat to medium-low and simmer for 5 minutes. Stir in the cilantro.

4. Meanwhile, make the salsa. In a small bowl, mix the mango, cilantro, orange juice, and vinegar.

5. To serve, spoon the beans over rice and top with the salsa.

Per serving: 278 cal, 14 g pro, 52 g car, 2 g fat, 0 mg chol, 873 mg sod

---

MAKE AHEAD • CLASSIC

COUNTRY-STYLE BAKED BEANS

Serves 8

Preparation time: 15 minutes plus soaking time for beans

Cooking time: 3 hours 30 minutes

This makes a generous side dish with fried chicken or grilled spareribs. Or add some small chunks of ham to the beans and serve with rice and cornbread for a main course. If time is short, try the hurry-up variation.

1 pound dried pinto beans
1 bay leaf
2 cloves garlic, peeled and smashed
4 slices bacon, cut into 1-inch pieces
2 medium-size onions, chopped
1 medium-size green bell pepper, chopped
2 cups bottled barbecue sauce
1 cup beer, apple juice, or water
¼ cup packed light brown sugar

1. In a large saucepan, combine the beans with cold water to cover and let soak overnight. Or boil for 2 minutes, then remove the pan from the heat and let stand, covered, 1 hour.

2. Drain the water from the beans and add enough cold water to cover the beans by 2 inches. Add the bay leaf and garlic. Bring to a boil, reduce the heat to low, and simmer for 2 hours, or until the beans are tender but still hold their shape. Drain. Discard the bay leaf and garlic.

3. Heat the oven to 350°F. In a Dutch oven, cook the bacon, onion, and bell pepper over medium-high heat, stirring occasionally, for about 10 minutes, or until the bacon is golden and the vegetables are softened. Drain off all but about 1 tablespoon of drippings.

▶

VARIATION

HURRY-UP BBQ BAKED BEANS

• In a large deep skillet, cook the bacon, onion, and bell pepper over medium-high heat, stirring occasionally, for about 10 minutes, or until the bacon is golden and the vegetables are softened. Drain off all but ½ tablespoon of drippings.

• Stir in 2 cans (28 ounces each) baked beans, ½ cup barbecue sauce, and ½ cup beer or apple juice. Bring to a boil, then simmer for 10 minutes, stirring frequently.

Serves 6. Per serving: 356 cal, 16 g pro, 61 g car, 8 g fat, 24 mg chol, 1,420 mg sod

•EASY • 30 MINUTES

4. Add the drained beans, barbecue sauce, beer, and brown sugar. Bake uncovered for 1½ hours, stirring occasionally, until bubbly and thickened.

Per serving: 318 cal, with beer or water, 330 cal with juice, 15 g pro, 59 g car with beer, 56 g car with juice or water, 5 g fat, 4 mg chol, 578 mg sod

EASY

WILD RICE WITH MUSHROOMS

Serves 4 to 6
Preparation time: 15 minutes
Cooking time: 1 hour

Wild rice has a certain cachet, elevating an ordinary meal to lofty new heights.

1½ cups chicken broth
1¾ cups water
⅔ cup wild rice, rinsed
1 tablespoon butter or margarine
2 teaspoons olive oil
2 slender leeks, white parts only, rinsed, cut lengthwise,
    and sliced thin crosswise
2 cups (6 ounces) white mushrooms, cleaned and sliced
½ teaspoon ground black pepper
¼ teaspoon salt

1. In a medium-size saucepan, bring the chicken broth, water, and rice to a gentle boil over high heat. Reduce the heat to medium. Cover and simmer for 40 to 45 minutes, or until the grains are tender but still chewy and almost doubled in size. Drain in a colander set over a medium-size bowl; reserve the liquid and set aside.

2. In a medium-size skillet, melt the butter with the oil over medium-high heat. Stir in the leeks and cook, stirring often, for 3 minutes, or until beginning to soften.

3. Add the mushrooms and cook, stirring often, for about 3 minutes, or until beginning to soften. Reduce the heat to low. Cover and cook for about 5 minutes, or until the vegetables release their liquid.

4. Add the rice and ¾ cup of the reserved liquid. Stir thoroughly and simmer uncovered for 5 to 8 minutes, or until almost all the liquid is absorbed. Serve right away.

Per serving: 152 cal, 5 g pro, 23 g car, 5 g fat, 6 mg chol with butter, 0 mg chol with margarine, 442 mg sod

MAKE AHEAD

The cooled baked beans can be refriger-ated in an airtight container up to 1 week. Reheat on the range top or in the microwave.

COOK'S TIP

Wild rice needs to be thoroughly rinsed before using. The best way to do this is to put the rice into a bowl and add enough cold water to cover it by about 4 inches. Stir it a couple of times and then let stand. Any debris will rise to the surface and can then be poured off.

EASY • MAKE AHEAD

MIXED GRAINS & FRUIT PILAF

Serves 6
Preparation time: 10 minutes
Cooking time: 56 minutes

The grains in this recipe can be found in health-food stores and some super-markets. Others, such as triticale, barley, and rye, may be used instead of spelt, wheat, or rice. If cooking times aren't given on packages, boil each variety separately (not in one pot as in this recipe) in plenty of water until firm-tender and still slightly chewy, then drain the grains in a colander and rinse under cold water.

6 cups water
½ cup spelt berries or wheat berries
    (3½ ounces)
⅓ cup plus 1 tablespoon Wehani rice
    (aromatic long-grain brown rice) or
    regular long-grain brown rice (3¼ ounces)
⅓ cup millet
⅓ cup Zante currants
    (look for them near raisins in most supermarkets)
⅓ cup snipped or chopped dried apricots
¼ cup olive oil
¼ cup orange juice
¼ teaspoon ground cumin
¾ teaspoon salt
¼ cup chopped fresh cilantro or parsley
¼ cup toasted slivered almonds

1. In a large saucepan, bring the water and spelt berries to a boil over high heat. Reduce the heat to medium and boil gently, uncovered, for 12 minutes.

2. Stir in the rice and boil gently for 22 minutes more, skimming the foam off the surface of the water occasionally.

3. Stir in the millet and cook for about 12 minutes more, or until all the grains are firm-tender and still slightly chewy.

4. Drain in a colander, rinse under cold running water, and drain well.

5. Transfer the grains to a large serving bowl. Add the currants, apricots, oil, juice, cumin, and salt. Toss until mixed and evenly moistened. Stir in the cilantro and toasted almonds.

Per serving: 312 cal, 6 g pro, 44 g car, 13 g fat, 0 mg chol, 279 mg sod

EASY

GRANOLA

Makes 4 1/2 cups
Preparation time: 10 minutes
Baking time: 25 minutes plus 1 hour to cool

Making granola is so easy that you will wonder why you never made your own before. It's scrumptious served with fresh fruit and yogurt, or as a topping for muffins, or just eaten plain. Granola lends itself to many variations. Add chopped dried apples or apricots, or use toasted pecans or hazelnuts in place of the almonds.

⅓ cup vegetable oil
⅓ cup honey
4 cups old-fashioned oats
¼ cup wheat germ
⅓ cup sliced almonds
¾ cup raisins

1. Heat the oven to 300°F. Line a jelly roll pan or baking sheet with sides with foil.

2. In a large bowl, mix the oil and honey. Add the oats, wheat germ, and almonds, stirring to coat.

3. Spread the mixture evenly over the prepared pan. Bake, stirring occasionally, for 20 to 25 minutes, or until golden brown.

4. Remove the pan from the oven. Stir in the raisins. Let cool for 1 hour. Store in an airtight container at room temperature up to 2 weeks.

Per serving: 315 cal, 8 g pro, 46 g car, 12 g fat, 0 mg chol, 4 mg sod

GRAINS FOR BREAKFAST

◆ Liven up oatmeal by sautéing 1 cup peeled orange sections and ¼ cup raisins, ¼ cup orange juice, and 1 tablespoon honey. Spoon on top of hot oatmeal.

◆ For a cold chewy cereal, in a medium-size bowl, soak 1 cup bulgur and ¹/2 cup each raisins and chopped dried apricots in 2 cups water or milk overnight in the refrigerator. To serve, top with vanilla yogurt, brown sugar, and cut-up fresh fruit such as apples, oranges, or strawberries.

◆ For a comforting hot cereal, soak 1 cup bulgur, ¹/2 cup raisins, and ¼ cup packed light brown sugar in 3 cups milk overnight in the refrig- erator. In the morning, bring the cereal to a boil in a nonstick saucepan and simmer uncovered for 8 to 10 minutes.

◆ For a pretty presentation, layer granola in parfait glasses with sliced fresh fruit such as kiwi, straw- berries, and banana and plain low-fat yogurt.

EASY • 30 MINUTES

FALAFEL IN PITA

Serves 4
Preparation time: 20 minutes
Cooking time: 9 minutes

Falafel is a Middle Eastern burger that traditionally combines ground chick-peas and fava beans instead of ground beef with the delicate flavor of spices native to the Mediterranean. Try falafel as a delicious and healthy alternative to meat dishes. Look for falafel mix in the rice and grains section of your supermarket.

1 box (6 ounces) falafel vegetable burger mix
1¼ cups water
1 cup plain low-fat yogurt
1½ tablespoons creamy peanut butter
½ teaspoon ground cumin
2 cups shredded lettuce
1 large ripe tomato, halved, seeded, and diced
½ medium-size cucumber, peeled and diced
3 tablespoons vegetable oil
4 (6- to 7-inch) pita breads, ½ inch sliced off to expose pocket

1. In a large bowl, mix the falafel and water until blended. Let stand for 10 minutes for the water to be absorbed.

2. Meanwhile, in a small bowl, mix ¼ cup of the yogurt, the peanut butter, and cumin until smooth. Gently stir in the remaining yogurt with a rubber spatula until blended.

3. In a medium-size bowl, gently mix the lettuce, tomato, cucumber, and 2 tablespoons of the yogurt mixture.

4. Form the falafel mixture into 12 small patties, using about 1 heaping tablespoon for each.

5. In a large nonstick skillet, heat the oil over medium-high heat. Add the patties and cook for 3 to 4 minutes on each side, or until crisp and brown. Remove to paper towels to drain.

6. Stuff each pita pocket with about ½ cup of the lettuce mixture. Add 3 falafel patties, then top with the remaining salad and a dollop of the yogurt mixture. Serve right away.

Per serving: 470 cal, 24 g pro, 65 g car, 16 g fat, 3 mg chol, 1,098 mg sod

FLAVOR UP PLAIN RICE: 10 WAYS TO DOCTOR ORDINARY RICE WITH TASTY FLAVOR BOOSTERS

If you've got leftover plain rice that just seems too plain, choose one of the following rice flavor boosters. You're sure to find one to go with whatever you're serving . For each of these variations, just stir the chosen ingredients into 3 cups of hot cooked rice. Or, if the rice is cold (and you're not making variation 10), stir in the ingredients, then heat on the range top or in the microwave (add 3 to 4 tablespoons of water if rice seems dry). Each recipe makes 4 servings.

◆ A 6-ounce jar of marinated artichoke hearts (including the marinade) and 1/4 cup grated Parmesan cheese.
Per serving: 262 cal, 7 g pro, 46 g car, 5 g fat, 4 mg chol, 315 mg sod

◆ About 1/2 cup chopped cooked ham, 8 green olives, sliced, and 1/2 teaspoon dried thyme leaves, crumbled.
Per serving: 239 cal, 8 g pro, 43 g car, 3 g fat, 10 mg chol, 453 mg sod

◆ Drain 1 can (about 16 ounces) red kidney beans (or black beans). Add to the rice along with 1/2 cup salsa and 1/2 cup shredded Cheddar cheese.
Per serving: 346 cal, 14 g pro, 58 g car, 6 g fat, 15 mg chol, 552 mg sod

◆ For quick rice salad, remove peel and pith from 2 navel oranges. Cut out sections. Add to warm or cold rice along with 1/4 cup chopped red onion or scallions. Toss gently with 3 tablespoons vinaigrette dressing.
Per serving: 249 cal, 5 g pro, 53 g car, 2 g fat, 0 mg chol, 112 mg sod

◆ Heat a 10-ounce package of frozen sliced okra with a 14 1/2-ounce can of stewed tomatoes. Stir in the rice and heat.
Per serving: 246 cal, 6 g pro, 54 g car, 1 g fat, 0 mg chol, 266 mg sod

◆ Three cups shredded lettuce, 1/4 cup sliced scallions, and 3 tablespoons teriyaki sauce.
Per serving: 219 cal, 6 g pro, 47 g car, 1 g fat, 0 mg chol, 525 mg sod

◆ Cook and drain a 10-ounce package frozen spinach (squeeze out as much water as you can). Mix with the rice. Add 1/4 cup milk and 1/8 teaspoon grated nutmeg.
Per serving: 225 cal, 7 g pro, 46 g car, 1 g fat, 2 mg chol, 63 mg sod

◆ About 1/2 cup chopped dried apricots and 1 teaspoon ground cumin.
Per serving: 239 cal, 5 g pro, 53 g car, 1 g fat, 0 mg chol, 6 mg sod

◆ Cook, drain, and crumble 2 strips of bacon. Add to the rice along with 1 cup frozen green peas. Heat until the peas are thawed.
Per serving: 244 cal, 7 g pro, 48 g car, 2 g fat, 3 mg chol, 94 mg sod

◆ For a crunchy, refreshing rice salad, add 1 chopped sweet apple, 1/2 cup celery, and 1/3 cup mayonnaise-type dressing to cold rice and toss.
Per serving: 297 cal, 5 g pro, 53 g car, 7 g fat, 5 mg chol, 154 mg sod

PIZZAS
& BREADS

> *"Open thine eyes, and thou*
> *shalt be satisfied with bread."*
> PROVERBS, 20:13

When it comes to meal planning, the breads in this chapter offer a tempting variety of options. Homemade pizza is always a favorite, and making it at home allows you to create just the kind you or your family likes best. Warm batches of flaky biscuits or fragrant muffins are a delightful addition with a minimum of effort to almost any meal, while sweet coffee cakes and whole-grain quick breads can be interpreted as making a good thing even better. And nothing compares to the aroma of home-baked yeast loaves. The range of recipes offered in this chapter demonstrates the diverse role of bread in meals and in between.

PIZZA DOUGH

Makes four 12-inch pizzas
Preparation time: 20 minutes plus 1½ hours
to rise and rest

Once you begin making your own pizza, you will always want to continue. The dough is easy and keeps well in the freezer. This recipe can be made in a food processor with a capacity of at least 8 cups or halved for a smaller machine. If you don't want to make your own pizza dough, you can use 10-ounce tubes of refrigerated pizza dough, a 16-ounce box of hot-roll mix (pizza directions are on the box), frozen pizza dough, or purchased fresh dough. Some pizza parlors will even sell you some of their own. Frozen and fresh dough usually comes in 16-ounce loaves or batches. Cut them in half and use 8 ounces per pizza.

To bake the pies, you'll need a 12-inch round pizza pan or a large cookie sheet. Dark, heavy pans are best because they absorb heat quickly and evenly for a crisp, browned crust.

1¼ cups warm water (105°F to 115°F)
1 envelope (¼ ounce) active dry yeast
1 teaspoon granulated sugar
5 cups all-purpose or bread flour, or as needed
2 large eggs
2 teaspoons salt
Olive oil
Topping of choice

1. In a small bowl, mix the water, yeast, and sugar and let stand for about 10 minutes, or until foamy.

2. Food Processor Method: In a food processor, combine 5 cups of flour, the eggs, and salt. Turn the processor on and pour the yeast mixture through the feed tube in a steady stream. Process until the dough cleans the sides of the bowl, then process for 45 seconds longer (this takes the place of kneading), or until the dough is smooth and elastic.

Hand or Electric Mixer method: In a large bowl, combine the yeast mixture and eggs. Mix in 5 cups of flour and the salt and stir or beat with an electric mixer until the dough pulls away from the sides of the bowl. Turn the dough out onto a lightly floured surface and knead for 5 to 10 minutes, or until smooth and elastic.

3. Put the dough into a large oiled bowl, turning to coat. Cover with

VARIATION

WHOLE WHEAT PIZZA DOUGH

Substitute 2 cups of whole wheat flour for 2 cups of the all-purpose flour and proceed as directed from step 1.

• EASY • MAKE AHEAD

Ⓜ**AKE AHEAD**

Wrap flattened balls of dough in plastic wrap and refrigerate up to 2 days (dough may rise a bit). Use directly from the refrigerator. To freeze: Wrap the flattened balls of dough in plastic wrap, then put into a zipper-type food storage bag and freeze up to 3 months. Thaw at room temperature 1½ hours, or until workable.

plastic wrap and let rise in a warm, draft-free place for about 1 hour, or until doubled in volume.

4. Punch down the dough and divide into 4 equal pieces. Shape the pieces into balls. Lightly cover the dough with a kitchen towel and let rest for 30 minutes so it will be easier to handle. (The dough will rise but not double in volume.)

5. For each pizza: Brush a 12-inch round pizza pan or a large baking sheet with 1 teaspoon olive oil or spray with olive oil cooking spray. Place the dough on a lightly floured surface. With floured hands, pat into a 6-inch round. Stretch or roll out the dough with a rolling pin into an 11-inch ▶

PIZZA TOPPINGS

EASY

VEGETABLE-PESTO PIZZA

◆ Heat the oven to 500°F. Leaving a 1-inch edge, spread the pizza dough with 2 tablespoons homemade or purchased pesto sauce. Sprinkle with ½ cup shredded mozzarella or provolone cheese. Top with 12 thin slices yellow squash, 12 thin slices plum tomatoes, and 1 cup very small, slightly undercooked broccoli florets. Sprinkle with ½ cup sliced scallions and another ½ cup shredded mozzarella or provolone.
◆ Bake for 10 to 15 minutes, or until the edge of the crust is browned and crisp.

Serves 2. Per serving: 549 cal, 22 g pro, 72 g car, 20 g fat, 83 mg chol, 833 mg sod

EASY

BLT PIZZA

◆ Heat the oven to 500°F. Brush the pizza dough with 1½ teaspoons olive oil. Leaving a 1-inch edge, sprinkle with ¾ cup shredded mozzarella cheese and 6 slices crumbled crisp-cooked bacon. Top with 12 thin slices plum tomatoes and ¼ cup shredded mozzarella.
◆ Bake for 10 to 15 minutes, or until the edge of the crust is browned and crisp.
◆ Meanwhile, toss 1 cup shredded romaine lettuce with 1 tablespoon mayonnaise. Before serving, top the pizza with the lettuce mixture.

Serves 2. Per serving: 686 cal, 28 g pro, 64 g car, 35 g fat, 118 mg chol, 1,127 mg sod

EASY

CALIFORNIA PIZZA

◆ Heat the oven to 500°F. Brush the pizza dough with 1½ teaspoons olive oil. Leaving a 1-inch edge, sprinkle with ⅓ cup shredded mozzarella cheese and 4 slices crumbled crisp-cooked bacon. Top with 12 thin slices plum tomatoes, 4 thin slices red onion with rings separated, 1 large seeded bell pepper sliced in rings, ¼ cup crumbled goat cheese, and another ⅓ cup shredded mozzarella.

◆ Bake for 10 to 15 minutes, or until the edge of the crust is browned and crisp.

Serves 2. Per serving: 623 cal, 26 g pro, 68 g car, 27 g fat, 106 mg chol, 1,002 mg sod

EASY

BBQ CHICKEN PIZZA

◆ Cut a skinless, boneless chicken breast half into ½-inch chunks. Marinate the chicken in 1½ tablespoons bottled barbecue sauce for at least 1 hour.
◆ Heat the oven to 500°F. Leaving a 1-inch edge, spread the pizza dough with 3 tablespoons of bottled barbecue sauce. Sprinkle with ¼ cup shredded smoked Gouda cheese, then ½ cup shredded mozzarella cheese. Top with the marinated chicken, ½ cup chopped red onion, 3 tablespoons chopped cilantro, and another ¼ cup shredded mozzarella.
◆ Bake for 10 to 15 minutes, or until the edge of crust is browned.

Serves 2. Per serving: 603 cal, 36 g pro, 70 g car, 19 g fat, 135 mg chol, 1,171 mg sod

circle. Lift onto the prepared pan and press the dough to the edges of the pizza pan or into a 12-inch circle on the baking sheet. Add the topping of your choice and bake on the lowest oven rack. Cut into wedges with a pizza wheel or knife and serve warm.

EASY • MAKE AHEAD • CLASSIC

SAUSAGE & CHEESE CALZONE

Serves 4 to 8
Preparation time: 30 minutes plus 1½ hours to rise and rest
Baking time: 20 minutes

Originating in Naples, Italy, calzones are stuffed pizzas that resemble a large turnover. Some are filled with meats and vegetables and others with cheese and herbs. This savory filling combines Italian sausage with sweet bell pepper, onion, mushrooms, and cheese. Calzones make a great dinner, especially if they are made ahead and frozen. They can be reheated and served with a salad for a quick and hearty weekday meal.

1 recipe Pizza Dough (see page 294)

SAUSAGE AND CHEESE FILLING

1 pound sweet Italian sausages, skins removed (about 2 cups)
1 medium-size onion, chopped (about 1 cup)
1 medium-size red bell pepper, seeded and chopped (about 1 cup)
4 ounces white mushrooms, cleaned and sliced (about 1½ cups)
10 ounces mozzarella cheese, chopped coarse (about 2 cups)
3 tablespoons minced fresh parsley
¼ teaspoon crushed hot red pepper flakes

1. Prepare the pizza dough according to the recipe.
2. In a medium-size skillet, cook the sausage and onion over medium heat for about 5 minutes, stirring to break up the meat. Add the bell pepper and mushrooms and cook for 5 minutes more, stirring often, or until the sausage is cooked through and vegetables are soft. Remove with a slotted spoon to a large bowl. Stir in the mozzarella, parsley, and red pepper flakes.
3. Heat the oven to 450°F. Brush 2 baking sheets with olive oil or spray with olive oil cooking spray
4. Divide the dough into 4 pieces. Take one piece of the dough and with floured hands press it into a 6-inch round. Stretch or roll it out with a rolling pin into a 12-inch circle.

VARIATION

MINI CALZONES

• Divide one piece of the dough into 8 equal pieces and roll each into a 6-inch circle. Divide the filling evenly between the circles and fill and seal as directed.
• Bake for about 10 minutes, or until golden and crisp on the outside.

Per serving: 393 cal, 18 g pro, 20 g car, 27 g fat, 84 mg chol, 691 mg sod

• EASY • MAKE AHEAD

MAKE AHEAD

Wrap the cooled baked calzones in plastic wrap, then foil, and freeze up to 1 month. Thaw in the refrigerator or microwave and reheat in a 350°F oven for about 20 minutes.

5. Leaving a ½-inch edge, spread a quarter of the filling over half of the dough. Dampen the edges with water. Fold the dough in half to enclose the filling; seal the edges with a fork. Repeat with the remaining dough and filling.

6. With a large spatula, carefully transfer the calzones to the prepared baking sheets. Bake for 20 minutes, or until golden and crisp on the outside. Serve warm.

Makes 4 calzones. Per half calzone: 393 cal, 18 g pro, 20 g car, 27 g fat, 84 mg chol, 691 mg sod

CHILI BEAN PITA PIZZAS

Serves 4
Preparation time: 10 minutes
Baking time: 12 minutes

If time is short, bottled salsa can also be used for this recipe.

4 (7- to 8-inch) round pita pockets, plain or whole wheat

1 (16-ounce) can chili with beans
1 cup shredded jalapeño Monterey Jack cheese
½ cup chopped tomato
½ cup chopped red onion
¼ cup diced avocado (optional)
¼ cup chopped fresh cilantro leaves
2 teaspoons fresh lime juice
¼ teaspoon salt
¼ cup sour cream

1. Heat the oven to 400°F.
2. Place the pita breads on a large baking sheet. Spread about ½ cup of chili over each pita bread and sprinkle with the shredded cheese.
3. Bake for 10 to 12 minutes, or until heated through and the pitas are crisp on the bottom.
4. In a small bowl, mix the tomato, onion, avocado, cilantro, lime juice, and salt.
5. Remove the pita pizzas from the oven. Top with sour cream and salsa. Serve warm.

Makes 4 pizzas. Per pizza: 510 cal, 22 g pro, 66 g car, 19 g fat with plain pita, 21 g fat with whole wheat pita, 56 mg chol, 1,384 mg sod

---

PITA BREAD PIZZAS

These pizzas are fun and easy to make, and the possibilities for experimenting are endless. Always keep a packet of pita breads in the freezer and keep ingredients handy so you can make these quick snacks any time.

EASY • 30 MINUTES • LOW FAT

HAM & CHEESE PITA PIZZAS

Serves 4
Preparation time: 10 minutes
Baking time: 12 minutes

These individual pizzas are a snap to make, and kids will love them for lunch.

4 (7- to 8-inch) round pita pockets, plain or whole wheat

1 cup tomato pizza sauce
1 cup shredded mozzarella cheese
½ cup finely chopped ham
¼ teaspoon crushed hot red pepper flakes (optional)

1. Heat the oven to 400°F.
2. Place the pita breads on a large baking sheet. Spread ¼ cup of pizza sauce over each pita bread. Sprinkle each with ¼ cup of shredded cheese, 2 tablespoons of diced ham, and a pinch of red pepper flakes.
3. Bake for 10 to 12 minutes, or until heated through and the pitas are crisp on the bottom. Serve warm.

Makes 4 pizzas. Per pizza: 375 cal, 18 g pro, 53 g car, 10 g fat with plain pita,
12 g fat with whole wheat pita, 32 mg chol, 1,047 mg sod

EASY • 30 MINUTES • LOW FAT

TOMATO–PESTO PITA PIZZAS

Serves 4
Preparation time: 15 minutes
Baking time: 12 minutes

For this easy-to-make treat, look for ready-made pesto in the refrigerated pasta section of your supermarket.

4 (7- to 8-inch) round pita pockets, plain or whole wheat

6 tablespoons ready-made pesto sauce
1 cup shredded fresh mozzarella cheese
4 ripe plum tomatoes, sliced
4 teaspoons grated Parmesan cheese

1. Heat the oven to 400°F.

2. Place the pita breads on a large baking sheet. Spread 1½ tablespoons of pesto sauce over each pita. Top each with ¼ cup of shredded cheese, 1 sliced tomato, and 1 teaspoon of Parmesan.

3. Bake for 10 to 12 minutes, or until heated through. Serve warm.

Makes 4 pizzas. Per pizza: 442 cal, 16 g pro, 52 g car, 19 g fat with plain pita, 20 g fat with whole wheat pita, 25 mg chol, 673 mg sod

---

EASY • 30 MINUTES • LOW FAT

CHICKEN NACHO PIZZA

Serves 4

Preparation time: 10 minutes

Baking time: 15 minutes

Packaged, fully baked Italian flatbreads are available in most supermarkets.

1 large (16-ounce) fully baked Italian flatbread shell, or a 10½-ounce
    partially baked pizza crust
1 can (about 15 ounces) pinto beans, drained and rinsed
2 tablespoons water
2 tablespoons bottled barbecue sauce
¼ teaspoon salt
3 ripe plum tomatoes, each cut crosswise into 6 slices
1 cup shredded nonfat mozzarella cheese
8 ounces (about 8) chicken tenderloins (tenders), white tendon cut out
    and tenderloins thinly sliced crosswise
1 can (about 4 ounces) chopped mild green chiles, drained
¼ cup chopped red onion

1. Heat the oven to 450°F. Place the bread on a baking sheet.

2. In a medium-size bowl, mash the pinto beans with the water, 1 tablespoon of barbecue sauce, and the salt. Spread the mixture over the bread to within 1 inch of the edge. Top with the tomatoes and ½ cup of the cheese.

3. In a medium-size bowl, toss the chicken with the chilies and the remaining 1 tablespoon of barbecue sauce. Scatter this mixture over the cheese.

4. Sprinkle with the chopped onion and the remaining ½ cup of the cheese.

5. Bake for 15 minutes, or until the chicken is cooked through and the cheese is melted and bubbly. Cut the pizza into wedges and serve warm.

Per serving with flatbread: 502 cal, 40 g pro, 65 g car, 7 g fat, 48 mg chol, 1,420 mg sod.
With pizza crust: 357 cal, 34 g pro, 50 g car, 5 g fat, 38 mg chol, 1,289 mg sod

---

QUICK FLAT-BREAD TOPPINGS

◆ Grilled or sautéed vegetables such as eggplant, bell peppers, onion, and zucchini

◆ Mozzarella, prosciutto, and chopped olives

◆ Fresh tomatoes, smoked mozzarella, and basil

◆ Swiss cheese and sliced, canned artichoke hearts

◆ Shredded Mozzarella, fontina, gorgonzola, and grated Parmesan

◆ Tomato sauce, drained, canned minced clams, and chopped fresh parsley

◆ Monterey Jack cheese, green bell pepper, and sausage

◆ Fontina cheese and caramelized onions

◆ Tomato sauce, spinach, and feta cheese

◆ Goat cheese, basil, and pine nuts

GARLIC ROSEMARY FOCACCIA

Serves 8

Preparation time: 25 minutes plus 1½ hours to rise

Baking time: 18 minutes

Focaccia is one of Italy's oldest breads—a simple yeast dough similar to pizza but without a heavy topping. Today's cook can easily make this flatbread at home and serve it with soup, salad, pasta, or as a finger food with cocktails. If time is short, you can use ready-made pizza dough instead of making the dough from scratch.

1¼ cups warm water (105°F to 115°F)

1 tablespoon honey

1 package (¼ ounce) active dry yeast

3 tablespoons olive oil

2 teaspoons salt

1½ teaspoons dried rosemary leaves, crumbled

1 cup whole wheat flour

3 cups all-purpose flour, or as needed

GARLIC TOPPING

3 tablespoons olive oil

2 teaspoons minced fresh garlic

1 teaspoon fennel seeds

1. In a large bowl, mix the water and honey until the honey has dissolved. Sprinkle the yeast over the liquid and let stand for about 5 minutes, until the mixture is foamy.

2. Stir in the olive oil, salt, and rosemary.

3. Beat in the whole wheat flour and enough of the all-purpose flour to form a soft dough.

4. Turn the dough out onto a lightly floured surface and knead for 5 to 10 minutes, or until smooth and elastic. Put the dough in a large oiled bowl, turning to coat. Cover with plastic wrap and let rise in a warm, draft-free place for about 1 hour, or until doubled in volume.

5. Punch down the dough and knead lightly. Let rest for 5 minutes. Divide the dough into two equal pieces. Lightly grease two baking sheets. Put one piece of dough onto each of the prepared baking sheets. Using a rolling pin or the palms of your hands, flatten each piece to form an oval disk approximately 12 x 10 inches. Make four or five indentations with a thumb in the dough.

VARIATION

GORGONZOLA FOCACCIA

Omit the garlic topping. Prepare the dough through step 5. Brush each oval with 1 tablespoon of olive oil. Sprinkle evenly with ½ cup crumbled gorgonzola or other blue-veined cheese. Proceed as directed from step 7.

Per wedge: 176 cal, 4 g pro, 25 g car, 7 g fat, 4 mg chol, 334 mg sod

• MAKE AHEAD

OLIVE FOCACCIA

Omit the garlic topping and add ½ cup chopped black or green olives to the dough while kneading. Brush each oval with 1 tablespoon olive oil and bake as directed.

Per wedge: 166 cal, 4 g pro, 25 g car, 6 g fat, 0 mg chol, 313 mg sod

• MAKE AHEAD

MAKE AHEAD

Prepare the dough
and let rise once as
directed. Punch down
the dough, place in an
airtight plastic bag,
and freeze for up to
1 month. Thaw in the
refrigerator. Proceed
with the recipe from
dividing the dough in
step 5.

6. Make the topping: In a small bowl, mix the oil and garlic. Brush the mixture over the two ovals. Sprinkle each oval with ½ teaspoon fennel seeds.

7. Let stand until the dough looks puffy, about 20 minutes. Meanwhile, heat the oven to 425°F.

8. Bake the focaccia for 15 to 18 minutes, or until golden brown (rotate the baking sheets halfway through the baking time so the baking will be even). Transfer the focaccia to a cutting board. Cut into wedges to serve warm.

Makes 16 wedges. Per wedge: 170 cal, 4 g pro, 25 g car, 6 g fat, 0 mg chol, 276 mg sod

---

MAKE AHEAD

TOMATO, ONION, & HERB BREAD

Makes 2 loaves
Preparation time: 30 minutes plus 3 hours to rise
Baking time: 40 minutes

This bread is especially pretty when decorated with fresh sage leaves. The tomatoes, Italian seasoning, and onion give it a fragrance reminscent of Mediterranean foods. The recipe works nicely for individual rolls, too.

1 can (about 16 ounces) whole tomatoes, undrained
2 envelopes (¼ ounce each) active dry yeast
5 teaspoons granulated sugar
6 cups all-purpose flour, or as needed
½ cup finely chopped onion
2 tablespoons Italian herb seasoning
1½ teaspoons salt
1 teaspoon celery seeds
½ teaspoon coarsely ground black pepper
6 tablespoons butter or margarine, at room temperature
White of 1 large egg
2 teaspoons water
For decoration: fresh sage leaves (optional)

MAKE AHEAD

Wrap the cooled baked
loaves in plastic wrap,
then in foil, and freeze
up to 3 months; thaw
at room temperature.
Or store tightly wrapped
at room temperature up
to 4 days.

1. Purée the undrained tomatoes in a blender or a food processor. Pour into a small saucepan and heat over medium heat until warm (105°F to 115°F). Remove the pan from the heat. Stir in the yeast and the sugar. Let stand for about 10 minutes, or until foamy.

2. In a large bowl, mix the 6 cups of flour, the onion, Italian seasoning, salt, celery seeds, and pepper. Stir in the tomato mixture and the butter, mixing until the flour is evenly moistened (the mixture will be in coarse ▶

shreds). Squeeze the shreds together to form a ball.

3. Turn out onto a lightly floured surface. With floured hands, knead the dough for 5 minutes, or until smooth and elastic.

4. Clean the bowl and oil it lightly. Put the dough into the bowl, turning to coat. Cover with greased plastic wrap and let rise in a warm, draft-free place for about 1½ to 2 hours, or until doubled in volume.

5. Lightly grease a baking sheet. Punch down the dough and divide in half. Shape each half into a round loaf. Place the loaves 5 inches apart on the prepared baking sheet. In a small bowl, beat the egg white and water together with a fork. Brush the egg-white mixture over the loaves. Dip the sage leaves in the egg white mixture and arrange decoratively on the loaves.

6. Loosely cover the loaves with greased plastic wrap or a kitchen towel and let rise in a warm place for no more than 1 hour, or just until doubled in volume. Meanwhile, heat the oven to 375°F.

7. Remove the plastic wrap and bake the loaves for 35 to 40 minutes, or until they sound hollow when the bottom is tapped. Transfer the loaves to a wire rack and cool completely.

Each loaf makes 12 slices. Per slice: 155 cal, 4 g pro, 26 g car, 4 g fat, 8 mg chol with butter, 0 mg chol with margarine, 205 mg sod with butter, 209 mg sod with margarine

---

MAKE AHEAD • CLASSIC

ANADAMA BREAD

Makes 2 loaves
Preparation time: 20 minutes plus 1 hour 15 minutes to rise
Baking time: 1 hour

Anadama refers to the sweet and savory flavor combination of cornmeal and molasses used frequently by the Colonists for bread making. Here's a quick version of this classic yeast bread. It requires no kneading and only one rising. This bread is wonderful served plain or toasted and makes a great accompaniment to soups, salads, and stews.

1 cup plus 6 teaspoons yellow cornmeal, preferably stone ground
2 teaspoons salt
2½ cups boiling water
1 envelope (¼ ounce) active dry yeast
½ cup warm water (105°F to 115°F)
½ cup molasses
¼ cup vegetable oil
6 cups all-purpose flour, or as needed

VARIATION

TOMATO HERB ROLLS

• Follow the recipe through step 4.

• Punch down the dough, divide it into 24 equal pieces, and shape into balls. Place about 3 inches apart on greased baking sheets. Brush with the egg white and decorate each with a small sage leaf if desired.

• Loosely cover with greased plastic wrap or a kitchen towel and let rise for about 40 minutes, or just until doubled in volume.

• Bake at 375°F for 18 to 20 minutes, or until the rolls begin to brown. Transfer to a wire rack and cool completely.

Makes 24 rolls. Per roll: 155 cal, 4 g pro, 26 g car, 4 g fat, 8 mg chol with butter, 0 mg chol with margarine, 205 mg sod with butter, 209 mg sod with margarine

• MAKE AHEAD

1. Lightly grease two 1½-quart ovenproof bowls. (The breads will be baked in bowls.) Coat each with 2 teaspoons of the cornmeal, shaking out any excess.

2. In a medium-size bowl, stir 1 cup of cornmeal and the salt into the boiling water. Let stand for 10 to 15 minutes, or until thickened and lukewarm.

3. In a large bowl, sprinkle the yeast over the warm water. Stir, then let stand for about 10 minutes, or until foamy. Stir in the molasses, oil, and the cornmeal mixture.

4. Beat in 5 cups of flour with an electric mixer set on low until well blended and smooth. Gradually beat in the remaining 1 cup flour with a wooden spoon.

5. Divide the batter between the prepared baking bowls. Sprinkle the tops with the remaining 2 teaspoons of cornmeal. Let rise uncovered in a warm, draft-free place for about 1 hour and 15 minutes, or until doubled in volume. Meanwhile, heat the oven to 375°F.

6. Bake the loaves for 55 to 60 minutes, or until they are well browned and start to pull away from sides.

7. Turn the loaves out onto a wire rack and cool completely.

Each loaf makes 12 slices. Per slice: 185 cal, 4 g pro, 35 g car, 3 g fat, 0 mg chol, 187 mg sod

BREAK BREAD MORE OFTEN

Some myths die hard, like the one that says bread is fattening. Nothing could be further from the truth. Bread and other grain foods like pasta, cereal, and rice are satisfying and low in fat and sugar, and may well be a dieter's best friend. Moreover, generous amounts increase fiber intake, which reduces the risk of certain kinds of cancer, lowers blood cholesterol, keeps blood-sugar levels in check, and provides a bevy of B vitamins too.

Nutrition experts recommend eating six to eleven servings of grain foods daily, but according to a recent survey, for most people a mere three servings is more typical.

Six to eleven servings sounds like a whopping amount, but really isn't. A single slice of whole wheat bread; half a bagel or English muffin; ¾ cup of ready-to-eat cereal; or half a cup of cooked pasta or rice each counts as a serving. Here are some easy ways to boost grain intake:

◆ Include bread in every meal: toast for breakfast, crackers for lunch, and rolls for dinner.

◆ Eat at least two servings of grain foods at meals, without fatty spreads like margarine or cream cheese. (Preserves and apple butter are good fat-free spreads.) Don't forget to count pasta and rice, either hot or in chilled salads.

◆ Tote a bagel or rice cake in your purse to stave off hunger between meals. (If you have a sweet tooth, make it a cinnamon-raisin bagel.)

◆ Enjoy a bowl of whole-grain cereal with skim milk as a late-night snack.

◆ Add toasted bread cubes (croutons) to bowls of soup and tossed salads.

◆ Use bread crumbs or bread cubes as a topping for casseroles.

HONEY–NUT STICKY BUNS

Makes 14 buns
Preparation time: 30 minutes plus 1 hour 50 minutes to rise
Baking time: 50 minutes

You won't miss the fat in this recipe! For appearance and for extra flavor, we added a cinnamon sugar swirl to the dough. Using a black steel muffin pan to bake these buns will give them a deeper golden color.

DOUGH

1¾ cups warm skim milk (105°F to 115°F)
1 envelope (¼ ounce) active dry yeast
¼ cup granulated sugar
5 cups all-purpose flour, or as needed
¼ cup calorie-reduced margarine (in a tub), melted
Whites of 2 large eggs

¼ cup plus 2 teaspoons calorie-reduced margarine (in a tub)
¾ cup plus 2 tablespoons honey
½ cup plus 4 teaspoons chopped walnuts
¼ cup granulated sugar
2 teaspoons ground cinnamon

1. Make the dough: In a medium-size bowl, mix the milk, yeast, and ½ teaspoon of sugar. Let stand for 10 minutes, or until foamy.

2. Meanwhile, in a large bowl, mix the remaining sugar and the flour.

3. Make a well in the center of the flour mixture. Pour in the yeast mixture, margarine, and egg whites. Stir with a wooden spoon until the flour is incorporated and a soft dough forms (the dough will pull away from the side of the bowl).

4. Turn the dough out onto a lightly floured surface. Knead for 5 to 10 minutes, or until smooth and elastic, sprinkling the surface with more flour if sticky.

5. Clean the bowl and spray with vegetable oil spray. Put the dough in the bowl, turning to coat. Cover with plastic wrap and let rise in a warm, draft-free place about 1 hour, or until doubled in volume.

6. Grease twelve 2½-inch muffin cups and two 6-ounce custard cups.

7. Place 1 teaspoon of margarine in the bottom of each cup. Next add 1 tablespoon of honey and 2 teaspoons of walnuts to each cup.

8. In a small bowl, mix the ¼ cup sugar and cinnamon.

9. Punch down the dough and knead in the bowl several times. Turn out

onto a lightly floured surface and roll with a rolling pin into a 21 x 12-inch rectangle. Sprinkle the dough with the cinnamon sugar. Starting with a long side, roll the dough tightly, jelly roll style. Cut crosswise into 14 equal pieces.

10. Arrange the pieces, cut side down, in the prepared muffin cups. Cover lightly with a kitchen towel. Let rise in a warm, draft-free place for about 50 minutes or until doubled in volume. Meanwhile, heat the oven to 350°F.

11. Place the muffin pan and custard cups on a baking sheet to catch any drips. Place in the oven and bake for 35 to 40 minutes, or until golden brown.

12. Invert the muffin pan and custard cups onto a baking sheet. Slowly lift up the pan and cups, allowing any excess honey to drip onto buns. Let cool for 15 minutes. Serve warm.

Per bun: 342 cal, 7 g pro, 62 g car, 8 g fat, 1 mg chol, 95 mg sod

---

30 MINUTES • MAKE AHEAD

PARMESAN–HERB BISCUITS

Makes 12 to 14 biscuits
Preparation time: 15 minutes
Baking time: 15 minutes

These moist, tender, melt-in-your-mouth biscuits are a welcome change for breakfast as well as being the perfect meal accompaniment. When filled with sausage or ham, these biscuits can become a meal in themselves. They are best served hot from the oven, but they can also be frozen and reheated.

2 cups all-purpose flour
¼ cup grated Parmesan cheese
1 tablespoon baking powder
½ teaspoon salt
¼ teaspoon ground white pepper
4 tablespoons (½ stick) cold unsalted butter, cut into small pieces
1 tablespoon chopped fresh herbs, such as sage, thyme or oregano
1 tablespoon snipped fresh chives or minced scallion tops
¾ cup milk

1. Heat the oven to 450°F. Have a baking sheet ready.

2. Hand method: In a medium-size bowl, mix the flour, cheese, baking powder, salt, and pepper. Add the butter and cut in with a pastry blender until the mixture resembles coarse crumbs. Stir in the herbs. Add the milk and stir just until blended. Do not overmix.

Food processor method: Put the dry ingredients in a food processor ▶

MAKE AHEAD

Wrap cooled baked biscuits in plastic wrap, then put into a plastic zipper-type freezer bag. Store them at room temperature up to 2 days or freeze up to 3 months. To reheat, unwrap the biscuits and rewrap in foil. Heat in a 300°F oven for about 8 minutes (20 minutes if frozen), or until heated through.

and pulse on and off briefly to mix. Add the butter and pulse on and off until the mixture resembles coarse crumbs. Add the herbs and pulse on/off to blend. Add the milk and pulse on/off just until dough gathers into moist clumps—do not overmix.

3. On a lightly floured surface, knead the dough for 10 to 15 seconds. With a lightly floured rolling pin, roll the dough out to ½ inch thickness. Cut out biscuits with a 2½-inch round biscuit cutter. (If the cutter sticks to the dough, dip it in flour and tap off the excess before each cut.) Gather scraps, reroll, and cut (but only once—overhandling will make biscuits tough).

4. Place the biscuits close together on an ungreased baking sheet for biscuits with soft sides, or 1 inch apart for biscuits with crisper sides. Bake for 12 to 15 minutes, or until golden brown. Serve warm or at room temperature.
Per biscuit: 118 cal, 3 g pro, 16 g car, 5 g fat, 13 mg chol, 233 mg sod

EASY • 60 MINUTES • MAKE AHEAD

WHOLE WHEAT ORANGE BISCUITS

Makes 12 biscuits
Preparation time: 15 minutes
Baking time: 20 minutes

Whole wheat flour gives these light and fluffy biscuits a slightly nutty flavor. Here the biscuits are made into squares, so they are easier to cut than the traditional round ones and there's no rerolling of scraps.

1 cup all-purpose flour
1 cup whole wheat flour
¼ cup granulated sugar
1 tablespoon baking powder
¼ teaspoon baking soda
½ teaspoon ground cinnamon
6 tablespoons cold butter or margarine, cut into small pieces
1 cup plus 1 tablespoon plain low-fat yogurt
1 tablespoon grated orange peel

1. Heat the oven to 375°F. Have a baking sheet ready.
2. In a large bowl, mix both flours, 3 tablespoons of sugar, the baking powder, baking soda, and cinnamon until blended. Cut in the butter with a pastry blender until the mixture resembles coarse crumbs. Add 1 cup of yogurt and the orange peel and stir just until blended.

MAKE AHEAD

Wrap the cooled baked biscuits in plastic wrap, then put into a plastic zipper-type freezer bag. Store them at room temperature up to 2 days or freeze up to 3 months. To reheat, unwrap the biscuits and rewrap in foil. Heat in a 300°F oven for about 8 minutes (20 minutes if frozen).

3. Transfer the dough to a well-floured surface and knead 4 or 5 times. Roll out the dough with a floured rolling pin or pat out with fingers into a 7-inch square. (The dough will be about ¾ inch thick.)

4. With a lightly floured sharp knife, cut the dough into 12 rectangles.

5. Place the biscuits close together on an ungreased baking sheet for biscuits with soft sides, or 2 inches apart for biscuits with crisper sides. Brush the tops with the remaining yogurt and sprinkle with the remaining 1 tablespoon of sugar. Bake for 18 to 20 minutes, or until the tops begin to turn golden brown. Serve warm or at room temperature.

Per biscuit: 153 cal, 4 g pro, 21 g car, 6 g fat, 17 mg chol with butter, 1 mg chol with margarine, 221 mg sod with butter, 230 mg sod with margarine

---

EASY • 30 MINUTES • MICROWAVE

RAISIN SCONES

Makes 12 scones
Preparation time: 15 minutes
Baking time: 8 minutes

Serve these scones warm, split open, and spread with butter or jam.

2½ cups all-purpose flour
2 tablespoons granulated sugar
1 teaspoon ground cinnamon
½ teaspoon ground nutmeg
½ teaspoon salt
1 tablespoon baking powder
¼ teaspoon baking soda
½ cup (1 stick) cold butter or margarine, cut into small pieces
½ cup sour cream
½ cup milk
1 large egg, slightly beaten
½ cup dark raisins

CINNAMON SUGAR
2 tablespoons granulated sugar
1 teaspoon ground cinnamon

1. In a medium-size bowl, mix the flour, sugar, spices, salt, baking powder, and baking soda until blended.

2. Cut in the butter with a pastry blender until the flour mixture ▶

resembles coarse crumbs. Stir in the remaining ingredients, except for the cinnamon sugar, until a soft dough forms.

3. Place half the dough onto a 10- to 12-inch round microwave-safe plate. Pat with lightly floured fingertips into an 8-inch round.

4. Make the cinnamon sugar: In a small bowl, mix the sugar with the cinnamon. Sprinkle the dough with half the sugar mixture.

5. With a sharp knife, cut the dough into 6 wedges. Place the plate on a microwave-safe trivet or inverted saucer. Microwave on High for 3 to 4 minutes, turning the plate ½ turn once, until the top looks almost dry (a few moist spots will dry upon standing).

6. Transfer the scones to a wire rack to cool. Repeat with the remaining dough. Serve the scones warm or at room temperature.

Per scone: 232 cal, 4 g pro, 30 g car, 11 g fat, 44 mg chol with butter, 23 mg chol with margarine, 334 mg sod with butter, 345 mg sod with margarine

MAKE AHEAD

ORANGE–PECAN MINI–SCONES

Makes 72 scones
Preparation time: 20 minutes plus 8 hours to chill
Baking time: 14 minutes

Serve these miniature scones with butter or honey for breakfast, or afternoon tea, or as an accompaniment to fruit soups or salads.

1 cup pecan pieces
3¾ cups all-purpose flour
1¼ cups packed light or dark brown sugar
1 tablespoon baking powder
1 cup (2 sticks) cold butter or margarine, cut into small pieces
1½ tablespoons grated orange peel
⅓ cup milk
2 large eggs
1 teaspoon vanilla extract
For decoration: 72 large pecan pieces

1. Hand method: Finely chop the nuts. In a large bowl, mix the flour, sugar, and baking powder until blended. Cut in the butter with a pastry blender until the mixture resembles coarse crumbs. Stir in the nuts and orange peel. In a small bowl, whisk the milk, eggs, and vanilla until blended. Stir into the flour mixture just until a soft dough forms.

Ⓜ AKE AHEAD

Store the baked scones in an airtight container at room temperature up to 2 days or freeze up to 3 months.

Food processor method: In a food processor, finely chop the pecans with 4 to 5 quick on/off pulses. Transfer the nuts to a small bowl. Add the flour, sugar, and baking powder to the food processor and pulse on/off just to mix. Add the butter and pulse on/off about 10 times, or until coarse crumbs form. Add the nuts and orange peel. In a small bowl, whisk the milk, eggs, and vanilla until blended. With the motor running, pour the milk mixture through the feed tube and process just until the dough pulls away from the side of bowl. Do not overmix.

2. Divide the dough into four equal pieces and pat out to 1-inch-thick disks. Wrap the disks in plastic and refrigerate at least 8 hours or up to 3 days.

3. To bake: Heat the oven to 350°F. Have two baking sheets ready. Working with one piece of dough at a time (keep the remainder refrigerated), pat out to ¾-inch thickness on a lightly floured surface. Cut out the scones with a 1¼-inch round cookie cutter, dipping the cutter in flour and shaking off the excess after each cut. Place the scones 1½ inches apart on ungreased baking sheets. (Scraps may be gently pressed together and cut, but only once or the resulting scones will be tough.) Repeat with the remaining dough.

4. Lightly brush the scones with water, then top each with a pecan piece. Refrigerate the scones for 10 minutes before baking.

5. Bake for 11 to 14 minutes, or until bottoms are lightly browned and tops look dry. Transfer the scones to a wire rack to cool. Serve warm or at room temperature.

Per scone: 77 cal, 1 g pro, 9 g car, 4 g fat, 13 mg chol with butter, 6 mg chol with margarine, 52 mg sod

ALL ABOUT HONEY

BUYING AND STORING GUIDE

◆ As a rule, the lighter the color of the honey the milder the flavor.

◆ Select mild honeys, such as clover or alfalfa, for use in recipes with delicate flavors.

◆ Use more distinctly flavored honeys, such as orange or sage, in spreads or other recipes where a more pronounced flavor is desired.

◆ Store at room temperature even after opening.

◆ If honey crystallizes, remove the lid and place the jar in warm water until the crystals dissolve, or in a microwave in an uncovered microwave-safe jar or container on High, stirring every 30 seconds, until the crystals dissolve. Don't let the honey boil or scorch.

COOKING TIPS

◆ Honey is sold by weight. The contents of a 12-ounce jar will fill an 8-ounce (1 cup) glass measure.

◆ Honey has more sweetening power than sugar, so it's best to use it in recipes that call for it specifically. If you want to experiment with honey as a sugar substitute, start by using it in place of up to half the sugar called for in the recipe. (When doing this with baked goods, decrease the amount of liquid by ¼ cup per cup of honey used and reduce the oven temperature by 25° to prevent overbrowning.)

◆ Keep honey from sticking to measuring cups by spraying cups with nonstick cooking spray. Or if oil is used in the recipe, measure it before the honey.

---

60 MINUTES • LOW FAT

HONEY–OATMEAL SODA BREAD

Makes 1 loaf
Preparation time: 20 minutes
Baking time: 40 minutes

Soda bread is associated with Irish cooking, and it is often served with a cup of tea. This classic bread is leavened with baking soda, hence the name. Before it is baked, a cross is cut in the top of the dough. Tradition has it that this cross was meant to keep the Devil away. Soda bread, similar in texture to a biscuit, makes an inviting breakfast when spread with jam or marmalade. It also goes nicely with stew or a main-dish soup.

2 cups all-purpose flour
1 cup plus 1 tablespoon quick-cooking oats
1½ teaspoons baking soda
½ teaspoon salt
1 cup plus 1 tablespoon buttermilk
2 tablespoons honey
1 tablespoon butter, melted

1. Heat the oven to 375°F. Lightly grease a baking sheet.

2. In a medium-size bowl, mix the flour, 1 cup of oats, the baking soda, and salt until well blended.

3. In a small bowl, whisk 1 cup buttermilk, the honey, and butter until well blended. Add this mixture to the dry ingredients, stirring just until moistened and blended.

4. Turn the dough out onto a lightly floured surface and knead 5 to 6 times, then shape it into a ball. Place it on the prepared baking sheet and pat into an 8-inch round.

5. Brush the top of the loaf with the remaining buttermilk and sprinkle with the remaining oats. With a sharp knife, score a cross in the dough.

6. Bake for 35 to 40 minutes, or until the loaf is golden brown and sounds hollow when the bottom is tapped. Transfer the loaf to a wire rack to cool. Serve warm or at room temperature.

Makes 12 slices. Per slice: 135 cal, 4 g pro, 25 g car, 2 g fat, 3 mg chol, 282 mg sod

---

WHICH FLOUR?

The protein level of flour is the basis for selecting the proper flour to use for breads. Check the information under Nutritional Facts. Flours with 12 to 14 grams of protein per cup are best for yeast breads; those with 9 to 11 grams of protein per cup are better for muffins and quick breads. Bread flour, with a high protein count, is specifically formulated for yeast breads.

VARIATION

RAISIN CARAWAY SODA BREAD

Stir ½ cup golden raisins and ½ teaspoon caraway seeds into the flour mixture and proceed with the recipe as directed.

Per slice: 153 cal, 4 g pro, 29 g car, 2 g fat, 3 mg chol, 283 mg sod

• 60 MINUTES
• LOW FAT

EASY • 60 MINUTES

SKILLET JALAPEÑO CORNBREAD

Serves 8
Preparation time: 12 minutes
Baking time: 30 minutes

This recipe uses buttermilk to produce a moist and delicious cornbread that's light on fat but not on flavor. It is best served on the day it is made, preferably warm from the oven. Serve it with soups, stews, or chili, or just eat it as a snack.

1½ cups yellow cornmeal
1 cup all-purpose flour
2 tablespoons granulated sugar
1½ teaspoons baking powder
½ teaspoon baking soda
¼ teaspoon salt
2 cups buttermilk or plain low-fat yogurt, stirred to liquefy
1 cup fresh, canned, or thawed frozen corn
3 tablespoons vegetable oil
3 medium-size jalapeño peppers, seeded and chopped fine
12 fresh sage leaves (optional)

1. Heat the oven to 400°F. Place a 9- to 10-inch ovenproof skillet in the oven.

2. In a large bowl, mix the cornmeal, flour, sugar, baking powder, baking soda, and salt until blended.

3. Stir in the buttermilk, then the corn, oil, and jalapeños until well blended.

4. Remove the hot skillet from the oven and lightly coat with vegetable oil cooking spray. Pour in the batter and arrange the sage leaves on top.

5. Bake for 30 minutes, or until a toothpick inserted in the center comes out clean. Cool in the skillet. Serve slightly warm.

Makes 8 wedges. Per wedge: 260 cal, 7 g pro, 43 g car, 6 g fat with buttermilk, 7 g fat with yogurt, 3 mg chol, 306 mg sod with buttermilk, 281 mg sod with yogurt

COCONUT–BANANA BREAD

Makes 1 loaf
Preparation time: 15 minutes
Baking time: 50 minutes plus cooling

The addition of coconut gives a chewy texture and tropical flavor to this old-fashioned favorite. It's a great way to use bananas that have ripened too much. In fact, this bread is so good it's worth letting a few bananas turn brown so you have an excuse to make it. For a decorative touch, sprinkle the top of the loaf with a little extra coconut before baking.

1½ cups all-purpose flour
½ cup toasted wheat germ
1 teaspoon baking powder
1 teaspoon baking soda
¼ teaspoon salt
½ cup (1 stick) butter, at room temperature
½ cup packed light brown sugar
2 large eggs
3 medium-size ripe bananas, peeled and mashed (1½ cups)
½ cup plain low-fat yogurt
1 cup flaked coconut

1. Heat the oven to 350°F. Grease a 9 x 5-inch loaf pan.

2. In a medium-size bowl, mix the flour, wheat germ, baking powder, baking soda, and salt.

3. In a large bowl, beat the butter and sugar with an electric mixer until pale and fluffy. Add the eggs one at a time, beating well after each addition. Beat in the bananas and yogurt until blended.

4. With a rubber spatula, gently stir in the flour mixture just to blend. Stir in the coconut.

5. Scrape the batter into the prepared pan. Bake for about 50 minutes, or until a toothpick inserted near the center comes out clean. Set the pan on a wire rack to cool for 10 minutes. Turn the bread out onto the rack and let cool completely before slicing.

Makes 16 slices. Per slice: 191 cal, 4 g pro, 25 g car, 9 g fat, 42 mg chol, 230 mg sod

NO CRACKS

It's okay for quick-bread loaves (leavened with baking powder or soda) to crack along the center of the top surface while baking; this only indicates that the bread expanded while baking. To eliminate the crack for appearance's sake, let the batter rise slightly in the loaf pan for 20 minutes at room temperature before baking.

MAKE AHEAD

Wrap the cooled baked bread in plastic wrap and store at room temperature up to 1 week. To freeze, put the wrapped bread in a plastic zipper-type freezer bag or double wrap with foil and freeze up to 1 month. Thaw at room temperature.

EASY • MAKE AHEAD

ZUCCHINI LEMON BREAD

Makes 1 loaf
Preparation time: 15 minutes
Baking time: 50 minutes plus cooling

Here's a good way to use the abundant zucchini supply that gardeners and farm stands always have at the end of the season. Because zucchini adds moisture to quick breads and muffins, they remain fresh up to 1 week. This bread is delicious for breakfast and makes a great healthy snack for kids.

1 cup all-purpose flour
1⅓ cups whole wheat flour
2 teaspoons baking powder
½ teaspoon baking soda
¼ teaspoon salt
¼ teaspoon ground ginger
¼ teaspoon ground nutmeg
2 large eggs
3 tablespoons vegetable oil
1 cup sugar
2 tablespoons lemon juice
1 cup packed shredded zucchini (1 medium zucchini)
1 tablespoon grated lemon peel

1. Heat the oven to 350°F. Grease a 9 x 5 inch loaf pan.

2. In a large bowl, mix both flours, the baking powder, baking soda, salt, ginger, and nutmeg.

3. In a medium-size bowl, beat the eggs, oil, sugar, and lemon juice until well blended. Stir in the zucchini and lemon peel.

4. Add the zucchini mixture to the flour mixture, stirring just until moist. Spoon the batter into the prepared pan.

5. Bake for 45 to 50 minutes, or until a toothpick inserted near the center comes out clean. Set the pan on a wire rack to cool for 10 minutes. Turn the bread out onto the rack and cool completely.

Makes 16 slices. Per slice: 148 cal, 3 g pro, 26 g car, 4 g fat, 27 mg chol, 143 mg sod

VARIATION

WHOLE WHEAT ZUCCHINI LEMON MUFFINS

• Grease twelve 2½-inch muffin cups or line them with foil (not paper) liners. Fill the cups ¾ full with the batter.

• Bake at 375°F for 15 to 20 minutes, or until a toothpick inserted into the center comes out clean.

• Set the pan on a wire rack to cool for 5 minutes. Turn the muffins out onto the rack and cool completely.

Makes 12 muffins. Per muffin: 204 cal, 4 g pro, 35 g car, 6 g fat, 35 mg chol, 191 mg sod

• EASY • MAKE AHEAD

MAKE AHEAD

Wrap the cooled baked bread in plastic wrap and store at room temperature up to 1 week. To freeze, put the wrapped bread in a plastic zipper-type freezer bag or double wrap with foil and freeze up to 1 month.

APRICOT NUT BREAD

Makes 1 loaf
Preparation time: 15 minutes
Baking time: 13 minutes plus 10 minutes to stand

Although this is technically a bread, the apricots impart such a naturally sweet flavor you can serve it as you would a cake. For extra flavor, serve with raspberry or strawberry jam. Use a light touch when mixing the dry and wet ingredients together. They should be mixed just until the dry ingredients are moistened. Don't overbeat or the bread will be dense and tough.

1½ cups dried apricots (8 ounces), snipped into small pieces
1 cup water
2½ cups all-purpose flour
½ cup granulated sugar
1 tablespoon baking powder
½ teaspoon baking soda
½ teaspoon salt
1 cup buttermilk
1 large egg, lightly beaten
2 tablespoons vegetable oil
½ cup pecans, chopped coarse

1. Lightly grease a 2-quart microwave-safe Bundt pan.

2. In a 4-cup microwave-safe measure, combine the apricots and water. Microwave uncovered on High for 3 to 4 minutes, stirring once, until the apricots are tender. Drain and reserve the apricots; discard the liquid.

3. In a medium-size bowl, mix the flour, sugar, baking powder, baking soda, and salt. Stir in the buttermilk, egg, and oil until just blended. Stir in the nuts and apricots. Spread the batter evenly in the prepared pan.

4. Place the pan on a microwave-safe trivet or inverted saucer. Microwave uncovered on High for 8 to 9 minutes, rotating the pan ¼ turn twice, until a toothpick inserted near the center of the bread comes out clean. Remove the pan from the microwave and let stand directly on a heatproof surface for about 10 minutes. Invert the bread onto a wire rack to cool completely.

Makes 16 slices. Per slice: 180 cal, 4 g pro, 31 g car, 5 g fat, 14 mg chol, 221 mg sod

COOK'S TIP

If you do not have a Bundt pan, use a deep 2-quart microwave-safe casserole or baking dish with a greased straight-sided glass jar or bottle, at least 4 inches high and 2 inches in diameter. Place the jar, open end up, in the center of the casserole. Spread the batter in the casserole and proceed with the recipe as directed. After baking, allow the bread to settle for 10 minutes before removing the jar and inverting the bread to cool.

EASY • 30 MINUTES

BASIC MUFFIN BATTER

Makes 12 muffins
Preparation time: 10 minutes
Baking time: 17 minutes plus cooling

Muffins lend themselves to every variation in the book, but why look up a different recipe each time you want something different? Here's a basic recipe, with four scrumptious variations, that can take you to the limits of your culinary imagination. Choose Apple-Almond, Spicy Mincemeat, Chocolate-Cream and Cinnamon, Cranberry, Cranberry Upside-Down, or Pumpkin-Streusel muffins, or be creative and invent a variation of your own.

2 cups all-purpose flour
2 teaspoons baking powder
1 teaspoon baking soda
½ teaspoon salt
½ cup (1 stick) butter or margarine, at room temperature
½ cup granulated sugar
2 large eggs
½ cup buttermilk

1. Get out the additional ingredients you need for the variation you've chosen (see Muffin Variations, page 316).

2. Heat the oven to 375°F. Grease twelve 2½-inch muffin cups or line with foil (not paper) baking cups.

3. In a small bowl, combine the flour, baking powder, baking soda, and salt.

4. In a large bowl with an electric mixer, beat the butter and sugar until pale and fluffy. Beat in the eggs and buttermilk until blended. Stir in the flour mixture just until blended.

5. Follow the directions for the variation you have chosen and divide the batter among the muffin cups.

6. Bake for 15 to 17 minutes, or until a toothpick inserted into the center of a muffin comes out clean. Set the pan on a wire rack to cool for 5 minutes. Turn the muffins out onto the rack and cool completely.

MUFFIN VARIATIONS

APPLE-ALMOND MUFFINS

◆ Crumble 1 can (8 ounces) or 1 roll (7 ounces) almond paste (marzipan) on top of the basic batter and stir in with 1 cup of finely chopped peeled apple.

◆ Divide the batter among the muffin cups and top each with 2 thin slices of apple. Bake as directed. Brush the muffin tops with 2 tablespoons of warmed honey and cool as directed.

Per muffin: 309 cal, 6 g pro, 39 g car, 15 g fat, 56 mg chol with butter, 36 mg chol with margarine, 379 mg sod with butter, 390 mg sod with margarine

SPICY MINCEMEAT MUFFINS

◆ Stir 1 cup mincemeat (from a jar) and ¼ teaspoon ground allspice into the basic batter.

◆ Divide the batter among the muffin cups. Bake and cool as directed.

Per muffin: 250 cal, 4 g pro, 37 g car, 10 g fat, 57 mg chol with butter, 36 mg chol with margarine, 339 mg sod

CHOCOLATE-CREAM AND CINNAMON MUFFINS

◆ Add 1 teaspoon ground cinnamon to the flour mixture in step 2 of the basic muffin batter recipe. Stir 1 cup of melted semisweet chocolate chips into the batter after adding the flour

and buttermilk. Divide the batter among the muffin cups. Cut 4 ounces of light cream cheese (Neufchâtel) into small pieces and divide among the muffins, gently pressing into the batter. Sprinkle with 2 tablespoons sugar mixed with ½ teaspoon ground cinnamon. Bake and cool as directed.

Per muffin: 299 cal, 5 g pro, 37 g car, 15 g fat, 61 mg chol with butter, 40 mg chol with margarine, 422 mg sod with butter, 433 mg sod with margarine

CRANBERRY MUFFINS

◆ Mix ¾ cup whole-berry cranberry sauce, ¼ cup chopped pecans, 2 tablespoons granulated sugar, and ¾ teaspoon grated nutmeg into the basic batter.

◆ Divide the batter among the muffin cups and top each with 1 pecan half. Bake and cool as directed.

Per muffin: 259 cal, 4 g pro, 34 g car, 12 g fat, 56 mg chol with butter, 36 mg chol with margarine, 382 mg sod with butter, 394 mg sod with margarine.

CRANBERRY UPSIDE-DOWN MUFFINS

◆ Thoroughly grease muffin pan cups (do not line with paper cups). Mix ¾ cup whole-berry cranberry sauce, ¼ cup chopped pecans, 2 tablespoons granulated sugar, and ¼ teaspoon grated nutmeg until well blended.

◆ Divide the mixture among the muffin cups. Press 1 pecan half, top side down, into the cranberries. Add ½ teaspoon grated nutmeg to the flour in step 2 of the basic batter. Divide the batter among the muffin cups and spread gently to cover the cranberries. Bake as directed. Turn out the muffins after cooling in the pan for 15 minutes.

Per muffin: 251 cal, 4 g pro, 34 g car, 11 g fat, 57 mg chol with butter, 36 mg chol with margarine, 277 mg sod

PUMPKIN-STREUSEL MUFFINS

◆ Make the streusel topping: In a small bowl, mix 3 tablespoons cold butter or margarine, cut into small pieces, with ⅓ cup all-purpose flour, 3 tablespoons light or dark brown sugar, and ⅓ cup finely chopped pecans until crumbly. Set the topping aside.

◆ In a medium-size bowl, mix ⅔ cup solid-pack pumpkin, ¼ cup packed light or dark brown sugar, 2 tablespoons molasses, 1 teaspoon pumpkin-pie spice, and 1 teaspoon freshly grated orange peel until well blended. Stir into the basic batter.

◆ Divide the batter among the muffin cups and top with streusel topping. Bake and cool as directed.

Per muffin: 305 cal, 4 g pro, 40 g car, 15 g fat, 64 mg chol with butter, 36 mg chol with margarine, 412 mg sod with butter, 427 mg sod with margarine

EASY • 30 MINUTES • MICROWAVE

CURRANT BRAN MUFFINS

Makes 6 to 12 muffins
Preparation time: 10 minutes
Cooking time: 4 minutes

Start the day out right with these quick and easy bran muffins. Studded with walnuts and currants, they will inspire even the busiest member of your family to make time for breakfast. A currant, like a raisin, is a dried grape, the tiny Zante grape. If stored in an airtight container in a cool, dry place, currants and raisins will keep indefinitely.

1 cup all-purpose flour
½ cup whole wheat flour
1 teaspoon baking soda
1 teaspoon ground cinnamon
½ teaspoon ground ginger
½ teaspoon salt
1 cup plain low-fat yogurt
¼ cup vegetable oil
1 large egg
¼ cup packed dark brown sugar
⅓ cup Zante currants

1. Line each cup of a microwave-safe muffin pan or six 6-ounce custard cups with 2 paper (not foil) baking cups.

2. In a food processor, combine both flours, baking soda, cinnamon, ginger, and salt. Process a few seconds to mix.

3. Add the yogurt, oil, egg, and sugar and process until smooth, scraping down the sides of the container once.

4. Sprinkle the currants over the batter. Pulse the processor on/off 4 or 5 times, just until the currants are mixed in.

5. Fill the prepared cups half full, using about 2 tablespoons batter for each.

6. Arrange the custard cups in a circle in the microwave oven. Microwave uncovered on High for 2 to 3 minutes, rearranging the cups or rotating the muffin pan ¼ turn twice, until the tops spring back when gently pressed. (The tops of the muffins may have a few moist spots, which will dry during the standing time.)

7. Remove the muffins from the pan (discard outer paper liners) or cups and set on a wire rack. Let stand for 3 minutes. Serve warm.

Per muffin: 152 cal, 3 g pro, 21 g car, 7 g fat, 19 mg chol, 217 mg sod

STREUSEL COFFEE CAKE

Serves 10

Preparation time: 20 minutes

Baking time: 1 hour

A cinnamon-spiced streusel crowns this moist and tender cake. It is baked in a springform pan (with a removable bottom) so it can be presented without disrupting the topping. Light or nonfat sour cream may be used in place of the regular sour cream.

STREUSEL TOPPING

⅔ cup all-purpose flour

⅔ cup packed light brown sugar

¾ teaspoon ground cinnamon

⅛ teaspoon ground nutmeg

¼ cup (½ stick) cold butter, cut into small pieces

½ cup toasted walnuts, chopped (optional)

2 cups all-purpose flour

1½ teaspoons baking powder

¾ teaspoon baking soda

¼ teaspoon salt

½ cup (1 stick) butter, at room temperature

¾ cup granulated sugar

2 large eggs

1½ teaspoons vanilla extract

1 cup sour cream

1. Heat the oven to 350°F. Lightly grease a 9-inch springform pan.

2. Make the streusel: In a medium-size bowl, mix the flour, brown sugar, cinnamon, and nutmeg. Cut in the butter with a pastry blender until the mixture resembles coarse crumbs.

3. In another medium-size bowl, mix the flour, baking powder, baking soda, and salt.

4. In a large bowl, beat the butter and sugar with an electric mixer until pale and fluffy. Beat in the eggs one at a time, beating well after each addition. Beat in the vanilla. Gently stir in the flour mixture alternately with the sour cream, beginning and ending with the flour, until well blended.

5. Spread half of the mixture over the bottom of the prepared pan. Sprinkle with ½ cup of streusel. Spread the remaining batter over the top of

MAKE AHEAD

Store the baked, cooled coffee cake in an airtight container at room temperature for 1 day or refrigerate up to 5 days.

the streusel. Add the walnuts to the remaining streusel mixture and sprinkle it over the top of the cake. With the back of a spoon, lightly pat the topping into the batter.

6. Bake for 55 minutes to 1 hour, or until a cake tester inserted near the center of the cake comes out clean. Set the pan on a wire rack to cool for 10 minutes, then remove the sides of the pan. Let cool for 30 minutes before serving.

Makes 10 slices. Per slice: 428 cal, 6 g pro, 56 g car, 20 g fat, 90 mg chol, 393 mg sod

---

MAKE AHEAD • CLASSIC

APPLE–ALMOND COFFEE CAKE

Serves 8

Preparation time: 20 minutes

Baking time: 1 hour and 15 minutes plus cooling

This coffee cake layered with apples and almonds is sweet enough for dessert, although it is also delicious with morning coffee or afternoon tea.

2 medium-size Granny Smith, Braeburn, Golden Delicious, or
    Winesap apples
2 cups all-purpose flour
2¼ teaspoons baking powder
¼ teaspoon salt
½ cup (1 stick) butter or margarine, at room temperature
1 cup granulated sugar
½ cup milk
2 large eggs
1½ teaspoons vanilla extract
½ teaspoon almond extract
⅓ cup apple jelly, stirred over low heat until smooth
1 tablespoon sliced almonds

1. Heat the oven to 450°F. Lightly grease and flour an 8 x 3-inch springform pan. Shake out the excess flour.

2. Peel, quarter, and core the apples. Cut each apple quarter into ½-inch-thick wedges.

3. Electric mixer method: In a large bowl, mix the flour, sugar, baking powder, and salt until blended. Add butter and beat with the mixer on low until fine crumbs form. Add milk, then eggs and extracts, and beat on medium speed for 2 minutes, or until smooth.   ▶

VARIATION

PEAR-ALMOND COFFEE CAKE:

Omit the apples. Peel, core and slice 2 medium-size ripe pears such as Anjou or Bartlett. Proceed with the recipe from step 1, substituting the pears for the apples.

Per slice: 416 cal, 6 g pro, 66 g car, 15 g fat, 86 mg chol with butter, 55 mg chol with margarine, 350 mg sod with butter, 367 mg sod with margarine

• MAKE AHEAD

Food processor method: In a food processor, combine the flour, sugar, baking powder, and salt and pulse on/off 4 or 5 times to mix. Add the butter and process until very fine crumbs form. With the motor running, pour the milk, then the eggs and extracts through the feed tube. Process for 1 minute, scraping down the side of the bowl once, or until smooth.

4. Spread the batter in the prepared pan. Arrange the apple wedges overlapping slightly in a circular pattern over the batter. Brush the apples with half the apple jelly. Sprinkle the almonds around the edge and in the center.

5. Bake for 15 minutes. Reduce the oven temperature to 350°F. Bake for 50 to 60 minutes longer, or until a cake tester inserted near the center comes out clean. (The cake will rise higher in the center.)

6. Set the pan on a wire rack to cool for 15 minutes, then remove the side of the pan. Brush the top of the cake with the remaining apple jelly. Cool completely on the rack. Serve at room temperature.

Makes 8 slices. Per slice: 410 cal, 6 g pro, 65 g car, 15 g fat, 86 mg chol with butter, 55 mg chol with margarine, 350 mg sod with butter, 367 mg sod with margarine

---

EASY • 60 MINUTES • CLASSIC

POPOVER PANCAKE WITH PLUMS

Serves 4
Preparation time: 15 minutes
Baking time: 40 minutes

Known in some areas as a Dutch Baby, this spectacular breakfast pancake can also be served simply dusted with confectioners' sugar or with pancake syrup.

1 tablespoon vegetable oil
4 large eggs
⅔ cup all-purpose flour
⅔ cup milk
1½ tablespoons cold butter or margarine, cut into small pieces

SAUTÉED PLUMS
1 tablespoon butter or margarine
1½ pounds ripe black plums (such as Black Beauty, Black Amber, or Friar), pitted and cut into wedges (about 6 cups)
¼ cup granulated sugar
½ teaspoon ground cinnamon

Confectioners' sugar (optional)

MAKE AHEAD

Store the baked, cooled coffee cake in an airtight container at room temperature up to 3 days or refrigerate up to 5 days.

THE HEAT IS ON

Help to keep pancakes, waffles, and French toast warm by serving them with warmed maple syrup. Heat a glass container of maple syrup by placing it a pan of hot water over low heat, or pour the syrup into a pan and heat directly. To microwave, heat ½ cup of maple syrup on High for 30 to 60 seconds, stirring once.

1. Heat the oven to 450°F. Pour the oil into a 9-inch metal pie pan. Heat in the oven for 5 minutes.

2. Meanwhile, in a blender or a food processor, combine the eggs, flour, milk, and butter and process until well blended. Scrape down the side of the bowl and process for 30 seconds longer.

3. Pour the batter into the hot pan and bake without opening the oven door for 20 minutes, or until the pancake has puffed up high around the edges. Reduce the oven temperature to 350°F and bake for 20 minutes longer, or until the sides are crisp.

4. Meanwhile, prepare the plums. In a large skillet, melt the butter over medium-high heat. Add the plums, sugar, and cinnamon. Cook for 4 minutes, stirring often, until the plums are softened.

5. Remove the pancake from the oven and dust with confectioners' sugar. Spoon the plums into the center. Cut the pancake into wedges and serve warm from the pan.

Per serving: 406 cal, 11 g pro, 52 g car, 18 g fat, 238 mg chol with butter, 218 mg chol with margarine, 157 mg sod with butter, 167 mg sod with margarine

---

EASY • 30 MINUTES • MAKE AHEAD • CLASSIC

BUTTERMILK PANCAKES

Makes 12 pancakes
Preparation time: 10 minutes
Cooking time: 15 minutes

These are the most versatile of pancakes, lending themselves to many variations and toppings. The addition of buttermilk gives them a light, tender texture. This recipe can be easily doubled, so you can freeze some pancakes for another meal.

2 cups all-purpose flour
2 tablespoons granulated sugar
2 teaspoons baking powder
½ teaspoon salt
1½ cups buttermilk
¼ cup vegetable oil
2 large eggs
For topping: butter and maple syrup or honey

1. Heat the oven to 200°F. In a medium-size bowl, mix the flour, sugar, baking powder, and salt.

VARIATION

BERRY BUTTERMILK PANCAKES

Prepare the batter as directed, adding 2 cups of fresh or frozen small blueberries or raspberries to the batter. Cook as directed.

• **EASY • 30 MINUTES**
• **MAKE AHEAD**

▶

2. In a 4-cup measure, beat the buttermilk, oil, and eggs with a fork until blended. Add to the flour mixture and stir just until smooth.

3. Heat a lightly greased griddle or large heavy skillet over medium–high heat until hot, or until a few drops of water dance on the surface.

4. Stir the batter. For each pancake, pour about ¼ cup of batter onto the hot griddle. Cook for about 2 minutes, or until the tops are covered with bubbles and the edges look dry. (Before turning the pancakes, lift the edges to check that the undersides are golden brown.) Turn the pancakes and cook for 1 to 2 minutes more, or until the undersides are golden brown. Transfer the pancakes to a heatproof plate or baking sheet, loosely cover with foil, and keep warm in the oven. Repeat with the remaining batter.

Per pancake without topping: 159 cal, 4 g pro, 20 g car, 7 g fat, 37 mg chol, 216 mg sod

---

EASY • 30 MINUTES

OVEN–BAKED FRENCH TOAST

Serves 6
Preparation time: 10 minutes
Cooking time: 15 minutes

Serve this French toast with your favorite breakfast meat, fresh fruit, and a pitcher of warm pancake syrup or honey for a weekend breakfast. A "sunrise" drink (fill glasses with orange juice, then slowly add a couple of tablespoons of grenadine or red raspberry syrup to each) will make the occasion festive.

6 large eggs
1½ cups skim milk
1½ tablespoons confectioners' sugar
1 teaspoon vanilla extract
½ teaspoon ground cinnamon
12½-inch-thick slices firm white bread
2 tablespoons butter or margarine
Confectioners' sugar, for dusting

1. Adjust the oven racks so that one is in the lowest position and the other is in the middle. Heat the oven to 425°F. Lightly butter 2 jelly roll pans.

2. In a medium-size bowl, lightly beat the eggs with a fork. Stir in the milk, confectioners' sugar, vanilla, and cinnamon until blended.

3. Soak the bread, 1 slice at a time, in the egg mixture for about 5 minutes, or until absorbed. Place 6 soaked slices in each prepared pan. Cut the butter into small pieces and scatter over the bread.

Ⓜ AKE AHEAD

Wrap the cooled baked pancakes in plastic wrap, then place in an airtight bag and freeze up to 1 month. To serve, thaw and heat in a toaster oven or on a baking sheet in a 350°F oven for 6 minutes, or until hot. Or stack 3 frozen pancakes on a microwave-safe plate and microwave on High for 2 to 3 minutes.

4. Place 1 pan on each oven rack. Bake for 8 minutes. Turn each piece and switch the positions of the pans. Bake for 7 minutes more, or until the top is golden brown.

5. Remove the French toast to a serving platter. Dust with confectioners' sugar and serve right away.

Per serving: 295 cal, 12 g pro, 33 g car, 12 g fat, 228 mg chol with butter, 218 mg chol with margarine, 416 mg sod with butter, 422 mg sod with margarine

---

30 MINUTES • MAKE AHEAD

APPLE–OATMEAL WAFFLES

Makes 6 waffles
Preparation time: 15 minutes
Baking time: 8 minutes

These waffles, flavored with applesauce and cinnamon, are slightly chewy with the whole-grain richness of oats. Serve them with grilled ham slices for a quick weekday dinner. Make 2 batches and freeze the extra waffles, then just pop them in the toaster for breakfast.

1¼ cups all-purpose flour
¾ cup quick-cooking oats
1 teaspoon baking powder
½ teaspoon baking soda
1 cup buttermilk
2 large eggs, separated
½ cup unsweetened applesauce
2 tablespoons butter, melted
2 tablespoons light brown sugar
For topping: butter and maple syrup

1. In a large bowl, mix the flour, oats, baking powder, and baking soda.

2. In a medium-size bowl, whisk the buttermilk, egg yolks, applesauce, melted butter, and brown sugar until well blended.

3. Stir the buttermilk mixture into the dry ingredients just until combined. Let stand for 5 minutes.

4. Meanwhile, in a small bowl, beat the egg whites with an electric mixer until soft peaks form when the beaters are lifted. With a rubber spatula, gently stir (fold) the egg whites into the batter just until combined.

5. Heat a waffle iron. Lightly grease the grids of the iron. Pour ½ to ⅔ cup of the batter (or the amount recommended by the manufacturer) ▶

WHICH OATS?

Use the specific type of oat called for in a recipe.

◆ Rolled or old-fashioned oats: These oats are steamed, then flattened into flakes. They take the longest to cook, about 15 minutes, and have the firmest texture.

◆ Quick-cooking oats: These oats are cut into several pieces before steaming and flattening. They cook in about 5 minutes and have a tender texture.

◆ Instant oats: These oats are cut into very small pieces and pre-cooked, then dried. They cannot be substituted in any recipes calling for rolled or quick-cooking oats.

into the center of the grids, spreading almost to the corners. Close the lid and bake according to the manufacturer's instructions, or until the iron opens easily. Transfer the waffles to the oven, placing them directly on the oven rack so they will remain crisp. Repeat with the remaining batter.

6. Place the waffles on warm serving plates and top with butter and maple syrup. Serve right away.

Per waffle without topping: 249 cal, 8 g pro, 36 g car, 8 g fat, 83 mg chol, 242 mg sod

> ⓜ**AKE AHEAD**
>
> Wrap the cooled baked waffles individually in plastic, place in a zipper-type food storage bag, and freeze up to 3 months.

DRESS UP PANCAKES AND WAFFLES

The next time you serve pancakes or waffles, try some of these suggestions for perking them up:

◆ **Banana:** Add mashed banana and a little lemon juice and sugar to the batter and top with maple syrup or honey or sprinkle with a little confectioners' sugar.

◆ **Ham and Cheese:** Add grated sharp cheese and finely chopped baked ham to the batter and top with butter and maple syrup.

◆ **Zucchini Cheddar:** Add shredded zucchini and cheddar cheese to the batter and top with butter and syrup.

◆ **Honey Nut:** Add finely chopped pecans, walnuts, or toasted almonds and a little honey to the batter and top with maple syrup.

◆ **Spice:** Add a little cinnamon, ground allspice, and grated nutmeg to the batter and top with maple syrup or applesauce.

◆ **Apple:** Add finely chopped apple and a little brown sugar to the batter and top with butter and maple syrup

◆ **Bacon:** Add crumbled crisp bacon to the batter, top with maple syrup, and serve with eggs.

◆ **Corn:** Stir up a batch of packaged corn muffin mix and cook it in your waffle iron. Top with chili, salsa, or creamed chicken, or drizzle with syrup and serve with ham steaks.

Flavored butters (also called compound butters) will not only perk up any pancake up or waffle, but are just as sensational spread onto slices of warm bread or muffins. Prepare the butters as follows: In a medium-size bowl, mix the ingredients by hand or with an electric mixer. Use right away, or wrap with waxed paper and chill. Flavored butters also freeze well—up to 2 months wrapped in waxed paper.

◆ **Herb Butter:** 4 tablespoons minced fresh herbs (chives, oregano, thyme, parsley, basil) and 1/2 cup (1 stick) butter, at room temperature.

◆ **Fruit Butter:** 3 to 4 tablespoons fruit jam or preserves of choice with 1/2 cup (1 stick) unsalted butter, at room temperature.

◆ **Citrus Butter:** 2 teaspoons freshly squeezed orange or lemon juice, 1 teaspoon grated zest, and 1/2 cup (1 stick) butter, at room temperature.

◆ **Nut Butter:** 1/2 cup very finely chopped toasted nuts of choice (almonds, walnut, hazelnuts) and 1/2 cup (1 stick) butter, at room temperature.

◆ **Curried Chutney Butter:** 1/4 cup mango chutney, 1 teaspoon curry powder, and 1/2 cup (1 stick) butter, at room temperature.

◆ **Honey-Dijon Butter:** 2 tablespoons Dijon mustard, 1 tablespoon honey, and 1/2 cup (1 stick) butter, at room temperature.

◆ **Maple Syrup Butter:** 2 to 3 tablespoons pure maple syrup and 1/2 cup (1 stick) unsalted butter at room temperature.

◆ **Lemon-Parsley Butter:** 2 tablespoons chopped fresh parsley, 1 teaspoon lemon juice, and 1/2 cup (1 stick) butter, at room temperature.

◆ **Orange Marmalade Butter:** 1/4 cup orange marmalade and 1/2 cup (1 stick) unsalted butter, at room temperature.

◆ **Berry Butter:** 1/2 cup fresh or frozen raspberries, blueberries, or strawberries, 2 tablespoons confectioner's sugar, and 1/2 cup (1 stick) unsalted butter.

SOUPS

> *"Soup, beautiful soup"*
> LEWIS CARROLL

There is nothing more satisfying than a bowl of homemade soup. But don't be misled into thinking that it takes endless preparation and long, slow cooking to prepare. The recipes in this chapter use a wide range of fresh and prepared ingredients, canned broth, and some short-cut methods to create a selection of easy-to-prepare, flavorful soups.

In winter, choose one of the hearty meat or bean soups and serve with crusty bread for a complete meal. When you need an interesting starter, try a lighter cream soup or chowder. And when the days are hot, choose from the selection of chilled puréed soups. However you serve it, soup fits into many menus, from the central theme to a sumptuous supporting role.

SQUASH & BEEF SOUP

Serves 6 to 8
Preparation time: 10 minutes
Cooking time: 1 hour 20 minutes

In the autumn months, take advantage of the wonderful selection of winter squash available at produce stands and supermarkets and make this hearty and colorful soup. With crusty French bread, you have a meal in a bowl.

2 tablespoons vegetable oil
12 ounces well-trimmed boneless beef chuck, cut into ½-inch pieces
1½ cups chopped onions
1½ cups thinly sliced celery
2 pounds winter squash (buttercup, butternut, or kabocha), peeled, seeded, and cut into ½-inch chunks (6 cups)
1 can (28 ounces) whole tomatoes in juice, undrained
2 cups beef broth
1 cup water
1 teaspoon salt
1 teaspoon dried basil leaves, crumbled
¾ teaspoon dried oregano leaves, crumbled
¼ teaspoon ground black pepper
1 package (10 ounces) frozen corn kernels

1. In a 4- to 5-quart pot, heat 1 tablespoon of the oil over medium-high heat.

2. Add the beef and cook for about 6 minutes, stirring occasionally, or until browned on all sides. Remove with a slotted spoon to a plate.

3. Heat the remaining 1 tablespoon of oil in the pot. Add the onions and celery. Cook over medium-low heat for about 10 minutes, stirring occasionally to scrape up the browned bits on the bottom, or until the onion is soft.

4. Return the beef to the pot. Add the remaining ingredients except the corn. Cover and simmer for about 45 minutes, stirring occasionally, or until the beef is tender.

5. Add the corn, cover and simmer for 8 to 10 minutes, or until the corn is heated through.

Makes 11 cups. Per 1 cup: 150 cal, 9 g pro, 20 g car, 5 g fat, 20 mg chol, 361 mg sod

---

MAKE AHEAD

Cool the soup to room temperature, then refrigerate in an airtight container up to 3 days.

VARIATION

MICROWAVE SQUASH & BEEF SOUP

• Omit the oil. Put the onions and 1½ cups broth in a deep 3- to 4-quart microwave-safe casserole. Cover with the lid or vented plastic wrap. Microwave on High for 3 to 4 minutes, or until simmering.

• Stir in the beef and ¾ cup water. Cover and microwave on medium for 30 to 35 minutes, or until the meat is almost tender, stirring 3 times and making sure the meat is submerged in the liquid.

• Add the remaining ingredients except the tomatoes and corn. Cover and microwave for on high 6 to 8

minutes, stirring twice,
until the squash is
crisp-tender.
• Add the tomatoes
and corn. Cover and
microwave on High
for 5 to 6 minutes, stir-
ring twice, until the
vegetables are tender.
Let stand, covered, for
10 minutes.

Per 1 cup: 128 cal, 9 g
pro, 19 g car, 3 g fat, 20
mg chol, 361 mg sod

• LOW FAT
• MAKE AHEAD
• ONE POT

COOK'S TIP

To reduce the fat

content of canned

broth, store it in the

refrigerator so the fat

will congeal and be

easy to remove from

the surface before

using.

EASY • LOW FAT • ONE POT • CLASSIC

BEEF BORSCHT

Serves 4
Preparation time: 15 minutes
Cooking time: 2 hours 30 minutes

This soup, which originated in Russia and Poland, has many variations but will always include a healthy quantity of beets, giving it its vibrant color. Thick slices of dark rye are the traditional bread accompaniment, but any whole-grain variety will do.

1½ cups beef broth
1½ cups water
1 pound well-trimmed boneless beef chuck, cut into 1-inch pieces
1 large onion, chopped (1 cup)
2 medium-size all-purpose potatoes, cut into 1-inch chunks (2 cups)
2 cans (16 ounces each) sliced beets, drained
8 ounces green cabbage, coarsely shredded (4 cups)
½ teaspoon salt
½ teaspoon ground black pepper
1 tablespoon plus 1 teaspoon red wine vinegar
¼ cup chopped fresh dill
For garnish: sour cream and fresh dill sprigs (optional)

1. In a 5- to 6-quart pot, bring the broth, water, beef, and onion to a boil over medium-high heat. Reduce the heat to low. Cover and simmer for 1½ hours, stirring occasionally.

2. Stir in the potatoes. Cover and simmer for 20 to 30 minutes, stirring occasionally, or until the potatoes are almost tender.

3. Add the beets, cabbage, salt, pepper, and vinegar. Cover and simmer for 20 to 30 minutes, stirring occasionally, or until the beef and vegetables are tender when tested with a fork.

4. Remove the pan from the heat and stir in the dill. Ladle the soup into bowls and garnish with sour cream and dill sprigs. Serve right away.

Makes 8 cups. Per 2 cups: 313 cal, 27 g pro, 33 g car, 9 g fat, 74 mg chol, 750 mg sod

ASIAN MEATBALL SOUP

Serves 6
Preparation time: 15 minutes
Cooking time: 33 minutes

These meatballs taste like pork dumplings without the wrappers. When you serve the soup, set out bottles of soy sauce, dark Asian sesame oil, and hot-pepper sauce for those who'd like to add extra flavor. Bok choy is a variety of Chinese cabbage. It has long celery-like stalks and large green leaves.

MEATBALLS

12 ounces ground pork
2 tablespoons sliced scallions
2 teaspoons minced peeled fresh gingerroot
1 teaspoon minced fresh garlic
½ teaspoon salt

2 teaspoons vegetable oil
8 cups water
2 packages (3 ounces each) beef-flavor Oriental noodles with seasoning packet
2 medium-size carrots, halved lengthwise, cut into sticks
½ teaspoon minced peeled fresh gingerroot
½ teaspoon minced fresh garlic
1 pound bok choy, chopped coarse (8 cups)
1 cup sliced scallions
1 can (14 ounces) baby corn, drained and cut in half crosswise
1 teaspoon dark Asian sesame oil

1. Make the meatballs: In a medium-size bowl, mix the pork, scallions, gingerroot, garlic, and salt with your hands or a wooden spoon until blended. Form into 30 balls.

2. In a 5- to 6-quart pot, heat the oil over medium heat. Add the meatballs and cook for 8 to 10 minutes, turning often, or until browned on all sides and no longer pink in the centers. Remove with a slotted spoon to a plate. Pour off any fat from the pot.

3. Add the water, contents of the seasoning packets, the carrots, ginger, and garlic to the pot. Bring the mixture to a boil over medium-high heat. Reduce the heat to low. Cover and simmer for 10 to 15 minutes, or until the carrots are tender.

STORING SOUPS

Many soups taste much better the second or third day, giving the flavors time to fully develop. Store cooled soups in the refrigerator. Chilling some soups will thicken them. To thin, add some extra stock, broth, water, cream, milk, or vegetable juice that was used to make the soup.

4. Add the bok choy, scallions, baby corn, and sesame oil. Cover and simmer for 3 to 5 minutes, or until the bok choy is almost tender.

5. Break the noodles in half and add to the pot. Cover and simmer for 2 to 3 minutes, or until tender. Serve right away.

Makes 12 cups. Per 2 cups: 312 cal, 15 g pro, 26 g car, 16 g fat, 37 mg chol, 961 mg sod

---

EASY • LOW FAT • CLASSIC

CHICKEN NOODLE SOUP

Serves 6
Preparation time: 12 minutes
Cooking time: 55 minutes

This hearty main-dish soup has a homey, cooked-for-hours flavor even though it takes just one. If you like, remove the chicken skin before cooking.

1 (3¼-pound) broiler-fryer chicken, quartered
4 cups chicken broth
4 cups water
2 medium-size carrots, cut into 1-inch pieces
1½ cups sliced celery
1 cup coarsely chopped onion
1 package (8 ounces) broad egg noodles
¼ cup chopped fresh parsley

1. In a 4- to 5- quart pot, bring the chicken, chicken broth, and water to a boil over high heat. Reduce the heat to medium-low. Cover and simmer for 20 to 25 minutes.

2. Add the carrots, celery, and onion. Cover and simmer for 15 to 20 minutes, or until the chicken is no longer pink near the bone. Using a slotted spoon, remove the chicken to a plate. Skim off all the fat from the soup.

3. Stir in the noodles. Increase the heat to medium and cook uncovered for 8 to 10 minutes, or until the noodles are tender.

4. Meanwhile, when the chicken is cool enough to handle, remove and discard the skin. Pull the meat from the bones and tear into bite-size pieces. Stir the meat and parsley into the soup. Serve right away.

Makes 12 cups. Per 2 cups: 327 cal, 34 g pro, 34 g car, 7 g fat, 119 mg chol, 212 mg sod

30 MINUTES • CLASSIC

TORTILLA SOUP

Serves 6
Preparation time: 10 minutes
Cooking time: 20 minutes

A bowl of steaming soup is the traditional start to a Mexican meal. Tortilla soup is probably the most popular, possibly because it's one of the easiest to prepare. Full of chicken and vegetables and topped with crispy tortilla strips, this spicy soup makes an excellent opener to a simple entree.

10 corn tortillas
1 tablespoon vegetable oil
1 medium-size onion, minced (½ cup)
1 teaspoon minced fresh garlic
8 cups chicken broth
2 cups diced cooked chicken
½ teaspoon ground cumin
1 medium-size green bell pepper, seeded and cut into thin strips (1 cup)
2 tablespoons chopped fresh cilantro
2 medium-size tomatoes, peeled and chopped (2 cups)
1 medium-size avocado, peeled and diced (1 cup)
6 ounces Monterey Jack cheese, diced
¾ cup medium-spicy thick and chunky salsa
For garnish: sour cream (optional)

1. Heat the oven to 400°F. Spray both sides of the tortillas with vegetable oil cooking spray. Stack and cut into ½-inch-wide strips, then cut in half crosswise. Spread the strips evenly on an ungreased baking sheet and bake for 8 to 10 minutes, turning once, until crisp and brown. Remove the pan from the oven and set aside.

2. In a 4- to 6-quart pot, heat the oil over medium heat. Add the onion and garlic and cook over medium-low heat for 3 to 4 minutes, stirring often, or until softened.

3. Add the broth, chicken, and cumin. Bring to a rapid boil over high heat. Add the bell pepper. Reduce the heat to medium and boil gently for 5 minutes, or until the pepper is crisp-tender. Stir in the cilantro.

4. Divide the tortilla strips, tomatoes, avocados, cheese, and salsa among 6 bowls. Ladle the soup into the bowls and garnish with sour cream. Serve right away.

Makes 12 cups. Per 2 cups: 414 cal, 28 g pro, 31 g cal, 23 g fat, 72 mg chol, 741 mg sod

FREEZING SOUPS

Most soups can be frozen in airtight freezer containers for up to 3 months. Thaw in the refrigerator and slowly reheat to avoid overcooking the ingredients. For quick serving, freeze soup in individual portions and reheat in the microwave oven.

WHITE BEAN & CABBAGE SOUP

Serves 6

Total time: 1 hour 30 minutes plus soaking

MAKE AHEAD

Cool the soup to room temperature, then refrigerate in an airtight container for up to 1 week.

COOK'S TIP

To stretch the servings, add extra chicken broth and chopped cooked chicken, ham, or kielbasa to the soup when reheating.

Soup gains significance in the autumn and winter months, when it often ceases to be a first course and becomes a hearty one-dish meal—and this recipe surely fits the bill. Serve with a spinach and bacon salad for a comforting fireside supper.

1½ cups (10 ounces) dried small white or navy beans, picked over and soaked (see Bean Cuisine, page 341)
2 tablespoons olive oil
2 cups coarsely chopped onions
2 tablespoons minced fresh garlic
½ teaspoon dried rosemary leaves, crumbled
¼ teaspoon dried thyme leaves, crumbled
3½ cups chicken broth
3 cups water
3 medium-size russet potatoes (about 1 pound), scrubbed
1 small head green cabbage, cored
3 medium-size carrots
¾ teaspoon salt
½ teaspoon ground black pepper

1. Rinse and drain the soaked beans.

2. In a heavy 5-quart pot, heat the oil over medium heat. Add the onions and garlic and cook for about 7 minutes, stirring often, until soft. Add the rosemary and thyme and stir for 30 seconds to release the flavors. Add the broth, water, and beans. Cover and bring to a boil over high heat. Reduce the heat to medium-low and simmer for 40 minutes, or until beans are nearly tender.

3. Meanwhile, cut the unpeeled potatoes into ½-inch chunks. Coarsely chop the cabbage and dice the carrots.

4. Add the vegetables, salt, and pepper to the pot. Bring to a boil over medium-high heat. Reduce the heat to medium-low. Cover and simmer for 35 minutes, or until beans and vegetables are very tender.

5. Remove the pan from the heat and, with a potato masher or the back of a slotted spoon, mash some beans and vegetables to thicken the soup. Serve right away.

Makes 12 cups. Per 2 cups: 343 cal, 16 g pro, 60 g car, 7 g fat, 0 mg chol, 388 mg sod

EASY • LOW FAT • MAKE AHEAD • ONE POT

GREEK LENTIL SOUP

Serves 8

Preparation time: 15 minutes

Cooking time: 1 hour 20 minutes

Oregano and mint are favorite herbs in Greek cooking. Here they combine with lentils, tomatoes, and spinach for a substantial soup the family will love. Serve with a couscous salad and whole wheat pita.

2 tablespoons olive oil

2 cups chopped onions

½ cup chopped celery with leaves

2 tablespoons minced fresh garlic

8 cups water

3½ cups beef broth

2½ cups (1 pound) dried lentils, sorted and rinsed
  (see Bean Cuisine, page 341)

½ cup medium pearl barley

1 can (about 16 ounces) whole tomatoes in juice, undrained

1½ teaspoons salt

½ teaspoon ground black pepper

½ teaspoon dried mint leaves, crumbled

¼ teaspoon dried oregano leaves, crumbled

1 package (10 ounces) frozen chopped spinach

For garnish: plain yogurt (optional)

1. In a heavy 5- to 6-quart pot, heat the oil over medium heat. Add the onions, celery, and garlic. Cook for about 8 minutes, stirring occasionally, until softened.

2. Add the water, broth, lentils, and barley. Bring to a boil over high heat. Reduce the heat to low. Cover and simmer for 1 hour, or until the lentils and barley are tender.

3. Drain the juice from the canned tomatoes into the pot. Chop and add the tomatoes, salt, pepper, mint, and oregano. Bring to a boil over medium-high heat. Reduce the heat to low and simmer uncovered for 5 minutes.

4. Add the spinach and break up the frozen block with a wooden spoon. Simmer uncovered for 5 to 7 minutes, or until spinach is heated through.

5. Ladle the soup into bowls and garnish with a spoonful of yogurt. Serve right away.

Makes 16 cups. Per 2 cups: 311 cal, 20 g pro, 51 g car, 4 g fat, 0 mg chol, 548 mg sod

MAKE AHEAD

Cool the soup to room temperature, then refrigerate in an airtight container for up to 1 week.

COOK'S TIP

A cup of this soup, reheated, makes a great sauce for a bowl of cooked couscous or rice.

BLACK BEAN SOUP WITH SALSA

Serves 5

Total time: 2 hours plus soaking

MAKE AHEAD

Cool the soup to room temperature, then refrigerate in an airtight container for up to 1 week. The salsa can be made up to 1 day ahead and refrigerated in an airtight container.

COOK'S TIP

Fill taco shells with shredded lettuce and top with reheated black bean soup, shredded Monterey Jack cheese, and salsa.

This Southwestern-inspired soup is served with a colorful salsa, which adds texture and a tangy flavor. If you like a milder flavor, reduce or eliminate the ground red pepper in the soup.

2½ cups (1 pound) dried black beans, picked over and soaked
  (see Bean Cuisine, page 341)
2 tablespoons olive oil
2 cups coarsely chopped onions
1 tablespoon minced fresh garlic
1 teaspoon cumin seeds
⅛ teaspoon ground red pepper (cayenne)
3½ cups low-sodium chicken broth
2 cups water

LIME–PEPPER SALSA
1 large red bell pepper, seeded and finely chopped (1½ cups)
1 medium-size onion, finely chopped (1 cup)
4 teaspoons fresh lime juice
⅛ teaspoon salt

1 can (16 ounces) whole tomatoes in juice, undrained
½ cup uncooked small pasta, such as tubettini
½ teaspoon salt

1. Rinse and drain the soaked beans.

2. In a heavy 5-quart pot, heat the oil over medium heat. Add the onions and garlic and cook for 3 to 5 minutes, stirring often, or until softened. Stir in the cumin and ground red pepper and cook, stirring often, for 30 seconds to release the flavors.

3. Add the beans, broth, and water. Cover and bring to a boil over high heat. Reduce the heat to low. Cover and simmer for 70 to 80 minutes, or until the beans are tender.

4. Meanwhile, make the lime-pepper salsa: In a medium-size bowl, mix the bell pepper, onion, lime juice, and salt. Cover with plastic wrap and refrigerate until ready to use. ▶

5. Drain the juice from the canned tomatoes into the pot. Chop the tomatoes and add along with the pasta and ½ teaspoon salt. Bring to a boil over medium-high heat, stirring occasionally. Reduce the heat to low and simmer uncovered for about 10 minutes, stirring occasionally, or until the pasta is tender.

6. Ladle the soup into serving bowls and garnish with a spoonful of salsa (or serve the salsa separately). Serve right away.

Makes 10 cups. Per 2 cups: 482 cal, 26 g pro, 81 g car, 9 g fat, 0 mg chol, 512 mg sod

---

EASY • LOW FAT • MAKE AHEAD • ONE POT

SPLIT PEA SOUP WITH SAUSAGE

Serves 5
Preparation time: 10 minutes
Cooking time: 1 hour

Split peas are one of the quickest-cooking dried legumes and are combined here with turkey kielbasa, barley, and spinach to make a soul-satisfying soup. If time is limited, use a thawed 10-ounce package of frozen chopped spinach, kale, or turnip greens instead of the fresh spinach.

8 ounces turkey kielbasa, cut in half lengthwise, then into ½-inch slices
4 cups chicken broth
4 cups water
1 cup (7 ounces) dried yellow or green split peas, picked over
 and rinsed (see Bean Cuisine, page 341)
1 cup medium pearl barley
¾ cup coarsely chopped onion
¾ cup chopped celery
¾ teaspoon dried thyme leaves, crumbled
1 pound fresh spinach, rinsed, thick stems removed, and leaves torn (8 cups)

1. In a 4- to 5-quart pot, cook the kielbasa over medium-high heat for 5 to 7 minutes, stirring often, or until lightly browned. Remove with a slotted spoon to a small bowl.

2. Put the broth, water, split peas, barley, onion, celery, and thyme into the pot. Bring to a boil over medium-high heat. Reduce the heat to medium-low and simmer uncovered for 40 to 45 minutes, or until barley is tender.

3. Stir in the cooked kielbasa and spinach and cook for 3 to 4 minutes, or until spinach is wilted.

Makes 10 cups. Per 2 cups: 388 cal, 26 g pro, 62 g car, 7 g fat, 31 mg chol, 570 mg sod

---

Ⓜ AKE AHEAD

Cool the soup to room temperature, then refrigerate in an airtight container for up to 1 week.

VARIATION

SPLIT PEA SOUP WITH HAM

Omit the kielbasa and spinach. Add ¾ cup finely chopped carrots along with the split peas and vegetables. Cook as directed, adding 8 ounces of diced ham for the last 5 minutes of cooking.

Per 2 cups: 399 cal, 25 g pro, 62 g car, 8 g fat, 26 mg chol, 721 mg sod

• EASY • LOW FAT
• MAKE AHEAD
• ONE POT

WARM AND COMFORTING Robust soups, such as this White Bean & Cabbage Soup (p.333) are great one-pot winter meals.

A warm and hearty soup can make a

nutritious meal-in-a-bowl. Served with a

whole grain bread and a tossed salad, the

soup provides a completely satisfying dinner.

Soup can also be a good source of fiber

if beans, grains, or vegetables are used.

EUROPEAN TREATS

Both Greek Lentil Soup (p.334), above, and Minestrone with Pesto (p.344), right, hail from the sunny Mediterranean. Power-packed and bursting with flavor, each of these soups makes a delicious one-pot meal.

BEAN CUISINE
Red Beans & Greens Soup (p.342) combines kale and two types of beans. The many flavors meld to produce a hearty, robust, Southern-style soup.

BEAN CUISINE

DELICIOUS, NUTRITIOUS BEANS
Hearty bean soups make simple and satisfying dinners. Just add bread and a little cheese and you have a complete meal.

It's common knowledge that beans are packed with protein, but they have a lot more going for them too. They're rich in vitamins and minerals and a great source of fiber —all for only 110 to 120 calories a 4-ounce serving. Beans are also low in fat and high in energy-boosting carbo-hydrates, and they have no cholesterol at all.

Not only are they good for you, they're good for your budget. Dollar for dollar they give you more protein than almost any other food, and they can be prepared in many tasty ways.

BEFORE YOU START:
◆ **Pick Over:** Measure out the amount of beans you need onto a tray or large plate and discard any pebbles that may be masquerading as beans. Then rinse in a colander under cold running water.
◆ **Soak:** Most dried beans, with the exception of split peas and lentils, need to be soaked before cooking in order to replace some of the moisture lost in the drying process. (Two cups of dried beans will yield 5 cups after soaking.) Choose the soaking method best suited to your needs:

Long method: Put beans in a large bowl or pot and add water to cover by 3 inches. Let soak at least 6 hours and up to 12 hours at room temperature, or as long as 3 days (covered) in the refrigerator. Drain and use as directed.

Short method: Put beans in a 2- to 3-quart saucepan (or the pot you will cook the soup in) and add water to cover by about 3 inches. Bring to a boil over high heat and boil for 2 to 3 minutes. Remove from the heat, cover, and let soak for 1 to 2 hours. Drain and use as directed.

TEX-MEX BEEF BEAN SOUP

Substitute 8 ounces extra-lean ground beef for the turkey and pro-ceed with the recipe as directed.

Per 1 cup: 303 cal, 16 g pro, 33 g car, 12 g fat, 28 mg chol, 1,051 mg sod

• EASY • 30 MINUTES
• ONE POT

`EASY • 30 MINUTES • ONE POT`

TEX-MEX TURKEY BEAN SOUP

Serves 4

Preparation time: 5 minutes

Cooking time: 20 minutes

In this soup, traditional Tex-Mex ingredients meld to produce a robust and hearty soup. Accompany it with warm cornbread for an easy one-dish sup-per. The recipe can also be easily doubled to feed a crowd.

2 teaspoons olive oil
8 ounces ground turkey
1 cup chopped onion
1½ cups water
1 can (16 ounces) refried beans
1 cup medium-spicy thick and chunky salsa
¼ teaspoon chili powder
¼ teaspoon ground cumin
6 taco shells
For garnish: shredded Cheddar cheese and
  shredded iceberg lettuce (optional)

▶

1. In a large saucepan, heat the oil over medium-high heat. Add the turkey and onion and cook, stirring often, or until the turkey is browned.

2. Add the water, refried beans, salsa, chili powder, and cumin. Bring to a boil over medium-high heat, stirring often. Reduce the heat to medium-low and simmer uncovered for 10 minutes, stirring occasionally.

3. Meanwhile, heat the taco shells as directed on the package and coarsely crush them.

4. Ladle the soup into bowls and top with the crushed taco shells. Garnish with cheese and lettuce. Serve right away.

Makes 5 cups. Per 1 cup: 290 cal, 15 g pro, 35 g car, 10 g fat, 33 mg chol, 1,062 mg sod

LOW FAT • ONE POT

RED BEANS & GREENS SOUP

Serves 6

Preparation time: 15 minutes plus soaking
Cooking time: 1 hour 45 minutes

This Southern-style soup can be spiced up with the addition of some cider vinegar and hot pepper sauce at the end of cooking. Serve with corn bread for a sensational supper.

1 cup (7 ounces) dried red kidney beans, picked over
  and soaked (see Bean Cuisine, page 341)
1 cup (6½ ounces) dried pink or pinto beans,
  picked over and soaked
4 cups water
3½ cups chicken broth
1 smoked ham hock (12 ounces)
2 large cloves garlic, peeled and halved
½ teaspoon ground black pepper
1 bay leaf (1½ inches long)
2 large onions
1 package (10 ounces) frozen chopped kale, turnip,
  or collard greens
¼ teaspoon salt

1. Rinse and drain the soaked beans.

2. In a heavy 5-quart pot, bring the water, broth, ham hock, garlic, pepper, and bay leaf to a boil over high heat. Reduce the heat to medium-low.

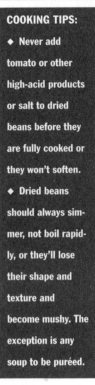

COOKING TIPS:

◆ Never add tomato or other high-acid products or salt to dried beans before they are fully cooked or they won't soften.

◆ Dried beans should always simmer, not boil rapidly, or they'll lose their shape and texture and become mushy. The exception is any soup to be puréed.

Cover and simmer for 30 minutes.

3. Meanwhile, slice the onions thin.

4. Add the beans to the pot. Bring to a boil over medium-high heat. Reduce the heat to medium-low. Cover and simmer for 45 to 50 minutes, or until the beans are tender. Remove the ham hock to a plate and cool until easy to handle.

5. Add the onions, frozen greens, and salt to the pot. Use a wooden spoon to break up the greens. Return the soup to a boil, reduce the heat to low, and simmer uncovered for 10 minutes, or until greens are heated through. Discard the bay leaf.

6. Remove the meat from the ham hock and cut into small pieces. Stir into the soup. Serve right away.

Makes 11½ cups. Per 1 cup : 163 cal, 12 g pro, 25 g car, 3 g fat, 8 mg chol, 275 mg sod

---

EASY • 30 MINUTES • ONE POT

VEGETABLE MINT SOUP

Serves 4

Preparation time: 10 minutes

Cooking time: 10 minutes

Here's a light springtime soup bursting with flavor. To keep the colors vibrant, be sure not to overcook the vegetables. Serve the soup with whole wheat rolls for an easy and economical meal.

5 cups chicken broth
1½ cups frozen mixed vegetables (peas, carrots, corn, lima beans, and green beans)
1 large tomato, halved, seeded, and diced (1½ cups)
2 tablespoons finely chopped chives or scallion tops
1 teaspoon chopped fresh mint leaves or ½ teaspoon dried mint leaves, crumbled
Ground black pepper to taste

1. In a medium-size saucepan, bring the broth, frozen vegetables, tomato, chives, and mint to a boil over medium-high heat.

2. Reduce the heat to medium-low and simmer for about 8 minutes, stirring occasionally, until the vegetables are tender. Season with the pepper. Serve right away.

Makes 8 cups. Per 2 cups: 89 cal, 7 g pro, 14 g car, 4 g fat, 0 mg chol, 182 mg sod

SNEAKY VEGETABLES

Soups are a great way to encourage nonvegetable eaters to eat their vegetables. Puréeing or cutting vegetables into small pieces will make them more palatable.

MINESTRONE WITH PESTO

Serves 7

Total time: 1 hour 20 minutes plus soaking

Here is a signature soup from Italy combining vegetables, pasta, and beans. Each region has its own version and this one, from Genoa, uses pesto, a pungent herb paste, as a traditional finish to the soup.

1 cup (7 ounces) dried white or red kidney beans, picked over
  and soaked (see Bean Cuisine, page 341)

4 cups water

3½ cups chicken broth

½ small head cauliflower

3 medium-size onions

3 medium-size carrots

1 medium-size zucchini

1 can (16 ounces) whole tomatoes in juice

1 cup uncooked elbow macaroni or small pasta shells

1 box (9 ounces) frozen cut Italian green beans

¾ teaspoon salt

¼ teaspoon ground black pepper

PESTO

1 cup loosely packed fresh basil leaves, or flat (Italian) parsley leaves and

1 teaspoon dried basil leaves, crumbled

2 tablespoons olive oil

1 tablespoon water

1 medium-size clove garlic

1. Rinse and drain the soaked beans and transfer to a heavy 5- to 6-quart pot. Add the water and broth. Cover and bring to a boil over high heat. Reduce the heat to medium-low and simmer uncovered until the beans are tender, about 55 minutes.

2. Meanwhile, coarsely chop the cauliflower and onions. Thinly slice the carrots. Cut the zucchini lengthwise into quarters, then cut crosswise into ¼-inch-thick slices.

3. Drain the juice from the canned tomatoes into the pot. Chop the tomatoes and add with the cauliflower, onions, and carrots. Bring the mixture to a boil over medium-high heat. Reduce the heat to low and simmer uncovered for about 10 minutes, or until the vegetables are tender.

 MAKE AHEAD

Do not add the pesto. Cool the soup to room temperature, then refrigerate in an airtight container for up to 1 week. Add the pesto just before serving.

COOK'S TIP

To stretch leftover soup, add tomato juice or extra broth when reheating and serve with a poached egg in each bowl.

4. Add the pasta, zucchini, green beans, salt, and pepper. Return the soup to a boil, reduce the heat to low, and simmer for 10 minutes.

5. Meanwhile, put all the pesto ingredients in a blender or a food processor and process until very finely chopped.

6. Remove the pot from heat and stir the pesto into the soup. Serve right away.

Makes 14 cups. Per 2 cups: 174 cal, 14 g pro, 46 g car, 6 g fat, 0 mg chol, 428 mg sod

---

SALT IN YOUR SOUP

Canned broth is a convenient alternative for homemade stock but it is high in sodium (salt). If this is of concern to you, use low-salt or unsalted versions in order to have control over the seasonings. As a general rule, always taste the soup first before adding extra seasoning. To rescue oversalted soups, add a thinly sliced, peeled medium-size potato to the soup and simmer for about 10 minutes to absorb the salt, then remove the potato.

EASY • 30 MINUTES • MICROWAVE

MICROWAVE CREAM OF BROCCOLI SOUP

Serves 4

Preparation time: 7 minutes

Cooking time: 20 minutes plus 3 minutes to stand

Jazz up this soup with chopped fresh dill and toasted slivered almonds and follow with a main course of broiled fish or chicken and a crisp salad for a delicious and informal meal.

1 package (10 ounces) frozen chopped broccoli
2 tablespoons butter or margarine
1 tablespoon finely chopped onion
¼ cup all-purpose flour
½ teaspoon salt
¼ teaspoon ground black pepper
2 cups 2% fat milk
1 cup chicken broth

1. Remove the outer wrapping and put the unopened package of broccoli in the microwave oven on a paper towel. Microwave on High for 3 to 4 minutes, or until just thawed.

2. Put the butter and onion in a 2- to 3-quart microwave-safe bowl or deep casserole. Microwave uncovered on High for 1½ to 2 minutes, stirring once, until the onion is tender.

3. Stir in the flour, salt, and pepper, then gradually whisk in the milk and chicken broth, stirring until smooth. Cover with a lid or vented plastic wrap and microwave on High for 8 to 10 minutes, whisking 2 or 3 times, until smooth and slightly thickened.

4. Open the package over the sink and gently press the broccoli to squeeze out the excess moisture. Add the broccoli to the soup. ▶

5. Cover and microwave on High for 3 to 4 minutes, stirring once, until the broccoli is tender and the soup is bubbly. Let stand for 3 minutes.

6. Pour the soup into a blender or food processor and process until puréed. Serve right away.

Makes 4 cups. Per 1 cup: 167 cal, 7 g pro, 15 g car, 9 g fat, 25 mg chol with butter, 10 mg chol with margarine, 664 mg sod

---

`EASY • 60 MINUTES • LOW FAT • ONE POT`

CAULIFLOWER & PASTA SOUP

Serves 6

Preparation time: 15 minutes

Cooking time: 30 minutes

Ready-made pizza bread dough, available at most large supermarkets, makes a quick and tasty accompaniment to this soup. Brush it with olive oil, sprinkle with fresh or dried rosemary, and bake according to the package directions. Cut the bread into wedges and serve with the soup for an Italian-style meal.

2 tablespoons olive oil

12 ounces all-purpose potatoes, scrubbed and cut into ½-inch chunks (2 cups)

1 large onion, halved and sliced thin (1 cup)

2 teaspoons minced fresh garlic

1 small head cauliflower, cut into florets (3 cups)

4 cups chicken broth

4 cups water

1 can (about 16 ounces) whole tomatoes in juice, drained and cut into small pieces

8 ounces orecchiette ("little ears" in Italian) or small shell-shaped pasta (about 2 cups)

1 cup canned chick-peas, rinsed and drained

Freshly ground black pepper to taste

For garnish: chopped fresh basil and grated Romano cheese (optional)

1. In a 3- to 4-quart pot, heat the oil over medium heat. Add the potatoes, onion, and garlic and cook for 4 minutes, stirring often, until the onion is soft.

2. Add the cauliflower and cook for 2 minutes more, stirring often. Add the broth, water, tomatoes, pasta, and chick-peas.

3. Bring the mixture to a boil over medium-high heat. Reduce the heat to low. Cover and simmer for 15 minutes, stirring occasionally, until the pasta

COOK'S TIP

Refrigerate the leftover soup in an airtight container for up to 1 week. To stretch the servings, add tomato juice or puréed whole tomatoes with a little of their juice and more rinsed canned chick-peas to the soup when reheating.

is firm-tender. Season the soup with the pepper.

4. Ladle the soup into bowls and garnish with chopped basil and grated cheese. Serve right away.

Makes 12 cups. Per 2 cups: 310 cal, 12 g pro, 52 g car, 8 g fat, 0 mg chol, 269 mg sod

---

60 MINUTES • ONE POT • CLASSIC

FRENCH ONION SOUP

Serves 4

Preparation time: 15 minutes

Cooking time: 45 minutes

At the famous Les Halles market in Paris, onion soup was the staple diet of both the late-night workers and Parisian party revelers. The market is no longer in existence, but the soup lives on.

2 tablespoons butter or margarine
3 large onions, sliced thin (4 cups)
1 tablespoon all-purpose flour
1 teaspoon paprika
½ teaspoon salt
½ teaspoon ground black pepper
2 cans (10½ ounces each) condensed beef broth, undiluted
1½ cups water
1 bay leaf
6 slices French bread (about ½ inch thick)
1½ cups shredded Swiss cheese

1. In a large heavy saucepan, melt the butter over medium heat. Add the onions, stirring to coat. Cover and cook for 20 minutes, stirring occasionally, or until the onions are very soft and beginning to caramelize.

2. In a small bowl, mix the flour, paprika, salt, and pepper. Stir the mixture into the onions until well blended.

3. Whisk in the broth and water. Add the bay leaf. Bring to a boil over high heat. Reduce the heat to low and simmer uncovered for 20 minutes.

4. Heat the broiler. Toast the bread under the broiler on both sides. Ladle the soup into ovenproof bowls set on a baking sheet. Place a slice of toasted bread in each bowl and top with ¼ cup of cheese. Broil for 2 minutes, or until the cheese is melted. Serve right away.

Makes 6 cups. Per 1 cup: 270 cal, 14 g pro, 25 g car, 13 g fat, 36 mg chol with butter, 26 mg chol with margarine, 1,171 mg sod

MEDITERRANEAN SEAFOOD SOUP

Serves 4
Preparation time: 10 minutes
Cooking time: 1 hour

This fish soup has a delicate flavor that will satisfy the heartiest of appetites. It's great for entertaining becausethe base can be prepared a few hours ahead and the seafood added just before serving. Toasted French bread spread with garlic butter makes a wonderful accompaniment.

2 tablespoons olive oil
1 large yellow or red bell pepper, seeded and chopped coarse (1½ cups)
1 large onion, quartered and sliced thin
1 tablespoon minced fresh garlic
3 cups water
1 can (about 28 ounces) crushed tomatoes
½ cup dry white wine or chicken broth
½ teaspoon dried thyme leaves, crumbled
½ teaspoon dried basil leaves, crumbled
½ teaspoon salt
⅛ teaspoon crushed hot red pepper flakes
1 cup uncooked white long-grain rice
8 ounces bay scallops (or sea scallops, cut in half)
8 ounces cod fillet, cut into bite-size pieces
For garnish: chopped fresh parsley (optional)

1. In a 4- to 5-quart pot, heat the oil over medium-high heat. Add the bell pepper, onion, and garlic and cook for 8 to 10 minutes, stirring often, until lightly browned.

2. Add the water, tomatoes, wine, thyme, basil, salt, and red pepper flakes. Bring the mixture to a boil over medium-high heat. Reduce the heat to low. Cover and simmer for 10 to 15 minutes.

3. Stir in the rice. Cover and simmer for 15 to 20 minutes, or until the rice is tender.

4. Add the scallops and cod. Cover and simmer for 2 to 4 minutes, or until the seafood is opaque in the center.

5. Ladle the soup into bowls and garnish with chopped parsley. Serve right away.

Makes 8 cups. Per 2 cups: 421 cal with wine, 404 with broth, 26 g pro, 55 g car, 9 g fat, 43 mg chol, 730 mg sod

60 MINUTES • ONE POT • CLASSIC

HEARTY HALIBUT CHOWDER

Serves 6
Preparation time: 15 minutes
Cooking time: 40 minutes

This recipe calls for halibut, but any mild-flavored, firm-fleshed fish such as cod, tilefish, grouper, or snapper can be used instead.

2 tablespoons unsalted butter or margarine
1 large onion, chopped fine (1½ cups)
2 large all-purpose potatoes, scrubbed and diced (2 cups)
2 teaspoons minced fresh garlic
6 cups chicken broth
1 can (8 ounces) stewed tomatoes, chopped
2 cups shredded carrots
1¾ cups milk
¼ cup heavy cream
2 pounds halibut fillets or steaks (about 1 inch thick), skinned, boned, and cut into 1-inch pieces
½ cup shredded Cheddar cheese
½ teaspoon salt
Freshly ground black pepper to taste
¼ teaspoon crushed hot red pepper flakes
For garnish: chopped fresh chives or scallion tops (optional)

1. In a 4-quart pot, melt the butter over medium heat. Add the onion and cook for 5 minutes, stirring often, until softened.
2. Stir in the potatoes and garlic. Reduce the heat to low. Cover and simmer for about 7 minutes, stirring occasionally, until the potatoes are just tender.
3. Add the chicken broth and bring to a boil over medium-high heat. Stir in the tomatoes and carrots. Reduce the heat to low. Cover and simmer for 10 minutes.
4. Gradually stir in the milk and cream, then the halibut. Return the soup to a simmer and cook uncovered for 10 minutes, or until the fish is barely opaque in center.
5. Remove the pan from the heat and stir in the cheese, salt, black pepper, and red pepper flakes.
6. Ladle the soup into bowls and garnish with chives or scallion tops.

Makes 12 cups. Per 2 cups with butter: 423 cal, 42 g pro, 24 g car, 19 g fat, 92 mg chol, 590 sod. With margarine: 389 cal, 42 g pro, 24 g car, 15 g fat, 82 mg chol, 589 mg sod

SOUP & SANDWICH COMBINATIONS

A bowl of soup and a sandwich is often a quick and easy solution to meal planning, especially if you are organized and make the soup in advance. It's also a great way to have an evening meal when everyone is on different schedules.

VEGETABLE MINT SOUP (page 343) and
◆ Egg salad and watercress on toasted English muffins
◆ Finely chopped ham with sweet pickle relish in whole wheat pita pockets

CREAM OF BROCCOLI SOUP (page 345) and
◆ Thinly sliced roast beef, tomato, onion, prepared horseradish, and Worcestershire sauce on French bread rolls
◆ Thinly sliced meat loaf, tomato, and mayonnaise on toasted sourdough bread

COLD LEEK & POTATO SOUP (page 358) and
◆ Chive biscuits with smoked ham and mango chutney

◆ Thinly sliced cucumber, tomato, and red onion layered on whole wheat bread, topped with Cheddar and broiled

HEARTY HALIBUT CHOWDER (page 349) and
◆ Avocado slices, bacon bits, bean sprouts, and chopped tomato in pita pockets
◆ Roast turkey and guacamole on pumpernickel

GAZPACHO (page 353) and
◆ Grilled ham, Brie, and mustard on raisin pumpernickel
◆ Sliced mozzarella, tomato, and basil pesto on crisp grinder or hero rolls

MINESTRONE WITH PESTO (page 344) and
◆ Thinly sliced prosciutto or ham and provolone cheese layered on slices of large Italian bread and broiled

GREEK LENTIL SOUP (page 334) and
◆ Warm ratatouille and shredded Monterey Jack in whole wheat pita pockets

---

EASY • 30 MINUTES • ONE POT

CORN & SALMON CHOWDER

Serves 4

Preparation time: 5 minutes

Cooking time: 15 minutes

Easy and inexpensive, this soup contains canned salmon, potatoes, corn, and frozen lima beans. It can be prepared in about 20 minutes, but it tastes as if it had been simmering on the stove for hours. Serve the chowder as a main course accompanied with biscuits or cornbread, or as a first course with grilled fish or chicken.

2 cans (10¾ ounces each) condensed golden corn soup

2 ⅔ cups milk

1 package (10 ounces) frozen baby lima beans

1 can (about 16 ounces) whole white potatoes, drained

1 can (about 7½ ounces) red or pink salmon, drained

⅓ cup sliced scallions

VARIATION

CORN & SHRIMP CHOWDER

Omit the salmon and add 8 ounces of shelled cooked shrimp to the soup just before serving.

Per 2 cups: 518 cal, 28 g pro, 72 g car, 13 g fat, 133 mg chol, 1,645 mg sod

•EASY • 30 MINUTES • ONE POT

1. In a large saucepan, bring the soup and milk to a boil over medium-high heat.

2. Stir in the lima beans. Reduce the heat to medium-low and simmer for 5 minutes, stirring occasionally.

3. Meanwhile, cut the potatoes into small chunks. Break the salmon into small pieces, removing any skin and bones.

4. Add the potatoes, salmon, and scallions to the pan. Cook for 5 to 7 minutes, stirring occasionally, or until the lima beans are tender. Serve right away.

Makes 8 cups. Per 2 cups: 528 cal, 25 g pro, 72 g car, 15 g fat, 42 mg chol, 1,751 sod

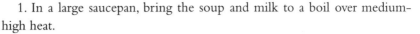

EASY • 60 MINUTES • MICROWAVE

MICROWAVE VEGETABLE CLAM CHOWDER

Serves 4

Preparation time: 15 minutes

Cooking time: 27 minutes plus 5 minutes to stand

Offer up this hearty chowder during the week, when time is at a premium. Serve it with ready-to-bake breadsticks or toasted English muffins.

1 slice bacon
½ teaspoon curry powder
½ teaspoon salt
⅛ teaspoon ground black pepper
1 can (10¾ ounces) condensed chicken broth, undiluted
12 ounces all-purpose potatoes, scrubbed and chopped fine (2 cups)
1 medium-size carrot, shredded coarse (1 cup)
1 medium-size onion, chopped (½ cup)
1 can (6½ ounces) minced clams, drained and liquid reserved
1 can (12 ounces) evaporated milk
2 tablespoons chopped fresh parsley

1. Put the bacon into a 3-quart microwave-safe bowl or deep casserole. Cover loosely with a paper towel. Microwave on High for 1 minute, or until crisp. Remove the bacon to a paper towel to drain.

2. Stir in the curry powder, salt, and pepper, then the broth, potatoes, carrot, onion, and reserved clam liquid.

3. Cover with a lid or vented plastic wrap. Microwave on High for 20 to 22 minutes, stirring carefully two or three times with a wooden spoon, until the vegetables are tender.

▶

MICROWAVE DISHES

Don't use metal, aluminum foil, or dishes with metal rims in the micro-wave; metal causes sparking. Nonmetal materials such as heatproof glass or ceramic, which allow the micro-waves to pass through them, are good for microwave cooking and they remain cool enough to handle. Plastics not designed for the microwave may melt or become misshapen.

4. Add the evaporated milk and clams. Cover and microwave on High for 3 to 4 minutes, stirring once, until the milk and clams are hot.

5. Remove the bowl from the microwave oven and let stand covered for 5 minutes, then stir in the parsley.

6. To serve, ladle the soup into bowls, crumble the bacon, and sprinkle some over each serving.

Makes 4 cups. Per 1 cup: 306 cal, 19 g pro, 31 g car, 12 g fat, 48 mg chol, 932 mg sod

EASY • 30 MINUTES • ONE POT

CRAB SOUP

Serves 4
Preparation time: 5 minutes
Cooking time: 15 minutes

The creamy texture of this favorite soup does not come from heavy cream, but rather from a combination of skim milk and flour that thickens the soup without adding any extra fat.

¼ cup (½ stick) butter or margarine
¼ cup chopped celery
¼ cup all-purpose flour
6 drops hot-pepper sauce
5 cups skim milk
16 ounces fresh or imitation crabmeat (3½ cups)(See Cook's Tip)
¼ cup sliced scallions

1. In a large saucepan, melt the butter over medium heat. Add the celery and cook for 3 minutes, stirring often, until crisp-tender. Add the flour and stir over low heat until frothy. Cook for about 3 minutes, stirring often to prevent browning. Add the hot-pepper sauce.

2. Gradually stir in the milk. Increase the heat to medium and bring the mixture to a boil. Immediately reduce the heat so the sauce simmers.

3. Add the crabmeat, return to a simmer, and cook for about 3 minutes, or until the crab is heated through. Stir in the scallions. Serve right away.

Makes 9 cups. Per 2 cups: 570 cal, 55 g pro, 34 g car, 23 g fat, 241 mg chol with butter, 191 mg chol with margarine, 967 mg sod

COOK'S TIP

Crabmeat can be purchased frozen, pasteurized (which requires refrigeration), and canned. Canned crabmeat is sold as claw, lump, or flaked meat. Imitation crabmeat (or surimi) is sold in sticks, chunks, flakes, or nuggets. For information on surimi, see "Surimi Savvy," page 353.

SURIMI SAVVY

Whether it's a crab, lobster, scallop, or shrimp look-alike, imitation shellfish is made from real fish—usually Alaskan white pollock—that's minced and repeatedly rinsed to wash away color, odor, and fat. But the thick, creamy paste that results—the Japanese, who devised the method more than a thousand years ago, call it surimi —also has no flavor. It's the addition of some real shellfish, shellfish extract, or flavoring, plus starch, egg white, sugar, salt, and preservatives, that makes the imitation taste like the real thing. And once the flavored surimi has been shaped, colored, and steamed, the fully cooked shellfish substitute is packaged, frozen, and shipped on its way.

Nutritionally, surimi compares more closely to the fish it's made from than the shellfish it resembles. Formulas vary from one manufacturer to another, but for people who are watching cholesterol intake, surimi is lower than real shellfish. Because of the salt added during processing, though, it's also higher in sodium. Given the high cost of fresh crabmeat, shrimp, scallops and lobster, surimi has become a viable and tasty alternative.

VARIATION

SPICY GAZPACHO

Prepare the recipe as directed, adding 2 tablespoons minced green chiles or jalapeños, ¼ cup chopped fresh cilantro, and 2 tablespoons fresh lime juice.

Per 1 cup: 49 cal, 2 g pro, 11 g car, 0 g fat, 0 mg chol, 115 mg sod

• EASY • LOW FAT
• MAKE AHEAD

EASY • LOW FAT • MAKE AHEAD • CLASSIC

GAZPACHO

Serves 4 to 6
Preparation time: 30 minutes plus chilling

Hailing from the Andalusian region of southern Spain, this soup is open to many interpretations, but most recipes recommend serving it well chilled. Traditionally, small bowls containing extra chopped vegetables, hard-cooked eggs, and bread cubes are passed separately as garnishes. Not only is this soup low in fat, it has lots of vitamins A and C. Serve it with whole wheat pitas stuffed with lean ham, cheese, and watercress for a nutritious no-cook meal.

2 medium-size ripe tomatoes, seeded and chopped fine (2 cups)
1 large red bell pepper, seeded and chopped fine (1½ cups)
1 medium-size unpeeled cucumber, seeded and chopped fine (1 cup)
1 small red onion, chopped fine (½ cup)
1 tablespoon minced fresh garlic
1 can (about 11½ ounces) 8-vegetable juice (about 1½ cups)
2 tablespoons red wine vinegar
For garnish: plain yogurt and chopped fresh cilantro (optional)

1. In a large bowl, mix all the ingredients. Cover with plastic wrap and refrigerate to chill thoroughly before serving.
2. To serve, ladle the chilled soup into mugs or serving bowls and garnish with a dollop of yogurt and chopped cilantro.

Makes 5½ cups. Per 1 cup: 26 cal, 2 g pro, 10 g car, 0 g fat, 0 mg chol, 215 mg sod

CANTALOUPE–PEACH SOUP

Serves 4

Preparation time: 15 minutes plus chilling (optional)

Fruit soups, a Slavic and Scandinavian tradition, are perfect to serve during the summer months. This refreshing soup will make a wonderful first course or a light and unusual dessert served with gingersnaps. To cut down on chilling time, start with thoroughly chilled fruit.

1 small ripe cantaloupe, peeled, seeded, and cut into small chunks (5 cups)
2 large ripe peaches, peeled and cut into small chunks (1½ cups)
½ cup buttermilk
¼ teaspoon ground ginger
For garnish: chopped fresh mint, blueberries, or raspberries (optional)

1. In a blender or food processor, combine the cantaloupe, peaches, buttermilk, and ginger and process until puréed. Serve immediately or transfer to a medium-size bowl, cover with plastic wrap, and refrigerate until thoroughly chilled.
2. Ladle the soup into mugs or bowls and garnish with chopped fresh mint and berries.

Makes 4 cups. Per 1 cup: 110 cal, 3 g pro, 15 g car, 1 g fat, 1 mg chol, 50 mg sod

CREAMY BEET SOUP

Serves 5

Preparation time: 10 minutes plus chilling (optional)

Pickled beets impart their brilliant color and plain yogurt contributes a pleasant tang and creamy texture to this blissfully quick and easily prepared soup. Serve it as a flavorful and healthful first course followed by grilled chicken or pork.

1 jar (16 ounces) sliced pickled beets, undrained
2 cups plain low-fat or nonfat yogurt
1 cup chicken broth
For garnish: yogurt and chopped fresh dill (optional)

THE FINAL FLOURISH

Top off soup with one or more of the following garnishes:

♦ Fresh herb sprigs or chopped leaves

♦ Grated or shredded cheese

♦ Toasted nuts

♦ Sour cream or yogurt

♦ Wafer-thin slices of lemon, lime, or orange

♦ Watercress or bean sprouts

♦ Scallion slices, strips, or brushes

♦ Shredded flour tortillas

♦ Crumbled tortilla chips

♦ Julienne strips of ham

♦ Crumbled crisp bacon

♦ Finely chopped bell pepper

1. In a blender or food processor, combine the beets, yogurt, and broth and process until puréed. Serve immediately or transfer to a medium-size bowl, cover with plastic wrap, and refrigerate until thoroughly chilled.

2. Ladle the soup into mugs or bowls and garnish with yogurt and dill.

Makes 5 cups. Per 1 cup: 118 cal, 6 g pro, 21 g car, 2 g fat, 3 mg chol, 328 mg sod

EASY • 30 MINUTES • LOW FAT • MAKE AHEAD

CURRIED SQUASH SOUP

Serves 4 to 6

Preparation time: 5 minutes plus chilling (optional)

This soup takes advantage of frozen winter squash. It can be made spicy or mild depending on the type and amount of curry powder used. For a creamier soup, add a little heavy cream to it before serving.

2 (12-ounce) packages frozen winter squash, thawed
1¾ cups chicken broth
1 cup applesauce
1 tablespoon curry powder, or to taste
½ teaspoon minced fresh garlic
For garnish: diced apple and chopped fresh cilantro (optional) ▶

SOUP ACCOMPANIMENTS

The next time you serve soup, try one of these tasty accompaniments instead of serving crackers.

CHILI PITAS

Heat the broiler. In a small bowl, mix 2 tablespoons olive oil, 3/4 teaspoon chili powder, 3/4 teaspoon ground cumin, 1/8 teaspoon salt, and 4 drops hot-pepper sauce. Brush both sides of six 3- to 4-inch pita breads with the mixture. Broil the pitas for 1 to 2 minutes per side until lightly browned and puffed.

Makes 6. Per pita: 120 cal, 3 g pro, 16 g car, 5 g fat, 0 mg chol, 203 mg sod

CHEESE TOASTS

Heat the broiler. Slice a small baguette (about 12 inches long) into 1/4-inch-thick slices. In a small bowl, mix 1 cup grated Parmesan cheese and 1/2 cup mayonnaise. Spread the mixture over one side of each bread slice. Broil for 1 to 2 minutes, or until the topping bubbles and edges are toasted.

Makes 48 slices. Per slice: 37 cal, 1 g pro, 3 g car, 2 g fat, 3 mg chol, 73 mg sod

CRISPY CROUTONS

Heat the oven to 350°F. Cut 3 slices of day-old white bread into 1/2-inch squares. Toss the bread cubes with 2 tablespoons olive oil until absorbed. Spread on an ungreased baking sheet. Bake for 5 to 7 minutes, stirring twice, until golden brown and crisp.

Makes about 1 cup. Per 1/4 cup: 110 cal, 2 g pro, 9 g car, 8 g fat, 0 mg chol, 101 mg sod

1. In a blender or food processor, combine the squash, chicken broth, applesauce, curry powder, and garlic and process until puréed. Serve at room temperature or transfer to a medium-size bowl, cover with plastic wrap, and refrigerate until thoroughly chilled.

2. Ladle the soup into mugs or bowls and garnish with diced apple and chopped fresh cilantro.

Makes 5½ cups. Per 1 cup: 118 cal, 3 g pro, 28 g car, 1 g fat, 0 mg chol, 41 mg sod

MAKE AHEAD

CHILLED BUTTERMILK SOUP

Serves 8
Preparation time: 15 minutes plus chilling
Cooking time: 15 minutes

Tart, tangy, and very refreshing, buttermilk is invaluable in cooking and baking and is especially suited to chilled soups. As an added bonus, it gives the soup a rich creamy texture without a lot of fat.

2 tablespoons unsalted butter or margarine
1½ cups chopped onion
3 medium-size apples (about 1 pound), peeled, cored, and chopped coarse
  (3¼ cups)
1½ cups chicken broth
1½ cups water
2½ cups buttermilk
1 medium-size cucumber, peeled, seeded, and chopped fine
1 medium-size tomato, peeled, seeded, and chopped fine
1 cup cooked fresh corn kernels, cut from
  2 medium-size cobs
1½ teaspoons salt
For garnish: sliced cucumber, chopped red bell pepper, and dill sprigs
  (optional)

1. In a large skillet, melt the butter over medium heat. Add the onions and cook for 4 to 5 minutes, stirring often, until softened.

2. Add the apples, broth, and water. Bring the mixture to a boil over medium-high heat. Reduce the heat to low and simmer uncovered for 8 to 10 minutes, or until the apples are tender. Remove the skillet from the heat and cool to room temperature.

3. Transfer the mixture in batches to a blender or food processor and

blend or process until puréed. Transfer the purée to a medium-size bowl.

4. Stir in the buttermilk, cucumbers, tomato, corn, and salt. Cover with plastic wrap and refrigerate until thoroughly chilled.

5. Ladle the soup into mugs or bowls and garnish with cucumber, bell pepper, and dill.

Makes 8½ cups. Per 1 cup: 121 cal, 4 g pro, 19 g car, 4 g fat, 10 mg chol with butter, 3 mg chol with margarine, 491 mg sod

---

EASY • 30 MINUTES • LOW FAT • MAKE AHEAD

MINTED GREEN PEA SOUP

Serves 4

Preparation time: 5 minutes plus chilling

This refreshing soup makes a dazzling light starter to a spring menu. For a heartier version, add some diced ham or hard-cooked egg to it before serving.

1 package (16 ounces) frozen green peas, slightly thawed
1 cup chicken broth
1 cup buttermilk or plain nonfat yogurt
1 scallion, chopped coarse
¼ cup fresh mint leaves
½ teaspoon salt
For garnish: crumbled feta cheese or shredded carrots (optional)

1. In a blender or a food processor, combine the peas, chicken broth, buttermilk, scallion, mint leaves, and salt and process until puréed. Serve at room temperature or transfer to a medium-size bowl, cover with plastic wrap, and refrigerate until thoroughly chilled.

2. Ladle the soup into mugs or bowls and garnish with feta cheese or carrots.

Makes 4½ cups. Per 1 cup: 110 cal, 8 g pro, 18 g car, 1 g fat, 2 mg chol, 430 mg sod

ABOUT BUTTERMILK

Contrary to its name, today's buttermilk contains no butter. Originally, it was the milk residue left after cream was churned into butter. Today, buttermilk is made by adding bacterial cultures to skim or part-skim milk. The cultures convert the sugar into lactic acid, producing a tart flavor and smooth, creamy consistency. Pure cultured buttermilk without any additives or thickeners, also called Bulgarian-style buttermilk, has the best flavor. Buttermilk can also be purchased in powdered form, which is great to keep on hand because it has a long shelf life. One cup of buttermilk has about 100 calories and less than 2 grams of fat.

COLD LEEK & POTATO SOUP

Serves 8

Preparation time: 15 minutes plus chilling
Cooking time: 30 minutes plus cooling

Created by a French chef living in New York who was nostalgic for his mother's home-cooking, this classic cold soup is also known as vichyssoise. It is the perfect choice for a summer menu because it can be prepared in advance and refrigerated until ready to serve. Although it is traditionally served cold, this soup can also be enjoyed piping hot.

2 tablespoons butter or margarine
2 medium-size cloves garlic, crushed
1 pound leeks, trimmed, halved lengthwise, rinsed well, drained, and
    chopped (5 cups)
1 pound all-purpose potatoes, peeled and chopped (2½ cups)
6 cups chicken broth
¼ teaspoon salt,
¼ teaspoon ground black pepper
1 cup half-and-half
For garnish: chopped fresh chives or scallion tops (optional)

1. In a large saucepan, melt the butter over medium–low heat. Add the garlic and leeks and cook for 8 to 10 minutes, stirring often, or until soft.

2. Add the potatoes, broth, salt, and pepper. Bring the mixture to a boil over high heat. Reduce the heat to medium–low. Cover and simmer for 15 to 20 minutes, stirring occasionally, or until the potatoes are tender. Remove the pan from the heat and cool slightly.

3. Process the soup in batches in a blender or food processor until puréed. Pour the purée to a bowl and stir in the half-and-half. Cover with plastic wrap and refrigerate for 4 hours or overnight.

4. Ladle the soup into serving bowls and garnish with chopped chives or scallion tops.

Makes 9 cups. Per 1 cup: 141 cal, 5 g pro, 18 g car, 8 g fat, 17 mg chol with butter, 10 mg chol with margarine, 189 mg sod

VARIATION

MICROWAVE LEEK & POTATO SOUP

● Put the butter, garlic, and leeks in a deep 3-quart microwave-safe container. Cover with a lid or vented plastic wrap. Microwave on High for 8 to 10 minutes, stirring twice, until the garlic is tender.

● Add the potatoes, broth, and salt and pepper. Cover and microwave on High for 20 to 24 minutes, stirring three times, until the potatoes are tender.

● Remove from the microwave oven and let cool to room temperature. Process the mixture in batches in a blender or food processor. Chill as directed.

Per 1 cup: 141 cal, 5 g pro, 18 g car, 8 g fat, 17 mg chol with butter, 10 mg chol with margarine, 189 mg sod

• MAKE AHEAD
• ONE POT

MAKE AHEAD

The soup can be refrigerated in an airtight conatiner up to 3 days.

SALADS

> *"The greatest dishes*
> *are very simple dishes."*
> BRILLAT-SAVARIN

Salads have taken on a new importance in our diet, and part of the reason is their flexibility. They can easily feature meats, fish, fruits, grains, or vegetables; can be served warm or cold; and can effortlessly become the focal point of a meal, especially during the warm-weather months. Most salads are light and use fresh ingredients, making them the spotlight of healthy eating. And because there's such a wide selection of ingredients available all year round, the variations are endless.

The following pages contain a mixture of salads. Some can be main courses, while others make great side dishes or first courses. We also have recipes for dressings that can be used on a variety of salads.

60 MINUTES

MICROWAVE

LOW FAT

MAKE AHEAD

CLASSIC

SALAD DRESSINGS

VEGETARIAN MAIN DISHES

FRUITY TWIST

POTLUCK PICNIC

LOW FAT • MAKE AHEAD

CURRIED CHICKEN SLAW

Serves 4

Preparation time: 20 minutes plus 1 hour to chill

Colorful and crunchy with a hint of curry flavor, this salad is a great picnic or barbecue dish. Use leftover chicken or turkey if you have it, or poach a chicken breast in chicken broth, then cool and cut in small pieces. Serve with whole wheat pita pockets.

CURRY DRESSING

1 cup plain nonfat yogurt

1 tablespoon reduced-fat or nonfat mayonnaise

2 to 3 teaspoons curry powder

3 tablespoons fresh lemon juice

Ground black pepper to taste

1 tablespoon Dijon mustard

2 tablespoons minced shallot

1½ cups chopped cooked chicken breast

¼ cup frozen peas, thawed

¼ cup shredded carrot

⅛ teaspoon celery seed

1 tablespoon golden raisins (optional)

1 cup shredded red cabbage

¼ cup chopped green apple

¼ cup chopped scallions

¼ cup chopped celery

For garnish: 4 large red cabbage leaves, 8 cherry tomato halves, and
   1 tablespoon chopped fresh parsley (optional)

1. Make the dressing: In a large serving bowl, whisk the yogurt, mayonnaise, curry powder, lemon juice, pepper, mustard, and shallot until well blended.

2. Add the chicken, peas, carrot, celery seed, raisins, cabbage, apple, scallions, and celery, tossing to coat. Cover and refrigerate for 1 hour for the flavors to develop.

3. Place each cabbage leaf on a serving plate so it curves up to form a cup. Mound the salad inside and garnish with cherry tomatoes and parsley. Serve right away.

Per serving: 162 cal, 21 g pro, 12 g car, 3 g fat with reduced-fat mayonnaise, 2 g fat with with nonfat mayonnaise, 46 mg chol, 224 mg sod

MAKE AHEAD

The salad can be prepared ahead and refrigerated in an airtight container up to 2 days. Serve chilled or at room temperature.

WARM FIESTA CHICKEN SALAD

Serves 2

Preparation time: 10 minutes plus 10 minutes to stand
Cooking time: 8 minutes

A Mexican inspiration, this satisfying warm salad is nearly a meal in itself. Just add corn bread for a quick and delicious meal.

LIME VINAIGRETTE
2½ tablespoons olive oil
1½ tablespoons fresh lime juice
¼ teaspoon minced garlic
¼ teaspoon salt
⅛ teaspoon ground black pepper
⅛ teaspoon ground cumin

½ pound skinless, boneless chicken breasts
1 teaspoon olive oil
1 can (about 8 ounces) black beans, drained and rinsed
4 ounces romaine lettuce, cut into thin strips (3 cups)
½ small red bell pepper, cut into thin strips (½ cup)
2 tablespoons chopped fresh cilantro

1. Make the vinaigrette: In a large serving bowl, whisk the oil, lime juice, garlic, salt, pepper, and cumin until well blended.

2. Put the chicken breasts on a large plate. Drizzle 1 tablespoon of the vinaigrette over the breasts and turn to coat. Let stand for 10 minutes.

3. In a large nonstick skillet, heat the oil over medium-high heat. Add the chicken and cook for 3 to 4 minutes on each side, or until golden brown and no longer pink in the center. Remove the skillet from the heat.

4. Add the beans, lettuce, bell pepper, and cilantro to the bowl with the dressing. Toss gently to mix and coat. Arrange the mixture on a serving platter.

5. Slice the chicken into thin strips. Arrange the chicken strips over the salad and drizzle with the pan drippings. Serve right away.

Per serving: 377 cal, 32 g pro, 15 g car, 21 g fat, 66 mg chol, 533 mg sod

---

READY-TO-GO SALAD FIXINGS

Get the fresh ingredients from supermarket salad bars so you don't have to chop and slice. For variety, here are some other quick salad ideas from things in your pantry:

◆ Open a jar of pickled beets or one of 3-bean salad, top with chopped hard-cooked eggs and chopped fresh parsley.

◆ Mix drained cans of corn and kidney beans. Toss with bottled ranch or Italian dressing.

◆ Toss a drained can of artichoke hearts or hearts of palm with bottled vinaigrette dressing.

CHICKEN SALAD WITH MELON

Serves 4

Preparation time: 18 minutes

Grilled chicken accented by fresh melon and cucumber makes a lively summer main-dish salad. Although the recipe calls for cantaloupe, you can experiment with some of the more exotic melon varieties, such as Crenshaw, Persian, or Honeyloupe. Offer it with warmed French bread for a weekend lunch or light dinner.

TARRAGON DRESSING

¼ cup plain nonfat yogurt

¼ cup reduced-fat or nonfat mayonnaise

2 teaspoons chopped fresh tarragon, or ¾ teaspoon
  dried tarragon leaves, crumbled

¼ teaspoon salt

3 cups 1-inch chunks ripe cantaloupe (from 1-pound melon)

1 medium-size English (seedless) cucumber, quartered lengthwise
  and cut into ¼-inch pieces (2 cups)

4 grilled chicken breast halves, cut into thin strips

1. Make the dressing: In a large serving bowl, whisk the yogurt, mayonnaise, tarragon, and salt until well blended.

COOK'S TIP

Grill or broil skinless, boneless chicken breast halves for 5 to 6 minutes on each side, or until no longer pink in the center. Let cool, then cut in strips.

MAKE IT A MEAL

Right now, somewhere in your kitchen, there's a main-dish salad waiting to happen. The trick is to look in places where you'd least expect to find it.

◆ ON THE LEFTOVERS SHELF Plain rice, pasta, couscous all make great salad starters. Simply toss what you have on hand with chopped vegetables and a vinaigrette.

◆ IN THE PANTRY A can of tuna or salmon...drained kidney beans, black beans, or chick-peas...canned caponata (a marinated eggplant appetizer) or ham chunks—any of these can be tossed with salad greens and/or chopped vegetables and a simple dressing.

◆ ON THE GRILL If you're grilling dinner, get started on another meal by cooking extra chicken, steak, shrimp, or skewered vegetables (they'll keep refrigerated for several days). To serve, toss with fresh greens and a vinaigrette dressing.

◆ IN THE BREADBOX If you have stale bread on hand, don't throw it to the birds. Soak chunks of it in just a little water, then squeeze out the excess. Toss with chopped tomato, red onion, garlic, and a vinaigrette dressing (flavored with basil if you've got it), and you've produced what the Italians call panzanella .

2. Add the melon, cucumber, and chicken. Toss gently to mix and coat. Serve right away.

Per serving: 239 cal with reduced-fat mayonnaise, 209 cal with nonfat mayonnaise, 29 g pro, 15 g car, 6 g fat with reduced-fat mayonnaise, 4 g fat with nonfat mayonnaise, 73 mg chol, 341 mg sod with reduced-fat mayonnaise, 326 mg sod with nonfat mayonnaise

MAKE AHEAD

The vegetables can all be prepared, packed in plastic food storage bags or airtight containers, and refrigerated up to 24 hours ahead. The honey-yogurt dressing can be prepared and refrigerated in an airtight container up to 2 days. Assemble the salad just before serving.

EASY • 30 MINUTES • MAKE AHEAD

TURKEY WALDORF SALAD

Serves 4 to 6
Preparation time: 20 minutes

This salad was created in the 1890s at the famous Waldorf Hotel in New York and originally contained only apples, celery, and mayonnaise. It has gone through many changes and adaptations during the years. In this version, other ingredients have been added to create a main-dish salad. It's also a good way to use leftover cooked turkey or chicken.

HONEY-YOGURT DRESSING
⅓ cup plain nonfat yogurt
3 tablespoons cider vinegar
2 tablespoons mayonnaise
4 teaspoons honey
½ teaspoon salt

3 cups diced cooked turkey
1½ cups chopped celery
2 large Red Delicious apples, unpeeled, quartered,
   cored, and diced
½ cup chopped scallions
Lettuce leaves (optional)
⅔ cup chopped walnuts

1. Make the dressing: In a large serving bowl, whisk the yogurt, vinegar, mayonnaise, honey, and salt until well blended.

2. Add the turkey, celery, apples, and scallions, tossing gently to coat.

3. Arrange the lettuce leaves on individual serving plates. Spoon the salad mixture on top of the lettuce and sprinkle with some of the chopped walnuts. Serve right away.

Per serving: 360 cal, 28 g pro, 22 g car, 19 g fat, 68 mg chol, 358 mg sod

THAI BEEF SALAD

Serves 4

Preparation time: 15 minutes

Cooking time: 7 minutes

If you were following a Thai cookbook, you would be adding 10 times the chopped jalapeño pepper called for here! Grilling steak over the weekend? Throw on an extra one, then use it in this salad during the week.

12 ounces well-trimmed flank steak

THAI DRESSING
¼ cup fresh lime juice
2 tablespoons vegetable oil
2 teaspoons granulated sugar
1½ teaspoons seeded and finely chopped jalapeño pepper
½ teaspoon minced garlic
½ teaspoon salt

4 cups bean sprouts (8 ounces)
1½ cups thinly sliced red bell pepper
1½ cups thinly sliced cucumber
¼ cup chopped fresh mint leaves
8 cups loosely packed torn romaine or other lettuce
For garnish: chopped peanuts (optional)

1. Heat a gas grill to medium-high, prepare a charcoal fire, or heat a broiler. Grill or broil the steak 4 to 6 inches from the heat source for 5 to 7 minutes, turning once, for medium-rare. Remove the steak to a cutting board and let stand for 5 minutes, then slice thin across the grain.

2. Make the dressing: In a large serving bowl, whisk the lime juice, oil, sugar, jalapeño, garlic, and salt until well blended.

3. Add the steak, sprouts, bell pepper, cucumber, and mint to the dressing, tossing to mix and coat.

4. Line a serving platter with the lettuce. Spoon the salad mixture on top, then garnish with peanuts. Serve right away.

Per serving: 265 cal, 22 g pro, 15 g car, 14 g fat, 43 mg chol, 343 mg sod

60 MINUTES

WILTED SPINACH
& PORK SALAD

Serves 4

Preparation time: 20 minutes

Cooking time: 16 minutes plus 5 minutes to stand

Mango lends a tropical flavor to this main-dish salad. If fresh mango is not available, use canned instead. Serve it with whole-grain bread for a simple supper on a cool night.

12 ounces fresh spinach leaves, well rinsed and divided

1 pound pork tenderloin, halved crosswise

1 teaspoon chopped fresh rosemary, or ½ teaspoon dried rosemary
    leaves, crumbled

½ teaspoon salt

½ teaspoon ground black pepper

4 tablespoons olive oil

2 medium-size onions, sliced thin (1½ cups)

¼ cup balsamic vinegar

2 tablespoons maple syrup

1 medium-size ripe mango, peeled and sliced thin

1. Put the spinach leaves in a large serving bowl and set aside. Rub the pork tenderloin with the rosemary and ¼ teaspoon of salt and pepper.

2. In a large skillet, heat 1 tablespoon of oil over medium-high heat. Add the pork and brown on all sides. Reduce the heat to medium. Cover and cook for 8 to 10 minutes, or until the meat is barely pink in the center (a meat thermometer should register 160°F when inserted into the center). Remove the meat to a cutting board and let stand for 5 minutes, then slice thin on the diagonal.

3. Meanwhile, put another 2 teaspoons of oil in the skillet. Add the onion and cook, stirring often, for 5 to 6 minutes, or until golden. brown. Stir in the remaining oil, the vinegar, maple syrup, and the remaining salt and pepper. Immediately pour this mixture over the spinach leaves, tossing to coat.

4. Add the pork and mango and toss gently to mix. Serve right away.

Per serving: 378 cal, 27 g pro, 24 g car, 20 g fat, 75 mg chol, 401 mg sod

ANTIPASTO PLATTER

Serves 2

Preparation time: 15 minutes

This is warm-weather eating at its easiest. Mix and match fresh and pantry ingredients at your convenience. (Try canned white beans, anchovies, marinated artichoke hearts, mushrooms, and so on.) Serve with olive oil and wine vinegar for drizzling and French or Italian bread. This recipe can easily be multiplied to feed more than two.

1 jar (4 ounces) whole pimientos, drained and cut into strips
⅔ cup pitted large black olives
1 can (6½ ounces) solid light tuna in olive oil, undrained
1 medium-size ripe tomato, sliced
1 small cucumber, peeled and sliced thin
4 ounces mozzarella cheese, sliced
Freshly ground black pepper

1. Mix the pimientos and olives on a serving platter and drizzle with the oil from the tuna.

2. Arrange the tuna, tomato, cucumber, and cheese on the platter. Sprinkle with pepper and serve right away.

Per serving: 437 cal, 35 g pro, 12 g car, 29 g fat, 80 mg chol, 1,127 mg sod

MARINATED SEAFOOD SALAD

Serves 12

Preparation time: 20 minutes plus at least 3 hours to chill

Cooking time: 4 minutes

Containing an array of luscious seafood, this salad is best made the day of serving. Squid, often known by its Italian name, calamari, can be purchased fresh or frozen, either whole or as cleaned bodies with tentacles removed. You can also use 1 pound of shredded imitation crabmeat (or surimi) instead of the squid if you prefer.

ADJUST THE COLOR

All green all the time spells dull. Punch up your salads with sliced radishes, cucumber, red or yellow peppers, and black olives.

VARIATION

SEAFOOD SALAD PROVENÇAL

• Omit the dressing and prepare the seafood as directed.
• In a small bowl, mix 1 cup of reduced-fat or nonfat mayonnaise, 1 tablespoon tomato paste, 1 tablespoon drained capers, 1 tablespoon snipped chives, 1 tablespoon fresh lemon juice, and 1 teaspoon minced garlic until well blended.
• Toss the dressing with the seafood and serve chilled or at room temperature.

Per serving: 156 cal, 19 g pro, 7 g car, 5 g fat, 147 mg chol, 312 mg sod. With nonfat mayonnaise: 116 cal, 19 g pro, 6 g car, 1 g fat, 147 mg chol, 292 mg sod

• 30 MINUTES
• LOW FAT

DRESSING

¼ cup tarragon or white wine vinegar
1 tablespoon fresh lemon juice
1 tablespoon Dijon mustard
1 teaspoon salt
½ teaspoon ground black pepper
¾ cup vegetable oil
1 cup chopped celery
½ cup sliced sweet miniature gherkins
¼ cup chopped fresh parsley

1 pound medium-size shrimp, shelled and deveined
1 pound bay scallops
1 pound cleaned small squid, bodies cut into ¼-inch-thick rings, tentacles in small pieces
For garnish: lettuce leaves and lemon wedges

1. Make the dressing: In a large bowl, whisk together the vinegar, lemon juice, mustard, salt, and pepper. Whisk in the oil in a thin stream until well blended. Stir in the celery, onion, gherkins, and parsley.

2. Bring a large saucepan of water to a boil over high heat. Add the shrimp, reduce the heat to low, and simmer for 1½ to 2 minutes, or just until opaque. Remove with a slotted spoon to a cutting board and let cool.

3. Return the water to a gentle boil. Add the scallops and squid and cook for 1 to 2 minutes, or just until opaque. Remove with a slotted spoon to the bowl with the dressing.

4. Cut the shrimp in half lengthwise. Add to the bowl, tossing gently to coat. Cover and refrigerate for at least 3 hours, up to 8 hours.

5. Serve chilled on lettuce leaves with lemon wedges.

Per serving: 440 cal, 19 g pro, 61 g car, 15 g fat, 147 mg chol, 2,065 mg sod

---

EASY • 30 MINUTES • LOW FAT • MAKE AHEAD

DILLED CRAB SALAD

Serves 4
Preparation time: 15 minutes
Cooking time: 1 minute

The flavor of fresh dill is unmistakable and bears little resemblance to that of the dried herb available in jars. Serve this salad with crisp crackers, toasted bagel slices, or flatbread.

▶

8 ounces sugar snap peas, trimmed and, if large, cut in half
    crosswise (3 cups)
12 ounces imitation crabmeat, in bite-size pieces
1 medium-size cucumber, halved lengthwise, and sliced thin
    (2 cups)
1 small red bell pepper, seeded and sliced thin (1 cup)
1 small red onion, halved and sliced thin (½ cup)
1 bunch fresh dill weed, snipped or chopped fine (½ cup)
⅓ cup bottled reduced-fat ranch dressing
⅓ cup nonfat sour cream
4 large Boston lettuce leaves
For garnish: fresh dill sprigs (optional)

1. In a medium-size saucepan of boiling water, cook the sugar snap peas
for 1 minute, or until bright green. Drain and rinse under cold running
water. Drain well and transfer to a large serving bowl.

2. Add the crabmeat, cucumber, bell pepper, onion, and dill. Toss gently to
mix thoroughly.

3. In a small bowl, mix the ranch dressing and sour cream. Pour the dressing mixture over the salad. Toss to mix and coat.

4. Arrange the lettuce leaves on a serving platter. Mound the salad on the
lettuce. Garnish with dill sprigs and serve right away.

Per serving: 232 cal, 17 g pro, 22 g car, 8 g fat, 32 mg chol, 351 mg sod

---

EASY • 30 MINUTES • MAKE AHEAD

SALMON & PASTA SALAD

Serves 4
Total time: 30 minutes

In a hurry for a delicious meal? Pasta and canned salmon make an quick and
economical combination. Round out the meal with a cup of soup and some
crusty bread.

LEMON–DILL DRESSING
⅓ cup vegetable oil
3 tablespoons fresh lemon juice
½ teaspoon minced garlic
1 tablespoon chopped fresh dill, or
    ½ teaspoon dried dill weed
½ teaspoon salt

VARIATION

**DILLED SHRIMP
SALAD**

Substitute 12 ounces
cooked medium-size
shrimp, shelled and de-
veined, for the crab and
proceed as directed.

Per serving: 232 cal,
22 g pro, 16 g car, 8 g
fat, 172 mg chol, 420
mg sod

• EASY • 30 MINUTES
• LOW FAT
• MAKE AHEAD

MAKE AHEAD

The salad mixture can
be prepared and
refrigerated in an air-
tight container for up
to 24 hours. The
dressing can be
prepared and refri-
gerated in an airtight
container for up to
1 week. Assemble the
salad just before
serving.

MAKE AHEAD

Put the dressing
ingredients into a
small jar, cover tightly,
and shake to blend.
Refrigerate up to 3
days. Bring to room
temperature and shake
before using. Cook the
pasta and store in an
airtight container up
to 1 day. Assemble
the salad just before
serving.

8 ounces (4 cups) rotini pasta, cooked, rinsed under cold running water,
and drained
3 cups coarsely chopped iceberg lettuce
1 large cucumber, halved lengthwise and sliced thin (2 cups)
1½ cups cherry tomatoes, halved
1 small red onion, quartered and sliced thin (½ cup)
1 can (15 ounces) pink salmon, drained and skin removed

1. To make the dressing: In a large serving bowl, whisk the oil, lemon
juice, garlic, dill, and salt until well blended.
2. Add the cooked pasta, lettuce, cucumber, tomatoes, and onion. Toss to
mix and coat.
3. With a rubber spatula, gently stir in the salmon. Serve right away.
Per serving: 528 cal, 28 g pro, 50 g car, 24 g fat, 34 mg chol, 718 mg sod

EASY • 60 MINUTES • MAKE AHEAD

PESTO PASTA SALAD
Serves 4
Total time: 45 minutes

Pesto and pasta is a delicious combination. Traditionally it is made with basil,
although you can use a mixture of other herbs as given here. It is also available
ready-made in some large supermarkets.

1 pound fusilli (spiral-shaped) pasta
1 bag (16 ounces) frozen mixed vegetables (broccoli,
carrots, and red bell pepper)

PESTO
1 cup packed fresh basil leaves
½ cup packed fresh Italian (flat-leaf) parsley
¼ cup grated Romano or Parmesan cheese
¼ cup olive oil
¼ cup chicken broth
¼ cup walnut pieces
1 medium-size clove garlic, crushed and peeled
½ teaspoon salt
¼ teaspoon ground black pepper

For garnish: fresh basil leaves (optional)

MAKE AHEAD

The pesto can be made
ahead and refrigerated
in an airtight container
up to 1 week or frozen
up to 1 month. Bring
to room temperature
before using.

▶

1. Bring a large pot of lightly salted water to a boil. Add the pasta and cook according to the package directions. Drain, rinse under cold running water, and drain again. Transfer to a large serving bowl.

2. Cook the frozen vegetables according to the package directions; drain well and place in the serving bowl.

3. Make the pesto: In a blender or a food processor, combine the basil, parsley, Romano, olive oil, chicken broth, walnuts, garlic, salt, and pepper. Blend or process until smooth.

4. Scrape the pesto into the bowl with the pasta and vegetables and toss to mix and coat. Garnish with fresh basil leaves. Serve at room temperature.

Per serving: 716 cal, 24 g pro, 111 g car, 23 g fat, 5 mg chol, 837 mg sod

---

EASY • 30 MINUTES

GREEK PASTA SALAD

Serves 4
Preparation time: 15 minutes
Cooking time: 10 minutes

If you are short on time, use frozen broccoli instead of fresh and bottled red wine vinaigrette dressing to make this recipe.

8 ounces wagon wheel or other small pasta (3 cups)
½ large bunch of broccoli, stems peeled and cut into chunks,
   florets cut into bite-size pieces (3¼ cups)

RED WINE VINAIGRETTE
⅓ cup olive oil
2 tablespoons red wine vinegar
1 teaspoon minced garlic
½ teaspoon salt
½ teaspoon ground black pepper

1 can (about 16 ounces) chick-peas, drained and rinsed
1 jar (about 6½ ounces) pimientos, drained and cut into thin strips
4 ounces feta cheese, crumbled (1 cup), (optional)

1. Cook the pasta according to package directions, adding the broccoli 2 to 3 minutes before the pasta is done. Drain in a colander, cool under cold running water, and drain again.

2. Make the vinaigrette: In a large serving bowl, whisk the oil, ▶ *p. 377*

PASTA PERFECT

◆ Cooked pasta is a wonderful ingredient to add to salads, especially if you are feeding a crowd. It will happily bulk up the other ingredients for little extra cost.

◆ Cooked pasta has no obvious taste of its own and blends with all the other flavors and textures in the salad bowl.

◆ Cooked pasta has a habit of absorbing all the dressing in the salad very quickly. Be sure to put the two together just prior to serving and toss well to coat.

SALAD MEALS
Warm Fiesta
Chicken Salad
(p.363)
combines the
distinctive South-
western flavors
of lime, cilantro,
and cumin.

QUICK AND EASY CUISINE

Feta cheese, made from goat's milk, adds a definite accent to this Greek Pasta Salad (p. 372), left. Served with sesame rolls, it makes a simple weeknight snack. Tofu is the secret ingredient in this low-fat, high-protein Enlightened Caesar Salad (p. 392), above.

Consisting of so many ingredients and served in a variety of ways, salads resist definition. The creativity of the salad maker is usually the determining factor.

OFF THE GRILL
A grilled salad? You bet. Eggplant is mixed with a variety of vegetables in this Roasted Eggplant Salad (p.379). It can be enjoyed as a main dish or an accompaniment to grilled steaks or chicken.

vinegar, garlic, salt, and pepper until well blended.

3. Add the pasta and broccoli, then the chick-peas, pimientos, and feta cheese. Toss to mix and coat. Serve right away.

Per serving: 478 cal, 14 g pro, 60 g car, 21 g fat, 0 mg chol, 429 mg sod

---

EASY • MAKE AHEAD

BLACK BEAN & CORN SALAD

Serves 10

Preparation time: 20 minutes plus at least 1 hour to chill

Jicama (pronounced HEE-ka-mah) is often referred to as Mexican potato. It is equally good eaten raw, as in this salad, or cooked. Look for a large bulbous root with a thin brown skin and peel just before using. If jicama is not available, use sliced celery instead.

DRESSING
½ cup olive oil
3 tablespoons cider vinegar
2 teaspoons minced garlic
1 teaspoon ground cumin
1 teaspoon salt
1 teaspoon granulated sugar
½ teaspoon ground red pepper (cayenne)

3 cans (about 16 ounces each) black beans drained and rinsed
2 cups diced peeled jicama
1 can (about 15 ounces) whole-kernel corn, drained
½ cup finely chopped red bell pepper
½ cup chopped fresh cilantro

1. Make the dressing: In a large serving bowl, whisk the oil, vinegar, garlic, cumin, salt, sugar, and red pepper until well blended.

2. Add the beans, jicama, corn, bell pepper, and cilantro. Toss to mix and coat. Cover and refrigerate at least 1 hour for the flavors to develop. Serve chilled.

Per serving: 220 cal, 6 g pro, 24 g car, 12 g fat, 0 mg chol, 558 mg sod

---

Ⓜ AKE AHEAD

The salad can be prepared and refrigerated in an airtight container up to 1 day, or 2 days ahead with the dressing and salad ingredients stored separately. Assemble the salad just before serving.

CRUNCHY BULGUR SALAD

Serves 8

Total time: 15 minutes plus 25 minutes to stand

Bulgur—cracked wheat kernels that have been steamed, dried, and crushed—is a great grain to have on hand because it requires very little preparation. It has a tender yet chewy texture that lends itself perfectly to salads as well as meat or vegetable pilafs. Serve this salad with grilled fish or poultry.

 4 cups water
 2 cups bulgur
 1½ cups plain low-fat or nonfat yogurt
 1½ teaspoons whole cumin seeds
 1 teaspoon salt
 ⅛ teaspoon crushed red pepper flakes
 1 teaspoon minced garlic
 3 medium-size cucumbers (about 1¼ pounds), sliced thin
 ½ cup sliced thin radishes

 1. In a medium-size saucepan, bring the water to a boil over high heat. Add the bulgur, cover, and remove from the heat. Let stand for 20 to 25 minutes, or until the bulgur is soft but still chewy. Drain well.

 2. In a large serving bowl, mix the yogurt, cumin seeds, salt, red pepper flakes, and garlic until well blended.

 3. Add the bulgur, cucumbers, and radishes. Toss to mix and coat. Serve right away.

Per serving: 159 cal, 7 g pro, 32 g car, 1 g fat, 3 mg chol, 315 mg sod

MAKE AHEAD

The salad can be
prepared ahead and
refrigerated in an
airtight container up
to 3 days.

COOK'S TIP

If a cucumber has been
waxed, it should be
peeled before using.

MEDITERRANEAN CHICK–PEA SALAD

Serves 4

Preparation time: 20 minutes

Chick-peas are used extensively in the Mediterranean in both hot and cold dishes. In this salad, other typically Mediterranean ingredients such as olives, tomatoes, feta cheese, and basil combine to make a stylish main-dish salad. Serve with lavash (a type of cracker bread) or crusty bread.

MAKE AHEAD

Put the dressing

ingredients into a

small jar, cover tightly,

and shake to blend.

Refrigerate up to 3

days. Bring to room

temperature and shake

before using. Prepare

the salad ingredients

and refrigerate covered

up to 1 day. Assemble

and dress the salad

just before serving.

BALSAMIC VINAIGRETTE

¼ cup olive oil

¼ cup balsamic vinegar

½ teaspoon minced garlic

½ teaspoon salt

¼ teaspoon ground black pepper

1 can (16 ounces) chick-peas, drained and rinsed

1 package (9 ounces) frozen French-cut green beans, thawed and drained

12 medium-size pitted black olives

1 cup thinly sliced peeled cucumber

12 cherry tomatoes, quartered, or 1½ cups diced plum tomatoes

4 ounces feta cheese, crumbled (1 cup)

¼ cup loosely packed fresh basil leaves, stacked and cut in strips, or

   1 tablespoon dried basil

1. Make the vinaigrette: In a large serving bowl, whisk the oil, vinegar, garlic, salt, and pepper until well blended.

2. Add the chick-peas, green beans, olives, cucumber, tomatoes, feta cheese, and basil. Toss to mix and coat. Serve right away.

Per serving: 322 cal, 10 g pro, 22 g car, 23 g fat, 25 mg chol, 822 mg sod

EASY • 60 MINUTES • LOW FAT • MAKE AHEAD

ROASTED EGGPLANT SALAD

Serves 4 to 6

Preparation time: 10 minutes

Cooking time: 25 to 50 minutes

Also called "poor man's caviar," this salad makes a nice side dish for a roast leg of lamb; or serve it spooned over pita bread or crackers.

1 large eggplant (1¼ to 1½ pounds)

1 teaspoon vegetable oil

1 medium-size ripe tomato, diced (about ½ cup)

¼ cup diced roasted red peppers or pimientos (from a jar)

¼ cup chopped fresh parsley

2 tablespoons sliced scallions

2 teaspoons fresh lemon juice

¼ teaspoon salt

⅛ teaspoon ground black pepper

MAKE AHEAD

The eggplant can be

roasted up to 24

hours ahead. Cut the

flesh into chunks

and refrigerate in an

airtight container.

Assemble the salad

just before serving.

▶

1. Rub the eggplant with oil.

To grill: Heat a gas grill to medium-high or prepare a charcoal fire. Put the whole eggplant on a lightly oiled grill rack 4 to 6 inches above the hot coals. Cover with the grill lid or a foil tent. Grill for 20 to 25 minutes, turning several times, until the eggplant collapses and is very soft (the skin may split—that's okay). Let stand until cool enough to handle.

To bake: Heat the oven to 400°F. Put the eggplant in a baking dish and bake for 45 to 50 minutes, or until very soft. Remove from the oven and let stand until cool enough to handle.

2. Slit the skin and scrape the flesh into a large bowl.

3. Cut the flesh into chunks (or process with several on/off turns in a food processor until chunky). Transfer the eggplant to a serving bowl and stir in the remaining ingredients. Serve at room temperature.

Per serving: 54 cal, 2 g pro, 10 g car, 1 g fat, 0 mg chol, 146 mg sod

TOSS IT

When tossing a salad, use two large spoons or a pair of salad servers and mix with an up-and-over motion, in much the same way that you would fold beaten egg whites into a batter.

EASY • 60 MINUTES • CLASSIC

ITALIAN TOMATO & BREAD SALAD

Serves 10

Preparation time: 15 minutes plus 30 minutes to marinate

Panzanella, as this classic Italian dish is called, is a time-honored way to use up dried bread. It's wonderful in late summer when vegetable gardens and farmers markets are brimming with vine-ripened tomatoes.

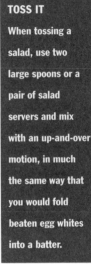

1 small loaf crusty Italian bread (about 12 ounces), cut into
   ½-inch-thick slices
½ cup olive oil
¼ cup red wine vinegar
1½ teaspoons salt
1 teaspoon minced garlic
½ teaspoon ground black pepper
2¾ pounds firm ripe tomatoes (about 8 medium-size),
   cut into large chunks
½ cup thinly sliced red onion
1 cup thinly sliced fresh basil leaves
For garnish: basil leaves (optional)

1. Put the bread slices in a large bowl. Add cold water to cover. Let the bread soak for 10 minutes.

2. Meanwhile, in another large bowl, whisk the oil, vinegar, salt, garlic, and pepper until well blended.

3. Drain the bread and press out the excess water. Tear into small pieces and add to the oil and vinegar mixture.

4. Add the tomatoes and onion. Toss to mix and coat. Let stand at room temperature for at least 30 minutes for the flavors to blend.

5. Stir in the sliced basil just before serving. Garnish with basil leaves and serve right away.

Per serving: 223 cal, 4 g pro, 25 g car, 12 g fat, 0 mg chol, 541 mg sod

---

EASY • 30 MINUTES • MAKE AHEAD

SESAME GREEN BEAN SALAD

Serves 8
Preparation time: 10 minutes
Cooking time: 14 minutes

MAKE AHEAD

Put the dressing ingredients into a small jar, cover tightly, and shake to blend. Refrigerate up to 3 days. Bring to room temperature and shake before using. The beans can be cooked and the radishes sliced up to 1 day before serving, refrigerate separately.

There are two types of sesame oil. One is light in color with a very mild taste and can be used in cooking interchangeably with vegetable oil. The darker Asian sesame oil used in this recipe has a much stronger taste and is used in moderation and only as a flavoring. Serve this salad as a side dish with chicken, turkey, or beef.

3 tablespoons sesame seeds
2 pounds green beans, trimmed and cut crosswise in half
¼ cup water

SESAME DRESSING
¼ cup vegetable oil
2 tablespoons cider vinegar
1 tablespoon dark Asian sesame oil
1 teaspoon Dijon mustard
1 teaspoon granulated sugar
¾ teaspoon salt
½ teaspoon minced garlic

1 bunch red radishes, trimmed, halved (if large), and sliced thin (1 cup)

1. In a large nonstick skillet, toast the sesame seeds over medium-low heat for 1 to 2 minutes, stirring often, until lightly browned. Scrape the ▶

sesame seeds into a small bowl.

2. In the same skillet, combine the beans and water. Cover and steam over medium-low heat for 10 to 12 minutes, or until tender. Drain in a colander and rinse under cold running water. Drain well.

3. Meanwhile, make the dressing: In a large serving bowl, whisk the oil, vinegar, sesame oil, mustard, sugar, salt, and garlic until well blended.

4. Add the beans and radishes. Toss to mix and coat. Sprinkle with the toasted sesame seeds. Serve right away.

Per serving: 131 cal, 2 g pro, 9 g car, 10 g fat, 0 mg chol, 231 mg sod

---

EASY • MAKE AHEAD

CORN & AVOCADO SALAD

Serves 8

Preparation time: 20 minutes plus 1 hour to chill

Prepare this salad in the summer months when local sweet corn and tomatoes are at their peak. It will make a festive and colorful accompaniment to grilled chicken or turkey.

VINAIGRETTE DRESSING
½ cup vegetable oil
3 tablespoons red wine vinegar
1 tablespoon Dijon mustard
½ teaspoon granulated sugar
½ teaspoon salt

4 cups cooked fresh corn kernels, cut from 8
   medium-size cobs
2 medium-size ripe tomatoes, cut into 1½-inch
   pieces (2½ cups)
1 small red onion, quartered and sliced thin
2 medium-size ripe avocados, halved, pitted, peeled,
   and cut into 1½-inch pieces

1. Make the dressing: In a large serving bowl, whisk the oil, vinegar, mustard, sugar, and salt until well blended.

2. Add the corn, tomatoes, and onion. Toss to mix and coat well. Cover and refrigerate for 1 hour for the flavors to develop.

3. Just before serving, gently stir in the avocados. Serve right away.

Per serving: 311 cal, 4 g pro, 29 g car, 23 g fat, 0 mg chol, 207 mg sod

Ⓜ AKE AHEAD

Put the dressing ingredients into a small jar, cover tightly, and shake to blend. Refrigerate up to 3 days. Bring to room temperature and shake before using. Toss it with the corn, tomatoes, and onion at least 1 hour, or up to a day, before serving. Add the avocados just before serving.

POTATO–PICKLE SALAD

Serves 6 to 8
Preparation time: 20 minutes plus 1 hour to chill
Cooking time: 15 minutes

MAKE AHEAD

Prepare the salad and refrigerate in an airtight container up to 2 days ahead.

COOK'S TIP

Potatoes of equal size will cook in the same amount of time. Cook potatoes for a salad just to the firm-tender stage. Overcooked potatoes absorb too much dressing and become mushy.

Chopped dill pickles and dill pickle juice lend a tangy zip to this potato salad. Be sure to add the dressing while the potatoes are still warm so they absorb more flavor.

2 pounds medium-size red-skinned potatoes (about 10), scrubbed and cut into ¾-inch chunks (7 cups)

DILL PICKLE DRESSING
½ cup reduced-fat sour cream
½ cup reduced-fat mayonnaise
1 tablespoon Dijon mustard
1 tablespoon prepared white horseradish
1 tablespoon dill pickle juice
1 teaspoon granulated sugar
½ teaspoon salt
½ teaspoon ground black pepper

2 small Kirby (pickling) cucumbers, scrubbed, halved lengthwise, and thinly sliced crosswise (1½ cups)
⅔ cup chopped red onion
⅓ cup finely chopped dill pickle

1. Bring a large pot of water to a boil. Add the potatoes, cover, and cook over medium heat for 12 to 15 minutes, or until firm-tender. Drain and let cool until warm.

2. Meanwhile, make the dressing: In a large serving bowl, whisk the sour cream, mayonnaise, mustard, horseradish, pickle juice, sugar, salt, and pepper until well blended.

3. Stir in the cucumber, red onion, pickle, and warm potatoes. Gently toss to mix and coat.

4. Cover and refrigerate for at least 1 hour for the flavors to develop. Serve chilled or at room temperature.

Per serving: 196 cal, 4 g pro, 31 g car, 6 g fat, 6 mg chol, 529 mg sod

WARM GERMAN POTATO SALAD

Serves 8

Preparation time: 10 minutes

Cooking time: 27 minutes plus 5 minutes to stand

There are two rules for a perfect potato salad. Don't overcook or undercook the potatoes and try not to swamp them in dressing. They should just be coated lightly. This warm potato salad is wondeful with German-style sausages, baked ham, or pork chops.

12 small red-skinned potatoes, scrubbed (2 pounds)

3 slices bacon

¾ cup beef or chicken broth

½ cup cider vinegar

1 tablespoon cornstarch

1 tablespoon granulated sugar

½ teaspoon salt

¼ teaspoon celery seed

¼ teaspoon ground black pepper

½ cup chopped onion

1 jar (4 ounces) pimientos, drained and chopped

1. Prick each potato 2 or 3 times with a fork. Arrange in a circle on a paper towel in the microwave oven. Microwave on High for 12 to 14 minutes, rearranging the potatoes once, until almost tender. Remove from the microwave and let stand for about 5 minutes, or until tender.

2. While the potatoes are standing, put the bacon in a 2-quart microwave-safe bowl. Cover with a paper towel and microwave on High for 4 to 4½ minutes, rotating the bowl ¼ turn once, until the bacon is crisp. Remove the bacon and pat dry with paper towels. Discard the bacon fat and wipe the bowl clean.

3. In the same bowl, whisk together the broth, vinegar, cornstarch, sugar, salt, celery seed, and pepper until blended. Stir in the onion. Microwave uncovered on High for 6 to 8 minutes, whisking every 2 minutes, until thick and bubbly.

4. Cut the potatoes into 1½-inch pieces. Add to the broth mixture along with the pimientos and toss to mix and coat. Crumble the bacon over the top. Serve warm.

Per serving: 127 cal, 3 g pro, 25 g car, 1 g fat, 2 mg chol, 340 mg sod

A QUARTET OF SALAD DRESSINGS

Try any of these dressings on your favorite mixture of greens.

CILANTRO-YOGURT DRESSING

Makes 2¼ cups
Preparation time: 20 minutes

1 cup loosely packed fresh cilantro
¼ cup cholesterol-free egg substitute
¼ cup fresh lime juice
2 medium cloves garlic, crushed and peeled
1 medium-size jalapeño pepper, seeded
  and coarsely chopped
1 teaspoon salt
1 cup olive oil
½ cup plain low-fat yogurt

1. In a blender or food processor, mix the cilantro, egg substitute, lime juice, garlic, jalapeño, and salt. Blend or process until smooth.
2. With the machine running, add the oil in a slow, steady stream until thickened. Stir in the yogurt.
3. Refrigerate in an airtight container up to 2 weeks

Per 2 tablespoons: 114 cal, 1 g pro, 1 g car, 12 g fat,
0 mg chol, 133 mg sod

TOMATO FRENCH DRESSING

Makes 2 cups
Preparation time: 10 minutes

½ cup red wine vinegar
3 tablespoons tomato paste
1 tablespoon Dijon mustard
1 tablespoon sugar
2 teaspoons minced garlic
½ teaspoon salt
¼ teaspoon ground black pepper
1 cup olive oil

1. In a blender or food processor, mix the vinegar, tomato paste, mustard, sugar, garlic, salt, and pepper and blend or process until smooth.
2. With the machine running, add the oil in a slow steady stream until well blended and thickened.
3. Refrigerate in an airtight container up to 2 weeks.

Per 2 tablespoons: 128 cal, 0 g pro, 2 g car, 14 g fat,
0 mg chol, 115 mg sod

CREAMY ROASTED PEPPER DRESSING

Makes 2⅔ cups
Preparation time: 20 minutes

1 jar (7 ounces) roasted red peppers, drained and
  patted dry
¼ cup cholesterol-free egg substitute
2 tablespoons red wine vinegar
2 medium-size scallions, cut into small pieces
1 teaspoon salt
½ teaspoon dried basil leaves
1½ cups olive oil

1. In a blender or food processor, mix the peppers, egg substitute, vinegar, scallions, salt, and basil. Blend or process until smooth.
2. With the machine running, add the oil in a slow steady stream until smooth and thickened.
3. Refrigerate in an airtight container up to 2 weeks.

Per 2 tablespoons: 141 cal, 0 g pro, 1 g car, 15 g fat,
0 mg chol, 111 mg sod

CREAMY ITALIAN DRESSING

Makes 2¼ cups
Preparation time: 10 minutes

1 cup buttermilk
1 cup 1% fat cottage cheese
¼ cup grated Parmesan cheese
3 tablespoons vegetable oil
1 tablespoon cider vinegar
1 teaspoon garlic powder
1 teaspoon dried basil leaves, crumbled
1 teaspoon prepared mustard
¼ teaspoon salt
¼ teaspoon ground black pepper

1. In a blender or food processor, mix the buttermilk, cottage cheese, Parmesan, oil, vinegar, garlic powder, basil, mustard, salt, and pepper and blend or process until smooth.
2. Refrigerate in an airtight container up to 2 weeks.

Per 2 tablespoons: 41 cal, 2 g pro, 1 g car, 3 g fat, 2 mg
chol, 120 mg sod

BEYOND THE GREEN

◆ If you're cooking rice or pasta, cook extra and refrigerate it. (You might want to toss leftover pasta with oil to keep it from clumping.) Later in the week, use it as the basis for a filling salad to serve with a light meal. Add one or more cut-up raw or cooked vegetables (carrots, green peas, sugar snap peas, broccoli, radishes, cucumber) and a dressing.

◆ Add drained and rinsed canned beans or chick-peas to greens, rice, or pasta.

◆ Drain plain beets (from a can or a jar) before tossing with herb vinaigrette and some sliced onions, if you wish. Beets are also delicious with sliced oranges.

◆ Toss sliced cucumbers (peeled or not) with plain yogurt seasoned with salt, pepper, and dill or chopped fresh cilantro.

◆ Toss strips of roasted red peppers (from a jar, often found in the Italian section of the market) with marinated artichoke hearts and the marinade. No additional dressing is needed.

◆ Arrange sliced, peeled seedless oranges on plates with sliced red onion and sprinkle with a citrus vinaigrette. Add drained and rinsed canned black beans for a more filling salad. Refreshing with spicy Tex-Mex food.

◆ Toss cooked sliced carrots (cook double for dinner) with an oil-and-vinegar dressing and refrigerate for a delicious salad three or four nights later.

◆ Mix drained canned (or fresh) orange segments with vinaigrette dressing. Sprinkle with snipped chives or sliced green onion. Add chopped walnuts if desired.

EASY • 30 MINUTES • MAKE AHEAD

MEXICAN CHILI BEAN COLESLAW

Serves 6

Preparation time: 20 minutes

This slaw is at its most crunchy when freshly made. However, if prepared a day ahead and refrigerated, it will soften somewhat, and the flavors will mellow and blend. It's great either way.

MAKE AHEAD

Prepare the salad and refrigerate in an airtight container up to 3 days.

MEXICAN DRESSING
½ cup reduced-fat mayonnaise
½ cup bottled taco sauce
2 tablespoons cider vinegar
1 tablespoon granulated sugar
1 teaspoon ground cumin

6 cups loosely packed finely shredded green cabbage
2 large carrots, shredded coarse (2 cups)
3 medium-size scallions, sliced thin
1 can (about 16 ounces) red kidney beans, drained and rinsed
2 medium-size jalapeño peppers, seeded
   and minced (3 tablespoons)

1. Make the dressing: In a large serving bowl, whisk the mayonnaise, taco sauce, vinegar, sugar, and cumin until well blended.

2. Add the cabbage, carrots, scallions, beans, and jalapeños. Toss to mix and coat. Refrigerate until ready to serve. Serve chilled or at room temperature.

Per serving: 166 cal, 6 g pro, 26 g car, 5 g fat, 0 mg chol, 431 mg sod

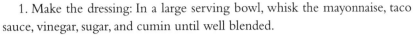

SPICY ASIAN SLAW

Serves 4

Preparation time: 20 minutes plus overnight to chill

Start this unusual salad a day ahead so the cabbage and scallions have time to absorb the flavors of the sweet and spicy dressing. It makes an excellent side dish for pork, chicken, or turkey. Look for hot chili oil in the Asian food section of your supermarket.

DRESSING
1 tablespoon granulated sugar
1 tablespoon rice or cider vinegar
½ teaspoon salt
½ teaspoon ground black pepper
2 tablespoons vegetable oil
2 teaspoons dark Asian sesame oil
1 teaspoon hot-chili oil

4½ cups shredded green cabbage (about 9 ounces)
½ cup sliced scallions
1 package (3 ounces) chicken or pork-flavor
  Oriental noodles with seasoning packets
½ cup water
¼ cup toasted slivered almonds
1 tablespoon toasted sesame seeds

1. Make the dressing: In a large serving bowl, whisk the sugar, vinegar, salt, and pepper until the sugar dissolves. Whisk in the oils until well blended.

2. Add the cabbage and scallions. Toss to mix and coat. Cover and refrigerate overnight (the mixture will wilt and decrease in volume).

3. About 4 hours before serving, crumble the uncooked noodles over the cabbage mixture. Sprinkle with the seasonings (from packets), add the water, and toss to mix well. Cover and refrigerate. The noodles will soften as ▶

Run on the shortest spin cycle. The lettuce will be dry and the case will be damp enough to keep the greens crisp in the refrigerator for hours.

they absorb the moisture.

4. Just before serving, add the almonds and sesame seeds and toss to mix.

Per serving: 285 cal, 5 g pro, 24 g car, 20 g fat, 0 mg chol, 753 mg sod

---

EASY • LOW FAT • MAKE AHEAD

MOLDED GAZPACHO SALAD

Serves 8

Total time: 20 minutes plus at least 3 hours to chill

This light and healthful salad makes a cool and refreshing addition to almost any meal. And any leftovers make a delicious low-calorie snack.

2 envelopes (¼ ounce each) unflavored gelatin
3¼ cups tomato juice or 8-vegetable juice
2 tablespoons cider vinegar
2 tablespoons fresh lemon juice
2 teaspoons Worcestershire sauce
½ teaspoon garlic powder
1 cup chopped green bell pepper
1 cup chopped cucumber
1 cup thinly sliced celery with leaves
1 cup thinly sliced scallions
For garnish: lamb's lettuce (mâche) or other greens (optional)

1. Have eight 6-ounce molds or one 6-cup mold ready.

2. In a large saucepan, sprinkle the gelatin over 1 cup of the tomato juice. Let stand for 1 to 2 minutes to soften the gelatin. Cook over low heat, stirring constantly with a rubber spatula, for about 3 minutes, or until the gelatin is completely dissolved and the liquid is almost boiling.

3. Stir in the remaining 2¼ cups tomato juice, the vinegar, lemon juice, Worcestershire sauce, and garlic powder. Refrigerate for 45 minutes, or until thickened to the consistency of unbeaten egg whites, stirring 3 times.

4. Stir in the bell pepper, cucumber, celery, and scallions. Ladle the mixture into the molds. Refrigerate for at least 3 hours, or until firm.

5. Dip the molds in warm, not hot, water. Invert the molds onto serving plates. Shake from side to side to release the gelatin. Garnish with lettuce. Serve right away.

Per serving: 39 cal, 3 g pro, 8 g car, 0 g fat, 0 mg chol, 391 mg sod with tomato juice, 340 mg sod with 8-vegetable juice

---

MAKE AHEAD

The salad can be refrigerated in the mold(s) up to 2 days. Unmold just before serving.

VARIATION

MICROWAVE MOLDED GAZPACHO SALAD

Sprinkle the gelatin over 1 cup of tomato juice in a 2-quart microwave-safe bowl. Let stand for 1 to 2 minutes for gelatin to soften. Microwave on High for 3 minutes, stirring once, until the gelatin is completely dissolved. Proceed as directed.

Per serving: 39 cal, 3 g pro, 8 g car, 0 g fat, 0 mg chol, 391 mg sod with tomato juice, 340 mg sod with 8-vegetable juice

• EASY • LOW FAT
• MAKE AHEAD

SPINACH & BACON SALAD

Serves 6
Preparation time: 30 minutes
Cooking time: 10 minutes

Fresh spinach leaves, crisp bacon, and a hard-cooked egg are a classic combination. The spinach should be crisp, well dried, and cold before you add the dressing to this salad. The leaves can be torn, placed in a plastic bag, and refrigerated for several hours before serving. The salad makes a filling accompaniment to a bowl of soup or a sandwich.

6 slices bacon, cut into 2-inch pieces
1 large egg, hard-cooked and shelled
3 tablespoons fresh lemon juice
1 teaspoon Dijon mustard
½ teaspoon Worcestershire sauce
¼ teaspoon salt
¼ teaspoon ground black pepper
⅓ cup olive oil
1½ pounds fresh spinach, well rinsed, leaves and tender stems
    torn into bite-size pieces (6 cups packed)
1 cup packaged garlic croutons
¼ cup sliced scallions
¼ cup grated Parmesan cheese

1. In a medium-size skillet, cook the bacon until crisp. Remove to paper towels and drain.

2. Remove and finely chop the egg white. Save for garnish.

3. In a blender or food processor, mix the egg yolk, lemon juice, mustard, Worcestershire sauce, salt, and pepper and blend or process until smooth. With the motor running, add the oil in a slow, steady stream until well blended and thickened. Pour into a large bowl.

4. Add the spinach, bacon, croutons, and scallions. Toss to mix and coat. Sprinkle with the Parmesan cheese and chopped egg white. Serve right away.
Per serving: 230 cal, 8 g pro, 10 g car, 18 g fat, 43 mg chol, 461 mg sod

WASH AHEAD

Washing greens need not be a daily chore. Separate the leaves and soak them in ice water for 10 to 20 minutes to fill the cells with water. Drain the leaves, then dry them well in a salad spinner. Refrigerate in zipper-type food storage bags with a few paper towels to absorb any remaining water. Squeeze out as much air as possible before closing the bags to extend the life of the greens.

An alternative is to line a large bowl with paper towels, add the washed, well-dried greens, then cover the bowl tightly with clear plastic wrap.

EASY • 30 MINUTES

CALIFORNIA SALAD

Serves 6 to 8

Preparation time: 20 minutes

By combining greens and fruits, this salad provides a great contrast in color, texture, and flavor. Choose one of the variations and get a whole new salad.

MUSTARD VINAIGRETTE

⅓ cup vegetable oil

3 tablespoons red wine vinegar

1½ teaspoons Dijon mustard

½ teaspoon minced garlic

½ teaspoon salt

Ground black pepper to taste

10 loosely packed cups mixed greens

1 medium-size grapefruit, peeled and segmented

2 medium-size oranges, peeled and segmented

1 small avocado, peeled, pitted, and cut into chunks

1 cup peeled jicama sticks

1 small red onion, sliced thin

1. Make the vinaigrette: In a large serving bowl, whisk the oil, vinegar, mustard, garlic, salt, and pepper until well blended.

2. Add the greens and toss to mix and coat.

3. Add the grapefruit, oranges, avocado, jicama, and onion. Toss to coat. Serve right away.

Per serving: 189 cal, 3 g pro, 15 g car, 14 g fat, 0 mg chol, 195 mg sod

EASY • 30 MINUTES • MAKE AHEAD

WATERCRESS–GRAPEFRUIT SALAD

Serves 6

Preparation time: 20 minutes

The tang of fresh grapefruit and the crunchy, peppery zip of watercress make this a healthful salad that's a joy to eat. Great served with broiled fish or chicken and cooked pasta.

VARIATIONS

FLORIDA SALAD

Put the dressing in a large serving bowl. Add the greens, 2 peeled and segmented grapefruits, 1 cucumber, halved lengthwise and thinly sliced, 2/3 cup thinly sliced radishes, and 1/2 cup thinly sliced scallions. Serve right away.

Per serving: 140 cal, 2 g pro, 11 g car, 11 g fat, 0 mg chol, 195 mg sod

• EASY • 30 MINUTES

PEAR-ROQUEFORT SALAD

Put the dressing in a large serving bowl. Add the greens and 3 large pears, peeled and cut into bite-size pieces, 1/4 cup toasted pine nuts or almonds, 4 ounces crumbled Roquefort cheese, and 1/2 cup chopped scallions. Serve right away.

Per serving: 251 cal, 7 g pro, 18 g car, 18 g fat, 15 mg chol, 485 mg sod

• EASY • 30 MINUTES

MAKE AHEAD

Put the dressing

ingredients into a small

jar, cover tightly, and

shake to blend.

Refrigerate up to 3

days. Bring to room

temperature and shake

before using. Prepare

and refrigerate the

greens and the grape-

fruit up to 1 day ahead.

Peel and slice the

avocado just before

assembling.

DRESSING

2 tablespoons olive oil

2 tablespoons vegetable oil

1½ tablespoons distilled white vinegar

¼ teaspoon minced garlic

¼ teaspoon dry mustard

8 ounces watercress, thick stems removed (about 4 loosely
  packed cups)

3 ounces romaine lettuce, torn into bite-size pieces
  (about 2 loosely packed cups)

2 large grapefruit, preferably pink (about 1 pound each),
  peeled, white membrane removed, divided into segments
  (about 1½ cups)

1 large avocado (8 ounces), halved, pitted, peeled, and
  cut crosswise into thin slices

¼ cup sliced scallions

1. Make the dressing: In a large serving bowl, whisk both the oils, the vinegar, garlic, and mustard until well blended.

2. Add the watercress and romaine. Toss to mix and coat. Line serving plates or a serving platter with the tossed greens.

3. Arrange alternating slices of grapefruit and avocado on top of the greens. Sprinkle with the scallions. Serve right away.

Per serving: 157 cal, 2 g pro, 9 g car, 13 g fat, 0 mg chol, 19 mg sod

IT'S EASY BEING GREEN

Who says it's not easy being green? Now, with all the colorful salad leaves available, preparing a salad with a variety of colors, textures, and flavors is easier than ever before. And a salad of mixed greens complements just about any meal.

◆ Start with about 9 cups of common greens (romaine, iceberg, green and red leaf lettuce) cut or torn into bite-size pieces. Then add 1 cup of the following more exotic greens:

◆ For a peppery, pungent taste, arugula (also known as rocket) or watercress. To prepare: Cut off arugula roots and wash and dry leaves. Pluck sprigs of watercress off thick stems. The thin stems can be chopped and eaten.

◆ For a pleasantly bitter flavor, add a small amount of escarole or chicory (curly endive), Belgian endive, or radicchio. A little bit goes a long way. To prepare: Tear escarole

or chicory into bite-size pieces. Discard any wilted outer leaves of Belgian endive, then cut into chunks and separate leaves. Or pull off leaves individually, cutting the thick base as necessary to loosen. Tear or cut radicchio.

◆ For a soft buttery taste add Boston or Bibb lettuce. To prepare: Just break leaves off from roots.

◆ Serve mixed greens with a dressing of your choice.

ENLIGHTENED CAESAR SALAD

Serves 8

Preparation time: 20 minutes
Cooking time: 10 minutes

Traditional Caesar dressing is made with raw egg, which sadly today may contain harmful salmonella bacteria. In this version, nutritious tofu has been substituted without altering the dressing's creamy consistency.

CAESAR DRESSING

1 package (10½ ounces) soft tofu (soybean curd), (about 1¼ cups), drained
½ cup olive oil
¼ cup fresh lemon juice
1 can (2 ounces) flat anchovy fillets packed in olive oil, undrained
2 tablespoons red wine vinegar
2 tablespoons grated Parmesan cheese
1 tablespoon Dijon mustard
1 teaspoon minced garlic
½ teaspoon ground black pepper

CROUTONS

½ an 8-ounce loaf French or Italian bread
3 tablespoons olive oil
2 large cloves garlic, peeled and crushed

1¼ pounds romaine lettuce, cut or torn into bite-size pieces (12 cups)
¼ cup grated Parmesan cheese

1. Make the dressing: In a blender or food processor, mix the tofu, oil, lemon juice, anchovies, vinegar, Parmesan, mustard, garlic, and pepper. Blend or process until smooth. Refrigerate until ready to use.

2. Make the croutons: Cut the crust from the bread. Cut the bread into cubes. In a large, heavy skillet, heat the oil and garlic over medium heat for about 5 minutes, or until the garlic is golden. Discard the garlic. Add the bread cubes and cook, stirring occasionally, for 3 to 5 minutes, or until lightly browned. Remove with a slotted spoon to paper towels.

3. Put ⅔ cup of the dressing into a large serving bowl. Add the lettuce and toss to coat. Add the croutons and cheese. Toss again. Serve right away.

Per serving: 283 cal, 7 g pro, 11 g car, 23 g fat, 6 mg chol, 416 mg sod

---

ABOUT TOFU

Tofu (also known as soybean curd) has become more readily available as it has come to be accepted as an excellent form of nutrition and not just a health food staple. Soybeans are cooked and the "milk" is extracted. This is then curdled and drained in a similar way to making cheese, and the solids (curds) formed into tofu cakes. Some cakes are firmer than others, depending on the amount of liquid (whey) that is extracted. The finished texture is smooth and creamy yet firm enough to slice or cube.

Soybean tofu is an economic form of protein that is cholesterol free and an excellent source of calcium and vitamins.

VEGETABLES

> *"What I say is that, if a fellow really likes potatoes, he must be a pretty decent sort of fellow."*
> A. A. MILNE

With their ever-increasing variety, year-round availability, and healthful appeal, vegetables have taken on a new importance in our diets. Naturally low in fat and high in vitamins and fiber, they offer endless options to today's nutrition-conscious consumers.

Supermarkets now offer a vast selection of vegetables including unusual greens and lettuces, fresh wild mushrooms, and regional American specialties such as okra, chile peppers, and tomatillos. In addition, local farmers' markets across the country supply us with a bounty of seasonal produce.

So if you haven't done so already, start making a variety of vegetables a highlight of your family's meals.

LEMON ASPARAGUS & CARROTS

Serves 6
Preparation time: 25 minutes
Cooking time: 15 minutes

Asparagus and carrots look particularly attractive when served together. Cloaked in a lemon butter sauce, they may be served as a side dish or a first course.

    2 pounds carrots, quartered and cut
        into ¼-inch sticks about 1½ inches long
    1 pound asparagus, woody stems broken off, spears cut into pieces
        about 1½ inches long
    2 tablespoons butter or margarine
    ½ teaspoon grated lemon peel
    2 tablespoons fresh lemon juice
    ½ teaspoon salt
    ½ teaspoon ground black pepper

1. In a large deep skillet, bring 1 inch of water to a boil. Add the carrots. Reduce the heat to medium. Cover and simmer for 4 to 6 minutes, or until crisp-tender. Remove the carrots with a slotted spoon to a colander.

2. Add the asparagus to the water in the skillet. Cover and simmer for 6 minutes, or until crisp-tender. Pour the asparagus and water into the colander.

3. In the same skillet, melt the butter over medium heat. Add the lemon peel, lemon juice, salt, and pepper. Return the carrots and asparagus to the skillet. Stir for 1 to 2 minutes, or until well coated and heated through. Serve right away.

Per serving: 110 cal, 3 g pro, 17 g car, 4 g fat, 10 mg chol with butter, 0 mg chol with margarine, 278 mg sod

GREEN BEAN CASSEROLE

Serves 6
Preparation time: 5 minutes
Cooking time: 35 minutes

This green bean casserole uses fat-free cream of mushroom soup and onion melba rounds to reduce fat but not flavor.

ⓜ AKE AHEAD

You can cook the carrots and asparagus up to 1 day ahead. Refrigerate them separately in airtight containers.

ⓒ OOK'S TIP

When buying fresh asparagus, choose spears that are firm and brittle, not limp, with tightly closed buds. Stalks about ½ inch in diameter are best; any stalks that are thicker than your finger may be tough. Store asparagus upright with the cut ends in about 1 inch of water, or wrap cut ends in damp paper towels and place the asparagus in a plastic bag. Refrigerate up to 1 week.

1 can (10¾ ounces) reduced-fat condensed cream
of mushroom soup
½ cup water
1 teaspoon soy sauce
⅛ teaspoon ground black pepper
1 bag (20 ounces) or 2 boxes (9 ounces each) frozen cut green beans,
thawed and drained
1¾ cups crushed fat-free onion melba rounds (about 27 rounds)

1. Heat the oven to 350°F. In a 1½-quart casserole, mix the soup, water, soy sauce, and pepper. Stir in the green beans and 1 cup of the crushed melba rounds.

2. Cover and bake for 20 to 25 minutes, or until hot. Uncover, sprinkle with the remaining crushed melba rounds, and bake for 8 to 10 minutes more, or until the topping is browned.

Per serving: 106 cal, 4 g pro, 20 g car, 1 g fat, 4 mg chol, 350 mg sod

EASY • 30 MINUTES • LOW FAT • MAKE AHEAD

CHINESE–STYLE GREEN BEANS

Serves 8
Preparation time: 7 minutes
Cooking time: 13 minutes

Ⓜ AKE AHEAD

The beans can be steamed up to one day ahead and refrigerated tightly covered.

Soy sauce, sesame oil, garlic, and fresh ginger contribute an aromatic flourish to these steamed green beans.

1 pound green beans, ends trimmed
2 tablespoons soy sauce
2 tablespoons water
1 teaspoon cornstarch
1 teaspoon brown sugar
1 teaspoon dark Asian sesame oil
¼ teaspoon crushed red pepper flakes
2 teaspoons vegetable oil
1 teaspoon minced fresh garlic
1 teaspoon minced peeled fresh gingerroot

1. Place the beans in a vegetable-steamer basket in a large pot over boiling water. Cover tightly and steam for 6 minutes, or until crisp-tender. Cool under cold running water. Drain. ▶

2. In a small bowl, mix the soy sauce, water, cornstarch, sugar, sesame oil, and red pepper flakes until the cornstarch is dissolved.

3. In a large Dutch oven, pot, or wok, heat the vegetable oil over medium-high heat.

4. Add the green beans and stir-fry for 3 minutes, or until the beans are very hot and start to char in spots. Add the garlic and ginger and stir-fry for 2 minutes.

5. Pour in the soy sauce mixture. Toss the beans for 1 minute, until evenly coated and glazed. Serve right away.

Per serving: 37 cal, 1 g pro, 5 g car, 2 g fat, 0 mg chol, 261 mg sod

---

60 MINUTES • CLASSIC

STEAMED ARTICHOKES WITH HERB VINAIGRETTE

Serves 4

Preparation time: 20 minutes

Cooking time: 25 to 40 minutes

Steaming is a good way to cook fresh artichokes because it locks in flavor and nutrients. When buying artichokes, look for ones that are dark green, feel heavy for their size, and are resilient when gently squeezed. Store unwashed artichokes in a plastic bag in the refrigerator up to 4 or 5 days. Serve this dish as an appetizer or main course.

4 medium-size globe artichokes (about 8 ounces each)
Lemon juice
1 tablespoon olive oil
1 medium-size lemon, cut in half

HERB VINAIGRETTE
2 tablespoons white wine vinegar
½ cup olive oil
2 tablespoons minced fresh herbs such as tarragon, basil, or dill
Pinch salt and pepper

1. Cut off the stems so the artichokes will stand upright and slice off ¼ to ⅓ from the top.

2. Break off and discard small leaves from the bottom. Snip off thorny leaf tips. Rub cuts with lemon juice to prevent discoloration.

3. Stand the artichokes in a deep large saucepan. Add 3 inches of water, the

VARIATION

STEAMED ARTICHOKES WITH LEMON BUTTER

Prepare the artichokes as directed. In a small saucepan, melt ¼ cup butter. Remove the pan from the heat and whisk in ¼ cup of fresh lemon juice and ⅛ teaspoon ground black pepper. Serve as directed.

Per serving: 175 cal, 5 g pro, 16 g car, 12 g fat, 31 mg chol, 245 mg sod

• 60 MINUTES
• CLASSIC

HOW TO EAT AN ARTICHOKE

◆ Pull off the leaf tip and dip the base into the sauce.

◆ Pull the base of the leaf between the teeth, scraping off the fleshy pulp. Leave the inedible part of the leaf on the plate and continue, one leaf at a time, down to the inedible center artichoke leaves.

◆ Scrape away (use a fork or spoon) the leaves along with the fuzzy choke to reveal the heart, or artichoke bottom.

◆ Cut the artichoke heart into chunks, dip into the sauce and eat.

oil, and the lemon halves, squeezing the juice into the pan. Cover, bring to a boil, and boil gently for 25 to 40 minutes, or until an artichoke leaf near the center pulls out easily.

4. Meanwhile, make the vinaigrette: In a small bowl, whisk together the vinegar and oil until well blended. Stir in the herbs and salt and pepper.

5. Remove the artichokes with a slotted spoon. Drain upside down in a colander.

6. To serve, put each artichoke on a serving plate with a small bowl of the vinaigrette.

Per serving: 311 cal, 5 g pro, 15 g car, 28 g fat, 0 mg chol, 162 mg sod

---

60 MINUTES • MICROWAVE • LOW FAT

SWEET-&-SOUR BEETS & GREENS

Serves 6
Preparation time: 14 minutes
Cooking time: 21 minutes

The sweetness of fresh beets and the slightly tangy flavor of beet greens make this dish a wonderful accompaniment to pork roasts or game. Beet greens are an excellent source of vitamin A and calcium.

DRESSING
½ cup fat-free red wine vinegar dressing
1 tablespoon minced scallions
1 tablespoon honey
1 tablespoon cider vinegar
½ teaspoon grated lemon peel
¼ teaspoon celery seed
¼ teaspoon ground black pepper

1 bunch (2 pounds) large beets with greens
3 tablespoons water

1. Make the dressing: In a small bowl, mix the vinegar dressing, scallions, honey, cider vinegar, lemon peel, celery seed, and pepper until well blended.

2. Cut the greens from the beets, leaving 1 inch of stems attached. Cut the leaves from the stems. Cut the stems into 1-inch pieces and tear the leaves into bite-size pieces.

3. Wash the stems and leaves separately. Set aside.

▶

4. Wash the beets and put into a deep 2 ½- to 3-quart microwave-safe casserole with 2 tablespoons of water. Cover with a lid or vented plastic wrap. Microwave on High for 12 to 14 minutes, turning the beets once, until tender when pierced in the middle. Drain in a colander. When the beets are cool enough to handle, slip off the skins and 1-inch stems and discard.

5. While the beets cool, put the cut stems in the same casserole with the remaining 1 tablespoon of water. Cover and microwave on High for 3 to 4 minutes, or until crisp-tender. Add the leaves, cover, and microwave on High for 2 to 3 minutes, or until wilted and just tender. Gently stir, then let stand while cutting up beets.

6. Put ½ cup of the dressing into a medium-size bowl. Cut the beets into ½-inch pieces, add to the dressing, and stir to coat. Arrange in the center of a serving platter.

7. Toss the stems and leaves with the remaining dressing and surround the beets. Serve right away or chill up to 3 hours and serve cold.

Per serving: 55 cal, 2 g pro, 12 g car, 0 g fat, 0 mg chol, 389 mg sod

EASY • 30 MINUTES

BROCCOLI VINAIGRETTE

Serves 4
Preparation time: 15 minutes
Cooking time: 5 minutes

This easy-to-prepare broccoli dish, tossed with sun-dried tomatoes, toasted almonds, and a vinaigrette, is served at room temperature and makes an excellent accompaniment to grilled chicken or pork.

1 large head broccoli (about 1 pound)
¼ cup sun-dried tomato bits
2 tablespoons olive oil
2 tablespoons red wine vinegar or cider vinegar
¼ teaspoon minced fresh garlic
¼ teaspoon ground black pepper
⅛ teaspoon salt
1 tablespoon toasted slivered almonds (optional)

1. Cut the broccoli into florets. Peel the stems, cut in half lengthwise, then cut crosswise into ½-inch-thick slices.

2. Bring a large saucepan of water to a boil over high heat. Put the dried tomato bits in a medium-size bowl. Add ¼ cup of the boiling water and set aside.

COOK'S TIP

When storing broccoli, be sure it has plenty of air circulation. Putting it in a plastic bag will cause humidity to build up and the broccoli to decay quickly. Wrap the broccoli in a damp kitchen towel or place in a perforated plastic bag and refrigerate up to 3 days.

3. Add the broccoli stems to the boiling water and boil for 2 minutes. Add the florets and boil for 2 to 3 minutes more, or until bright green and the stems and florets are crisp-tender. Drain well.

4. Add the oil, vinegar, garlic, pepper, and salt to the dried tomatoes and water. Whisk until well blended. Add the broccoli and almonds, tossing to coat. Serve at room temperature.

Per serving: 97 cal, 3 g pro, 8 g car, 7 g fat, 0 mg chol, 95 mg sod

---

60 MINUTES • MAKE AHEAD

SCALLOPED BROCCOLI & CAULIFLOWER

Serves 6

Preparation time: 35 minutes

Cooking time: 25 minutes

This colorful vegetable dish makes a wonderful accompaniment to baked ham or roast turkey, especially for a holiday celebration.

2 cups broccoli florets
2½ cups small cauliflower florets

CHEESE SAUCE
1 tablespoon butter or margarine
1 tablespoon all-purpose flour
½ cup chicken broth
½ cup milk
½ cup shredded Cheddar cheese
⅛ teaspoon white or ground red pepper
   (cayenne)

1. In a large saucepan, bring ½ inch of water to boil. Add the cauliflower florets. Cover, reduce the heat to medium-low, and simmer for 6 to 9 minutes, or until firm-tender when pierced. Drain, rinse with cold water, and drain again. Repeat with the broccoli florets, but cook for only 3 to 5 minutes, or until crisp-tender.

2. Make the sauce: In a medium-size saucepan, melt the butter over medium heat. Add the flour and whisk until blended and bubbly. Gradually add the broth and milk, whisking constantly to prevent lumps. Bring to a simmer and cook for 1 minute, or until thickened. Add the cheese and pepper. Whisk until the cheese melts.

▶

MAKE AHEAD

The vegetables and cheese sauce can be prepared up to 1 day ahead. Place the vegetables in a plastic bag and refrigerate. Pour the sauce into a container, cool it slightly, then place waxed paper or plastic wrap directly on the surface to keep a skin from forming. Bring the vegetables to room temperature and heat in the sauce.

3. Add the vegetables and stir gently to coat. Reduce the heat to medium-low. Cover and heat for 5 minutes, stirring once, until heated through. Serve right away.

Per serving: 98 cal, 6 g pro, 7 g car, 6 g fat, 18 mg chol with butter, 13 mg chol with margarine, 190 mg sod

EASY • 30 MINUTES • CLASSIC

SAUTÉED BROCCOLI RABE

Serves 4

Preparation time: 15 minutes

Cooking time: 10 minutes

Broccoli rabe, also called rapini, rapa, rape, and raab, looks and even cooks a bit like broccoli, but the flavor may remind you of kale, turnip greens, or mustard greens. It is packed with iron, calcium, potassium, and vitamins A, C, and K.

1¼ pounds broccoli rabe
1 tablespoon olive oil
1 teaspoon minced fresh garlic
½ teaspoon salt

1. Remove ½ inch from the bottom of the broccoli rabe stems. Stack the leaves and cut them crosswise into 1-inch pieces. You should have about 14 loosely packed cups.

2. In a deep large, preferably nonstick skillet, heat the oil over medium heat. Add the garlic and cook, stirring once or twice, for 30 seconds to 1 minute, or until its aroma is released.

3. Stir in the salt and add the broccoli rabe (if not all of it fits, let the first batch cook down, then add the rest). If the pan seems dry on the bottom, add 2 to 3 tablespoons of water to prevent scorching. Cover and cook for 6 to 7 minutes, stirring and turning occasionally with 2 spoons, just until the leaves are wilted and the stems are crisp-tender. Cook for 2 minutes more, or until the liquid is almost evaporated. Serve right away.

Per serving: 64 cal, 4 g pro, 6 g car, 4 g fat, 0 mg chol, 338 mg sod

---

COOK'S TIP

Look for broccoli rabe with crisp, dark green leaves, small, firm, unsplit stems, and florets with few or no yellow flowers. Store broccoli rabe in the refrigerator up to 4 days, loosely wrapped in plastic to retain moisture and vitamins.

EASY • 30 MINUTES • LOW FAT

GARLIC–BRAISED BRUSSELS SPROUTS

Serves 4
Preparation time: 10 minutes
Cooking time: 15 minutes

Brussels sprouts are a member of the cabbage family and look like miniature heads of cabbage. They are high in vitamins A and C and are a good source of iron. Prolonged storage of Brussels sprouts often intesifies the flavor, so it's best to use them within two days of purchase.

½ cup water
1 tablespoon butter or margarine
1 tablespoon minced fresh garlic
1 teaspoon minced peeled fresh gingerroot
⅛ teaspoon salt
⅛ teaspoon ground black pepper
1 container (about 10 ounces) Brussels sprouts,
   trimmed and quartered lengthwise

1. In a medium-size saucepan or lidded skillet, bring the water, butter, garlic, ginger, salt, and pepper to a simmer.
2. Add the Brussels sprouts. Cover and simmer for about 8 minutes, or until tender. Uncover and boil for 1 to 2 minutes more, or until most of the liquid has evaporated. Serve right away.

Per serving: 57 cal, 2 g pro, 7 g car, 3 g fat, 8 mg chol with butter, 0 mg chol with margarine, 118 mg sod

THERE'S SAFETY IN BROCCOLI

Scientists have long suspected that eating broccoli and other cruciferous vegetables (cabbage, cauliflower, Brussels sprouts) would deter cancer, but now the proof is in. Researchers have found that these vegetables contain a potent anti-cancer compound called sulphoraphane, which stimulates the body's natural defenses to render cancer-causing chemicals harmless. The researchers are not yet sure how well the anticancer agent in these vegetables stands up under all cooking methods, but microwaving is fine. Nor do the researchers know how much is needed to protect against cancer. For the time being, though, eating five servings of fruits and vegetables a day—at least one of which is broccoli or one of its cruciferous cousins—is an excellent idea. One caveat: Don't count dishes such as broccoli soufflé or quiche as a full serving. They actually contain very little broccoli (and are high in fat to boot).

CABBAGE & NOODLES

Serves 8

Total time: 30 minutes

Here is a hearty cold-weather dish that goes well with ham, chicken, or beef.

4 ounces medium-wide egg noodles

2 slices bacon, diced

1 tablespoon butter or margarine

1 tablespoon olive oil

1 medium-size onion, sliced thin

½ teaspoon minced fresh garlic

¼ cup chicken broth

¼ cup dry white wine or additional chicken broth

¼ teaspoon salt

¼ teaspoon ground black pepper

1½ pounds green cabbage, shredded (9 cups)

1 teaspoon poppy seeds

1. Bring a large pot of water to a boil. Add the noodles and cook according to the package directions. Drain well.

2. Meanwhile, in a large skillet, cook the bacon over medium heat until crisp. Remove with a slotted spoon to paper towels. Wipe the skillet clean.

3. In the same skillet, melt the butter with the oil over medium heat. Add the onion and cook, stirring often, for 6 to 7 minutes, or until the onion is softened. Add the garlic and cook, stirring often, for 1 minute.

CABBAGE QUICK FIXES

Shred cabbage by cutting the head lengthwise in quarters and removing the hard white core with a large knife. Slice the quarters crosswise or grate them on the coarse side of a grater. Then . . .

◆ Stir into canned stewed tomatoes and heat until the cabbage wilts.

◆ Add cider vinegar and brown sugar to taste. Stir-fry in a small amount of oil with garlic and fresh or ground ginger.

◆ Toss 4 cups raw with 1 thinly sliced onion, ¼ cup cider vinegar, 1 tablespoon granulated sugar, and salt and pepper to taste. Chill at least 1 hour. Drain and serve.

◆ Cook along with noodles during the last 5 minutes in the same pot. Drain and toss with oil, lemon juice, poppy seeds, and salt and pepper.

◆ Make a zesty coleslaw with thinly sliced green and red bell peppers and purple onion. Stir a bit of Dijon mustard, dill, hot-pepper sauce, and freshly ground pepper into your usual coleslaw dressing.

◆ Mix shredded cabbage with fresh pineapple chunks, fresh chopped mint, and mayonnaise.

4. Add the broth, wine, salt, and pepper. Bring to a boil and boil for 1 minute.

5. Add the cabbage. Stir over medium–high heat for 3 to 5 minutes, or until crisp-tender.

6. Stir in the bacon, then the noodles and poppy seeds. Cook just until the noodles are heated through. Serve right away.

Per serving: 126 cal, 4 g pro, 17 g car, 5 g fat, 17 mg chol, 159 mg sod with wine, 190 mg sod with broth

EASY • 60 MINUTES • LOW FAT

RED CABBAGE WITH APPLES

Serves 8
Preparation time: 15 minutes
Cooking time: 20 minutes

Red cabbage and apples accented by a sweet and sour mixture of brown sugar and vinegar are a traditional German combination of flavors. Serve this dish alongside bratwurst or with any pork or beef dish.

1 tablespoon solid vegetable shortening
1 head red cabbage (about 2 pounds),
   cored and thinly shredded (11 cups)
½ cup plus 2 teaspoons water
1 large Granny Smith or other tart cooking apple,
   cored and coarsely chopped
1 tablespoon packed light brown sugar, or to taste
1 teaspoon salt
¼ teaspoon pepper
2 teaspoons all-purpose flour
1 tablespoon cider vinegar

1. In a large pot, melt the shortening over medium heat. Add the cabbage and ¼ cup of water. Cover and cook for 5 to 7 minutes, stirring occasionally, until wilted.

2. Stir in ¼ cup of water, the apple, brown sugar, salt, and pepper. Cover and cook for 7 to 10 minutes, stirring often, until the cabbage is almost tender.

3. Meanwhile, in a small cup, mix the flour with the remaining 2 teaspoons of water. Stir in the vinegar. Add to the cabbage, stirring to coat. Cook and stir for 2 to 3 minutes, or until slightly thickened. Serve right away.

Per serving: 61 cal, 1 g pro, 11 g car, 2 g fat, 0 mg chol, 286 mg sod

CLASSIC

FRESH CORN TAMALES

Serves 6

Preparation time: 1 hour

Cooking time: 30 minutes

Tamales are a popular Mexican dish consisting of a cornmeal mixture and various fillings enclosed in a corn husk packet and steamed. These tamales are much lower in fat than their traditional counterparts. They are delicious served as a main dish with chunky salsa or taco sauce.

7 large ears fresh corn with husks

1⅓ cups yellow cornmeal

3 tablespoons corn oil or canola oil

1½ tablespoons sugar

1½ teaspoons baking powder

1 teaspoon salt

1 pound cooked chicken or turkey breast, cut into 2½ x ¼-inch strips

2 cans (4 ounces each) whole green chiles, drained and cut into 12 pieces

1 (6-ounce) chunk Monterey Jack cheese, cut into 12 strips

1. Carefully remove the husks from the corn and reserve. Discard the silk. Cut the kernels off the corn cobs into a large bowl (for about 5 cups of kernels). Reserve the cobs for steaming the tamales.

2. Put the kernels into a food processor, or in batches into a blender, and process to a coarse purée.

3. Pour the purée into a large bowl. Stir in the cornmeal, oil, sugar, baking powder, and salt. Let stand for 15 minutes.

4. For each tamale, select 2 wide or 3 smaller corn husks. Arrange them side by side, placing the tip end of one husk by the wide end of the one next to it, to make a rectangle. In the center of each husk rectangle, place ⅓ cup of the corn mixture and spread it into a 3½-inch square. Repeat with the remaining corn husks and corn mixture.

5. Divide the chicken into 12 equal portions and put 1 portion into the center of each corn mixture with 1 piece of green chile and 1 strip of cheese.

6. Carefully roll up the husks lengthwise, enclosing the filling in the corn mixture, then continue to wrap the uncoated portion of the husk around the outside of the tamale. Tear extra corn husks (use the thinner, inside husks) in long strips and use to tie the ends of the tamale closed. Repeat the procedure to make remaining tamales.

7. Arrange the corn cobs on the bottom of a wide 5- to 6-quart pot or

Dutch oven. Add enough water to come ¾ of the way up the sides of the corn cobs. Stack the tamales on tops of the corn cobs so they don't touch the water. Bring the water to a boil. Reduce the heat to medium. Cover and steam for 30 minutes, or until the tamales feels firm all around (the corn mixture will resemble corn bread).

8. Place 2 tamales on each serving plate. Slide off the corn husk ties. Open up the tamales and serve right away.

Per serving with chicken: 554 cal, 36 g pro, 54 g car, 23 g fat, 97 mg chol, 957 mg sod.
With turkey: 513 cal, 37 g pro, 54 g car, 18 g fat, 93 mg chol, 931 mg sod

---

EASY • 60 MINUTES • CLASSIC

BUTTER–CRUMBED CAULIFLOWER

Serves 4
Preparation time: 10 minutes
Cooking time: 25 minutes

In this dish, cauliflower florets are first blanched then cooked with butter and bread crumbs until golden and crisp. Cauliflower, a member of the cabbage family, is a good source of vitamin A and iron.

1 head cauliflower (about 1½ pounds), cut into florets
2 tablespoons cider vinegar
2 tablespoons butter or margarine
¼ teaspoon salt
¼ teaspoon ground black pepper
2 tablespoons packaged seasoned bread crumbs
1 tablespoon chopped fresh parsley
Grated Parmesan cheese (optional)

1. Bring a large saucepan of water to a boil. Add the vinegar and cauliflower and boil for 6 to 8 minutes, or until crisp-tender. Drain well.

2. In a medium-size skillet, melt the butter over medium heat. Add the cauliflower and season with the salt and pepper. Cook, stirring often, for 4 to 5 minutes, or until lightly golden. Add the bread crumbs, tossing to coat. Cook over medium-low heat, stirring often, for about 3 minutes, or until the bread crumbs are crisp and golden.

3. Stir in the parsley and Parmesan cheese and serve right away.

Per serving: 82 cal, 2 g pro, 7 g car, 6 g fat, 16 mg chol with butter, 0 mg chol with margarine, 308 mg sod

---

COOK'S TIP

When purchasing cauliflower, choose a firm, compact head with a crisp, creamy white curd. (The white portion of cauliflower is called the curd.) Store in the refrigerator in a perforated plastic bag up to 4 days.

60 MINUTES • MAKE AHEAD

CARROT & RUTABAGA PURÉE

Serves 6

Preparation time: 15 minutes

Cooking time: 30 minutes

Fragrant with fresh ginger, this light and delicate vegetable purée is a perfect partner with roast turkey at Thanksgiving.

1 cup water
1½ pounds carrots, cut into 2-inch pieces (3½ cups)
1¼ pounds rutabaga (yellow turnip), peeled and cut into 1-inch pieces (3½ cups)
2 tablespoons butter or margarine
1 to 2 teaspoons minced peeled fresh gingerroot
½ to ¾ teaspoon salt
¼ teaspoon ground black pepper
2 tablespoons chopped fresh parsley

1. In a large saucepan, bring the water to a boil. Add the carrots and rutabaga. Reduce the heat and boil gently for about 20 minutes, or until the vegetables are tender. Drain any liquid into a small dish.

2. In the same pan, melt the butter with the ginger over medium heat.

3. Put the vegetables into a food processor. Process until almost smooth, scraping down the side of the bowl as needed. Add the butter mixture and season with salt and pepper. Process until smooth. Scrape the purée into a serving bowl and sprinkle with the parsley.

Per serving: 118 cal, 2 g pro, 19 g car, 4 g fat, 10 mg chol with butter, 0 mg chol with margarine, 332 mg sod

MAKE AHEAD

The purée can be prepared ahead and refrigerated in an airtight container up to 3 days. Reheat in a saucepan over low heat, stirring often, until heated through.

EASY • 60 MINUTES • LOW FAT

SPICY LIME CORN ON THE COB

Serves 4

Preparation time: 10 minutes

Cooking time: 45 minutes

In this dish, husked corn on the cob is seasoned with lime juice, chili powder, cumin, and cilantro, then wrapped in foil and grilled or oven roasted. The piquant flavors of the seasoning accent the corn's sweetness. ▶ *p. 413*

GREENS
Mustard Greens, Corn, & Ham Cakes (p.417) is nourishing because it includes crucifer-ous vegetables.

The next time you see a farm stand on the side of the road, stop and see what they have to offer. But be warned: Once you've bought fresh vegetables from the source, supermarket produce won't look as good as it used to.

MAIN DISH VEGETABLES
Baked Potatoes with topping (p.425), above, and Vegetable Pancakes with Tomato-Basil Cream (p.435), right, are two excellent ways to enjoy fresh vegetables as an entree.

SOUTH OF THE BORDER
For a Mexican meal, try Fresh Corn Tamales (p.406), filled with chicken or turkey and chiles.

3 tablespoons fresh lime juice
2 teaspoons olive oil
¾ teaspoon chili powder
½ teaspoon ground cumin
4 ears fresh corn
2 tablespoons chopped fresh cilantro
For garnish: lime wedges (optional)

1. Heat a gas grill to medium, prepare a charcoal fire, or heat the oven to 400°F. Tear off 4 large sheets of foil large enough to wrap the corn individually.

2. In a small bowl, mix the lime juice, oil, chili powder, and cumin. Remove the husks and silk from the corn. Place one ear of corn in the center of each sheet of foil. Spoon the lime mixture over the corn, turning to coat evenly. Sprinkle each ear with the cilantro.

3. Bring the longer sides of the foil together over the corn; fold the foil down loosely in folds, allowing space for heat circulation and expansion. Fold up the short ends of the foil; crimp to seal. Place the foil packets on the grill and cover with a grill lid or bake for 40 to 45 minutes, or until the corn is tender.

4. To serve, place the foil packets on serving plates. Fold back the foil, turn the corn to coat with the juices, and garnish with lime wedges.

Per serving: 103 cal, 3 g pro, 19 g car, 3 g fat, 0 mg chol, 19 mg sod

EASY • 60 MINUTES • LOW FAT

FENNEL WITH PARMESAN

Serves 4
Preparation time: 10 minutes
Cooking time: 50 minutes

Fennel's licorice flavor becomes light and delicate when cooked. Fennel is high in vitamin A and is a good source of calcium, phosphorus, and potassium.

2 large bulbs fennel (about 1 pound each), trimmed and halved lengthwise
½ cup chicken broth
2 tablespoons grated Parmesan cheese
2 tablespoons packaged bread crumbs
⅛ teaspoon ground black pepper

1. Heat the oven to 375°F. Butter a shallow baking dish. Place the fennel, cut side down, in the dish. Pour in the chicken broth.

2. Cover tightly with foil and bake for 35 to 40 minutes, or until the ▶

fennel can be pierced through with a fork without any resistance.

3. In a small bowl, combine the Parmesan, bread crumbs, and pepper. Turn the fennel so the cut sides are up. Sprinkle with the Parmesan mixture. Bake uncovered for 10 minutes, or until the crumbs are lightly browned. Serve right away with the pan juices.

Per serving: 54 cal, 3 g pro, 6 g car, 2 g fat, 5 mg chol, 313 mg sod

60 MINUTES • CLASSIC

RATATOUILLE

Serves 6
Preparation time: 20 minutes
Cooking time: 40 minutes

This vegetable stew from the south of France is delicious as a hot or cold side dish or a filling for omelets. Or serve it with bread and cheese for a main course.

¼ cup olive oil

2 large onions, halved and sliced thin

3 large cloves garlic, sliced thin

1 firm eggplant (about 1 pound), cut into
   1-inch cubes (about 5 cups)

1 pound small zucchini, cut in half lengthwise, then cut crosswise into
   ½-inch-thick pieces (about 3½ cups)

1 each small red, green, and yellow bell peppers (or use 3 of one color),
   halved, seeded, and cut into 1-inch strips (3 cups)

1½ pounds ripe plum tomatoes, quartered lengthwise, seeded,
   and cut into 1-inch chunks (about 3 cups)

1 tablespoon chopped fresh thyme, or 1 teaspoon dried thyme leaves,
   crumbled

1½ teaspoons chopped fresh marjoram, or ½ teaspoon
   dried marjoram leaves, crumbled

1½ teaspoons salt

½ teaspoon ground black pepper

1. In a large saucepan, heat 1 tablespoon of oil over medium heat. Add the onions and garlic. Cover and cook over medium-low heat for 10 minutes, stirring twice, until almost tender but not browned.

2. Meanwhile, in a large nonstick skillet, heat 2 tablespoons of oil until hot but not smoking. Add the eggplant and cook for 5 minutes, tossing several times, until lightly browned. Add the remaining 1 tablespoon oil, the zucchini, and the

peppers, and cook for 5 minutes, or until the vegetables are crisp-tender.

3. Add to the onion mixture. Cook, uncovered, over medium-low heat for 15 minutes, stirring gently 2 or 3 times.

4. Add the tomatoes, thyme, marjoram, salt, and pepper. Cook for 5 minutes, or until the vegetables are tender but still hold their shape. Serve hot or at room temperature.

Per serving: 178 cal, 4 g pro, 22 g car, 10 g fat, 0 mg chol, 568 mg sod

MAKE AHEAD • CLASSIC

SICILIAN STUFFED EGGPLANT

Serves 4
Preparation time: 30 minutes
Baking time: 55 minutes

The warm flavors of the Mediterranean come through in this hearty eggplant dish, which makes a pleasing main dish served with polenta and a tossed salad.

2 small to medium-size eggplants (1½ pounds each)
1½ teaspoons salt
3 tablespoons olive oil
1 cup finely chopped onion
1 tablespoon minced fresh garlic
⅔ cup packaged plain bread crumbs
½ cup golden raisins
¼ cup pine nuts or slivered almonds
¼ cup grated Parmesan cheese
¼ cup minced fresh parsley
2 tablespoons fresh lemon juice

1. Halve the eggplants lengthwise. Run a small sharp knife ½ inch in from the edges of the cut side of each eggplant. Scoop out the insides of the eggplants with a spoon and reserve, leaving ½-inch-thick shells. Sprinkle 1 teaspoon of salt into the eggplant shells and invert on paper towels while preparing the filling.

2. Heat the oven to 350°F.

3. Make the filling: Coarsely chop the reserved scooped-out eggplant. In a large skillet, heat 2 tablespoons of oil over medium heat. Add the onion, garlic, and chopped eggplant and cook, stirring often, for 5 minutes, or until the onion is softened. Remove the skillet from the heat and stir in the remaining ingredients with the remaining salt.

▶

---

4. Place the eggplant shells, cut side up, in a 13 x 9-inch baking pan. Mound the filling in each shell. Drizzle with the remaining 1 tablespoon of oil. Pour water into the pan to a depth of ½ inch. Cover tightly with foil and bake for 40 minutes.

5. Remove the foil and bake for 10 to 15 minutes more, or until the edges of the eggplant are tender and the bread crumbs are very lightly browned. Serve hot or at room temperature.

Per serving: 315 cal, 8 g pro, 36 g car, 17 g fat, 4 mg chol, 806 mg sod

30 MINUTES

KALE WITH RAISINS
& ALMONDS

Serves 8 to 10
Preparation time: 10 minutes
Cooking time: 16 minutes

Kale is easily identified by the bluish-gray tint on its ruffled leaves. It is more mildly flavored than most greens and is a good source of calcium, potassium, and vitamins A and C. Here kale is given a taste twist when combined with apple juice, raisins, and almonds.

¼ cup slivered almonds
2 pounds fresh kale, rinsed, stems removed, and leaves chopped
   (20 cups)
½ cup water
½ cup apple juice
¼ cup golden raisins
2 tablespoons butter or margarine

1. Toast the almonds in a large, preferably nonstick skillet over medium heat for 7 to 8 minutes, stirring often. Scrape into a small bowl.

2. Add the kale and water to the skillet (if greens don't all fit, let some cook down, then add the rest). Cover and cook for 4 to 5 minutes, stirring and turning occasionally with 2 spoons, until the leaves are just wilted and most of the liquid is evaporated.

3. Stir in the apple juice and raisins. Cook uncovered for 2 to 3 minutes, stirring often, until the apple juice is almost evaporated. Remove the skillet from the heat and stir in the butter, then almonds. Serve right away.

Per serving: 94 cal, 3 g pro, 12 g car, 5 g fat, 7 mg chol with butter, 0 mg chol with margarine, 56 mg sod

COOK'S TIP

To store kale, snap off and discard any exceptionally large stems, put in a plastic bag, and refrigerate up to 3 days. When ready to use, rinse the leaves in lukewarm—not cold—water, to remove any grit or sand.

MUSTARD GREENS, CORN, & HAM CAKES

Serves 4 to 6
Preparation time: 15 minutes
Cooking time: 18 minutes (6 minutes per batch)

Usually sharp mustard greens are mild-flavored in these skillet cakes. If using frozen chopped mustard greens, it's important that they be thawed and squeezed dry before using. Serve these savory cakes as a main course with cooked rice.

1 cup milk
1 large egg
1 package (8½ to 12 ounces) corn-muffin mix
2 tablespoons vegetable oil
8 ounces ham, cut into ¼-inch pieces (1⅔ cups)
1 pound fresh mustard greens, well rinsed and chopped (about 12 cups),
    or 1 package (10 ounces) frozen chopped mustard greens, thawed and
    squeezed dry
1 cup fresh, canned, or thawed frozen corn kernels
½ cup plain low-fat yogurt
½ cup bottled salsa

1. In a medium-size bowl, whisk together the milk and egg. Whisk in the corn muffin mix until evenly moistened (the batter will be slightly lumpy).

2. In a large, preferably nonstick skillet, heat 1 tablespoon of the oil. Add the ham and cook for 2 to 3 minutes, stirring often, until any moisture evaporates. Add the fresh greens, stirring 3 or 4 times, until wilted and any moisture evaporates.

3. Stir the ham and greens (or thawed frozen greens if using) and corn into the batter.

4. Wipe the skillet clean with paper towels. Put ½ teaspoon of oil in the skillet and heat over medium heat. Drop the batter by ⅓ cupfuls and spread to form 4-inch-wide cakes. Cook for 2 to 3 minutes on each side, or until lightly browned. Remove to a serving platter and keep warm. Repeat with the remaining oil and batter.

5. Serve with the yogurt and salsa.

Makes 12 cakes. Per 3 cakes with fresh ham: 606 cal, 24 g pro, 72 g car, 27 g fat, 96 mg chol, 1,914 mg sod. With canned ham: 594 cal, 21 g pro, 75 g car, 24 g fat, 42 mg chol, 2,034 mg sod

COOK'S TIP

If you're using fresh mustard greens, choose bunches with small, light-colored leaves. This means the greens are young and therefore the most tender and mild-flavored. Store mustard greens unwashed in a plastic bag in the refrigerator up to 2 days.

BRAISED MUSHROOMS

Serves 6

Preparation time: 15 minutes plus 20 minutes to soak
Cooking time: 50 minutes

Dried porcini and fresh white mushrooms are slow-cooked to produce a flavorful and succulent side dish that is wonderful with veal chops, steaks, or chicken.

½ ounce dried porcini mushrooms (about ½ cup)
1 cup hot water
3 tablespoons olive oil
1 teaspoon minced fresh garlic
1½ pounds white mushrooms, cut in half (8 cups)
¼ teaspoon salt
¼ teaspoon ground black pepper

1. Put the porcini mushrooms into a small bowl and cover with the hot water. Let soak for about 20 minutes, or until soft (if porcini feel sandy after soaking, rinse them in lukewarm water). Line a strainer with a paper towel and place over a small bowl. Pour the soaking liquid through the strainer to catch any sand. You should have about ¾ cup soaking liquid.

2. In a large skillet, heat the oil over medium heat. Add the garlic and cook over medium-low heat for 2 to 3 minutes, stirring often, until softened.

3. Add the white mushrooms, porcini, porcini soaking water, salt, and pepper. Stir over medium-high heat for 1 to 2 minutes, or until coated and simmering. Reduce the heat to low.

4. Partially cover and cook for 40 to 45 minutes, stirring occasionally, until deep golden brown. If any liquid remains in pan, increase the heat to high and cook until it evaporates.

Per serving: 96 cal, 3 g pro, 7 g car, 7 g fat, 0 mg chol, 96 mg sod

MAKE AHEAD

**The braised
mushrooms can be
prepared up to one day
ahead and refrigerated
in an airtight container.
Slowly reheat on the
stove over low heat.**

HONEY–BAKED RED ONIONS

Serves 6

Preparation time: 15 minutes
Baking time: 1 hour 5 minutes

This vegetable dish is delicious served hot or at room temperature.

COOK'S TIP

This dish can be prepared with other mild-tasting onions, such as Vidalia, Maui, or Walla Walla.

3 large red onions (about 2 pounds), peeled and cut in half crosswise
¼ cup water

GLAZE
⅓ cup honey
3 tablespoons butter or margarine, melted
1 teaspoon paprika (preferably sweet Hungarian)
1 teaspoon ground coriander
½ teaspoon salt
⅛ teaspoon ground red pepper (cayenne)
For garnish: sprigs fresh parsley (optional)

1. Heat the oven to 350°F.
2. Arrange the onions, cut sides down, in one layer in an ungreased baking dish. Sprinkle with the water, cover with foil, and bake for 30 minutes.
3. Meanwhile, make the glaze. In a medium-size bowl, mix the honey, butter, paprika, coriander, salt, and red pepper until well blended.
4. Turn the onions cut sides up. Spoon half the glaze over them. Bake uncovered for 15 minutes. Baste with the remaining glaze and bake for 15 to 20 minutes more, or until the onions are tender when pierced.

Per serving: 164 cal, 2 g pro, 28 g car, 6 g fat, 16 mg chol with butter, 0 mg chol with margarine, 263 mg sod

---

EASY • 30 MINUTES

GREEN PEAS WITH TOMATOES & MINT

Serves 8
Preparation time: 8 minutes
Cooking time: 15 minutes

Chopped fresh mint adds a refreshing dash to this simple, colorful side dish.

3 tablespoons olive oil
¾ cup finely chopped onion
1 cup coarsely chopped, seeded, and peeled plum tomatoes (fresh or canned)
2 packages (10 ounces each) frozen green peas, thawed
½ teaspoon salt
¼ teaspoon ground black pepper
2 tablespoons chopped fresh mint, basil, or parsley

▶

1. In a large saucepan, heat the oil over medium heat. Add the onion and cook, stirring often, for 5 to 7 minutes, until golden brown.

2. Stir in the tomatoes and cook for 3 minutes, then stir in the peas, salt, and pepper.

3. Cover and cook for 4 to 5 minutes, stirring once or twice, until the peas are hot.

4. Remove the pan from the heat. Stir in the mint and serve right away.

Per serving: 110 cal, 4 g pro, 12 g car, 5 g fat, 0 mg chol, 219 mg sod

EASY • 30 MINUTES

ASIAN SNOW PEAS

Serves 4
Preparation time: 15 minutes
Cooking time: 3 minutes

This stir-fry makes a wonderful accompaniment to lamb, chicken, or pork. Look for canned straw mushrooms and water chestnuts in the Asian food section of your supermarket.

⅓ cup chicken broth
1 tablespoon soy sauce
1 tablespoon rice vinegar
1 teaspoon minced peeled fresh gingerroot
2 tablespoons vegetable oil
8 ounces snow peas, strings removed
1 can (8 ounces) sliced water chestnuts, drained (½ cup)
1 can (8 ounces) straw mushrooms, drained (½ cup)

1. In a small bowl, mix the chicken broth, soy sauce, vinegar, and ginger.

2. In a wok or large heavy skillet, heat the oil over high heat until hot but not smoking. Add the snow peas and stir-fry for 30 seconds.

3. Add the chicken broth mixture and cook, stirring constantly, for about 1½ minutes, or until most of the liquid has evaporated. Add the water chestnuts and mushrooms and stir-fry for 30 seconds to 1 minute, or until heated through. Serve right away.

Per serving: 113 cal, 3 g pro, 9 g car, 7 g fat, 0 mg chol, 480 mg sod

ROASTED STUFFED PEPPERS

Serves 4 to 8
Preparation time: 25 minutes
Cooking time: 35 minutes

ⓜAKE AHEAD

Prepare the stuffed peppers through step 4. Cover with plastic wrap and refrigerate up to 2 days. Bring to room temperature, remove plastic wrap, and proceed as directed.

Freshly roasted red bell peppers impart a rich, sweet flavor to this dish. The stuffed peppers can be served as a side dish or as a meatless main course. If serving them as an entree, round the meal out with sautéed white beans, a mixed green salad, and bread.

½ cup uncooked long-grain white rice
4 medium bell peppers (red, green, and/or yellow),
   halved lengthwise, seeds and membranes removed
1 tablespoon olive oil
½ cup finely chopped onion
2 teaspoons minced fresh garlic
1 small eggplant (about 1 pound), diced (2 cups)
1 large zucchini or yellow squash (about 8 ounces),
   shredded (about 1½ cups)
1 large carrot, shredded (about 1 cup)
¼ teaspoon dried oregano leaves, crumbled
2 tablespoons chopped fresh basil
½ cup shredded fontina cheese (2 ounces)
¼ cup grated Parmesan cheese
¼ teaspoon salt
¼ teaspoon ground black pepper

1. Adjust the oven rack to the center of the oven. Heat the broiler. Cook the rice according to the package directions.

2. Meanwhile, arrange the bell peppers, cut sides down, in a shallow baking pan, and coat with vegetable oil cooking spray. Broil for 5 minutes on each side, or until lightly charred. Remove the pan from the oven and reduce the oven temperature to 375°F.

3. In a large nonstick skillet, heat the oil over medium heat. Add the onion and cook for 2 minutes, stirring often, until softened. Add the eggplant and garlic and cook for 5 minutes, stirring often. Add the zucchini, carrot, and oregano and cook for 5 minutes more, stirring often, until tender.

4. Stir in the rice, basil, fontina, 2 tablespoons of Parmesan, the salt, and pepper. Fill the roasted pepper halves with the vegetable mixture.

5. Loosely cover with foil and bake for 25 minutes. Remove the foil, ▶

sprinkle with the remaining Parmesan, and bake for 5 to 10 minutes more, or until lightly browned.

Makes 8 peppers. Per pepper: 138 cal, 5 g pro, 19 g car, 5 g fat, 10 mg chol, 181 mg sod

---

EASY • 60 MINUTES

ROASTED GARLIC MASHED POTATOES

Serves 6

Total time: 1 hour

If skin's your thing, don't peel the potatoes. Mash the skins along with the spuds (but be sure they've been scrubbed well). Or peel the potatoes ahead and keep them covered with water to prevent discoloring.

1 small head garlic

10 large baking or all-purpose potatoes (5 pounds), peeled (or not) and quartered

1⅓ cups milk

1 stick (½ cup) butter or margarine, cut into pieces, at room temperature

2 teaspoons salt

½ teaspoon ground black pepper

1. Heat the oven to 325°F.

2. Slice about ¾ inch from the top of the garlic head. Wrap the head in foil. Bake directly on the oven rack for 45 minutes, or until the cloves are softened. Or peel the garlic cloves, boil, and mash with the potatoes.

3. Meanwhile, cook the potatoes in a large pot of boiling water to cover for 25 to 30 minutes, or until tender when tested with a fork. Drain and return the potatoes to the pot.

4. Unwrap the roasted garlic. Press the uncut ends of the garlic cloves to squeeze the garlic paste over the potatoes.

5. Add the milk, butter, salt, and pepper. Mash or whip with an electric mixer until blended.

Per serving: 490 cal, 10 g pro, 68 g car, 21 g fat, 59 mg chol with butter, 9 mg chol with margarine, 1,122 mg sod with butter, 1,149 mg sod with margarine

---

POTATO TIPS

◆ **Buying:** Choose fairly clean, smooth, firm potatoes. For even cooking, pick potatoes that are about the same size. Select regular shapes to save on waste in peeling. Do not select potatoes with wrinkled skins, soft dark spots, cut surfaces, or green areas. Green spots means exposure to light; cut the spot off before cooking to eliminate any bitterness.

◆ **Storing:** Potatoes are more fragile than they appear, so you should handle them carefully to prevent bruising. Keep potatoes in a cool, dry, dark, and well-ventilated place. White potatoes will keep for several weeks. Sweet potatoes do not keep as well and should be stored only up to one week.

**MICROWAVE
SLIM-SCALLOPED
POTATOES**

• Coat a large
microwave-safe baking
dish with vegetable oil
cooking spray and
arrange the potatoes
as directed.

• In a 2-quart
microwave-safe bowl,
microwave the butter
on High for 1 minute,
or until melted. Stir in
the onion and ¼ tea-
spoon thyme. Cover
with waxed paper and
microwave on High for
2 to 3 minutes.

• Stir in the flour, salt,
and pepper. Whisk in
the milk. Microwave on
High for 5 to 7 minutes,
whisking once, until
thickened. Pour over
the potatoes.

• Cover with vented
plastic wrap and
microwave on High for
22 to 24 minutes,
rotating the dish ¼ turn
3 times, until the pota-
toes are almost tender.
Sprinkle the cheese on
top. Let stand for 10
minutes, or until the
cheese is melted.

Per serving: 152 cal, 4 g
pro, 23 g car, 5 g fat, 12
mg chol with butter, 5
mg chol with margarine,
211 mg sod

• EASY • 60 MINUTES

EASY

SLIM–SCALLOPED POTATOES

Serves 8
Preparation time: 10 minutes
Cooking time: 1 hour 5 minutes

If scalloped potatoes seem too rich, try this lightened-up version that skimps on fat but not on flavor. This dish is a favorite accompaniment with roasts and baked ham. Gruyère and Swiss cheese can also be used instead of Jarlsberg.

> 2 pounds russet potatoes, peeled and sliced ⅛ inch thick
> 2 tablespoons butter or margarine
> 1 medium-size onion, chopped
> ½ teaspoon dried thyme leaves, crumbled
> ½ teaspoon salt
> ½ teaspoon ground black pepper
> 3 tablespoons all-purpose flour
> 2 cups skim milk
> ½ cup shredded Jarlsberg cheese (2 ounces)

1. Heat the oven to 350°F. Coat a 13 x 9-inch baking dish with vegetable-oil cooking spray. Arrange the potato slices slightly overlapping in a single layer in the dish.

2. In a medium-size saucepan, melt the butter over medium-low heat. Stir in the onion, thyme, salt, and pepper. Cook for 4 to 5 minutes, stirring occasionally, until the onion is softened. Stir in the flour until frothy. Let the mixture bubble for about 2 minutes, stirring often to prevent browning. Gradually stir in the milk until well blended. Increase the heat to medium and simmer until the sauce is thick, stirring constantly. Spread the sauce over the potatoes.

3. Cover the dish with foil. Bake for 45 minutes, or until the potatoes are tender when pierced with a fork. (Sauce may look curdled, but that's okay.) Sprinkle the cheese over the top. Bake uncovered for about 10 minutes more, or until the cheese is melted and the sauce is bubbly. Let stand for 5 minutes before serving.

Per serving: 152 cal, 4 g pro, 23 g car, 5 g fat, 12 mg chol with butter, 5 mg chol with margarine, 211 mg sod

MAKE AHEAD • CLASSIC

TWICE–BAKED POTATOES

Serves 9
Total time: 1 hour 45 minutes

These crispy potato shells filled with mashed potatoes are sure to be a family favorite. They can be served with almost any meat or poultry entree.

6 medium-size russet potatoes, scrubbed
½ cup milk
¼ cup (½ stick) butter or margarine
1 large egg, lightly beaten
6 tablespoons grated Parmesan cheese
¼ cup snipped fresh chives or finely chopped scallion tops
¼ teaspoon salt
¼ teaspoon ground black pepper
Pinch of nutmeg
Paprika

1. Heat the oven to 400°F. Pierce the potatoes in several places with a fork. Place on a baking sheet or oven rack. Bake for 50 to 60 minutes, or until the potatoes feel soft when squeezed. Remove the potatoes from the oven and let cool for 15 minutes.

2. Halve the potatoes lengthwise. Using a teaspoon, scoop out the pulp into a large bowl, leaving a ¼-inch-thick shell. Reserve the 9 best shells. (See Cook's Tip.)

3. In a medium-size saucepan, combine the milk and butter and heat over medium heat until the butter melts. Pour the mixture over the potato pulp and mash (or beat with electric mixer) until almost smooth. Add the egg, 3 tablespoons of Parmesan cheese, the chives, salt, pepper, and nutmeg. Mash until smooth (some small lumps may remain).

4. Fill the potato shells using about ⅓ cup of the mashed potato mixture for each shell. Sprinkle the potatoes with the remaining 3 tablespoons of Parmesan cheese and a little paprika.

5. Reduce the oven temperature to 350°F. Arrange the potatoes on a baking sheet. Bake for 30 minutes, or until puffed and lightly golden.

Makes 9 halves. Per half: 163 cal, 5 g pro, 20 g car, 7 g fat, 42 mg chol with butter, 28 mg chol with margarine, 200 mg sod

 COOK'S TIP

Freeze the remaining shells and use for fried or stuffed potato skins. For creamy-smooth potatoes, beat them with an electric mixer. Don't use a food processor—it can make them very gummy.

 MAKE AHEAD

The potatoes can be assembled through Step 4 up to one day ahead. Arrange on a baking sheet or in a pan, cover with plastic wrap, and refrigerate. Bring the potatoes to room temperature before baking.

VARIATION

SWEET POTATO OVEN-FRIES

Peel 2 large sweet potatoes, cut into ¼-inch-thick sticks, and proceed as directed.

Per serving: 93 cal, 1 g pro, 20 g car, 1 g fat, 0 mg chol, 146 mg sod

- **EASY • 30 MINUTES**
- **LOW FAT**

EASY • 30 MINUTES • LOW FAT

OVEN-FRIES

Serves 4

Preparation time: 5 minutes

Cooking time: 25 minutes

Now you can enjoy the taste of French fries without having to fry them. These potato sticks become crisp and crunchy from baking in the oven. They can be cooked simultaneously with oven-fried or baked chicken.

> 2 large baking potatoes, peeled and cut into
>   ¼-inch-thick sticks
> ¼ teaspoon salt
> ¼ teaspoon ground black pepper

1. Place an oven rack in the top third of the oven. Heat to 450°F. Coat a large wire cake rack with vegetable oil cooking spray and place on a baking sheet.

2. Put the potato sticks in a bowl. Toss and spray with cooking spray until lightly coated. Arrange the potatoes in a single layer on the wire rack.

3. Bake for 18 to 20 minutes, or until the tops of the potato sticks are golden. Remove from the oven. Turn the potatoes over with a spatula. Return to the oven and bake for 5 to 7 minutes more, or until golden and crisp. (Watch carefully; the potatoes may bake unevenly.) Toss with salt and pepper.

Per serving: 74 cal, 2 g pro, 15 g car, 1 g fat, 0 mg chol, 140 mg sod

---

PERFECT BAKED POTATOES

Scrub potatoes well and pierce with a fork. Bake at 400°F about 45 minutes for 6-ounce potatoes, or up to 70 minutes for really big potatoes. Or arrange one inch apart on a microwave-safe paper towel. Count on 8 minutes for four 6-ounce potatoes, longer for more potatoes—or larger ones. To open, cut an X just through the skin on top, then push the ends toward the center to open. Try one of the following toppings:

♦ **Reuben:** Top baked potatoes with corned beef, Russian dressing, sauerkraut, and Swiss cheese strips. Broil until cheese melts.

♦ **Chili Head:** Top with heated canned chili, shredded Cheddar cheese, and a sprinkling of sliced scallions.

♦ **Surfside:** Top with drained canned salmon or tuna, snipped fresh dill, and heated frozen creamed spinach.

♦ **Smoky Joe:** Thin slices of smoked sausage pan-fried with sliced onions. Drizzle with horseradish sauce.

♦ **Shanghai Spud:** Spoon on heated canned chicken chow mein and sprinkle with peanuts.

♦ **Finnish Up:** Herring in cream sauce and a sprinkling of chopped chives.

♦ **Deli:** Whipped cream cheese, sliced smoked salmon, and a little bit of chopped red onion.

♦ **Garden Variety:** Shredded zucchini and carrots mixed with yogurt, chopped scallions, and a pinch of curry powder.

MASHED SWEET POTATOES & APPLES

Serves 6

Total time: 55 minutes

Sweet potatoes are not actually potatoes at all, but members of the morning glory family. Here, the potatoes are mashed with sautéed apple and onion and flavored with a little grated nutmeg. Serve this dish with roast chicken, turkey, or pork.

> 2 pounds sweet potatoes
> 1½ tablespoons butter or margarine
> ½ cup chopped onion
> 2 large Granny Smith apples, peeled, cored, and coarsely
>   chopped (2½ cups)
> 2½ tablespoons water
> ¼ teaspoon salt
> ¼ teaspoon ground black pepper
> ¼ teaspoon grated nutmeg
> For garnish: sprigs of fresh dill or parsley (optional)

1. Bring a large pot of water to a boil. Add the sweet potatoes and boil gently for 30 to 35 minutes, or until tender. Drain and let cool slightly.

2. Meanwhile, in a large skillet, melt 1 tablespoon of butter over medium heat. Add the onion and cook, stirring occasionally, for 6 to 8 minutes, or until golden and tender. Add the apples and water. Cover and cook over medium-low heat for 10 to 15 minutes, stirring occasionally, until tender.

3. Peel the potatoes (pull or slip off skin), cut into chunks, and put into a large bowl.

4. Add the remaining butter, the salt, pepper, nutmeg, and apple mixture. Mash until smooth, then spoon into a serving dish. Garnish with sprigs of fresh dill or parsley. Serve right away.

Per serving: 172 cal, 2 g pro, 35 g car, 3 g fat, 8 mg chol with butter, 0 mg chol with margarine, 136 mg sod

COOK'S TIP

Sweet potatoes are easier to peel after boiling.

MAKE AHEAD

The recipe can be made up to 3 days ahead, spooned into a greased 2½- to 3-quart baking dish, covered, and refrigerated. To serve, reheat, covered, in a 375°F oven for 25 to 30 minutes.

EASY • 60 MINUTES

ORANGE–SCALLION SWEET POTATO PACKETS

Serves 4
Preparation time: 15 minutes
Cooking time: 40 minutes

Slices of sweet potato are drizzled with orange-scallion butter and folded into foil packets. These vegetable packets are perfect for entertaining because they can be made early in the day, they can be either grilled or baked just before serving.

ORANGE–SCALLION BUTTER
½ stick (¼ cup) butter or margarine
1 tablespoon minced scallions
½ teaspoon freshly grated orange peel
¼ teaspoon salt
¼ teaspoon ground black pepper

4 medium-size sweet potatoes (about 8 ounces each),
    scrubbed and cut crosswise into ¼-inch-thick slices

1. Heat a gas grill to medium, prepare a charcoal fire, or heat the oven to 350°F.
2. Make the orange-scallion butter: In a small saucepan, melt the butter over medium heat. Stir in the scallions, orange peel, salt, and pepper.
3. Put four 12-inch squares of foil on the counter. Put 1 sliced potato near the bottom of each piece of foil and drizzle with the orange-scallion butter. Toss the potatoes to coat evenly. Fold the foil over the potatoes, bring the edges together, and double fold all sides to seal.
4. To grill, place the packets on the grill 4 to 6 inches above the coals. Grill for 35 to 40 minutes, shaking the packet 2 or 3 times and turning over once, until the potatoes are tender. (To test for doneness, pierce through the foil with a skewer or long-tined fork.)

To bake, place the packets directly on the oven rack. Bake for 35 to 40 minutes. (No need to shake or turn packets.) Serve right away.

Per serving: 341 cal, 4 g pro, 55 g car, 12 g fat, 31 mg chol with butter, 0 mg chol with margarine, 282 mg sod with butter, 299 mg sod with margarine

SQUASH CHEDDAR BAKE

Serves 7

Preparation time: 10 minutes

Cooking time: 40 minutes

Serve with a crisp green salad and dark bread. You can also bake this in a 9-inch pie plate for 35 to 40 minutes. Winter squash is a good source of vitamins A, B, and C, plus potassium, calcium, and iron. It comes frozen, too, in chunks or puréed, which can save a lot of peeling and cooking time.

1 tablespoon butter or margarine

1 cup chopped onion (1 large)

3 large eggs

3 cups mashed cooked winter squash
   (from about 3 pounds buttercup, butternut, or kabocha)

½ cup milk

1 cup shredded sharp Cheddar cheese (4 ounces)

1 teaspoon salt

2 tablespoons chopped fresh dill, or ½ teaspoon dried dillweed

¼ teaspoon ground black pepper

For garnish: fresh dill sprigs (optional)

1. Heat the oven to 350°F. Lightly grease seven 6-ounce ramekins or custard cups and place on a baking sheet.

2. In a medium-size skillet, melt the butter over medium heat. Add the onion and cook over medium-low heat for 8 to 10 minutes, stirring occasionally, until golden and tender.

3. Meanwhile, in a large bowl, beat the eggs with a fork. Stir in the squash, milk, ½ cup of cheese, the salt, dill, and pepper, then the onion mixture.

4. Ladle into the prepared ramekins. Sprinkle the tops with the remaining ½ cup cheese.

5. Bake for 25 to 30 minutes, or until a toothpick inserted into the centers comes out clean. Set the ramekins on a wire rack to cool for 5 minutes. Garnish with fresh dill sprigs.

Per serving: 186 cal, 8 g pro, 12 g car, 12 g fat, 119 mg chol with butter, 111 mg chol with margarine, 469 mg sod

MICROWAVE SQUASH CHEDDAR BAKE:

• Lightly grease seven 6-ounce microwave-safe ramekins. Put the butter and onion in a 1½-quart microwave-safe bowl. Cover and microwave on High for 4 to 5 minutes, or until the onion is softened, stirring once.

• Remove the bowl from the oven. Beat in the eggs. Stir in ½ cup of cheese, then the remaining ingredients except for the garnish. Ladle the mixture into the prepared ramekins.

• Arrange in a circle in the microwave oven. Cover with waxed paper. Microwave on High for 5 to 7 minutes, rearranging the cups and rotating ½ turn twice, until the tops are slightly puffed. Sprinkle the tops with the remaining cheese. Let stand for 5 minutes, or until the cheese is melted.

Per serving: 186 cal, 8 g pro, 12 g car, 12 g fat, 119 mg chol with butter, 111 mg chol with margarine, 488 mg sod

• 30 MINUTES

EASY • 30 MINUTES

SQUASH & PEPPER SKILLET GRATIN

Serves 4

Preparation time: 15 minutes

Cooking time: 14 minutes

Gratin is French for "crust" and refers to any dish with a browned or crusty topping of bread crumbs or cheese. This recipe uses a trio of zucchini, yellow summer squash, and red bell pepper for a colorful presentation. It is quickly prepared in a skillet and makes a good accompaniment with almost any meat or poultry main dish.

2 teaspoons vegetable oil

2 teaspoons butter or margarine

2 slices whole wheat bread, processed into crumbs
 with blender or food processor (¾ cup)

2 small zucchini (5 ounces each), quartered lengthwise,
 cut crosswise into 1½-inch pieces

2 small yellow summer squash (5 ounces each),
 quartered lengthwise, cut crosswise into 1½-inch pieces

1 medium-size red bell pepper, cut into thin strips

1¼ cups chopped onion

1 tablespoon fresh thyme leaves, chopped,
 or ½ teaspoon dried thyme leaves, crumbled

¾ teaspoon salt

¼ teaspoon ground black pepper

1. In a large skillet, heat 1 teaspoon each of oil and butter over medium-high heat. Add the bread crumbs and cook, stirring constantly for 3 to 4 minutes, or until crisp. Scrape into a small bowl.

2. Wipe the skillet with a paper towel. Heat the remaining 1 teaspoon each of oil and butter over medium-high heat. Add the vegetables and stir-fry for 7 to 8 minutes, or until crisp-tender. Add the thyme, salt, and pepper. Stir-fry for another 30 seconds. Spoon into a serving bowl. Stir in half the bread crumbs. Sprinkle the remaining crumbs over the top. Serve right away.

Per serving: 120 cal, 4 g pro, 17 g car, 5 g fat, 5 mg chol with butter, 0 mg chol with margarine, 514 mg sod

HOW TO COOK WINTER SQUASH

ACORN, DELICATA, SWEET DUMPLING
(about 1 pound):

Cut in half. Discard seeds and strings. Do not peel.

TO STEAM: Place cut side down in colander or steamer basket over ½ to ¾ inch boiling water. cover and steam about 20 minutes until tender when pierced.

TO BAKE: Cut a small slice from bottom so halves don't wobble. Place bottom down in baking pan. Add ¼ cup water. Cover and bake in a 400°F over about 30 minutes until tender when pierced.

TO MICROWAVE: Omit water. Arrange halves bottom down in shallow microwave-safe baking dish. Cover with vented plastic wrap. Microwave on High 7 to 9 minutes until almost tender, rotating dish ½ turn once. Let stand covered 5 minutes or until tender.

BUTTERNUT (2 to 2½ pounds):

Cut in half. Discard seeds and strings. Do not peel.

TO STEAM: Peel, cut in half, discard seeds and strings and cut squash in 2-inch chnunks. Put into a colander or steamer basket over ½ to ¾ inch boiling water. Cover and steam 8 to 10 minutes until tender.

TO BAKE: Do not peel. Halve lengthwise and place cut side up in baking pan. Add ¼ cup water. Cover and bake in a 400°F oven 40 to 45 minutes.

TO MICROWAVE: Do not peel. Pierce whole squash in 4 or 5 places with tip of small knife. Place on paper towel. Microwave on High 6 to 7 minutes. Turn over. Microwave 6 to 7 minutes longer or until easily pierced and yields to gentle pressure. Let stand 5 minutes. Cut in half lengthwise, discard seeds and strings. Scoop out flesh.

HUBBARD, BUTTERCUP, KABOCHA
(about 3 pounds):

Do not peel. Cut squash in half. Discard seeds and strings, then cut each half in 4 wedges.

TO STEAM: Arrange wedges cut side down in colander or steamer basket, overlapping if necessary. Place over ½ to ¾ inch boiling water. Cover and steam about 12 minutes until tender.

TO BAKE: Arrange wedges in single layer cut side up in shallow baking pan. Add ¼ cup water. Cover and bake in a 400°F oven 40 to 45 minutes until tender.

TO MICROWAVE: Do not peel. Cut squash in half and discard seeds and strings. Follow directions for acorn squash except add 2 tablespoons water and microwave 8 to 10 minutes, rearranging halves once.

SPAGHETTI SQUASH (2 to 2½ pounds):

Do not peel. Leave squash whole.

TO STEAM: Put squash into a large pot with enough water to cover it when held down. Bring to a boil. Cover and cook 35 to 40 minutes over medium heat until tender when pierced. Drain. When cool enough to handle, cut in half lengthwise and discard seeds and strings. With fork, scrape out spaghetti-like strands.

TO BAKE: Place whole in shallow baking pan. Add ¼ cup water. Cover and bake in a 400°F oven about 45 minutes. Cut in half lengthwise and discard seeds and strings. With fork, scrape out spaghetti-like strands.

TO MICROWAVE: Follow directions for butternut squash. Cut in half lengthwise and discard seeds and strings. With fork, scrape out spaghetti-like strands.

`EASY • 60 MINUTES • MAKE AHEAD`

SPAGHETTI SQUASH WITH CHILI–TOMATO SAUCE

Serves 4

Total time: 1 hour

Spaghetti squash is so called because its sweet-tasting flesh separates into spaghetti-like strands when scraped with a fork after cooking. Topping it with a tomato-based sauce, as given here, turns it into an easy-to-prepare main course.

MAKE AHEAD

The chili-tomato sauce
can be prepared
ahead. Let cool, then
refrigerate airtight up
to 3 days. Reheat on
the rangetop or in the
microwave.

VARIATION

**MICROWAVE
SPAGHETTI SQUASH
WITH CHILI-TOMATO
SAUCE**

• Microwave the
squash as directed
"How to Cook Winter
Squash," page 430.
• Crumble the beef
into a 1-quart micro-
wave-safe bowl. Cover
with waxed paper and
microwave on High for
2 to 3 minutes, stirring
twice to break up
meat, until it loses its
pink color.
• Stir in the sauce and
chili powder. Cover and
microwave on High for
3 to 4 minutes more,
stirring until the sauce
is thickened and hot.
Proceed as directed.

Per serving: 368 cal,
16 g pro, 26 g car,
22 g fat, 57 mg chol,
694 mg sod

• EASY • 30 MINUTES
• MAKE AHEAD

1 spaghetti squash, about 2½ pounds
¼ cup water
8 ounces lean ground beef
1¾ cups spaghetti sauce
1 teaspoon chili powder
½ cup shredded sharp Cheddar cheese

1. Heat the oven to 400°F. Pierce the squash in several places with the tip of a small knife.

2. Place the squash in a shallow baking pan. Add the water. Cover with foil and bake for 45 minutes, or until the squash gives to gentle pressure and can easily be pierced. Let stand until cool.

3. Meanwhile, in a medium-size skillet, cook the beef over medium-high heat, stirring occasionally to break up the meat, until it is no longer pink.

4. Stir in the sauce and chili powder. Cover and simmer over medium heat for 5 to 7 minutes, stirring twice, until slightly thickened.

5. Halve the squash lengthwise. Remove the seeds and strings. With a fork, scrape out the spaghetti-like strands onto a serving platter.

6. Spoon the sauce over the squash and sprinkle with cheese. Serve right away.

Per serving: 368 cal, 16 g pro, 26 g car, 22 g fat, 57 mg chol, 694 mg sod

EASY

VEGETABLE CASSEROLE

Serves 6
Preparation time: 10 minutes
Baking time: 1 hour

This casserole can be served hot or at room temperature.

¼ cup olive oil
2 large all-purpose potatoes (about 1 pound),
    scrubbed and sliced ¼ inch thick (about 3½ cups)
2 small red, yellow, or green bell peppers,
    seeded and sliced ½ inch thick (2½ cups)
2 large ripe tomatoes (about 1 pound), cored and sliced
¼ inch thick (about 2 ½ cups)
2 teaspoons minced fresh garlic
½ teaspoon salt
½ teaspoon ground black pepper
½ teaspoon dried oregano leaves, crumbled

▶

1. Heat the oven to 375°F.

2. Spread 1 tablespoon of the oil over bottom of a shallow 1½- to 2-quart baking dish. Layer half the potatoes, slightly overlapping if necessary, in the dish. Top with 1¼ cups of bell peppers, then 1¼ cups sliced tomatoes. Drizzle with 1 tablespoon of oil. Sprinkle with 1 teaspoon garlic and ¼ teaspoon each salt, pepper, and oregano. Repeat the layers using the remaining ingredients.

3. Bake, uncovered, for 50 minutes to 1 hour, or until the vegetables are tender. Serve right away.

Per serving: 164 cal, 3 g pro, 19 g car, 9 g fat, 0 mg chol, 195 mg sod

---

EASY • 30 MINUTES

MINTED CHERRY TOMATOES

Serves 4

Preparation time: 5 minutes

Cooking time: 15 minutes

A sprinkling of sugar brings out the flavor of the cherry tomatoes. If the tomatoes you purchased are firm and underripe, store them in a brown paper bag at room temperature for 1 to 2 days during which they will ripen.

2 pints (12 ounces each) cherry tomatoes
2 tablespoons olive oil
½ teaspoon granulated sugar
¼ cup fresh mint, basil, parsley, or dill, or
   1 teaspoon dried mint, oregano, or tarragon
¼ teaspoon salt
Ground black pepper to taste
2 scallions

1. Heat the oven to 350°F.

2. Rinse and stem the cherry tomatoes. Put into a baking pan. Toss with the oil, sugar, dried herbs (if using), salt, and pepper.

3. Bake for about 15 minutes. Meanwhile, mince the fresh herbs (if using) and trim and thinly slice the scallions. Toss with the baked tomatoes. Serve right away.

Per serving: 100 cal, 2 g pro, 9 g car, 7 g fat, 0 mg chol, 152 mg sod

COOK'S TIP

Chop leftover tomatoes and add to soups, pasta sauces, or stews, or purée with some chicken broth and serve as a pasta sauce.

60 MINUTES • MAKE AHEAD

TOMATO GRATIN

Serves 6

Preparation time: 15 minutes

Baking time: 45 minutes

This delicious gratin can be baked and served immediately, or assembled and refrigerated overnight before baking. It uses sourdough bread, which is now available sliced in supermarkets. Serve with a salad for light brunch, or as a side dish with dinner.

8 slices sourdough sandwich bread, toasted

2½ pounds large, ripe tomatoes, cut into ¼-inch-thick slices

½ teaspoon minced fresh garlic

¼ cup snipped fresh chives

½ teaspoon salt

Ground black pepper

4 ounces soft goat cheese or crumbled feta cheese

1 tablespoon olive oil

2 ½ tablespoons grated Parmesan cheese

1. Heat the oven to 350°F. Lightly coat a shallow 2-quart baking dish with olive oil cooking spray.

2. Arrange 4 slices of bread over the bottom of the baking dish, tearing to fit. Top with half the tomato slices. ▶

TERRIFIC TOMATOES

TOMATO TIPS

◆ Think of tomatoes as fruit (they are actually berries). Buy them a few days ahead and let them ripen at home— just as you would bananas or avocados. Try to eat them at their peak; overage tomatoes lose nutrients.

◆ Choose smooth, unblemished ones that feel heavy for their size and have firm, not mushy, flesh. Pear-shaped Italian plum tomatoes are best for sauce-making. They have less water and more sugar than other tomatoes.

◆ Never refrigerate tomatoes. Cold temperatures kill flavor and stop the ripening process in its tracks. Instead, leave unripe tomatoes in a basket on a counter, stem side up and away from direct sunlight (which destroys vitamins A and C). Or put them in a closed paper bag or special ripening bowl to speed up the process.

MAKING THE MOST OF SUMMER TOMATOES

There's always an abundance of luscious varieties of tomatoes in the summer. Enjoy them as much as possible while they're at their peak in lots of simple, speedy ways:

◆ Serve cherry tomatoes with dip for a refreshing starter.

◆ Sauté a mix of cherry and pear tomatoes in a little olive oil just until the skins start to split for a fast side dish.

◆ Cut large tomatoes into thick slices and alternate on a platter with slices of mozzarella cheese and whole or slivered fresh basil leaves. Drizzle with olive oil.

3. Sprinkle the garlic over the tomatoes, then sprinkle with half the chives. Season with salt and pepper.

4. Crumble the goat cheese over the chives and drizzle with half the oil.

5. Top with the remaining bread slices, pressing firmly to fit.

6. Arrange the remaining tomato slices on top, then sprinkle with the remaining chives, the Parmesan cheese, and additional pepper to taste. Drizzle with the remaining 1½ teaspoons oil.

7. Bake for 40 to 45 minutes, or until the cheese on top is golden and the tomatoes are soft.

Per serving: 214 cal, 8 g pro, 27 g car, 9 g fat, 10 mg chol with goat cheese, 18 mg chol with feta, 511 mg sod with goat cheese, 652 with feta

Ⓜ AKE AHEAD

Prepare the casserole through step 6. Cover and refrigerate up to 1 day. Bake for 45 to 50 minutes, or until the top is golden and the tomatoes are soft.

EASY • LOW FAT • CLASSIC

ROASTED ROOT VEGETABLES

Serves 8
Preparation time: 20 minutes
Cooking time: 45 minutes

Roasting vegetables concentrates their flavors and natural sweetness. You can use any or all of the vegetables listed.

3 large red potatoes (1 pound), scrubbed and cut into 2-inch chunks
1 small (about 1 pound) rutabaga (yellow turnip),
    peeled and cut into 1½-inch chunks
2 medium-size red onions, peeled and quartered lengthwise
3 medium-size white turnips (1 pound), peeled or scrubbed and quartered
4 medium-size carrots, quartered lengthwise
2 parsnips, quartered lengthwise
1 tablespoon olive oil
1 tablespoon minced fresh thyme leaves,
    or 1 teaspoon dried thyme leaves, crumbled
1½ teaspoons salt
½ teaspoon coarsely ground pepper

1. Heat the oven to 375°F. Have ready 2 large baking pans with sides (to fit side-by-side on lower oven rack if roasting meat on upper rack).

2. Toss the cut vegetables with the oil, thyme, salt, and pepper to coat. Spread in a single layer in the pans. Roast for 45 minutes, stirring and turning vegetables two or three times, until tender and lightly browned.

Per serving: 145 cal, 3 g pro, 30 g car, 2 g fat, 0 mg chol, 477 mg sod

VEGETABLE PANCAKES WITH TOMATO–BASIL CREAM

Serves 4
Preparation time: 25 minutes
Cooking time: 22 minutes

This recipe is perfect to make in the summertime when farmer's markets are full of fresh vegetables. The pancakes are made with shredded zucchini, yellow squash, and carrots. Serve them as a main course with thin slices of "frizzled," or pan-broiled, ham.

TOMATO–BASIL CREAM
1 large ripe tomato, halved, seeded, and chopped (1 cup)
½ cup nonfat sour cream
2 tablespoons chopped fresh basil
¼ teaspoon salt
¼ teaspoon ground black pepper

VEGETABLE PANCAKES
4 large eggs
8 ounces zucchini, shredded fine (2 cups)
8 ounces yellow summer squash, shredded fine (2 cups)
1 medium-size carrot, shredded fine (½ cup)
⅓ cup packaged plain bread crumbs
⅓ cup packed basil, chopped fine
⅓ cup grated Parmesan cheese
1 small onion, grated (¼ cup)
¼ teaspoon salt
¼ teaspoon ground black pepper

1. Make the cream: In a medium-size bowl, mix the tomato, sour cream, basil, salt, and pepper until blended. Cover and refrigerate until ready to serve.

2. Heat the oven to 200°F.

3. Make the pancakes: In a large bowl, beat the eggs with a fork. Stir in the remaining ingredients until well blended (you should have 3 cups).

4. Coat a large nonstick skillet with vegetable-oil cooking spray and place over medium-low heat. Pour ¼ cup of the vegetable mixture into the skillet, spreading to a 3½-inch-wide pancake. Add 2 more pancakes to the skillet. Cook the pancakes for 2½ to 3 minutes on each side.

5. Remove the pancakes to a baking sheet and keep warm in the ▶

oven while preparing the remaining pancakes.

6. Put three pancakes on each serving plate and spoon ¼ cup tomato-basil cream on the side. Serve right away.

Per serving: 212 cal, 14 g pro, 19 g car, 9 g fat, 218 mg chol, 566 mg sod

HOW TO GRILL VEGETABLES

PREPARING THE VEGETABLES:

◆ Bell peppers, cut in half lengthwise, stems and seeds removed. 3 medium-size bell peppers (1 pound) yield 2 cups bite-size pieces

◆ Eggplant, unpeeled, sliced lengthwise 1/2-inch thick. 1 medium-size eggplant (1 pound) yields 2 1/2 cups bite-size pieces

◆ Mushrooms, whole and wiped clean. 1 pound mushrooms yields 2 1/2 cups whole

◆ Red onions, skin removed, cut in half lengthwise with root ends left intact. 4 medium-size (1 pound) yield 2 1/2 cups cut in eighths

◆ Zucchini, cut in half lengthwise. 3 medium-size (1 pound) yield 2 cups bite-size pieces

◆ Yellow squash, cut in half lengthwise. 3 medium-size yellow squash (1 pound) yield 2 cups bite-size pieces

GRILL METHOD:

◆ Heat a gas grill to medium/medium-high, or prepare a charcoal fire.

◆ Brush the vegetables with olive oil. Place in a hinged grilling basket or on a piece of thick-gauge metal mesh. Grill 4 to 6 inches from the heat source 10 to 20 minutes, turning once, until the vegetables are tender and slightly charred.

◆ Cut the vegetables into bite-size pieces if desired and serve right away.

NON-GRILL METHOD:

◆ Heat a cast-iron stove-top grill pan on a stove burner over medium-high heat for 5 minutes or until a drop of water flicked onto the surface evaporates immediately. Reduce the heat to medium low.

◆ Pan-grill the vegetables for 9 to 11 minutes, turning once, until tender and slightly charred. To speed up cooking of halved onions, bell peppers, and squash, put a skillet or other heavy pan on top to press them down as they cook.

STORING:

Put each type of vegetable into a separate gallon-size plastic zipper-type bag or container with lid. Add 1/2 cup olive oil and 1 crushed clove garlic to each (the garlic flavor gets more intense the longer the vegetables are stored). Squeeze excess air out of bags. Tightly seal and refrigerate up to 1 week. Bring to room temperature before using.

12 QUICK FIXES WITH GRILLED VEGETABLES

◆ Top cooked pizza with a colorful assortment of grilled vegetables.

◆ Skewer chunks of grilled red bell peppers, eggplant, or zucchini and leftover lamb. Serve at room temperature.

◆ Toss with leftover rice and bottled Italian dressing or your favorite vinaigrette for a delicious rice salad.

◆ Split a round loaf of Italian bread, pull out some of the inside, fill with an assortment of grilled vegetables, then drizzle with oil and red wine vinegar. Cut into wedges to serve.

◆ Top cooked burgers with grilled mushrooms and red bell pepper.

◆ Chop the grilled vegetables, then spread on slices of grilled eggplant and roll up from the narrow end.

◆ Stir chopped grilled onion, bell pepper, and zucchini into baked beans just before serving.

◆ Sandwich slices of smoked mozzarella cheese and grilled red bell peppers between slices of crusty Italian or sourdough bread.

◆ Add chopped grilled vegetables to spaghetti sauce. Heat and serve over hot pasta.

◆ Purée grilled eggplant and use as a dip for pita triangles.

◆ Add chopped grilled vegetables and feta cheese to mixed greens for a substantial salad.

◆ Toss grilled vegetables with cooked pasta and Italian dressing.

DESSERTS

> *"Had I but one penny in the world,*
> *thou should have it for gingerbread."*
> WILLIAM SHAKESPEARE

Most people don't need to be told twice to clear the table to make way for dessert. In fact, the word comes from *desservir*, which is French for "to clear away." Dessert is an integral part of any menu and imparts a satisfying sense of completion.

The recipes in this chapter are not difficult nor do they require any special skills. The best part is that almost all of them can be made ahead. With any recipe, the secret to success is to follow the instructions closely. Be sure to read the recipe carefully before you begin to make certain you have the proper ingredients and equipment on hand. And most of all—save room for dessert!

MAKE AHEAD

DEEP CHOCOLATE HAZELNUT CAKE

Serves 24

Preparation time: 25 minutes plus 8 hours to chill

Baking time: 1 hour 20 minutes

For admirers of rich chocolate cake, this flourless confection studded with hazelnuts and topped with chocolate whipped cream will be a winner. The cake uses a combination of semisweet and unsweetened chocolate to deliver an intense punch. The light whipped cream icing provides a contrast in flavor and texture.

CHOCOLATE HAZELNUT CAKE

1½ cups hazelnuts

⅔ cup (10 tablespoons plus 2 teaspoons) butter or margarine (not spread)

6 (1-ounce) squares semisweet chocolate, or 1 cup (6 ounces) semisweet chocolate chips

2 (1-ounce) squares unsweetened chocolate

⅔ cup granulated sugar

4 large eggs, at room temperature

3 tablespoons hazelnut liqueur, or 1 teaspoon pure vanilla extract

For garnish: fresh raspberries (optional)

CHOCOLATE WHIPPED CREAM

1 cup heavy (whipping) cream

1 tablespoon unsweetened cocoa powder

1 tablespoon granulated sugar

½ teaspoon pure vanilla extract

1. Heat the oven to 350°F. Lightly grease a 9 x 5-inch loaf pan. Line the bottom with foil and grease the foil.

2. Spread the hazelnuts on a baking sheet. Bake for 10 to 12 minutes, or until the nuts are toasted, stirring once. Let cool slightly.

3. Rub the nuts between your hands or in a kitchen towel to remove most of the skins. Reserve 24 whole hazelnuts for garnish. Coarsely chop the remaining nuts.

4. Meanwhile, in a small saucepan, melt the butter and both chocolates over low heat, stirring often until smooth. Remove the pan from the heat and let cool until slightly warm.

MAKE AHEAD

The cooled baked cake can be refrigerated airtight up to 2 weeks, or frozen up to 3 months. Thaw in the refrigerator.

5. Fill a baking pan with hot tap water to a depth of 1 inch. Place the pan in the oven.

6. In a large bowl, beat the sugar and eggs with an electric mixer on high speed for 12 to 15 minutes, or until very pale, thick, and tripled in volume. Reduce the mixer speed to low and beat in the liqueur. With a rubber spatula, gently stir (fold) in the chocolate mixture and chopped hazelnuts until no streaks remain. Pour the mixture into the prepared loaf pan. Cover tightly with greased foil.

7. Place the loaf pan in the center of the pan of water in the oven. Bake for 1 hour and 10 minutes, or until a toothpick inserted near the center comes out clean.

8. Remove the loaf pan from the water, uncover, and place on a wire rack to cool for 30 minutes. (The cake will sink about 1 inch.) Invert the pan onto the rack, remove the pan and foil. Let cool completely. Wrap the loaf airtight. Refrigerate for at least 8 hours, or until completely firm.

9. To serve, make the whipped cream. In a small bowl, beat the cream, cocoa, sugar, and vanilla with an electric mixer until stiff peaks form when the beaters are lifted.

10. Unwrap the cake and place on a serving plate. Spoon the whipped cream into a pastry bag fitted with an open star tip. Pipe the sides and top with whipped cream and decorate with raspberries and the reserved hazelnuts. Cut into thin slices with a sharp knife.

Makes 24 slices. Per slice: 213 cal, 3 g pro, 13 g car, 18 g fat, 63 mg chol with butter, 49 mg chol with margarine, 63 mg sod with butter, 75 mg sod with margarine

CAKE CLINIC

Even the best bakers have problems periodically. If you experience difficulties baking cakes, try to identify the problem, then consult this chart for possible answers.

PROBLEM	POSSIBLE CAUSE(S)
Cake cracks	Oven too hot
Cake falls	Underbaking; old leavening; too much or too little liquid; oven not hot enough
Cake is dense and tough	Overbeating after flour is added; not enough fat
Cake crumbles when sliced	Too much fat; too much sugar
Cake has holes	Too many or too large eggs; not enough sugar; oven too hot batter mixed improperly
Cake peaks in the center	Overbeating after flour is added; oven too hot

LEMON LAYER CAKE

Serves 10

Preparation time: 30 minutes plus 1 hour to chill

Baking time: 40 minutes

This layer cake is tart, tangy, and just fabulous, with lots of creamy icing.

LEMON CAKE

1½ cups all-purpose flour

1 teaspoon baking powder

½ teaspoon salt

6 tablespoons fresh lemon juice

2 teaspoons pure vanilla extract

Peel from 2 medium-size lemons, removed with a vegetable peeler

1 cup granulated sugar

1 cup (2 sticks) unsalted butter or margarine (not spread),
   at room temperature

3 large eggs

LEMON FROSTING

Peel from 1 medium-size lemon, removed with a vegetable peeler

⅓ cup granulated sugar

2 (8-ounce) packages cream cheese, at room temperature

2 tablespoons fresh lemon juice

1. Heat the oven to 350°F. Lightly grease an 8-inch springform pan or two 8-inch layer cake pans. Line the bottom(s) with waxed paper and lightly grease the paper. Dust the pan(s) with a little of the flour and shake out any excess.

2. In a small bowl, mix the flour, baking powder, and salt.

3. In another small bowl, mix the lemon juice and vanilla.

4. In a food processor or blender, process the lemon peel and sugar until the peel is finely ground. Transfer to a large bowl, add the softened butter, and beat the with an electric mixer until pale and fluffy. Beat in the eggs one at a time, beating well after each addition. On low speed, beat in the flour alternately with the lemon juice, beginning and ending with flour and adding ⅓ to ¼ with each addition. Pour the batter into the prepared pan(s).

5. Bake for about 40 minutes, or until the top springs back when gently pressed and a toothpick inserted near the center comes out clean. Set the pan(s) on a wire rack to cool for 20 minutes. Invert the cake onto the rack and peel off the waxed paper.

Ⓜ AKE AHEAD

The cooled baked layer cakes can be stored airtight at room temperature up to 2 days, or frozen up to 3 months. Thaw at room temperature.

6. Make the frosting: In a food processor or blender, process the lemon peel and sugar until the peel is finely ground. In a medium-size bowl, beat the cream cheese, lemon juice, and sugar mixture with an electric mixer until smooth (all this may be done in the food processor). Cover with plastic wrap and refrigerate for about 1 hour, or until firm but spreadable.

7. To assemble: Using a long serrated knife, slice the cake into 3 layers or slice the 2 cakes in half horizontally to make 4 thin layers. Frost the cake with the frosting, using about ⅓ cup between the layers. Frost the outside, then refrigerate until ready to serve.

Makes 10 slices. Per slice: 526 cal, 7 g pro, 44 g car, 36 g fat, 163 mg chol with butter, 114 mg chol with margarine, 315 mg sod with butter, 526 mg sod with margarine

LEMON–STRAWBERRY ANGEL CAKE

Serves 12
Preparation time: 18 minutes plus at least 2 hours to chill
Baking time: 30 minutes

This light-as-a-feather treat with layers of lemon and strawberry filling in an angel food cake is bound to become one of your favorites.

1 box (16 ounces) white angel food cake mix

TART LEMON FILLING
1 tablespoon grated lemon peel
¾ cup fresh lemon juice
2 large eggs
Yolks from 4 large eggs
⅔ cup granulated sugar

STRAWBERRY FILLING
1 pint (12 ounces) fresh strawberries, rinsed, hulled, and chopped coarse
½ cup granulated sugar
½ cup water
3 tablespoons cornstarch

1 cup heavy (whipping) cream
1 tablespoon granulated sugar
For garnish: halved strawberries and mint leaves (optional)

ⓂAKE AHEAD

The cake and fillings can be made a day ahead, but it's best to fill the cake no more than 6 hours before serving and to add the final touches shortly before bringing it to the table.

1. Prepare the cake mix, bake, and cool according to the package directions.

2. Make the lemon filling: In a medium-size heavy nonaluminum saucepan, whisk the lemon peel, lemon juice, eggs, egg yolks, and sugar until well blended. Heat over low heat for about 5 minutes, stirring often, until hot. When the mixture begins to thicken, stir constantly. Cook gently (don't boil or it will curdle) for about 3 minutes, or until the filling thickly coats the back of a metal spoon. Strain the mixture through a fine sieve set over a medium-size bowl. Place a piece of plastic wrap flat on the surface to prevent a skin from forming; refrigerate for at least 2 hours. The filling will thicken as it cools.

3. Make the strawberry filling: Put the chopped strawberries into a small heavy saucepan and mash them into a chunky purée. In a small bowl, mix the sugar, water, and cornstarch until blended. Stir this mixture into the berries and cook over medium heat until boiling. Reduce the heat to low and simmer, stirring constantly, for 1 minute, or until thickened and glossy. Cool slightly, then place plastic wrap directly on the surface and refrigerate for at least 2 hours.

4. To assemble: Using a long serrated knife, slice the cake horizontally into 3 layers. Put one layer on a flat serving plate and spread with strawberry filling. Top with second cake layer. Gently spread with the lemon filling. Top with the remaining cake layer.

5. In a small bowl, beat the cream and sugar with an electric mixer until stiff peaks form when the beaters are lifted. Frost the top of the cake with the whipped cream and garnish with berries and mint.

Makes 12 slices. Per slice: 200 cal, 3 g pro, 26 g car, 10 g fat, 133 mg chol, 21 mg sod

---

EASY • MAKE AHEAD

TURTLE CAKE

Serves 18
Preparation time: 15 minutes
Baking time: 1 hour

This is one of those easy and delicious cakes that you will make time and time again. It keeps well and is a great addition to picnics or backyard barbecues.

1 bag (about 14 ounces) vanilla caramels
1 can (about 5 ounces) evaporated (not sweetened condensed) milk
1 box (18¼ ounces) German chocolate cake mix with pudding
    (use mix that calls for vegetable oil)
¾ cup (1½ sticks) butter or margarine (not spread), at room temperature
1 bag (12 ounces) semisweet chocolate chips
2 cups pecans, chopped

▶ *p. 449*

WHAT'S UP? BAKING POWDER AND BAKING SODA

◆ Baking soda starts working as soon as it gets wet, so once a batter is mixed, bake it right away.

◆ Baking powder is double-acting, or has two rising ingredients. The first is triggered by moisture and the second by heat. That means you can delay baking after the batter or dough has been mixed.

◆ It you are suspicious about your baking powder, test it by putting ½ teaspoon in ¼ cup hot water. If the water bubbles like mad, it still works.

DECADENCE
Easily made Turtle Cake (p.444) is a delectable combination of chocolate, vanilla caramels, and pecans.

A IS FOR APPLE
Rum-Raisin
Poached Apples
(p.480), left, and
old-fashioned
Apple Strudel
(p.475), above,
are two fine ways
to enjoy this fruit
for dessert.

DAZZLING
Impress your dinner guests by serving this Strawberry Vanilla Terrine (p.489) for dessert. They'll never guess how easy it was to make.

MAKE AHEAD

The cooled baked cake

can be refrigerated

airtight up to 1 week.

1. Heat the oven to 350°F. Line a 13 x 9-inch baking pan with foil and lightly grease the foil.

2. In a small saucepan, heat the caramels and milk over low heat, stirring occasionally, for about 10 minutes, or until the caramels melt.

3. Using an electric mixer, prepare the cake mix according to the package directions, using only half the oil called for on the box. Beat on low speed for 1 minute. Add the butter, increase the mixer speed to high, and beat for 2 minutes more, or until the batter is thick and smooth.

4. Spread half the batter (about 3 cups) into the prepared pan. Bake for 12 to 14 minutes, or until the cake starts to puff up around the edges (the middle will still be slightly wet).

5. Pour the caramel mixture over the cake and spread to the edges of the pan with a rubber spatula. Sprinkle with 1 cup of the chocolate chips and 1 cup of the pecans. Spoon the remaining cake batter over the top and carefully spread to the edges.

6. Bake for 35 to 45 minutes more, or until the cake puffs up above the sides of the pan, springs back when gently pressed, and starts to pull away from the sides of pan. Set the pan on a wire rack to cool.

7. Meanwhile, melt the remaining 1 cup of chocolate chips. Spread over the cooled cake. Sprinkle with the remaining pecans. Let cool completely.

Makes 18 rectangles. Per rectangle: 474 cal, 5 g pro, 55 g car, 28 g fat, 25 mg chol with butter, 4 mg chol with margarine, 322 mg sod with butter, 333 mg sod with margarine

QUICK DESSERT FIXES

When you crave a sweet ending—but don't have the time or energy to make one—satisfaction may be closer than you think.

◆ Drizzle grapefruit with grenadine syrup. For adults, sprinkle with bitters. Or sprinkle grapefruit halves with brown sugar and broil just until the sugar bubbles.

◆ Freeze (in a dish or unopened can) a can of crushed pineapple in syrup. Cut into chunks and purée in a food processor for a refreshing ice.

◆ Top store-bought lemon sorbet with crumbled gingersnaps.

◆ Top sliced bananas with honey yogurt and low-fat granola.

◆ Serve fresh strawberries with melted chocolate or chocolate sauce for dipping.

◆ Toss canned mandarin orange segments with fresh or canned pineapple chunks. Sprinkle with coconut.

◆ Toast slices of angel food cake. Serve with thawed strawberries in syrup and whipped cream or topping.

◆ Spoon hot or cold applesauce over vanilla ice cream. Sprinkle with cinnamon.

◆ Heat frozen waffles. Top with preserves and ice cream.

◆ Sandwich mint chocolate chip ice cream between two graham crackers.

◆ Spoon whole-berry cranberry sauce over sliced oranges.

◆ Stuff pitted dates with peanuts and roll in confectioners' sugar. (Or just serve the dates and nuts as munchies with apple wedges.)

◆ Serve dried figs with hazelnuts and fresh pears. Pears are good with blue cheese and walnuts too (but kids may prefer Cheddar or American cheese and apples).

◆ Keep tubs of tapioca or rice pudding (from the deli) in the refrigerator. Top with apricot preserves or quick-thaw frozen berries.

◆ Top packaged lemon pudding with blueberry pourable fruit.

EASY • 60 MINUTES

CASHEW–HONEY GINGERBREAD

Serves 9

Preparation time: 10 minutes

Baking time: 32 minutes

Here is a cake that you mix, bake, and serve all in the same pan.

1⅔ cups all-purpose flour
⅓ cup packed light brown sugar
1¼ teaspoons ground ginger
1 teaspoon baking soda
½ teaspoon grated nutmeg
½ teaspoon salt
¼ teaspoon ground allspice
½ cup water
⅓ cup vegetable oil
⅓ cup mild-flavored honey
1 large egg

CASHEW–HONEY TOPPING

3 tablespoons butter or margarine (not spread)
¼ cup mild-flavored honey
½ cup chopped unsalted cashews

1. Heat the oven to 350°F.

2. In an ungreased 8-inch square baking pan, combine the flour, sugar, ginger, baking soda, nutmeg, salt, and allspice. Stir with a fork until well blended.

3. Add the remaining ingredients except for the topping. Stir until smooth.

4. Using a rubber spatula, scrape any ingredients clinging to the sides, corners, and bottom of the pan into the batter.

5. Bake for 25 to 30 minutes, or until a toothpick inserted near the center comes out clean.

6. Meanwhile, make the topping. In a small saucepan, melt the butter over medium heat. Remove the pan from the heat. Stir in the honey and cashews.

7. Remove the pan from the oven. Turn the oven to "broil."

8. Spoon the topping over the hot cake. Broil for 1 to 2 minutes, or just until the nuts turn golden brown.

9. Set the cake in the pan on a wire rack to cool. Cut into 9 squares.

Makes 9 squares. Per square: 337 cal, 4 g pro, 46 g car, 16 g fat, 34 mg chol with butter, 24 mg chol with margarine, 313 mg sod with butter, 319 mg sod with margarine

VARIATION

MICROWAVE CASHEW-HONEY CAKE

● Mix the batter in an 8- or 9-inch square microwave-safe baking dish. (Be sure the baking dish is also broiler-proof.)

● Microwave on High for 6 to 8 minutes, rotating the dish ¼ turn once, until a toothpick inserted near the center comes out clean. (If using a transparent pan, lift it and check the bottom. The cake should look dry.) There will be a few moist spots on the surface of the cake. These will dry while the cake is cooling.

● Cool the cake in the pan on a heatproof surface for 15 minutes, or until the sides of the cake have pulled slightly away from the edges of the pan. Prepare the topping and proceed as directed.

Makes 9 squares. Per square: 337 cal, 4 g pro, 46 g car, 16 g fat, 34 mg chol with butter, 24 mg chol with margarine, 313 mg sod with butter, 319 mg sod with margarine

● EASY • 60 MINUTES

EASY • 60 MINUTES • LIGHT • MAKE AHEAD

CHOCOLATE MINT SQUARES

Serves 24

Preparation time: 20 minutes

Baking time: 30 minutes

Though you won't be able to taste it, ordinary applesauce takes over the job of fat to provide moistness in this scrumptious chocolatey cake.

CHOCOLATE CAKE

1 cup evaporated (not sweetened condensed) skim milk

¾ cup unsweetened cocoa powder

1 cup unsweetened applesauce

1 tablespoon pure vanilla extract

2 cups all-purpose flour

1½ cups granulated sugar

½ teaspoon baking powder

½ teaspoon baking soda

½ teaspoon salt

Whites from 4 large eggs, at room temperature

MINT TOPPING

1 envelope nondairy whipped topping mix (from a 2.6-ounce box of two)

3 tablespoons evaporated (not sweetened condensed) skim milk

2 cups confectioners' sugar

2 teaspoons peppermint extract

1. Heat the oven to 350°F. Grease a 13 x 9-inch baking pan.

2. In a medium-size saucepan, heat the evaporated milk until barely simmering. Remove the pan from the heat and whisk in the cocoa until thickened and almost smooth (some tiny lumps will remain). Let stand for 2 to 3 minutes to cool slightly. Whisk in the applesauce and vanilla extract.

3. In a large bowl, mix the flour, 1¼ cups of the granulated sugar, the baking powder, baking soda, and salt.

4. In a medium-size bowl, beat the egg whites with an electric mixer until thick and foamy. Gradually beat in the remaining ¼ cup of granulated sugar until stiff peaks form when the beaters are lifted.

5. Pour the cocoa mixture over the flour. Stir just until blended.

6. With a rubber spatula, gently stir about ¼ of the egg whites into the flour mixture. Gently stir (fold) in the remaining egg whites until no ▶

VARIATION

CREAMY CUPCAKES

• Prepare the cake batter as directed. Line eighteen 2½-inch muffin pan cups with paper cups. Fill each with ⅓ cup batter. Bake at 350°F for 20 to 25 minutes. Cool.

• Meanwhile, prepare one 4-serving-size package (3 ounces) instant French vanilla pudding and pie filling according to package directions, using the 1 ¾ cups evaporated skim milk instead of 2 cups whole milk. Refrigerate until set, about 1 hour.

• With a thin sharp knife, slice off tops of the cupcakes. Spread cut sides of the tops with about 1½ tablespoons pudding each. Replace the tops. Sift confectioners' sugar stirred through a sieve over the cupcakes.

Makes 18 cupcakes. Per cupcake: 183 cal, 6 g pro, 40 g car, 1 g fat, 2 mg chol, 236 mg sod

• EASY • LIGHT

white streaks remain. Pour the batter into the prepared pan.

7. Bake for 25 to 30 minutes, or until a toothpick inserted near the center comes out clean and/or edges of the cake begin to pull away from the sides of the pan. Set the pan on a wire rack to cool.

8. Meanwhile, make the topping. In a medium-size bowl, beat the topping mix and evaporated milk with an electric mixer on low speed until smooth and the graininess disappears. Beat in the confectioners' sugar and peppermint extract, gradually increasing the mixer speed to high. Beat until frosting is thick and smooth.

9. Spread the frosting evenly over the top of cake. Let the frosting set until firm before cutting cake into squares.

Makes 24 squares. Per square: 162 cal, 3 g pro, 36 g car, 1 g fat, 1 mg chol, 109 mg sod

---

60 MINUTES • MAKE AHEAD • CLASSIC

CARROT CAKE

Serves 16

Preparation time: 20 minutes

Baking time: 35 minutes

This carrot cake contains crushed pineapple for added moistness.

CARROT CAKE

¼ cup walnuts

2 cups all-purpose flour

1 tablespoon ground cinnamon

2 teaspoons baking powder

1 teaspoon baking soda

1 teaspoon salt

1¼ cups granulated sugar

½ cup vegetable oil

2 large eggs plus whites from 3 large eggs

2 teaspoons pure vanilla extract

5 medium-size carrots, shredded fine (3 cups)

2 (8-ounce) cans crushed pineapple packed in
   juice, well drained

LIGHT CREAM CHEESE FROSTING

1 tub (8 ounces) fat-free cream-cheese product

2 envelopes (1.3 ounces each) whipped topping mix (in dry form)

1 teaspoon pure vanilla extract

MAKE AHEAD

The frosted cake can be refrigerated airtight up to 1 week.

MAKE AHEAD

The iced cake can be refrigerated airtight up to 1 week. Serve chilled or at room temperature.

1. Heat the oven to 350°F. Spray a 13 x 9-inch baking pan with vegetable oil cooking spray.

2. Make the cake: Spread the nuts in a baking pan. Bake for 10 minutes, stirring once, until toasted. Cool, then chop fine.

3. Meanwhile, in a small bowl, mix the flour, cinnamon, baking powder, baking soda, and salt.

4. In a large bowl, whisk the sugar, oil, eggs, egg whites, and vanilla until well blended. Stir in the flour mixture, then the carrots and pineapple. Pour the batter into the prepared baking pan.

5. Bake for 30 to 35 minutes, or until a toothpick inserted near the center comes out clean and the cake begins to pull away from the sides of the pan. Set the pan on a wire rack to cool completely.

6. Meanwhile, make the frosting: In a medium-size bowl, beat the cream cheese, topping mix, and vanilla with an electric mixer until no longer grainy.

7. Spread the frosting on top of the cooled cake. Sprinkle with the nuts.

Makes 18 rectangles. Per rectangle: 272 cal, 6 g pro, 39 g car, 10 g fat, 28 mg chol, 380 mg sod

---

EASY • 60 MINUTES • LIGHT • CLASSIC

PINEAPPLE UPSIDE–DOWN CAKE

Serves 8
Preparation time: 20 minutes
Baking time: 35 minutes

There's no fat in this cake, and very little in the topping.

TOPPING
1 tablespoon butter or margarine (not spread)
3 tablespoons packed light brown sugar
7 slices juice-packed canned pineapple (reserve ⅓ cup juice)
7 pecan halves

CAKE
1 cup all-purpose flour
1½ teaspoons baking powder
⅛ teaspoon salt
2 large eggs, separated
⅓ cup granulated sugar

1. Heat the oven to 350°F.

▶

2. Put the butter in a 9-inch round cake pan and place in the oven to melt. Stir in the brown sugar and 1 teaspoon of the reserved pineapple juice. Arrange the pineapple slices in the bottom of the pan and place a pecan half, curved side down, in the center of each.

3. In a small bowl, mix the flour, baking powder, and salt.

4. In a medium-size bowl, beat the egg yolks with an electric mixer until well blended. Gradually add the granulated sugar and beat until thick and pale.

5. Beat in the remaining pineapple juice, then stir in the flour mixture.

6. With clean, dry beaters, beat the egg whites in another medium-size bowl until stiff peaks form when the beaters are lifted. With a rubber spatula, gently stir (fold) the egg whites into the flour mixture. Carefully pour the batter into the cake pan and spread evenly.

7. Bake for 25 to 30 minutes, or until a toothpick inserted near the center comes out clean. Set the pan on a wire rack and cool for 5 minutes. Loosen the edges of the cake with a knife, then invert onto a serving plate.

Makes 8 slices. Per slice: 176 cal, 3 g pro, 34 g car, 3 g fat, 57 mg chol with butter, 53 mg chol with margarine, 160 mg sod

---

MAKE AHEAD

CHOCOLATE MOUSSE ROLL

Serves 8

Preparation time: 20 minutes plus 2 hours 30 minutes to chill

Baking time: 10 minutes

Cake rolls are surprisingly easy to make. The chocolate mousse filling given here is light and luscious.

CHOCOLATE CAKE

⅔ cup all-purpose flour
¼ cup plus 2 tablespoons unsweetened cocoa powder
¾ teaspoon baking powder
Whites from 3 large eggs, at room temperature
2 large eggs, at room temperature
⅔ cup granulated sugar

MOUSSE FILLING

1 cup heavy (whipping) cream
½ cup confectioners' sugar
¼ cup unsweetened cocoa powder
For garnish: confectioners' sugar (optional)

Ⓜ AKE AHEAD

Once rolled up with the kitchen towel, the cooled baked cake can be refrigerated up to 24 hours. To freeze, unroll it when cool and roll up again without the towel. (Always roll from the same end.) Wrap in plastic and again in foil. Freeze up to 1 month. Before unrolling and filling, unwrap and bring to room temperature.

VARIATION

COFFEE-HAZELNUT ROLL

- Prepare the cake as directed.
- In a medium-size bowl, beat 1 cup heavy (whipping) cream, 2 tablespoons granulated sugar, 1 tablespoon instant coffee powder or granules, and ½ teaspoon vanilla extract with an electric mixer until stiff peaks form when the beaters are lifted. With a rubber spatula, gently stir (fold) in ½ cup toasted chopped hazelnuts or almonds. Fill and serve as directed.

Per slice: 304 cal, 6 g pro, 33 g car, 18 g fat, 94 mg chol, 95 mg sod

- MAKE AHEAD

1. Heat the oven to 375°F. Grease the bottom and sides of a 15½ x 10½-inch jelly roll pan. Line with waxed paper and grease the paper.

2. Make the cake: In a small bowl, mix the flour, ¼ cup of the cocoa, and the baking powder until blended.

3. In a large bowl, beat the egg whites, whole eggs, and sugar with an electric mixer on high speed for 8 to 10 minutes, or until thick and tripled in volume. Sprinkle the flour mixture over the top. With a rubber spatula, gently stir (fold) the flour into the egg mixture just until blended. Spread the batter into the prepared pan.

4. Bake for 10 minutes, or until the cake springs back when gently pressed in the center. Set the pan on a wire rack to cool for 10 minutes. Meanwhile, spread a clean cloth kitchen towel on a countertop. Using a small strainer, sift the remaining 2 tablespoons of cocoa over the towel, covering an area the size of the cake.

5. Invert the cake onto the towel. Remove the pan and peel off the waxed paper. Starting at a narrow end, roll up the cake and the towel. Set on a wire rack to cool completely. (The cake must be at room temperature before you unroll and fill it.)

6. Meanwhile, make the filling: In a large bowl, beat the cream, confectioners' sugar, and cocoa with an electric mixer until stiff peaks form when the beaters are lifted.

7. Gently unroll the cake; remove the towel. Spread the mousse to within 1 inch of all edges. Reroll gently, starting at the same end as before. Transfer the roll, seam side down, to a serving platter. Serve right away or cover loosely and refrigerate until ready to serve.

8. Just before serving, sift confectioners' sugar over the top of the cake. Cut the cake roll into slices with a serrated knife.

Makes 8 slices. Per slice: 280 cal, 6 g pro, 37 g car, 14 g fat, 94 mg chol, 95 mg sod

---

MAKE AHEAD • CLASSIC

BEST-EVER DEVIL'S FOOD CAKE

Serves 10
Preparation time: 25 minutes plus 2 hours to chill
Baking time: 30 minutes

Over the years, the kitchens at Woman's Day have turned out truckloads of fabulous recipes. Among our all-time favorites is this one for a traditional, delicious chocolate cake. It is said that this confection is named after the devilishly reddish tint the cocoa gives the cake.

▶

DEVIL'S FOOD CAKE

2 cups all-purpose flour

⅔ cup unsweetened cocoa powder

1¼ teaspoons baking soda

¼ teaspoon baking powder

½ teaspoon salt

⅔ cup (10 tablespoons plus 2 teaspoons) unsalted butter
    or margarine (not spread), at room temperature

1⅔ cups granulated sugar

3 large eggs

1 teaspoon pure vanilla extract

1½ cups milk

WHIPPED CREAM TOPPING

2 cups heavy (whipping) cream

1⅓ cups (8 ounces) semisweet chocolate chips

For garnish: fresh raspberries (optional)

1. Adjust the oven racks to divide the oven into thirds. Heat the oven to 350°F. Grease three 8-inch round cake pans. Line the bottoms with waxed paper and grease the paper. Sprinkle with flour and rotate the pans to coat the bottoms and sides. Shake out the excess.

2. Make the cake: In a medium-size bowl, mix the flour, cocoa, baking soda, baking powder, and salt.

3. In a large bowl, beat the butter, sugar, eggs, and vanilla with an electric mixer until fluffy. On low speed, beat in the flour mixture alternately with the milk just until blended, beginning and ending with the flour. (The mixture will look slightly curdled.) Pour the batter into the prepared pans (about 2 cups in each).

4. Stagger the pans on the oven racks and bake, switching the position of the pans once to ensure even layers, for about 30 minutes, or until a toothpick inserted near the centers comes out clean. Set the pans on wire racks to cool for 10 minutes. Invert the cakes onto the racks, remove the pans, and peel off the paper. Turn the cakes right side up and cool completely.

5. Make the topping: In a medium-size saucepan, heat the cream over medium heat until boiling. Add the chocolate chips. Remove the pan from the heat and stir with a rubber spatula until melted and smooth. Transfer to a large bowl and refrigerate for about 2 hours, stirring twice, just until chilled. (If the mixture gets too cold, it will be too stiff to beat properly.) Beat the mixture with an electric mixer just until soft peaks form when the beaters are lifted. (The cream will continue to thicken after a few minutes at room temperature, so be careful not to overbeat or it will turn curdy and grainy. Should

MAKE AHEAD

The cooled baked layer cakes can be stored airtight at room temperature up to 2 days, or frozen up to 3 months. Thaw at room temperature.

COOK'S TIP

Avoid opening the oven door during the first 15 minutes of baking. This lowers the oven temperature, which may cause the cake to fall.

this happen, you can salvage it by remelting, rechilling, and rebeating.)

6. To assemble, trim the top of the cake layers with a long serrated knife, cutting off any raised areas. Place 1 cake layer on a serving plate. Spread 1 cup of chocolate cream evenly over the layer. Top with another cake layer and 1 more cup of chocolate cream. Top with the remaining cake layer. Reserve some of the cream for piping decorations, then frost the sides and top with a thin layer of chocolate cream.

7. Put the reserved chocolate cream in a pastry bag with an open star tip. Pipe a border around the bottom and top edges of the cake. Refrigerate until ready to serve. Garnish with fresh raspberries.

Makes 10 slices. Per slice: 671 cal, 9 g pro, 74 g car, 41 g fat, 168 mg chol with butter, 134 mg chol with margarine, 337 mg sod with butter, 479 mg sod with margarine

---

EASY • MAKE AHEAD

TOASTED ALMOND COCONUT CAKE

Serves 16
Preparation time: 20 minutes
Baking time: 50 minutes

Here's a delicious moist cake with a delightfully crunchy texture. It's very simple to make and looks particularly festive when baked in a fluted pan.

> 1½ cups sweetened flaked coconut
> 1 cup (4 ounces) whole natural almonds, coarsely chopped
> 1½ cups all-purpose flour
> 1 teaspoon baking soda
> ½ teaspoon salt
> 1 cup plain yogurt
> ¾ cup granulated sugar
> ½ cup (1 stick) butter or margarine (not spread), melted
> 2 large eggs
> ½ teaspoon almond extract
> For decoration: 4 (1-ounce) squares semisweet chocolate,
>   melted (optional)

1. Heat the oven to 350° F. Grease a 10-cup Bundt or fluted tube pan.

2. Spread the coconut and almonds on a jelly roll pan or baking sheet with sides. Bake for 12 to 15 minutes, stirring 3 times, until the coconut is lightly browned. Set the pan on a wire rack to cool completely. Reserve ▶

Ⓜ AKE AHEAD

The cooled baked cake can be stored airtight at room temperature up to 5 days, or frozen up to 1 month. Thaw at room temperature. Decorate just before serving.

½ cup of the nut mixture for decoration

3. Meanwhile, in a large bowl, mix the flour, baking soda, and salt.

4. In a medium-size bowl, whisk the yogurt, sugar, melted butter, eggs, and almond extract until smooth. Stir this mixture into the flour mixture just until blended. Stir in the remaining coconut-almond mixture.

5. Spread the batter into the prepared pan. Bake for 30 to 35 minutes, or until a toothpick inserted near the center of the cake comes out clean. Set the pan on a wire rack to cool for 20 minutes. Invert the cake onto the rack, remove the pan, and cool completely.

6. To decorate, drizzle with the melted chocolate and sprinkle with the reserved coconut-almond mixture.

Makes 16 slices. Per slice: 227 cal, 4 g pro, 24 g car, 13 g fat, 43 mg chol with butter, 28 mg chol with margarine, 242 mg sod with butter, 251 mg sod with margarine

---

EASY • CLASSIC

MARBLE POUND CAKE

Serves 12
Preparation time: 15 minutes
Baking time: 1 hour 20 minutes

This simple cake keeps well and is a great idea for buffet tables. For an extra special treat, top with a scoop of ice cream and hot fudge or chocolate sauce.

2⅓ cups all-purpose flour
1½ teaspoons baking powder
¼ teaspoon salt
2 sticks (1 cup) butter or margarine (not spread), at room temperature
1⅔ cups granulated sugar
5 large eggs
1½ teaspoons almond extract
3 ounces semisweet chocolate chips (½ cup), melted
For garnish: confectioners' sugar (optional)

1. Heat the oven to 325°F. Grease and lightly flour a 10-cup Bundt or fluted tube pan.

2. In a small bowl, mix the flour, baking powder, and salt.

3. In a large bowl, beat the butter with an electric mixer until smooth. Add the sugar and beat until pale and fluffy.

4. Add the eggs one at a time, beating well after each addition. Beat in the almond extract.

CAKE PERFECT

◆ Be sure all ingredients are at room temperature, especially eggs. (If eggs are cold, immerse in warm water before you crack them.)

◆ To distribute spices and flavorings evenly in a batter, beat them with the butter and sugar.

◆ Stir dry ingredients well. Otherwise, all the leavening agent will end up in one place.

◆ To avoid disasters and infinite frustration, don't experiment with the size of your cake pan. Use what the recipe calls for.

◆ Add nuts to batter at the very last moment and they'll keep their texture.

◆ The batter should fill the pan from 1/2 to 3/4 full, depending on the cake.

5. With the mixer on low speed, beat in the flour mixture until smooth.

6. Put about 1½ cups of the batter into a small bowl. Stir in the melted chocolate until well blended.

7. Alternately put large spoonfuls of white and chocolate batter into the prepared pan. Swirl gently with a thin knife to marbleize the batter slightly. Tap the pan on the countertop to remove any air bubbles.

8. Bake for 1 hour and 20 minutes, or until a toothpick inserted near the center of the cake comes out clean. Set the pan on a wire rack to cool for 20 minutes. Invert the cake onto the rack and cool completely. Just before serving, sift confectioners' sugar over the top.

Makes 12 slices. Per slice: 408 cal, 6 g pro, 53 g car, 20 g fat, 130 mg chol with butter, 89 mg chol with margarine, 289 mg sod with butter, 311 mg sod with margarine

LIGHT • MAKE AHEAD • CLASSIC

LIGHT & CREAMY CHEESECAKE

Serves 8

Preparation time: 20 minutes plus at least 3 hours to chill

Baking time: 9 minutes

The creamy cheese filling is made of low-fat cottage cheese, buttermilk, and gelatin, lower in fat, cholesterol, and calories than the traditional version.

CRUST

1 cup graham cracker crumbs (fourteen 2½-inch square crackers)

¼ cup finely chopped pecans

3 tablespoons granulated sugar

3 tablespoons vegetable oil spread, melted

FILLING

2 envelopes (¼ ounce each) unflavored gelatin

2 cups buttermilk

½ cup granulated sugar

1 tablespoon lemon juice

16 ounces (2 cups) small-curd 1 percent fat cottage cheese

1 pint (about 12 ounces) strawberries, rinsed and patted dry (optional)

1 kiwifruit, peeled and sliced thin (optional)

1. Heat the oven to 350°F.

2. Make the crust: In a small bowl, mix the crumbs, pecans, sugar, and ▶

oil spread until well blended. Press the mixture evenly over the bottom and up the inside of an 8-inch springform pan.

3. Bake for 7 to 9 minutes, or until lightly browned. Set the pan on a wire rack and cool to room temperature.

4. Meanwhile, in a small saucepan, sprinkle the gelatin over ½ cup of the buttermilk. Let stand for 1 minute to soften. Stir over low heat for 2 to 3 minutes, or until almost boiling and the gelatin is completely dissolved.

5. Pour the mixture into a food processor or blender. Add the remaining buttermilk, the sugar, and lemon juice and process until blended. Add the cottage cheese and process until smooth. Pour into the cooled crust. Chill for at least 3 hours, or until firm.

6. Before serving, garnish the top with the strawberries and kiwifruit.

Makes 8 slices. Per slice: 257 cal, 16 g pro, 36 g car, 4 g fat, 5 mg chol, 418 mg sod

CANNOLI CHEESECAKE

Serves 16

Preparation time: 15 minutes plus at least 8 hours to chill
Baking time: 1 hour 30 minutes

In this ricotta and chocolate chip takeoff on the popular Italian pastry, most of the chips end up as a layer on the bottom of the cake.

CHEESECAKE

1 container (3 pounds) whole-milk ricotta cheese (6 cups)
7 large eggs
1¼ cups granulated sugar
½ cup all-purpose flour
1 tablespoon vanilla extract
1½ teaspoons grated orange peel
⅓ cup mini semisweet chocolate chips

TOPPING

3 tablespoons apricot preserves
3 small navel oranges, peel and white pith cut off, then sliced
   into thin rounds
¼ cup shelled pistachio nuts, skins rubbed off

1. Fill a roasting pan or a 13 x 9-inch baking pan with hot tap water to a depth of 1 inch. Place the pan on an oven rack in the center of the oven.

Heat the oven to 350°F.

2. Lightly grease and flour an 8-inch springform pan. Tap out the excess flour. Wrap the outside of the pan with heavy-duty foil, molding it tightly around the pan to prevent water from seeping in.

3. In a food processor, process the ricotta cheese, scraping down the sides once or twice, until smooth.

4. In a large bowl, whisk the eggs, sugar, flour, vanilla, and orange peel until blended. Stir in the ricotta until blended and smooth.

5. Pour the batter into the prepared pan and spread evenly. Sprinkle the chocolate chips over the top. Carefully place the pan into the pan of hot water. Bake for 1½ hours, or until the top is golden and the cake pulls away slightly from the side of the pan (the middle may still jiggle slightly when pressed gently).

6. Turn off the oven and prop the oven door open about 1 inch. Let the cake cool in the oven for about 45 minutes. Remove the pan from the water, then remove the foil. Set the pan on a wire rack to cool completely. Cover and refrigerate for at least 8 hours, or overnight.

7. Up to 3 hours before serving, run a long thin knife around the edge of the pan to loosen the cake. Remove the sides of the pan. Brush the top of the cake with half the melted preserves. Top with a layer of orange slices and brush with the remaining preserves. Sprinkle with the pistachio nuts.

Makes 18 slices. Per slice: 309 cal, 14 g pro, 30 g car, 15 g fat, 136 mg chol, 101 mg sod

EASY • 30 MINUTES • MAKE AHEAD

PASTRY FOR SINGLE-CRUST PIE

Makes one 9-inch pie crust
Preparation time: 15 minutes

Here's a great all-purpose pie dough recipe that can be used for either a single- or double-crust pie (see Variation). Make up several batches of the dough at one time, then freeze it so you'll have it readily on hand. For tips on making a perfect pie crust, see page 465.

1 cup all-purpose flour
2 tablespoons granulated sugar
¼ cup solid vegetable shortening
1½ tablespoons butter or margarine (not spread), chilled and cut
    into small pieces
3 tablespoons ice cold water

Ⓜ AKE AHEAD

The pastry dough can be wrapped tightly and frozen up to 3 months. Thaw at room temperature.

▶

1. To make the dough in a food processor: Process the flour, sugar, vegetable shortening, and butter with on/off turns until coarse crumbs form. With the motor running, add the water. Process just until the dough leaves the sides of the bowl. Remove the blade, then the dough.

To make the dough by hand: In a medium-size bowl, mix the flour and sugar. With 2 knives, cut in the shortening and butter until the mixture resembles coarse crumbs. Sprinkle with the water, 1 tablespoon at a time, stirring with a fork after each addition until the mixture clumps together to form a dough.

2. Press the dough into a ball, then flatten into a 1-inch-thick round.

3. If not using immediately, wrap and refrigerate up to 3 days.

MAKE AHEAD • CLASSIC

STRAWBERRY RHUBARB PIE

Serves 8

Preparation time: 30 minutes

Baking time: 50 minutes

The tart refreshing flavor of rhubarb combined with sweet, juicy strawberries makes a strikingly colorful and tasty pie. If you're not expert at crimping pie crust, you'll love making this—you simply fold the pastry over the filling.

STRAWBERRY RHUBARB FILLING

3 tablespoons cornstarch
3 tablespoons fresh lemon juice
½ teaspoon ground cinnamon
Pinch of ground cloves
10 ounces fresh rhubarb (without leaves) cut into 1-inch pieces (2 cups),
   or 1 pound frozen rhubarb, thawed and well drained
1 pint (12 ounces) ripe strawberries, rinsed, drained, hulled, and halved
   lengthwise (2 cups)
1 cup granulated sugar

Pastry for single-crust pie (page 461)
¼ cup strawberry preserves
1 tablespoon confectioners' sugar

1. Heat the oven to 450°F. Make the filling: In a large bowl, mix the cornstarch, lemon juice, cinnamon, and cloves until blended. Add the rhubarb, strawberries, and sugar. Toss to mix. Let stand at room temperature for 15

VARIATION

PASTRY FOR DOUBLE-CRUST PIE

● **Double all ingredients for the single-crust pie except for the sugar. Increase sugar to 3 tablespoons. Prepare the dough as directed.**

● **Divide the dough in half. Press each half into a ball, then flatten into a 1-inch-thick round. If using immediately, wrap half in plastic wrap or waxed paper to prevent drying while working with other half. If not using immediately, wrap individually and refrigerate up to 3 days or freeze up to 3 months.**

● **EASY • 30 MINUTES**
● **MAKE AHEAD**

MAKE AHEAD

The cooled baked pie can be refrigerated airtight up to 3 days.

minutes, stirring occasionally, until the fruits release some of their juices and the sugar is almost completely dissolved.

2. Roll out the pastry on a lightly floured surface with a lightly floured rolling pin into a 12-inch-diameter circle. Trim the ragged edges. Line a 9-inch pie plate with the dough.

3. Spoon the filling into the crust. Fold the dough around the edge of the pie plate over the filling, letting it form folds naturally.

4. Bake for 10 minutes. Reduce the heat to 350°F and bake for 35 to 40 minutes more, or until the crust is golden and the filling bubbles.

5. Set the pan on a wire rack. Spoon the preserves over the filling. (Preserves will melt from the heat of the pie and glaze the filling.) Let cool for at least 30 minutes. Serve warm or chilled. Just before serving, sift confectioners' sugar over the crust.

Makes 8 slices. Per slice: 302 cal, 2 g pro, 55 g car, 9 g fat, 6 mg chol with butter crust, 0 mg chol with margarine crust, 29 mg sod

---

MAKE AHEAD • CLASSIC

LEMON PIE

Serves 8
Preparation time: 40 minutes
Baking time: 40 minutes

Garnish the pie with dollops of sweetened whipped cream and add a border of halved or sliced fresh strawberries or very thin slices of fresh lemon.

SHORTBREAD CRUST
1½ cups all-purpose flour
2 tablespoons granulated sugar
½ teaspoon salt
½ cup vegetable oil
2 tablespoons milk

LEMON FILLING
Grated peel from 1 large lemon (about 1½ teaspoons)
3 tablespoons fresh lemon juice
2 tablespoons all-purpose flour
1 tablespoon butter or margarine, melted
1 cup milk
1 cup granulated sugar
3 large eggs, yolks and whites separated, at room temperature

COOK'S TIP

When grating citrus peel for a dessert, use the smallest openings on a grater and grate only the colored part of the peel.

1. Heat the oven to 325°F.

2. Make the crust: In a medium-size bowl, mix the flour, sugar, and salt until blended. Add the oil and milk. Stir with a fork until well blended.

3. Gather the dough into a ball and flatten into a 1-inch-thick round. Press the dough evenly over the bottom and up the sides of an ungreased 9-inch pie plate. Press the edge into a standing rim and flute or crimp.

4. Make the filling: In a large bowl, whisk the lemon peel, lemon juice, flour, and melted butter until smooth. Whisk in the milk, sugar, and egg yolks until blended.

5. In a medium-size bowl, beat egg whites with an electric mixer until stiff peaks form when the beaters are lifted. With a rubber spatula, gently stir (fold) the egg whites into the yolk mixture. Pour the filling into the crust.

6. Bake for 40 minutes, or until a toothpick inserted near the center comes out clean and the top of the filling is golden.

7. Set the pie on a wire rack to cool completely. Serve at room temperature or chilled.

Makes 8 slices. Per slice: 385 cal, 6 g pro, 50 g car, 18 g fat, 88 mg chol with butter, 84 mg chol with margarine, 193 mg sod

---

CLASSIC

OLD–FASHIONED APPLE PIE

Serves 8
Preparation time: 30 minutes
Baking time: 45 minutes

There's a suprise layer of brown sugar nestled at the bottom of this pie. Delicious served warm with vanilla ice cream or frozen yogurt.

Pastry for double-crust pie (page 462)

APPLE FILLING
⅔ cup packed light or dark brown sugar
3 tablespoons all-purpose flour
¾ teaspoon ground cinnamon
⅛ teaspoon grated nutmeg
3 pounds Golden Delicious or Granny Smith apples, peeled, cored, and
    cut into ½-inch-thick slices (9 cups)
1 tablespoon lemon juice
1 large egg, slightly beaten
1 tablespoon granulated sugar

M AKE AHEAD

The cooled baked pie can be refrigerated air tight up to 2 days.

1. Place the oven rack in the lowest position. Heat the oven to 425°F.

2. Roll out half the dough on a lightly floured surface with a lightly floured rolling pin into a 12-inch circle. Line a 9-inch pie pan with the dough.

3. Make the filling: In a large bowl, mix the brown sugar, flour, cinnamon, and nutmeg. Add the apples and lemon juice. Toss gently to mix and coat. Spread the filling into the crust, slightly mounding the apples in the center. Scrape any juices in the bowl over the apples.

4. Roll out the remaining dough into a 12-inch circle. Place over the filling. Press the edges together and roll up to form a rim. Flute or crimp the edges to seal.

5. Brush the pie with the egg, then sprinkle with the granulated sugar. Cut small slits in the top crust for steam to escape.

6. Bake for 20 minutes. Reduce the oven temperature to 375°F and bake for 20 to 25 minutes more, or until the crust is golden brown and the fruit is tender when pierced through a slit. (If the top crust browns too quickly, drape a piece of foil loosely over the pie.)

7. Set on a wire rack to cool. Serve warm or at room temperature.

Makes 8 slices. Per slice: 462 cal, 5 g pro, 72 g car, 18 g fat, 38 mg chol with butter crust, 27 mg chol with margarine crust, 63 mg sod

PERFECT PIE CRUSTS

◆ Measure carefully. Too much flour toughens a crust; too much liquid makes it soggy; too much fat makes it greasy and crumbly.

◆ Use a chopping motion to cut fat into the flour with two knives or a pastry blender.

◆ Sprinkle, don't pour, ice cold liquid over the dry ingredients one tablespoon at a time. Toss gently (don't stir) with a fork just until dough clumps together.

◆ Chilling pastry makes it easier to handle, but let it stand at room temperature until soft enough to roll.

◆ When rolling out pastry between two sheets of waxed paper, sprinkle the countertop with a few drops of water first to keep the paper from sliding. Flip the pastry occasionally and lift off the top sheet to smooth out any wrinkles.

◆ Don't stretch pastry to fill a pie plate or tart pan. Roll it out gently about 2 inches wider than the top of the plate or pan.

◆ What's the difference in using a glass, stainless steel, aluminum, or black metal pie pan? Depending on how they absorb and conduct heat, each will have a different effect on the pastry. Aluminum, which has a dull finish, is the best choice because it absorbs heat quickly and retains it. Glass pie pans are also good because they conduct the heat evenly and offer the advantage of seeing the color of the crust before removing the pie from the oven. Shiny metal surfaces, such as stainless steel, should be avoided because they deflect heat. Also, avoid using black metal, which absorbs heat too quickly and will overbrown pie crusts.

◆ For a crisp bottom crust and to keep the rim or top crust from overbrowning, bake a pie in the lower third of the oven.

◆ If a prebaked shell cracks on the bottom, seal it with a paste made of flour and water. Return the shell to the oven for a few minutes to dry the "glue."

FRENCH CHERRY PIE

Serves 12
Preparation time: 20 minutes
Baking time: 35 minutes

Make the meringue crust for this pie on a cool dry day, and don't fill it more than 30 minutes before serving or it will lose its crispness.

MERINGUE CRUST

Whites of 4 large eggs, at room temperature
1 cup granulated sugar
1 teaspoon baking powder
1 teaspoon cider vinegar
1 teaspoon pure vanilla extract
¾ cup chopped pecans
14 saltine crackers, crushed fine (½ cup)

FILLING

4 ounces cream cheese (½ cup), at room temperature
½ cup confectioners' sugar
1 cup whipping cream
1 teaspoon pure vanilla extract
1 can (about 21 ounces) cherry pie filling

1. Heat the oven to 325°F.

2. Make the crust: In a large bowl, beat the egg whites with an electric mixer until soft peaks form when the beaters are lifted. Beat in the baking powder, vinegar, and vanilla. With a rubber spatula, gently stir (fold) in the pecans and saltines.

3. Gently spread the mixture into an ungreased 9-inch square baking pan. Bake for 30 to 35 minutes, or until the top looks dry and lightly browned. Set the pan on a wire rack and cool completely.

4. Meanwhile, make the filling: In a large bowl, beat the cream cheese and confectioners' sugar with an electric mixer until smooth.

5. In a medium-size bowl, beat the cream and vanilla with an electric mixer (no need to wash the beaters) until soft peaks form when the beaters are lifted. Whisk this mixture into the cream cheese mixture until smooth.

6. Spread the cream cheese filling over the crust, then cover with the cherry pie filling. To serve, spoon onto serving plates.

Makes 12 slices. Per slice: 311 cal, 3 g pro, 41 g car, 16 g fat, 38 mg chol, 145 mg sod

MAKE AHEAD

The meringue crust can be prepared through step 3. Store, loosely covered, at room temperature up to 3 days.

VARIATION

APRICOT TARTS

• Heat the oven to 375°F. In a shallow 3-quart baking dish, mix 6 cups sliced pitted ripe apricots (about 2 pounds), ¼ cup sugar, and 3 tablespoons fresh lemon juice. Bake uncovered for 8 to 10 minutes, stirring once, until the apricots release some of their juices.

• Stir in 1 cup apricot jam, large chunks broken up, and ⅓ cup orange juice. Cool to room temperature. Fill the tart shells with the fruit mixture, or cover and refrigerate up to 2 days and serve chilled.

Per tart: 280 cal, 3 g pro, 46 g car, 11 g fat, 42 mg chol with butter, 18 mg chol with margarine, 106 mg sod with butter, 194 mg sod with margarine

• 60 MINUTES
• MAKE AHEAD

60 MINUTES • MAKE AHEAD

PLUM TARTS

Serves 12
Preparation time: 28 minutes
Baking time: 32 minutes

This easy pastry recipe makes 12 individual servings. For a party, double the pastry recipes and make both toppings (see Variation) and let guests choose or double up on one topping for a simply wonderful dinner finale.

TART PASTRY
1½ cups all-purpose flour
¼ cup granulated sugar
½ teaspoon salt
½ cup cold unsalted butter or margarine, cut into small pieces
2 tablespoons cream or milk
Yolk from 1 large egg

PLUM TOPPING
3 pounds ripe plums, halved, pitted, and cut in ½-inch-thick wedges
   (about 8 cups)
1 cup granulated sugar
2 tablespoons lemon juice
¼ teaspoon ground cinnamon

1. Heat the oven to 375°F.

2. To make the pastry in a food processor: Process the flour, sugar, and salt to blend. With the machine running, drop the butter through the feed tube and process with on/off turns until the mixture resembles fine crumbs. In a small bowl, beat the cream and egg yolk with a fork until blended. With the machine running, pour this mixture through the feed tube and process until the dough leaves the side of the bowl clean.

To make by hand: In a medium-size bowl, mix the flour, sugar, and salt. Cut in the butter with 2 knives until the mixture resembles fine crumbs. In a small bowl, beat the cream and egg yolk with a fork until blended. Stir this mixture into the crumb mixture until the dough forms a ball and leaves the side of the bowl clean.

3. Divide the dough into 12 equal pieces. Roll each piece into a ball. Press each ball evenly over the bottoms and up the sides of lightly greased muffin pan cups or 3 x 1-inch tart pans. Place on a baking sheet and bake at 375° F for 15 to 17 minutes, or until the pastry looks dry and pale ▶

golden brown. Set on a wire rack to cool completely. Carefully remove the tart shells from the pans.

4. Meanwhile, make the topping: In a shallow 3-quart baking dish, mix all the ingredients. Bake for 12 to 15 minutes, stirring once, or until the plums release some of their juices. Cool to room temperature and spoon the topping into the tart shells.

Makes 12 tarts. Per tart: 285 cal, 3 g pro, 47 g car, 11 g fat with cream, 10 g fat with milk, 42 mg chol with butter, 18 mg chol with margarine, 95 mg sod with butter, 183 mg sod with margarine

MAKE AHEAD

CHOCOLATE PECAN TART

Serves 12
Preparation time: 20 minutes
Baking time: 1 hour

This chewy, fudgelike tart—more like candy than cake—makes a spectacular dessert or gift for the true chocoholic.

PECAN CRUST
15 pecan shortbread cookies, crushed fine (1¾ cups)
2 tablespoons butter or margarine, at room temperature
1 cup pecans, coarsely chopped

CHOCOLATE FILLING
1 cup packed light brown sugar
⅓ cup granulated sugar
⅓ cup (5⅛ tablespoons) butter or margarine
2 tablespoons milk
2 (1-ounce) squares unsweetened
   chocolate, cut into pieces
1 tablespoon all-purpose flour
1 teaspoon pure vanilla extract
2 large eggs

1. Heat the oven to 325°F.
2. Make the crust: Put the crumbs and butter in a medium-size bowl. Using 2 knives or your fingertips, work the butter evenly into crumbs. Press the mixture over the bottom and up the inside of a ungreased 9-inch tart pan with a removable bottom. Scatter the pecans over the bottom.

MAKE AHEAD

Prepare the dough as directed in step 1. Wrap airtight and refrigerate up to 1 week, or freeze for up to 3 months. Thaw at room temperature and proceed as directed. The cooled baked fruit topping can refrigerated airtight up to 2 days.

M AKE AHEAD
Wrap airtight and store
at room temperature
up to 1 week,
refrigerate up to 2
weeks, or freeze up to
3 months.

3. Bake for 8 to 10 minutes, or until the crust is set and the pecans are lightly toasted. Set the pan on a wire rack to cool.

4. Meanwhile, make the filling. In a medium-size saucepan, heat both sugars, the butter, and milk over medium-low heat for 5 minutes, stirring often, until the sugars dissolve and the mixture is smooth. Remove the pan from the heat and stir in the chocolate until melted and smooth. Stir in the flour and vanilla. Add the eggs, one at a time, stirring after each until well blended. Pour the mixture into the prepared crust.

5. Bake for 45 minutes, or until the filling is set and the top forms a thin crust. Set on a wire rack to cool completely. Remove the side of the pan and cut the tart into wedges. Serve at room temperature.

Makes 12 slice. Per slice: 348 cal, 4 g pro, 37 g car, 22 g fat, 55 mg chol with butter, 36 mg chol with margarine, 146 mg sod

EASY • LIGHT • CLASSIC

TIRAMISÙ

Serves 12

Total time: 30 minutes plus at least 4 hours to chill

Tiramisù, the Italian dessert whose name means "a pick-me-up," is a cousin of the trifle. It is usually made with mascarpone cheese and Italian biscotti with a high calorie count to match. Here the fat and calories are dramatically reduced, without sacrificing flavor. You can make this up to two days ahead.

1 cup water
2 tablespoons instant coffee granules
1 tablespoon granulated sugar

FILLING
1 container (8 ounces) nonfat vanilla yogurt
¾ cup (half a 12-ounce tub) light cream cheese (pasteurized process cream-cheese product), at room temperature

1 purchased 15-ounce fat-and-cholesterol-free chocolate loaf cake
2 tablespoons unsweetened cocoa powder

1. In a 2-cup measure or bowl, mix the water, coffee granules, and sugar and stir until the sugar dissolves.

2. Make the filling: In a medium-size bowl, beat the yogurt and cream cheese with an electric mixer until creamy and smooth.

▶

3. Using a serrated knife, cut the cake in half lengthwise between the top and bottom. Cut each half crosswise into 14 slices.

4. Cover the bottom of a shallow 9- to 10-inch serving bowl or deep-dish pie plate with the 16 smallest cake slices. Overlap the remaining slices in a border around the edge of the dish.

5. Slowly pour the coffee mixture over the cake until all the slices are moistened. Pour the filling into the center and spread evenly to the cake slices around the edge. Cover with plastic wrap and refrigerate for at least 4 hours, or until the filling sets.

6. Up to 2 hours before serving: Using a small strainer, sift the cocoa over the filling. With the back of a table knife, score a diamond pattern in the cocoa. Serve chilled.

Makes 12 servings. Per serving: 141 cal, 4 g pro, 26 g car, 3 g fat, 8 mg chol, 256 mg sod

---

LIGHT • MAKE AHEAD

LEMON SPONGE PUDDING

Serves 8
Preparation time: 20 minutes
Baking time: 55 minutes

As it bakes, this dessert separates into two layers: a luscious, smooth pudding covered by a light, airy cake. If you like a very tart lemony flavor, increase the lemon juice to ⅓ cup.

2 large eggs, whites and yolks separated, at room temperature,
2 tablespoons plus ¾ cup granulated sugar
3 tablespoons butter or margarine, at room temperature
3 tablespoons all-purpose flour
1 cup milk
2 teaspoons grated lemon peel
¼ cup fresh lemon juice

1. Fill a roasting pan or 13 x 9-inch baking pan half full of hot tap water and place on an oven rack in the center of the oven. Heat the oven to 350°F.

2. In a medium-size bowl, beat the egg whites with an electric mixer until foamy. Gradually beat in 2 tablespoons of sugar until stiff peaks form when the beaters are lifted.

3. In another medium-size bowl with an electric mixer (no need to wash the beaters), beat the yolks, remaining ¾ cup granulated sugar, the butter, and flour until blended and smooth. With the mixer on low speed, gradually

WHIPPING CREAM HINTS

◆ Heavy cream will whip faster if cream, beaters, and bowl are well chilled.

◆ Eliminate splatter when whipping cream this way: Measure a piece of plastic wrap large enough to cover the bowl, make a hole in the center and push the blade stems through and into the beater.

◆ Freeze dollops or piped rosettes of sweetened whipped cream on a flat, waxed paper–covered plate. When hard, pop them into a plastic bag and freeze until needed (or up to two months). Use to garnish cakes, puddings, and other desserts.

beat in the milk, lemon peel, and lemon juice just until blended.

4. With a rubber spatula, gently stir (fold) the whites into the yolk mixture until no white streaks remain. Pour the batter into a ungreased deep 1½-quart baking dish or soufflé dish.

5. Carefully place the baking dish in the center of the pan of hot water. Bake for 50 to 55 minutes, or until the top is golden brown and a toothpick inserted near the center comes out clean.

6. Remove the pan from the water and set on a wire rack to cool. Serve warm or at room temperature.

Per serving: 173 cal, 3 g pro, 26 g car, 7 g fat, 69 mg chol with butter, 57 mg chol with margarine, 77 mg sod

EASY • 60 MINUTES • MAKE AHEAD

CHOCOLATE BREAD–PUDDING CUPS

Serves 6
Preparation time: 20 minutes
Baking time: 40 minutes

French schoolchildren have long adored the combination of bread and chocolate, and so will you and your family. If you like chocolate paired with banana, try the variation.

2 large eggs
2¼ cups milk
½ cup granulated sugar
1 teaspoon pure vanilla extract
18 (½-inch-thick) slices from a loaf of French or
    Italian bread (no larger than 3 inches in diameter)
6 tablespoons semisweet chocolate chips

1. Fill a 13 x 9-inch baking pan half full of hot tap water and place on an oven rack in the center of the oven. Heat the oven to 325°F.

2. In a medium-size bowl, whisk the eggs to blend yolks and whites. Whisk in the milk, sugar, and vanilla until well blended.

3. For each pudding: Place 1 slice of bread on the bottom of six 6-ounce custard cups or individual soufflé dishes. Sprinkle each with ½ tablespoon of chocolate chips, add 2 slices of bread, overlapping to fit, and sprinkle with another ½ tablespoon of chips. Pour about ½ cup milk mixture over each and press down the bread so the slices begin to absorb the milk mixture. ▶

Ⓜ️AKE AHEAD

The cooled baked pudding can be covered airtight and refrigerated up to 5 days.

VARIATION

BANANA CHOCOLATE BREAD-PUDDING CUPS

Mash 2 medium-size ripe bananas. Whisk the bananas with the eggs. Reduce the milk to 2 cups. Proceed as directed.

Per cup: 350 cal, 10 g pro, 60 g car, 9 g fat, 82 mg chol, 337 mg sod

• EASY • 60 MINUTES
• MAKE AHEAD

4. Carefully place the cups in the pan of hot water. Bake for 35 to 40 minutes, or until the edges of the bread are very lightly browned and a knife inserted near the centers comes out clean.

5. Remove the cups from the water and set on a wire rack to cool. Serve warm or at room temperature.

Per serving: 321 cal, 9 g pro, 52 g car, 9 g fat, 84 mg chol, 341 mg sod

---

EASY • MAKE AHEAD • CLASSIC

ALMOND RICE PUDDING

Serves 8
Preparation time: 10 minutes
Cooking time: 1 hour 25 minutes

Soft, creamy, and soothing, rice pudding is a dessert you never outgrow. A topping of sliced almonds, sugar, and nutmeg is sprinkled over the pudding before it bakes, leaving a crunchy crust.

1½ cups water
¾ cup uncooked white rice (not converted)
4 large eggs
4 cups milk
⅔ cup granulated sugar
2 teaspoons pure vanilla extract
1 teaspoon almond extract
1 cup dark raisins

TOPPING
⅓ cup sliced almonds
1 teaspoon granulated sugar
¼ teaspoon grated nutmeg

1. In a medium-size saucepan, bring the water and rice to a boil. Reduce the heat to low. Cover and simmer for 18 to 20 minutes, or until the water is absorbed and the rice is tender. Let cool.

2. Heat the oven to 325°F. Lightly grease a shallow 2-quart baking dish.

3. In a large bowl, whisk the eggs to blend the yolks and whites. Whisk in the milk, sugar, and both extracts until well blended. Stir in the rice and raisins. Pour the mixture into the prepared baking dish.

4. Make the topping: In a small bowl, mix the almonds, sugar, and nutmeg. Sprinkle the topping over the pudding.

ⓜAKE AHEAD

The cooled baked puddings can be covered airtight and refrigerated up to 5 days.

ⓜAKE AHEAD

The cooled baked pudding can be covered and refrigerated up to 5 days.

EGGSACTLY

◆ Separating eggs is hard enough, so don't do it when they're warm; it goes much better when they're ice cold. And use an egg separator, which helps protect against harmful bacteria that may be on the shell.

◆ Although eggs separate better when cold, egg whites will beat to a higher volume when at room temperature.

◆ When beating egg whites, be sure the beaters and bowl are absolutely free of fat. Otherwise, your whites will never beat up fully.

◆ You can freeze egg whites in an airtight container up to 3 months. Thaw the whites and pour into a measuring cups. Count 1 egg white to the liquid ounce: 1 cup (8 fluid ounces) = 8 egg whites.

5. Bake for 55 to 60 minutes, or until a knife inserted near the center comes out clean. (The center may still jiggle but will become firm on standing.) Remove to a wire rack to cool. Serve warm or at room temperature.
Per serving: 330 cal, 10 g pro, 53 g car, 9 g fat, 123 mg chol, 95 mg sod

---

MAKE AHEAD

BANANA CARAMEL CUSTARD

Serves 10
Preparation time: 20 minutes plus at least 8 hours to chill
Baking time: 1 hour 20 minutes

This custard is a great dessert for entertaining because it can be made ahead. It also can be easily doubled and baked in two loaf pans for a large group.

1¼ cups sugar
2 medium-size slightly overripe bananas, peeled and cut into pieces
8 large eggs
2 cans (12 ounces each) evaporated (not sweetened condensed) milk
2 teaspoons pure vanilla extract
½ teaspoon grated nutmeg
¼ teaspoon salt
For garnish: strawberries (optional)

1. Fill a roasting pan or a 13 x 9-inch baking pan half full of hot tap water and place on an oven rack in the center of the oven. Heat the oven to 350°F.

2. In a small heavy saucepan, heat ½ cup of the sugar over medium heat for about 5 minutes, swirling the pan occasionally until the sugar has melted and turns golden brown. (Watch the sugar carefully after it liquefies. If it gets too dark it will taste burned.) Immediately pour the mixture into a 9 x 5-inch loaf pan so the sugar (caramel) covers the bottom of the pan completely.

3. In a large bowl, beat the banana and remaining ¾ cup of sugar with an electric mixer on high speed until completely liquefied with no lumps. Or process in a food processor. Beat in the eggs (or process) until well blended. (If using a food processor, scrape the mixture into a large bowl.)

4. Add the evaporated milk, vanilla, nutmeg, and salt. Beat with a mixer on low speed or stir just until blended. Pour the mixture into the loaf pan. (Don't worry if the caramel cracks.)

5. Carefully the place the baking pan in the center of the pan of hot water. Bake for 1 hour and 15 to 20 minutes, or until a knife inserted near the center comes out clean and the top is browned. Remove the pan ▶

from the water and set on a wire rack to cool completely. When cooled, cover and refrigerate for at least 8 hours.

6. To serve, run a thin knife around the inside edges of the custard. Invert a serving plate over the pan. Invert the pan and plate together. Lift the pan and allow the syrup to run onto the plate. Serve right away or cover loosely with plastic wrap and refrigerate until ready to serve. Cut into 10 slices.
Makes 10 slices. Per slice: 282 cal, 10 g pro, 39 g car, 10 g fat, 192 mg chol, 185 mg sod.

EASY • LIGHT • MAKE AHEAD • CLASSIC

CHOCOLATE MOUSSE

Serves 6
Total time: 20 minutes plus at least 1 hour to chill

Yes, you can make a great mousse without eggs, heavy cream, and high-fat chocolate, and here it is. Accompany this dessert with a crisp cookie or fresh strawberries for contrast.

½ cup evaporated (not sweetened condensed) 2 percent fat milk
1½ teaspoons unflavored gelatin
6 tablespoons water
¼ cup unsweetened cocoa powder
⅓ cup granulated sugar
1 teaspoon pure vanilla extract

1. Put the milk into a small bowl and place in the freezer for about 30 minutes, or until ice crystals begin to form around the edges.

2. Sprinkle the gelatin over 2 tablespoons of water in a cup. Let stand for 1 minute to soften.

3. Meanwhile, in a small heavy saucepan, mix the remaining 4 tablespoons of water, the cocoa, and sugar. Cook over medium-low heat for 2 to 3 minutes, stirring occasionally, until the sugar has dissolved. Reduce the heat to low, add the gelatin mixture, and stir until the gelatin is completely dissolved. Pour the mixture into a large bowl and let cool to room temperature.

4. Meanwhile, remove the milk from the freezer. Add the vanilla and beat with an electric mixer until stiff peaks form (about 5 minutes). Stir a spoonful into the gelatin mixture until blended, then gently stir (fold) in the remaining with a rubber spatula.

5. Spoon the chocolate mousse into dessert glasses and chill for 1 hour, or until set. Serve chilled.
Per serving: 73 cal, 3 g pro, 15 g car, 1 g fat, 3 mg chol, 24 mg sod

---

Ⓜ AKE AHEAD

Prepare the custard through step 5. Cover airtight and refrigerate up to 2 days. Proceed as directed.

Ⓜ AKE AHEAD

The mousse can be prepared ahead and refrigerated up to 2 days.

APPLE STRUDEL

Serves 12
Preparation time: 45 minutes
Baking time: 45 minutes

ⓜAKE AHEAD

Store tightly wrapped at room temperature overnight or freeze up to 1 month. Defrost wrapped strudel at room temperature and recrisp by reheating in a 400°F oven for 10 minutes.

Made with delicate phyllo dough, apple strudel is as satisfying for dessert as it is with a cup of coffee for breakfast. Phyllo dough (also called filo or strudel leaves) is found frozen in most supermarkets. It is generally packaged in 1-pound boxes. Thaw frozen dough in the refrigerator for 8 hours or overnight.

½ cup granulated sugar
⅓ cup finely chopped walnuts
¼ cup raisins
1 teaspoon grated fresh lemon peel
1 teaspoon ground cinnamon
1½ pounds Golden Delicious apples (about 5 medium-size), peeled, cored, and cut into ½-inch chunks
6 sheets (each 17 x 12 inches) phyllo pastry, thawed if frozen
½ cup (1 stick) butter or margarine, melted and cooled
6 cinnamon-honey graham crackers (double crackers), crushed fine
For garnish: confectioners' sugar (optional)

1. Heat the oven to 400°F. Grease a 15½ x 10½ x 1-inch jelly roll pan.
2. In a large bowl, mix the sugar, walnuts, raisins, lemon peel, and cinnamon. Add the apples, tossing to coat.
3. Put a kitchen towel on the work surface with one long side nearest you. Place 1 sheet of phyllo on the towel (keep the remaining phyllo covered with plastic wrap to prevent drying). Brush the entire surface with about 1 tablespoon of butter, then sprinkle with 1 tablespoon of graham cracker crumbs. Layer 5 more sheets in the same manner, brushing each with butter and sprinkling with crumbs.
4. Mound the apple mixture across the side of phyllo nearest you, 1½ inches in from the sides and ends. Fold the short ends of the phyllo over the filling. Using the towel as a guide, gently roll up the strudel tightly, enclosing the filling. Lift carefully (on the towel) and place, seam side down, on the prepared jelly roll pan. Brush the top with butter.
5. Bake for 35 to 40 minutes, or until golden. Set the pan with the strudel on a wire rack to cool.
6. Use 2 spatulas to transfer the strudel to a cutting board. Serve warm or at room temperature. Just before serving, sift confectioners' sugar over ▶

the top. Using a sharp knife, cut the strudel into 1-inch-thick slices.

Per serving: 204 cal, 2 g pro, 26 g car, 11 g fat, 21 mg chol with butter, 0 mg chol with margarine, 150 mg sod

---

EASY • 60 MINUTES

PEAR CUSTARD CRUMBLE

Serves 8

Preparation time: 15 minutes

Baking time: 35 minutes

Few things are as soothing as warm baked fruit. Top with custard and crumb topping and you've made a good thing even better. In this crumble, each pear half holds a hidden treasure of raspberry jam.

1 large egg
1 cup light sour cream or plain low-fat yogurt
2 tablespoons granulated sugar
1 tablespoon all-purpose flour
1 teaspoon pure vanilla extract
2 cans (about 16 ounces each) pear halves, drained and patted dry
   with paper towels
2 tablespoons seedless raspberry jam

TOPPING

¾ cup uncooked quick or old-fashioned oats
½ cup packed light or dark brown sugar
¼ cup (½ stick) butter or margarine (not spread), chilled and cut
   into small pieces

1. Heat the oven to 350°F.

2. In a medium-size bowl, whisk the egg, sour cream, sugar, flour, and vanilla until well blended.

3. Fill the hollow of each pear with ½ teaspoon of raspberry jam. Arrange the pears, jam side down, in a single layer in a 9- to 10-inch deep-dish pie plate.

4. Pour the sour cream mixture over the pears to cover. Bake for 15 minutes, or until the custard starts to set.

5. Meanwhile, make the topping. In a small bowl, mix the oats and brown sugar. Cut in the butter with 2 knives or your fingertips until the mixture is crumbly. Sprinkle the topping over the custard.

6. Bake for 15 to 20 minutes more, or until the filling is bubbly and the

topping is lightly browned. Set on a wire rack to cool. Serve warm or at room temperature.

Per serving with sour cream: 277 cal, 5 g pro, 43 g car, 11 g fat, 52 mg chol with butter, 37 mg chol with margarine, 83 mg sod. With yogurt: 245 cal, 4 g pro, 439 car, 7 g fat, 44 mg chol with butter, 28 mg chol with margarine, 102 mg sod

---

EASY • 60 MINUTES • CLASSIC

BLUEBERRY PLUM CRISP

Serves 8

Preparation time: 20 minutes

Baking time: 40 minutes

This old-fashioned favorite is best served warm or at room temperature. For a special treat, top it with vanilla ice cream or lightly sweetened whipped cream. You can also use fresh raspberries or blackberries in place f the blueberries.

1 pint (12 ounces) blueberries, rinsed and picked over
2 pounds plums (about 9 medium-size purple or red plums, or
  32 Italian prune plums), halved, pitted, and cut into ½-inch slices
2 tablespoons granulated sugar
1 tablespoon all-purpose flour
1 tablespoon fresh lemon juice
½ teaspoon ground cinnamon

TOPPING

¾ cup packed light brown sugar
⅔ cup all-purpose flour
6 tablespoons butter or margarine (not spread), chilled and cut into
  small pieces
¾ cup uncooked old-fashioned or quick-cooking oats

1. Heat the oven to 375°F. Put the blueberries, plums, granulated sugar, flour, lemon juice, and cinnamon into a 9-inch pie plate. Mix, then spread evenly.

2. To make the topping in a food processor: Process the brown sugar and flour to blend. Add the butter and process with on/off turns until coarse crumbs form. Transfer to a medium-size bowl and stir in the oats with a fork.

To make the topping by hand: In a medium-size bowl, mix the brown sugar and flour. Cut in the butter with 2 knives until the mixture resembles coarse crumbs. Stir in the oats with a fork.

▶

3. Sprinkle the topping evenly over the fruit, then press down gently. Bake for 35 to 40 minutes, or until the plums are tender when pierced, juices bubble, and the topping is crisp and lightly browned. Serve warm or at room temperature.

Per serving: 320 cal, 4 g pro, 57 g car, 10 g fat, 23 mg chol with butter, 0 mg chol with margarine, 105 mg sod

PEACH COBBLER WITH PRALINE BISCUITS

Serves 8

Preparation time: 20 minutes

Baking time: 25 minutes

This version of a truly American dessert consists of lightly spiced fresh peaches scented with anise and topped with praline-filled crescent dough spirals. It not only tastes great but looks spectacular as well. Praline is a Southern confection made of pecans, brown sugar, and butter. Here the ingredients are formed into a paste and used as a filling for the biscuits.

PRALINE BISCUITS

1 cup pecans

¼ cup packed dark brown sugar

3 tablespoons butter or margarine, cut into small pieces

1 tube (8 ounces) refrigerated crescent-roll dough

PEACH COBBLER

½ cup granulated sugar

1 tablespoon cornstarch

1 teaspoon anise seed

⅓ cup water

1½ teaspoons pure vanilla extract

4 pounds medium-size ripe peaches or nectarines, halved, pitted, and each half cut into 4 wedges (10½ cups)

1 tablespoon butter or margarine, cut into small pieces

1. Heat the oven to 400°F. Grease an 11 x 7-inch baking dish.

2. To make the biscuit topping with a food processor: Process the pecans and brown sugar using on/off turns until the pecans are very finely chopped. Add the butter and process just until the mixture forms a paste and pulls

etable shortening.

◆ Sour cream and yogurt should be measured the same way as solid vegetable shortening.

◆ Last but not least, measure any dry ingredients over waxed paper rather than the mixing bowl. It's easy to return spills to the containers and you won't have to start from scratch if something spills into the bowl.

away from the side of the bowl into a ball.

To make the biscuit topping by hand: Very finely chop the pecans. In a small bowl, mix and mash the pecans, brown sugar, and butter until blended to a paste.

3. Remove the crescent-roll dough from the tube and separate into 2 pieces at the perforation in the middle. Unroll each half into a 12 x 4-inch rectangle, pressing the perforations together.

4. Crumble half of the pecan mixture over each dough rectangle and press into an even layer. Starting from one long side, roll up the dough jelly roll style. Cut each roll crosswise into 8 pieces. Turn the pieces spiral-side up. Press down on each piece to flatten to an even ½-inch thickness (each will be about 2 inches across).

5. Make the cobbler: In a large pot, mix the sugar, cornstarch, and anise seeds until blended. Stir in the water and vanilla. Add the peaches and stir while bringing the mixture to a boil. Boil for 1½ minutes, or until the mixture thickens and the peaches are coated.

6. Pour the filling into the prepared baking dish and dot with butter. Arrange the biscuits over the peaches in 4 rows, 4 biscuits each, so they are barely touching.

7. Bake for 22 to 25 minutes, or until the biscuits are golden brown and the filling is bubbling. Set the pan on a wire rack to cool. Serve slightly warm.

Per serving: 401 cal, 4 g pro, 53 g car, 21 g fat, 16 mg chol with butter, 0 mg chol with margarine, 280 mg sod

THE BERRY BEST

What could be more wonderful than an unadorned bowl of perfectly fresh berries? Perhaps berries topped with a cloud of whipped cream or maybe awash in heavy cream or cold milk? Or how about sprinkled on ice cream or breakfast cereal, or plopped onto pancakes? That's only the beginning.

DIP TIPS

Serve whole large berries (with toothpicks for spearing) with bowls of
◆ Sour cream and brown sugar
◆ Honey, maple syrup, and finely chopped nuts

FRUIT AND BERRY COMBOS

◆ Melon chunks and blueberries sprinkled with coarsely chopped mint leaves

◆ Sliced bananas and strawberries with orange juice or sprinkled with cinnamon
◆ Fresh pineapple chunks and raspberries sprinkled with ground ginger (use a light touch) or with finely chopped fresh or crystallized ginger

BERRIES ON TOP

◆ Crown a brownie with a scoop of vanilla ice cream, mashed sweetened raspberries, and a generous sprinkling of mini semisweet chocolate chips.
◆ Fill a purchased ready-to-serve pie crust with ice cream or pudding. Top with a colorful mixture of fresh berries.
◆ Warm ready-made biscuits, split them, then fill and top with sliced strawberries and softly whipped cream.
◆ Spoon berries over rice pudding.
◆ Spoon mashed berries over slices of pound cake.

RASPBERRY RAVE

Serves 12

Total time: 12 minutes plus at least 8 hours to chill

This bright, tasty gelatin dish is a perfect for buffets.

2 packages (10 ounces each) frozen red raspberries in syrup, thawed
1 can (about 20 ounces) crushed pineapple packed in juice
1 cup boiling water
2 four-serving-size packages (3 ounces each) raspberry-flavored gelatin
1 cup, regular, reduced-fat, or nonfat sour cream
For garnish: strawberries, raspberries, blueberries, and mint sprigs (optional)

1. Drain the raspberries and pineapple in a sieve set over a 4-cup measure, pressing the fruit with the back of a spoon until you have 2 cups of liquid.

2. In a medium-size bowl, dissolve the gelatin in the boiling water. Stir in the 2 cups of fruit liquid, the drained fruit, and the sour cream until completely blended. Pour into an 8- to 10-cup Bundt pan or ring mold and refrigerate for at least 8 hours, or until firm.

3. To unmold: Moisten a serving plate with cold water (if gelatin lands off-center you can slide it to the middle). Dip the pan up to the rim in warm, not hot, water for about 10 seconds. Invert the moistened plate over the pan. Invert the pan and plate together and shake gently from side to side to release the gelatin. Repeat the process if the gelatin doesn't drop from the mold. Remove the pan gently. Refrigerate the gelatin until ready to serve.

Per serving: 171 cal with regular sour cream, 164 cal with reduced-fat sour cream, 144 cal with nonfat sour cream, 3 g pro, 34 g car, 4 g fat with regular sour cream, 3 g fat with reduced-fat sour cream, 0 g fat with nonfat sour cream, 8 mg chol, 0 mg chol with nonfat sour cream, 70 mg sod

RUM–RAISIN POACHED APPLES

Serves 4

Preparation time: 15 minutes

Cooking time: 20 minutes

Poached fruit is simple to prepare and makes for an elegant presentation. Enjoy these tender juicy apples as is or top with whipped cream *p. 485*

MAKE AHEAD

The mold can be prepared through step 2 and refrigerated up to 2 days. Unmold and serve as directed.

VARIATION

STRAWBERRY RAVE

Substitute 2 packages (10 ounces each) frozen strawberries in syrup for the frozen raspberries, and 2 four-serving-size packages of strawberry-flavored gelatin for the raspberry-flavored gelatin. Proceed as directed.

Per serving: 168 cal with regular sour cream, 161 cal with reduced-fat sour cream, 141 cal with nonfat sour cream, 3 g pro, 34 g car, 4 g fat with regular sour cream, 3 g fat with reduced-fat sour cream, 0 g fat with nonfat sour cream, 8 mg chol, 0 mg chol with nonfat sour cream, 83 mg sod

• EASY • MAKE AHEAD
• LIGHT

KEEP COOL
Since everyone likes cake with ice cream, this Peach Melba Ice Cream Cake (p.488) makes a great grand finale.

When the mood strikes for something sweet, choose

from one of the many desserts featured here. There's

something for every occasion.

SWEET TREATS
Deep Chocolate
Hazelnut Cake
(p.440), above, or
Blueberry Plum
Crisp (p.477),
right, proves
there's always
room for dessert.

FROZEN ASSETS These luscious Individual Ice Cream Bombes (p.491) are made with ice cream and chocolate-covered cherries.

or ice cream. They can also be served over pound cake or gingerbread.

2 cups water

¾ cup granulated sugar

½ teaspoon grated nutmeg

2 tablespoons dark rum, or ½ teaspoon each rum and vanilla extract

4 Golden Delicious or other all-purpose apples (about 1½ pounds), peeled, quartered, and cored

½ cup raisins

1. In a large deep skillet, bring the water, sugar, and nutmeg to a boil. Boil for 5 minutes, stirring occasionally, until slightly reduced in volume.

2. Add the rum and apples. Cover and simmer over low heat for 10 to 15 minutes, gently stirring two or three times, until the apples are tender.

3. Remove the skillet from the heat. Stir in the raisins. Serve warm.

4. Spoon the poached apples with some of the sauce and raisins into serving bowls and serve warm.

Per serving: 300 cal with dark rum, 288 cal with rum and vanilla, 1 g pro, 73 g car, 1 g fat, 0 mg chol, 3 mg sod

---

EASY • 30 MINUTES • LIGHT • MAKE AHEAD

CHERRIES SUPREME

Serves 6

Preparation time: 10 minutes

This is a very simple dessert—nothing more than fresh sweet cherries and a creamy dip scented with allspice. Allspice highlights the flavor of fresh cherries. Try some in your next cherry pie.

1 cup part-skim ricotta cheese

3 tablespoons granulated sugar

¼ teaspoon ground allspice

1 pound fresh sweet cherries with stems

For garnish: fresh mint leaves (optional)

1. In a food processor or a blender, process the ricotta, sugar, and allspice until smooth. Scrape into a small bowl or bowls. Decorate with mint.

2. Serve as a dip with the cherries.

Per serving with 2 tablespoons dip: 130 cal, 5 g pro, 20 g car, 4 g fat, 13 mg chol, 51 mg sod

Ⓜ AKE AHEAD

The dip can be prepared ahead and refrigerated airtight up to 3 days. Serve chilled or at room temperature.

EASY • 60 MINUTES • LIGHT

BLUEBERRY NECTARINE CUPS

Serves 6

Preparation time: 15 minutes plus 30 minute to chill

You can enjoy this dish for breakfast as well as dessert.

1 pint fresh blueberries (about 2 cups)
3 medium-size ripe nectarines, cut into thin wedges
¼ cup orange juice
1 tablespoon fresh lemon juice
1 container (8 ounces) low-fat vanilla yogurt (1 cup)
6 tablespoons granola

1. In a medium-size bowl, gently mix the blueberries, nectarines, orange, and lemon juice. Refrigerate for 30 minutes, or until chilled.
2. Spoon the fruit mixture into 6 dessert glasses. Top with yogurt and sprinkle with granola.

Per serving: 145 cal, 4 g pro, 26 g car, 2 g fat, 2 mg chol, 32 mg sod

---

EASY • 60 MINUTES • MICROWAVE • LIGHT

PINEAPPLE FOSTER

Serves 8

Preparation time: 15 minutes

Cooking time: 11 minutes plus 5 minutes to stand

Serve this takeoff on Bananas Foster warm with scoops of vanilla ice cream.

1½ cups packed light brown sugar
½ cup maple or maple-flavor syrup
1 tablespoon pure vanilla extract
1 teaspoon ground cinnamon
¼ teaspoon grated nutmeg
1 fresh ripe pineapple (3 pounds), peeled, cored, and cut into 1-inch spears

1. In a deep 2-quart microwave-safe casserole, mix all the ingredients except the pineapple.
2. Microwave uncovered on High for 2 to 3 minutes, stirring once, until the sugar has dissolved.

SUGAR, SUGAR

◆ Light and dark brown sugars are different—dark brown sugar has more molasses added. If a recipe simply calls for brown sugar, use dark if you prefer a stronger molasses flavor.

◆ Confectioners' sugar is a much finer sugar than granulated and contains a trace of cornstarch. You can substitute 1¾ cups confectioners' sugar for each cup of granulated sugar in most cake recipes.

**BE BRAVE—
MICROWAVE**

◆ When it comes
to baking, your
microwave can
come in handy.
Here are some
helpful uses:

◆ To soften brown
sugar, place the
sugar in a covered
microwave-safe
dish and microwave
on Low for 1 to 2
minutes per cup.

◆ To melt choco-
late, place the
chocolate squares
or chips in a
microwave-safe
bowl. Microwave on
High, stirring after
1 minute (the
chocolate won't
look melted yet). If
necessary give it
another zap.

◆ To soften cold
butter, microwave it
on Medium (50
percent power) for
20 to 25 seconds
per stick.

3. Add the pineapple and turn to coat. Microwave on High for 6 to 8 minutes, stirring twice, until the sauce is slightly thickened and the pineapple is very tender.

4. Remove the dish from the microwave and let stand on a heatproof surface for 5 minutes.

5. To serve, put a scoop of ice cream on a serving plate, arrange pineapple spears alongside, and drizzle the sauce over all.

Per serving: 257 cal, 0 g pro, 65 g car, 0 g fat, 0 mg chol, 19 mg sod

EASY • 30 MINUTES • LIGHT

TROPICAL FRUIT PLATTER

Serves 10

Preparation time: 25 minutes

Guests can add sugar, lime, and coconut as they wish. Once cut, the melon will keep just fine for at least 8 hours if tightly wrapped and refrigerated.

½ watermelon (about 12 pounds), quartered lengthwise and cut into
　1-inch-thick slices
½ large pineapple (about 1¾ pounds), quartered lengthwise, cored,
　and cut into 1-inch-thick slices
¾ cup sweetened flaked coconut
½ cup granulated sugar
2 limes, each cut into 8 wedges

1. Arrange the watermelon and pineapple slices on a large serving platter.

2. Put the coconut, sugar, and lime wedges in separate serving bowls. Serve alongside.

Per serving: 180 cal, 2 g pro, 39 g car, 3 g fat, 0 mg chol, 21 mg sod

EASY • MAKE AHEAD

FRUIT & ICE CREAM PIE

Serves 8

Preparation time: 20 minutes plus at least 4 hours to freeze

For a slimmed-down version of this pie, use low-fat frozen vanilla yogurt and light whipped topping. Crown the pie with whatever fresh fruits and berries you wish.

▶

1 (10-ounce) package quick-thaw frozen raspberries in light syrup,
    thawed and drained (reserve ¼ cup syrup)
1 (12-ounce) jar seedless red raspberry jam (1 cup)
1 quart (4 cups) vanilla ice cream, slightly softened
1 (6-ounce) ready-to-fill graham-cracker or chocolate-flavored crumb
    crust (save the plastic lid)
2 cups frozen nondairy whipped topping, thawed, or 2 cups slightly
    sweetened whipped cream
2 cups mixed fresh fruits, whole or cut up (we used raspberries,
    blueberries, strawberries, kiwifruit, cherries, and orange slices)

1. In a small bowl, stir the drained raspberries into ¾ cup of the jam.

2. Drop tablespoonfuls of the raspberry mixture and heaping soupspoon-fuls of ice cream alternately onto the pie crust. Smooth the surface with a spatula, mounding the filling slightly in the center. Cover with the plastic lid and freeze for at least 4 hours, until firm.

3. Meanwhile, in another small bowl, whisk the reserved raspberry syrup into the remaining ¼ cup of raspberry jam to make a sauce. Pour into a small pitcher, cover, and refrigerate.

4. To serve, spread the whipped topping over the pie. Top with the fruit. Serve with the sauce.

Makes 8 slices. Per slice with nondairy whipped topping: 450 cal with graham-cracker crust, 470 cal with chocolate crust, 4 g pro, 75 g car, 17 g fat, 29 mg chol, 201 mg sod with graham-cracker crust, 175 mg sod with chocolate crust. With whipped cream: 484 cal with graham-cracker crust, 505 cal with chocolate crust, 5 g pro, 74 g car, 22 g fat, 62 mg chol, 207 mg sod with graham-cracker crust, 181 mg sod with chocolate crust

Ⓜ AKE AHEAD

The pie can be
prepared through
step 2 and frozen up
to 1 week.

EASY • LIGHT • MAKE AHEAD

PEACH MELBA
ICE CREAM CAKE

Serves 8

Preparation time: 20 minutes plus at least 5 hours to freeze

This dish makes a great summer dessert because the cake insulates the frozen center, so it doesn't melt so fast.

1 purchased ring-shaped angel food cake (about 13 ounces)
1 pint frozen low-fat raspberry yogurt or raspberry sherbet,
    softened slightly
¼ cup raspberry pourable fruit

FRUIT TOPPING

2 medium-size fresh peaches, pitted and cut into small chunks
1 cup fresh raspberries
½ cup raspberry pourable fruit

MAKE AHEAD

The cake can be
prepared through
step 3 and frozen up
to 2 days. Decorate
with the topping just
before serving.

1. Place the cake, top side down, on a plate. Using a long serrated knife, slice a ½-inch layer from the top of the cake, lift the slice off in one piece, and reserve.

2. Using a small serrated knife, cut a trench in the cake ½ inch in from the inner and outer edges to within ½ inch of the bottom. Carefully remove the center with a grapefruit knife, small spoon, or with your fingers without breaking through the sides or bottom.

3. Spoon 1 cup of frozen yogurt into the trench. Press gently into an even layer with the back of a spoon. Drizzle with the pourable fruit. Top with the remaining frozen yogurt. Cover with the reserved top of the cake and gently press down.

4. Freeze for 1 hour, then wrap loosely and freeze for at least 4 more hours, or overnight.

5. Make the topping: In a medium-size bowl, gently mix the peaches, raspberries, and pourable fruit.

6. To serve, remove the cake from the freezer and invert it onto a serving plate. Spoon the fruit topping into the center. Serve right away.

Makes 8 slices. Per slice with yogurt: 252 cal, 6 g pro, 56 g car, 1 g fat, 2 mg chol, 397 mg sod. With sherbert: 261 cal, 4 g pro, 60 g car, 1 g fat, 2 mg chol, 386 mg sod

---

EASY • LIGHT • MAKE AHEAD

STRAWBERRY VANILLA TERRINE

Serves 8

Preparation time: 15 minutes plus at least 5 hours to freeze

If you can't find individual "luncheon-size" jelly roll cakes, try a larger jelly roll. Just cut off as many ½-inch-thick slices as you need to line the pan. When using a glass loaf dish, be sure to chill it thoroughly in the freezer before assembling the terrine.

MAKE AHEAD

The terrine can be
prepared through
step 4 and frozen up
to 2 weeks. Serve as
directed.

4 (7-ounce) individual luncheon-size jelly roll cakes, each cut in 4 slices
1 pint frozen vanilla low-fat yogurt or vanilla ice cream, softened slightly
1 pint strawberry ice cream or frozen low-fat strawberry yogurt, softened slightly
For decoration: fresh raspberries (optional)

▶

1. Line a 9 x 5-inch loaf pan with foil, letting enough foil extend above the sides of the pan to cover the top when filled.

2. Arrange 8 jelly roll slices on the bottom of the pan. Line each long side of the pan with 4 more slices.

3. Spoon the vanilla ice cream into the cake-lined pan. Press the ice cream into an even layer with the back of a spoon. Top with a layer of strawberry ice cream.

4. Fold the foil tightly over the top of the loaf. Freeze for at least 5 hours, or overnight.

5. To serve, fold back the foil. Loosen the ends of the loaf from the pan with a thin knife. Holding the foil, carefully lift the loaf from the pan. Invert onto a serving plate. Peel off the foil. Surround with the raspberries and serve right away.

Per serving with frozen yogurt: 202 cal, 4 g pro, 36 g car, 5 g fat, 5 mg chol, 84 mg sod.
With ice cream: 226 cal, 3 g pro, 33 g car, 10 g fat, 25 mg chol, 102 mg sod.

EASY • MAKE AHEAD

CAPPUCCINO TORTE

Serves 12

Preparation time: 15 minutes plus at least 5 hours to freeze

This ice cream confection is a delicious combination of chocolate and coffee ice cream with a crunchy chocolate wafer cookie center.

2 pints coffee ice cream or frozen low-fat coffee yogurt, softened slightly
15 chocolate wafer cookies, crushed (see Cook's Tip)
2 pints chocolate ice cream or frozen low-fat chocolate yogurt,
   softened slightly
¾ cup heavy (whipping) cream
2 teaspoons granulated sugar
For decoration: ground cinnamon and chocolate coffee-bean candies
   (optional)

1. Spread the coffee ice cream evenly over the bottom of an 8-inch spring-form pan. Sprinkle with the wafer crumbs. Spoon the chocolate ice cream on top. Press the ice cream into an even layer with the back of a spoon.

2. Cover with plastic wrap and freeze for at least 5 hours, or overnight.

3. Just before serving, in a small bowl, beat the cream and sugar with an electric mixer until stiff peaks form.

4. To serve, run a thin long knife around the pan and remove the side.

COOK'S TIPS

◆ To crush cookies, crumble with the fingers or place in a plastic bag and crush with a rolling pin or the bottom of a saucepan. Do not crush fine.

◆ Make clean cuts on an ice cream cake by dipping the knife in hot water between slices.

MAKE AHEAD

The torte can be
prepared through step
2 and frozen up to
2 weeks. Serve as
directed.

Spoon a border of whipped cream around the top of the torte, sprinkle with the cinnamon, and decorate with the candies. Serve right away.

Makes 12 slices. Per slice with ice cream: 270 cal, 4 g pro, 29 g car, 16 g fat, 55 mg chol, 118 mg sod. With yogurt: 229 cal, 6 g pro, 34 g car, 8 g fat, 27 mg chol, 86 mg sod

---

EASY • MAKE AHEAD

INDIVIDUAL ICE CREAM BOMBES

Serves 8

Preparation time: 20 minutes plus 3 hours to freeze

You won't believe how easy these elegant desserts are to make. And everyone will wonder how you got the candy treasure inside.

8 semisweet or milk chocolate–covered cherries with cream or
 liquid centers
1 quart vanilla or other flavor ice cream (or use frozen yogurt)
½ cup hardening chocolate ice cream topping

MAKE AHEAD

The bombes can be
prepared through
step 6 and frozen up
to 2 weeks.

1. Line a baking sheet with waxed paper. Place the cherries on the waxed paper. Use a medium-size ice cream scoop to scoop out the ice cream, then level off the excess with a metal spatula or knife.

2. Invert the full scoop over the cherry, making sure it's centered. Slowly press the ice cream down until the rim of the scoop hits the waxed paper. Release the ice cream from the scoop. Repeat with the remaining candies and ice cream.

3. Freeze the bombes on the baking sheet for 3 hours, or until firm.

4. Remove from the freezer. Peel off the waxed paper and place on a wire rack set over a baking sheet.

5. Pour the chocolate topping over each bombe to cover. Topping that falls onto the baking sheet can be scraped back into the jar and reused.

6. Freeze the bombes in a waxed paper–lined airtight container until ready to serve.

7. To serve, cut the bombes in half and place 2 halves, cut-side up, on serving plates.

Per serving: 294 cal, 3 g pro, 37 g car, 16 g fat, 29 mg chol, 89 mg sod. With yogurt: 261 cal, 5 g pro, 39 g car, 10 g fat, 5 mg chol, 86 mg sod

LEMON COCONUT BARS

Makes 16 squares
Preparation time: 20 minutes
Baking time: 50 minutes

These tangy layered lemon bars are simple to prepare and simply delicious—which makes them appealing for entertaining. The shortbread cookie crust is topped with a sweet-tart, chewy mixture of lemon juice and coconut.

CRUST
1 cup all-purpose flour
½ cup granulated sugar
½ cup (1 stick) unsalted butter
   or margarine (not spread), at room temperature,
   cut into small pieces

TOPPING
2 large eggs
⅔ cup granulated sugar
2 tablespoons all-purpose flour
3 tablespoons fresh lemon juice
2 teaspoons grated lemon peel
1½ cups unsweetened flaked coconut

1. Heat the oven to 350°F. Line a 8- or 9-inch square baking pan with foil so the ends extend over two sides of the pan. Lightly grease the foil.

2. Make the crust: In a medium-size bowl, mix the flour and sugar. Add the butter and, using your fingers, rub into the flour mixture until coarse crumbs form.

3. Press the mixture evenly over the bottom of the pan. Bake for 15 to 20 minutes, or until the top looks golden.

4. Make the topping: In a large bowl, beat the eggs, sugar, flour, and lemon juice with an electric mixer until well blended.

5. With the mixer on slow speed, beat in the lemon peel and coconut just until blended. Spread the topping over the crust.

6. Bake for 25 to 30 minutes, or until the edges are golden. Set the pan on a wire rack to cool completely. Lift the foil by the ends to a cutting board. Cut into squares.

Per square: 192 cal, 2 g pro, 23 g car, 11 g fat, 42 mg chol with butter, 27 mg chol with margarine, 11 mg sod with butter, 77 mg sod with margarine

MAKE AHEAD

The cooled baked lemon squares can stored airtight in the refrigerator up to 1 week or frozen up to 3 weeks.

MINI MINT BROWNIE CUPS

Makes 36 cups
Preparation time: 20 minutes
Baking time: 25 minutes

These super-moist brownie cupcakes will appeal to children and adults alike. The recipe calls for semisweet mint chocolate chips, but you can also use just plain semisweet chips.

1 cup (2 sticks) butter or margarine (not spread)
1 bag (10 ounces) semisweet mint-chocolate chips (1⅔ cups)
1 cup granulated sugar
4 large eggs
1 cup all-purpose flour

1. Heat the oven to 350°F. Arrange 36 doubled mini-muffin paper or foil baking cups (1¼ inch measured across the bottoms) on 2 jelly roll pans or baking sheets with sides.
2. In a medium-size saucepan, melt the butter over medium-low heat. Add the chocolate chips and stir until melted and smooth. Remove the pan from the heat.
3. Stir in the sugar. Add the eggs and stir briskly until blended. Stir in the flour until blended.
4. Fill the baking cups ¾ full. Bake for 20 to 25 minutes, or until the tops look cracked and a toothpick inserted into the center has moist crumbs. Set the baking sheets on wire racks to cool completely.
Per cup: 129 cal, 2 g pro, 13 g car, 8 g fat, 37 mg with butter, 24 mg with margarine, 63 mg sod

MAKE AHEAD

The cooled baked brownie cupcakes can be stored, at room temperature, in an airtight container up to 1 week, or frozen up to 3 months.

MAKE AHEAD

The cooled baked brownies can be stored airtight at room temperature up to 3 days. Ice just before serving.

ICED BUTTERMILK BROWNIES

Makes 24 brownies
Preparation time: 20 minutes plus 2 hours to chill
Baking time: 35 minutes

Not as dense as fudgy brownies, these bars have more in common with a rich chocolate cake. They're great to make for a crowd because they keep fresh and moist up to 5 days. ▶

BROWNIES

¾ cup (1½ sticks) butter or margarine (not spread)

¾ cup water

⅓ cup unsweetened cocoa powder

1½ cups granulated sugar

⅓ cup buttermilk

2 large eggs

1½ teaspoons pure vanilla extract

1½ cups all-purpose flour

1½ teaspoons baking soda

ICING

⅓ cup (5 tablespoons plus 1 teaspoon) butter or margarine
  (not spread)

¼ cup buttermilk

¼ cup unsweetened cocoa powder

¾ cup confectioners' sugar

1. Heat the oven to 350°F. Lightly grease a 13 x 9-inch baking pan.

2. Make the brownies: In a medium-size saucepan, melt the butter over medium heat. Remove the pan from the heat and whisk in the water and cocoa until smooth. Whisk in the sugar, buttermilk, eggs, and vanilla until well blended and smooth.

3. In a medium-size bowl, mix the flour and baking soda. Whisk in the cocoa mixture until blended. (The batter will be thin.) Pour the batter into the prepared pan.

4. Bake for 30 to 35 minutes, or until a toothpick inserted near the center comes out clean and the edges begin to pull away from the sides of the pan. Set the pan on a wire rack and cool for 10 minutes.

5. Meanwhile, make the icing. In a medium-size saucepan, melt the butter over medium heat. Add the buttermilk and cocoa and bring to a boil, whisking until smooth.

6. Remove the pan from the heat and whisk in the confectioners' sugar until no lumps remain.

7. Pour the icing over the brownies. Spread evenly with a metal spatula. Chill for at least 2 hours, or until the icing has set. Cut into squares.

Per brownie: 180 cal, 2 g pro, 24 g car, 9 g fat, 40 mg chol with butter, 18 mg chol with margarine, 180 mg sod

---

COOKIE BAKING TIPS

◆ Use only stick butter or margarine, not whipped, tub-types or corn oil spread (which comes in a stick like margarine).

◆ Use an oven thermometer to check oven temperature and adjust temperature setting if necessary.

◆ Make sure there are at least two inches between the baking sheet and oven sides and door, so air can circulate properly.

◆ Always place dough on a cool baking sheet, it will spread on a hot one.

◆ Bake only one baking sheet at a time, using the middle oven rack.

◆ Check cookies at minimum baking time. One minute can make a difference. More important than baking time, however, is how a cookie looks and feels.

ORANGE–GINGER DIAMONDS

Makes 42 cookies
Preparation time: 15 minutes
Baking time: 20 minutes

MAKE AHEAD

The cooled baked

cookies can be stored

in an airtight container

in the refrigerator up

to 1 week or frozen up

to 1 month.

A lovely combination of tart and sweet, these bar cookies have a buttery brown sugar crust flavored with crystallized ginger and a thin layer of creamy orange custard. Make two batches and freeze one—this way you will never be caught short by unexpected guests.

CRUST
¾ cup (1½ sticks) butter or stick margarine (not spread),
   at room temperature, cut into small pieces
½ cup packed light brown sugar
2 tablespoons chopped crystallized ginger
2 cups all-purpose flour

TOPPING
4 large eggs
1½ cups granulated sugar
¼ cup all-purpose flour
½ teaspoon baking powder
2 tablespoons grated orange peel
¼ cup fresh orange juice
3 tablespoons fresh lemon juice
For garnish: confectioners' sugar, drained canned mandarin
   orange segments (optional)

1. Heat the oven to 350°F. Line a 13 x 9-inch baking pan with foil, letting the foil extend over the ends. Grease the foil.

2. Make the crust: In a large bowl, beat the butter, sugar, and ginger with an electric mixer until smooth. With the mixer on low speed, gradually add the flour. Beat just until blended. Pat the crust mixture evenly into the bottom of the prepared pan.

3. Bake for 15 to 20 minutes, or until the top looks dry and lightly golden.

4. Meanwhile, make the topping. In a medium-size bowl, beat the eggs and sugar with an electric mixer for about 2 minutes, or until pale and fluffy. With the mixer speed on low, add the flour and baking powder. Beat on high speed for 1 minute, or until thick. Beat in the orange peel and orange and lemon juices.

▶

5. Pour the filling over the crust. Bake for 25 to 30 minutes, or until the topping is set and golden. Set the pan on a wire rack to cool completely.

6. To cut, lift the foil by the ends onto a cutting board. Make 9 diagonal cuts about 1½ inches apart. Repeat in diagonally opposite direction. You'll have 42 whole diamond shapes plus 20 small triangles. Shortly before serving, sift confectioners' sugar over the cookies and top with mandarin orange segments.

Per cookie: 103 cal, 1 g pro, 16 g car, 4 g fat, 29 mg chol with butter, 20 mg chol with margarine, 49 mg sod

EASY • 60 MINUTES • LIGHT • MAKE AHEAD

RAISIN–WALNUT OATMEAL COOKIES

Makes 34 cookies
Preparation time: 20 minutes
Baking time: 12 minutes per batch

These chewy cookies are so full of good old-fashioned oatmeal-spice flavor that they are sure to become a standard in your home.

1 cup all-purpose flour
1 teaspoon ground cinnamon
½ teaspoon baking powder
½ teaspoon baking soda
¼ teaspoon salt
½ cup (1 stick) butter or margarine (not spread), at room temperature
½ cup granulated sugar
½ cup packed light brown sugar
1 large egg
1 teaspoon pure vanilla extract
1¼ cups quick-cooking oats
½ cup raisins
¾ cup chopped pecans or walnuts

1. Heat the oven to 375°F. In a small bowl, mix the flour, cinnamon, baking powder, baking soda, and salt.

2. In a large bowl, beat the butter, both sugars, the egg, and vanilla with an electric mixer until creamy. With the mixer on low speed, gradually add flour mixture. Beat just until blended. Beat in the oats, raisins, and nuts.

3. Roll heaping measuring tablespoonfuls of the dough into balls. Place 2 inches apart on ungreased baking sheets.

MAKE AHEAD

The dough may be stored in the refrigerator tightly wrapped up to 3 days, or frozen up to 3 months. There are two ways to freeze the dough: Drop the dough by tablespoonfuls onto a baking sheet; freeze; then put into a freezer container. Bake frozen, adding about 2 minutes to the baking time. The cookies won't spread as much as they would if the dough were at room temperature. Or pat dough flat (for faster thawing) and freeze in an airtight container. Thaw in the refrigerator before shaping and baking.

4. Bake for 10 to 12 minutes, or until the cookies are light golden brown.

5. Cool the cookies on the baking sheet for 1 minute before removing to wire racks to cool completely. Store the cookies in an airtight container up to 1 week, or freeze up to 3 months.

Per cookie: 97 cal, 1 g pro, 13 g car, 5 g fat, 14 mg chol with butter, 6 mg chol with margarine, 74 mg sod

---

EASY • 60 MINUTES • MAKE AHEAD

PEANUT BUTTER CRISSCROSS COOKIES

Makes 60 cookies
Preparation time: 15 minutes
Baking time: 12 minutes per batch

These old-fashioned cookies make great lunchbox or after-school treats.

1½ cups all-purpose flour
½ teaspoon baking soda
½ cup (1 stick) butter or margarine (not spread),
   at room temperature
1 cup chunky peanut butter
½ cup packed light brown sugar
½ cup granulated sugar
1 large egg
1 teaspoon pure vanilla extract

1. Heat the oven to 375°F. In a small bowl, mix the flour and baking soda.

2. In a large bowl, beat the butter and peanut butter with an electric mixer until creamy. Add both sugars and beat until fluffy. Beat in the egg and vanilla until well blended. With the mixer on low speed, gradually add the flour mixture. Beat just until blended.

3. Roll heaping teaspoonfuls of dough into balls. Place 1½ inches apart on ungreased cookie sheets. Flatten with a fork, making a crisscross design.

4. Bake for 10 to 12 minutes, or until browned.

5. Cool the cookies on the baking sheet for 1 minute before removing to wire racks to cool completely.

6. Store the cookies in an airtight container at room temperatureup to 1 week, or freeze up to 3 months.

Per cookie: 65 cal, 1 g pro, 7 g car, 4 g fat, 8 mg chol with butter, 4 mg chol with margarine, 49 mg sod

---

Ⓜ AKE AHEAD

The dough may be stored in the refrigerator tightly wrapped up to 3 days, or frozen up to 3 months. To freeze the dough: Drop the dough by teaspoonfuls onto a baking sheet; freeze; then put into a freezer container. Bake frozen, adding about 2 minutes to the baking time. The cookies won't spread as much as at room temperature. Or pat the dough flat and freeze in an airtight container. Thaw in the refrigerator before shaping and baking.

CHOCOLATE–PECAN COOKIES

Makes 22 cookies
Preparation time: 15 minutes
Baking time: 17 minutes per batch

Bars of Swiss dark chocolate, coarsely chopped, and pecans transform the familiar chocolate chip cookie into a luscious upscale version.

⅔ cup (10 tablespoons plus 2 teaspoons) butter or stick margarine
   (not spread), at room temperature
⅔ cup granulated sugar
½ cup packed dark brown sugar
1 large egg
1 teaspoon pure vanilla extract
1½ cups all-purpose flour
3 bars (3 ounces each) Swiss dark chocolate, chopped into ½-inch pieces
⅔ cup coarsely chopped pecans

1. Heat the oven to 325°F. Lightly grease 2 baking sheets.

2. In a large bowl, beat the butter, both sugars, the egg, and vanilla with an electric mixer until fluffy. With the mixer on low speed, gradually add the flour. Beat just until blended. Stir in the chopped chocolate and pecans.

3. Drop heaping tablespoonfuls of dough 2½ inches apart onto the prepared baking sheets. Bake for 17 minutes, or until the edges of the cookies are lightly browned and the tops look dry.

4. Cool the cookies on the baking sheets on a wire rack for 5 minutes before removing to the racks to cool completely. Store airtight.

Per cookie: 215 cal, 2 g pro, 25 g car, 12 g fat, 25 mg chol with butter, 10 mg chol with margarine, 66 mg sod

MAKE AHEAD

The cooled baked cookies can be stored airtight at room temperature up to 1 week.

COOKIE MAILING TIPS

◆ Mail your cookie container inside a sturdy mailing carton big enough to leave a space all around the container for cushioning.
◆ Cushion the box with crumpled newspaper, plastic bubble wrap, foam pellets, or shredded paper.
◆ Don't use popcorn, cereal, or other edibles for fillers. They attract insects and pick up noxious fumes en route.

◆ Use shoe boxes for cookies if you run out of tins. Cookies must be well cushioned inside their container.
◆ Mark the carton "Open immediately" or "Fragile."
◆ Close the carton and shake before sealing. If the cookie container rattles, add more cushioning.
◆ Highly decorated cookies should be wrapped individually in plastic, then in bubble wrap.

CHOCOLATE PEANUT BUTTER BARS

Makes 36 bars
Preparation time: 15 minutes plus 2 hours to chill

These no-bake bar cookies are a cinch to make and kids will love them.

2 cups confectioners' sugar
2 cups graham cracker crumbs
1 cup smooth peanut butter
½ cup (1 stick) plus 2 tablespoons butter or margarine (not spread), melted
1 bag (12 ounces) semisweet or milk chocolate chips (2 cups), melted

1. In a medium-size bowl, mix the sugar, crumbs, peanut butter, and melted butter until well blended. Scrape the mixture into an ungreased 13 x 9-inch baking pan and press into an even layer. Spread the melted chocolate over the top.

2. Refrigerate for at least 2 hours, or until the chocolate is set. Let stand at room temperature for 20 minutes before cutting into bars with a sharp knife.

Per bar: 174 cal with milk chocolate, 168 cal with semisweet chocolate, 3 g pro, 19 g car, 10 g fat, 9 mg chol with butter, 0 mg chol with margarine, 110 mg sod

BEAR SQUARES

Makes 24 squares
Preparation time: 10 minutes
Cooking time: 5 minutes

Not only are these cookies quick and easy, they are also no-bake.

6 cups (7½ ounces) crisp rice cereal
4 cups (6 ounces) miniature marshmallows
½ cup raisins
¼ cup smooth or chunky peanut butter
3 tablespoons stick margarine (not spread)
24 bear-shaped chocolate graham crackers

1. Lightly grease a 13 x 9-inch baking pan. In a large bowl, mix the ▶

Sidebar

MAKE AHEAD

These bar cookies can be made ahead and refrigerated tightly covered up to 1 week.

HONEY—HOW SWEET IT IS

Here are some tips for replacing granulated sugar with honey

◆ Reduce any liquid called for in the recipe by 1/4 cup for each cup of honey used.

◆ Add 1/4 to 3/4 teaspoon baking soda for each cup of honey used.

◆ Lower the oven temperature by 25 degrees to prevent overbrowning.

cereal, 1 cup of the marshmallows, and the raisins.

2. In a medium-size saucepan, combine the peanut butter, margarine, and the remaining 3 cups of marshmallows. Stir over low heat until completely melted and smooth. Immediately pour the mixture over the cereal mixture and stir until well blended. (The mixture will leave the sides of the bowl.)

3. Scrape the mixture into the prepared pan and press into an even layer. While still warm, place the bear-shaped cookies waist-deep into the cereal mixture, spacing them about 1½ inches apart. Let cool before cutting.

Per square: 98 cal, 2 g pro, 17 g car, 3 g fat, 0 mg chol, 140 sod

---

EASY • 30 MINUTES

WALNUT–BUTTERSCOTCH FUDGE

Makes 64 squares
Preparation time: 5 minutes
Cooking time: 15 minutes

For a change of taste, make this easy fudge with other flavored chips such as semisweet, mint-chocolate, peanut butter, or even vanilla-milk chips.

⅔ cup evaporated (not sweetened condensed) milk
1 jar (7 ounces) marshmallow fluff or creme
1 cup granulated sugar
¼ cup (½ stick) butter or margarine (not spread)
1 bag (12 ounces) butterscotch chips (2 cups)
1½ teaspoons pure vanilla extract
1 cup walnuts, chopped

1. Line an 8-inch square pan with foil, letting the ends extend over the pan on 2 sides.

2. In a medium-size, preferably nonstick saucepan, combine the evaporated milk, marshmallow fluff, sugar, and butter. Bring to a boil over medium-high heat, stirring constantly to prevent scorching. Reduce the heat to medium and boil for 5 minutes, stirring constantly.

3. Remove the pan from the heat. Stir in the chips until melted. Stir in the vanilla and walnuts until blended. Pour the mixture into the prepared pan. Chill for about 2 hours, or until firm.

4. Lift the foil by the ends onto a cutting board. Cut into squares. Store in an airtight container in the refrigerator up to 2 weeks.

Per square: 72 cal, 1 g pro, 10 g car, 4 g fat, 3 mg chol with butter, 1 mg chol with margarine, 17 mg sod

 VARIATION

ROCKY ROAD FUDGE

Reduce the walnuts to ½ cup. When you stir in the nuts, add ½ cup dark raisins and ½ cup mini marshmallows. Proceed as directed.

Per square: 71 cal, 1 g pro, 11 g car, 3 g fat, 3 mg chol with butter, 1 mg chol with margarine, 17 mg sod

• EASY • 30 MINUTES
• LIGHT

ENTERTAINING

"To invite a person into your house is to take charge of his happiness for as long as he is under your roof."
BRILLAT-SAVARIN

Anyone can entertain, but it's no secret that when the host or hostess is relaxed and enjoying the party, everyone else usually has a great time too. All it takes is a little advance planning, organization, and some proven menus and recipes.

The best way to get organized is with specific lists. Make a shopping list and shop in stages. Prepare a detailed list of food preparation and cooking steps for each recipe, beginning as many days in advance as possible.

Of course, entertaining always revolves around food. This chapter will illustrate that it's just as easy to cook for many guests as it is for just a few. You'll find a wide array of party formats, from a leisurely Sunday brunch for six to a buffet party for twenty, plus a variety of theme menus including a Tex-Mex Fiesta and a Tropical Party.

Entertaining is never effortless, but combine these menus and recipes with a relaxed and organized approach and you'll entertain easily, successfully, and be able to enjoy your guests from the beginning of the party to the end.

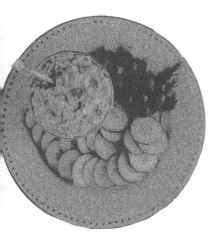

TEX-MEX FIESTA FOR 12

For a blue-ribbon Tex-Mex buffet, you will need lots of bowls and some hungry friends. The best part of this menu is that everyone can get involved in both the work and the fun. Set the table with a brightly colored cloth, mats or runners. Earthenware serving pieces will enhance the Mexican theme. Arrange the foods on the buffet table in the order they will be needed: taco shells, tortillas, hot chili-beef filling, toppings, hot rice, bean salad, and beverages.

TEX-MEX FIESTA

SALSA BEAN DIP

Serves 10 to 20
Preparation time: 15 minutes plus 1 hour to chill

Serve this dip with tortilla chips and cut-up fresh vegetables. The recipe can be halved to serve fewer people.

2 cans (about 15 ounces each) black beans or red kidney beans,
   drained and rinsed
2 cups medium-spicy thick and chunky salsa
½ cup chopped green bell pepper
½ cup chopped red bell pepper
4 jalapeño peppers, seeded and chopped
½ cup chopped pitted black olives
6 scallions, chopped
1 teaspoon ground cumin
1 teaspoon granulated sugar
½ teaspoon coarsely ground black pepper
½ cup chopped fresh cilantro
1 cup sour cream
For garnish: chopped red and green bell pepper, black olives,
   and scallions (optional)

1. In a large bowl, coarsely mash the beans. Stir in all the remaining ingredients except for the sour cream and garnish.

2. Cover and refrigerate for at least 1 hour for the flavors to blend.

3. To serve, stir the dip and spoon it into a serving bowl. Spoon the sour cream over the dip and sprinkle with garnish.

Makes 5 cups. Per 2 tablespoons: 36 cal, 1 g pro, 4 g car, 2 g fat, 3 mg chol, 173 mg sod

---

MENU

Salsa Bean Dip

Guacamole

Shredded Chili-Beef Burritos & Tacos

Mexican Three-Bean Salad

Yellow Rice*

Orange-Ginger Diamonds (page 495)

Cranberry Sangria

*Recipe not provided

GUACAMOLE

Serves 12

Preparation time: 20 minutes

Make a double batch of this recipe and serve half as an appetizer dip for tortilla chips and the other half as a taco or burrito topping. For a more assertive flavor, add some minced jalapeño pepper. The guacamole can be made up to 3 hours ahead.

> 4 ripe avocados (about 9 ounces each)
> 3 to 4 tablespoons fresh lemon or lime juice
> ¾ teaspoon salt
> ¼ teaspoon ground black pepper
> ½ teaspoon minced fresh garlic
> 1 large tomato, halved, seeded, and diced

1. Halve the avocados, remove the pits, and scoop out the pulp with a spoon into a medium-size nonaluminum bowl.

2. Mash the pulp coarsely with a fork while adding the lemon juice, salt, pepper, and garlic. Gently stir in the tomato.

3. Serve the guacamole right away or cover airtight with plastic wrap and refrigerate up to 3 hours.

Makes 3 cups. Per ¼ cup: 105 cal, 1 g pro, 6 g car, 10 g fat, 0 mg chol, 145 mg sod

VEGETABLE DIPPERS FROM A TO Z

Asparagus (blanched, see note)

Beans, green, pole, or wax beans, whole or cut into 3-inch lengths (raw or blanched)

Belgian endive leaves (raw)

Broccoli florets (raw or blanched)

Carrot sticks (raw or blanched)

Cauliflower florets (raw or blanched)

Celery sticks (raw)

Cucumber rounds or spears (raw)

Endive (Belgian) spears (raw)

Fennel sticks (raw)

Jicama rounds or sticks (raw)

Knob celery rounds or sticks (raw)

Kohlrabi rounds or sticks (raw or blanched)

Mushroom caps or halves (raw)

New potato slices (cooked)

Onion rings or strips (raw sweet onions or blanched yellow)

Peppers, bell or Italian, strips (raw)

Radishes, red or white, whole if small; cut in sticks or rounds if large (raw)

Snow Peas (raw or blanched)

Sugar-snap peas (raw or blanched)

Tomatoes, red cherry or small pear or tearcrop (raw)

Vidalia onions, rings or strips (raw)

Water chestnut slices (raw or canned)

Yellow squash rounds or sticks (raw)

Zucchini rounds or sticks (raw)

BLANCHING VEGETABLES

To blanch (or partially cook) fresh vegetables, bring a large pot of water to a boil. Add the vegetables and boil until barely crisp-tender. Remove at once with a slotted spoon to a bowl of ice water. Drain well.

SHREDDED CHILI–BEEF FILLING (FOR BURRITOS & TACOS)

Serves 12
Preparation time: 15 minutes
Cooking time: 3 hours 15 minutes plus 45 minutes to stand

The preferred Mexican way to use meat in chili is to pot-roast a chunk of it and then shred it as given here. The result is a delicious filling for burritos and tacos (see page 508).

1 boneless beef chuck roast, about 5 pounds, trimmed of visible fat
    and tied in several places to hold meat together
2 bay leaves (2 inches long)
3 cups beef broth
⅓ cup red wine vinegar
¼ cup plus 1 tablespoon chili powder
1½ tablespoons minced fresh garlic
2 teaspoons ground cumin
2 teaspoons dried oregano leaves, crumbled
1½ cups finely chopped onions
1 can (16 ounces) crushed tomatoes
1 can (7 ounces) chopped green chiles
For garnish: chopped cilantro (optional)

1. In a 5- or 6-quart heavy pot or Dutch oven, combine the beef, 1 cup of water, and the bay leaves. Bring to a boil. Reduce the heat to medium-low. Cover and simmer for 30 minutes, turning the meat twice.

2. Meanwhile, in a 4-cup measure or a bowl, mix the broth, vinegar, chili powder, garlic, cumin, and oregano.

3. Uncover the pot, increase the heat to high, and boil for 5 minutes, or until the liquid is reduced to about 2 tablespoons of a thick glazelike sauce. Turn the meat with a fork to coat.

4. Add the broth mixture to the pot. Bring to a boil. Reduce the heat to medium-low. Cover and simmer for 1½ hours, turning the meat twice.

5. Add the onions and tomatoes. Cover and simmer for 1 hour more, or until the meat is fork-tender and shreds easily.

6. Remove the pot from the heat. Remove the meat to a cutting board or large plate. Cover loosely with foil and let stand for 45 minutes, or until cool

MAKE AHEAD

You can make this taco and burrito filling up to 2 days ahead. To reheat, add ½ cup water to the pot, cover, and cook over low heat, stirring occasionally, until the meat is hot.

enough to handle.

7. Meanwhile, skim the fat from the sauce and remove and discard the bay leaves. Bring the sauce to a boil. Reduce the heat to medium and boil gently for 12 minutes, stirring often, until the sauce is chunky and reduced by almost half. Remove the pot from the heat.

8. Untie the beef. Using your fingers or two forks, pull the meat apart into bite-size shreds and add, with the green chiles, to the sauce in the pot. Stir until the meat is evenly moistened.

Makes 8 cups, enough for 24 tacos or small burritos. Per 1/3 cup: 113 cal, 16 g pro, 4 g car, 4 g fat, 43 mg chol, 351 mg sod

---

TEX-MEX FIESTA

MEXICAN THREE–BEAN SALAD

Serves 12

Preparation time: 20 minutes plus at least 3 hours to chill

This salad uses a combination of black beans, white beans, kidney beans, and red bell pepper for a lively presentation. Cilantro adds a Southwestern flavor.

DRESSING
1/4 cup olive oil
3 tablespoons red wine vinegar
3/4 teaspoon salt
1/2 teaspoon ground black pepper

1 can (about 16 ounces) black beans, rinsed and drained well
1 can (about 16 ounces) small white beans, rinsed and drained well
1 can (about 16 ounces) red kidney beans, rinsed and drained well
1 large red bell pepper, seeded and diced
1 cup thinly sliced scallions
1/2 cup loosely packed cilantro leaves, chopped fine

1. Make the dressing: In a large serving bowl, mix the oil, vinegar, salt, and pepper until blended.

2. Add the beans, pepper, scallion, and cilantro. Toss to mix and coat. Cover and refrigerate for at least 3 hours for the flavors to develop. Stir before serving.

Per 1/2 cup: 114 cal, 5 g pro, 12 g car, 5 g fat, 0 mg chol, 308 mg sod

MAKE AHEAD

This salad can be prepared and refrigerated airtight up to 3 days. Stir before serving.

CRANBERRY SANGRÍA

Serves 12

Preparation time: 10 minutes

Serve this refreshing nonalcoholic drink in a punch bowl and it will look as festive as it tastes. You can also use cran-apple or cran-raspberry juice as a substitute for the cranberry.

4 cups ice cubes

7 cups cranberry-juice cocktail

5 small peaches or nectarines, cut in chunks

1 sliced lemon

5 cups club soda

1. Put the ice cubes into a punch bowl or large pitcher. Add the cranberry juice. Stir in the peaches and lemon slices.

2. Just before serving, stir in the club soda. Serve right away.

Makes 12 cups. Per 1 cup: 103 cal, 0 g pro, 27 g car, 0 g fat, 0 mg chol, 24 mg sod

TACOS AND BURRITOS

Tacos are crisp U-shaped shells made of deep-fried corn tortillas that have a filling spooned into them. Toppings are then sprinkled or spooned on. Ready-to-heat taco shells can be bought in the Mexican food section of the supermarket.

Burritos are soft flour tortillas that are wrapped, egg-roll style, around a filling. Find flour tortillas in the produce section or dairy case of most supermarkets.

Heat taco shells and soft tortillas before serving. Heating brings out the flavor and crispness of taco shells; it makes tortillas soft, and easy to fold. To heat taco shells in the oven: Separate the shells and arrange them on a paper-towel-lined cookie sheet. Heat them at 200°F for 15 minutes. To heat in a microwave oven: Separate the shells and fan 10 or 12 at a time into a circle on a paper-towel-lined large round microwave-safe plate. Microwave on High for 1 minute. Rotate dish ¼ turn and microwave on High for 1 minute more.

To warm flour tortillas in the oven: Wrap a stack in foil and heat at 325°F for 10 to 15 minutes. To warm in a microwave: Poke several holes in the plastic wrapper of purchased tortillas and microwave on High for 1 to 1 ½ minutes. Or stack 4 to 6 and wrap in moist paper towels, then microwave on High for 10 to 20 seconds. Keep the shells or tortillas warm in napkin-lined and covered baskets or warmed platters covered with cloth napkins.

How to fill tacos: Show beginners how to spoon some beef filling into a warmed taco shell on a plate, and then add a few or all of the toppings, ending with salsa. Eat out of hand and have napkins available.

To assemble a burrito: Put a warm flour tortilla on a plate and scatter some shredded lettuce in the center. Top with 2 heaping spoonfuls of beef filling and a few or all of the toppings. Fold the bottom of the tortilla over the filling, then fold the sides in and roll up. Eat out of hand, or top with guacamole, sour cream, and salsa and use knife and fork.

MEDITERRANEAN PARTY FOR 20

Here's a reason to celebrate: This festive meal can be prepared ahead, can be served at any time of the day, and is easy on the budget. The cooking of the sunny Mediterranean region centers on olives and olive oil, garlic, tomatoes, and eggplant—all of which underscore this lively menu. Read the recipes carefully and work up a schedule to have everything done in advance. You can designate one day to finish all the cooking or spread it out over a couple of days. Give your table a casual country look with potted geraniums and ceramic serving pieces.

MENU

Olive & Eggplant Bites

Outside-in Pizza (Calzone)

Tomato, Broccoli, & White Bean Salad

Banana Caramel Custard (page 473)

Lemonade Iced Tea

MAKE AHEAD

The olive-eggplant mixture is best made a day ahead. The cucumber and carrots can also be sliced, wrapped, and refrigerated a day ahead.

MEDITERRANEAN PARTY

OLIVE & EGGPLANT BITES

Serves 20
Preparation time: 15 minutes
Cooking time: 50 minutes

The flavor of roasted garlic is rich, mellow, and slightly sweet—a far cry from raw garlic. Roasting also softens the cloves so they can be turned into a paste. This spread is also good on crackers or toasted pita bread wedges.

1 medium-size eggplant (1¼ pounds), rinsed, trimmed,
    and halved lengthwise
1 whole head (about 2 ounces) garlic
¾ cup green salad olives, chopped coarse
2 stalks celery, halved lengthwise and sliced thin crosswise (1 cup)
3 tablespoons cider vinegar
1 teaspoon granulated sugar
¼ teaspoon crushed hot red pepper flakes
2 medium-size cucumbers (10 ounces each), scrubbed and cut into
    ¼-inch-thick rounds
2 large carrots (6 ounces each), peeled and cut diagonally into
    ⅛-inch-thick rounds

1. Heat the oven to 425°F. Lightly coat a broiler-pan rack with vegetable oil cooking spray. (Or use a cake rack positioned on a shallow baking pan; spray the rack.)
2. Place the eggplant halves, cut sides down, on the rack. Slice off and ▶

discard about ½ inch from the top (opposite the root end) of the garlic. Wrap the garlic in a small square of aluminum foil and place on the rack. Transfer to the oven and roast the eggplant and garlic for 45 to 50 minutes, or until the eggplant is soft and wrinkled. Let stand until cool.

3. Using a spoon, scoop the eggplant from the skin into a medium-size bowl. Cut the garlic in half crosswise. Wrap and refrigerate half the garlic to use in the tomato, broccoli, and white-bean salad (recipe follows). Squeeze the remaining half of garlic into the bowl with the eggplant. Mash to a paste with a potato masher, or process the eggplant and garlic in a food processor until smooth.

4. Stir in the olives, celery, vinegar, sugar, and hot pepper flakes. Cover and refrigerate until ready to serve.

5. To serve, put 1 teaspoon of the eggplant mixture on each cucumber and carrot slice. Arrange on a platter.

Per serving: 26 cal, 1 g pro, 5 g car, 1 g fat, 0 mg chol, 135 mg sod

---

MEDITERRANEAN PARTY

OUTSIDE–IN PIZZA (CALZONE)

Serves 24

Preparation time: 45 minutes

Baking time: 30 minutes

These make-ahead pizzas, also known as calzone are perfect for casual entertaining. Any leftovers make a great lunch or quick dinner served with a mixed green, or bean salad.

2 pounds Italian sausage (sweet or hot), casings removed
8 medium-size onions, cut into thin wedges (10 cups)
4 cans (about 10 ounces each) refrigerated pizza dough
2 jars (about 11 ounces each) pimientos or roasted red peppers, drained, patted dry with paper towels, and cut into strips
1 pound Muenster cheese, shredded (4 cups)
2 tablespoons olive oil
4 teaspoons dried rosemary leaves, crumbled

1. Position oven racks to divide oven into thirds. Heat the oven to 400°F.

2. In a large, deep, preferably nonstick skillet, cook the sausage over medium-high heat for 5 to 6 minutes, or until browned, stirring to break up lumps. Drain the sausage, reserving 1 tablespoon of fat.

3. In the same skillet, cook the onions in the reserved fat over medium

MAKE AHEAD

The outside-in pizzas may be prepared one day before serving. If making ahead, bake 5 minutes less than directed, let cool completely on wire racks, then wrap airtight and refrigerate. Reheat on baking sheets 5 to 10 minutes in a 400°F oven.

heat for 7 to 8 minutes, or until softened and slightly browned. (You may need to do this in two batches.)

4. Tear off a 15-inch-long piece of aluminum foil, place on a work surface, and lightly spray with vegetable oil cooking spray. Unroll one pizza dough onto the foil. Pat out to a 15 x 10-inch rectangle.

5. Starting ½ inch in from one of the short sides (and leaving ½ inch at the sides), distribute ¼ of the sausage over half the dough. Top the sausage with ¼ of the onions, pimiento strips, and cheese.

6. Moisten the edges of the dough with water. Fold the other half of the dough over the filling, using the foil as an aid, then peel back the foil. Press the edges of the dough to seal, then crimp with a fork.

7. Brush the top with ½ tablespoon of oil and sprinkle with 1 teaspoon of rosemary. Prick the top of the dough with a fork in several places to allow steam to escape.

8. Repeat steps 4 through 7 with the remaining pizza dough, sausage, onions, pimientos, and cheese.

9. Using the foil edges as an aid, slide each pizza onto a baking sheet. Bake for 25 to 30 minutes, switching the baking sheets on the oven racks halfway through baking. The pizzas should be golden brown and crusty. Remove the pizza from the foil to wire racks. Serve hot or at room temperature. Cut each pizza in 6 pieces to serve.

Per serving: 331 cal, 15 g pro, 30 g car, 16 g fat, 40 mg chol, 642 mg sod

MEDITERRANEAN PARTY

TOMATO, BROCCOLI, & WHITE BEAN SALAD

Serves 20
Preparation time: 20 minutes
Cooking time: 2 minutes

If it seems as if there's not enough dressing for so much salad, don't worry. The tomatoes will add just the right amount of liquid.

MUSTARD DRESSING
½ cup vegetable oil
¼ cup cider vinegar
2 tablespoons Dijon mustard
½ head roast garlic (reserved from recipe for Olive & Eggplant Bites, page 509)
2 teaspoons salt

MAKE AHEAD

You can mix the dressing up to five days ahead and cook the broccoli up to two days ahead. Cover both airtight and refrigerate.

▶

2 bunches (1¼ pounds each) broccoli, cut into florets, stems peeled
and cut into 1-inch pieces (14 cups)
4 cans (19 ounces each) white kidney beans, drained and rinsed
1 medium-size red onion (6 ounces), chopped (1 cup)
2 cups fresh basil leaves, rinsed and chopped (1 cup)
2½ pounds tomatoes (about 6 ripe medium-size), cut into 1-inch chunks
(7 cups)

1. Bring a large pot of water to a boil.

2. Meanwhile, make the dressing. In a small bowl, combine the oil, vinegar, and mustard. Squeeze the softened garlic cloves from the ½ head of roast garlic. Add the salt and whisk until well blended, or put all the ingredients into a food processor or blender and process until smooth.

3. Add the broccoli to the boiling water and boil for about 2 minutes, or until bright green and crisp-tender. Cool under cold running water and drain well.

4. In a very large bowl or pot, combine the broccoli, beans, onion, basil, tomatoes, and dressing. Toss to coat and mix. Serve at room temperature.

Per serving: 79 cal, 2 g pro, 6 g car, 6 g fat, 0 mg chol, 382 mg sod

MEDITERRANEAN PARTY

LEMONADE ICED TEA

Serves 8 to 10
Preparation time: 15 minutes

There are infinite variations to this recipe depending on the type of tea you use. Experiment with Earl Grey for a delicate perfumed flavor, or try a spice or herb blend.

8 cups water
12 tea bags
1 can (12 ounces) frozen concentrated lemonade
Granulated sugar (optional)

1. In a medium-size saucepan, bring 4 cups of water to a rapid boil. Put the tea bags into a heatproof large pitcher or bowl and pour the boiling water over them. Let steep for 5 minutes.

2. Remove the tea bags and add 4 cups of cold water. Stir in the lemonade concentrate until blended. Add sugar to taste. Serve over ice.

Makes 4½ cups syrup. Per 2 tablespoons without sugar: 101 cal, 0 g pro, 26 g car, 0 g fat, 0 mg chol, 9 mg sod

COOK'S TIP

As a garnish for iced tea, perch slices of carambola (starfruit) on the rims of the glasses. If you can't find starfruit, use slices of peeled kiwifruit or strawberries.

SUNDAY BRUNCH FOR 6

Brunch, the leisurely blend of breakfast and lunch, is the perfect meal for an unstructured Sunday, and this easy, casual menu follows suit. The menu can be made ahead and only requires that you reheat the tomato, scallion, and smoked ham pie. Set a cozy table and let the season dictate the decor.

SUNDAY BRUNCH

GAZPACHO COCKTAIL

Serves 6
Preparation time: 10 minutes

For a spicy and refreshing drink, try this combination of vegetable juice and cucumber. To turn this cocktail into a Bloody Mary, add a splash of vodka.

1 large cucumber, peeled and cut into small chunks
½ cup fresh lemon or lime juice
1½ teaspoons red wine vinegar
½ to 1 teaspoon hot-pepper sauce
6 cups 8-vegetable juice
Ground black pepper to taste

1. In a food processor or blender, combine the cucumber, lemon juice, vinegar, and hot-pepper sauce. Process until smooth.
2. Pour the vegetable juice into a large pitcher. Add the cucumber mixture, season with the pepper, and mix well. Serve over ice.
Makes 6½ cups. Per 1 cup: 60 cal, 2 g pro, 13 g car, 0 g fat, 0 mg chol, 787 mg sod

SUNDAY BRUNCH

TOMATO, SCALLION, & SMOKED HAM PIE

Serves 6
Preparation time: 22 minutes
Baking time: 52 minutes plus 15 minutes to cool

This savory pie is easy to make and packs a flavorful punch. To serve more people, simply make two or more pies.

▶

1 refrigerated ready-to-use pie crust
1 bunch (about 6) medium-size scallions, sliced thin (¾ cup)
6 thin slices (about 2 ounces) low-fat smoked ham, cut into thin strips
½ cup (2 ounces) shredded reduced-fat Cheddar or Swiss cheese
3 medium-size plum tomatoes, cut into ¼-inch-thick slices and seeded
4 large eggs
2 cups milk
¼ teaspoon ground red pepper (cayenne)
¼ teaspoon salt
Pinch of grated nutmeg

1. Heat the oven to 400°F.

2. Unfold the pie crust and pat into a 12-inch circle. Set a 9-inch pie plate on a baking sheet. Line the pie plate with the pastry, pressing firmly over the bottom and up the side. Fold the edges under and crimp or flute. Prick the pastry all over with a fork. Bake for 8 minutes, or until the entire crust looks dry. Remove to a wire rack to cool.

3. Meanwhile, coat a nonstick skillet with olive or vegetable oil cooking spray and heat over medium heat until hot. Add the scallions and ham and cook, stirring often, for 5 minutes, or until the ham is browned and the scallions are tender. Remove the skillet from the heat.

4. Sprinkle the cheese over the bottom of the prepared crust, then top with the scallion mixture and the tomato slices.

5. In a medium-size bowl, whisk the eggs lightly; add the milk, pepper, salt, and nutmeg and whisk until blended. Pour the mixture into the crust. Bake for 20 minutes. Reduce the heat to 325°F and bake for 32 minutes more, or until a knife inserted near the center comes out clean.

6. Remove to a wire rack to cool for 15 minutes before serving.

Makes 6 slices. Per slice: 309 cal, 13 g pro, 22 g car, 18 g fat, 173 mg chol, 555 mg sod

ⒸOOK'S TIP

To reduce the fat from 18 grams to 10 grams per slice of this pie, use three 8-inch tortillas instead of the refrigerated pie crust. Lightly spray a 9-inch pie plate with vegetable oil cooking spray and place 1 tortilla on the bottom of the plate. Cut the other 2 tortillas into 1½-inch-wide strips, about 3 inches long. Arrange the tortilla strips around the edge of the plate, overlapping slightly. Do not prebake, just fill and bake as directed.

SUNDAY BRUNCH

CONFETTI RICE

Serves 6
Preparation time: 30 minutes
Cooking time: 20 minutes

Chock-full of fresh vegetables, this rice dish is as pretty to look at as it is to eat. If time is short, use fresh onion and red pepper and replace the remaining fresh vegetables with 1 package (10 ounces) frozen mixed vegetables. This dish can be served warm or at room temperature.

1½ cups water

1 cup chicken broth

1 cup long-grain white rice

1 tablespoon butter or margarine

1 tablespoon olive oil

⅔ cup diced carrots

½ cup finely chopped onion

½ cup diced red bell pepper

2 ounces green beans, ends trimmed, cut crosswise on the diagonal into ¼-inch-long pieces (½ cup)

1 small zucchini, quartered lengthwise, seeded, and diced (⅔ cup)

1 small yellow squash, quartered lengthwise, seeded, and diced (⅔ cup)

2 teaspoons chopped fresh thyme leaves, or ¾ teaspoon dried thyme leaves, crumbled

¾ cup grated Parmesan cheese

¼ teaspoon salt

¼ teaspoon ground black pepper

M AKE AHEAD

You can dice the vegetables, bag them separately, and refrigerate them up to 2 days ahead. Or prepare the entire recipe, refrigerate, then reheat in the microwave when ready to serve.

1. In a large saucepan, bring the water and chicken broth to a boil. Stir in the rice. Reduce the heat to medium-low, cover, and simmer for 15 to 20 minutes, or until most of the liquid is absorbed and the rice is tender. Remove the pan from the heat. Let stand for 5 minutes, or until all the liquid is absorbed.

2. Meanwhile, in a large skillet, melt the butter with the oil over medium heat. Stir in the carrots, onion, bell pepper, and green beans. Cover and cook over medium-low heat for 5 to 6 minutes, or until crisp-tender. Stir in the zucchini, yellow squash, and thyme. Cover and cook for 3 to 4 minutes, or until the vegetables are tender. Remove the skillet from the heat.

3. Transfer the rice to a serving bowl. Stir in the cheese, then the vegetables, salt, and pepper.

Per serving: 108 cal, 5 g pro, 5 g car, 8 g fat, 13 mg chol with butter, 8 mg chol with margarine, 469 mg sod

SUNDAY BRUNCH

FRESH FRUIT COMPOTE

Serves 6

Preparation time: 30 minutes plus at least 2 hours to chill

Star fruit, also called carambola, reveals a five-pointed star when sliced crosswise. It has a sweet-tart flavor and is completely edible. If you can't find star fruit, use kiwifruit instead.

▶

2 medium-size white or pink grapefruit (about 2 pounds), peel
and white pith removed
2 medium-size navel oranges (about 12 ounces), peel and white pith
removed
1½ cups red seedless grapes
1 star fruit (carambola), sliced thin
2 tablespoons honey
½ teaspoon pure vanilla extract

1. Working over a serving bowl to catch the juices, cut along both sides of
the membranes dividing the grapefruit and orange sections, letting the segments
fall into the bowl. Squeeze the juice from the membranes into the bowl.

2. Add the remaining ingredients. Toss to mix and coat. Cover and refrigerate for at least 2 hours. Serve chilled.

Per serving: 87 cal, 1 g pro, 22 g car, 0 g fat, 0 mg chol, 2 mg sod

ENTERTAINING COUNTDOWN

Use this list as a general guideline and checklist for creating a workable and pleasurable party.

3 TO 4 WEEKS AHEAD:
◆ Decide on style of party.
◆ Make the guest list. Write invitations or telephone guests.
◆ Recruit any extra help if necessary.

2 WEEKS AHEAD:
◆ Plan the menu and make the cooking schedule.
◆ Make the shopping list.
◆ Check your supply of chairs, glasses, and utensils, and arrange to buy (if you're using paper products) or borrow or rent what you don't have (churches, schools, community centers can be good source for borrowing tents and chairs).

1 WEEK AHEAD:
◆ Plan decorations (including

tablecloths, candles, place settings etc.) and purchase (except flowers).
◆ Take stock of bar and beverage supplies: liquor, wine, beer, mixers, soft drinks, juices.
◆ Shop for nonperishable food and staples.
◆ Check for outdoor outlets and buy extension cords if you need to plug in coffee makers or other appliances outdoors.

3 DAYS AHEAD:
◆ Clean up the yard if you are entertaining outdoors.

2 DAYS AHEAD:
◆ Cook the dishes that can be made ahead.
◆ Start making extra ice and store it in plastic bags in the freezer.
◆ Clear counters of all appliances and other items you won't need for the party.

1 DAY AHEAD:
◆ Buy any remaining food (perishables) and flowers.
◆ Wash salad greens (if using), dry well, and store in plastic bags.
◆ Get out platters and serving dishes and plan which food will go where.
◆ Select CD's, tapes, or records for music.

MORNING OF PARTY:
◆ Finish cooking.
◆ Set up tables and chairs.
◆ Rig up speakers if you need to play music outdoors.
◆ Chill beverages.
◆ Set out garbage cans.
◆ Spray for bugs if you are entertaining outdoors.
◆ Tie a balloon in front of the house to identify it if you've invited guests who have never visited.
◆ Set the table(s) and put up decorations.

SIMPLY SALAD
Mixed Greens
with Blue Cheese
& Walnuts
(p.522) is a per-
fect way to serve
a first course for
dinner: simple but
elegant.

Buffets are a hassle-free way to entertain a large group of people. Everything is set out so that the guests can serve themselves.

IT'S FIESTA TIME
This Tex-Mex Fiesta for 12 features Guacamole (p.504), burritos and tacos with Shredded Chili-Beef Filling (p.506), Mexican Three-Bean Salad (p.507), and yellow rice.

COMPANY'S COMING
Jamaican Jerk Chicken (p.525), above, is the star of a Tropical Buffet for 20, while Pasta with Shrimp & Artichokes (p.523), left, is the big event at a Dinner Party for 8.

DINNER PARTY FOR 8

You don't have to spend all day putting together a dinner party that's smashing. With this easy menu you can get everything ready in 2½ hours and spend more time with guests and less time in the kitchen. The table setting can be dressed up or down depending on the occasion. If it's a special occasion, set the dining room table with a starched cloth and china. A casual gathering of friends could be enjoyed in the kitchen or on the deck.

DINNER PARTY

ROASTED EGGPLANT SPREAD

Serves 8 to 12
Preparation time: 10 minutes
Cooking time: 30 minutes plus at least 8 hours to chill

This robust spread tastes better when it's made in advance so the flavors can mellow. Serve with pita triangles or toasted bread rounds and/or raw carrot and celery sticks.

2 large eggplants (2 pounds each), pierced in several places with a fork
¼ cup fresh lemon juice
¼ cup nonfat sour cream
¼ cup creamy peanut butter
1 tablespoon olive oil
1½ teaspoons minced fresh garlic
1½ teaspoons ground cumin
1½ teaspoons salt
¾ teaspoon hot-pepper sauce
For garnish: pimiento (optional)

1. Heat the broiler. For easy cleanup, cover the broiler pan rack with foil.
2. Place the eggplants on the broiler-pan rack. Broil 4 inches from the heat source for 30 minutes, turning every 5 minutes, until charred, wrinkled, and very soft. Let cool completely.
3. Cut off the stem ends. Remove the charred skins. Cut the pulp into large chunks and place in a colander set in the sink. Press the eggplant with a potato masher or large spoon to squeeze out the excess liquid.
4. Put the pulp into a food processor or blender. Add the remaining ingredients and process to a purée. Transfer to a 1½-quart serving bowl ▶

or mound on a plate. Cover and refrigerate for at least 2 hours or up to 3 days. Before serving, garnish with stars cut from pimiento.

Makes 4 cups. Per 1/3 cup: 80 cal, 3 g pro, 9 g car, 4 g fat, 0 mg chol, 318 mg sod

DINNER PARTY

SMOKED TROUT SPREAD

Serves 8

Preparation time: 20 minutes plus at least 2 hours to chill

Smoked trout can be found in the deli or seafood section of your supermarket. Serve this easy, luscious spread on crackers, sliced cucumbers, or sliced radishes.

   1 whole smoked trout (about 10 ounces) head, tail, skin, and bones
      removed (see Cook's Tip)
   8 ounces light cream cheese (Neufchâtel), at room temperature
   3 tablespoons snipped fresh dill
   2 tablespoons fresh lemon juice
   1 tablespoon drained white horseradish
   1/4 teaspoon salt
   For garnish: snipped fresh dill (optional)

   1. Break the trout into small pieces. For a smooth spread, put the trout, cream cheese, dill, lemon juice, horseradish, and salt into a food processor and turn on/off several times. For a chunkier spread, mix all the ingredients except the dill in a medium-size bowl just until blended.

   2. Cover with plastic wrap and refrigerate for at least 2 hours. Sprinkle with dill just before serving.

Makes 2 cups. Per 1/4 cup: 85 cal, 7 g pro, 2 g car, 5 g fat, 27 mg chol, 338 mg sod

DINNER PARTY

MIXED GREENS WITH BLUE CHEESE & WALNUTS

Serves 8

Preparation time: 15 minutes

Use an assortment of greens for flavor and texture. Many stores now sell packaged mixed greens. It's a more expensive alternative, but when you're in a hurry, it can be a real time-saver.

COOK'S TIP

There's no trick to skinning a trout. Hold the skin at one end and pull—it should come off in one piece. The bones should also lift out in one piece. Rub your hands with a cut lemon and salt to remove any fishy smell.

MAKE AHEAD

The spread can be prepared and refrigerated airtight up to 3 days.

DRESSING

6 tablespoons olive oil
¼ cup red wine vinegar
½ teaspoon salt
¼ teaspoon ground black pepper

12 cups torn mixed greens (try combinations of romaine and Bibb
   lettuce, watercress, radicchio, and Belgian endive)
¾ cup walnuts, lightly toasted and broken into large pieces
4 ounces blue cheese, crumbled (¾ cup)

1. Make the dressing: In a small bowl, whisk the oil, vinegar, salt, and pepper until blended, or place the ingredients into a small jar, cover tightly, and shake until blended.
2. In large serving bowl, combine the greens, walnuts, and blue cheese. Add the dressing and toss to mix and coat.
Per serving: 226 cal, 6 g pro, 5 g car, 21 g fat, 11 mg chol, 347 mg sod

DINNER PARTY

PASTA WITH SHRIMP & ARTICHOKES
Serves 8
Preparation time: 15 minutes
Cooking time: 20 minutes

Welcome family and friends with this easy but elegant pasta dish. To save time, buy frozen, peeled and deveined shrimp. This recipe can also be easily doubled to serve more guests.

1 pound linguine
2 tablespoons olive oil
1 pound large shrimp, shelled and deveined (thawed if frozen)
2 teaspoons minced fresh garlic
½ teaspoon salt
½ teaspoon ground black pepper
1½ cups chicken broth
1 package (9 ounces) frozen artichoke hearts, in halves and quarters
8 ounces fresh plum tomatoes, chopped coarse (1½ cups)
½ cup chopped parsley
2 tablespoons butter or margarine

▶

1. Bring a large pot of lightly salted water to a boil. Add the pasta and cook according to the package directions. Drain in a colander.

2. Meanwhile, in a large skillet, heat the oil over medium heat. Add the shrimp and 1 teaspoon of garlic. Cook for 3 to 5 minutes, stirring often, until the shrimp turn opaque but are still translucent in the center. Remove the shrimp with a slotted spoon to a bowl.

3. Add the remaining garlic, the salt, pepper, and chicken broth to the skillet. Bring to a boil and cook for 3 to 5 minutes to reduce the liquid slightly.

4. Stir in the artichoke hearts and tomatoes and cook, stirring occasionally, for 5 to 7 minutes, or until the artichoke hearts are tender.

5. Add the shrimp to the artichoke mixture and cook for about 2 minutes, or until the mixture is hot and the shrimp are no longer translucent in the center. Remove the skillet from the heat. Stir in the parsley and butter.

6. Pour the shrimp mixture over the hot pasta and toss to mix. Garnish with parsley sprigs and serve right away.

Per serving: 341 cal, 18 g pro, 47 g car, 9 g fat, 78 mg chol with butter, 70 mg chol with margarine, 640 mg sod

---

M AKE AHEAD

Up to 1 day ahead: Prepare the recipe through step 5 and cook the pasta, rinse with cold water, and drain. Toss with 2 tablespoons of olive oil, cover, and refrigerate separately from the shrimp mixture. Before serving, add the pre-cooked pasta to a pot of boiling water and let stand 1 minute until hot. Drain.

SIMPLE SETTINGS

Simple innovative table decorations don't need to be time-consuming or creativity-taxing to add the perfect final touch to your party. Two rules to keep in mind are: (1) keep it simple and (2) guests should always be able to see each other across the table. Make sure your centerpiece is below eye level, or at least not so full that you can't see through to the other side.

PLACE SETTING IDEAS:

◆ Fresh herbs are an easy and romantic way to dress up a place setting. Tie tiny bunches of sturdy herb sprigs with green garden twine, raffia, or thread. Set the miniature bouquets at each place or tie them around napkins.

◆ Other small decorations to put in front of each place setting could be miniature topiaries, delicate bouquets in small glass vases, and small seashells and/or coral.

CENTERPIECE IDEAS:

◆ A hurricane lamp set in the center of a twig wreath.

◆ Several plain short glass candle holders placed in a row down the center of the table.

◆ A cluster of richly colored fruits or vegetables.

◆ A cluster of small glass bottles each filled with a single bloom.

◆ A group of small potted flowering plants.

◆ A basket filled with fruit or vegetables, either different kinds and colors or monochrome.

◆ Unusual flower vases such as teapots; placing a small flowering plant inside a small antique bird cage; a tin watering can; crocks; a glass bowl of water with floating flowers.

◆ A cluster of candleholders at varying heights.

◆ A basket filled with fresh herbs.

◆ A twig wreath filled with fresh grapes.

TROPICAL BUFFET FOR 20

This menu is perfect for warm-weather entertaining because the food can be made ahead. You'll be happy not to have to heat up the kitchen on the day of the party and you'll have more time to relax with guests. Here's a chance to really have fun with decorations. Transport your guests to the tropics with lush fresh or paper flowers such as bird of paradise or hibiscus, and play CDs or tapes of lively steel band music.

TROPICAL BUFFET

JAMAICAN JERK CHICKEN

Serves 20
Preparation time: 5 minutes plus at least 8 hours to marinate
Cooking time: 25 minutes

"Jerking" is a traditional Jamaican way of preserving and cooking meat. This entree makes for great party fare because you can prepare it up to three days ahead. If you prefer, you can remove the skin before marinating.

JERK SAUCE
1 large onion, quartered
¼ cup distilled white vinegar
¼ cup vegetable oil
3 tablespoons granulated sugar
2 tablespoons paprika
2 tablespoons dried thyme leaves, crumbled
1 tablespoon ground red pepper (cayenne)
1 tablespoon salt
2 teaspoons grated nutmeg
1½ teaspoons ground allspice

40 chicken drumsticks (about 10 pounds)
For garnish: sliced lemons (optional)

1. Make the jerk sauce: In a food processor, combine the onion, vinegar, oil, sugar, paprika, thyme, pepper, salt, nutmeg, and allspice. Process until blended and smooth (you should have 1½ cups of the marinade).
2. Pour half the marinade into a large zipper-type food-storage bag. ▶

Add half the drumsticks. Seal the bag and turn several times to coat the chicken. Repeat in another zipper-type bag with the remaining marinade and drumsticks. Refrigerate for at least 8 hours or up to 3 days. Turn the bags occasionally to redistribute the marinade.

3. Heat the oven to 475°F. Line 4 baking sheets (with sides) with foil for easy cleanup. Arrange the drumsticks in a single layer in the pans and discard any leftover marinade. Bake for 20 to 25 minutes, or until golden and no longer pink in center. Serve garnished with sliced lemons.

Per serving with skin: 263 cal, 29 g pro, 3 g car, 15 g fat, 98 mg chol, 344 mg sod.
Without skin: 187 cal, 26 g pro, 3 g car, 7 g fat, 84 mg chol, 334 mg sod

`TROPICAL BUFFET`

S E S A M E   P A S T A   S A L A D

Serves 20

Preparation time: 25 minutes plus at least 1 hour to chill

Dark, amber-colored sesame oil, made from toasted sesame seeds, contributes a characteristic flavor to this pasta salad. Look for it in Asian markets, specialty food shops, or in the Asian section of large supermarkets.

2 pounds rotini pasta

SESAME DRESSING
1½ cups reduced-calorie or regular mayonnaise
⅓ cup water
3 tablespoons soy sauce
1½ tablespoons minced peeled fresh gingerroot
1 tablespoon dark Asian sesame oil
1 tablespoon distilled white vinegar

2 medium-size cucumbers (10 ounces each), quartered lengthwise
   and sliced thin crosswise (2½ cups)
1 cup coarsely chopped carrots
½ cup sliced radishes (quarter large slices)

1. Bring a large pot of lightly salted water to a boil. Add the pasta and cook according to the package directions. Drain in a colander, rinse under cold running water, and drain again. (There will be about 16 cups cooked pasta.)

2. Meanwhile, make the dressing. In a medium-size bowl, whisk together the mayonnaise, water, soy sauce, ginger, sesame oil, and vinegar until well blended.

Ⓜ AKE AHEAD

You can prepare the dressing up to 5 days ahead and the salad ingredients up to 2 days ahead. Toss all together up to 8 hours before serving.

3. In a large bowl, combine the pasta, cucumbers, carrots, and radishes. Add the dressing and toss to mix and coat. Cover with plastic wrap and chill for at least 1 hour (or up to 8 hours) for the flavors to develop.

Per serving with reduced-calorie mayonnaise: 231 cal, 6 g pro, 37 g car, 6 g fat, 6 mg chol, 413 mg sod. With regulor mayonnaise: 301 cal, 6 g pro, 36 g car, 15 g fat, 10 mg chol, 410 mg sod

---

TROPICAL BUFFET

CARIBBEAN SLAW

Serves 20

Preparation time: 25 minutes plus at least 1 hour to chill

MAKE AHEAD

You can get all the chopping done and make the dressing up to 3 days ahead. Toss everything together up to 4 hours before serving.

Fresh oranges and cilantro added to shredded green and red cabbage give this colorful coleslaw a tropical flavor. It needs to be made at least 1 hour ahead so the flavors can blend.

DRESSING

½ cup distilled white vinegar
⅓ cup granulated sugar
¼ cup vegetable oil
¼ cup orange juice (fresh or reconstituted frozen)
2 teaspoons salt
2 teaspoons ground black pepper

CARIBBEAN SLAW

1 head (3 pounds) green cabbage, cored and shredded (15 cups)
1 head (2 pounds) red cabbage, cored and shredded (10 cups)
5 navel oranges (1¾ pounds), peeled, sliced thin crosswise, and cut into quarters (3 cups)
1 bunch cilantro, chopped coarse (2 cups)

1. Make the dressing: In a small bowl, whisk together the vinegar, sugar, oil, orange juice, salt, and pepper; or place the ingredients into a jar, cover, and shake until blended.

2. Make the slaw: In a large bowl, combine the cabbages, oranges, and cilantro. Add the dressing and toss to mix and coat. Cover with plastic wrap and refrigerate for at least 1 hour for the flavors to develop.

Per serving: 75 cal, 1 g pro, 12 g car, 3 g fat, 0 mg chol, 235 mg sod

TROPICAL BUFFET

FRUIT PUNCH

Serves 20

Preparation time: 15 minutes

This refreshing nonalcoholic punch can be made several hours before serving. For a festive presentation, make an ice ring for your punch bowl using more fruit juice. It looks nice and won't water down the punch as it melts.

6 cups apricot nectar
6 cups pineapple juice
3 cups orange juice
4½ cups ice-cold ginger ale or champagne
For garnish: orange and lemon slices (optional)

1. In a large punch bowl, mix the apricot nectar, pineapple juice, and orange juice.
2. Add the ginger ale. Garnish with orange and lemon slices.

Makes 20 cups. Per 1 cup: 116 cal with ginger ale, 134 cal with champagne, 0 g pro, 28 g car, 0 g fat, 0 mg chol, 6 mg sod

VARIATION

RUM PUNCH

Add ½ cup dark rum to the punch.

Per 1 cup: 126 cal with ginger ale, 149 cal with champagne, 0 g pro, 26 g car, 0 g fat, 0 mg chol, 6 mg sod

BUG CONTROL FOR OUTDOOR ENTERTAINING

They're the worst kind of uninvited guests, diving into drink cups and walking across plates. Worse yet, many of them bite. Here's some nonchemical, environmentally sound ammunition to battle the bugs.

Yellow Jackets, Wasps, and Bees:
◆ Keep garbage cans and serving dishes covered, and don't leave empty cups, plates, or drink cans around.
◆ If you have fruit trees, don't leave ripe or rotting fruit on the ground.
◆ Drink from cups with lids and straws.
◆ Avoid wearing perfume or other fragrances, which attracts bugs.
◆ Make a simple trap by filling a glass or plastic jug with a few inches of sweet fruit juice. Once pests are in, getting out is almost impossible.
Mosquitoes:
◆ Get rid of stagnant water around the yard. Mosquitoes need only a pint—as much water as may collect in a watering can—in which to lay their eggs.
◆ An open bottle of citronella oil will clear mosquitoes from a room; citronella candles, which are scented with the oil and available at hardware or camping supply stores, work well outside.
◆ Put a bucket of water (with a generous addition of liquid dish soap) in the yard. Female mosquitoes can't get out when they land on the water to lay eggs.

BACKYARD PICNIC FOR 12

Here's a simple menu that celebrates the ease of summertime entertaining. Pack up a basket with this movable feast and find a sunny spot—even if it's in your own backyard. Use bright colors for tablecloths, napkins, and flowers to reflect the flavor of summer and the casual mood.

BACKYARD PICNIC

CHILLED TOMATO–DILL SOUP

Serves 12
Preparation time: 20 minutes plus 3 hours to chill
Cooking time: 25 minutes

Summer appetites respond to simply prepared foods like this chilled tomato soup. It's not only delicious but also low in fat.

8 medium-size ripe tomatoes (about 4¾ pounds), cut into wedges
7 cups chicken broth
4 large onions, cut into large chunks (4 cups)
3 cloves garlic
2 tablespoons tomato paste
2 teaspoons salt
½ teaspoon ground black pepper
2 cups buttermilk
½ cup snipped fresh dill
For garnish: chopped tomatoes, fresh dill (optional)

1. In a large nonaluminum pot, bring the tomatoes, broth, onions, garlic, tomato paste, salt, and pepper to a boil over high heat, stirring two or three times.

2. Reduce the heat to low. Cover and simmer for 15 to 20 minutes, stirring three or four times, until the onions are softened. Remove the pot from the heat.

3. With a slotted spoon, remove the solids from the pot in batches to a food processor or blender. Process until smooth.

4. Pour the purée into a large bowl. Stir in the broth from the pot, the buttermilk, and dill. Cover and refrigerate for at least 3 hours, or until thoroughly chilled. Garnish each serving with chopped tomato and dill.

Per serving: 97 cal, 5 g pro, 16 g car, 2 g fat, 2 mg chol, 1,033 mg sod

MAKE AHEAD

The soup can be refrigerated up to 4 days.

MARINATED TURKEY BREAST WITH PEACH CHUTNEY

Serves 12

Preparation time: 15 minutes plus at least 3 hours to marinate
Cooking time: 45 minutes plus 10 minutes to stand

This turkey breast can be grilled or broiled and served warm or cold. Juicy ripe peaches, mango chutney, and scallions combine to make an especially delicious accompaniment.

MARINADE
⅔ cup plain low-fat yogurt
¼ cup soy sauce
¼ cup dark Asian sesame oil
¼ cup cider vinegar
2 teaspoons crushed hot red pepper flakes
2 teaspoons minced fresh garlic

2 skinless, boneless turkey breast halves (about 2½ pounds each)

PEACH CHUTNEY
3 cups fresh or thawed frozen, chopped peaches
1 cup bottled mango chutney
½ cup minced scallions

1. Make the marinade: In a large bowl, whisk together the yogurt, soy sauce, sesame oil, vinegar, hot pepper flakes, and garlic until blended.

2. Put the turkey breast halves on a cutting board and cover with plastic wrap. Gently pound with a meat mallet or rolling pin to 1½-inch thickness. Place the turkey in a shallow dish and spread all the surfaces with the marinade. Cover and refrigerate for at least 3 hours.

3. Meanwhile, prepare the chutney. In a medium-size nonaluminum bowl, mix the peaches, mango chutney, and scallions until well blended. Cover with plastic wrap and let stand at room temperature until ready to serve.

4. Heat a gas grill to medium, prepare a charcoal fire, or heat the broiler. Grill or broil the turkey 6 inches from the heat source for 25 minutes. Turn and baste the turkey with the marinade. Grill or broil for about 20 minutes more, or until the meat is opaque in the center of the thickest part, or a meat thermometer inserted into the thickest part registers 175°F to 180°F.

5. To serve, transfer the turkey to a cutting board. Cover loosely with a foil

ⓂAKE AHEAD

The turkey breasts can be marinated up to 24 hours before cooking.

tent. Let stand for 8 to 10 minutes. Slice and arrange on a serving platter. Serve with the peach chutney.

Per serving: 333 cal, 47 g pro, 21 g car, 6 g fat, 126 mg chol, 477 mg sod

BACKYARD PICNIC

GREEN BEAN SALAD

Serves 12
Preparation time: 30 minutes
Cooking time: 10 minutes

Green beans are also called snap beans because of the noise they make when broken sharply to test for freshness. They are available year round.

3 pounds green beans, ends trimmed
2 medium-size red bell peppers, seeded and cut into thin strips
1 cup finely chopped red onion
⅔ cup bottled Dijon vinaigrette or Italian dressing
½ teaspoon salt
½ teaspoon ground black pepper

1. Bring a large pot of water to a boil over high heat. Cook the beans in the boiling water for 8 to 10 minutes, or until crisp-tender. Drain and plunge the beans into cold water; drain again.

2. In a large bowl, toss the beans with the bell pepper, onion, dressing, salt, and pepper. Cover and refrigerate until ready to serve, or up to 45 minutes.

Per serving: 94 cal with Dijon vinaigrette, 101 cal with Italian dressing, 2 g pro, 10 g car, 6 g fat, 0 mg chol, 269 mg sod with Dijon vinaigrette, 202 mg sod with Italian dressing

SUMMER ENTERTAINING TIPS

Making the yard a special spot for day or night doesn't have to be expensive or time-consuming.

◆ String Christmas-tree lights—small white ones are particularly pretty—in a tree or bush or along roof eaves.

◆ Make luminarias by half filling lunch-size brown-paper bags with sand. Roll over a 1- to 2-inch cuff around the top and put a votive candle (in a glass container) in each bag. Space the bags along a walkway or outdoor stair. Light candles just before guests arrive.

◆ Soft music outside is a terrific touch. (Maybe people will even slow-dance under the stars.) Seclude a tape player—attached to an indoor/outdoor extension cord if necessary—behind a bush. Or put stereo speakers (thread cords through windows) in a dark corner. Be thoughtful about noise levels if there are neighbors nearby.

HARVEST DINNER FOR 8

No matter where you live, the coming of fall brings a longing for more robust flavors. Here's a sensational all-purpose dinner menu that makes for a perfect autumn Saturday night dinner party or Sunday family dinner. Take advantage of the season's bounty of colorful produce for table decoration.

HARVEST DINNER

BUTTERNUT SQUASH SOUP

Serves 8

Preparation time: 20 minutes

Cooking time: 40 minutes

A cornucopia of winter squash is now commonly seen in the produce section of supermarkets—and despite its name, is generally available year-round. Winter squash is identifiable by its hard skin (summer squash is soft-skinned). And while these squash may vary in shape and size, all have pale-yellow to orange-colored flesh and a similar flavor and texture. The many varieties can be used interchangeably in recipes that call for them to be puréed, as in this soup.

2 tablespoons butter or margarine

2 cups chopped onion

2 medium-size butternut squash (about 4 pounds) peeled, seeded, and cut into 1-inch chucks (8 cups)

4 medium-size Granny Smith apples, cored, peeled, and cut into small pieces (4 cups)

7 cups chicken broth

1½ teaspoons salt

½ teaspoon ground black pepper

½ cup plain low-fat yogurt

1. In a large pot, melt the butter. Add the onion and cook over medium-low heat for 8 to 10 minutes, or until softened.

2. Add the squash, apples, broth, salt, and pepper. Bring to a boil over medium-high heat. Cover, reduce the heat to medium-low, and simmer for 20 to 25 minutes, stirring occasionally, until the squash is tender. Remove the pan from the heat and let cool.

3. In a food processor or blender, process the mixture in batches until

MENU

Butternut Squash Soup

Muddy-Water Pork Loin

Gingered Wild Rice Salad

Steamed Green Beans or Brussels Sprouts*

Apple Strudel (page 475)

Wine recommendation:
Cabernet Sauvignon or Merlot

*Recipe not provided

M AKE AHEAD

The soup can be prepared through step 4. Cool completely, then refrigerate in an airtight container up to 2 days. Reheat and proceed as directed.

smooth. Return to the pot and reheat.

4. Ladle into serving mugs and top each serving with a spoonful of yogurt, swirled with the tip of a knife.

Per serving: 193 cal, 5 g pro, 35 g car, 5 g fat, 9 mg chol with butter, 1 mg chol with margarine, 1,336 mg sod.

HARVEST DINNER

MUDDY–WATER PORK LOIN

Serves 8

Preparation time: 25 minutes plus overnight to marinate
Cooking time: 2½ hours plus 15 minutes to stand

The name may sound unappetizing, but wait until you taste this lean, succulent pork roast. It can be slow-roasted on the grill or in the oven.

MUDDY–WATER MARINADE
¾ cup olive oil
⅓ cup red wine vinegar
¼ cup lemon juice
¼ cup water
1 tablespoon dried oregano leaves, crumbled
1 teaspoon salt
1 teaspoon coarsely ground pepper
½ teaspoon paprika

1 (3-pound) boned and tied pork loin, with a thin layer of fat
For garnish: fresh sprigs of oregano (optional)

1. Make the marinade: In a shallow glass or ceramic baking dish, mix the oil, vinegar, lemon juice, water, oregano, salt, pepper, and paprika until well blended. Let stand at room temperature for 20 minutes.

2. Add the pork, turning to coat. Cover and refrigerate overnight, turning 3 or 4 times.

3. Put a 15½ x 10½ x 3½-inch disposable foil drip pan in the bottom of a barbecue. Arrange briquettes or lava rocks around all sides of the pan. Pour 1 inch of water into the pan. Adjust the grill 4 to 6 inches above the hot coals. If using a gas grill, set to medium-low.

4. Remove the pork from the marinade and place on the grill over the drip pan. Cover the grill with a grill lid or foil tent. Grill the pork for about 30 minutes, or until it begins to brown on the underside. Turn and grill ▶

for 1½ to 2 hours longer, turning the roast every 20 minutes, or until a meat thermometer inserted in the thickest part of the veal loin not touching the fat registers 160°F. Replenish the water in the drip pan and add more briquettes as necessary.

4. Transfer the pork to a cutting board and let stand for 15 minutes. Remove the strings and slice the meat thin. Arrange on a serving platter and garnish with fresh oregano.

Per serving: 497 cal, 30 g pro, 0 g car, 41 g fat, 118 mg chol, 174 mg sod

---

HARVEST DINNER

GINGERED
WILD RICE SALAD

Serves 8 to 10
Preparation time: 20 minutes
Cooking time: 50 minutes

Known for its nutty flavor, wild rice isn't really rice at all, but rather a marsh grass native to the northern Great Lakes region. Because of its labor-intensive harvesting process, it can be quite expensive. Fortunately, when paired with other ingredients such as the orzo and vegetables used here, a little wild rice can go a long way.

WILD RICE SALAD

1 package (8 ounces) cultivated wild rice, rinsed
8 ounces snow peas, trimmed
1 box (16 ounces) orzo (rice-shaped pasta)
2 large yellow or red bell peppers, seeded and diced (3 cups)
¾ cup finely chopped red onion
1 bunch large radishes (about 8), cut into thin strips

GINGER DRESSING

⅔ cup cider vinegar
½ cup olive oil
⅓ cup minced fresh parsley
¼ cup minced peeled fresh gingerroot
2 teaspoons salt
1½ teaspoons Dijon mustard
1 teaspoon ground black pepper

For garnish: fresh sprigs of parsley (optional)

COOK'S TIP

To roast the pork loin, put it on a rack in a large roasting pan. Roast in a 400°F oven uncovered 1 ½ to 2 hours, or until a meat thermometer registers 160°F.

MAKE AHEAD

Put the dressing ingredients into a small jar and cover tightly. Shake to blend mixture. Refrigerate up to 3 days. Bring to room temperature and shake before using. Prepare the salad ingredients, wrap separately, and refrigerate up to 1 day or less. Assemble and dress the salad up to 2 hours before serving.

1. Make the salad: Bring a large saucepan of water to a boil over high heat. Add the wild rice and cook for 50 minutes, or until grains are tender but still chewy and almost doubled in size. Drain in a colander, cool under cold running water, and drain again. Transfer the rice to a large bowl.

2. Meanwhile, in a large pot, bring 3 quarts of water to a boil. Add the snow peas and cook for 30 seconds, or until bright green. Scoop out the snow peas with a small strainer and cool under cold running water.

3. Add the orzo to the boiling water and cook for 10 minutes, or until firm-tender. Drain in a colander, cool under cold running water, and drain again. Add the orzo to the rice in the bowl.

4. Cut the snow peas crosswise into ¼-inch-wide strips. Add to the rice mixture.

5. Add the bell peppers, onion, and radishes to the bowl, tossing to mix.

6. Make the dressing: In a blender or food processor, put the vinegar, oil, parsley, ginger, salt, mustard, and pepper and blend or process until smooth. Pour the dressing over the salad, tossing to mix and coat. Serve chilled or at room temperature.

Per cup: 415 cal, 12 g pro, 64 g car, 13 g fat, 0 mg chol, 520 mg sod

MAKING A CHEESE BOARD

◆ Buy cheese from different groups (see Cheese Primer, page 684) for color, texture, and flavor contrasts. If you're serving them as an hors d'oeuvre or dessert, plan on two or three kinds for a small group, adding more variety for a larger party.

◆ What you serve the cheeses on doesn't have to be a board. It may be a slab of marble, a large platter, even a lined wicker tray. Or you may want to put out each type of cheese on its own plate and label it, depending on how many kinds you are planning on serving. Try lining cheese serving platters with clean grape or lemon leaves or paper cheese leaves available at specialty cookware stores.

◆ Group stronger cheeses away from milder ones so the aromas and flavors don't mix. Leave enough cutting space between the cheeses so they don't get smeared into each other. Make sure each has its own knife or spreader.

◆ For best flavor, cheeses should be served at room temperature. Remove them from the refrigerator 30 minutes to 1 hour ahead. For a more attractive platter and to prevent cheese from drying out, don't precut it but rather let guest cut their own servings.

◆ Plain crackers or thin slices of French bread are always a good choice to serve with cheese. The idea is not to choose anything with a strong flavor that will compete with the cheese. Raw vegetables will let guests clear their taste buds between cheeses.

◆ For dessert, apples, pears, and grapes go well with almost any kind of cheese. You may make up individual plates for each guest or put out the fruit and cheese on large platters and let guests experiment with their own combinations.

◆ For a large party, arrange two or three separate cheese boards. Put out one to start, and when that's been demolished, call up the reserves.

WINTER DINNER PARTY FOR 12

The holiday season is the perfect time to host an elegant dinner party. It's a time when family and friends are visiting, everything looks festive, and everyone wants to share the warmth of the season. Because the season makes so many other demands, we created a menu that's easy on the cook. Most everything can be made ahead, and the beef tenderloin can be roasting unattended while you and your guests enjoy hors d'oeuvres. For extra ease, serve the menu buffet-style so everyone can help themselves.

WINTER DINNER PARTY

ENDIVE WITH MANDARIN SHRIMP

Serves 12

Preparation time: 30 minutes plus at least 8 hours to marinate

Cooking time: 4 minutes

Small elongated heads of Belgian endive, also called French endive and witloof chicory, are made up of smooth, creamy white, spear-shaped leaves that have a pleasantly bitter taste. In this recipe, the individual whole leaves make an edible and attractive container for marinated shrimp and mandarin oranges.

MARINADE

1 teaspoon grated orange peel
½ cup fresh orange juice
2 tablespoons finely chopped red onion
1 tablespoon dark Asian sesame oil
½ teaspoon crushed hot red pepper flakes
½ teaspoon minced fresh garlic

2 teaspoons vegetable oil
1 pound raw medium-size shrimp (about 36), shelled and deveined
3 Belgian endives (about 7 ounces each)
1 can (11 ounces) mandarin oranges, drained
For garnish: chopped red onion (optional)

1. Make the marinade: In a large zipper-type food-storage bag or a nonaluminum bowl, mix the orange peel and juice, the onion, sesame oil, hot

---

COOK'S TIP

To separate endive leaves, cut a slice off the root end, then pull off leaves one at a time.

MAKE AHEAD

The shrimp can be
prepared through step
2 up to one day ahead.
Proceed as directed.

pepper flakes, and garlic and shake or stir until blended.

2. In a large nonstick skillet, heat the oil over medium-high heat. Add the shrimp and cook for 1 to 2 minutes, stirring constantly, until pink. Remove the skillet from the heat. Cover and let stand for 1 minute, or until the shrimp are cooked through. Add the shrimp to the marinade. Cover and refrigerate for at least 8 hours or up to 24 hours.

3. Up to 2 hours before serving, arrange the endive leaves spoke-fashion on a serving platter. Place 1 shrimp and 1 orange section on the base of each leaf. Sprinkle with the onion. Cover loosely with plastic wrap and refrigerate until ready to serve.

Per serving : 68 cal, 8 g pro, 5 g car, 2 g fat, 58 mg chol, 61 mg sod

WINTER DINNER PARTY

BLACK–TIE POTATOES

Serves 12
Preparation time: 20 minutes
Cooking time: 20 minutes

COOK'S TIP

Cut the potatoes in half
with a very sharp knife
so the skin doesn't tear.

The classic combination of potatoes, sour cream, and caviar makes an exquisite hors d'oeuvre that your guests will never forget. And the presentation is gorgeous! Since this dish is served as finger food, try to buy very small potatoes, preferably red-skinned, so one potato half makes a bite-size serving.

18 very small (about 1½ inches in diameter) red-skinned potatoes,
    well-scrubbed
½ cup sour cream
1 jar (4 ounces) red or black lumpfish caviar or yellow whitefish roe
    (or some of all three)

MAKE AHEAD

You may cook the
potatoes up to 1 week
ahead and refrigerate
them tightly covered.

1. Cook the potatoes in water to cover for 15 to 20 minutes, or until firm-tender. Drain and cool.

2. Two or three hours before serving, cut the potatoes in half and arrange cut side up on a serving platter. Cover loosely and refrigerate.

3. Just before serving, top each potato half with a dab of sour cream, then a small amount of caviar.

Per serving: 101 cal, 3 g pro, 16 g car, 3 g fat, 38 mg chol, 268 mg sod with caviar, 12 mg sod with roe

BEEF TENDERLOIN WITH MUSHROOM GRAVY

Serves 12

Total time: 55 minutes

Tenderloins are lean and tender and are served rare or medium-rare to retain the juices. The mushroom gravy makes a delectable accompaniment and classic presentation.

1 whole beef tenderloin roast (about 4 pounds), trimmed
1 tablespoon olive oil
½ teaspoon ground black pepper

MUSHROOM GRAVY

2 tablespoons vegetable oil
¼ cup all-purpose flour
2½ cups beef broth
½ cup dry white wine or water
12 ounces white mushrooms, cleaned and sliced thin
2 teaspoons chopped fresh rosemary,
    or 1 teaspoon dried rosemary leaves, crumbled
½ teaspoon salt
½ teaspoon ground black pepper

For garnish: sprigs of fresh rosemary (optional)

1. Heat the oven to 500°F. Rub the beef with the oil and sprinkle with the pepper. Place diagonally on a 15½ x 10½-inch jelly roll pan, tucking the thin end under for even cooking.

2. Roast for 25 to 30 minutes, or until a meat thermometer inserted into the center of the thickest part registers 135°F for rare.

3. Meanwhile, make the gravy. In a large skillet, heat the oil over medium-high heat. Add the flour and whisk for 2 to 4 minutes, or until a dark golden color.

4. Slowly whisk in the broth and wine, then the mushrooms, rosemary, salt, and pepper. Reduce the heat to medium-low and cook for 10 to 15 minutes, stirring occasionally, until slightly thickened.

5. Remove the meat from the oven, cover loosely with foil, and let stand for about 10 minutes, or until a meat thermometer registers 140°F. The meat will continue cooking and the slicing will be easier.

COOK'S TIP

Beef tenderloin is an elegant cut of meat and is perfect for entertaining: it cooks quickly, slices easily, and can be served with a sauce or alone.

6. Slice ¼ inch thick and arrange on a serving platter. Garnish with rosemary sprigs and serve with the mushroom gravy.

Per serving: 295 cal, 32 g pro, 2 g car, 16 g fat, 94 mg chol, 503 mg sod

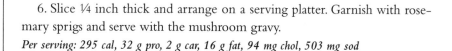

WINTER DINNER PARTY

GARLICKY BAKED TOMATOES

Serves 12
Preparation time: 10 minutes
Cooking time: 15 minutes

When serving these succulent tomatoes with beef tenderloin, pop them into the oven when you remove the meat. They also go well with roasted chicken, turkey, or lamb.

6 medium-size ripe tomatoes, cut in half
1 container (about 5 ounces) creamy garlic-flavored cheese,
　　at room temperature
¼ cup packaged seasoned bread crumbs

1. Heat the oven to 450°. Lightly grease a jelly roll pan or other large pan with sides.

2. Arrange the tomatoes, cut sides up, in the pan. Spread about 2 teaspoons of the cheese over each half.

3. Lightly sprinkle with the bread crumbs. Bake for 12 to 15 minutes, or until the crumbs are golden. Serve right away.

Per serving: 63 cal, 2 g pro, 5 g car, 4 g fat, 12 mg chol, 116 mg sod

HASSLE-FREE PARTY IDEAS

♦ **Coffee and Dessert:** Offer a few desserts and a variety of flavored instant coffees along with regular and decaffeinated. Set out bowls of ground cinnamon, chopped chocolate, and whipped cream so guests can dress up their coffee.

♦ **Bring-a-Dish:** Plan a menu loosely, based around a main dish or theme, like Italian or Chinese cuisine. Guests each bring a dish and everyone helps with serving.

♦ **Salad-Bar Buffet:** Put out a large bowl of greens, bowls of fixings, and homemade or bought dressings. For a more substantial meal, add bread and a platter of cheese and cold cuts.

♦ **Box Lunch:** Buy cake boxes at your bakery. Put a sandwich, bag of chips, assorted crudités, a napkin, and cookies in each. No dishes, cutlery, or table needed, just beverage glasses.

♦ **Wine and Cheese:** Serve a few cheese—from mild to sharp—with crusty bread and crackers and fresh cut-up fruit. Ask your wine merchant to help you select appropriate wines.

POTLUCK PARTIES

When it comes to entertaining a large crowd, nothing is easier than a potluck buffet. Here, the guests all bring a dish to create a varied and interesting menu. In general, potluck dishes should have wide appeal, and those that can be served at room temperature are an advantage. Here are some tips for a successful potluck party:

♦ Don't serve overly spicy or unfamiliar foods.
♦ Don't include such items as seafood, delicate greens, and cut vegetables that wilt quickly if food will sit at room temperature for long periods. Perishability is always a concern.
♦ Don't try very fancy appetizers or complicated pastries—anything that's time-consuming or requires lots of experienced hand labor.
♦ Don't opt for out-of-season produce or expensive ingredients. Why serve a rhubarb crisp in October when apples are plentiful and cheap?
♦ Don't serve food that can't be cooked in available facilities. Few church kitchens, for example, are equipped to broil or bake large amounts of food.
♦ Especially if you're outdoors in hot weather (85°F and above), don't let perishable food sit out for more than one hour.
♦ If possible, serving dishes should contain smaller portions. You can't change the size of a baking dish, but for something like chicken salad, it is better to put out a relatively small amount to begin with. Keep the rest chilled in another serving bowl—ready to go when the first dish is empty. It's also useful for an organizer to assign certain foods to guests so you don't end up with too much of the same thing.

Here are a few potluck favorites:

ALL AMERICAN POTATO SALAD

Peel 5 pounds all-purpose potatoes and cut into 1-inch pieces. Boil the potatoes in a large pot for 12 minutes, or until firm-tender, not mushy. Drain and cool slightly. In a large bowl mix 1 cup mayonnaise, 1/3 cup chicken broth, 2 tablespoons coarse-grain Dijon mustard, 2 cups chopped celery, 3 chopped hard-cooked eggs, 1/3 cup chopped scallions, and 1/2 teaspoon each salt and pepper. Add the potatoes and toss gently to coat. Makes 14 servings. Per serving: 237 cal, 5 g pro, 23 g car, 14 g fat, 70 mg chol, 280 mg sod

BAKED BEANS

In a large bowl, mix 2 (40 ounces) cans pork and beans, 1 pound light brown sugar, 2 cups chopped onion, 1/4 cup coarse-grain Dijon mustard and 1/4 cup Worcestershire sauce. Pour the mixture into a shallow 3-quart casserole or baking dish and top with 6 slices of bacon. Bake at 325°F. for 1 1/2 to 2 hours, or until the juices have thickened. Makes 20 servings. Per serving: 229 cal, 4 g pro, 43 g car, 6 g fat, 12 mg chol, 558 mg sod

CREAMY PINEAPPLE-GELATIN SALAD

In a large saucepan, bring 2 (20-ounce) cans crushed pineapple with juice to a boil. Remove the pan from the heat. Stir in 2 (8-serving size) packages of orange-flavored gelatin until dissolved. Let cool. Stir in 4 cups buttermilk, then fold in 2 (8 ounce tubs) thawed, frozen whipped topping until no clumps remain. Stir in 2 cups chopped pecans. Pour into two 13 x 9 x 2-inch baking pans. Cover and refrigerate for a least 4 hours, or until firm. Cut into squares and serve on lettuce-lined plates garnished with orange segments. Makes 24 servings. Per serving: 220 cal, 4 g pro, 28 g car, 11 g fat, 2 mg chol, 85 mg sod

HAM AND LENTIL SALAD

In a large saucepan, bring 2 cups dried lentils and 6 cups water to a boil. Cover, reduce the heat to low, and simmer for 20 to 25 minutes, or until tender, but not mushy. Drain in a colander and rinse under cold water. In a large bowl, whisk together 2/3 cup olive oil, 1/4 cup red wine vinegar, 1/4 cup creamy mustard spread (like Dijonnaise), 1 teaspoon salt, and 1/2 teaspoon pepper. Add 6 medium-size tomatoes, cut into chunks, 1 pound Virginia ham, cut into strips, 2 cups sliced cucumber, 2 cups corn kernels, and the lentils. Toss to mix and coat. Makes 8 servings. Per serving: 503 cal, 28 g pro, 43 g car, 26 g fat, 33 mg chol, 1,248 mg sod with fresh or frozen corn, 1,388 mg sod with canned corn

CELEBRATIONS

*"Small cheer and a great welcome
makes a merry feast."*
WILLIAM SHAKESPEARE

In our hectic, fast-paced lives, sometimes the only time we have to slow down and enjoy family and friends is during a holiday or special celebration. And food often becomes the foundation of these occasions.

Cooking for these events can be a delight, if you can join your guests in the dining room and not be worried about what's happening in the kitchen. The menus in this chapter will give you peace of mind because much of the preparation can be done in advance and at a leisurely pace. Preparing food ahead takes careful thought and a master plan. To help the cook, we've devised a planning timetable for each menu. Follow it carefully and you will succeed without a hitch.

On the following pages you will find complete menus for Easter, Passover, Thanksgiving, Christmas, and Hanukkah. Let the menu suggestions, planning schedules, and table-setting tips inspire you to relax and enjoy the celebration.

EASTER DINNER FOR 12

This Easter feast is a salute to spring. To reflect the gentle warmth of this season, set the table with soft pastel colors. Rely on spring flowers such as tulips, irises, and lilies loosely arranged in a clear glass vase for a centerpiece, or fill a shallow basket with colored eggs and set out small terra-cotta pots of miniature daffodils or grape hyacinths.

EASTER DINNER

SPRING VEGETABLE SOUP

Serves 12
Preparation time: 15 minutes
Cooking time: 45 minutes

This creamy, colorful soup, bursting with the fresh flavor of fresh asparagus, is delicious chilled as well as hot.

2 cups water
2¼ pounds (2 bunches) fresh asparagus, woody ends broken off, spears cut into 2-inch lengths, and tips reserved
6 cups chicken broth
1½ cups thinly sliced carrots
1½ cups chopped onion
¾ cup thinly sliced celery
1 teaspoon minced fresh garlic
¾ teaspoon dried tarragon leaves, crumbled
¾ teaspoon salt
1¼ cups milk
1 cup half-and-half
2 tablespoons fresh lemon juice

1. In a large saucepan, bring the water to a boil. Add the asparagus tips to the water and boil for 45 seconds, or until bright green and crisp-tender. Drain, rinse under cold running water, and drain again. Wrap the asparagus and refrigerate for garnish.

2. In the same pan, combine the chicken broth, asparagus pieces, carrots, onion, celery, garlic, tarragon, and salt. Bring to a boil. Reduce the heat to low. Cover and simmer for 30 to 35 minutes, or until the vegetables are very tender.

3. Remove the pan from the heat and cool slightly. Process in batches in a

MENU

Spring Vegetable Soup

Lemon-Herb Roast Leg of Lamb

Roasted Onions & Shallots

Parmesan Potato Casserole

Honey Snow Peas & Carrots

Herb Rolls*

Almond-Macaroon Easter Nests

Spice Cake with Strawberries

Wine recommendation:
Cabernet Sauvignon
or
dry California Zinfandel

*Recipe not provided

food processor or blender until smooth.

4. Return to the saucepan and stir in the milk and half-and-half. Heat until simmering (do not boil). Remove the pan from the heat and stir in the lemon juice.

5. Ladle into serving bowls and garnish with the asparagus tips.

Per serving: 82 cal, 4 g pro, 7 g car, 4 g fat, 11 mg chol, 671 mg sod

EASTER DINNER

LEMON–HERB ROAST LEG OF LAMB

Serves 12 with leftovers
Preparation time: 20 minutes
Cooking time: 2 hours 15 minutes plus 15 minutes to stand

Rosemary, garlic, and lemon—three of spring's essential flavors—are also classic seasonings for lamb, while roasted onions and shallots make a delicious garnish. Lamb is at its best when cooked rare to medium-rare.

3 large garlic cloves, peeled
1 tablespoon fresh rosemary leaves,
    or 2 teaspoons dried rosemary leaves, crumbled
1 teaspoon grated lemon peel
½ teaspoon salt
Freshly ground black pepper
⅓ cup fresh lemon juice
1 bone-in leg of lamb, about 8 pounds, trimmed of excess fat
2 tablespoons olive oil
1 cup low-sodium beef broth or water

PAN GRAVY
2 tablespoons all-purpose flour
2 cups low-sodium beef broth
1 tablespoon fresh lemon juice
Freshly ground pepper to taste

For garnish: small sprigs of fresh rosemary (optional)

1. Heat the oven to 450°F.
2. Chop the garlic, rosemary, lemon peel, salt, and ½ teaspoon of pepper together with a large knife until the mixture is paste-like. Scrape into a ▶

small bowl. Stir in 2 teaspoons of the lemon juice.

3. With the tip of a small knife make about 12 deep slits on each side of the lamb. Using a small measuring spoon, push about ¼ teaspoon of the garlic mixture into each slit.

4. Rub the lamb with the oil, then sprinkle with pepper. Place on a rack in a large roasting pan. Pour in the 1 cup of beef broth.

5. Roast for 15 minutes. Spoon the remaining lemon juice over the meat, then reduce the temperature to 350°F. Roast for 1½ to 2 hours more, basting 3 times with the pan juices, to desired doneness (For rare: 130°F on a meat thermometer inserted in thickest part not touching fat or bone; 140°F for medium and 150°F for medium-well).

6. Remove the lamb to a serving platter. Cover loosely with a foil tent to keep warm. Let stand for 15 minutes. (As the meat rests, the juices redistribute and the internal temperature should rise about 10 degrees.)

7. Meanwhile, make the gravy: Spoon off and discard all but 2 tablespoons of fat from juices in the roasting pan. Whisk in the flour until smooth, scraping up the browned bits from the bottom of the pan. Gradually whisk in the beef broth and lemon juice until blended. Place the pan over medium-high heat. Bring to a boil, reduce the heat to low, and simmer for 5 minutes, whisking several times, until the gravy is thickened. Stir in the pepper. (Makes 2 cups.)

8. To serve, insert small sprigs of rosemary into the slits in the roast. Serve the pan gravy from a sauceboat at the table.

Per serving: 340 cal, 30 g pro, 3 g car, 23 g fat, 108 mg chol, 169 mg sod

COOK'S TIP

To make a smoother gravy, stir the flour into the pan drippings and add the liquid off the heat, then cook as directed.

EASTER DINNER

ROASTED ONIONS & SHALLOTS

Serves 12
Preparation time: 20 minutes
Cooking time: 1 hour

Roasting onions and shallots brings out their sweet flavor. This dish is the perfect accompaniment to roasted meats or poultry because they can both cook simultaneously.

1½ pounds small white onions (about 24), peeled
1½ pounds large shallots (about 24), peeled
2 tablespoons vegetable oil

1. Heat the oven to 350°F.

2. In a shallow roasting pan or baking dish, combine the onions and shallots. Add the oil and stir to coat.

3. Place on the lowest rack in the oven and roast for about 1 hour, stirring once or twice, until browned and tender.

Per serving: 75 cal, 2 g pro, 13 g car, 2 g fat, 0 mg chol, 11 mg sod

EASTER DINNER

PARMESAN POTATO CASSEROLE

Serves 12

Preparation time: 30 minutes

Baking time: 50 minutes

These wonderfully simple potatoes are mashed with Parmesan cheese and fresh parsley, then baked until the top is golden brown. Other fresh herbs, such as chives or chervil, can also be used for this dish. To save on calories, use low-fat milk and reduced-calorie margarine.

12 medium-size all-purpose potatoes (4 pounds), peeled and quartered
½ cup (1 stick) butter or margarine
1 cup milk
3 large eggs, lightly beaten
½ cup grated Parmesan cheese
¼ cup chopped fresh parsley
1 teaspoon salt
½ teaspoon ground black pepper

1. Heat the oven to 350°F. Lightly grease a shallow 3-quart casserole or baking dish.

2. Cook the potatoes in a large pot of boiling water to cover for 15 to 20 minutes, or until tender when tested with a fork. Drain and return the potatoes to the pot.

3. Add the butter to the potatoes and mash until the butter melts. Add the milk, eggs, cheese, parsley, salt, and pepper. Mash or whip with an electric mixer until smooth (some small lumps may remain). Spoon the potatoes into the prepared dish.

4. Bake uncovered for 45 to 50 minutes, or until the top is puffed and golden. Serve right away.

Per serving: 207 cal, 6 g pro, 22 g car, 11 g fat, 79 mg chol with butter, 59 mg chol with margarine, 365 mg sod

---

Ⓜ️AKE AHEAD

The casserole can be assembled up to 1 day ahead and refrigerated. Bring to room temperature before baking.

HONEY SNOW PEAS & CARROTS

Serves 12
Preparation time: 20 minutes
Cooking time: 13 minutes

Snow peas, popular in Chinese cooking, are delicious when combined with carrots and coated with a honey glaze. They are available in most supermarkets year round, with peak supplies in the spring.

1 pound carrots, sliced thin (6 cups)
1¼ pounds fresh snow peas, strings removed (7½ cups)
5 tablespoons honey
1½ teaspoons cornstarch
¼ teaspoon salt
5 tablespoons butter

1. Bring a large pot of water to a boil. Add the carrots and boil for 5 to 6 minutes, or until crisp-tender. Add the snow peas and boil for 1 to 2 minutes more, or until the carrots are tender and the snow peas are crisp-tender.
2. Meanwhile, in a small bowl, mix the honey, cornstarch, and salt.
3. Drain the vegetables, rinse under cold running water, and drain again,
4. In the same pot, melt the butter over medium heat. Stir in the honey mixture. Stir for 1 to 2 minutes, or until thickened slightly.
5. Add the carrots and snow peas and toss to mix and coat. Stir for 2 to 3 minutes, or until the vegetables are hot and glazed. Serve right away.

Per serving: 106 cal, 2 g pro, 15 g car, 5 g fat, 13 mg chol, 109 mg sod

ALMOND–MACAROON EASTER NESTS

Serves 12 to 20
Preparation time: 15 minutes plus 45 minutes to chill
Baking time: 17 minutes per batch

Coconut macaroons tinted with food coloring and crowned with pastel sugar-coated almonds are pretty and fun at the same time. They make the perfect cookie for an Easter celebration.

COOK'S TIP

If you're using the
same baking sheet to
bake several batches of
cookies, be sure to let
it cool before adding
more dough. Otherwise
the cookies will melt
and spread too much.

2 cups all-purpose flour
1 tablespoon baking powder
¼ teaspoon salt
¾ cup (1½ sticks) butter or margarine, at room temperature
1 (8-ounce) brick (not tub) light cream cheese (Neufchâtel),
    at room temperature
1 cup granulated sugar
¾ teaspoon almond extract
1 package (7 ounces) sweetened flaked coconut
Red and yellow liquid food coloring
About 120 pastel-colored sugar-coated almonds

1. In a medium-size bowl, mix the flour, baking powder, and salt until well blended.

2. In a large bowl, beat the butter and cream cheese with an electric mixer until well blended. Add the sugar and almond extract. Beat for 2 minutes, or until fluffy.

3. With the mixer on low speed, gradually beat in the flour mixture and 1 cup loosely packed coconut until well blended. Cover and refrigerate for 45 minutes, or until firm enough to handle.

4. Meanwhile, put ½ cup loosely packed coconut into each of two glass jars and the remaining ½ cup into a medium-size bowl. Add 1 drop of red food coloring to one jar and 1 drop of yellow food coloring to the other. Close the lids and shake vigorously until the coconut is evenly tinted. Add to untinted coconut and toss to mix.

5. Heat the oven to 350°F. Divide the chilled dough in half and put half back into the refrigerator. Roll slightly rounded tablespoonfuls of dough into balls (you'll have 20). Roll each into the coconut until lightly coated. Place the coated balls on baking sheets, spacing them about 2 inches apart. Press 1 almond into each (the other 2 almonds are added after the dough spreads while baking). Bake for 12 minutes. Remove from the oven and gently press 2 more almonds into each cookie close to the first one, to resemble eggs in a nest. Bake for 4 to 5 minutes more, or until the edges are firm and the coconut starts to turn golden.

6. Set the sheets on wire racks to cool for 5 minutes before removing the cookies to the racks to cool completely. Repeat with the remaining dough.

Makes 40 cookies. Per cookie: 157 cal, 2 g pro, 20 g car, 8 g fat, 12 mg chol with butter, 3 mg chol with margarine, 128 mg sod

SPICE CAKE WITH STRAWBERRIES

Serves 8
Preparation time: 20 minutes
Baking time: 35 minutes

This cake gets its flavor from a fragrant combination of ginger, cinnamon, and allspice. A simple and plain filling of fresh berries and vanilla pudding makes a luscious complement.

SPICE CAKE

1½ cups all-purpose flour
1 teaspoon baking soda
1 teaspoon ground cinnamon
1 teaspoon ground ginger
½ teaspoon ground allspice
½ teaspoon salt
1 cup packed light brown sugar
1 cup water
⅓ cup vegetable oil
1 tablespoon fresh lemon juice

FILLING AND SAUCE

1 package (4-serving size) instant vanilla pudding
1½ cups milk
1 pint (12 ounces) strawberries, rinsed, hulled, and sliced
3 tablespoons fresh lemon juice
½ teaspoon freshly grated lemon peel

For garnish: confectioners' sugar, small whole strawberries (optional)

1. Heat the oven to 350°F. Lightly grease an 8-inch round cake pan.

2. Make the cake: In a medium-size bowl, mix the flour, baking soda, cinnamon, ginger, allspice, and salt.

3. In another medium-size bowl, whisk the brown sugar, water, oil, and lemon juice until blended. Pour into the flour mixture and whisk until blended. Pour into the prepared pan.

4. Bake 30 to 35 minutes until a pick inserted in the center of the cake comes out clean. Let cool in the pan on a wire rack for 10 minutes. Loosen the edges with a knife and invert on a wire rack to cool completely.

5. Meanwhile, make the filling and sauce. Prepare the pudding mix with

COOK'S TIP

Do not wash or hull the strawberries until you are ready to use them. To hull, use a small sharp knife to remove the leafy portion at the top.

the 1½ cups of milk according to the package directions. Let stand for 5 minutes to thicken. Remove ⅔ cup of the mixture to a medium-size bowl and stir in the sliced strawberries (this is the filling). Stir the lemon juice and peel into the remaining pudding mixture (this is the sauce).

6. To assemble: Using a long serrated knife, slice the cake into 2 layers. Put the bottom half on a serving plate and spread with the filling. Top with the remaining layer. Sift the confectioners' sugar over the top. Put the sauce in a separate small bowl to ladle onto the cake slices.

Makes 8 slices. Per slice: 362 cal, 4 g pro, 62 g car, 11 g fat, 6 mg chol, 507 mg sod

EASTER DINNER PLANNING TIMETABLE

3 TO 4 WEEKS AHEAD:
- Make the guest list and write invitations or telephone guests.

1 TO 2 WEEKS AHEAD:
- Order the leg of lamb.
- Shop for nonperishable food.
- Plan the table setting and centerpiece.

3 DAYS AHEAD:
- Bring out china, serving dishes, and serving utensils. Polish silver if necessary.

2 DAYS AHEAD:
- Shop for perishables.
- Make spring vegetable soup; leave out the milk and half-and-half until you are ready to serve.
- Make almond-macaroon Easter nests. Store in an airtight container at room temperature.
- Make spice cake, but don't fill it. Wrap the cake in the pan and store at room temperature.
- Make the garlic paste for the lamb. Cover tightly and refrigerate.

1 DAY AHEAD:
- Assemble the parmesan potato

casserole. Cover and refrigerate.
- Buy any flowers.
- Pick up the meat and refrigerate.
- Prepare the snow peas and carrots and refrigerate separately in zipper-type bags.
- Set the table.
- Select CDs, tapes, or records for music.

EASTER MORNING:
- Prepare the lamb with the garlic paste, rub with the oil, and sprinkle with pepper. Cover and refrigerate.
- Peel the shallots and onions.
- Make the filling and sauce for the spice cake. Fill the cake and sift with confectioners' sugar. Transfer the sauce to a bowl and set aside in a cool place.
- Arrange the macaroons on a serving plate.
- Chill beverages.

ABOUT 2½ HOURS BEFORE SERVING:
- Start roasting the lamb.
- Combine the snow peas and carrots through step 3. Set aside. Mix the honey mixture and set aside.
- Bring the Parmesan potato

casserole to room temperature.
- Set up beverages. Fill the creamer for coffee and refrigerate.

ABOUT 1 HOUR BEFORE SERVING:
- Baste the lamb. Roast the onions and shallots.
- Bake the potato casserole.
- Transfer the soup to a saucepan. Add the milk and half-and-half. Set aside.
- Set out the butter.

30 MINUTES BEFORE SERVING:
- Check the lamb for doneness. Stir the onions and shallots.
- Warm the rolls.

JUST BEFORE SERVING:
- Reheat the soup over low heat, stirring occasionally.
- Put the lamb on a serving platter, garnish with rosemary sprigs, and cover loosely with foil.
- Make the gravy and transfer to a sauceboat. Keep warm.
- Transfer the onions and shallots to a serving dish.
- Finish off the snow peas and carrots and transfer to a serving dish.
- Place the warmed rolls in a basket.

PASSOVER DINNER FOR 8

This ritual Jewish dinner, known as the seder, is rooted in centuries of tradition and ceremony. Here's a contemporary yet traditional menu to commemorate this week-long celebration.

MENU

Gefilte Fish Terrine

Red Horseradish

Roast Capon with Pan Gravy

Baby Carrots with Mint

Mashed Potatoes with Browned Onions

Lemon Sponge Cake

PASSOVER DINNER

GEFILTE FISH TERRINE

Serves 12

Preparation time: 20 minutes plus at least 8 hours to chill

Cooking time: 10 minutes

Here is an elegant way to serve bottled gefilte fish as a first course. Gefilte fish is made from ground fish fillets—usually carp, pike, or whitefish—vegetables, eggs, matzo meal, and seasonings. The mixture is formed into balls or patties and simmered in fish stock.

3 envelopes unflavored regular or kosher gelatin

2½ cups water

2 jars (24 ounces each) gefilte fish (no sugar added) in jellied broth

2 medium-size carrots, cut into long thin matchsticks

1 medium-size zucchini, cut into long thin matchsticks

1 medium-size yellow summer squash, cut into long thin matchsticks

For garnish: lettuce leaves (optional)

1. In a small bowl, sprinkle the gelatin over ½ cup cold water. Let stand for about 2 minutes to soften.

2. Drain the gefilte fish in a strainer set over a medium-size saucepan to catch the jellied broth.

3. Bring the broth to a boil. Stir in the softened gelatin. Reduce the heat to medium-low and simmer for 1 to 2 minutes, stirring with a rubber spatula 2 or 3 times, until the gelatin dissolves and no granules remain on the spatula. Remove the pan from the heat and stir in the remaining 2 cups of water.

4. Pour a thin layer of the gelatin mixture into a 9 x 5-inch loaf pan or an 8-cup terrine. Refrigerate or place in the freezer briefly just until set. Let the remaining gelatin cool until slightly warm.

5. Meanwhile, bring a large saucepan of water to boil. Add the carrots. Reduce the heat to low and simmer, covered, for 4 minutes. Add the zucchini and squash, cover, and simmer for 3 minutes more, until the ▶*p. 557*

MAKE AHEAD

The terrine can be prepared ahead through step 7. Cover with plastic wrap and refrigerate up to 2 days. Unmold and serve as directed.

HOLIDAY TREAT
Serve Apple-
Almond Coffee
Cake (p.319) with
coffee and tea on
Christmas or
Easter morning.

Celebrations tend to become annual events. Vary the

menus and every year the celebration will become a

new experience.

SPRING BREAK
Salute Easter with
a Roast Leg of
Lamb (p.545),
above, and pretty
Almond-Macaroon
Easter Nests
(p.548), right.

SOMETHING SPECTACULAR
Cheese Soufflé (p.257) makes a dramatic and elegant presentation on special occasions. And it's easier to make than you'd think.

vegetables are tender. Drain, rinse, drain again, then spread on paper towels.

6. Arrange the vegetable sticks and the gefilte fish lengthwise in 2 rows over the gelatin in the pan, about ¼ inch from the sides of the pan. Add the remaining gelatin mixture until the pan is filled. Refrigerate for at least 8 hours. Cover with plastic wrap when the gelatin has set.

7. To unmold, run a knife around the inside edge of the pan. Place a serving plate upside down on the pan, then invert both. Shake gently from side to side to release the mold (dip the bottom of the pan in warm, not hot, water if necessary). Remove the pan.

8. To serve, cut the terrine into slices. Serve with red horseradish (recipe follows) or plain horseradish on lettuce-lined plates.

Per serving: 111 cal, 12 g pro, 11 g car, 2 g fat, 34 mg chol, 603 mg sod

PASSOVER DINNER

RED HORSERADISH

Serves 12

Preparation time: 10 minutes

MAKE AHEAD

The horseradish will keep in the refrigerator up to 3 months.

Compared to the bottled variety, freshly grated horseradish is potent stuff. Turn your head away when opening the food processor, or the horseradish fumes will make your eyes tear.

8 ounces fresh horseradish root, peeled and cut into small chunks
1 can or jar (16 ounces) julienne-cut or sliced beets, drained
¼ cup distilled white vinegar
1 tablespoon granulated sugar
1 teaspoon salt

1. In a food processor, process the horseradish chunks until finely chopped.

2. Add the beets, vinegar, sugar, and salt. Turn the processor on/off several times until the beets are finely chopped.

3. Refrigerate in a tightly covered container until ready to use.

Makes 2 cups. Per 1 tablespoon: 10 cal, 0 g pro, 2 g car, 0 g fat, 0 mg chol, 91 mg sod

ROAST CAPON WITH PAN GRAVY

Serves 8 with leftovers
Preparation time: 30 minutes
Cooking time: 2 hours 30 minutes

Capon (a male chicken neutered while young) is plump, meaty, and especially flavorful. You could use a large roasting chicken or a small turkey instead.

1 capon, about 10 pounds, thawed if frozen, rinsed and patted dry,
   neck and giblets reserved
1 teaspoon salt
½ teaspoon ground black pepper
3 tablespoons margarine, at room temperature
10 sprigs fresh thyme
1 small lemon, washed
4 cups water
2 cups low-sodium chicken broth
1 rib celery with leaves, cut into 3-inch-long pieces
1 small onion, unpeeled and quartered
1¼ tablespoons potato starch
⅛ teaspoon ground red pepper (cayenne)
For garnish: fresh thyme (optional)

1. Heat the oven to 450°F.
2. Remove and discard the excess fat from the capon neck and body cavities. Rub inside and out with the salt and pepper.
3. Insert your fingers between the skin and meat on the breast and legs and gently the loosen skin. Rub 1½ tablespoons of margarine under the skin. Gently tuck the thyme sprigs under the skin on the breast and legs.
4. Prick the lemon all over. Place in the body cavity.
5. Tie the legs together with kitchen twine and, if you wish, fold the wing tips under the back.
6. Place the capon, breast side up, on a rack in a large roasting pan. Tuck the neck skin under the back or close the opening with a skewer. Smear the remaining 1½ tablespoons of margarine over the skin. Pour 1 cup of water into the pan.
7. Roast for 10 minutes. Reduce the oven temperature to 325°F. Roast for 1¾ to 2¼ hours more, basting occasionally with pan juices, until a meat thermometer inserted into the thickest part of a thigh not touching the bone

registers 170°F to 175°F and the juices run clear when thigh is pierced.

8. Meanwhile, put the reserved neck and all the giblets except the liver (save for another use) into a medium-size saucepan. Add the remaining 3 cups of water, the chicken broth, celery, and onion. Bring to a boil. Reduce the heat to medium-low and simmer, uncovered, for about 1¼ hours, or until the broth is reduced to 2 cups. Strain the broth. Discard the neck and giblets.

9. Untie the capon legs, if tied, and remove the skewers or trussing thread. Lift the capon, tilting it slightly so juices from the cavity run into the roasting pan, and transfer it to a serving platter. Cover loosely with a foil tent to keep warm. Let stand for 15 to 30 minutes for juices to redistribute.

10. Make the gravy: Pour the pan juices into a 4-cup measure. Skim off 2½ tablespoons of fat and return it to the roasting pan. Skim off and discard the remaining fat from the pan juices. Add enough giblet broth to measure 2½ cups. Whisk the potato starch into the fat until smooth, scraping up the browned bits in the bottom of the pan. Gradually whisk in the broth until blended. Place the roasting pan over medium-high heat. Bring to a boil. Reduce the heat to low and simmer for 5 minutes, whisking several times, until the gravy is thickened. Stir in the red pepper. (Makes 2½ cups.)

11. Serve the pan gravy from a sauceboat at the table.

Per serving: 257 cal, 26 g pro, 5 g car, 15 g fat, 73 mg chol, 401 mg sod

---

PASSOVER DINNER

BABY CARROTS WITH MINT

Serves 8
Preparation time: 20 minutes
Cooking time: 25 minutes

Look for bags of cleaned ready-to-cook baby carrots, 1 to 5 inches long, in your market. To chop mint, stack leaves and cut lengthwise in thin strips, then cut crosswise.

2 pounds baby carrots, peeled or scrubbed and trimmed
2 tablespoons olive oil
½ teaspoon minced garlic
½ teaspoon salt
¼ cup chopped fresh mint

1. In a deep large skillet, bring 1 quart of water to a boil. Add the carrots, cover, and cook over medium-high heat for 10 to 15 minutes, or until ▶

COOK'S TIP

When buying fresh mint, look for leaves that are free of any brown spots. Crush a leaf in the palm of your hand; the fragrance should be full-bodied, not weak and hard to detect.

tender. Drain in a colander.

2. In the same skillet, heat the oil over medium heat. Add the garlic and cook over low heat for 1 to 2 minutes, stirring occasionally, until tender but not browned.

3. Add the carrots and salt and stir over medium-high heat for 1 to 2 minutes, or until the carrots are hot and coated with garlic oil. Remove the skillet from the heat and stir in the mint. Serve right away.

Per serving: 74 cal, 1 g pro, 10 g car, 4 g fat, 0 mg chol, 172 mg sod

---

PASSOVER DINNER

MASHED POTATOES WITH BROWNED ONIONS

Serves 8
Preparation time: 15 minutes
Cooking time: 30 minutes

These full-flavored potatoes are easy to prepare and can be served as part of a kosher meat menu because they don't use butter, milk, or cream. Be sure to use a potato masher or electric mixer for mashing, not a food processor, which makes the potatoes gluey.

3 pounds medium-size (about 9) all-purpose potatoes, peeled
⅔ cup margarine
2 cups chopped onion
1 teaspoon salt
½ teaspoon ground black pepper
¼ cup chopped fresh parsley

1. Cook the potatoes in a large saucepan in water to cover for 20 to 30 minutes, or until tender when tested with a fork.

2. Meanwhile, in a large skillet, melt 3 tablespoons of the margarine over medium heat. Add the onion and cook over medium-low heat for 8 to 10 minutes, stirring occasionally, until softened. Increase the heat to medium and cook for 5 to 7 minutes more, stirring occasionally, until golden.

3. Drain the potatoes, reserving 1 cup of the cooking liquid, and return them to the pan. Add the reserved cooking liquid, the remaining margarine, the salt and pepper.

4. Mash or whip with an electric mixer until blended (some small lumps may remain). Stir in the onions and parsley.

Per serving: 254 cal, 3 g pro, 27 g car, 15 g fat, 0 mg chol, 464 mg sod

COOK'S TIP

The potatoes can be cut up several hours before cooking. To prevent them from darkening, keep them submerged in water.

LEMON SPONGE CAKE

Serves 16
Preparation time: 25 minutes
Baking time: 45 minutes

MAKE AHEAD

The sponge cake
can be prepared in
advance, wrapped
airtight, and stored at
room temperature up
to 3 days or refriger-
ated up to 1 week.

This light-as-a-feather cake uses matzo cake meal instead of flour. Have all
the ingredients measured and ready before beating the egg whites so that the
separated whites don't stand too long.

7 large eggs, whites and yolks separated, at room temperature
¼ teaspoon salt
1½ cups granulated sugar
1 tablespoon grated lemon peel
½ teaspoon grated nutmeg
¼ cup fresh lemon juice
1 cup matzo cake meal, or finely grind in a blender
    1 cup plus 2 tablespoons matzo meal

TOPPING
⅓ cup apricot jam
3 tablespoons honey
1 cup sliced unblanched (skins still on) almonds

1. Heat the oven to 350°F.
2. In a large bowl, beat the egg whites and salt with an electric mixer on
medium speed until foamy and white. Add 2 tablespoons of the sugar, 1
tablespoon at a time, beating after each addition. Increase the mixer speed to
high and add 2 more tablespoons of sugar, 1 at a time. Continue beating
until stiff, glossy peaks form when the beaters are lifted.
3. In a medium-size bowl, combine the egg yolks, the remaining 1¼ cups
sugar, the lemon peel, and nutmeg. Beat with an electric mixer (no need to
wash beaters) at high speed for 2 to 3 minutes, or until the yolks are thick
and pale.
4. Reduce the mixer speed to low and beat in the lemon juice just until
blended, then the matzo meal just until blended, stopping the mixer once or
twice to scrape down the sides of the bowl with a rubber spatula.
5. Gently stir (fold) about ¼ of the egg whites into the yolk mixture just
until blended. Gently stir (fold) the mixture into the remaining whites just
until no white streaks remain (the batter will be very thick). Scrape into an
ungreased 10-inch tube pan. Smooth the top. ▶

6. Bake for 40 to 45 minutes, or until the top is lightly browned and a toothpick inserted into the cake comes out clean. Invert the pan on a wire rack and let the cake cool completely.

7. Run a thin sharp knife around the inside edges of the pan and tube. Invert the cake onto a serving plate and shake sharply to release the cake.

8. Make the topping: In a small saucepan, stir the jam over low heat until melted. Remove the pan from the heat. Stir in the honey until blended. Put the almonds into a small bowl. Pour the jam mixture through a strainer over the almonds. Gently stir the almonds with a rubber spatula until coated. Spoon the nut mixture over the top of cake.

9. To serve, slice with a serrated knife.

Makes 16 slices. Per slice: 206 cal, 5 g pro, 36 g car, 5 g fat, 93 mg chol, 66 mg sod

PASSOVER DINNER PLANNING TIMETABLE

3 TO 4 WEEKS AHEAD:
- Make the guest list and write invitations or telephone guests.
- Check supply of chairs, glasses, dishes, and utensils and arrange to borrow or rent what you don't have.

1 WEEK AHEAD:
- Order the capon.
- Make the shopping list. Shop for nonperishable food.
- Prepare the red horseradish. Cover tightly and refrigerate.
- Plan the table setting and centerpiece.
- Bring out china, serving dishes, and serving utensils.
- Polish silver if necessary.
- Be sure to have haggadahs ready if you plan to use them.

2 DAYS AHEAD:
- Shop for perishable food. Pick up the capon (if it's frozen, place in the refrigerator to thaw).

- Make the sponge cake. Store wrapped at room temperature.
- Make the gefilte fish terrine. Cover tightly and refrigerate.

1 DAY AHEAD:
- Buy any flowers.
- Prepare the carrots. Store in a zipper-type bag in the refrigerator.
- Make the giblet broth for the pan gravy. Cool, cover, and refrigerate.
- Set the table.
- Select CD's, tapes, or records for music.
- Start making extra ice. Chill beverages.

3 HOURS BEFORE SERVING:
- Prepare and roast the capon.
- Peel the potatoes. Keep covered in water. Chop the onions and parsley.
- Unmold the gefilte fish terrine onto a lettuce-lined serving platter. Cover and refrigerate.
- Transfer the red horseradish to a

serving bowl. Cover loosely with plastic wrap and refrigerate.
- Place the lemon sponge cake on a serving plate. Make the topping and spoon over the cake.

1 HOUR BEFORE SERVING:
- Baste the capon.
- Prepare the mashed potatoes and browned onions. Keep warm.
- Cook the carrots and drain. Chop the mint and garlic.

JUST BEFORE SERVING:
- Finish the carrots and tranfer to a serving dish.
- Transfer the roasted capon to a serving platter. Cover loosely with foil.
- Make the gravy and transfer to a sauceboat. Keep warm.
- Put the potatoes into a serving dish.
- Gently warm the topping for the lemon sponge cake, if necessary, and spoon over the cake.

OLD–FASHIONED THANKSGIVING DINNER FOR 12

MENU

Mulled Cider

Roast Turkey

Cornbread, Sausage, & Onion Stuffing

Foolproof Giblet Gravy

Streusel Sweet Potatoes

Corn Pudding

Green Beans with Shallot Butter

Carrots with Grapes & Dill

Fresh Cranberry-Orange Relish

Scallion-Cheddar Rolls

Pumpkin Cheesecake

Apple, Date, & Pecan Pie

Wine recommendation: Zinfandel or California Chardonnay

"Let's be thankful for all we have, for all we feel, for all whom we love, and for all who love us. Let's look forward to meeting here again next year with friendship, good cider, and a fine turkey."—George Greene

To make Thanksgiving dinner memorable and enjoyable for everyone (including the cook), we've developed a menu that can be prepared in stages. Follow the timetable on page 575 and you'll save frazzled nerves and last-minute panics as never before. What's more, you'll actually look forward to eating what you've made.

OLD-FASHIONED THANKSGIVING

MULLED CIDER

Serves 12
Preparation time: 5 minutes
Cooking time: 35 minutes

As this punch simmers it will fill the house with a rich, spicy fragrance. To make mulled cranberry-cider, use 8 cups of apple cider with 4 cups of cranberry juice cocktail.

12 cups (3 quarts) apple cider
3 cinnamon sticks
4 whole cloves
3 strips orange peel, removed with a vegetable peeler
1 cup dark rum (optional)
For garnish: orange slices, whole cloves, cinnamon sticks

1. In a large pot, combine the cider, cinnamon sticks, cloves, and orange peel. Bring to a boil over medium-high heat. Reduce the heat and simmer uncovered for 25 to 35 minutes.

2. Line a strainer with cheesecloth and set it over a clean large saucepan. Strain the cider mixture into the pan and keep warm.

3. When ready to serve, put 1 to 2 tablespoons rum into mugs, then fill to the rim with the hot cider. Garnish and serve.

Makes 13 cups. Per 1 cup: 118 cal, 0 g pro, 29 g car, 0 g fat, 0 mg chol, 8 mg sod

ROAST TURKEY

Serves 12
Preparation time: 30 minutes
Cooking time: 4½ hours

Plan to have the turkey done 30 to 45 minutes before rest of meal. Once cooked, a whole turkey will stay warm for at least 1 hour. See "Turkey Roasting Chart," page 565, for turkey weights and cooking times.

1 (12- to 16-pound) whole turkey, fresh or frozen, thawed
Salt
Ground black pepper
Cornbread, Sausage, & Onion Stuffing (see page 565)
Vegetable oil
Chicken broth

1. Heat the oven to 325°F. Remove the giblets, neck, and any fat from the turkey body and neck cavities. Discard the fat. Dry the turkey inside and out with paper towels. Sprinkle the cavities with salt and pepper.

2. Lightly spoon some of the stuffing into the neck cavity. Fold the skin flap under the back and fasten with skewers. Loosely stuff the body cavity and close with turkey lacers or skewers, or sew shut with a trussing needle. Tie or clamp legs together. Twist the wing tips under the back. Rub the skin with oil, salt, and pepper.

3. Place the turkey, breast side up, on a rack in a shallow roasting pan. Insert a meat thermometer into the center of a thigh next to the body (not touching bone). Pour 1 cup of chicken broth into the pan. Roast for 3½ to 4½ hours, basting the bird every 30 to 40 minutes with pan juices, adding more broth or water if pan seems dry. If the breast starts to get too brown, cover loosely with a foil tent.

4. Two-thirds through roasting time, untie the drumsticks so the heat can penetrate the body cavity.

5. About 1 hour before the turkey should be done, start checking the meat thermometer for doneness. When the thermometer reads 180° to 185°F in thigh and the center of the stuffing registers 165°F (to check stuffing insert thermometer through body cavity and leave for 5 minutes), remove the turkey to a serving platter or carving board. Let rest for at least 30 minutes for juicier meat and easier carving.

Per 4-ounce serving without skin or stuffing: 191 cal, 33 g pro, 0 g car, 5 g fat, 87 mg chol, 84 mg sod. With skin: 230 cal, 32 g pro, 0 g car, 10 g fat, 93 mg chol, 103 mg sod

TURKEY ROASTING CHART

Because turkey body shapes differ, these cooking times are approximate. The times are based on open-pan roasting of a chilled turkey (with a starting internal temperature of 40°F) in a 325°F oven.

WEIGHT (POUNDS)	UNSTUFFED (HOURS)	STUFFED (HOURS)
8 to 12	2¾ to 3	3 to 3½
12 to 14	3 to 3¾	3½ to 4
14 to 18	3¾ to 4¼	4 to 4¼
18 to 20	4¼ to 4½	4¼ to 4¾
20 to 24	4½ to 5	4¾ to 5¼

OLD-FASHIONED THANKSGIVING

CORNBREAD, SAUSAGE, & ONION STUFFING

Serves 12 to 18
Total time: 35 minutes

If you don't want to cook the stuffing in the bird, you can bake it after the turkey has been cooked.

14 cups packaged cornbread stuffing mix or homemade
    cornbread cubes (see page 565)
1 package (about 16 ounces) sweet Italian-style turkey sausage,
    removed from casings
2 tablespoons vegetable oil
3 cups chopped onions
2 cups chopped celery
¾ cup chopped parsley
⅓ cup chopped fresh sage leaves, or 2½ tablespoons dried sage leaves,
    crumbled
1 teaspoon salt
1 teaspoon ground black pepper
1 can (13¾ ounces) chicken broth

1. Put the cornbread cubes into a very large bowl or pot.
2. In a deep large skillet, cook the sausage over medium–high heat, stirring and breaking up the chunks, until browned. Add the sausage with the drippings to the cornbread. ▶

3. Put the oil in the skillet, then add the onions and celery. Cook the vegetables over medium heat for 5 to 7 minutes, stirring often, until crisp-tender. Stir in the parsley, sage, salt, and pepper. Add to the cornbread-sausage mixture. Toss gently to mix. Sprinkle with the broth and mix again.

4. Stuff the neck and body cavities of the turkey. Or bake the stuffing in a covered well-greased baking dish for about 30 minutes, then uncover and bake 15 minutes more, or until browned.

Makes 18 cups, enough to stuff an 18- to 20- pound bird. Per 1 cup: 244 cal, 10 g pro, 30 g car, 10 g fat, 12 mg chol, 720 mg sod

---

OLD-FASHIONED THANKSGIVING

FOOLPROOF GIBLET GRAVY

Serves 12
Preparation time: 15 minutes
Cooking time: 45 minutes

Nothing tastes better than roast turkey with homemade gravy. Here's a recipe that's sure to become part of your holiday menu repertoire.

Turkey neck and giblets (refrigerate liver until needed)
6 cups chicken broth
2 large onions, sliced
1 cup sliced carrots
1 cup dry white wine or water
½ cup celery leaves
6 tablespoons butter or margarine, at room temperature
¾ cup all-purpose flour
Turkey drippings
Salt to taste
Ground black pepper to taste

1. Cut the turkey neck and heart in half. Put into a large saucepan along with the gizzard and the chicken broth, onions, carrots, wine, and celery leaves. Bring to a boil, reduce the heat, and simmer gently, uncovered, for 1 ½ hours. Add the liver and simmer for 30 minutes more, or until the gizzard is very tender.

2. Remove the giblets to a cutting board. Strain the broth into a large cup measure, pressing the vegetables to extract as much liquid as possible. Discard the vegetables. Add extra water to the broth if needed to make 6 cups. Chop the giblets and neck meat. Refrigerate in covered container.

HOMEMADE CORNBREAD FOR STUFFING

♦ In a large bowl, mix 2½ cups all-purpose flour, 1½ cups yellow cornmeal, ¼ cup granulated sugar, 4 teaspoons baking powder, 1 teaspoon baking soda, and 1 teaspoon salt. Stir in 2 cups plain nonfat yogurt or buttermilk, ⅓ cup vegetable oil, and 4 large egg whites until fairly smooth.

♦ Spread the mixture in a greased 15½ x 10½-inch jelly-roll pan. Bake at 400°F for 20 minutes, or until a toothpick inserted into the center comes out clean.

♦ Set the pan on a wire rack to cool. Leave the cornbread uncovered for 8 hours or overnight to dry out. Cut into ½-inch cubes. Store airtight at room temperature up to 1 week.

M AKE AHEAD

Prepare the gravy
through step 4 up to
3 days ahead. Place
waxed paper or plastic
wrap directly on the
surface to keep a skin
from forming; refrig-
erate. Reheat before
continuing with step 5.

3. Mash the butter and flour with a fork or the back of a spoon until blended to a paste. Break it into 4 chunks.

4. In a medium-size saucepan, bring the broth to a boil, reduce the heat to low, and gradually whisk in the flour mixture, 1 chunk at a time, until well blended. Whisk until thickened and boiling. Boil for 3 minutes to cook out any floury taste.

5. After the turkey is removed from the roasting pan: Pour the pan drippings into a 2-cup glass measure. Spoon the fat from the top and discard. Add enough water to equal 2 cups. Pour the mixture back into the roasting pan. Stir in the giblets and neck meat. Heat over medium-low heat, scraping up the brown bits on the bottom of the pan, until hot. Season to taste with salt and pepper.

Per ¼ cup: 82 cal, 6 g pro, 4 g car, 4 g fat, 49 mg chol, 281 mg sod

OLD-FASHIONED THANKSGIVING

STREUSEL SWEET POTATOES

Serves 12
Preparation time: 50 minutes
Baking time: 45 minutes

Sweet potatoes are a Thanksgiving classic. Here they are baked with maple syrup and orange juice and served with a crunchy, sweet streusel topping. To save on calories, use reduced-calorie margarine and pancake syrup.

3½ pounds medium-size sweet potatoes, peeled
¾ cup maple pancake syrup
⅓ cup orange juice
¼ cup (½ stick) butter or margarine, cut into small pieces

STREUSEL TOPPING
¼ cup all-purpose flour
3 tablespoons packed light brown sugar
½ teaspoon ground cinnamon
⅓ cup pecans, chopped coarse

1. Heat the oven to 325°F. Lightly grease a shallow 1½-quart baking dish or casserole.

2. Cook the potatoes in a large pot of boiling water for 20 to 30 minutes, or until firm-tender when tested with a fork. Drain and cool under cold water. Cut in ½-inch-thick slices. Arrange the slices in the prepared ▶

dish in concentric circles, overlapping the slices slightly.

3. In a small bowl, mix ½ cup of the pancake syrup with the orange juice. Pour over the potatoes. Dot with 1 tablespoon butter. Cover tightly with foil.

4. Bake for 20 to 30 minutes, or until hot and the potatoes have absorbed some liquid.

5. Make the topping: In a medium-size bowl, mix the flour, brown sugar, and cinnamon. With 2 knives, cut in the remaining 3 tablespoons butter until the mixture resembles very coarse crumbs. Stir in the chopped pecans. Refrigerate if making ahead.

6. Remove the potatoes from the oven. Uncover and sprinkle with the streusel topping. Bake uncovered for 15 minutes more, or until the topping is bubbly and lightly browned. Pour over the remaining ¼ cup pancake syrup. Serve right away.

Per serving: 234 cal, 2 g pro, 43 g car, 7 g fat, 10 mg chol with butter, 0 mg chol with margarine, 58 mg sod

OLD-FASHIONED THANKSGIVING

CORN PUDDING

Serves 12
Preparation time: 10 minutes
Baking time: 45 minutes

A cross between custard and cornbread, this old-fashioned side dish is updated with the addition of hot-pepper sauce and minced red bell pepper. To save on calories, use 8 egg whites instead of 4 whole eggs and two 12-ounce cans of evaporated skimmed milk instead of fresh whole milk. Any leftovers can be sliced and pan-fried for a tasty breakfast treat.

3 cups milk
4 large eggs
1 bag (28 ounces) frozen whole-kernel corn, thawed (4¾ cups)
⅓ cup minced red bell pepper
⅓ cup minced onion
1 teaspoon salt
10 drops hot-pepper sauce

1. Heat the oven to 325°F. Lightly grease a shallow 2-quart baking dish.
2. In a large saucepan, heat the milk just until boiling.
3. Meanwhile, put the eggs and 2 cups of the corn in a food processor or blender. Blend until almost smooth.

Ⓜ AKE AHEAD

The potatoes can be assembled up to 1 day ahead and refrigerated, tightly covered. Bring to room temperature before baking. The streusel topping can be made up to 1 week ahead.

Ⓜ AKE AHEAD

The bell pepper and onion can be minced 1 day ahead.

4. Add the remaining corn, the bell pepper, onion, salt, and hot pepper sauce to the hot milk. Remove the pan from the heat and stir in the egg mixture.

5. Pour into the prepared dish. Bake uncovered for 45 minutes, or just until firm to the touch. Serve right away.

Per serving: 123 cal, 6 g pro, 17 g car, 4 g fat, 79 mg chol, 239 mg sod

OLD-FASHIONED THANKSGIVING

GREEN BEANS WITH SHALLOT BUTTER

Serves 12
Preparation time: 20 minutes
Cooking time: 18 minutes

MAKE AHEAD

Trim the beans 1 day
ahead and make the
shallot butter up to 5
days ahead.

Tossed with shallots, butter, and chopped fresh parsley, the green beans are quick and easy to prepare. Be sure not to overcook the beans, or they will lose their bright green color. To save on calories, use reduced-calorie margarine.

½ cup (1 stick) butter or margarine
1 tablespoon olive oil
⅔ cup thinly sliced shallots or white part of scallions
½ teaspoon salt
½ teaspoon ground black pepper
3 pounds fresh green beans, ends trimmed
⅓ cup chopped fresh parsley
For garnish: toasted slivered almonds (optional)

1. In a small skillet, melt ¼ cup (½ stick) butter with the oil over medium heat. Add the shallots and cook for 7 to 9 minutes over low heat, stirring occasionally, until very tender. Stir in the remaining butter and the salt and pepper. Remove the skillet from the heat.

2. Cook the green beans uncovered in a large pot of boiling water for 5 to 7 minutes, until crisp-tender. Drain well and transfer to a serving bowl.

3. Add the shallot butter and parsley. Toss to mix and coat.

4. Garnish with toasted almonds and serve right away.

Per serving: 116 cal, 2 g pro, 9 g car, 9 g fat, 21 mg chol with butter, 0 mg chol with margarine, 182 mg sod

CARROTS WITH GRAPES & DILL

Serves 12

Preparation time: 20 minutes
Cooking time: 12 minutes

Carrots and grapes may seem like an unusual pair, but they make a colorful and tasty combination. To save on calories, use reduced-calorie margarine.

3 pounds carrots, peeled or scraped and cut into 1½-inch chunks
   (8 cups)
¼ cup (½ stick) butter or margarine
2 cups seedless grapes, preferably red
½ teaspoon salt
¼ cup snipped fresh dill or chopped parsley

1. Cook the carrots uncovered in a large pot of boiling water for 8 to 10 minutes, or until crisp-tender. Drain. (Refrigerate in plastic bags if cooking early. Bring to room temperature before proceeding.)

2. In a large saucepan, melt the butter over medium heat. Add the carrots and stir until well coated. Stir in the grapes and salt. Cook for 2 minutes, or until hot. Sprinkle with the dill.

Per serving: 88 cal, 1 g pro, 13 g car, 4 g fat, 10 mg chol with butter, 0 mg chol with margarine, 168 mg sod

FRESH CRANBERRY–ORANGE RELISH

Serves 12

Preparation time: 15 minutes plus at least 1 hour to chill

This uncooked relish is made special by adding chopped fresh oranges. Serve with roast turkey, chicken, or pork.

1 navel orange (about 8 ounces), unpeeled and cut into small chunks
1 bag (12 ounces) cranberries, washed and stemmed
¾ cup granulated sugar
For garnish: orange twist and whole cranberries (optional)

Ⓜ AKE AHEAD

The relish can be made up to 1 week ahead. Refrigerate in an airtight container.

1. Process the orange, cranberries, and sugar in a food processor using on/off turns until finely chopped.

2. Cover and chill for at least 1 hour. Spoon the relish into a serving dish and garnish with an orange twist and whole cranberries.

Makes 3 cups. Per ¼ cup: 69 cal, 0 g pro, 18 g car, 0 g fat, 0 mg chol, 1 mg sod

OLD-FASHIONED THANKSGIVING

SCALLION–CHEDDAR ROLLS

Serves 24
Preparation time: 20 minutes plus 20 minutes to rise
Baking time: 15 minutes per batch

MAKE AHEAD

The rolls can be made
up to 6 hours ahead.
Wrap in aluminum foil
and warm in the oven
before serving.

These rolls, enhanced with Cheddar cheese and scallions, are quick and easy to prepare because they begin with hot-roll mix. This is a terrific recipe to have on hand for any celebration because it can be easily adapted to any menu by substituting for the cheese and scallions and omitting the celery seeds. Be sure to serve the rolls warm.

1 cup finely chopped scallions
4 ounces Cheddar cheese, shredded (1 cup)
1 teaspoon celery seeds
1 teaspoon ground black pepper
2 boxes (16 ounces each) hot-roll mix

1. Grease 3 large baking sheets.

2. Add the scallions, cheese, celery seeds, and pepper to the dry hot-roll mix, then prepare the mix according to the package directions.

3. Divide the dough into thirds. Working with one third at a time, cut each third into 24 pieces. Roll each piece into a ball and arrange, with sides touching, in 2 curves (12 balls each) on a prepared baking sheet. Repeat with remaining dough.

4. Cover loosely with greased plastic wrap and let rise in a warm place (80°F to 85°F) for 20 minutes, or until almost doubled in volume.

5. Heat the oven to 375°F. Uncover the rolls and bake 1 sheet at a time for 15 minutes, or until golden brown. Set the sheet(s) on a wire rack.

6. To serve, tear the baked strips apart and serve warm from a bread basket.

Makes 72 rolls. Per roll: 58 cal, 2 g pro, 9 g car, 2 g fat, 9 mg chol, 100 mg sod

PUMPKIN CHEESECAKE

Serves 18
Preparation time: 15 minutes
Baking time: 1 hour 20 minutes plus 6 hours to chill

One taste of this velvety smooth dessert and you'll never believe that it is substantially lower in fat and calories than a traditional cheesecake.

GRAHAM CRACKER CRUST

⅓ cup reduced-calorie margarine, at room temperature
2 cups graham-cracker crumbs (from about 15 double crackers)

PUMPKIN FILLING

1 container (24 ounces) nonfat cottage cheese (3 cups)
1 tub (12 ounces) light process cream-cheese product
1¼ cups packed light brown sugar
2 large eggs
Whites from 2 large eggs
1 can (16 ounces) solid-pack pumpkin
2 tablespoons cornstarch
2 teaspoons pumpkin-pie spice
1 teaspoon pure vanilla extract

For garnish: caramelized pecan halves (see Cook's Tip)

1. Lightly grease the bottom and sides of a 9 x 3-inch springform pan.

2. Make the crust: In a medium-size bowl, mix the margarine and graham cracker crumbs until evenly moistened. Press the moistened crumbs over the bottom and 2 inches up the side of the prepared pan.

3. Heat the oven to 325°F. Make the filling: In a food processor or blender, process the cottage cheese and cream-cheese product for about 2 minutes, scraping down sides 2 or 3 times, until thick and smooth. Add the brown sugar and process until the sugar dissolves. Add the eggs and egg whites and process just until blended. Transfer the mixture to a large bowl. Stir in the pumpkin, cornstarch, spice, and vanilla until well blended and smooth. Pour into the prepared crust.

4. Bake for 1 hour 20 minutes, or until the top of the cake looks set (the center may jiggle and the top crack). Turn the oven off. Let the cake cool in the oven for 2 hours.

5. Remove the cheesecake from the oven. Set on a wire rack to cool com-

MAKE AHEAD

You can make the cheesecake and caramelize the pecans up to 4 days ahead.

COOK'S TIP

To make caramelized pecan halves: Arrange 20 pecan halves 1 inch apart on a foil-lined cookie sheet. Cook ½ cup sugar in a small dry saucepan over medium-low heat, stirring occasionally, until melted and dark amber in color. Slowly pour over the pecans. Let cool until hard. Break apart.

pletely. Cover and refrigerate in the pan for at least 6 hours, or up to 4 days.

6. To serve, run a knife around the inside edge of the pan. Remove the pan sides. Place the cake on a serving plate. Garnish with pecans.

Makes 18 slices. Per slice: 219 cal, 9 g pro, 31 g car, 7 g fat, 35 mg chol, 381 mg sod

OLD-FASHIONED THANKSGIVING

APPLE, DATE, & PECAN PIE

Serves 8
Preparation time: 30 minutes
Baking time: 40 minutes

This pie is delicious the day it's made but even better the next day, when the flavor of the dates has had time to develop. Serve with softly whipped cream.

Dough for single-crust pie (page 461)
2 large eggs
1 tablespoon pure vanilla extract
⅔ cup packed light or dark brown sugar
½ cup all-purpose flour
½ teaspoon baking powder
1 pound apples, peeled, quartered, cored,and chopped
   into ½-inch pieces (3 cups)
⅔ cup (3½ ounces) snipped dates
⅔ cup pecans; coarsely chop about half

1. On a lightly floured surface with a lightly floured rolling pin, roll out the dough into a 12-inch circle. Line a 9-inch pie plate with the dough. Turn the edge under and flute or crimp.

2. Place the oven rack in the lowest position. Heat the oven to 375°F.

3. In a large bowl, beat the eggs until blended. Brush about 1 teaspoon of the eggs on the edge of the dough.

4. Add the vanilla, sugar, flour, and baking powder to the remaining eggs. Stir until well blended. Stir in the apples, dates, and pecans. Spread in the lined pie plate.

5. Bake for 35 to 40 minutes, or until lightly browned and a toothpick inserted near the center comes out clean.

6. Set the plate on a wire rack to cool. Serve at room temperature. Keeps well up to 3 days.

Makes 8 slices. Per slice: 389 cal, 5 g pro, 58 g car, 16 g fat, 59 mg chol with butter, 53mg chol with margarine, 78 mg sod

THANKSGIVING DINNER PLANNING TIMETABLE

3 TO 4 WEEKS AHEAD:
- Make out guest list. Write invitations or telephone guests.
- Check supply of chairs, dishes, glasses, utensils, and arrange to borrow or rent what you don't have.

1 TO 2 WEEKS AHEAD:
- Order the turkey to be sure you get the size you want. Make sure it fits in the refrigerator and oven.
- Make shopping list. Shop for nonperishable food.
- Plan the table settings and centerpiece.

SATURDAY BEFORE THANKSGIVING:
- Pick up the turkey if frozen.
- Get out the china, serving dishes, and serving utensils. Polish silver if necessary.

MONDAY BEFORE THANKSGIVING:
- Shop for perishable food.
- Put the frozen turkey in the refrigerator to thaw.
- Make the giblet gravy. Refrigerate.
- Prepare the fresh cranberry-orange relish. Refrigerate in a covered serving bowl.
- Make the streusel for the streusel sweet potatoes. Refrigerate.

TUESDAY BEFORE THANKSGIVING:
- Make the shallot butter for the green beans. Cover and refrigerate.
- Prepare the homemade cornbread for the stuffing.

- Chop the onions, celery, parsley, and sage for the cornbread stuffing. Refrigerate.
- Mince the bell pepper and onion for the corn pudding. Refrigerate.
- Make the pumpkin cheesecake (if serving). Cool in the pan, cover, and refrigerate.
- Make the apple, date, and pecan pie. Store covered at room temperature.
- Start making extra ice.

THE DAY BEFORE THANKSGIVING:
- Buy any flowers.
- Pick up the turkey if fresh. Refrigerate.
- Pull the grapes from stems for the carrots.
- Trim the green beans.
- Cook the carrots. Store in plastic bags.
- Prepare streusel sweet potatoes through step 3.
- Set dinner table and arrange the centerpiece.
- Make the pumpkin pie (if serving). Store covered in the refrigerator.
- Chill beverages.
- Select CDs or tapes for music.

THANKSGIVING MORNING:
- Make the stuffing and stuff the turkey. Spoon the extra stuffing into a baking dish.
- Start roasting a 12- to 16-pound turkey so it will be done 45 minutes before dinner. Check the turkey roasting chart (page 565) for roasting time if bird is smaller or larger.
- Snip the dill for the carrots.

- Remove the cooked carrots from the refrigerator.
- Make the scallion-cheddar rolls.

2 HOURS BEFORE SERVING:
- Bring the sweet potatoes to room temperature.
- Prepare the corn pudding.
- Fill a creamer for coffee and refrigerate.
- Make the cider and set aside.

45 MINUTES BEFORE SERVING:
- Transfer the turkey to a serving platter. Cover lightly with foil.
- Bake the corn pudding.
- Bake the streusel sweet potatoes.
- Set out the butter.
- Warm the cider and serve to guests while waiting for dinner.

30 MINUTES BEFORE SERVING:
- Heat the giblet gravy. Add the turkey drippings.
- Finish cooking the green beans with shallot butter.
- Finish cooking the carrots with grapes and dill.
- Set the pumpkin pie out at room temperature or transfer the cheesecake to a serving plate.

JUST BEFORE SERVING:
- Garnish the turkey platter and the cranberry-orange relish.
- Put all of the food into serving dishes and set out.
- Pour the gravy into a gravy boat.

JUST BEFORE SERVING DESSERT:
- Make the orange whipped cream for the pumpkin pie (if serving).

ONE-HOUR THANKSGIVING DINNER FOR 6

If you haven't got all day to make Thanksgiving dinner, you can still put a feast on the table. Follow the step-by-step directions in the proper sequence and, chances are, you'll even have a few spare minutes to freshen up before you serve the soup.

MENU

Mugs of Corn Chowder

Turkey Breast with Mushroom Gravy
Pecan Stuffing
Orange Mashed Sweet Potatoes
Vegetable Casserole
Cran-Pineapple Relish

Pumpkin Pie*
Fresh Fruit Bowl*
Nuts in Shell*

*Recipe not provided

THE NIGHT BEFORE:

◆ Set the table and get out all the necessary serving dishes and utensils. Arrange a fresh fruit bowl with nuts (don't forget a nutcracker) and place on the table as the centerpiece. Line up non-perishable food in order of use on kitchen counter.

ONE HOUR BEFORE DINNER:

◆ Heat the oven to 350°F. Empty two 16-ounce bags of mixed vegetables such as cauliflower, broccoli, and red peppers) into a shallow baking dish. Sprinkle with packaged seasoned bread crumbs and dot with butter. Cover and place in the oven.

◆ Drain one 40-ounce can of yams (sweet potatoes). Put into a deep casserole and mash with ¼ cup each pancake syrup and orange juice, 2 tablespoons butter, and ½ teaspoon each nutmeg and salt. Cover and place in the oven.

◆ Stack 1½ pounds of ¼-inch-thick slices of cooked turkey breast (from the deli section) in the middle of a large sheet of foil, sprinkling each slice with a little dried sage. Top with 1 tablespoon of butter. Wrap airtight and place in a shallow baking dish. Place in the oven.

◆ Mix one 16-ounce can of whole-berry cranberry sauce with one 8-ounce can of crushed pineapple. Cover and refrigerate.

◆ Slice 3 scallions (for the soup) and prepare parsley sprigs for garnish.

◆ Prepare one 6-ounce box of range-top stuffing mix according to package directions, adding ½ cup of pecans with the stuffing.

◆ Prepare 2 cans of condensed cream of corn soup with milk according to the package directions. Stir in the sliced scallions and place the saucepan over low heat.

◆ Mix and heat two 12-ounce jars of turkey gravy and one 4-ounce can of sliced mushrooms.

◆ Uncover the vegetable dish. Return to the oven to brown the crumbs.

◆ Just before dinner: Pour the soup in mugs. Serve in the living room.

◆ Just before dinner: Put the bowl of cranberry relish on the table. Remove the turkey from the oven and carefully open the foil. Arrange the slices in the middle of a large serving platter. Spoon the juices from the foil, then some gravy over the turkey. Spoon the stuffing on one side of the turkey and the mixed vegetables on the other side. Garnish with parsley sprigs. Pour the remaining gravy into a sauceboat and serve at the table.

◆ For dessert, serve purchased pumpkin pie with whipped cream and set out bowls of fresh fruit and nuts in shells. Accompany with coffee and tea.

CHRISTMAS BUFFET
FOR 12 OR 24

This bountiful holiday buffet includes a wide array of dishes that are as easy on the eyes as they are on the cook. It will be a pleasure to host because the recipes can be made ahead, require a minimum of last-minute fuss, and are served at room temperature. Another helpful feature is that the menu can be adapted to serve twelve or twenty-four. For decoration, just tie some gold ribbons on your sideboard, or drape a table in a white cloth and decorate it with holly leaves and candles at different heights.

CHRISTMAS BUFFET

HAM WITH
APPLE–MUSTARD GLAZE

Serves 12 with leftovers
Total time: 1 hour 20 minutes plus 10 minutes to stand

The spiral-cut fully cooked ham for this recipe is machine-sliced on the bone for easy serving. It's available in many supermarkets. For 24 servings, buy a 14- to 18-pound whole ham, double the glaze recipe, and increase the baking time by 8 minutes per pound of ham.

APPLE–MUSTARD GLAZE
½ cup (6 ounces) apple jelly
1 tablespoon Dijon mustard
1 tablespoon bourbon (optional)
1½ teaspoons lemon juice
⅛ teaspoon ground cloves

1 (7- to 9-pound) shank-portion spiral-cut ham
For garnish: fresh pineapple wedges (optional)

1. Make the glaze: Melt the jelly in a small saucepan or in microwave. Remove the pan from the heat. Whisk in the mustard, bourbon, lemon juice, and cloves until well blended. Cool to room temperature.

2. Heat the oven to 350°F.

3. Stand the ham, cut side down, in a roasting pan (this seals in moisture and keeps slices from separating during heating). Bake for about 1 hour (8 minutes per pound). Remove the ham from the oven. Increase the oven temperature to 450°F. Brush the ham with the glaze and return to the oven

MENU

Ham with Apple-Mustard Glaze

Turkey Breast with Garlic-Herb Mayonnaise

Angel Biscuits

Cheddar Scalloped Potatoes

Marinated Sesame Vegetables

Pasta Seafood Salad

Fennel & Orange Salad

Romaine Salad with Cucumber Dressing

Brandied Cranberry Relish

English Trifle

Christmas Cookies: Spritz Wreaths Lebkuchen Spiced Raisin Chews

---

Spirited Cranberry Punch

Light Eggnog

for 5 to 7 minutes more, or until glazed. Remove from the oven and let stand for 10 minutes before serving.

4. To serve, place the ham on its side on a serving platter. Gently fan the slices out from the bone. Surround with pineapple wedges.

Per serving: 163 cal, 18 g pro, 11 g car, 5 g fat, 45 mg chol, 1,058 mg sod

CHRISTMAS BUFFET

TURKEY BREAST WITH GARLIC–HERB MAYONNAISE

Serves 12

Preparation time: 50 minutes

Cooking time: 1 hour

The turkey breasts are butterflied (split down the center and flattened), spread with a paste of walnuts and herbs, then rolled up.. For 24 servings, double the recipe.

WALNUT–PARSLEY PASTE

1½ cups Italian (flat-leaf) parsley leaves

1 cup walnut pieces

¼ cup fresh lemon juice

2 tablespoons olive oil

2 large cloves garlic, coarsely chopped

1 teaspoon salt

½ teaspoon dried thyme leaves

½ teaspoon ground black pepper

2 large skinned and boned turkey breast halves
   (about 2½ pounds each)

2 tablespoons vegetable oil

1 can (about 14 ounces) chicken broth

GARLIC–HERB MAYONNAISE

1 medium-size head garlic

2 teaspoons olive oil

½ cup Italian (flat-leaf) parsley leaves

1½ cups mayonnaise

1 tablespoon fresh lemon juice

¼ teaspoon ground black pepper

▶

1. Make the walnut-parsley paste: In a food processor or blender process the parsley, walnuts, lemon juice, olive oil, garlic, salt, thyme, and pepper, scraping down the sides of the container a few times, until thick and smooth.

2. To butterfly the turkey: Hold the turkey breast half flat on a work surface with one hand. Starting from the thickest side, cut through the meat horizontally to within ½ inch of the opposite side. Repeat with the other breast half. Open each half like a book. Place between sheets of heavy-duty plastic wrap or waxed paper and pound with a meat mallet or the bottom of a heavy skillet to a uniform ¾-inch thickness.

3. Spread each breast half with the walnut paste to within ½ inch of the edges and, starting from one long side, tightly roll up. Tuck the ends in and skewer with toothpicks. Tie in several places with kitchen twine.

4. Heat the oven to 350°F. Put the oil in a heavy roasting pan or a shallow rangetop-to-oven baking dish large enough to hold the two turkey rolls without crowding. Placing the pan across two burners, heat the oil over medium-high heat until it looks ripply. Add the turkey rolls and brown on all sides. Remove the pan from the heat, let the oil cool slightly, then pour the broth around the turkey. Cover the pan tightly with foil. Bake for 1 hour, or until a meat thermometer inserted into the middle registers 170°F and the meat is no longer pink in the center.

5. Meanwhile, make the mayonnaise. Slice about ½ inch off the top of the garlic. Place on a 6-inch square of foil, drizzle with oil, and wrap in the foil to seal completely. Bake at 350°F for 1 hour, or until the cloves are tender when pierced through the foil. Cool in the foil.

6. Remove the turkey rolls to a plate. Cool completely. (If not serving right away, cover and refrigerate. Remove from the refrigerator about 1 hour before serving to bring the turkey to room temperature.)

7. Unwrap and separate the garlic cloves, and squeeze the soft garlic from the root ends into a food processor or blender. Add the remaining ingredients. Process, scraping down the sides of the container a few times, until the mayonnaise is pale green. Refrigerate tightly covered until ready to serve.

8. Shortly before serving, cut each breast into 18 slices. Arrange on a serving platter. Serve with the Garlic-Herb Mayonnaise.

Per serving with 2 tablespoons mayonnaise: 535 cal, 49 g pro, 5 g car, 35 g fat, 134 mg chol, 576 mg sod

FESTIVE FOOD:

Here are some ways to turn something simple into something special:

◆ Make an ice ring for your punch bowl, using fruit juice or even sherbert instead of water. It looks nice and it won't water down the punch.

◆ To decorate the rim of a large serving platter, spray it with vegetable oil cooking spray, then sprinkle with one of the following: curry powder, paprika, fresh or dried chopped dill, or chopped fresh parsley. All of this can be done ahead of time.

◆ Keep a sugar shaker (from a cookware store) filled with confectioners' sugar and at the ready in the

CHRISTMAS BUFFET

ANGEL BISCUITS

Serves 12

Preparation time: 20 minutes plus 2½ hours to rise and 3 hours to chill

Baking time: 24 minutes

These biscuits are light as air. Cut them out with cookie cutters or into squares. For 24 servings, double the recipe.

1 package (¼ ounce) active dry yeast
¼ cup granulated sugar
¼ cup warm water (105°F to 115°F)
5½ cups all-purpose flour
1 tablespoon baking powder
1 teaspoon baking soda
1 teaspoon salt
2 cups buttermilk or plain low-fat yogurt
¼ cup (½ stick) butter or margarine, melted and
    cooled slightly

1. In a small bowl, mix the yeast, ½ teaspoon of the sugar, and the water. Let stand for 10 minutes, or until foamy.

2. Meanwhile, in a large bowl, mix the remaining sugar with the flour, baking powder, baking soda, and salt until well blended.

3. Make a well in the center of the flour mixture. Pour in the yeast mixture, buttermilk, and butter. Stir with a wooden spoon until a soft dough forms.

4. Turn the dough out onto a lightly floured surface. Knead gently about 10 times. Gather the dough into a ball.

5. Wipe the bowl clean, then lightly coat with vegetable-oil cooking spray. Add the dough, turn to grease the top, then cover the bowl with plastic wrap. Let rise in a warm, draft-free place for 1½ hours, or until doubled in volume.

6. Punch down the dough. Cover and refrigerate for at least 3 hours.

7. To bake: On a lightly floured surface roll out the dough with a rolling pin to ⅜-inch thickness. Cut the dough with 2-inch angel or star-shaped cookie cutters or, using a pizza wheel or knife, trim the sides straight and cut into 2-inch squares. Reroll and cut the scraps. Place 1 inch apart on ungreased baking sheets, cover loosely, and let rise in a warm, draft-free place for 1 hour, or until doubled in volume.

8. Adjust the oven racks to divide the oven in thirds. Heat the oven to 425°F. Bake 1 sheet on each rack, switching positions halfway through baking, for 10 to 12 minutes, or until the biscuits are light golden. ▶

9. Set the baking sheets on wire racks to cool. Serve the biscuits warm or at room temperature.

Makes 50 biscuits. Per biscuit: 68 cal, 2 g pro, 12 g car, 1 g fat, 3 mg chol with butter, 0 mg chol with margarine, 119 mg sod with buttermilk, 115 mg sod with yogurt

CHRISTMAS BUFFET

CHEDDAR SCALLOPED POTATOES
Serves 12
Preparation time: 25 minutes
Cooking time: 1 hour 10 minutes

These cheddary potatoes are a proven favorite. Another way to enjoy the casserole is to add a layer of thinly sliced baked ham between the potato layers. For 24 servings, double the recipe and bake in 2 dishes.

3½ pounds baking potatoes (about 7 large), peeled and sliced
⅛ inch thick (10 cups)
4 ounces Cheddar cheese, shredded (1 cup)
½ cup sliced scallions
1 teaspoon salt
½ teaspoon ground black pepper
2 tablespoons all-purpose flour
3 cups milk

1. Heat the oven to 350°F. Grease a shallow 3-quart baking dish.
2. Layer half the potatoes over the bottom of the prepared dish. Sprinkle with half the cheese, half the scallions, and half the salt and pepper. Cover with the remaining potatoes.
3. Put the flour into a small bowl. Whisk in the milk until blended. Pour the mixture evenly over the potatoes. Sprinkle with the remaining cheese, scallions, salt, and pepper.
4. Bake uncovered for 1 hour to 1 hour 10 minutes, or until the potatoes are very tender and the top is lightly browned.

Per serving: 155 cal, 6 g pro, 21 g car, 5 g fat, 18 mg chol, 278 mg sod

MAKE AHEAD

The baked biscuits can be frozen in an airtight container up to 1 month.

COOK'S TIP

Russet or Idaho potatoes, which are long with rounded ends and rough brown skin, are considered baking potatoes.

**6 NO-COOK LOW-
CAL BUFFET
HORS D'OUEVRES:**

They're quick to fix,
too.

◆ Fill mushroom
caps with salsa.

◆ Dip canned
shrimp in lemon
juice and snipped
dill and stuff
into split cherry
tomatoes.

◆ Spear cherry
tomatoes and
pepperoncini (pick-
led Tuscan peppers)
on picks.

◆ Stuff bite-size
pieces of celery or
spears of Belgian
endive with
Neufchâtel cheese
and sprinkle with
red caviar.

◆ Skewer zucchini
slices on picks with
canned smoked
oysters.

◆ Put rolled caper-
filled anchovies
into bell-pepper
wedges.

CHRISTMAS BUFFET

MARINATED SESAME VEGETABLES

Serves 12
Preparation time: 30 minutes plus 4 hours to chill
Cooking time: 14 minutes

Here is one the easiest and prettiest ways to serve vegetables for a party. The sesame dressing, gives them an Asian essence. For 24 servings, double the recipe.

1½ bunches (about 1¾ pounds) broccoli, cut into florets and stems cut
    into bite-size pieces
8 large carrots, cut diagonally into thin slices

SESAME DRESSING
1 cup vegetable oil
½ cup red wine vinegar
⅓ cup Dijon mustard
¼ cup dark Asian sesame oil
1½ tablespoons minced fresh garlic
1½ teaspoons salt
¾ teaspoon granulated sugar
¾ teaspoon ground black pepper

2 medium-size (1 pound) summer squash, halved lengthwise and cut
    crosswise into thin slices (4½ cups)
2 medium-size (1 pound) red bell peppers, seeded and cut into 1-inch
    pieces (3 cups)

1. Bring a large pot of water to a boil. Add the broccoli and boil for 5 to 6 minutes, or until crisp-tender. Scoop out with a slotted spoon and plunge into cold water. Drain very well. Repeat the procedure in the same boiling water with the carrots, cooking them for 7 to 8 minutes.
2. Make the dressing: In a large serving bowl, whisk together the oil, vinegar, mustard, sesame oil, garlic, salt, sugar, and pepper until well blended.
3. Add the vegetables, except the broccoli, and toss to mix and coat well. Cover and refrigerate for at least 4 hours, stirring every few hours.
4. Just before serving, stir in the broccoli.

Per serving: 269 cal, 3 g pro, 14 g car, 23 g fat, 0 mg chol, 469 mg sod

CHRISTMAS BUFFET

PASTA SEAFOOD SALAD

Serves 12
Preparation time: 15 minutes
Cooking time: 12 minutes

This salad has a zesty mayonnaise dressing that teams well with the pasta and seafood. For a more colorful dish, use tricolor pasta shells or rotini. For 24 servings, double the recipe.

1 pound medium-size pasta shells
4 ounces fresh snow peas, strings removed, cut in half (1¼ cups)

DRESSING
1 cup mayonnaise
2 tablespoons fresh lemon juice
1 tablespoon Dijon mustard
¼ teaspoon salt
⅛ teaspoon ground red pepper (cayenne)

8 ounces imitation crabmeat, large chunks torn into bite-size
    pieces (1¾ cups)
½ cup chopped red onion
½ cup chopped fresh cilantro

1. Bring a large pot of lightly salted water to a boil. Add the pasta and cook according to the package directions. Drain, rinse under cold running water, and drain again.

2. Meanwhile, bring a medium-size saucepan of water to a boil. Add the snow peas and boil for 1 to 2 minutes, or until bright green. Drain, plunge into cold water, and drain again.

3. Make the dressing. In a large bowl, mix the mayonnaise, lemon juice, mustard, salt, and pepper until well blended.

4. Add the pasta, snow peas, crabmeat, onion, and cilantro. Stir gently to mix and coat. Serve right away or cover and refrigerate and remove about 30 minutes before serving.

Per serving: 295 cal, 7 g pro, 32 g car, 15 g fat, 14 mg chol, 474 mg sod

FENNEL & ORANGE SALAD

Serves 12

Preparation time: 20 minutes

Fennel, also known as finocchio or anise, is a crunchy vegetable that tastes like licorice and looks like a bunch of celery with a fat bottom. Use the wispy leaves to flavor and garnish the salad. For 24 servings, double the recipe.

DRESSING

⅓ cup olive oil

¼ cup orange juice

2 tablespoons distilled white vinegar

½ teaspoon salt

FENNEL & ORANGE SALAD

2 fennel bulbs (1½ pounds), root ends and tough stalks cut off,
   bulbs cut in half lengthwise, then sliced into narrow strips (6 cups)

2 navel oranges, peel and white pith removed, cut into segments

¼ cup thinly sliced red onion

¼ cup chopped fennel leaves

For garnish: fennel leaves (optional)

1. Make the dressing: In a large serving bowl, whisk together the oil, orange juice, vinegar, and salt.

2. Make the salad: Add the fennel, oranges, onion, and fennel leaves to the bowl. Toss to mix and coat.

3. Garnish the salad with fennel leaves just before serving.

Per serving: 74 cal, 1 g pro, 5 g car, 6 g fat, 0 mg chol, 132 mg sod

ROMAINE SALAD WITH CUCUMBER DRESSING

Serves 12

Preparation time: 15 minutes

To keep this salad fresh and crunchy, don't dress it before serving, but offer the dressing in a pitcher so the guests can pour their own. For 24 servings, double the recipe.

▶

CUCUMBER DRESSING

1 medium-size cucumber, peeled, halved lengthwise, seeded,
   and cut into chunks
1 small onion, peeled and quartered
⅓ cup vegetable oil
½ cup plain low-fat or nonfat yogurt
3 tablespoons cider vinegar
2 teaspoons granulated sugar
2 teaspoons caraway seeds (optional)
1 teaspoon salt
½ teaspoon ground black pepper

1 large head (1¾ pounds) romaine lettuce, rinsed and torn
   into bite-size pieces (12 cups)
1 bag (6 ounces) red radishes, trimmed and sliced thin (1¾ cups)

1. Make the dressing: In a food processor, combine the cucumber, onion, oil, yogurt, vinegar, sugar, caraway seeds, salt, and pepper. Process until creamy. Pour into a serving pitcher, cover, and refrigerate.

2. To serve, toss the lettuce and radishes in a large serving bowl. Stir the dressing and serve from the pitcher.

Per serving: 77 cal, 2 g pro, 4 g car, 6 g fat, 1 mg chol with low-fat yogurt, 0 mg chol with nonfat yogurt, 199 mg sod

> **COOK'S TIP**
>
> Cresent-shaped caraway seeds have a nutty, slightly sweet flavor that is reminiscent of anise. These give rye bread its distinctive flavor and aroma. Store caraway seeds in a cool, dark place up to 6 months.

CHRISTMAS BUFFET

BRANDIED CRANBERRY RELISH

Serves 12
Preparation time: 5 minutes
Cooking time: 1 hour

This cranberry relish, spiked with apple brandy, is excellent with both ham and turkey. For 24 servings, double the recipe.

2 cups fresh cranberries, rinsed and stemmed, or frozen cranberries,
   thawed
1 cup granulated sugar
¼ cup apple brandy

1. Heat the oven to 300°F. Grease a shallow 2-quart baking dish.
2. Spread the cranberries in the prepared dish. Sprinkle evenly with the

(nocnust.
Quiche
potato salad

sugar. Cover and bake for 50 to 60 minutes, stirring twice, until the sugar is completely dissolved. Uncover and stir in the brandy.

3. Pour the mixture into a jar or airtight container. Cool completely, then cover and refrigerate for at least 3 hours.

Makes 1⅓ cups. Per 2 tablespoons: 105 cal, 0 g pro, 25 g car, 0 g fat, 0 mg chol, 0 mg sod

CHRISTMAS BUFFET

ENGLISH TRIFLE

Serves 12

Preparation time: 15 minutes plus at least 4 hours to chill
Cooking time: 12 minutes

A decadent combination of custard, sponge cake, fruit, and sherry wine, all topped with whipped cream, makes a traditional and dreamy finish to the buffet. For 24 servings, double the recipe and serve in 2 dishes.

CUSTARD
½ cup granulated sugar
2 tablespoons cornstarch
¼ teaspoon salt
1 large egg, lightly beaten
2 cups milk
1½ teaspoons pure vanilla extract

1 small sponge cake layer, angel food cake, or poundcake
  (about 11 ounces), cut into ½-inch-thick slices
½ cup cream sherry wine, or orange juice
1 pint fresh raspberries, or 1 package (10 ounces) frozen raspberries
  in syrup
3 cups lightly sweetened whipped cream

1. Make the custard: In a medium-size saucepan, mix the sugar, cornstarch, and salt. Stir in the egg, then slowly whisk in the milk. Bring to a boil over medium heat, stirring often. Boil for 1 minute or until thickened. Remove the pan from the heat and stir in the vanilla. Let cool to warm.

2. To assemble the trifle, line the bottom and sides of a 2-quart clear-glass trifle dish or bowl with half the cake slices. Sprinkle with ¼ cup of the sherry and half the raspberries if using fresh, all if using frozen. Pour the warm custard over the berries. Top with the remaining cake. Sprinkle with the remaining sherry. Cover and refrigerate for at least 4 hours, or overnight. ▶

COOK'S TIP

For 3 cups of whipped cream, you'll need 1½ cups of heavy or whipping cream. You can also use 1 (8 ounce) container of thawed frozen whipped topping instead of whipped cream.

3. To serve, top with the whipped cream and sprinkle with the remaining fresh berries.

Per serving with sponge cake: 256 cal with fresh raspberries, 270 cal with frozen raspberries, 4 g pro, 33 g car with fresh raspberries, 37 g car with frozen raspberries, 12 g fat, 83 mg chol, 145 mg sod

SPRITZ WREATHS

Serves 12 to 24
Preparation time: 30 minutes
Baking time: 6 minutes per batch

You can make these cookies in many shapes besides wreaths, using a cookie press, spritz gun, or pastry bag.

1½ cups (3 sticks) unsalted butter or margarine (not spread),
   at room temperature
1 cup granulated sugar
1 large egg
1 tablespoon pure vanilla extract
1 teaspoon almond extract
3½ cups all-purpose flour
Green liquid food coloring (optional)
For decoration: candy stars, red cinnamon hearts (optional)

1. Heat the oven to 400°F.

2. In a large bowl, beat the butter and sugar with an electric mixer until pale and fluffy. Beat in the egg, vanilla, and almond extract. With the mixer on low speed, beat in the flour until well blended.

3. Add the food coloring, a small amount at a time, beating well after each addition, until the dough is bright green.

4. Spoon 1 cup of the dough at a time into a cookie press or pastry bag fitted with a large star tip. Press the dough into 2-inch wreaths 1 inch apart on ungreased baking sheets. Decorate with candy stars and red cinnamon hearts.

5. Bake for 5 to 6 minutes, or until the bottoms are just barely browned. Set the sheets on wire racks to cool for 2 to 3 minutes before removing the cookies to the racks to cool completely. Store in an airtight container at room temperature up to 2 weeks.

Makes 72 cookies. Per cookie: 69 cal, 1 g pro, 8 g car, 4 g fat, 13 mg chol with butter, 3 mg chol with margarine, 2 mg sod with butter, 46 mg sod with margarine

M AKE AHEAD

The cooled, baked cookies can be frozen airtight up to 3 months. Thaw at room temperature.

LEBKUCHEN

Serves 12 to 24
Preparation time: 45 minutes
Baking time: 10 minutes per batch

Bake these traditional spicy German honey cookies at least 1 week ahead to give the flavors time to mellow. Glazed with a lemon wash, they make a wonderful addition to any Christmas cookie selection.

⅔ cup honey
1 cup packed light or dark brown sugar
2 tablespoons water
2 tablespoons butter or margarine (not spread)
3½ cups all-purpose flour
½ teaspoon baking soda
½ teaspoon salt
½ teaspoon ground ginger
½ teaspoon grated nutmeg
1 teaspoon ground cinnamon
1 cup slivered blanched almonds
½ cup chopped candied orange peel
1 tablespoon grated orange peel

GLAZE
1 cup confectioners' sugar
2 tablespoons hot water
1 tablespoon fresh lemon juice

For decoration: sliced unblanched almonds, red and green
   candied cherries (optional)

1. In a medium-size saucepan, bring the honey, brown sugar, water, and butter to a boil. Remove the pan from the heat and cool to room temperature.

2. Heat the oven to 400° F. Lightly grease baking sheet(s).

3. In a large bowl, mix the flour, baking soda, salt, and spices. Stir in the slivered almonds, the candied and grated orange peel, and then the honey mixture until well blended. Divide the dough in half.

4. On a lightly floured surface with a lightly floured rolling pin, roll half the dough at a time into a 12 x 9-inch rectangle. With a floured knife, make 4 lengthwise, then 9 crosswise cuts. Place the cut rectangles ½ inch apart ▶

COOK'S TIP

Know your oven. Check the temperature occasionally with an oven thermometer and adjust for variances while baking. Even a few degrees can mean overbaked or under-baked cookies.

on the prepared baking sheet(s).

5. Bake for 9 to 10 minutes, or until pale brown and still soft. Set the sheets on wire racks to cool.

6. Meanwhile, make the glaze. In a small bowl, mix the confectioners' sugar, water, and lemon juice until well blended. Brush the glaze over the tops of the cooled cookies. Decorate with sliced almonds and candied cherries. Let stand for about 1 hour, or until the glaze sets. Store airtight at room temperature with waxed paper between the layers up to 2 weeks.

Makes 48 cookies. Per cookie: 102 cal, 2 g pro, 20 g car, 2 g fat, 1 mg chol with butter, 0 mg chol with margarine, 44 mg sod

---

CHRISTMAS BUFFET

SPICED RAISIN CHEWS

Serves 24 to 36

Preparation time: 30 minutes

Baking time: 10 minutes per batch

The freshly ground pepper is an especially nice touch in these cookies.

2 cups all-purpose flour
2 teaspoons ground cinnamon
1 teaspoon ground cloves
½ teaspoon baking powder
½ teaspoon baking soda
½ teaspoon salt
½ teaspoon ground black pepper
1 box (about 15 ounces) raisins
1 cup slivered almonds
¼ cup chopped citron
3 large eggs
2 cups packed light brown sugar
For decoration: confectioners' sugar (optional)

1. In a medium-size bowl, mix the flour, cinnamon, cloves, baking powder, baking soda, salt, and pepper until blended.

2. In a food processor, process the raisins, almonds, and citron using on/off pulses until finely chopped. Add to the flour mixture and mix well (with hands is easiest).

3. In a large bowl, beat the eggs and brown sugar with an electric mixer for 10 minutes, or until thick and pale. With a wooden spoon, stir ▶ *p. 593*

Ⓜ AKE AHEAD

The cooled, baked raisin chews can be frozen airtight up to 3 months. Thaw at room temperature.

SIDE EFFECTS
Carrots with
Grapes & Dill
(p.570) and
Green Beans with
Shallot Butter
(p.569) add color
to your
Thanksgiving.

GIVE THANKS
Serve a Roast Turkey (p.564), left, with Cornbread-Stuffing (p.565) and baked Corn Pudding (p.568)—or even Parmesan Potato Casserole (p.547), all below.

PUMPKIN AND SWEET POTATOES
Add creamy Pumpkin Cheese-cake (p.572), above, and crunchy Streusel Sweet Potatoes (p.567), left, to your Thanksgiving menu for a little creative flair.

in the raisin-flour mixture and mix well (dough will be stiff). Cover and chill for 1 hour, or until firm enough to handle.

4. Heat the oven to 350°F. Lightly grease baking sheet(s).

5. With floured hands, form level tablespoons of the dough into 1-inch balls. Place 2 inches apart on the prepared baking sheet(s).

6. Bake for 10 minutes, or until the cookies are brown on the bottom but still soft on top. Set the sheets on wire racks to cool before removing the cookies to the racks to cool completely. Refrigerate airtight up to 1 month. Roll the edges in confectioners' sugar before serving.

Makes 72 cookies. Per cookie: 71 cal, 1 g pro, 14 g car, 1 g fat, 9 mg chol, 36 mg sod

---

CHRISTMAS BUFFET

SPIRITED CRANBERRY PUNCH

Preparation time: 10 minutes

Serves 24

This holly-red punch is equally good without the vodka. Pour the well-chilled ingredients into the punch bowl just before serving. A fun way to serve the punch is to hang small candy canes over the rims of the punch cups.

2 bottles (48 ounces each) cranberry juice cocktail (12 cups),
   or 2 cans (12 ounces each) frozen cranberry juice cocktail concentrate,
   reconstituted and chilled
1 bottle (48 ounces) cranberry-raspberry drink (6 cups), or 1 can
   (12 ounces) frozen cranberry-raspberry drink concentrate,
   reconstituted and chilled
1 bottle (33.8 ounces) ginger ale (4 cups), chilled
1 bottle (750 ml) nonalcoholic sparkling white grape juice (2½ cups),
   chilled
1½ cups vodka (optional), chilled
For garnish: cranberries, small cinnamon sticks, and orange, lemon, and
   lime slices (optional)

1. In an 8-quart or larger punch bowl, mix the cranberry juice, cranberry-raspberry drink, ginger ale, white grape juice, and vodka.

2. Add the cranberries, cinnamon sticks, and citrus slices.

Makes 26 cups. Per 1 cup: 128 cal, 0 g pro, 32 g car, 0 g fat, 0 mg chol, 10 mg sod

LIGHT EGGNOG

Serves 12 to 24
Preparation time: 5 minutes plus at least 2 hours to chill and freeze
Cooking time: 15 minutes

A favorite way to toast the holidays is with rich and creamy eggnog, which is as high in calories (from the cream) as it is delicious. Our solution is to use fresh skim milk and evaporated skim milk. It's safe to use fresh eggs here because they are cooked, but if you're watching cholesterol use egg substitute instead.

2 quarts (8 cups) skim milk
¾ cup plus 2 tablespoons granulated sugar
⅛ teaspoon grated nutmeg
4 whole eggs, or 8 ounces cholesterol- and fat-free egg substitute
Whites from 2 large eggs
½ cup light rum (optional)
2 teaspoons pure vanilla extract
1 cup evaporated skim milk
For garnish: grated nutmeg (optional)

1. In a medium-size heavy saucepan, mix the skim milk, sugar, and nutmeg. Stir over medium heat until bubbles appear around the edge. Remove the pan from the heat.

2. In a medium-size bowl, whisk together the eggs (or egg substitute) with the egg whites until well blended. Slowly whisk in 2 cups of the scalded milk mixture. Return the mixture to the saucepan. Stir over medium-low heat for about 8 minutes, or until the mixture is just under the boiling point (200°F) and is lightly thickened.

3. Remove the pan from the heat. Stir in the rum and vanilla. Refrigerate the eggnog for at least 2 hours.

4. One hour before serving: Pour the evaporated skim milk into a small bowl and place in the freezer for 45 minutes, or until it starts to freeze around the edges. Beat with an electric mixer until foamy. Add 2 tablespoons of sugar and beat for 5 minutes, or until stiff peaks form when the beaters are lifted. Gently stir (fold) the mixture into the eggnog. Pour into a punch bowl. Sprinkle lightly with nutmeg.

Makes 12 cups. Per ½ cup serving: 80 cal, 5 g pro, 13 g car, 1 g fat, 37 mg chol, 70 mg sod. With egg substitute: 73 cal, 5 g pro, 13 g car, 0 g fat, 2 mg chol, 76 mg sod

COOK'S TIP

Freshly grated nutmeg has more full-bodied flavor and aroma than its ground counterpart. Whole nutmeg is sold in most supermarkets. Look for nutmeg graters in cookware or gourmet stores.

CHRISTMAS BUFFET PLANNING TIMETABLE

1 MONTH AHEAD:

- Make the guest list. Write invitations or telephone guests.
- Make the angel biscuits and the Christmas cookies. Freeze in airtight containers.
- Order the ham and turkey breasts.
- Plan the table setting and any decorations. Check serving dishes and serving utensils. Order any rental items or line up items to borrow such as linens, glasses, silverware, china, tables, coffeepot, etc.

2 WEEKS AHEAD:

- Make shopping list. Shop for nonperishable food.
- Make the brandied cranberry relish. Refrigerate in an airtight container.

1 WEEK AHEAD:

- Make the apple-mustard glaze, garlic herb mayonnaise, and sesame dressing for the marinated vegetables. Refrigerate, tightly covered.

3 DAYS AHEAD:

- Shop for perishable food.
- Make the dressing for the fennel and orange salad, romaine salad, and pasta seafood salad. Refrigerate, tightly covered.

2 DAYS AHEAD:

- Prepare the vegetables for the marinated sesame vegetables. Refrigerate separately in zipper-type bags.
- Prepare the ingredients for the fennel and orange salad. Reserve fennel leaves. Refrigerate

separately in zipper-type bags.
- Grate the cheese and chop the scallions for the cheddar scalloped potatoes. Cover and refrigerate.
- Remove the cookies from the freezer and let thaw at room temperature.
- Decorate the house.
- Select CD's, tapes, or records for music.

1 DAY AHEAD:

- Buy any flowers.
- Butterfly and flatten the turkey breasts. Wrap in plastic and refrigerate.
- Make the walnut-parsley paste. Cover tightly and refrigerate.
- Prepare the pasta seafood salad. Cover and refrigerate.
- Prepare the ingredients for the Romaine Salad. Refrigerate separately in zipper-type bags.
- Bring the dressing for the marinated sesame vegetables to room temperature. Assemble the vegetables, except for the broccoli. Cover and refrigerate.
- Prepare the English trifle through step 2. Cover tightly and refrigerate.
- Remove the biscuits from the freezer and thaw at room temperature.
- Make the eggnog through step 3.
- Set the buffet table. Chill beverages. Make extra ice.

THE MORNING OF THE PARTY:

- Assemble and cook the turkey breasts.
- Prepare the cheddar scalloped potatoes.

- Arrange the biscuits on a baking sheet for reheating.
- Arrange the cookies on serving plates.
- Transfer the garlic-herb mayonnaise, cucumber dressing, and brandied cranberry relish to serving bowls. Refrigerate.
- Bring the dressing for the fennel and orange salad to room temperature.
- Chill the punch ingredients.

ABOUT 1 HOUR BEFORE SERVING:

- Glaze and bake the ham.
- Finish and set out the marinated sesame vegetables.
- Assemble and set out the fennel and orange salad.
- Finish the English trifle and refrigerate until ready to serve.
- Cover the cheddar scalloped potaotes with foil and warm in the oven.
- Slice the turkey rolls and arrange on a serving platter. Cover with plastic wrap and set out with the garlic-herb mayonnaise.
- Finish making the eggnog.

JUST BEFORE SERVING:

- Make the punch and set out.
- Arrange the ham on a serving platter and garnish with pineapple wedges.
- Warm the biscuits and place in baskets.
- Set out the pasta seafood salad, cheddar scalloped potatoes, romaine salad with cucumber dressing, brandied cranberry relish, cookies, punch, and eggnog.

HANUKKAH CANDLE–LIGHTING PARTY FOR 10

Family and friends will enjoy this Hanukkah menu, which includes latkes, the traditional potato pancakes, served with applesauce. A festive holiday such as this deserves an equally festive but easy-to-prepare menu.

HANUKKAH PARTY

SMOKED FISH MOUSSE

Serves 10 to 16
Preparation time: 30 minutes plus at least 3 hours to chill
Cooking time: 3 minutes

Your guests will think you splurged on smoked salmon to make this mousse—and why not let them!

1 envelope unflavored kosher gelatin
¾ cup cold water
1 can (about 15 ounces) red salmon, drained (reserve ¼ cup of liquid)
8 ounces smoked whitefish
½ cup reduced-fat mayonnaise
2 tablespoons fresh lemon juice
2 tablespoons minced onion
2 teaspoons prepared white horseradish
¾ teaspoon salt
¾ teaspoon hot-pepper sauce
For garnish: fresh chives or thin strips of scallion (optional)

1. In a small saucepan, sprinkle the gelatin over the water. Let stand for 1 minute. Stir over low heat with a rubber spatula for 2 to 3 minutes until the granules completely dissolve and the mixture is clear. Remove the pan from the heat.

2. Remove the skin and any bones from the salmon and whitefish. Put the fish into a food processor. Add the mayonnaise, lemon juice, onion, horseradish, salt, and hot pepper sauce. Process until smooth. Add the gelatin and process until blended.

3. Pour the mixture into a 4½- to 5-cup shallow serving bowl. Cover and refrigerate for at least 3 hours, or until firm.

 MAKE AHEAD

The fish mousse can be prepared and refrigerated, tightly covered, up to 5 days ahead of time.

4. Garnish with chives or scallions and serve with crackers and/or slices of cucumber.

Makes 4 cups. Per ¼ cup: 71 cal, 8 g pro, 2 g car, 3 g fat, 14 mg chol, 431 mg sod

VARIATION

HERB POTATO LATKES

• In a food processor, combine the potatoes, onion, salt, and 1 teaspoon of white vinegar and process until finely chopped. Line a colander or strainer with cheesecloth. Set it into a large bowl and pour the potato mixture into it. Twirl the cheesecloth into a pouch and let the mixture drain into the bowl for 10 to 15 minutes.

• Pour off the liquid from the bowl, but leave the white potato starch that will have settled on the bottom. Stir into the potato mixture: 2 tablespoons of all-purpose flour (omit the matzo meal), the eggs, and 1 teaspoon of chopped fresh sage or thyme (or ⅓ teaspoon dried) into the starch. Cook as directed.

Makes 30 pancakes. Per 3 pancakes without topping: 189 cal, 3 g pro, 24 g car, 9 g fat, 42 mg chol, 24 mg sod

---

HANUKKAH PARTY

POTATO LATKES

Serves 10
Preparation time: 20 minutes
Cooking time: 7 minutes per batch

These crispy potato pancakes make a delicious side dish with beef or poultry, or turn them into a simple but satisfying non-meat meal topped with sour cream and applesauce.

5 russet (baking) potatoes, peeled and quartered
1 large onion, quartered
2 large eggs
¼ cup matzo meal or all-purpose flour
1 teaspoon salt
½ teaspoon ground black pepper
Vegetable oil for frying
For topping: applesauce (optional)

1. In a food processor, finely chop the potatoes and onion. Add the eggs, matzo meal, salt, and pepper. Process until potatoes are very finely chopped (the mixture will look like bottled horseradish).

2. In a large skillet, heat ¼ inch of oil over medium-high heat until hot but not smoking. Drop heaping tablespoonfuls of the potato mixture into the oil. Cook for 6 to 7 minutes, turning once, until the pancakes are golden on both sides. Drain on paper towels. Serve right away or keep warm in a 200°F oven.

Makes 30 pancakes. Per 3 pancakes without topping: 195 cal, 3 g pro, 27 g car, 9 g fat, 42 mg chol, 243 mg sod

BRISKET OF BEEF WITH VEGETABLES

Serves 10
Preparation time: 20 minutes
Cooking time: 2 hours 20 minutes

This brisket tastes so good it's hard to believe how simple it is to make. It's good on the day it's made and even better one or two days later. Try to find first-cut brisket, which is leaner with only a thin layer of fat on one side.

1 beef brisket, about 5 pounds, fat trimmed to ¼ inch
2 teaspoons minced fresh garlic
1½ teaspoons salt
½ teaspoon ground black pepper
2 large onions, cut into large chunks (2 cups)
1 pound carrots, peeled and cut into 2-inch pieces (2 cups)
1 pound parsnips, peeled and cut into 2-inch pieces (2¼ cups)
1 cup dry red wine or low-sodium beef broth

1. Heat the oven to 500°F.

2. Rub the brisket with the garlic, salt, and pepper. Place it, fat side up, in a large roasting pan.

3. Roast for 15 to 20 minutes, or until browned. Reduce the oven temperature to 350°F.

4. Remove the brisket from the pan. Scatter the onions over the bottom of the pan. Place the brisket on top of the onions. Scatter the carrots and parsnips around the brisket. Add the wine to the pan. Cover the pan with a lid or foil.

5. Bake for 2 hours, or until the meat is tender. Remove the meat to a cutting board and cut across the grain in thin slices. Arrange on a serving platter. Add the carrots and parsnips and cover with foil to keep warm.

6. Make the gravy: Skim off and discard the fat from the pan juices. Put the juices and onions into a food processor or blender (in batches if necessary) and process until smooth. Makes about 1½ cups of gravy.

7. Spoon some of the gravy over the meat. Serve the remaining gravy in a sauceboat at the table.

Per serving: 685 cal, 40 g pro, 11 g car, 53 g fat, 156 mg chol, 444 mg sod with wine, 606 mg sod with broth

MAKE AHEAD

The brisket can be prepared through step 5, but do not remove the meat and vegetables from the pan. Let cool, then cover and refrigerate up to 2 days. To serve, remove the congealed fat, meat, carrots, and parsnips from the pan. Slice the meat and prepare the gravy as directed. Return the gravy, carrots, parsnips, and meat to the pan or to a Dutch oven and reheat in the oven or on the range top.

CHOCOLATE–ORANGE ANGEL CAKE

Serves 12

Preparation time: 30 minutes

Baking time: 40 minutes

Ⓜ AKE AHEAD

The cake can be made up to 1 week ahead and stored airtight in the refrigerator, or up to 3 days ahead and stored airtight at room temperature.

This delightfully light and tender high-rise cake is practically fat-free and not overly sweet. Flavored with cocoa, grated orange rind, and orange extract, it can be served as is or with fresh berries and cut-up fruit. It is important not to grease the cake pan when making an angel food cake. The batter must be able to cling to the sides.

1½ cups superfine granulated sugar
1 cup cake flour (not self-rising)
2 teaspoons ground cinnamon
¼ teaspoon salt
2 teaspoons grated orange peel
⅓ cup unsweetened Dutch-processed cocoa powder
¼ cup boiling water
1 teaspoon orange extract
Whites from 15 large eggs, at room temperature
1½ teaspoons cream of tartar
For garnish: confectioners' sugar (optional)

1. Heat the oven to 375°F. Have a 10- x 4-inch angel food pan ready.

2. In a small bowl, mix ¾ cup of the sugar, the flour, cinnamon, and salt. Spoon the mixture into a fine-mesh strainer over a piece of waxed paper. Add the orange peel and toss gently to mix.

3. In a medium-size bowl, whisk the cocoa into the boiling water until blended. Stir in the orange extract.

4. In a large bowl with an electric mixer, beat the egg whites until foamy. Add the cream of tartar and beat until soft peaks form. Slowly add the remaining ¾ cup of sugar and beat until stiff peaks form. Stir about 1 cup of the egg whites into the cocoa mixture.

5. Sift about ¼ cup of the flour mixture over the beaten egg whites remaining in the bowl and gently and thoroughly fold in, using a rubber spatula or large balloon-type whisk. Repeat with the remaining flour mixture, adding about ¼ cup at a time. Gently and thoroughly fold in the cocoa mixture.

6. Pour the batter into a 10 x 4-inch angel food cake pan. Run a knife through the batter to remove air pockets. ▶

7. Bake in the center of the oven for 40 minutes, or until a toothpick inserted in the center of the cake comes out clean and the cake springs back when gently pressed. (The cake will rise above the pan while baking, then sink slightly while cooling.)

8. Invert the pan onto its raised feet or hang the pan upside down over the neck of a bottle and cool completely (several hours or overnight). Run a thin knife around the edge of the cake to loosen it from the pan and tube. Invert the cake onto a serving plate.

9. To serve, lightly sift confectioners' sugar over the top of the cake and slice with a serrated knife.

Makes 12 slices. Per slice: 161 cal, 6 g pro, 34 g car, 1 g fat, 0 mg chol, 131 mg sod

HANUKKAH CANDLE-LIGHTING PARTY PLANNING TIMETABLE

3 TO 4 WEEKS AHEAD:
- Make the guest list. Write invitations or telephone guests.
- Plan the table setting and any decorations. Check serving dishes and serving utensils. Order any rental items or line up items to borrow such as linens, glasses, silverware, china, tables, coffeepot, menorah, etc.
- Order the brisket.

1 TO 2 WEEKS AHEAD
- Make shopping list. Shop for nonperishable food.

3 DAYS AHEAD:
- Bring out china, serving dishes, and serving utensils. Polish silver if necessary.
- Pick up meat.
- Shop for perishable food.

- Make the smoked fish mousse. Cover and refrigerate.

2 DAYS AHEAD:
- Make the brisket and refrigerate.
- Make the chocolate-orange angel cake.

1 DAY AHEAD:
- Buy any flowers.
- Set the table. Chill beverages. Make extra ice.
- Select CDs, tapes, or records for music.

THE MORNING OF THE PARTY:
- Make the potato latkes. Drain on paper towels and set on wire racks at room temperature.
- Make a cucumber and tomato salad and refrigerate.

ABOUT 1 HOUR BEFORE SERVING:
- Finish the brisket of beef.
- Set the angel cake on a platter and sift with confectioners' sugar.
- Warm the latkes in a 200°F oven.
- Put the applesauce for the latkes into a serving dish.
- Set out the cucumber and tomato salad at room temperature.

JUST BEFORE SERVING:
- Garnish the smoked fish mousse and set out with crackers or cucumber rounds.
- Slice the brisket and arrange on a serving platter with the vegetables.
- Pour the gravy into a sauceboat. Keep warm.
- Slice the challah and place in a basket.
- Arrange the latkes on a platter.

COOK ONCE
EAT TWICE

> *"The most remarkable thing about my mother*
> *is that for thirty years she served us*
> *nothing but leftovers. The original meal*
> *has never been found."*
> CALVIN TRILLIN

There has always been a slight stigma attached to the idea of serving leftovers at a meal. However, planning for leftovers not only gives you the luxury of having at your fingertips one or two more delicious meals in the refrigerator or freezer, it also saves on time and money. And there are some dishes that actually taste better the second time around.

The selection of recipes in this chapter relies on a combination of double-duty ingredients and convenience. It's a simple concept. Shop and cook once to have two or three home-cooked meals ready to go. Here's how it works: The juicy grilled London broil left over from Sunday's dinner can be recycled as quick and simple sesame beef stir-fry on Tuesday, then frozen to be served the following week as deviled beef hash. So instead of telling them it's leftovers for dinner, just produce one of these fabulous meal plans and wait for the applause.

POACHED TURKEY BANQUET

Turkey Breast with Vegetables & Lime, 604
Turkey Pasta Salad, 605
Turkey, Tomato, & Cheese Casserole, 605

TWIN ROASTED CHICKENS

Moroccan Roast Chicken, 606
Citrus Chicken Salad with Walnuts, 607

QUICK & EASY CHICKEN

Chicken Fajitas, 607
Chicken, Cabbage, & Corn Salad, 617

LONDON BROIL MEDLEY

Grilled London Broil & Vegetables, 617
Sesame Beef Stir-Fry, 618
Deviled Beef Hash, 619

OFF THE GRILL

Deviled Steaks with Stuffed Pitas, 619
Pita & Beef Salad, 620

ONE POT PLUS

Corned Beef Dinner, 621
Reuben Sandwiches, 621

ROAST PORK TRIO

Roast Fresh Ham, 622
Tropical Pork Salad, 623
Pork Sandwiches Cubano, 624

LAMB CLASSICS

Braised Lamb Shanks with White Beans, 624
Greek Lamb & Pasta Pie, 625

LIGHT & EASY FISH

Poached Halibut with Cucumber & Tomato, 626
Halibut-Spinach Salad, 626

VEGETABLE DUO

Vegetable Stew with Couscous, 627
Vegetable & Tuna Pan Bagna, 628

POACHED TURKEY BANQUET

Poaching a turkey breast with vegetables is easy and yields a juicy, flavorful meal. The turkey leftovers are used in a tasty pasta salad and a savory tomato and cheese casserole.

POACHED TURKEY #1

TURKEY BREAST WITH VEGETABLES & LIME

Serves 4 with leftovers
Preparation time: 30 minutes
Cooking time: 1 hour 10 minutes

Adding potatoes, carrots, green beans, and a combination of lime juice and grated peel to the turkey while it cooks gives you an interesting one-pot meal.

1 cup chopped parsley (from 3 cups loosely packed leaves)
2 teaspoons minced fresh garlic
1½ teaspoons grated lime peel
½ teaspoon crushed hot red pepper flakes
½ teaspoon salt
2 tablespoons fresh lime juice
1 tablespoon olive oil
4- to 5-pound bone-in turkey breast, thawed if frozen
2 cups chicken broth
½ teaspoon anise or celery seeds
5 small red-skinned potatoes (12 ounces), scrubbed and quartered
5 medium-size carrots (12 ounces), peeled and cut into 2-inch-long chunks
12 ounces fresh green beans, trimmed and snapped into 2 or 3 pieces (3 cups)
For garnish: tomato wedges (optional)

1. In a food processor, combine ¾ cup of parsley, the garlic, lime peel, crushed red pepper, and salt and process until finely chopped (or chop fine with a large knife). Add 1 tablespoon of lime juice and the olive oil and process briefly (or stir) to make a paste.

2. Gently run your fingers under the turkey skin to separate it from the flesh, leaving the skin attached at one side. Lift the skin and spread the herb mixture over the flesh. Replace the skin and skewer in place to hold the herb mixture against the turkey.

3. Place the turkey, skin side up, in a large pot. Add the broth and anise seeds. Bring to a boil over medium-high heat. Reduce the heat to low. Cover and simmer for 55 minutes. Scatter the potatoes and carrots around the turkey. Cover and simmer for 10 minutes, then add the green beans around the turkey. Simmer for 5 minutes, or until the green beans are crisp-tender, the potatoes and carrots are tender, and the turkey juices run clear when the breast is pierced. (A meat thermometer inserted into the thickest part, not touching the bone, should register 170°F to 175°F.)

4. Remove the turkey to a cutting board, and let stand for 15 minutes, loosely covered. Reserve 1 cup each of carrots and green beans for meal 2. Place the remaining carrots and green beans on a heated serving platter and cover to keep warm.

5. Meanwhile, strain the poaching liquid into a 2-cup measure and blot the surface with paper towels to remove fat. Pour off ¼ cup broth, cover, and refrigerate for meal 2. Stir the remaining 1 tablespoon lime juice and ¼ cup chopped parsley into the broth.

6. To serve, remove the skewers from the turkey and discard the skin. Slice ⅓ of the breast (about 12 ounces) and add to the platter with vegetables for meal 1. Cut 16 thin 3-inch-long slices turkey (about 12 ounces) and freeze

in a single layer on a waxed paper-lined baking sheet until hard. Transfer the meat to a freezer bag, seal, and freeze up to 2 weeks for meal 3. Tear the remaining turkey into shreds (about 12 ounces; you should have 2 cups), cover, and refrigerate for meal 2.

7. Moisten the turkey on the platter with some of the lime broth. Garnish with tomato wedges. Serve with the remaining broth.

Per serving: 239 cal, 29 g pro, 23 g car, 3 g fat, 71 mg chol, 538 mg sod

1. Bring a large pot of lightly salted water to a boil. Add the pasta and cook according to the package directions. Drain, rinse under cold running water, and drain again.

2. Meanwhile, make the dressing. In a food processor or blender, combine the poaching liquid, vinegar, egg yolk, basil, scallions, pepper, and oil and process until smooth and creamy.

3. In a large serving bowl, mix the pasta, vegetables, and turkey. Add the dressing and toss.

Per serving: 530 cal, 32 g pro, 32 g car, 31 g fat, 124 mg chol, 237 mg sod

---

POACHED TURKEY #2

TURKEY PASTA SALAD

Serves 4
Preparation time: 15 minutes
Cooking time: 10 minutes

Here, leftover turkey is tossed with pasta and creamy basil dressing. Serve it with a cup of soup and Italian bread for an easy meal.

4 ounces farfalle (bow-tie) pasta (2 cups)

CREAMY BASIL DRESSING
¼ cup turkey poaching liquid (from meal 1)
¼ cup cider vinegar
Yolk of 1 hard-cooked large egg
½ cup loosely packed fresh basil leaves
¼ cup sliced scallions
½ teaspoon ground black pepper
½ cup olive oil

1 cup cooked green beans (from meal 1),
   cut into smaller pieces
1 cup cooked carrots (from meal 1),
   cut into smaller pieces
½ cup thinly sliced celery
2 cups (12 ounces) shredded cooked turkey
   (from meal 1)

POACHED TURKEY #3

TURKEY, TOMATO, & CHEESE CASSEROLE

Serves 4
Preparation time: 15 minutes plus
at least 3 hours to chill
Cooking time: 45 minutes

Start this casserole the day before serving.

2 teaspoons butter or margarine
1 loaf (8 ounces) Italian bread (14 inches
   long), ends cut off, loaf cut into sixteen ¾-
   inch-thick slices
1 large ripe tomato, cut in half, seeds removed,
   and each half cut into 8 thin slices
1 package (6 ounces) sliced Gouda, Cheddar,
   or Swiss cheese, each slice cut crosswise
   into thirds (18 strips)
16 frozen slices cooked turkey breast
   (from meal 1)
4 large eggs
1 ½ cups milk
1 tablespoon Dijon mustard
½ teaspoon paprika
¼ teaspoon ground black pepper
¼ cup sliced scallions

▶

1. Grease a 10 x 7-inch baking dish or casserole with the butter.

2. Stand 2 bread slices upright side by side against one short end of the prepared dish. Next, place a tomato slice against each slice of bread, then a cheese slice, and then a frozen turkey slice. Repeat until you have 2 long rows and the dish is filled. Tear the remaining 2 strips of cheese into small pieces and scatter over the top.

3. In a medium-size bowl, whisk together the eggs, milk, mustard, paprika, and pepper until smooth. Pour evenly into the dish. Sprinkle the scallions over the top.

4. Cover with plastic wrap and refrigerate for at least 3 hours or overnight (the turkey will thaw and the bread will soak up the egg mixture).

5. Heat the oven to 350°F. Uncover the casserole and bake for 40 to 45 minutes, or until the top is lightly browned and a toothpick inserted near the center comes out clean.

Per serving with Gouda: 585 cal, 51 g pro, 35 g car, 25 g fat, 350 mg chol with butter, 344 mg chol with margarine, 1,019 mg sod

QUICK FIXES FOR LEFTOVERS

Here are some ideas for perking up food the second time around:

◆ **Chili** — Leftover chili can be used as a topping for pasta, baked potatoes, or burgers.

◆ **Fish or shellfish**—Use leftover fish or shellfish to make a chowder full of potatoes and vegetables. Or mix in a food processor with some mayonnaise, herbs, and seasonings to use as a sandwich spread. You can also use fish or shellfish to liven up a salad.

◆ **Meats** — Make a casserole by mixing leftover meats with cooked egg noodles and a white sauce. Top with bread crumbs and bake until topping is lightly browned and sauce is bubbly. Or meats can also be added to a basic tomato sauce for pasta. Like fish, they also make for a great sandwich spread.

TWIN ROASTED CHICKENS

Something as simple as roasting two whole chickens at once is all it takes to have the makings for dual dinners, an exotic North African-style entrée and a lively main-dish salad.

ROASTED CHICKENS #1

MOROCCAN ROAST CHICKEN

Serves 4 with leftovers
Preparation time: 25 minutes
Cooking time: 1 hour 10 minutes plus
5 minutes to stand

This one-pot meal features a whole spice-roasted chicken accompanied by roasted root vegetables. Serve it with warmed pita bread or biscuits.

2 (4-pound) whole broiler-fryer chickens
⅓ cup chopped fresh cilantro
⅓ cup chopped fresh parsley
2 cloves garlic, chopped
2 tablespoons paprika
1 tablespoon cumin
2 teaspoons ground black pepper
1 teaspoon salt
1 tablespoon olive oil
2 large parsnips, peeled and cut into 2-inch lengths
2 large carrots, peeled, cut in half lengthwise, then in half crosswise
2 medium-size all-purpose potatoes, scrubbed and quartered
2 medium-size onions, quartered

1. Heat the oven to 425°F. Place the chickens, breast side up, on a rack in a large roasting pan.

2. In a small bowl, mix the cilantro, parsley, garlic, paprika, cumin, pepper, salt, and olive oil. Rub all but 2 tablespoons of the mixture over both chickens.

3. Roast the chickens for 30 minutes. Reduce the oven temperature to 350°F.

4. In a medium-size bowl, toss the parsnips, carrots, potatoes, and onions with the remaining spice mixture. Scatter the vegetables in the roasting pan. Roast for 35 to 40 minutes more, or until the drumsticks move easily, the juices run clear when a thigh is pierced with a sharp knife, and the vegetables are tender.

5. Remove 1 chicken and the vegetables to a serving platter and let stand for 5 minutes before carving and serving. Cool the remaining chicken completely. Remove and shred the meat, discarding the bones. Refrigerate in an airtight container up to 4 days, or freeze up to 3 months for meal 2.

Per serving: 746 cal, 59 g pro, 45 g car, 36 g fat, 181 mg chol, 474 mg sod

---

ROASTED CHICKENS #2

CITRUS CHICKEN SALAD WITH WALNUTS

Serves 4
Preparation time: 20 minutes

This second meal is not only fast and healthy but elegant as well. A main-dish salad featuring shredded roast chicken, juicy pieces of fresh orange, and mixed greens tossed with an orange infused dressing. Serve it with crusty peasant bread.

CITRUS DRESSING

⅓ cup fresh orange juice
2 tablespoons olive oil
¾ teaspoon salt
¼ teaspoon ground black pepper

CHICKEN SALAD WITH WALNUTS

4 cups torn mixed greens (such as arugula, frisée, romaine, radicchio, and endive)
Shredded chicken (from meal 1), at room temperature
2 navel oranges, peel and white pith removed, sectioned
½ cup thinly sliced red onion
¼ cup broken walnuts, toasted

1. Make the dressing: In a large serving bowl, whisk together the orange juice, oil, salt, and pepper until well blended.

2. Add the greens, chicken, orange sections, and onion, tossing to coat. Sprinkle with the walnuts. Serve right away.

Per serving: 475 cal, 50 g pro, 15 g car, 24 g fat, 145 mg chol, 563 mg sod

QUICK & EASY
CHICKEN

Marinated and broiled boneless, skinless chicken breasts serve as the base for two satisfying meals: Southwestern-inspired fajitas and a colorful and hearty chicken salad.

QUICK & EASY CHICKEN #1

CHICKEN FAJITAS

Serves 4 with leftovers
Preparation time: 15 minutes plus at least
30 minutes to marinate
Cooking time: 17 minutes

Start things off with a south-of-the-border bang: flour tortillas rolled around a trio of chicken, peppers, and onions and served with guacamole and sour cream. ▶

MARINADE

3 tablespoons fresh lime juice

2 tablespoons olive oil

1 teaspoon minced fresh garlic

½ teaspoon ground cumin

½ teaspoon dried oregano leaves, crumbled

½ teaspoon salt

¼ teaspoon ground black pepper

CHICKEN FAJITAS

7 chicken cutlets (about 5 ounces each) or boneless, skinless chicken breast halves, flattened to ½-inch thickness

4 medium-size onions

3 large red and/or green bell peppers

2 tablespoons olive oil

½ teaspoon salt

8 (8-inch) flour tortillas, stacked and wrapped in foil

Toppings: homemade guacamole (see Cook's Tip) or purchased frozen guacamole, thawed, and sour cream

1. Make the marinade: In a zipper-type food-storage bag, mix the lime juice, oil, garlic, cumin, oregano, salt, and pepper. Add the chicken, seal the bag, and turn until chicken is coated. Let marinate for 30 minutes at room temperature, or up to 8 hours in the refrigerator.

2. Meanwhile, halve the onions lengthwise and cut into long strips. Halve and seed the bell peppers and cut into thin strips.

3. In a deep large skillet or saucepan, heat the oil over medium-high heat. Add the onions and cook for about 3 minutes, stirring often, until softened.

4. Add the bell peppers and stir-fry for 2 minutes. Reduce the heat to medium-low, add the salt, cover, and cook for 4 to 5 minutes, stirring once, until the peppers are crisp-tender. Remove the skillet from the heat. Scoop 2 cups of the mixture into a bowl. Let cool, then cover

and refrigerate for meal 2. Spoon the remaining vegetable mixture onto a serving platter and cover with foil to keep warm.

5. Arrange the chicken cutlets in a single layer on a broiler-pan rack. Place foil-wrapped tortillas on the lowest oven rack. Broil the chicken 4 inches from the heat source for about 7 minutes, turning once, until just barely pink in the thickest part when cut with knife. Cool 3 cutlets briefly, then wrap and refrigerate for meal 2.

6. Let the remaining chicken stand for 3 minutes, then slice crosswise into thin strips. Add to the serving platter with the vegetable mixture.

7. To serve, remove the tortillas from the oven. Top the middle of each tortilla with chicken strips, pepper mixture, and a dollop of guacamole and sour cream. Fold the bottom of the tortilla to cover part of the filling, then fold in the sides.

Makes 8 fajitas. Per 2 fajitas without topping without toppings: 493 cal, 40 g pro, 50 g car, 14 g fat, 82 mg chol, 724 mg sod

ⒸOOK'S TIPS

◆ To make guacamole: Mash 1 ripe avocado (about 9 ounces) with 1 tablespoon lime juice. Add salt and pepper to taste.

◆ If you can't find chicken cutlets (thin slices of chicken breast) in your market, you can pound chicken breasts between sheets of waxed paper to about ½ inch thick with a meat mallet, rolling pin, or the bottom of a heavy skillet.

DOUBLE DUTY
This Chicken, Cabbage, & Corn Salad (p.617) uses extra broiled chicken and vegetables from Chicken Fajitas (p.607).

The strategy of cook once–eat twice goes beyond leftovers, with recipes and tips for extending today's cooking so you don't have to worry about it tomorrow.

DINNER ALFRESCO
Fire up the grill for Deviled Steaks with Stuffed Pitas (p.619), a warmweather meal of mustard-coated blade steaks and grilled vegetables.

**LIVELY
LEFTOVERS**
Reuben
Sandwiches
(p.621), below,
and Sandwiches
Cubano (p.624),
right, are great
ways to enjoy
corned beef and
roast pork for a
second round.

ON THE MESA
Chicken Fajitas
(p.607) are
Southwestern fare
that has become
popular in the last
few years.
Guacamole and
beer make fine
accompaniments.

The boom in Tex-Mex

cooking taking place

across the U.S. has

widened the choices of

ingredients available,

and markets are now

stocked with items such

as tortillas, cilantro,

fresh chile peppers, and

mesquite chips.

ENCORE
In this Pita & Beef Salad (p.620), leftover steak, vegetables, and lettuce in a lemon-mint dressing make a tasty summer salad.

CHICKEN, CABBAGE, & CORN SALAD

Serves 4
Total time: 20 minutes

Follow up the fajitas with a crisp salad, using that winning chicken-pepper-onion combination. Bread on the side makes it an incredibly easy one-dish meal.

DRESSING

2 tablespoons balsamic or cider vinegar
1 tablespoon olive oil
1 tablespoon water

3 cups finely shredded Napa cabbage (Chinese cabbage) or romaine lettuce
3 chilled, cooked chicken cutlets, torn into bite-sized strips (from meal 1)
2 cups chilled, cooked bell pepper and onion mixture, chopped coarse (from meal 1)
1 cup fresh, drained canned, or thawed frozen corn kernels
½ cup packed cilantro leaves, chopped

1. Make the dressing: In a large serving bowl, whisk together the vinegar, oil, and water until blended.
2. Add the remaining ingredients and toss to mix and coat.

Per serving: 290 cal, 28 g pro, 20 g car, 12 g fat, 62 mg chol, 334 mg sod

LONDON BROIL MEDLEY

Always popular, a large London broil has the added bonus of supplying you with the main ingredient for an excellent stir-fry and savory hash.

GRILLED LONDON BROIL & VEGETABLES

Serves 4 with leftovers
Preparation time: 15 minutes
Cooking time: 57 minutes plus
15 minutes to stand

In this easy-to-prepare meal, the meat and vegetables are all cooked on the grill—perfect for a warm-weather dinner.

2-inch-thick boneless beef top round steak (London broil), about 3 pounds
½ cup bottled barbecue sauce
4 large Italian frying peppers, halved lengthwise and seeded
2 medium-size zucchini (4 ounces each), halved lengthwise, then quartered
2 tablespoons olive or vegetable oil
2 medium-size ripe tomatoes, halved
2 teaspoons packaged seasoned bread crumbs
2 teaspoons grated Parmesan cheese

1. Heat a gas grill to medium, prepare a charcoal fire, or heat a broiler. Brush the steak all over with some of the barbecue sauce.
2. Place the steak on the grill or broiler-pan rack about 5 inches from the heat source. Grill or broil for 35 to 40 minutes, turning the steak and brushing with sauce 4 times, until a meat thermometer inserted in the thickest part ▶

registers 140°F (for medium-rare).

3. Remove the steak to a cutting board, cover loosely with foil, and let stand 15 minutes before slicing.

4. Meanwhile, lightly brush the frying peppers and zucchini with some of the oil. Place, cut sides down, on the grill or broiler-pan rack 4 to 6 inches from the heat source. Grill or broil for 10 minutes, turning twice and basting with remaining barbecue sauce, if desired, until the vegetables are crisp-tender. Remove to a serving platter and cover to keep warm.

5. Brush the cut sides of the tomatoes with the remaining oil. Place cut sides down on the grill, or cut sides up on the broiler-pan rack, 4 to 6 inches from the heat source. Grill or broil for 4 minutes, or until the edges are lightly browned. In a small bowl, mix the bread crumbs and Parmesan cheese. Turn the grilled tomatoes over and sprinkle with the bread crumb mixture. (If broiling the tomatoes, leave cut sides up for entire cooking time.) Grill or broil for 2 to 3 minutes more, or until the tomatoes are hot and very tender when pierced.

6. To serve, cut ⅓ of the steak diagonally across the grain into ¼-inch-thick slices. Arrange on a serving platter and surround with grilled vegetables. Finely dice enough of remaining steak to get 2 cups (about 12 ounces). Wrap well and freeze up to 2 weeks for meal 3. Wrap and refrigerate remaining piece (about 1 pound) for meal 2.

Per serving: 355 cal, 36 g pro, 10 g car, 18 g fat, 97 mg chol, 222 mg sod.

LONDON BROIL #2

SESAME BEEF STIR-FRY

Serves 4
Preparation time: 15 minutes
Cooking time: 3 minutes

The pleasure of stir-frying is that all the ingredients are cut in uniform pieces and therefore cook quickly and evenly. Serve with cooked rice and crusty bread or breadsticks.

SESAME DRESSING
¼ cup cider vinegar
1 tablespoon soy sauce
1 ¾ teaspoons ground ginger
1 teaspoon dry mustard
¼ teaspoon ground black pepper
3 tablespoons vegetable oil
1 ½ tablespoons dark Asian sesame oil
⅓ cup sliced scallions

1 tablespoon vegetable oil
1 large red, green, or yellow bell pepper
  halved, seeded, and cut in 1-inch squares
2 cups corn kernels, thawed if frozen
1 pound bok choy, stalks halved lengthwise,
  cut in 1-inch pieces (4 packed cups)
1 pound cooked London broil (from meal 1),
  cut diagonally across the grain in ¼-inch-
  thick slices then cut crosswise into ½-
  inch-wide strips
1 teaspoon toasted sesame seeds

1. Make the dressing: In a small bowl, whisk together the vinegar, soy sauce, ginger, mustard, and pepper. Gradually whisk in the oils until well blended. Stir in scallions.

2. In a wok or deep large skillet, heat the 1 tablespoon of vegetable oil over medium-high heat. Add the bell pepper and stir-fry for 30 to 60 seconds.

3. Add the corn and stir-fry for 30 seconds.

4. Add the bok choy and stir-fry for about 1 minute, or just until wilted.

5. Remove the pan from the heat and stir in the beef and about half the Sesame Dressing. Spoon onto serving plates.

6. Sprinkle with the sesame seeds. Serve the remaining dressing on the side.

Per serving: 524 cal, 40 g pro, 23 g car, 32 g fat, 96 mg chol, 510 mg sod

LONDON BROIL #3

DEVILED BEEF HASH

Serves 4
Preparation time: 10 minutes
Cooking time: 21 minutes

Thaw frozen beef and hash-brown potato patties overnight in the refrigerator. Serve with a mixed green salad.

  2 cups frozen finely diced cooked London broil (from meal 1), thawed
  4 patties (3 ounces each) frozen shredded hash browns, thawed and broken into small pieces
  ½ cup finely chopped green, red, or yellow bell pepper
  ½ cup sliced scallions
  2 tablespoons bottled barbecue sauce
  1 tablespoon Dijon mustard
  1 tablespoon butter or margarine
  2 tablespoons olive or vegetable oil

1. In a large bowl, mix the meat, hash browns, bell pepper, scallions, barbecue sauce, and mustard until well blended.

2. In a 10-inch nonstick skillet, melt the butter with the oil over medium-low heat. When the butter is foamy, add the hash mixture. Press down with a wide spatula into a flat round, covering the bottom of the skillet.

3. Cook uncovered, pressing down occasionally, for 10 minutes, or until the bottom is browned and crisp.

4. Turn the hash in clumps and press back into a round.

5. Cook, pressing down occasionally, for 10 minutes more, or until the bottom is browned and crisp.

6. Loosen the hash with the spatula, invert onto a serving plate, and cut into 4 wedges. Serve right away.

Per serving: 362 cal, 28 g pro, 19 g car, 19 g fat, 80 mg chol with butter, 72 mg chol with margarine, 330 mg sod

FROM THE GRILL

Head straight for the grill and get two meals out of one: Deviled Steaks with Stuffed Pitas and a Pita and Beef Salad.

FROM THE GRILL #1

DEVILED STEAKS WITH STUFFED PITAS

Serves 4 with leftovers
Preparation time: 12 minutes
Cooking time: 21 minutes

Boneless chuck top blade steaks are tender and great for grilling and broiling. They're easy to identify by the thin translucent line that runs down the center. Grilled steak is an excellent candidate for using aromatic wood chips such as mesquite or hickory. Soak the chips in water for 1 hour, then drain and add to the hot coals just before grilling.

▶

2 large yellow summer squash (1 pound),
  halved lengthwise

2 large red onions, each cut into 5 slices

1 tablespoon olive oil

12 boneless top blade steaks (about 3 ounces
  each), trimmed of fat

¼ cup creamy mustard spread

8 pita breads

1 large tomato, cut into bite-size chunks

½ cup fresh basil leaves, torn into pieces

½ teaspoon salt

Ground black pepper to taste

1. Heat a gas grill to medium, prepare a charcoal fire, or heat a broiler.

2. Lightly brush the squash and onions with oil. Place on the grill or broiler pan rack 4 inches from the heat source. Grill or broil for 12 minutes, turning once, until tender. Remove the grilled vegetables to a cutting board and cover with foil to keep warm.

3. Brush one side of the steaks with half the mustard spread. Grill or broil, mustard side down, for 4 to 5 minutes. Brush the tops of the steaks with the remaining mustard, turn over, and grill or broil for 3 to 4 minutes more for medium meat.

4. Remove 8 of the steaks to a serving platter and cover loosely with foil to keep warm. Cool the remaining 4 steaks, wrap with plastic, and refrigerate for meal 2.

5. Grill or broil all the pitas briefly until lightly toasted. Cool and store 4 in a plastic food bag for meal 2.

6. Cut the squash and onions into bite-size pieces. Toss in a medium-size bowl with the tomato, basil, salt, and ground pepper to taste.

7. Halve and split the pitas and stuff with squash mixture. Serve the stuffed pitas with the grilled steaks.

Per serving: 621 cal, 49 g pro, 54 g car, 23 g fat, 135 mg chol, 847 mg sod

---

FROM THE GRILL #2

PITA & BEEF SALAD

Serves 4

Total time: 15 minutes

For your command performance, toss pieces of torn pita bread, pregrilled steak, lettuce, and a handful of fresh vegetables into a main-dish salad with a distinctively grilled flavor. If bread in salad seems unusual, think of the toasted pieces of pita as giant croutons. Try it. You'll love it.

LEMON–MINT DRESSING

⅓ cup fresh mint leaves, chopped

¼ cup olive oil

2 tablespoons fresh lemon juice

1 teaspoon salt

½ teaspoon ground black pepper

4 chilled, grilled boneless top blade steaks
  (from meal 1)

3 cups loosely packed 1½-inch-wide strips
  romaine lettuce

4 toasted pita breads, torn into small pieces
  (from meal 1)

1 large tomato, cut into ½-inch pieces

½ long seedless cucumber (or 1 peeled
  regular cucumber), quartered lengthwise,
  then cut into ½-inch pieces

1. Make the dressing: In a large serving bowl, whisk together the mint, oil, lemon juice, salt, and pepper until well blended.

2. Cut the steaks in half on either side of the translucent line, then cut the halves crosswise into thin strips.

3. Add the steak strips and the remaining ingredients to the dressing. Toss to mix and coat.

Per serving: 481 cal, 27 g pro, 39 g car, 24 g fat, 68 mg chol, 994 mg sod

What could be easier or more delicious than a boiled corned beef dinner one night, then grilled reuben sandwiches on another?

ONE POT PLUS #1

CORNED BEEF DINNER

Serves 4 with leftovers
Preparation time: 25 minutes
Cooking time: 3 hours 25 minutes

This traditional boiled dinner also includes beets, which are cooked separately and then added to the platter.

- 1 medium-size onion, peeled and studded with 4 whole cloves
- 1 large carrot, cut into chunks
- 1 rib celery, cut into chunks
- 2 bay leaves (each 1½ inches long)
- 4-pound corned-beef brisket
- 4 small onions, peeled
- 1 small head green cabbage (1¼ pounds), cut into 6 wedges
- 8 small potatoes (about 1 pound), peeled
- 4 small parsnips (about 8 ounces), peeled and halved
- 3 large carrots, halved
- 4 small beets (about 12 ounces), freshly boiled and peeled (see Cook's Tip)
- Accompaniment: creamy Dijon-mustard spread or horseradish sauce (optional)

1. In an 8-quart pot, bring 4 quarts of water and the first 4 ingredients to a boil.

2. Add the brisket and bring to a simmer. Reduce the heat to medium-low and simmer (don't boil), partially covered, for about 3 hours.

3. Remove the brisket to a cutting board and cover loosely with foil to keep warm. Discard the onion, carrot, celery, and bay leaves from the cooking liquid.

4. Return the cooking liquid to a boil. Add the small onions and simmer for 5 minutes. Add the cabbage, potatoes, parsnips, and carrots and simmer for 20 minutes, or until tender.

5. Starting at the thickest end, slice the brisket thin on a slight diagonal across the grain. Cool half the slices, wrap, and refrigerate up to 4 days for meal 2. Put the remaining slices on a serving platter and surround with the vegetables.
Per serving: 496 cal, 27 g pro, 49 g car, 22 g fat, 111 mg chol, 1,393 mg sod

COOK'S TIP

To cook beets, scrub and trim but don't peel. Boil for 30 minutes, or until tender. Drain, cool slightly, then slip off skins under cold running water.

ONE POT PLUS #2

REUBEN SANDWICHES

Serves 4
Preparation time: 15 minutes
Cooking time: 20 minutes

These sandwiches are a snap made with leftover corned beef plus. Assemble them in the morning, then wrap and refrigerate until time to bake.

- 8 slices rye bread
- 4 teaspoons butter or margarine, at room temperature
- 4 slices (1 ounce each) Swiss cheese
- ½ cup bottled fat-free Russian dressing
- 1 pound sauerkraut, rinsed and well drained
- 1 pound thinly sliced corned beef (from meal 1)

▶

1. Adjust the oven rack to the lowest position. Heat the oven to 400°F. Spread one side of each of the bread slices with the butter.

2. Place 4 bread slices, buttered sides down, on a baking sheet. Cover each with 1 slice of cheese, 1 tablespoon of dressing, ¼ of the sauerkraut, ¼ of the corned beef, and another tablespoon of dressing. Cover with the remaining bread, buttered sides up.

3. Bake for about 20 minutes, turning the sandwiches once, until lightly toasted. Serve right away.

Makes 4 sandwiches. Per sandwich: 647 cal, 35 g pro, 46 g car, 35 g fat, 148 mg chol with butter, 137 mg chol with margarine, 2,380 mg sod

---

R O A S T   P O R K   T R I O

Save time and money with this easy menu plan: Cook a large cut of meat one night and turn the leftovers into a delicious tropical salad and hot sandwiches for later on in the week.

ROAST PORK #1

ROAST FRESH HAM

Serves 4 with leftovers
Preparation time: 15 minutes plus at least
4 hours to marinate
Cooking time: 3 hours 55 minutes plus
15 minutes to stand

Leg of pork, sometimes confusingly labeled "fresh ham," is one of the best buys in meat. Here it's prepared with a spice and herb rub and served with roasted potatoes, red onion, and yellow squash and homemade pan gravy.

SEASONING MIXTURE

3 tablespoons olive oil
1 tablespoon red wine vinegar
1 tablespoon minced fresh garlic
1½ teaspoons dried oregano leaves, crumbled
1 teaspoon salt
¾ teaspoon ground cumin
½ teaspoon ground black pepper

1 pork leg half, shank portion
 (about 7 pounds with bone)
2 large baking potatoes (8 ounces each), scrubbed and each cut lengthwise into 8 wedges
1 large red onion (8 ounces), cut into 8 wedges
12 ounces yellow summer squash, cut into 1-inch slices

PAN GRAVY

2 tablespoons fat from drippings
2 tablespoons all-purpose flour
¼ teaspoon ground black pepper
2 cups water or beef broth

1. Make the seasoning mixture: In a small bowl, mix the oil, vinegar, garlic, oregano, salt, cumin, and pepper until well blended.

2. With a very sharp long-bladed knife, score a diamond pattern on top of the roast, cutting through the rind and the underlying fat almost to the meat.

3. Brush the entire roast with the seasoning mixture. Place in a baking pan and cover with plastic wrap. Let marinate in the refrigerator at for least 4 hours, or overnight.

4. Heat the oven to 325°F. Unwrap the meat and transfer to a rack in a large roasting pan. Roast for 2 hours.

5. Add the potatoes and onion wedges to the roasting pan and brush with drippings. Roast for 1 hour, then add the squash, brush with drip-

pings, and roast for 45 minutes more (the meat should roast a total of 32 to 35 minutes per pound), or until a meat thermometer inserted into the thickest part (not touching the bone) registers 160°F and the vegetables are tender.

6. Remove the meat to a cutting board and cover loosely with foil (reserve the pan drippings for gravy). Let stand for 15 minutes before slicing. Arrange the vegetables on a serving platter and cover to keep warm.

7. Meanwhile, make the gravy. Drain off all but 2 tablespoons of fat from the drippings in the roasting pan. Sprinkle with the flour and pepper. Whisk over medium-high heat until smooth, scraping up the browned bits from the bottom of the pan. Gradually whisk in the water until blended. Bring to a boil. Reduce the heat to medium-low and simmer for 5 minutes, or until thickened, stirring 2 or 3 times.

8. Slice one-third of the pork and serve with the vegetables and 1 cup of the pan gravy for meal 1. Freeze the remaining cup of gravy for meal 3. Slice half the remaining pork thin (about 1 pound), wrap well, and freeze up to 2 weeks for meal 3. Shred the remaining meat (about 12 ounces, you should have 2 cups), cover, and refrigerate for meal 2.

Per serving with ¼ cup gravy: 507 cal with water, 512 cal with broth, 35 g pro, 30 g car, 28 g fat, 110 mg chol, 304 mg sod with water, 714 mg sod with broth

---

ROAST PORK #2

TROPICAL PORK SALAD

Serves 4

Preparation time: 20 minutes

Shredded cooked pork combined with chunks of avocado and papaya and tossed with a piquant orange dressing makes an easy-to-prepare and refreshing salad.

ORANGE–MINT DRESSING

1 teaspoon grated orange peel

¼ cup fresh orange juice

1 ½ tablespoons cider vinegar

¼ cup chopped fresh mint leaves, or 1 tablespoon dried mint leaves, crumbled

¾ teaspoon Dijon mustard

¼ teaspoon salt

¼ teaspoon ground black pepper

⅓ cup olive oil

2 cups (12 ounces) shredded cooked pork (from meal 1)

1 large ripe papaya (1 pound), peeled, halved, seeded, and cut into ½-inch chunks (2 cups)

1 ripe avocado (10 ounces), halved, pitted, peeled, and cut into ½-inch chunks (1½ cups)

1 small red onion, sliced thin (½ cup)

12 ounces chicory or romaine lettuce, torn into bite-size pieces (6 cups)

⅓ cup toasted sliced almonds

1. Make the dressing: In a large serving bowl, whisk together the orange peel, orange juice, vinegar, mint, mustard, salt, and pepper. Gradually whisk in the oil until well blended.

2. Add the remaining ingredients except for the chicory and almonds. Toss to mix and coat.

3. Mound the salad on a chicory-lined serving plate. Sprinkle with the almonds.

Per serving: 617 cal, 28 g pro, 21 g car, 48 g fat, 80 mg chol, 423 mg sod

PORK SANDWICHES CUBANO

Serves 4
Preparation time: 10 minutes
Cooking time: 20 minutes

For best flavor and texture, thaw the still-wrapped sliced cooked pork in the refrigerator (figure on at least 24 hours). Serve with a lettuce and tomato salad.

> 1 tablespoon olive oil
> 2 large onions, sliced thin (2 cups)
> 1/3 cup chopped fresh cilantro, basil, or parsley
> 1/4 teaspoon ground black pepper
> 1 cup frozen pan gravy (from meal 1), thawed
> 1 pound frozen sliced cooked pork (from meal 1), thawed
> 4 soft hero rolls (6 inches long), cut in half lengthwise
> For garnish: diced pimiento

1. In a large nonstick skillet, heat the oil over medium heat. Add the onions and cook for 12 to 15 minutes, stirring several times, until very tender and lightly golden. Stir in the cilantro and pepper. Transfer to a small bowl.

2. In the same skillet (no need to wash it) heat the gravy over medium-low heat. When very hot, add the pork slices and heat through.

3. Place hero rolls cut sides up, on individual plates.

4. Arrange the pork slices on the rolls. Top with the onion mixture.

5. Pour the gravy over the sandwiches and sprinkle with the pimiento.

Makes 4 sandwiches. Per serving: 680 cal, 39 g pro, 52 g car, 34 g fat, 110 mg chol, 738 mg sod with water, 1,198 mg sod with broth

LAMB CLASSICS

Lamb shanks are slow-cooked until they are tender and succulent, then combined with white beans for a hearty one-pot meal. The meat from two lamb shanks is shredded and mixed with some of the sauce for a Greek-style lamb and pasta pie.

BRAISED LAMB SHANKS WITH WHITE BEANS

Serves 4 with leftovers
Preparation time: 25 minutes
Cooking time: 2 hours

Accompany this slowly simmered feast with a simple green salad and a hearty red wine.

> 1 tablespoon olive oil
> 4 lamb shanks (12 to 14 ounces each)
> 2 cups chopped onion
> 1 can (28 pounces) whole tomatoes in juice
> 1 teaspoon dried rosemary leaves, crumbled
> 4 cloves garlic, peeled and crushed
> 2 cups beef broth
> 1 tablespoon all-purpose flour
> 1 can (about 15 ounces) white kidney beans, rinsed and drained
> For meal 2: 1/2 teaspoons ground cinnamon, 1/4 teaspoon ground black pepper, 1/4 teaspoon salt, pinch of allspice

1. In a 5-quart nonaluminum pot or Dutch oven, heat the oil over medium-high heat. Add the shanks in batches and brown on all sides, about 10 minutes. Remove to a plate.

2. Add the onion to the pot and cook for 5 minutes, stirring often, until softened. Return

the shanks to the pot.

3. Add the tomatoes, rosemary, and garlic. In a small bowl, mix the flour with 1 cup of broth until well blended. Stir into the pot with the remaining cup of broth. Cover and simmer for about 1 hour and 30 minutes, or until the meat is tender.

4. Remove 2 shanks and 2½ cups of liquid and set aside for meal 2.

5. Add the beans to the pot. Cover and simmer for 15 minutes more, or until heated through.

6. Shred the meat from the reserved shanks and combine with the reserved liquid. Stir in the cinnamon, black pepper, salt, and allspice. Cover tightly and refrigerate up to 3 days for meal 2.

Per serving: 433 cal, 35 g pro, 21 g car, 23 g fat, 99 mg chol, 789 mg sod

---

LAMB CLASSICS #2

GREEK LAMB & PASTA PIE

Serves 4

Preparation time: 25 minutes

Baking time: 45 minutes

This Greek version of macaroni and cheese uses shredded lamb and sauce from meal 1, ziti pasta, and a rich and creamy white sauce flavored with Parmesan cheese. The casserole can be assembled one day ahead and refrigerated, then baked just before serving.

8 ounces ziti pasta
2 tablespoons butter or margarine
¼ cup all-purpose flour
2 cups milk
2 large eggs, well beaten
2 tablespoon grated Parmesan cheese
¼ teaspoon salt
¼ teaspoon ground black pepper

Pinch grated or ground nutmeg
Shredded lamb mixture (from meal 1),
    at room temperature

1. Heat the oven to 350° F. Grease a shallow 2-quart baking dish.

2. Bring a large pot of water to a boil. Add the pasta and cook according to the package directions. Drain in a colander.

3. Meanwhile, in a medium-size saucepan, melt the butter over low heat. Add the flour, stirring until well blended. Cook, stirring constantly, for 2 to 3 minutes. Slowly whisk in the milk. Bring the mixture to a boil while whisking constantly. Cook for 10 minutes, whisking constantly, until thick and creamy. Remove the pan from the heat and let cool slightly.

4. Whisk in the eggs, then the Parmesan cheese, salt, pepper, and nutmeg.

5. Layer half the pasta in the prepared dish. Spread the lamb mixture over the pasta. Top with the remaining pasta. Spoon the white sauce over the pasta. Bake uncovered for 45 minutes, or until the top is golden brown. Let stand for 5 to 10 minutes before serving.

Per serving: 772 cal, 46 g pro, 64 g car, 36 g fat, 240 mg chol with butter, 224 mg chol with margarine, 1,132 mg sod

SAFEKEEPING

To prevent drying out or spoiling, cut up and then refrigerate or freeze meat for meals 2 and 3 as soon as possible—not more than 2 hours after cooking. Label clearly to protect from midnight snackers!

In next to no time, you will have made a poached halibut and vegetable dinner and have the makings for a delectable fish salad.

POACHED HALIBUT WITH CUCUMBER & TOMATO

Serves 2 with leftovers
Preparation time: 15 minutes
Cooking time: 15 minutes

The cucumber sits briefly in the poaching liquid, giving it extra flavor and tenderness. Serve this dish with cooked white or brown rice.

½ cup chopped red onion

⅓ cup water

⅓ cup dry white wine or chicken broth

1 tablespoon fresh lemon juice

¼ teaspoon salt

¼ teaspoon ground black pepper

2 halibut steaks, 1 inch thick (12 ounces each)

1 tablespoon olive oil

1 medium-size cucumber (8 ounces), peeled, seeded, and diced

1 medium-size tomato, diced

1½ teaspoons chopped fresh tarragon, or ¼ teaspoon dried tarragon leaves, crumbled

1. In a deep large skillet, mix the onion, water, wine, lemon juice, salt, and pepper. Add the halibut. Bring to a boil. Reduce the heat to low. Cover and simmer for 8 to 12 minutes, or until the fish is just opaque at its thickest part when tested with a fork.

2. Using two spatulas (so the fish doesn't fall apart), remove the steaks from the skillet. Put one on a serving platter and keep warm. Put the other on a plate, let cool, then wrap and refrigerate for meal 2.

3. Add the oil to the poaching liquid. Bring to a boil over high heat and boil for 1 to 2 minutes, or until reduced to ¼ cup. Remove the skillet from the heat. Stir in the cucumber, tomato, and tarragon.

4. Remove and discard the skin and bones from the warm fish. Spoon the warm cucumber mixture over the fish and serve right away.

Per serving: 283 cal with wine, 262 cal with broth, 31 g pro, 11 g car, 10 g fat, 44 mg chol, 362 mg sod with wine, 525 mg sod with broth

HALIBUT–SPINACH SALAD

Serves 2
Preparation time: 20 minutes

You can assemble this through step 4 several hours ahead. Just before serving, spoon over spinach leaves.

2 medium-size navel oranges

1 tablespoon raspberry or cider vinegar

¼ teaspoon Dijon mustard

¼ teaspoon salt

⅛ teaspoon ground white or black pepper

1½ teaspoons chopped fresh tarragon, or ¼ teaspoon dried tarragon leaves, crumbled

2 tablespoons olive oil

Half a medium-size red onion, sliced thin

1 poached halibut steak (from meal 1), skinned, boned, and broken into bite-size chunks

8 ounces fresh spinach, tough stems removed, well rinsed, drained, and torn into bite-size pieces (6 cups)

1. Grate ½ teaspoon of peel from 1 orange into a large bowl. Halve, then juice the orange (you'll need ¼ cup juice) into the bowl.

2. Add the vinegar, mustard, salt, pepper, and tarragon and whisk until well blended. Whisk in the olive oil.

3. Cut away the peel and white pith from the remaining orange. Cut crosswise into thin slices, then into small pieces.

4. Add to the bowl along with the onion and halibut. Gently stir with a large spoon to moisten.

5. To serve, mound the spinach on serving plates. Spoon the fish salad over the spinach.

Per serving: 346 cal, 32 g pro, 17 g car, 17 g fat, 44 mg chol, 427 mg sod

MORE QUICK FIXES

◆ **Potatoes** — Peel and slice leftover baked potatoes and make hash-browns or home-fries. Turn leftover mashed potatoes into potato croquettes: Form into patties. Dip into beaten egg, then bread crumbs. Chill for 30 minutes, then pan-fry in a little oil until golden brown on each side.

◆ **Poultry** — Like leftover fish and shellfish (see page 606), leftover poultry can be turned into a tasty sandwich spread, or used to top off a green salad. And like leftover meats (see page 606), it can be the starting point for a terrific casserole or pasta sauce. You can also mince leftover chicken and use for omelets or to stir into scrambled eggs.

◆ **Rice** — Make fried rice by sautéing leftover rice in a little oil with finely chopped vegetables, a small amount of minced fresh gingerroot, and a dash of soy sauce.

◆ **Soup** — Turn leftover soup into a curry sauce by pouring into a food processor or blender, adding curry powder and other seasonings, and blending until almost smooth. Serve over rice or egg noodles.

◆ **Vegetables** — Like fish, poultry, and meats, leftover vegetables can be used variously in sandwich spread, pasta sauce, or scrambled eggs. Or mince leftover vegetables and add to hamburger or meatloaf mixture.

VEGETABLE DUO

A vegetable stew that cooks in 15 minutes? And that's only the beginning. The second meal features a delightfully unusual sandwich.

VEGETABLE DUO #1

VEGETABLE STEW WITH COUSCOUS

Serves 4 with leftovers
Preparation time: 18 minutes
Cooking time: 15 minutes

Perfect for a summer dinner, this quick-cooking stew combines eggplant, zucchini, chick-peas, and feta cheese served over couscous.

   3 tablespoons olive oil
   1 large eggplant (1¼ pounds), cut into ½-inch chunks (about 7 cups)
   2 zucchini (1 pound), quartered lengthwise and cut into ½-inch pieces (3½ cups)
   2 cans (14½ ounces each) seasoned-for-pasta, cut-up tomatoes, undrained
   6 scallions, cut into ½-inch pieces
   1 tablespoon red wine vinegar
   1 teaspoon dried thyme leaves, crumbled
   1 teaspoon salt
   ½ teaspoon ground black pepper
   1 can (19 ounces) chick-peas, drained and rinsed
   4 ounces feta cheese, diced
   1 cup dry couscous, freshly prepared according to package directions

1. In a large pot, heat 2 tablespoons of oil over medium-high heat. Add the eggplant and cook, stirring often, for 4 minutes, ▶

or until lightly browned.

2. Add the zucchini and the remaining 1 tablespoon oil. Cook for 3 minutes, stirring once or twice.

3. Add 1 can of tomatoes, the scallions, vinegar, thyme, salt, and pepper. Cook, stirring often, for 5 minutes, or until the vegetables are tender and most of the liquid has evaporated. Scoop 2 cups of the stewed eggplant mixture into a medium-size bowl, cover, and refrigerate up to 2 days for meal 2.

4. Add the remaining can of tomatoes and the chick-peas to the pot. Cook, stirring often, for 2 minutes, or until heated through.

5. Remove the pot from the heat, stir in the feta cheese, and serve right away over hot couscous.

Per serving: 478 cal, 19 g pro, 68 g car, 16 g fat, 25 mg chol, 1,610 mg sod

COOK'S TIP

Couscous is made from ground wheat kernels (also called semolina flour) and water, rubbed into small pellets. In supermarkets, look for boxes of couscous near the rice. Natural-food stores and Middle Eastern shops sell it too.

VEGETABLE DUO #2

VEGETABLE & TUNA PAN BAGNA

Serves 4

*Preparation time: 8 minutes
plus at least 8 hours to chill*

Pan bagna, a sandwich famous in the Mediterranean region, literally means "bathed bread." You weight the loaf for several hours so that juices from the filling flow into it. The sandwich can be assembled in the morning or even the night before. What could be easier?

2 cans (6½ ounces each) light tuna in olive oil, undrained
2 tablespoons red wine vinegar
½ teaspoon minced fresh garlic
1 (8-inch) round loaf (about 16 ounces) Italian bread
1 jar (7 ounces) roasted sweet red peppers, drained
1 small bunch arugula or watercress
2 cups chilled stewed eggplant mixture (from meal 1)

1. Drain the oil from the tuna into a 1-cup glass measure. Discard all but ¼ cup of the oil. Add the vinegar and garlic and beat with a fork until well blended.

2. Cut the loaf in half horizontally. Pull some bread from the center of each half to form a hollow about 1 inch deep (you can save the bread you pulled out for bread crumbs). Spoon the oil mixture over both of the cut sides.

3. Place the bottom half of the bread on a large plate. Spoon the tuna, straight from cans, evenly over the bread. Top with a layer of roasted peppers, then the arugula. Spoon the eggplant mixture over the arugula and gently press into an even layer. Cover with the bread tops.

4. Wrap the loaf tightly in plastic wrap. Put it back on the plate, place in the refrigerator, and cover with another large plate. Place a large can or other heavy weight on top to press the sandwich down. Refrigerate for at least 8 hours, or overnight.

5. To serve, let stand at room temperature 30 minutes. Unwrap and cut into 8 wedges.

Makes 8 wedges. Per 2 wedges: 709 cal, 41 g pro, 98 g car, 20 g fat, 36 mg chol, 1,691 mg sod

INVESTMENT COOKING

"In cooking, as in all the arts, simplicity is the sign of perfection."
CURNONSKY

The WOMAN'S DAY kitchens have stirred up some remarkable things over the years, but nothing compares to the response we receive on our investment cooking strategies. The idea is simple: For just 3 to 4 hours in the kitchen (Sunday afternoons are perfect), you can whip up 44 to 56 servings of several different meals all ready for the freezer or refrigerator. Now, there's a worthy investment!

The benefits of cooking this way are many: You'll save money because of buying in bulk, eating out less often, and making fewer trips to the grocery store; you'll enjoy the satisfaction of knowing that your family is eating well; and you'll be able to save time and energy for needs outside of the kitchen.

Although it may sound daunting, it isn't. Everything you need to know is included here for each menu plan, from a shopping list to the required equipment. There are even alternatives for storing and freezing the dishes so you can decide when to serve them. Our only advice is to follow the instructions carefully, and to prepare the recipes in the order given. If you do, you'll be astounded at how simple it is.

BEFORE YOU BEGIN...

- If you can, do the shopping on one day and the cooking on the next.
- Read recipes through before starting.
- Begin by assembling all ingredients and equipment for each dish.
- To chop vegetables by hand, use a sharp chef's knife with a 6- or 8-inch blade and a sturdy cutting board.
- To chop vegetables in a food processor, first cut them into 1-inch chunks. Then process 1 cup at a time, using quick on/off turns until vegetables are desired size.
- Use one or two timers to remind you that something is the oven or on the stove for a certain length of time.
- Use any waiting time to prepare ingredients for another dish (measuring, opening cans, chopping, etc.).
- Reuse bowls and pans as much as possible to save counter and stove-top space.
- Clean up as you go along.

GROUND BEEF QUARTET

Servings: 44
Total time: 3 hours

Instead of chopping onions and garlic and mixing ground beef on four separate occasions, do enough at once to make four different recipes. Follow our step-by-step instructions and with minimal effort you'll end up with big pots of spicy chili and Asian meatball soup, a luscious meat lasagne, and two hearty meat loaves, all cooked and ready to serve or store.

SHOPPING LIST
Grocery items
Olive or vegetable oil
1 loaf light rye bread (with or without caraway seeds)
½ cup ketchup
Beef bouillon cubes (you will need 8 cubes)
16-ounce bag of dried lentils
2 cups white converted rice (13½ ounces)
8-ounce box no-boil lasagne noodles

Canned Foods
5 (28-ounce) cans crushed tomatoes in purée
4 (19-ounce) cans red kidney beans
3 (11-ounce) cans vacuum-packed corn

Herbs and Seasonings
Chili powder (you'll need ⅓ cup)
Dark Asian sesame oil
Ground cumin
Italian seasoning
Poultry seasoning
Salt

Meat
6 pounds lean ground beef
2 pounds ground turkey

Dairy
1 quart milk
1 dozen large eggs
15-ounce container part-skim ricotta cheese
8-ounce package part-skim shredded mozzarella cheese
Grated Parmesan cheese (you will need at least 3 ounces)

Produce
2 pounds onions
2 pounds bell peppers: green, yellow, or red
1 large bunch curly parsley
1 head fresh garlic
2-inch piece fresh gingerroot
1½ pounds bok choy

EQUIPMENT LIST
Food processor (optional)
Chef's knife with 6- to 8-inch blade
Standing mixer with paddle attachment (optional)
Cutting board
12-inch skillet
2 large bowls
1 medium-size bowl
8-quart pot
6-quart pot
2 (9 x 5-inch) loaf pans or heavy-duty foil pans
13 x 9-inch baking dish or heavy-duty foil pan
Measuring spoons
Nested measuring cups
Glass measuring cup
Cheese grater
Assorted freezer containers or heavy-duty zipper-type freezer bags
Heavy-duty aluminum foil, freezer wrap, or plastic wrap

TO BEGIN:

Chop and cook the aromatic vegetables (these will be used to flavor all the recipes in this plan).

1. Chop 2 pounds onions (you'll have about 6 cups), 2 pounds bell peppers (about 4 cups), and 1 large bunch curly parsley (5 cups of leaves will make about 2½ cups chopped).

2. In a large skillet, heat 3 tablespoons of oil. Add the onions and peppers and cook over medium-high heat 10 to 12 minutes, stirring occasionally, until almost tender. Remove the skillet from the heat. Stir in the parsley. You should have about 7 cups of cooked vegetables.

While the vegetables cook: Prepare the meat mixture.

1. In a large bowl, mix 6 pounds lean ground beef with 2 pounds ground turkey until blended. (If you have a heavy-duty mixer with a paddle attachment, mix the meat half at a time.)

2. Mince 10 large garlic cloves.

Now you're ready to prepare all four recipes. For the most efficient use of time and tools, make the recipes in the order given.

GROUND BEEF #1

MEAT LASAGNE

Serves 8

This delicious lasagne uses no-boil noodles. You can assemble and freeze the lasagne before baking, and you don't need to defrost it when you're ready to cook.

1. Heat the oven to 350°F (if you're going to bake lasagne right away).

2. Put 1 cup of aromatic vegetables in a large skillet. Add 1 pound (2 packed cups) of meat mixture, crumbling it with fingers; 1 tablespoon minced garlic; and 1 teaspoon Italian seasoning.

Cook over medium-high heat for 3 to 5 minutes, stirring occasionally, until the meat is no longer pink.

3. Stir in a 28-ounce can of crushed tomatoes to make a meat sauce. Spread 1 cup of meat sauce over the bottom of an ungreased 13 x 9-inch baking pan. Cover with 3 dry no-boil lasagne noodles (see Cook's Tip), being careful the noodles don't touch the edges of the dish.

4. Cover the noodles with 1 cup of meat sauce. Layer over the meat sauce half a 15-ounce container of part-skim ricotta cheese, ⅔ cup shredded part-skim mozzarella cheese, 2 tablespoons grated Parmesan cheese, 3 more noodles, and 1 cup meat sauce. Repeat layering once.

5. Sprinkle with ⅔ cup shredded mozzarella and 2 tablespoons grated Parmesan cheese.

6. Cover with foil and bake for 35 to 45 minutes, or until bubbly and the noodles are firm-tender.

7. Cool completely, then tightly cover with plastic wrap and refrigerate up to 3 days. Remove the plastic, loosely cover with foil, and heat at 350°F for 20 to 25 minutes, or until heated through. Or cover with plastic wrap, then heavy-duty aluminum foil, and freeze up to 2 months before baking. (Seal all wrapping securely so package is moisture-proof and vapor-proof.) When ready to bake, don't worry about thawing. Just increase the baking time by 30 to 40 minutes.

Per serving: 409 cal, 27 g pro, 31 g car, 19 g fat, 72 mg chol, 413 mg sod

COOK'S TIP

The new no-boil variety are good news for those who hate to boil lasagne noodles. The reason you leave room between the noodles and the sides of your pan is for the expansion that occurs with these unboiled noodles.

GROUND BEEF #2

MEAT LOAVES
Serves 16

Everybody loves meat loaf and our easy recipe makes two of these delicious entrees. Have one now and freeze the other for later.

1. Heat the oven to 350°F.
2. In a large bowl, beat 4 large eggs and 1½ cups milk until well blended.
3. Add 8 slices of light rye bread, torn into small pieces. Let soak for 2 to 3 minutes, then beat with a fork until a thin paste forms.
4. Stir in 2 cups of aromatic vegetables, ½ cup ketchup, 1 tablespoon each poultry seasoning and salt, and 1½ teaspoons minced garlic.
5. Add 4 pounds (8 packed cups) of meat mixture and mix until very well blended.
6. Pack the meat loaf mixture into two ungreased 9 x 5-inch loaf pans.

Bake, uncovered, for 1 hour, or until the meat loaves are firm to the touch and no longer pink in the center (about 165°F to 170°F on a meat thermometer). Pour off fat, let stand in pans 15 minutes, then remove from pans.

7. Cool the meat loaves completely, then tightly wrap and refrigerate up to 3 days. Remove the plastic, cover loosely with foil, and reheat at 300°F for 20 to 25 minutes, or until heated through. Or wrap in heavy-duty foil or freezer paper and freeze up to 4 months. Thaw in the refrigerator or microwave before reheating.
Makes 2 meat loaves. Per serving: 269 cal, 24 g pro, 14 g car, 23 g fat, 141 mg chol, 723 mg sod

GROUND BEEF #3

TEXAS CHILI
Serves 12

Chili is one of the great main dishes to have on hand. Freeze in serving-size portions, and they'll be ready in a snap.

1. In an 8-quart pot, put 2 cups of aromatic vegetables. Add 2 pounds (4 packed cups) of meat mixture, crumbling it with fingers; ⅓ cup chili powder; 2 tablespoons each ground cumin and minced garlic; and 2 teaspoons salt.
2. Cook over medium-high heat for 3 to 5 minutes, stirring occasionally, until the meat is no longer pink.
3. Stir in four 28-ounce cans crushed tomatoes, four 19-ounce cans red kidney beans, drained; and three 11-ounce cans vacuum-packed corn. Bring to a boil. Reduce the heat to medium low.
4. Cover and simmer for about 1½ hours, stirring occasionally, so the flavors blend and develop.
5. Cool the chili completely. Pack into airtight containers and refrigerate up to 1 week. Reheat on the range top. Or cool quickly by putting the pot in a sink full of cold water, then pack in airtight containers and freeze up to 4 months. Thaw in a covered saucepan over low heat. Increase the heat and cook until hot.
6. Serve with sour cream and chopped scallions. Accompany with rice or corn bread.
Per serving: 469 cal, 28 g pro, 56 g car, 17 g fat, 56 mg chol, 1,529 mg sod

GROUND BEEF #4

ASIAN MEATBALL SOUP

Serves 8

This lively flavored soup makes a hearty main dish that's good any time of year.

1. Put 2 cups of aromatic vegetables into a 6-quart pot. Mince one 2-inch piece of fresh gingerroot (you'll need 1 tablespoon plus 2 teaspoons).

2. Add 3½ quarts of water to the pot, along with 8 beef bouillon cubes, 1 pound of dried lentils (about 2½ cups), rinsed and picked over, 2 cups uncooked converted white rice, and 1 tablespoon each minced gingerroot and minced garlic. Bring to a boil, cover, and reduce the heat. Simmer for about 20 minutes, or until the lentils are almost tender.

3. Meanwhile, in a medium-size bowl, mix 1 pound (2 packed cups) of meat mixture and 2 teaspoons each minced gingerroot and minced garlic until well blended.

4. Form the meat into 24 small balls and stir into soup or drop by tablespoonfuls into soup.

5. Cover and simmer for 5 to 7 minutes, or until the meat loses its pink color.

6. Meanwhile, rinse 1½ pounds bok choy, then cut the stems and leaves crosswise into ½-inch-wide strips.

7. Stir the bok choy and 2 tablespoons dark Asian sesame oil into the soup. Simmer for 4 to 5 minutes, stirring 2 or 3 times, until the bok choy stems are crisp-tender.

8. Cool the soup completely and refrigerate in airtight containers up to 4 days. Reheat on the range top. Or freeze up to 3 months. Thaw in a covered saucepan over low heat. Increase the heat and cook until heated through.

Per serving: 585 cal, 32 g pro, 79 g car, 16 g fat, 42 mg chol, 976 mg sod

CONTEMPORARY CHICKEN CLASSICS

Servings: 46
Total time: 4 hours

With this investment plan, in about 4 hours you'll end up with 8 main-dish servings of chicken cacciatore, coq au vin, chicken potpie, chicken-vegetable soup, 10 chicken burritos, ready and waiting in the refrigerator or freezer, plus 4 servings of oven-fried Parmesan chicken for tonight's dinner.

SHOPPING LIST
Grocery items

Packaged plain bread crumbs
10 large (burrito size) flour tortillas
Long grain white rice (1 cup)
Chicken bouillon cubes (8 cubes)
Vegetable oil
Olive oil
All-purpose flour (½ cup)
4 (8½-ounce) boxes cornbread mix

Canned and jarred foods

2 (28-ounce) cans whole plum tomatoes in purée
1 (28-ounce) can crushed tomatoes
2 (16-ounce) cans refried beans

Herbs and Seasonings

1 bunch fresh dill (½ cup)
1 bunch fresh rosemary, or 2½ teaspoons dried
Bay leaves (4)
Black peppercorns
Salt
Ground black pepper
Italian seasoning
Chili powder
Dried oregano
Ground cloves

▶

Frozen items
1 (16-ounce) bag frozen peas
1 (16-ounce) bag frozen pearl onions

Meats
62 chicken thighs (about 20 pounds)
20 chicken drumsticks (about 5½ pounds)
Thick-sliced bacon (4 slices)

Dairy
Milk (you will need 2 cups plus amount needed
 for cornbread mix)
Eggs (4 for cornbread mix)
8 ounces Cheddar cheese
Grated Parmesan cheese (2 tablespoons)
Butter or margarine (1 stick)

Produce
20 ounces white mushrooms
18 large carrots (about 4½ pounds)
9 medium-size onions (about 3 pounds)
6 ribs celery (from 1 bunch)
5 medium-size zucchini (about 2½ pounds)
6 medium-size red bell peppers (about 2½
 pounds)
4 medium-size green bell peppers (about 2
 pounds)
3 medium-size jalapeño peppers
3 large baking potatoes
1 navel orange
1 bulb fresh garlic

Liquor
Dry red wine (you will need 3 cups)

EQUIPMENT LIST
Food processor (optional)
Chef's knife with a 6- or 8-inch blade
Cutting board
3 (8-quart) pots with lids
1 wide (5-quart) Dutch oven
2 wide large skillets

1 jelly roll pan, metal or heavy-duty aluminum
3 (2-quart) baking dishes or heavy-duty foil pans
3 (13 x 9-inch) baking dishes or heavy-duty
 foil pans
Colander
Large saucepan
Large bowl
Measuring spoons
Nested measuring cups
Glass measuring cup
Vegetable peeler
Wire whisk
Slotted spoon
Cheese shredder
Assorted freezer containers or heavy-duty
 zipper-lock freezer bags
Waxed paper, heavy-duty aluminum foil,
 plastic wrap

TO BEGIN:

1. Place one oven rack in the middle of the oven and the other in the lowest position. Heat the oven to 400°F. Remove the pearl onions and peas from the freezer to thaw.

2. Put 12 chicken thighs in a shallow baking pan and bake for 30 minutes (these will be part of the burrito filling).

3. Meanwhile, remove and discard the skin from 30 raw chicken thighs. Divide between two 8-quart pots. To each pot, add 2 quarts of water, 4 bouillon cubes, 1 bay leaf, and 6 black peppercorns.

4. Cut the tops off the 6 celery ribs. Cut 3 onions into quarters. Peel 12 whole carrots. Divide the celery ribs and tops, onions, and carrots between the pots.

5. Bring both pots to a boil over high heat, removing foam as it rises. Reduce the heat to medium-low, cover, and simmer for 45 minutes. Uncover and simmer for about 30 minutes more, or until the chicken is very tender. With a slotted spoon, remove the chicken to a bowl.

Remove the pots from the heat and set the broth aside.

MEANWHILE:

1. Peel the remaining carrots and cut in half lengthwise, then quarter crosswise. Cover and reserve for tonight's meal (oven-fried Parmesan chicken).

2. Halve 3 zucchini lengthwise, then slice crosswise (will be added to soup later). Quarter the remaining zucchini lengthwise, then cut in half crosswise. Cover and reserve for tonight's meal (oven-fried Parmesan chicken).

3. Slice the remaining onion thin.

4. Seed and cut the bell peppers into thin strips. Seed the jalapeños and slice thin. (Don't touch eyes, and wash hands well after cutting jalapeños.)

5. Mince 6 garlic cloves. Wrap and reserve 2 minced cloves for tonight's meal.

6. Heat 1 tablespoon of vegetable oil in each of 2 large skillets over medium-high heat. To each add half the sliced onion, bell pepper strips, and minced garlic. Cook, stirring often, for about 20 minutes, or until the vegetables are softened. Season each pan of cooked vegetables with ½ teaspoon salt and ground black pepper.

7. Meanwhile, remove the skin from the raw chicken drumsticks and the remaining chicken thighs.

8. Scrub the potatoes and reserve for tonight's meal (oven-fried Parmesan chicken).

Now you are ready to prepare all six recipes. For the most efficient use of time and tools, make them in the order given. However, if you're going to start cooking long before you want to serve tonight's dinner (oven-fried Parmesan chicken), read the note at the beginning of the recipe and finish making all the other chicken dishes (including the chicken potpie filling) before cooking tonight's dinner.

CHICKEN CLASSICS #1

CHICKEN CACCIATORE
Serves 8

Accompany this hearty and flavorful dish with pasta, a tossed green salad, and perhaps a glass of robust red wine.

1. In each of two 2-quart baking dishes, combine a 28-ounce can plum tomatoes, 1 cup of the chicken broth, 1 teaspoon of Italian seasoning, ½ teaspoon salt, ½ teaspoon ground black pepper, 2 strips of orange peel removed with a vegetable peeler, and 1 bay leaf.

2. Divide the cooked vegetables from 1 skillet between the baking dishes and stir to mix.

3. Arrange 4 uncooked chicken thighs and 4 uncooked drumsticks in each baking dish.

4. Bake on the middle oven rack (the thighs that you put in to bake earlier should be out by now) at 400°F for 1 hour and 10 minutes, stirring 3 or 4 times, until the chicken is opaque near the bone.

5. Cool completely, then cover with foil and refrigerate up to 3 days. Or pack into airtight freezer containers or zipper-type bags and freeze up to 3 months. Thaw in the refrigerator or microwave before reheating. Reheat at 350°F for 25 to 30 minutes, or until heated through.
Per serving: 309 cal, 34 g pro, 26 g car, 8 g fat, 121 mg chol, 997 mg sod

CHICKEN CLASSICS #2

COQ AU VIN
Serves 8

Flavored with red wine, bacon, and mushrooms, this chicken dish is based on a French classic. Serve with roasted potatoes, a simple vinaigrette-dressed salad, and crusty bread. ▶

1. Cut 4 slices thick-cut bacon into 1-inch pieces. In a large wide skillet, cook the bacon over medium heat. With a slotted spoon, remove the bacon to paper towels to drain, then divide between two 13 x 9-inch baking dishes.

2. Meanwhile, trim the mushrooms and cut into quarters.

3. Drain off all but 1 tablespoon of bacon drippings from the skillet. Brown 8 uncooked chicken thighs and 8 drumsticks in batches for about 2 minutes on each side. Divide the chicken between the baking dishes with the bacon.

4. Add the pearl onions to the skillet and cook over high heat, stirring often, until lightly browned. Divide the onions between the baking dishes.

5. Add the mushrooms to the skillet in batches and cook, stirring often, until golden. Divide the mushrooms between the baking dishes.

6. Add 1½ cups red wine, ½ cup chicken stock, 2 rosemary sprigs or 1 teaspoon dried, and ½ teaspoon salt to each baking dish and mix gently.

7. Bake both dishes on the lower oven rack, uncovered, for 40 minutes, or until the chicken is opaque near the bone.

8. Cool completely, then cover with foil and refrigerate up to 3 days. Or pack in airtight freezer containers and freeze up to 2 weeks. Thaw in the refrigerator or microwave before reheating. Reheat at 350°F for 20 to 25 minutes, or until heated through.

Per serving: 316 cal, 34 g pro, 8 g car, 10 g fat, 127 mg chol, 573 mg sod

CHICKEN BURRITOS
Serves 10

Individually wrapped burritos are nice to have on hand for a quick and filling lunch, dinner, or snack. Serve them topped with salsa (spicy if you dare), sour cream to temper the heat, and chopped fresh scallions.

1. In a wide 5-quart pot, mix a 28-ounce can of crushed tomatoes with 1 tablespoon chili powder, ½ teaspoon dried oregano, ¼ teaspoon salt, and a pinch of ground cloves. Bring the mixture to a boil. Reduce the heat to medium-low and simmer, uncovered, for about 20 minutes, or until thickened slightly.

2. Meanwhile, shred 8 ounces Cheddar cheese.

3. When the 12 roasted chicken thighs are cool enough to handle, remove the skin and shred the meat.

4. Add the shredded meat to the pot and simmer for 5 minutes more, or until the mixture is very thick.

5. Lay one flour tortilla flat on a counter top. Spread about ¼ cup of refried beans down the center. Top with ½ of the chicken mixture, ¼ cup cooked vegetables in the skillet, and ¼ cup shredded cheese. Fold the bottom of the tortilla over the filling, fold in the sides, and roll up. Repeat with the remaining 9 tortillas.

6. Individually wrap the burritos in foil for reheating in the oven, or in waxed paper for reheating in the microwave. Place the wrapped burritos in zipper-type food storage bags and refrigerate up to 3 days, or freeze up to 3 months. Thaw in the refrigerator or microwave before reheating.

7. Reheat foil-wrapped burritos in the oven at 350°F for 10 to 15 minutes, or until heated through and cheese is melted. Microwave waxed

paper–wrapped burritos on High for 2 to 3 minutes, turning once, until heated through and cheese is melted.

Makes 10 burritos. Per burrito: 554 cal, 38 g pro, 56 g car, 20 g fat, 91 mg chol, 1,041 mg sod

---

CHICKEN CLASSICS #4

CHICKEN–VEGETABLE SOUP

Serves 8

Soup fits nicely into these cooking plans because one of its most appealing attributes is that it almost always tastes better if made ahead.

1. Strain the broth from both pots through a colander or sieve set over a large bowl. Reserve the chicken thighs and carrots and discard the remaining solids. Reserve 2 cups of broth for the potpie. Wipe 1 pot clean and return the strained broth to it.

2. Bring the broth to a boil. Add 1 cup long-grain white rice and ½ teaspoon salt. Reduce the heat to medium-low and simmer uncovered for 15 minutes, or until the rice is almost tender.

3. Meanwhile, remove the meat from the chicken thighs and tear into bite-size pieces. Slice the cooked carrots. Finely chop ½ cup of fresh dill.

4. Add the sliced zucchini and 1½ cups of peas to the soup. Simmer for 5 minutes. Remove the pot from the heat.

5. Stir in half the chicken (about 5 cups), half the sliced carrots, and the dill.

6. Cool the soup quickly by putting the pot into a sink full of cold water. Pack into airtight containers and refrigerate up to 4 days or freeze up to 3 months. Thaw in a covered saucepan over low heat. Increase the heat and cook until hot.

Per serving: 434 cal, 39 g pro, 37 g car, 15 g fat, 113 mg chol, 953 mg sod

---

CHICKEN CLASSICS #5

OVEN–FRIED PARMESAN CHICKEN

Serves 4

Serve this simple oven meal of crispy, Parmesan-coated chicken and oven-roasted potatoes, carrots, and zucchini for tonight's dinner. The recipe can also be easily expanded to serve more. Note: If you start this cooking plan early in the day, refrigerate the uncooked chicken for the recipe and cover the pan of oiled potatoes and carrots until ready to assemble.

1. Heat the oven to 400°F. Lightly grease a jelly roll pan. Have ready a 13 x 9-inch baking pan.

2. In a small bowl, mix the reserved minced garlic with 1 tablespoon olive oil. Brush the mixture over 4 chicken thighs and 4 chicken drumsticks.

3. In a large zipper-type food-storage bag, mix ¾ cup packaged plain bread crumbs, 2 tablespoons Parmesan cheese, ½ teaspoon Italian seasoning, ½ teaspoon ground black pepper, and ¼ teaspoon salt. Add the chicken, seal the bag, and turn or shake to coat evenly.

4. Arrange the coated chicken pieces in the prepared jelly roll pan. Bake on the lower oven rack for about 40 minutes, turning every 10 minutes, until the chicken is opaque near the bone.

5. Meanwhile, cut the 3 potatoes into 6 wedges each.

6. In a medium-size bowl, combine the potato wedges and reserved sliced carrots and toss with 1 tablespoon olive oil. Spread the vegetables in the 13 x 9-inch baking dish.

7. Bake on the middle oven rack for 15 minutes. Add the zucchini and bake for 15 minutes more, or until the vegetables are tender.

Per serving: 530 cal, 40 g pro, 57 g car, 16 g fat, 123 mg chol, 536 mg sod

CHICKEN CLASSICS #6

CHICKEN POTPIE

Serves 8

This humble dinner pie uses cornbread for a topping, but you could use mashed potatoes, or biscuit dough instead.

1. In a large saucepan, melt 1 stick of butter or margarine over medium heat. Whisk in ½ cup of flour until well blended. Slowly whisk in 2 cups of milk until smooth. Stir in the reserved 2 cups of chicken broth, 2 teaspoons chopped rosemary or ½ teaspoon dried, and ½ teaspoon each salt and ground black pepper.

2. Bring to a boil while whisking constantly. Reduce the heat and simmer uncovered for about 5 minutes, or until thickened slightly.

3. Stir in the reserved 5 cups of shredded chicken (from chicken-vegetable soup recipe), sliced carrots, and the remaining pearl onions and peas. Simmer, stirring occasionally, for 8 to 10 minutes, until thickened.

4. Remove the pan from the heat and cool completely. Divide evenly between 2 airtight containers and refrigerate up to 3 days or freeze up to 3 months.

5. To serve, thaw potpie filling in the refrigerator or in the microwave. Heat the oven to 400°F.

6. Spoon the filling into a shallow 2-quart baking dish. Bake for about 20 minutes, or until heated through.

7. Meanwhile, for each pie, prepare 2 packages cornbread mix according to the package directions. Top the hot filling with spoonfuls of the cornbread batter.

8. Bake for another 20 minutes, or until the cornbread is golden and cooked through.

Per serving: 778 cal, 43 g pro, 71 g car, 35 g fat, 208 mg chol with butter, 177 mg chol with margarine, 1,062 mg sod

GLOBAL PORK PLUS

Servings: 56
Total time: 4 hours

You will be making a total of six recipes, including black bean soup, roast pork with vegetables, turkey cannelloni, a deviled pork casserole, fajita-style tacos, and open-face sandwiches.

SHOPPING LIST

Grocery items

3 (1-pound) bags dried black beans

Instant beef bouillon (6 tablespoons granules)

2 (8-ounce) boxes no-boil lasagne noodles

1 long loaf (16 ounces) soft Italian bread

8 ounces wide egg noodles

Cider vinegar (½ cup plus 2 tablespoons)

Dijon mustard (1½ tablespoons)

Taco-dinner kit (12 taco shells, seasoning, and sauce)

Vegetable oil

All-purpose flour (2 tablespoons)

Canned and jarred foods

2 (8-ounce) cans tomato sauce

1 (3-pound) jar spaghetti sauce with mushrooms

1 (10⅓-ounce) can beef broth

Freezer items

1 (16-ounce) bag frozen cut-leaf spinach

Seasonings

Caraway seeds

Garlic powder

Ground black pepper

Ground cumin

Grated nutmeg

Salt

Meat

1 boneless pork leg roast (shank half, about
   8 pounds), fat trimmed to ¼ inch, tied in
   several places
2 pounds ground turkey

Dairy

2 pounds (32 ounces) ricotta cheese
1 cup grated Parmesan cheese

Produce

3 pounds onions
2 pound baking potatoes
12 ounces carrots
8 ribs celery (from 1 bunch)
1 head (about 1½ pounds) green cabbage
3 Granny Smith apples
6 medium-size scallions
2 small red and/or green bell peppers

EQUIPMENT LIST

Roasting pan with rack
Meat thermometer
Food processor (optional)
Chef's knife with a 6- or 8-inch blade
Sharp carving knife
Cutting board
10-quart pot, or one 6-quart pot and one
   5-quart pot
4-quart pot
5 (12 x 8-inch) heavy-duty foil pans
13 x 9-inch baking pan
8-inch skillet
8-inch square baking pan
Colander
Potato masher
Measuring spoons
Nested measuring cups
Glass measuring cup
Assorted freezer containers or heavy-duty
   zipper-type freezer bags
Zipper-type sandwich bags

Waxed paper, heavy-duty aluminum foil,
   plastic wrap

TO BEGIN:

Start the pork roast.

1. Place one oven rack in the lowest position
and the other in the middle. Heat the oven to
450°F.

2. Get out the pork roast and rub all over
with 1 tablespoon oil, then sprinkle with 1 teaspoon each garlic powder and salt and ½ teaspoon pepper. Place on a rack in a roasting pan
and insert a meat thermometer into the thickest
part. Cover loosely with foil.

3. Roast on the middle rack for 30 minutes,
then reduce the oven temperature to 350°F and
roast 3½ hours, or until the meat thermometer
registers 160°F.

MEANWHILE:

Continue with preparations for all six recipes.

1. Get out your food processor (optional),
cutting board, chef's knife, the onions, potatoes,
carrots, celery, cabbage, apples, scallions, and bell
peppers.

2. Peel the onions and cut half of them in
two lengthwise, then lengthwise into thin strips
(4½ cups). Put into an 8-inch square baking
dish and toss with 1 tablespoon oil. Cover and
set aside. These will go into the oven after the
pork has cooked for 3 hours. (We'll tell you
when.) After roasting, they'll be added to the
fajita-style pork tacos and hot open-face pork
sandwiches.

3. Scrub the potatoes. Cut each into 6
wedges. Put into a 13 x 9-inch baking dish.
Halve the carrots lengthwise, then crosswise.
Add to the potatoes and toss with 1 tablespoon
oil. Cover and set aside. The potatoes and carrots
will go into the oven when the onions do.
They'll be served with the roast pork with
vegetables dinner. ▶

4. Cut the remaining onions and the celery into 1-inch chunks. Chop the onion chunks fine (in batches, with on/off turns, if using processor). You'll have 4½ cups. Mound on waxed paper. Chop celery fine. Mound on waxed paper.

5. Coarsely shred the cabbage. Bag and set aside.

6. Peel, halve, and core the apples. Cut into 1-inch chunks. Bag and set aside.

7. Slice the scallions. Bag and set aside.

8. Seed and cut the bell peppers into ½-inch pieces. Bag and set aside.

Now you're ready to prepare the cannelloni casserole from start to finish, and prepare the Cuban black-bean soup and deviled cabbage, noodles, and pork up to the point where the cooked pork is added. For most efficient use of time and tools, prepare recipes in the order given.

Be sure to watch the clock, because after the pork has cooked three hours, you need to put the potatoes, carrots, and onions in the oven to roast.

GLOBAL PORK #1

CUBAN BLACK BEAN SOUP

Serves 20

If you have a pot 10 quarts or larger, you can cook the soup in one pot instead of the two called for in the recipe.

1. Have ready a 6-quart and a 5-quart pot, or two of either size, on the back burners. Rinse 3 pounds dried black beans in a colander and pick over thoroughly to remove any foreign material. Put half the beans into each pot.

2. To each pot add 3 quarts of water, 1½ cups each chopped onions and celery, one 8-ounce can tomato sauce, 3 tablespoons instant beef-bouillon granules, 1 tablespoon garlic powder, 1½ teaspoons ground cumin, and ½ teaspoon pepper. Bring to a boil. Reduce the heat to low. Cover and simmer for 3 hours, stirring occasionally, until the beans are very tender but not disintegrating.

3. Mash some beans (not all) in the pots with a potato masher to thicken the soup.

Stop here. You now have to wait until the pork is ready before continuing.

4. After the cooked pork has cooled, dice enough, including browned sides and ends of roast, to make 3½ cups (about 1¼ pounds).

5. Stir half into each pot. Cool the soup completely. Refrigerate in airtight containers (in sizes to suit your family's needs) up to 5 days. Reheat on the range top. Or pack in freezer containers and freeze up to 4 months. Thaw in a covered saucepan over low heat. Increase the heat and cook, stirring occasionally, until heated through.

6. To serve, mound ½ cup hot cooked rice in each soup bowl. Add soup and a dash of vinegar or hot-pepper sauce. Garnish with cilantro sprigs and a lemon slice.

Per serving with rice: 440 cal, 26 g pro, 74 g car, 4 g fat, 26 mg chol, 479 mg sod

---

GLOBAL PORK #2

TURKEY CANNELLONI

Serves 20

No-boil lasagne noodles are wider and shorter than regular lasagne noodles. If no-cook noodles are unavailable, cook 20 manicotti shells as directed on the box and stuff them with the turkey mixture instead. You can freeze individual cannelloni (without sauce) on cookie sheets lined with plastic wrap. When the cannelloni are frozen, pack in freezer bags. Assemble in pans and add sauce before baking.

1. Have ready five 12 x 8-inch heavy-duty foil pans.

2. In a large bowl, soak 20 no-boil lasagne noodles in cool water for 20 minutes, or until soft.

3. Meanwhile, in a 4-quart pot, cook one 16-ounce bag frozen cut-leaf spinach in 1 cup water for 4 minutes, or until fully thawed. Drain in a colander. Press out the excess water with a potato masher.

4. Wipe out the pot. Heat 2 tablespoons of oil in the pot over medium-high heat. Add the remaining 1½ cups chopped onions and cook for 5 minutes, stirring often, until softened.

5. Crumble 2 pounds of ground turkey into the pot. Cook for 7 to 10 minutes, breaking up the turkey with a wooden spoon, until no longer pink. Remove the pot from the heat. Cool 5 minutes.

6. Stir in 2 pounds ricotta cheese, the spinach, 1 cup grated Parmesan cheese, 2 teaspoons garlic powder, 1 teaspoon each salt and pepper, and ½ teaspoon grated nutmeg until blended.

7. Drain the noodles and cut each in half crosswise.

8. Put a level ¼ cup of filling across the middle of each noodle and roll up.

9. Place seam-side down in foil pans, 8 per pan. Top each batch with 1 cup of bottled spaghetti sauce with mushrooms. Cover the pans with foil.

10. Refrigerate one or several pans up to 3 days. Bake (covered) for 30 minutes at 350°F, until bubbly. Or freeze, tightly wrapped and unbaked, up to 4 months. To serve, bake the frozen casserole (covered) for 1 hour at 350°F.

11. To serve, top with extra Parmesan cheese and accompany with a crisp green salad and breadsticks.

Makes 5 casseroles. Per serving: 344 cal, 20 g pro, 30 g car, 15 g fat, 59 mg chol, 541 mg sod

GLOBAL PORK #3

DEVILED CABBAGE, NOODLES, & PORK
Serves 4

Refrigerate the cooked cabbage mixture in the same bag you used to store the raw cabbage.

1. Wipe out the pot used to make cannelloni filling. In a small bowl, mix ½ cup plus 2 tablespoons cider vinegar, 1½ tablespoons Dijon mustard, and 1 teaspoon each caraway seeds and salt.

2. Heat 2 tablespoons of oil in the pot over medium-high heat. Add the shredded cabbage and stir-fry 3 to 4 minutes, or until wilted and crisp-tender. Stir in apple chunks and scallions.

3. Pour in the vinegar mixture and ⅓ cup water and bring to a boil. Reduce the heat to medium-low. Cover and simmer for 7 to 10 minutes, stirring occasionally, until the cabbage is tender. Let cool for 10 minutes.

4. Spoon the mixture into zipper-lock food-storage bags. Cool completely before sealing. Stop here. You now have to wait until the pork is ready before continuing.

5. After the cooked pork has cooled, cut enough in 1-inch-long, ¼-inch-wide strips to make 2¾ cups (about 1 pound). Add pork to cabbage mixture.

6. Refrigerate in airtight containers up to 3 days. Reheat on the range top. Or pack in freezer containers and freeze up to 4 months. Thaw in a covered saucepan over low heat. Increase the heat and cook, stirring occasionally, until heated through.

7. To serve, stir 8 ounces of freshly cooked and drained wide egg noodles and snipped fresh dill into the heated cabbage-pork mixture. A hearty pumpernickel bread goes well with this.

Per serving: 645 cal, 43 g pro, 70 g car, 22 g fat, 158 mg chol, 805 mg sod

FAJITA-STYLE PORK TACOS

Serves 4

For this recipe, the roast pork is diced and flavored with packaged taco-seasoning mix. This filling can also be used to make burritos in flour tortillas or served plain over rice or noodles.

1. Remove taco-seasoning-mix packet from taco-dinner kit. Put taco shells and sauce packet in cupboard until needed.

2. In a small skillet, heat 1 tablespoon oil over medium-high heat. Add the bell pepper chunks and cook 3 minutes. Stir in the taco-seasoning mix and 1 cup water. Bring to a boil. Reduce the heat to medium-low. Simmer uncovered for 7 minutes, stirring occasionally.

3. Remove the skillet from the heat. Let cool slightly and spoon into a 1-quart-size freezer container or zipper-type food-storage bag. Stop here. You now have to wait until the pork is ready before continuing.

4. After the cooked pork roast and roasted onions have cooled, dice 12 ounces pork (to make 2 cups) and measure ½ cup onion.

5. Stir the pork and onion into the bag containing the seasoning mixture.

6. Refrigerate up to 4 days. Reheat on the stove top. Or freeze up to 4 months. Thaw in a covered saucepan over low heat. Increase the heat and cook, stirring occasionally, until heated through.

7. To serve, heat the taco shells as directed on the taco-kit box. Fill the shells with shredded lettuce and the filling, then top with shredded Cheddar cheese. Serve with taco sauce included in the kit.

Makes 12 tacos. Per taco: 299 cal, 7 g pro, 25 g car, 20 g fat, 12 mg chol, 1, 534 mg sod

FINISH THE PORK ROAST AND ROASTED VEGETABLES:

1. By now the pork has been roasting for about 3 hours and it's time to put the pans with the potato and carrot mixture and the sliced onions on the oven rack under the pork. Roast for 1 hour, stirring once or twice, until vegetables are lightly browned and very tender.

2. When pork and vegetables are cooked, remove the pork to a cutting board (don't wash the roasting pan—you'll need it to make gravy), and put the baking dishes on a heatproof surface. Let everything cool for about 1 hour.

3. Meanwhile, make the pan gravy. Pour the drippings from the roasting pan into a 1-cup measure. Spoon 2 tablespoons of fat off the top and into the roasting pan. Discard the remaining fat (the clearer liquid on top of the dark juices in the cup).

4. Put the roasting pan across 2 burners (you may have to move one soup pot). Sprinkle 2 tablespoons of flour and ¼ teaspoon pepper over the fat in pan. Whisk over medium-high heat until smooth, scraping up the browned bits from the bottom of the pan. Gradually whisk in one 10¾-ounce can beef broth plus ¼ cup water until blended. Bring to a boil, reduce the heat and simmer for 5 minutes, or until thickened, stirring 2 or 3 times. Makes 2 cups.

5. Divide the pork. With a sharp carving knife, cut off and discard all the visible fat. (You should have about 5 pounds of cooked meat.) Trim off and save the browned sides and ends (this will be added to the soup). Score the top of the pork to divide into 5 equal pieces (the narrow end will have less meat than wide end). Starting at the widest end, cut about two-fifths (about 2 pounds) of the pork into thin slices. Wrap half for the roast pork with vegetables and the remaining slices for the hot open-face pork sandwiches (recipes follow). Cut the remaining pork into thirds, 1 pound (plus the browned

sides and ends) for the soup, 1 pound for the deviled cabbage, noodles, and pork, and 12 ounces for the fajita-style pork tacos.

ROAST PORK WITH VEGETABLES

Serves 4

After an afternoon of cooking, what could be better than sitting down to a dinner like this one?

1. Cover the baking dish of potatoes and carrots with foil. Reheat in 350°F oven for 20 minutes.

2. In a large skillet, reheat half the sliced pork in 1 cup of the gravy.

Per serving: 499 cal, 38 g pro, 47 g car, 17 g fat, 106 mg chol, 256 mg sod

---

HOT OPEN–FACE PORK SANDWICHES

Serves 4

The portions are wrapped individually so you can heat what you need at one time.

1. Have ready 4 quart-size containers or freezer bags (or, if serving within 3 days, assemble in 1 container).

2. Divide the remaining sliced pork into 4 portions and put each into a container with ¼ cup of the remaining roasted onions and ¼ cup of gravy.

3. Refrigerate up to 3 days. Reheat pork in a covered saucepan over low heat. Or freeze up to 4 months. Thaw in refrigerator. Add 1 tablespoon water for each portion and reheat pork in a covered saucepan.

4. To serve, cut a loaf of soft Italian bread crosswise into four pieces. Split and top with the pork mixture. Kaiser rolls can be used instead of the bread.

Makes 4 sandwiches. Per sandwich: 548 cal, 41 g pro, 49 g car, 19 g fat, 107 mg chol, 847 mg sod

ⓒOOK'S TIP

You can roast a 12- to 14-pound turkey or use 5 pounds of cooked skinless boned turkey meat instead of the roast pork. Rub the turkey with oil and season as directed for the pork. Roast, following directions on turkey wrapper. Let cool as directed for pork. Remove the skin and meat from the drumsticks and thighs. Cut up and use for the soup and tacos. Slice the breast meat to serve with the roast vegetables, hot sandwiches, and cabbage dish.

SIMPLE BEEF MEALS

Servings: 54
Total time: 3 hours

This plan starts with 8½ pounds of ground beef and in less than three hours gives you more than 50 servings of five different and delicious main dishes: pasta with meat sauce, chili, meatball soup, Salisbury steaks, and picadillo casseroles.

SHOPPING LIST
Grocery Items
Vegetable oil
Granulated sugar
Red wine vinegar
2 cups packaged plain bread crumbs
2-ounce box onion-soup mix
16 ounces tiny bow-tie or other pasta
  for soup

▶

Canned and jarred foods

4 (28-ounce) cans crushed tomatoes in purée

2 (about 19 ounce) cans kidney beans

15-ounce can tomato sauce

64 ounces chicken broth (8 cups)

2 (12-ounce) jars brown gravy

5-ounce jar pimiento-stuffed green olives
   (you'll need ½ cup sliced)

Freezer Items

1 (16-ounce) bag frozen cut-leaf spinach

Herbs and Seasoning

Chili powder

Ground cinnamon

Meat

8½ pounds ground beef

Dairy

10 ounces shredded Cheddar cheese

2 large eggs

10 (8-inch) flour tortillas

½ cup grated Parmesan cheese

Produce

2 pounds onions

2 pounds carrots

2 pounds zucchini

1 bulb fresh garlic

EQUIPMENT LIST

Food processor (optional)

Chef's knife with 6- to 8-inch blade

Cutting board

Two 8-quart pots

One 6-quart pot

2 to 3 large bowls

Two 9- or 10-inch deep pie plates or two
   9-inch shallow round baking dishes

Two 11 x 7-inch baking pans or heavy-duty
   foil pans

1 medium-size saucepan

Measuring spoons

Nested measuring cups

Glass measuring cup

Assorted freezer containers or heavy-duty
   zipper-lock freezer bags

Heavy-duty aluminum foil, freezer wrap, or
   plastic wrap

TO BEGIN:

Chop and cook the aromatic vegetables (these will be used to flavor all the recipes).

1. Chop 2 pounds onions (you'll have about 6 cups), 2 pounds carrots (6 cups), and 2 pounds zucchini (7 cups). Or cut the vegetables in 1-inch chunks, then process in a food processor, 1 cup at a time, using quick on/off turns, just until the vegetables are desired size.

2. In an 8-quart pot, heat ¼ cup of vegetable oil. Add the vegetables. Cook over medium-high heat 15 to 20 minutes, stirring 3 or 4 times, until almost tender. (You will have about 12 cups cooked vegetables.) Transfer the vegetables to a large bowl.

PREPARE THE MEAT SAUCE:

1. Mince 8 large garlic cloves (or use 4 teaspoons minced garlic from a jar).

2. In an 8-quart pot, put 3 pounds (6 packed cups) ground beef and 1 tablespoon minced garlic. Cook for 7 to 10 minutes over medium-high heat, breaking up the meat with a wooden spoon, stirring every minute or so, until the meat is no longer pink.

3. Stir in 6 cups of the cooked aromatic vegetables, four 28-ounce cans crushed tomatoes in purée, a 15-ounce can tomato sauce, and 2 teaspoons salt. Bring to a boil. Reduce the heat to medium-low.

4. Simmer uncovered for 15 to 20 minutes for the flavors to develop.

5. Remove from the pot: 7 cups for the meat

sauce and 8 cups for the picadillo casseroles, leaving 7 cups in the pot for the zesty chili (next recipe). Refrigerate the 7 cups plain meat sauce in airtight containers (in sizes that suit your family's needs) up to 5 days. Reheat on the range top. Or pack in freezer containers and freeze up to 4 months.

Now that the meat sauce is done, you're ready to prepare the other four recipes. For most efficient use of time and tools, make them in the order given.

MEAT SAUCE (FOR PASTA)

Serves 7

The full-bodied, flavorful meat sauce is a natural for serving over pasta and creates a satisfying dish that will send you back for more.

1. Reheat the refrigerated plain meat sauce on the range top, or thaw frozen meat sauce in a covered saucepan over low heat. Increase the heat and cook, stirring occasionally, until heated through.

2. To serve, spoon the plain meat sauce over hot pasta.

Makes 7 cups. Per 1 cup without pasta: 267 cal, 12 g pro, 15 g car, 18 g fat, 53 mg chol, 597 mg sod

FREEZING TIPS

To protect quality, package carefully to keep air out of food. Expel as much air as you can from plastic freezer bags before tying or sealing. Use freezer tape to double-seal even made-for-the-freezer lids. In rigid plastic containers leave 1/4-inch head space for expansion. Freeze in individual or 2- or 4-person servings. Label packages for easy identification.

ZESTY CHILI

Serves 7

Chili can be served as a topping for baked potatoes, a filling for tacos or burritos, over hot dogs and hamburgers, as well as eaten plain.

1. Drain two 19-ounce cans kidney beans. Stir into the 7 cups meat sauce left in the pot with 2 or more tablespoons chili powder.

2. Cool completely, then refrigerate chili in airtight containers up to 5 days. Reheat on the range top. Or pack into freezer containers and freeze up to 4 months. Thaw in a covered saucepan over low heat. Increase the heat and cook, stirring occasionally, until heated through.

3. Top with shredded Cheddar cheese, sour cream, and chopped raw onion and tomato.

Per serving without topping: 382 cal, 21 g pro, 33 g car, 19 g fat, 53 mg chol, 810 mg sod

PICADILLO CASSEROLES

Serves 12

This sweet and spicy casserole will be a favorite with kids and adults alike.

1. Heat the oven to 375°F (if you're going to eat casserole[s] right away).

2. Lightly grease two 9-or 10-inch deep-dish pie plates, or two 9-inch round shallow baking dishes.

3. In a large bowl, mix 8 cups of meat sauce, 1/2 cup sliced pimiento-stuffed green olives, 1 tablespoon granulated sugar, 2 tablespoons red-wine vinegar, 2 teaspoons chili powder, and 1 teaspoon ground cinnamon.

4. Spread 2/3 cup of the sauce in bottom of each baking dish. Cover each with a flour ▶

tortilla, spread each tortilla with ⅔ cup sauce and sprinkle with ¼ cup shredded Cheddar cheese. Top with another tortilla, ⅔ cup sauce, and ¼ cup cheese. Repeat these layers 3 more times, ending with cheese (the layers may extend above plate rim).

5. Cover each casserole with foil and refrigerate one or both casseroles up to 4 days. Bake for 30 to 35 minutes at 375°F until bubbly. Or freeze before baking up to 4 months. Bake frozen casserole[s] for 1 hour 45 minutes at 350°F.

Makes 2 casseroles. Per serving: 387 cal, 17 g pro, 28 g car, 23 g fat, 60 mg chol, 824 mg sod

---

SIMPLE BEEF #4

SALISBURY STEAKS WITH VEGETABLE GRAVY

Serves 16

You'll never tire of this homey dish. Serve it with mashed potatoes to pour the gravy over.

1. Heat the oven to 375°F.

2. In a large bowl, put 4 pounds (8 packed cups) of ground beef, 2 cups dried bread crumbs, 1 box (2 ounces) onion-soup mix, 2 large eggs, ½ cup water, and 1 tablespoon minced garlic. Mix until blended.

3. Pack the mixture into two ungreased 11 x 7 x 1½-inch baking pans. Bake for 20 to 25 minutes, or until firm to the touch and no longer pink in center. Cool.

4. Meanwhile, in a medium-size saucepan, mix 2 cups of aromatic vegetables, 2 jars (12 ounces each) of brown gravy, and 2 cups of water. Bring to a boil. Reduce the heat to medium and simmer for 5 minutes for the flavors to blend. Cool, then pour into two 4-cup containers.

5. Wrap the uncut Salisbury steak tightly in plastic wrap. Refrigerate one or both pans and gravy up to 3 days. Reheat, covered, for 20 to

25 minutes at 350°F. Cut into 8 portions before serving. Or wrap in plastic, then heavy-duty aluminum foil, and freeze up to 4 months. Unwrap, cover with foil, and reheat at 350°F for 35 to 45 minutes, or until heated through.

Per serving: 462 cal, 24 g pro, 16 g car, 33 g fat, 124 mg chol, 544 mg sod

---

SIMPLE BEEF #5

CHICKEN SOUP WITH TINY MEATBALLS

Serves 12

While the Salisbury steaks bake, finish up by making this delicious main-dish soup.

1. In a 6-quart pot, bring 8 cups chicken broth and 8 cups water to a boil.

2. Add 16 ounces tiny bow-tie pasta and cook for 5 minutes. Then add one 16-ounce bag frozen cut-leaf spinach. Simmer for 5 minutes more.

3. Meanwhile, in a large bowl, mix the remaining 1½ pounds ground beef (3 packed cups), ½ cup grated Parmesan cheese, and 1 teaspoon minced garlic until blended.

4. Form rounded teaspoonfuls of the meat mixture into small meatballs and stir into the soup, or drop by rounded teaspoonfuls directly into the soup.

5. Simmer for 5 to 7 minutes, or until the meat is no longer pink in center.

6. Stir in remaining 3 cups aromatic vegetables and heat through.

7. Cool the soup completely. Refrigerate in airtight containers up to 4 days. Or pack into freezer containers and freeze up to 4 months. Thaw in a covered saucepan over low heat. Increase the heat and cook, stirring occasionally, until heated through.

Per serving: 389 cal, 19 g pro, 34 g car, 19 g fat, 51 mg chol, 806 mg sod

BASTA PASTA
A robust tomato-based Meat Sauce (p.647) can be spun off into several Italian meals, including just a simple plate of pasta.

SMART MONEY
With the Simple Beef Meals plan, you can look forward to Chicken Soup with Tiny Meatballs (p.648), left, and Salisbury Steak (p.648), above.

Our investment cooking strategies are some of the most sensible kitchen time-savers around. Be sure to plan carefully and prepare the recipes in the order they are given in this chapter.

All the information you need to know about investment cooking is included here, from step-by-step
recipes and detailed shopping and equipment lists to
advice on storing and freezing.

FOOD SAVVY
After an afternoon of cooking, Hot Open-Face Pork Sandwiches (p.645), above, and Cuban Black Bean Soup (p.642), right, are ready and waiting.

INTERNATIONAL
Circle the globe
with these pork
entrees: Fajita-
Style Pork Tacos
(p.644), left, and
Deviled Cabbage,
Noodles, & Pork
(p.643), above.

Take the list of everything you'll need with you when you go shopping—be sure to check your cupboards first—so that you will have all the ingredients on hand as you prepare the meals.

MEXICANA
Flour tortilla layered with spicy meat sauce and cheese combine to make Picadillo Casseroles (p.647).

A YEAR OF
MENUS

"We must eat to live and live to eat."
HENRY FIELDING

Finally, an answer to the time-honored dilemma of what to cook for dinner: A year's worth of menus, from January through December, that includes an easy recipe or tip for each night. Our goal in putting together these menus is to cut corners on time and money while suggesting new ideas or new twists to faithful standbys.

You'll find many menus that call for cooking extra food one night (usually on the weekend) and using it for another meal during the week. There are many low-fat meals, some that take advantage of convenience foods, and others designed with kids in mind. And don't forget that store-bought prepared foods and foods from high-quality take-out establishments should not be considered a compromise and can be just the thing on nights when you are really short on time. All menus are given for 4 servings unless otherwise indicated.

	WEEK 1	WEEK 2	WEEK 3	WEEK 4	
SUNDAY	**Roast Chicken** (roast an extra chicken for Tuesday) **Saucepan Stuffing Brussels Sprouts Mixed Green Salad with Dijon Vinaigrette Hot Apple Wedges with Vanilla Ice Milk *** *Sauté peeled apple wedges in butter, sugar, and cinnamon until tender. Spoon over ice milk.*	**Baked Glazed Ham* Baked Sweet Potatoes Creamed Onions and Peas** (frozen) **Vanilla Pudding with Toasted Coconut** *Mix ½ cup orange marmalade, 2 tablespoons mustard, and 1 tablespoon each cider vinegar and molasses. Brush on ham during baking.*	**Meat Loaf** (bake enough for Tuesday) **Mashed Potatoes** (make enough for Monday) **Green Beans Baked Stuffed Apples*** *Stuff apples with raisins, chopped pecans, and brown sugar. Dot with butter. Bake in oven with meat loaf.*	**London Broil*** (make enough for tomorrow) **Buttered Orzo** (rice-shaped pasta) **Sautéed Zucchini with Thyme Marble Pound Cake** *Mix 2 tablespoons cider vinegar, 1 tablespoon olive oil, and ½ teaspoon Cajun or Creole seasoning. Rub on meat. Let stand for 30 minutes before broiling.*	
MONDAY	**Bow-Tie Pasta with Spinach and White Bean Sauce* Breadsticks Tossed Green Salad Fig-Bar Cookies** *Cook a 10-ounce box frozen chopped spinach. Stir in one 16-ounce can drained white beans and one 15½-ounce jar marinara sauce. Cook until hot.*	**Quick Lamb Curry on Rice with Condiments* Cucumber Spears Tangelos** *Add 2 cups diced cooked lamb (left over from Saturday) to curry sauce (mix). Cook for 5 minutes to heat and blend flavors. Spoon over cooked white rice. Serve with bowls of chutney, peanuts, raisins, and chopped apple.*	**Scallion and Cheese Omelets Fried Potato Patties* Shredded Carrot Salad with Italian Dressing Caramel Custard (mix)** *Season mashed potatoes with freeze-dried chives. Shape into patties. Coat with flour. Fry in butter or margarine until hot and browned.*	**Sliced Steak** (from Sunday) **Sandwiches with Lettuce, Tomato, and Mayonnaise on Rye Bread Crunchy Vegetable Salad* Fruited Gelatin** *Marinate one 16-ounce bag of partially thawed, frozen mixed vegetables in bottled creamy garlic dressing at room temperature 30 minutes, or until the vegetables are completely thawed.*	
TUESDAY	**Chicken Beijing with Flour Tortillas * Sugar Snap Peas** (frozen) **Sliced Pears and Almond Cookies** *Shred roast chicken from Sunday. Drizzle with bottled hoisin sauce, then heat under broiler. Roll up in warm tortillas with scallions.*	**Chicken Thighs Provençal* Crusty French Bread Pound Cake with Strawberries and Cream** *In a Dutch oven brown 2 pounds chicken thighs in oil. Slice and add 2 large onions and 2 green bell peppers, one 14½-ounce can stewed tomatoes, one 8-ounce can tomato sauce, and 1 teaspoon each dried thyme and basil. Cover and bake at 350°F for 1 hour.*	**Meat Loaf Tacos* Carrot Sticks Chocolate Pudding on a Stick** *Heat crumbled meat loaf (left over from Sunday) in taco sauce (canned). Fill taco shells with heated refried beans, meat-loaf mixture, shredded Cheddar cheese, shredded lettuce, and chopped tomatoes and onions.*	**Vegetable Soup** (canned) **Tuna, Noodle, and Broccoli Casserole* Tossed Green Salad Pineapple Chunks** *Add a 10-ounce package of well-drained thawed frozen chopped broccoli to your tuna casserole.*	
WEDNESDAY	**Eggplant Parmesan Garlic Bread Gremolata Green Beans * Broiled Grapefruit Halves** *Mix ¼ cup fresh minced parsley, 1 teaspoon grated lemon peel, and ½ teaspoon minced garlic. Toss with hot green beans.*	**Bell Pepper Frittata* Hash Brown Potatoes** (frozen) **Stewed Tomatoes Oatmeal Cookies** *Heat 2 tablespoons olive oil in a large nonstick skillet. Add 1 cup each thinly sliced onion and green bell pepper and 1 teaspoon minced garlic. Cook until tender. Pour in 6 beaten large eggs. Cook until eggs are just set.*	**Broiled Thin-Cut Pork Chops with Applesauce Braised Cabbage and Potatoes* Frozen Peach Yogurt** *Cut green cabbage and potatoes into wedges. Cook covered with 1 cup chicken broth for about 20 minutes, or until tender.*	**Chicken Potpies** (frozen) **Mixed Green Salad with Salsa Dressing* Chocolate Pudding** *Stir ¼ cup salsa into ½ cup bottled Ranch Dressing.*	
THURSDAY	**Lentil Soup** (canned) **Grilled Chili-Cheese Sandwiches on Whole Wheat Bread * Raspberry Gelatin with Sliced Bananas** *Drain one 4-ounce can whole green chilies. Assemble sandwiches with 1 chili between 2 cheese slices. Fry on griddle or in a skillet.*	**Broccoli Cheese Soup** (canned) **Pan-Fried Cajun Cubed Steaks with Sautéed Onions* Corn on the Cob** (frozen) **Chocolate Cake à la Mode** *Mix ¼ teaspoon each garlic powder, onion powder, paprika, and ground red pepper. Rub into steaks before frying.*	**Macaroni and Cheese* Sautéed Cherry Tomatoes Apple Wedges with Honey** *Make your favorite cheese sauce and instead of using elbow macaroni use cooked pasta shells. They catch more of the sauce.*	**Mugs of Corn Chowder Tortellini** (frozen) **with Spaghetti Sauce** (jarred) **Romaine, Radish, and Cucumber Salad Quick Plum Crumble*** *Put canned purple plums in individual serving bowls. Pour on warm half-and-half. Sprinkle with coarsely crumbled oatmeal cookies.*	
FRIDAY	**Deviled Fish and Chips* Green Beans Sliced Banana and Kiwifruit** *Mix ¼ cup mayonnaise or salad dressing, 2 tablespoons minced fresh onion, and 2 teaspoons mustard. Spread on 1 pound fish fillets. Bake in 500°F oven with frozen French fries for 15 minutes.*	**Halibut Steaks with Herb Butter Lemon-Pepper Potatoes* Zucchini Grapefruit Halves with Honey** *Mix drained canned potatoes with melted butter, lemon pepper, and paprika. Broil in foil-lined pan with fish and sliced zucchini.*	**Broiled Fish Steaks 10-Minute Brown Rice Sautéed Cucumbers with Dill* Grapes and Gingersnaps** *Peel, halve, and scoop the seeds from cucumbers. Cut into 1-inch chunks. Sauté in butter until tender. Season with salt, pepper, and dried dillweed.*	**Moroccan Burgers on Couscous* Sliced Cucumbers in Minted Yogurt Pecan Shortbread Cookies** *Pan-fry hamburgers and drain fat. Add bottled marinara sauce, frozen mixed vegetables, and a little ground cinnamon. Heat through. Serve over couscous. (Look for couscous near rice in your supermarket.)*	
SATURDAY	**Broiled Butterflied Leg of Lamb** (save leftovers for Monday) **Orzo Oregano* Broccoli Spears Anisette Toasts with Hot Chocolate** *Toss 8 ounces hot orzo (rice-shaped pasta) with 2 tablespoons each olive oil and chopped parsley, 1½ teaspoons oregano, and salt and pepper to taste.*	**Breaded Turkey Cutlets Tomato Risotto (mix) Green Beans Tossed Salad with Italian Dressing Cheese-stuffed Pears*** *Fill cored pear halves with a mixture of cream cheese and blue cheese.*	**Oven-Barbecued Chicken Drumsticks* Mashed Turnips Corn on the Cob** (frozen) **Hot Chocolate and Vanilla Wafer Cookies** *Before baking, toss drumsticks in bottled barbecue sauce mixed with Dijon mustard for extra spiciness.*	**Turkey Fajitas in Flour Tortillas with Salsa* Sliced Avocado with Lemon Green and Red Grapes** *Marinate 1 pound turkey breast steaks in 1 ½ tablespoons each lime juice and vegetable oil blended with ¼ teaspoon each salt and pepper for 1 hour in the refrigerator. Grill or broil the turkey for 5 minutes on each side. Slice into thin strips.*	

	WEEK 5	**WEEK 6**	**WEEK 7**	**WEEK 8**
SUNDAY	**Veal Roast** (slice leftovers for Tuesday) **Garlicky Mashed Potatoes* Baked Acorn Squash Warm Gingerbread** (mix) with **Whipped Cream** ˙Cook 1½ pounds peeled potatoes with 6 garlic cloves until tender. Drain and mash both with ¼ cup each olive oil and chopped parsley and 1 teaspoon salt.	**Cuban Pork Loin Roast*** (save leftovers for Wednesday) **Roast Potato Wedges Baked Acorn Squash Apple Crisp** ˙Rub the pork loin with lime juice, ground cumin, oregano, salt, and pepper before roasting.	**Roast Beef with Roasted Garlic Cloves*** (cook extra meat for Tuesday) **French Bread Pan-Roasted Potatoes Brussels Sprouts Fresh Pears** ˙Roast unpeeled garlic cloves in pan with beef. The inside of the clove cooks to a sweet, creamy paste.	**Roast Turkey Breast** (save some for Tuesday) **Rosemary Potato Wedges* Brussels Sprouts Chocolate Mousse** (mix) ˙Cut 4 potatoes into wedges. Toss with 1 tablespoon oil and 1 teaspoon each seasoned salt and dried rosemary. Roast with the turkey.
MONDAY	**Chunky Vegetable Soup** (canned) **Bean Burritos** (frozen) **Topped with Yogurt and Salsa Sliced Orange and Red Onion Salad with Lime–Olive Oil Dressing Mexican Sundaes*** ˙Stir ground cinnamon into chocolate sauce. Spoon over frozen coffee yogurt.	**Spaghetti and Meatballs** (make extra meatballs and freeze for week 8) **Italian Bread Mixed Green Salad with Italian Dressing Maple Grapes*** ˙Mix ½ cup plain low-fat yogurt with 2 tablespoons pancake syrup. Pour over red seedless grapes.	**Spinach & Mushroom Omelets Cheesy Grits* Cucumber–Cherry Tomato Salad with Dijon Vinaigrette Dressing Cinnamon Graham Crackers with Grape Jelly** ˙Stir shredded Cheddar cheese and sliced scallions into hot grits.	**Mexi-Burgers*** on Toasted **English Muffins Corn on the Cob** (frozen) **Avocado, Orange, and Onion Salad with French Dressing Hot Cocoa with Cinnamon** ˙Drain 4-ounce can chopped green chilies. Mix with 1 pound lean ground beef. Shape into patties and cook as usual. Serve with salsa.
TUESDAY	**Veal and Vegetable Stir-Fry* Cooked White Rice Lemon Yogurt** ˙Add diced veal (left over from Sunday) to one 14-ounce package frozen vegetables with Oriental sauce and prepare according to package directions.	**Oven-Barbecued Chicken Legs Corn on the Cob* Cucumber-Scallion Salad with Ranch Dressing Tangelos, Chocolate Chip Cookies** ˙Wrap corn in aluminum foil and bake alongside chicken legs.	**Cream of Celery Soup Roast Beef, Tomato, and Watercress Sandwiches on Whole Wheat Bread or Rolls* Carrot Sticks Frozen Fruit-Juice Bars** ˙Mix ¼ cup mayonnaise, 1 tablespoon prepared white horseradish, and 1 teaspoon mustard. Spread on sandwiches made with sliced roast beef (left over from Sunday).	**Turkey-Noodle Casserole* Green Beans Sliced Bananas in Pineapple Juice** ˙Use your favorite tuna-noodle casserole recipe; just substitute 2½ cups shredded cooked turkey (left over from Sunday) for the tuna.
WEDNESDAY	**Linguine with White Clam Sauce Garlic Bread* Mozzarella and Roasted Red Pepper Salad with Italian Dressing Fresh Pears, Nuts in Shell** ˙Rub sliced Italian bread with cut garlic clove. Drizzle with olive oil and sprinkle with salt and pepper. Broil until golden.	**Vegetable Soup** (canned or mix) **Pork and Black Bean Salad* Vanilla Pudding with Sliced Bananas** ˙Mix 2 cups shredded cooked pork (left over from Sunday) with one 16-ounce can drained black beans, 2 peeled and sliced navel oranges, and ½ cup sliced scallions. Toss with bottled vinaigrette dressing. Serve on lettuce.	**Bean Burritos** (frozen) with **Salsa and Sour Cream Romaine, Orange, and Red Onion Salad, Olive Oil and Lime Wedges Mexican Pudding Cups*** ˙Top prepared chocolate pudding with whipped topping. Sprinkle with cinnamon.	**Vegetarian Chili with Beans on Corn Bread with Sour Cream and Sliced Scallions Iceberg Lettuce Wedges with Thousand Islands Dressing* Flan or Custard** ˙Mix equal parts bottled ranch dressing and salsa. Serve over lettuce wedges.
THURSDAY	**Broiled Teriyaki Turkey Tenderloins* Mashed Sweet Potatoes Mixed Vegetables** (frozen) **Broiled Pineapple†** ˙Brush the tenderloins with teriyaki sauce before broiling. †Crumble brown sugar over pineapple, then broil.	**Pan-Broiled Lamb Chops Couscous** (mix) **Steamed Spinach Broiled Grapefruit*** ˙Drizzle pancake syrup over grapefruit halves. Broil until syrup is bubbly.	**Crab Cakes** (frozen) with **Chili Sauce** (jarred) **Waffle Fries** (frozen) **Carrot Slaw* Oatmeal Cookies** ˙Grate 3 large carrots and toss with bottled coleslaw dressing.	**Broiled Spicy Cod Fillets* with Chunky Salsa** (jarred) **Steamed Red Potatoes Cucumber Salad Raspberry Sherbet** ˙Mix 1 teaspoon each chili powder, garlic powder, ground cumin, and salt and ½ teaspoon ground black pepper. Rub the cod with a little oil, then the spice mixture before broiling.
FRIDAY	**Pizza** (takeout or frozen) **Mixed Green Salad with Italian Dressing Raspberry-Vanilla Floats*** ˙Pour raspberry ginger ale into tall glasses. Add a scoop of vanilla ice milk. Stir until foamy.	**Pan-Fried Flounder Fillets** (fresh or frozen) with **Lemon Wedges New Potatoes Steamed Whole Cauliflower* Strawberry Yogurt** ˙Remove the outer leaves of the cauliflower. Trim core. Bring 2 cups water to a boil in a large pot. Add the cauliflower. Steam for 20 minutes, or until fork tender.	**Macaroni and Cheese* Sautéed Cherry Tomatoes with Sliced Green Onions Lettuce Wedges with Vinaigrette Dressing Cinnamon Graham Crackers** ˙For added tang, stir a little prepared mustard or hot-pepper sauce into macaroni and cheese.	**Deviled Pork Cutlets* Mashed Butternut Squash Lettuce with French Dressing Fresh Pineapple Spears and Gingersnaps** ˙Thinly spread Dijon mustard on cutlets. Coat with seasoned bread crumbs. Pan-fry in oil for 2 to 3 minutes on each side, or until the center is barely pink.
SATURDAY	**Calves' Liver with Wheat-Germ Crust* Noodles Stroganoff** (mix) **Sautéed Spinach Ice-Cream Sandwiches** (bought) ˙Coat liver with mixture of wheat germ, ground black pepper, and dried marjoram or sage. Pan-fry in oil with sliced onions until golden.	**Pan-Fried Turkey Cutlets with Sage Butter* Long Grain and Wild Rice** (mix) **Steamed Broccoli Spears Sliced Apples and Cheddar Cheese** ˙Pan-fry cutlets in skillet. Remove. Add butter, dried sage, and lemon juice. When melted, pour over cutlets.	**Chicken Cutlets Italiano* Long Grain and Wild Rice** (mix) **Broccoli Spears Frozen Chocolate or Coffee Yogurt with Almond Cookies** ˙Before pan-frying, dip the chicken cutlets in beaten egg. Sprinkle with grated Parmesan cheese, then coat with seasoned bread crumbs.	**Eggplant Parmesan Sesame Breadsticks Mixed Green Salad with Dijon Vinaigrette Dressing Broiled Banana Splits*** ˙Bake whole unpeeled bananas in 325°F oven for 20 minutes. Slit bananas lengthwise and open slightly to form a boat. Top with vanilla ice cream and drizzle with honey.

WEEK 9	WEEK 10	WEEK 11	WEEK 12	
Roast Leg of Lamb* (save leftovers for Tuesday) **Orzo** (rice-shaped pasta) **Sautéed Zucchini with Garlic and Oregano** **Angel Food Cake with Strawberry Pourable Fruit** *Make several shallow slits in lamb and insert garlic slivers before roasting.	**Oven-Fried Chicken Thighs** **Baked Beans** **Cajun Coleslaw*** **Raspberry Sherbet** *Spice up deli coleslaw with ground red pepper, garlic and onion powder, paprika, and salt to taste.	Brunch **Broiled Grapefruit*** **Scrambled Eggs** **Pan-Fried Canadian Bacon** **Oat Bran Muffins** *Section halved grapefruit. Spread top of each with 1 tablespoon apricot or peach jam. Broil 3 to 5 inches from heat source until jam bubbles.	**London Broil** (cook extra for Tuesday) **Potatoes au Gratin** **Mixed Green Salad with Oil-Vinegar Dressing** **Almond-Cherry Parfaits*** *Mix 20-ounce can cherry pie filling and ½ teaspoon almond extract. Layer in parfait glasses with vanilla pudding. Top with toasted sliced almonds.	**SUNDAY**
Light Mushroom Soup* **Grilled Jack Cheese and Green-Chili Sandwiches** **Carrot and Celery Sticks** **Vanilla Frozen Yogurt with Sliced Bananas** *Cook 1 cup sliced mushrooms and ¼ cup sliced scallions in 2 cans (about 14 ounces) chicken broth until tender.	**Manicotti** (frozen) with **Marinara Sauce** (jarred) **Sesame Breadsticks** **Roasted Red Peppers** (jarred) **and Marinated Artichokes on Lettuce*** **Hot Cocoa and Oatmeal Cookies** *Dress salad with artichoke marinade left in jar.	**Turkey and Skillet Stuffing*** **Green Peas** **Lemon Sherbet with Melted Seedless Raspberry Jam** *Prepare stuffing mix in large skillet. Top with pieces of cooked and boned turkey, then gravy (from can or jar). Cover and heat gently until warmed through.	**Oven-Fried Chicken Drumsticks*** **Corn on the Cob** **Coleslaw** **Dutch Apple Yogurt** *Dip drumsticks in mixture of 1 egg white and 1 tablespoon water, then in seasoned instant mashed potato flakes. Bake at 425°F for 30 to 35 minutes, or until no pink remains.	**MONDAY**
Mediterranean Lamb Stew* **Couscous** (mix) **Spinach Salad with Vinaigrette Dressing** **Gingersnaps** *Heat 1 cup diced lamb (left over from Sunday) with drained 16-ounce can chick-peas, 14½-ounce can diced tomatoes in olive oil, and 7½-ounce can caponata (eggplant appetizer).	**Mugs of Onion Soup** (mix) **Tuna and White Bean Salad*** **Toasted Bagels** **Carrot and Bell Pepper Strips** **Grapes** *Make your favorite tuna salad recipe. Mix in one 16-ounce can drained white beans. Add more dressing if needed.	**Meat Loaf Squares*** **Scalloped Potatoes** (frozen) **Italian Green Beans** (frozen) **Grapes and Gingersnaps** *For speedier meat loaf, pat mixture into a square baking pan instead of a loaf pan. Bake in 350°F oven for 25 to 30 minutes or until done.	**Split-Pea Soup** (canned) **Sliced Steak** (left over from Sunday) **Sandwiches with Russian Dressing, Red Onion Slices, and Lettuce** **Cucumber Salad** **Plum Good*** *Mixed canned plums with a little ground ginger. Top with whipped topping and granola.	**TUESDAY**
Broiled Teriyaki Fish Fillets* **Cooked White Rice** **Oriental-Style Vegetables** (frozen) **Orange Sherbet** *Brush fish fillets with bottled teriyaki sauce before broiling.	**Broiled Ham Steaks** **Broiled Sweet Potato Wedges** **Broiled Zucchini Spears with Thyme** **Apple Pineapple Yogurt*** *Stir drained canned pineapple chunks into Dutch apple yogurt. Top with granola.	**Breaded Fish Fillets** (frozen) **on Buns with Lettuce and Tartar Sauce** **Fast Fries** (frozen) **Cherry Tomatoes** **Orange-Kiwi Sundaes*** *Peel and quarter 2 kiwifruit. Purée in blender. Melt ⅓ cup orange marmalade. Stir into purée. Chill. Serve over vanilla ice cream.	**Bean Tacos with Toppings*** **Spanish Rice** (mix) **Sliced Bananas in Orange Juice** *Spoon heated canned refried beans into packaged taco shells. Serve with shredded lettuce, sliced avocado, chopped onion and tomato, salsa, and sour cream.	**WEDNESDAY**
Saucy Meatball Dinner* **Buttered Green Beans** **Wide Egg Noodles** **Canned Plums and Granola Cookies** *Heat meatballs (from week 6) in mushroom gravy (jarred). Serve over noodles.	**Crunchy Catfish Fillets*** **Herb Rice** (mix) **Spinach** **Fig Bars** *Dip fillets in milk, then seasoned cornmeal. Bake in a 425°F oven 10 to 12 minutes, until lightly browned and opaque in center.	**Cheese Ravioli** (frozen) with **Tomato Sauce** (jarred) **Garlic Bread** **Mixed Green Salad with Italian Dressing** **Orange Cows*** *Put 2 scoops orange sherbet in each tall glass. Fill with orange-flavored soda. Serve with long spoons.	**Turkey Burgers on Buns with Lettuce, Onion, and Tomato Slices** **Three-Bean Salad** (jarred) **Broiled Pineapple*** *Arrange drained canned pineapple slices on broiler pan rack. Sprinkle with sugar. Broil 8 minutes or until sugar sizzles.	**THURSDAY**
Cheese Pizza* (takeout or frozen) **Mixed Green Salad with Dijon Vinaigrette Dressing** **Grapes and Oatmeal Cookies** *Save money by topping a takeout cheese pizza with your own leftover vegetables or sliced canned olives.	**Chicken Potpie** **Green, Red, and Blue Salad with Dijon Vinaigrette*** **Sliced Bananas in Black-Cherry Gelatin with Whipped Topping** *Crumble 2 ounces blue cheese over mixed salad greens and sliced red onion. Toss with dressing just before serving.	**Sautéed Chicken Livers** **Herbed Rice*** **Steamed Broccoli** **Fruited Gelatin** *Cook rice with chicken broth instead of water, a little thyme, and 1 bay leaf. Discard bay leaf when rice is cooked.	**Grapefruit Halves** **Creamy Herbed Scrambled Eggs*** **O'Brien Potatoes** (frozen) **Stewed Tomatoes** (canned) **Black Cherry Gelatin** *Beat 3 tablespoons softened cream cheese and 2 teaspoons dried herbs into 8 eggs. Scramble as usual.	**FRIDAY**
Pan-Fried Pork Chops **Potato Pancakes** (mix) **Pickled Red Cabbage** (jarred) **Mixed Green Salad** **Sweet and Crunchy Apple Wedges*** *Dip apple wedges in pancake syrup, then in low-fat granola.	**Wonton Soup** (canned) **Stir-Fried Beef and Vegetables*** **Rice or Chinese Noodles** **Orange Wedges and Almond Cookies** *Heat oil in large skillet or work. Add beef strips and stir-fry until browned. Add frozen Chinese-style vegetables with sauce and prepare as directed on package.	**Deviled Pork Cutlets*** **Mashed Potatoes** **Brussels Sprouts** **Canned Sliced Peaches** *Thinly spread creamy Dijon mustard sauce on cutlets. Coat with seasoned bread crumbs. Pan-fry in oil 2 to 3 minutes per side until center is barely pink.	**Seafood Macaroni and Cheese*** **Mixed Green Salad with Dijon Vinaigrette Dressing** **Vanilla Pudding** *Stir 8 ounces imitation crabmeat or a 6½-ounce can drained tuna into hot macaroni and cheese.	**SATURDAY**

662

	WEEK 13	WEEK 14	WEEK 15	WEEK 16
SUNDAY	**Baked Ham with Pineapple and Cloves** (save some for Wednesday) **Mashed Sweet Potatoes Steamed Broccoli Lemon Sherbet and Sliced Strawberries*** *Sprinkle sliced strawberries with 2 tablespoons sugar. Let stand 30 minutes to draw out juices.	**Pot Roast* with Potatoes, Onions, and Carrots** (cook enough meat and gravy for Tuesday) **Lettuce with Russian Dressing Stewed Rhubarb** (make enough for Tuesday) *A boneless beef shoulder roast is a tasty and economical cut. Have the butcher trim off excess fat and tie it.	**Broiled Lamb Chops Wheat Pilaf** (mix) **Italian-Style Cauliflower* Lemon Yogurt** *In a small saucepan, heat 3 tablespoons olive oil, 2 tablespoons balsamic vinegar or red wine vinegar, 1 teaspoon minced garlic, and 1/4 teaspoon salt. Simmer for 3 minutes. Pour over steamed cauliflower.	**Roast Citrus-Herb Chicken* Corn on the Cob Stir-Fried Snow Peas Brownies or Blondies** *Mix 2 tablespoons each oil, lemon juice, and lime juice; 1/4 teaspoon each dried thyme, rosemary, salt, and pepper. Brush on chicken during roasting.
MONDAY	**Pan-Fried Chicken Cutlets Boiled New Potatoes Asparagus Spears Apricots Melba*** *Slice fresh apricots over vanilla ice milk. Top with melted raspberry jam.	**Tuna Chowder* French Bread Lettuce and Tomato Wedges with Oil-Vinegar Dressing Brownies** *Cook 2 cups diced potatoes until tender. Drain. Add 2 cups milk, one 10¾ ounce can condensed cream of chicken soup, one 16-ounce can corn kernels, and one 6½-ounce can drained tuna. Heat, don't boil.	**Clam Chowder* Grilled Cheddar Cheese Sandwiches on Whole Wheat Bread Dill Pickle Spears Applesauce and Gingersnaps** *Look for large pots of chowder and other hearty soups at the prepared-food counter of your supermarket.	**8-Vegetable Juice Black Bean or Lentil Soup** (canned) over Bulgur with Sliced **Scallions Watercress Salad Pear Freeze*** *Freeze a can of pears. Dip can in warm water. Open both ends. Slide out contents and slice. Top with melted red currant jelly.
TUESDAY	**Spaghetti Squash Marinara* Sautéed Escarole with Garlic Sesame Breadsticks Rice Pudding** *Prick squash all over. Boil 35 minutes or until tender. Halve; discard seeds; scrape out squash strands with fork. Toss with marinara sauce.	**Hot Pot Roast** (left over from Sunday) **Heros** (Submarines) **with Spicy Gravy* Celery, Carrot, and Cucumber Sticks with Blue-Cheese Dressing Rhubarb-Orange Compote†** *Add prepared horseradish to leftover pot-roast gravy.	**Lemon-Pepper Turkey Fillets* Mashed Potatoes Green Beans Tangelos or Tangerines** *Before pan-frying, dip the turkey fillets in 3 tablespoons melted butter mixed with 2 tablespoons lemon juice, then in 1/2 cup flour mixed with 1 teaspoon each salt and lemon-pepper.	**Moo Shu Pork* Steamed Rice Broccoli Spears Honeydew Melon Wedges** *Cut pork cutlets into 1-inch strips. Pan-fry in a little oil until cooked through. Add bottled hoisin sauce and toss to coat. Sprinkle with sliced scallions. Roll in lettuce-lined warmed flour tortillas.
WEDNESDAY	**Grilled Ham** (left over from Sunday), **American Cheese, and Tomato Sandwiches on Rye Bread Three-Bean Salad** (jarred) **Cucumber Salad Cherry Sundaes*** *Top scoops of ice milk with canned cherry-pie filling.	**Tex-Mex Macaroni and Cheese* Tortilla Chips Lettuce Wedges Frozen Fruit Juice Bars** *Stir one 4-ounce can chopped green chilies and 1/4 cup jarred salsa into prepared macaroni and cheese.	**Apple Juice Spritzers Steamed Vegetable Platter with Cheese Sauce* Crusty French Bread Honey-Drizzled Fresh Pears** *Stir 1 cup shredded Cheddar cheese into 1 cup prepared white sauce (from mix). Season with 1 teaspoon each dry mustard and instant minced onion.	**Spinach Lasagne** (frozen from Week 13) **Onion Breadsticks Tossed Green Salad with Dijon Vinaigrette Peach Crunch*** *Top canned peaches with low-fat granola.
THURSDAY	**Adobo Chicken and Potatoes* Steamed Spinach Baked Apples** *Rub chicken pieces and red-skinned potatoes with olive oil. Sprinkle with adobo all-purpose seasoning and cumin. Bake as usual, basting chicken and potatoes with pan drippings.	**Knockwurst, Potato Wedges, and Sauerkraut Platter* Assorted Mustards Chunky Applesauce and Oatmeal Cookies** *Spread drained sauerkraut in a large non-aluminum skillet. Sprinkle with 1 teaspoon caraway seeds. Add knockwurst, potatoes, and 1 cup apple juice. Cover and cook until potatoes are tender.	**Picadillo over Corn Muffins* Tossed Green Salad with Oil-Vinegar Dressing Canned Peaches and Gingersnaps** *Sauté 1/2 cup chopped bell pepper in 1 tablespoon oil. Add two 15-ounce cans chili with beans, 1/3 cup raisins, and 2 tablespoons cider vinegar. Heat and spoon over corn muffins.	**Pan-Fried Ham Steaks Raisin Couscous* Kale** (Frozen) **Lemon Yogurt** *Add 1/2 cup raisins and 1/4 teaspoon ground cinnamon to couscous mix. Prepare as usual.
FRIDAY	**Manhattan Scallop Chowder* Oyster Crackers or Saltines Romaine-Radish Salad Grapes** *Heat 2 cans condensed vegetarian vegetable soup and 2 soup cans water. Stir in 12 ounces bay scallops and 1/2 teaspoon dried thyme. Heat through.	**Spicy Catfish Fillets* Corn on the Cob** (frozen) **Coleslaw** (deli) **Chocolate Pudding** *Lightly brush catfish with "hot" tomato ketchup and sprinkle with Creole seasoning before broiling.	**Teriyaki-Broiled Boneless Pork Chops* Couscous** (mix) **Buttered Green Peas Lemon Sherbet and Grapes** *Brush both sides of chops with bottled teriyaki sauce. Broil 3 to 4 minutes on each side or until no longer pink in center. Sprinkle with thinly sliced scallions.	**Down-Home Fish Fillets* Sautéed Yellow Summer Squash Cajun Stewed Tomatoes** (canned) **Pear Melba Sundae†** *Dip fillets in milk, then seasoned cornmeal before pan-frying. †Top vanilla frozen yogurt with canned pears and raspberry pourable fruit.
SATURDAY	**Spinach Lasagne** (make an extra pan and freeze for Week 16) **Tossed Salad with Italian Dressing Quick Tiramisù*** *Soak 8 slices pound cake in strong coffee. Stir 2 tablespoons cocoa powder into 2 cups non-dairy topping, thawed. Spread on slices. Stack 2 slices on each plate and dust with cocoa.	**Chicken Breast Cutlets* with Lemon Wedges Buttered Bow-Tie Pasta Broccoli Spears Lemon Meringue Pie** *Brush cutlets with olive oil and sprinkle with lemon-pepper seasoning and seasoned bread crumbs before frying.	**Ziti and Meatballs* Tossed Green Salad Papaya with Lime Wedges** *Mix 1 pound ground beef, 1 egg, and 1/4 cup each grated Parmesan cheese and seasoned bread crumbs. Shape into meatballs. Brown in oil, then simmer in bottled marinara sauce until cooked through.	**Flank Steak Garlic Bread Summer Squash, Mushroom, Onion, and Bell Pepper Kebabs Sweet and Sour Strawberry Cups*** *Arrange sliced strawberries in dessert cups. Top with sour cream and a sprinkling of brown sugar.

WEEK 17	WEEK 18	WEEK 19	WEEK 20	
Roast Pork (make enough for Tuesday) **Baked Sweet Potatoes Green Beans Cantaloupe-Blueberry Compote*** ˙Cut cantaloupe into chunks, sprinkle with sugar and ground ginger. Stir in blueberries.	**Ground Turkey Meat Loaf** (cook extra for Tuesday) **Baked Parmesan Potatoes* Collard Greens Coffee Ice Cream with Chopped Toasted Pecans** ˙Halve unpeeled potatoes lengthwise. Brush cut sides with olive oil. Sprinkle with Parmesan cheese and bake until tender.	**Broiled Peppery Pork Chops* Saucepan Stuffing** (mix) **Okra Ginger Ice Cream and Gingersnaps†** ˙Spread mustard over chops, sprinkle with coarsely ground black pepper, then broil. †Stir 2 tablespoons chopped crystallized ginger into 1 pint softened vanilla ice cream or frozen yogurt, then refreeze.	**Roast Leg of Lamb** (save leftovers for Tuesday) **Wheat Pilaf** (mix) **Sautéed Lettuce and Peas* Angel Food Cake with Sugared Strawberries** ˙Melt 2 tablespoons butter in a large skillet. Add 2 cups shredded romaine and 2 cups frozen green peas. Stir 3 to 4 minutes, until peas are hot and lettuce is crisp-tender.	SUNDAY
Angel-Hair Pasta* with White Clam Sauce (from can or jar) **Italian Bread Mixed Green Salad with Italian Dressing Vanilla Ice Milk** ˙To prevent pasta from clumping, add a few tablespoons oil to boiling water. Add pasta; stir until boiling again.	**Cranberry-Juice Cocktail Curried Eggs and Peas* on Whole Wheat Toast Sliced Tomatoes with Dijon Vinaigrette Chocolate Chip Cookies** ˙Prepare 2 cups white sauce. Add 1 tablespoon curry powder and 2 cups thawed green peas. Simmer for 3 minutes. Fold in 6 quartered hard-cooked eggs.	**Falafel** (mix)* **in Lettuce-Lined Pita Pockets with Sliced Tomato Cucumber and Onion Salad with Olive Oil and Lemon Juice Dressing Oranges** ˙Spray falafel patties with vegetable oil cooking spray. Bake at 350°F for 10 to 12 minutes. Top with low-fat plain yogurt and a little ground cumin.	**Chicken Potpie** (frozen) **Mixed Green Salad with Italian Dressing Rhubarb with Raspberry Gelatin*** ˙Mix 4 cups chopped fresh or 1 pound frozen rhubarb, 1 cup water, one 3-ounce package raspberry gelatin, and ¼ cup sugar in a large skillet. Cook, stirring occasionally, for 4 minutes, or until the rhubarb is tender. Chill until set.	MONDAY
Barbecued Pork* on Buns Corn on the Cob Coleslaw (deli) **Frozen grapes** ˙Shred leftover pork. Heat in saucepan over low heat with bottled barbecue sauce.	**Open-Face Hot Turkey Meat Loaf Sandwiches with Turkey Gravy* Italian Green Beans** (frozen) **Orange Wedges, Chocolate Cookies** ˙Heat meat-loaf slices (leftover from Sunday) in gravy from jar or mix.	**Cranberry Juice Cocktails Smoked Chicken, Potato, and Spinach Salad* Italian Bread Cantaloupe Chunks** ˙Cube cooked smoked chicken (deli). Toss with sliced white potatoes (canned), red onion, cucumber, torn spinach leaves, and bottled creamy-garlic dressing.	**Mediterranean Lamb Stew* Couscous** (mix) **Mixed Green Salad with Dijon Vinaigrette Dressing Gingersnaps** ˙Heat 1 cup diced lamb (left over from Sunday) with one 16-ounce can drained chick-peas, one 14½-ounce can diced tomatoes in olive oil, and one 7½-ounce can caponata (eggplant appetizer).	TUESDAY
Pan-Fried Turkey Cutlets Bulgur Pilaf (mix) **Sautéed Fresh Spinach* Strawberry Gelatin** ˙Wash spinach in warm, not cold, water to remove grit. Heat 1 teaspoon minced garlic in 1 tablespoon oil. Add spinach and stir-fry until wilted. Sprinkle with red wine vinegar.	**Calves' Liver Smothered with Bell Peppers and Onions Mashed Potatoes Mixed Green Salad with Ranch Dressing Rhubarb-Strawberry Compote*** ˙Slice strawberries into chilled stewed rhubarb.	**Turkey Kielbasa with Mustard Rye Bread Sauerkraut with Caraway Seeds Carrot and Celery Sticks Sweet and Crunchy Pear Wedges*** ˙Dip cored pear wedges in honey or chocolate syrup, then in your favorite ready-to-eat cereal.	**Carrot Rice Soup* Cottage Cheese and Fruit Platter Bran Muffins Iced Herb Tea** ˙Cook 3 cups sliced carrots in 3 cups chicken broth. Add 1 cup cooked rice. Purée in batches until smooth. Stir in 2 cups of milk. Heat through.	WEDNESDAY
Pizza As-You-Like-It* Romaine, Chick-Pea and Olive Salad with Italian Dressing Frozen Coffee Ice Milk ˙"Homemade" pizza is easier than ever. Look for refrigerated baked crust, canned crust, or packaged crust mix in your grocery store.	**Spaghetti Olé* French Bread Mixed Green Salad with Italian Dressing Canned Apricots and Almond Cookies** ˙Stir a little chili powder into your meat sauce for a south-of-the-border taste.	**Broiled Flounder Fillets Mushroom Risotto** (mix) **Sautéed Cucumbers with Dill* Raspberry Sherbet and Vanilla Wafer Cookies** ˙Peel cucumbers, halve lengthwise. Scrape out seeds with teaspoon. Slice thin. Cook in butter just until crisp-tender. Sprinkle with salt, pepper, and snipped fresh dill.	**Linguine with Double Clam Sauce* Garlic Bread Spinach Salad with Roasted Red Peppers** (jarred) **and Vinaigrette Dressing Coconut Macaroons** ˙Add a can of drained chopped clams and ½ cup chopped fresh parsley to a can of white or red clam sauce.	THURSDAY
Spanish or Western Omelets Green Chili Corn Bread* Avocado Wedges with Lemon Juice Dressing Lime Gelatin with Sliced Bananas ˙Prepare corn bread batter from mix. Stir 1 well-drained 4-ounce can chopped green chilies. Bake as directed. Serve hot.	**Crab Cakes** (frozen) **with Tartar Sauce Herbed Rice** (mix) **Sautéed Cherry Tomatoes Crunchy Blueberry-Banana Parfaits*** ˙Layer blueberry yogurt and sliced bananas in dessert glasses. Top with low-fat granola.	**Fettuccine with Marinara Spinach Sauce* Crusty French Bread Chicory, Red Onion, and Chick-Pea Salad with Italian Dressing Dutch-Apple Yogurt** ˙Heat 10-ounces package frozen chopped spinach until thawed. Add 15½-ounces jar marinara sauce and stir occasionally until hot.	**Spanish-style Scrambled Eggs* Potato Rounds** (frozen) **Lettuce Wedges with Oil-Vinegar Dressing Frozen Yogurt** ˙In nonstick skillet, sauté ½ cup each chopped onion and bell pepper in 1 tablespoon oil until tender. Stir in 1 cup chopped tomato and 6 beaten eggs. Cook until set.	FRIDAY
Asian Broiled Pork Tenderloins with Broiled Pineapple* Long-Grain and Wild Rice (mix) **Mixed Green Salad with Dijon Vinaigrette Dressing Iced Tea and Sugar Cookies** ˙Brush tenderloins and sliced pineapple with teriyaki sauce and vegetable oil before broiling.	**Pan-Fried Blade Steaks* Steamed Potatoes Peas and Corn** (frozen) **Melon Wedges** ˙Blade steaks are one of the most tender as well as inexpensive cuts of beef.	**Oven-Roasted Cornish Hens* Tossed Spinach Salad with Blue Cheese Dressing Carrot Cake** ˙Rub hens with rosemary, salt, and pepper. Roast with unpeeled whole garlic cloves. Squeeze tender cloves on French bread.	**Oriental Hoisin Pork Tenderloin* Cooked White Rice Stir-Fried Bok Choy Fresh Pineapple** ˙Brush tenderloins with hoisin sauce (jarred) during the last 10 minutes of baking. Serve extra sauce on side.	SATURDAY

	WEEK 21	WEEK 22	WEEK 23	WEEK 24
SUNDAY	**Roast Chicken** (shred 2 cups for Tuesday) **Potatoes au Gratin Steamed Green Beans Strawberries with Strawberry Cream Dip*** *Mix ½ cup light sour cream and ¼ cup strawberry fruit spread. Dip whole strawberries.	**Baked Ham Glazed with Apricot Preserves** (dice 2 cups ham for Tuesday and 1 cup for Thursday) **Roasted New Potatoes Glazed Carrots* Lemon Sorbet with Blueberry Pourable Fruit** *Stir 1 pound cooked, sliced carrots, ¼ cup orange juice, 2 tablespoons butter, and 1 tablespoon sugar over high heat until glazed.	**Braised Lamb Shanks with New Potatoes Steamed Acorn Squash Rings* Lettuce with French Dressing Strawberries à la Mode** *Steam or microwave the whole squash until slightly soft, then slice into rings and remove seeds.	**Roast Turkey Breast** (make enough for Tuesday) **Mashed Potatoes Peas and Carrots Old Glory Shortcake*** *Top homemade or purchased biscuits with a mixture of sweetened blueberries and sliced strawberries and a dollop of whipped topping.
MONDAY	**Cheese Enchiladas* Refried Beans Broccoli Spears Mexican Ice Cream Sodas†** *Sprinkle enchiladas with chopped fresh cilantro. †Scoop chocolate ice milk into tall glasses. Add a shot of chocolate syrup. Fill with club soda or seltzer. Sprinkle with ground cinnamon.	**Cheese Tortellini and Peas in Tomato-Cream Sauce* Tossed Salad with Oil-Vinegar Dressing Cantaloupe** *Heat 1 teaspoon minced garlic in 2 tablespoons oil. Add one 16-ounce can crushed tomatoes and 2 cups frozen green peas. Simmer for 5 to 6 minutes. Stir in ¼ cup heavy cream. Toss with 1 pound hot tortellini.	**Eggplant Parmesan** (frozen) **Garlic-Herb Bread* Tossed Salad with White Beans** (canned) **and Italian Dressing Biscotti** *Cook 2 cut-up cloves garlic in ¼ cup olive oil. Brush oil on cut halves Italian bread. Sprinkle with Italian herb seasoning and bake until hot.	**Tuna-Bean Salad* on Lettuce in Whole Wheat Rolls Sliced Tomatoes and Cucumbers Fig Bars and Lemonade** *Add rinsed and drained canned red kidney beans to tuna salad.
TUESDAY	**Chicken in Spanish Rice** (mix)* **Green Salad with Sugar Snap Peas Flan** (mix) *Five minutes before the rice is done, stir in the leftover shredded chicken.	**Jellied Consommé Ham, Cheese, and Broccoli Salad in Pitas* Pickled Beets** (jarred) **Frozen Yogurt** *Mix 2 cups diced ham (left over from Sunday), 1 cup shredded Swiss cheese, 2 cups chopped cooked broccoli, ½ cup chopped red onion, and ½ cup bottled slaw dressing. Stuff into whole wheat pitas.	**Linguine with Clam Sauce** (canned) **Marinated Artichokes** (jarred) **and Roasted Red Peppers** (jarred) **on Lettuce with Marinade from Artichokes Plum Melba Sundaes*** *Slice fresh plums over vanilla ice cream. Top with melted raspberry jam.	**Curried Turkey on Rice* Sugar Snap Peas Honeydew Melon and Lime Wedges** *Prepare one 2-ounce package curry sauce mix according to package directions. Stir in 3 cups diced turkey (left over from Sunday) and ⅓ cup raisins. Stir over low heat until turkey is hot.
WEDNESDAY	**Broiled Lamb Chops Buttered Lima Beans Braised Escarole* Cantaloupe** *Wash escarole, don't dry. Cook covered for 5 minutes until wilted. Stir in olive oil, minced garlic, salt, and pepper. Cook for 5 minutes more, or until tender.	**Roast Chicken Thighs Roast New Potatoes with Rosemary Roast Zucchini Halves Chocolate Egg Creams*** *New York's famous drink has no egg or cream. Mix 3 tablespoons each chocolate syrup and milk in a tall glass. Stirring, gradually fill the glass with cold seltzer water or club soda.	**Pan-Fried Veal Chops Risotto** (mix) **Sautéed Swiss Chard* Nectarines** *Rinse 1 pound chard. Stack leaves. Cut crosswise in 1-inch-wide ribbons. Fry 1 teaspoon minced garlic in 2 tablespoons oil. Add chard and cook until wilted. Sprinkle with vinegar.	**Cheese Ravioli with Vegetables and Pesto* Crusty Italian Bread Tossed Green Salad with Italian Dressing Fresh Papayas** *Sauté 1 cup each diced bell pepper and zucchini in 2 tablespoons oil until crisp-tender. Stir in 12 ounces cooked ravioli and ¼ cup pesto.
THURSDAY	**Sautéed Bay Scallops with Lemon and Basil Buttered Noodles Fresh Asparagus Apples with Peanut Dip*** *Stir 2 tablespoons peanut butter into ½ cup vanilla yogurt until smooth. Serve with apple wedges.	**8-Vegetable Juice Hunter's Eggs with Salsa* Toasted Bagels Tossed Green Salad with Roasted Red-Pepper Strips** (jarred) **and French Dressing Grapes** *Beat 6 eggs. Stir in 1 cup diced ham and ⅓ cup frozen chopped onion. Scramble as usual.	**Broiled Catfish Fillets Broiled Potato Wedges Coleslaw Banana-Caramel Sundaes*** *Slice bananas onto frozen vanilla yogurt. Drizzle with caramel sauce.	**Cubed Steaks with Herb Butter* Parsleyed Potatoes Steamed Broccoli Spears Plums** *Pan-fry steaks, remove to plate. In the same pan, melt 2 tablespoons butter or margarine with ½ teaspoon dried oregano. Serve over the steaks.
FRIDAY	**Spaghetti with Turkey Meat Sauce* Focaccia Mixed Green Salad Neapolitan Ice Cream** *Brown ground turkey and Italian turkey sausage removed from casing. Add bottled marinara sauce.	**Broiled Flounder Fillets with Tartar Sauce Rice Pilaf Sugar snap Peas* Honeydew Melon Wedges** *Sugar snap peas are delicious raw, but for extra flavor cook them in boiling water about 1 minute.	**Rotisserie Chicken*** (deli) **Macaroni Salad** (deli) **Tossed Salad Cantaloupe Chunks** *Look for whole roasted chicken at the supermarket deli counter or in the poultry section of the meat counter.	**Grilled Halibut Steaks* Corn on the Cob Sautéed Zucchini with Basil Kiwifruit Sorbet†** *Brush halibut with mixture of olive oil and minced garlic before grilling. †Process frozen kiwifruit in a blender with ¾ cup orange juice and 2 tablespoons sugar.
SATURDAY	**Barbecued Spareribs Corn on the Cob Tropical Coleslaw* Fresh Papaya** *Mix shredded cabbage with drained canned pineapple chunks and bottled poppy-seed dressing. Stir in chopped fresh cilantro.	**Hamburgers on Buns with Cucumber Sauce* French Fries** (frozen) **Pickled Beets** (jarred) **Butterscotch Pudding** *Mix ⅓ cup light mayonnaise, ¼ cup diced cucumber, and 1 tablespoon minced onion.	**Cheese Enchiladas Refried Beans** (canned) **Sliced Oranges, Radishes, and Scallions on Lettuce with Italian Dressing Mangoes*** *A ripe mango will be slightly soft to the touch. Cut unpeeled fruit in half from end to end around seed. Eat from skin with spoon.	**Chilled Beet Soup* Baked Chicken Drumsticks Buttered Egg Noodles Green Beans Brownies** *Drain one 1-pound can sliced beets. Purée in blender with 3 cups buttermilk and lemon juice, salt, and pepper to taste. Top with minced scallions or chives.

WEEK 25	WEEK 26	WEEK 27	WEEK 28	
Meat Loaf (bake extra for Tuesday) **Baked Sweet Potatoes Yellow Summer Squash Peach Coupes*** ˙Fill centers of fresh peach halves with a scoop apiece of vanilla ice milk.	**Grilled Butterflied Leg of Lamb** (save some for Wednesday) **with Mint Pesto* White Beans** (canned) **Spinach Salad with Vinaigrette Cherry Pie** ˙In blender or food processor purée 1 cup packed fresh mint leaves, ¼ cup olive oil, 2 tablespoons walnuts, 2 cloves garlic, and ½ teaspoon salt. Serve with lamb.	**Broiled Ham Steaks** (buy enough for Monday) **Broiled Sweet Potatoes** (canned) **and Pineapple Rings** (canned) **Mixed Green Salad with Blue Cheese Dressing Mint Julep Watermelon*** ˙Cut watermelon into chunks. Sprinkle with bourbon (optional) and chopped mint.	**Barbecued Chicken Buttermilk Biscuits** (mix) **Grilled Vegetables Coleslaw* Watermelon** ˙Add 1 cup each coarsely shredded carrots and jicama to your coleslaw for added color.	SUNDAY
Shrimp Skewers* Herbed Rice Steamed Spinach Fruit Salad ˙Skewer peeled and deveined raw large shrimp alternately with strips of bell peppers, scallions, and mushrooms. Brush with nonfat French dressing and broil until shrimp are opaque.	**Curried Chicken Salad* Pita Bread Lemonade, Oatmeal Cookies** ˙Mix 8 ounces plain nonfat yogurt, 2 tablespoons honey, and ¼ teaspoon curry powder with 2 cups shredded cooked chicken (left over from Saturday), 1½ cups pineapple chunks, ½ cup each chopped onions and raisins. Top with 2 tablespoons walnuts.	**Cantaloupe Wagon Wheel Pasta with Ham* Cherry Tomatoes and Black Olives** (canned) **Frozen Fruit-Juice Pops** ˙Heat one 10¾-ounce can condensed cream of mushroom soup, ¾ cup milk, and 2 cups diced ham. Pour over freshly cooked and drained pasta.	**Italian Vegetable Stew* Whole Wheat Rolls Orange Sherbet** ˙Brown 2 cups each diced potatoes and sliced onions in 2 tablespoons oil. Add 2 cups sliced zucchini, one 15-ounce can undrained tomatoes, 1 cup chicken broth, and 1 teaspoon oregano. Simmer covered 10 minutes. Break 8 eggs over stew. Cover and cook until firm.	MONDAY
Meat Loaf Marinara* Italian Bread Green Beans Vinaigrette Orange Sherbet Sodas ˙Heat one 15-ounce jar marinara sauce in a large skillet. Add 1 bell pepper cut into strips. Simmer until crisp-tender. Add sliced meat loaf and heat through.	**Crunchy Fish Sticks** (frozen) **with Tartar Sauce* Cottage Fried Potatoes** (frozen) **Succotash** (frozen) **Raspberry Bar Cookies** ˙Freshen the flavor of bottled tartar sauce with some chopped fresh dill and a squeeze of lemon or lime juice.	**Bean Burritos** (frozen) **with Guacamole** (frozen) **Spanish Rice** (mix) **Romaine Lettuce and Radish Salad with French Dressing Creamy Banana Pudding*** ˙Prepare a 4-serving package instant vanilla pudding as directed. Chill for 5 minutes. Fold in 1 cup each whipped topping and sliced bananas. Chill until ready to serve.	**Breaded Pork Chops with Chunky Applesauce Steamed Red New Potatoes Sugar Snap or Snow Peas Pineapple with Ginger Cream*** ˙Stir 1 tablespoon each honey and chopped candied ginger into ½ cup light sour cream. Spoon over fresh or canned pineapple chunks.	TUESDAY
Orzo Stuffed Peppers* Cucumber Spears Strawberries with Whipped Topping ˙Mix cooked orzo pasta with cheese. Moisten with marinara sauce. Spoon into pepper, top with more sauce. Cover and bake at 350°F for 45 minutes.	**Sliced Lamb** (left over from Sunday) **in Pitas with Cucumber-Mint Yogurt Sauce* Greek Salad** (deli) **Bananas and Sugar Cookies** ˙Peel 2 cucumbers and halve lengthwise. Scrape out the seeds. Slice thin. Mix ¾ cup plain yogurt with 1 tablespoon chopped fresh mint and ½ teaspoon each salt, sugar, and minced garlic. Add the cucumbers. Mix well.	**Baked Chicken Thighs Creole Rice** (mix) **Steamed Broccoli Spears Rhubarb with Raspberry Gelatin*** ˙In a large saucepan. mix 4 cups chopped fresh or frozen rhubarb, 1 cup water, one 3-ounce package raspberry gelatin, and ¼ cup sugar. Cook, stirring occasionally, for 4 minutes, or until the rhubarb is tender. Chill until set..	**Broiled Catfish Fillets* Summer Squash Herb Rice** (mix) **Brownies à la Mode** ˙Mix 1 tablespoon each soy sauce, Dijon mustard, vegetable oil, and honey. Brush on fillets and squash before broiling.	WEDNESDAY
Pan-Fried Pork Cutlets with Warm Applesauce Potatoes O'Brien (frozen) **Yellow Wax Beans Skinny Peach Shakes*** ˙In blender, whirl 1½ cups frozen peach yogurt or ice milk with 1½ cups skim milk and ¼ cup peach preserves until smooth.	**Swiss Cheese and Mushroom Omelets* Flaky Biscuits** (refrigerated) **Steamed Spinach Cantaloupe** ˙If you find omelets tricky to make, mix beaten eggs with cubed cheese and sautéed mushrooms and scramble the mixture instead.	**"Crab" Salad* in Pita Pockets Cherry Tomatoes and Marinated Artichoke Hearts on Lettuce† Gingersnaps** ˙Use shredded or flaked imitation crabmeat in the salad. †Mix halved cherry tomatoes with undrained artichoke hearts.	**Chicken Drumsticks* Zucchini Slices & Onion Wedges Garlic Bread Fresh Strawberries & Cream** ˙Brush chicken, zucchini, and onions with barbecue sauce before broiling.	THURSDAY
Tuna Salad Platter with Sliced Hard-Cooked Eggs, Black Olives, and Pickled Beets on Watercress Toasted Bagels Broiled Banana Boats* ˙Broil unpeeled ripe bananas 15 minutes, turning once. Split peels and sprinkle brown sugar inside, then a squeeze of lime juice. Serve in peel.	**Hot-Dog Reubens* Baked Beans Coleslaw Fruit Salad** ˙Cut a lengthwise slit in heated hot dogs. Place in buns. Spread with mustard. Top with sauerkraut, bottled Russian dressing, and Swiss cheese. Broil until cheese melts.	**Frankfurters on Buns Potato Chips Baked Beans Purple Cows*** ˙Drop scoops of vanilla ice cream into tall glasses. Fill with grape soda. Serve with straws and long spoons.	**Cheese Tortellini** (frozen) **with Marinara Sauce** (jarred) **Garlic Bread Tossed Salad with Italian Dressing Summer-Fruit Parfaits*** ˙In goblets, layer a mixture of sliced fresh fruit and berries with lemon yogurt.	FRIDAY
Grilled or Broiled Chicken Breasts (cook extra for Monday) **Boiled Potatoes Zucchini Fresh Nectarine Ices*** ˙Whirl 2 cups sliced nectarines in blender with ⅓ cup orange juice and 2 tablespoons sugar. Freeze in paper cups.	**Bay Scallops with Chives* Cooked White Rice Stewed tomatoes** (canned) **Sliced Strawberries and Bananas** ˙Melt 2 tablespoons butter in a skillet. Add the scallops and toss over high heat just until opaque. Stir in 2 tablespoons chopped fresh chives or scallions and 1 teaspoon lemon juice.	**Grilled or Broiled Flank Steak Spicy Corn on the Cob* Red Cabbage Slaw Blueberries with Milk, Sugar Cookies** ˙Stir ⅛ teaspoon ground red pepper into 2 tablespoons softened butter or margarine. Serve with corn.	**Meat Loaf** (bake enough for Monday) **Mashed Potatoes Hot Green Beans Vinaigrette* Chocolate Pudding** ˙Marinate ½ cup thinly sliced red onion in ½ cup bottled Italian dressing 15 minutes or until limp. Toss with 1 pound freshly cooked and drained green beans.	SATURDAY

	WEEK 29	WEEK 30	WEEK 31	WEEK 32
SUNDAY	**Brunch** **Scrambled Eggs with Scallions** **Hash-Brown Patties** (frozen) **Mandarin Oranges and Sliced Avocado on Romaine Lettuce with Oil-Vinegar Dressing** **Spiced Pineapple*** *Toss fresh pineapple chunks with sugar and ground cinnamon. Refrigerate for 1 hour.*	**Roast Chicken, New Potatoes, and Zucchini*** **Sliced Tomatoes** **Peach Shortcake** *Arrange cut-up chicken, halved potatoes, and sliced zucchini in baking pan. Brush with oil and sprinkle with rosemary, salt, and pepper before roasting.*	**Roast Pork Loin** (save leftovers for Tuesday) **Baked Potatoes** **Sautéed Summer Squash and Bell Pepper Strips** **Fresh Plum Ice*** *At least 6 hours before serving, purée 2 cups sliced plums, ½ cup orange juice, and 2 tablespoons sugar. Freeze in paper cups.*	**Barbecued Turkey Tenderloins** **Corn on the Cob** **Mixed Green Salad with Salsa-Ranch Dressing*** **Watermelon Wedges** *Mix ⅓ cup salsa with ⅓ cup ranch dressing.*
MONDAY	**Soft Meat-Loaf Tacos with Salsa and Cheese*** **Chili Beans** (canned) **Lettuce and Cucumber Salad with Oil-Vinegar Dressing** **Watermelon Slices** *Top warmed corn tortillas with thin slices meat loaf (left over from Saturday), salsa, and shredded Jack cheese. Fold tortillas.*	**Pan-Fried Pork Chops** **Sautéed Italian Peppers** **Orzo Salad*** **Chocolate-Chip Ice Cream** *Mix orzo (left over from Saturday) with 1 cup chopped tomato, ½ cup crumbled feta cheese, and 2 tablespoons each lemon juice and chopped dill.*	**Pasta with Roasted Pepper Sauce*** **Crusty Bread** **Tossed Salad with Oil and Vinegar Dressing** **Fruited Gelatin** *To make sauce, purée in blender one 7-ounce jar of roasted peppers, 1 cup nonfat sour cream, and 3 tablespoons grated Parmesan cheese. Toss with freshly cooked hot pasta.*	**Lentil Chili* with Sour Cream** **Garlic Bread** **Coleslaw** **Brownies** *Bring 1 cup lentils, 2 cups water and one 1 ¼-ounce package Sloppy Joe mix to a boil. Cover and simmer 18 minutes or until lentils are tender. Stir in 15-ounce can tomato sauce. Simmer 5 minutes more.*
TUESDAY	**Chicken Nuggets** (bought) **with Honey Mustard** **Corn Bread Sticks** (from refrigerated dough) **Sliced Tomato and Red Onion Salad with Spicy Dressing*** **Lemon Sherbet** *Add a few drops of hot-pepper sauce to bottled oil-vinegar dressing.*	**Macaroni Shells and Cheese** (mix) **with Broccoli*** **Shredded Iceberg Lettuce and Carrot Salad with Dijon Vinaigrette** **Peaches or Nectarines** *Add 10-ounce package frozen chopped broccoli to boiling water while cooking the macaroni.*	**Lively Leftovers** **Roast Pork Sandwiches** (left over from Sunday) **with Lettuce and Tomato on Whole Wheat Buns** **Creamy Cucumber Salad*** **Brownies or Blondies** *Thinly slice 1 large peeled seedless cucumber. Toss with cold plain yogurt, chopped fresh mint, garlic, and sugar to taste.*	**Spaghetti and Meatballs** **Italian Bread** **Chicory, Roasted Red Pepper** (jarred) **and White Bean Salad** **Lemon Ginger Ale Floats*** *Drop scoops of lemon sherbet into tall glasses. Fill with lemon-flavored ginger ale.*
WEDNESDAY	**Broiled Orange Roughy with Melted Butter** **Curried Rice** (mix) **Steamed Zucchini** **Minted Cantaloupe*** *Bring ¼ fresh lime juice, 3 tablespoons sugar, and 2 tablespoons chopped fresh mint to a boil. Remove the pan from the heat and let stand for 30 minutes. Strain and cool. Mix with 4 cups cantaloupe chunks.*	**Scallops Sautéed with Garlic** **Boiled Potatoes with Parsley and Carrots** **Watermelon Compote*** *Toss watermelon chunks with lime juice and a little sugar.*	**Spicy Chicken Wings*** **Potato Salad** (deli) **Bell Pepper and Celery Sticks with Blue Cheese Dressing** **Frozen Fruit Juice Bars** *Look for cooked seasoned chicken parts in your store's meat case.*	**Creamy Corn and Tomato Chowder*** **Ham Sandwiches with Lettuce and Horseradish Sauce** (jar) **on Pumpernickel Bread** **Health Salad** (deli) **Sliced Bananas in Pineapple Juice** *Stir 1 cup chopped tomato into heated canned creamy corn soup.*
THURSDAY	**Pizza Provençal*** **Mixed Green Salad with Italian Dressing** **Coconut Layer Cake** *Top frozen cheese pizza with bell pepper strips, sliced black olives, and scallions before baking. Sprinkle with chopped fresh basil before serving.*	**Broiled Peppered Flank Steak*** **with Sautéed Onions** (cook enough steak and onions for Saturday) **Broiled Potato Wedges** **Carrots and Peas** (frozen) **Strawberry Pie** *Press coarsely ground black pepper on steaks before broiling. Sprinkle cooked onions with vinegar and Worcestershire sauce.*	**Grilled Halibut Steaks with Peach-Mint Salsa*** **10-Minute Brown Rice** **Grilled Zucchini** **Honeydew and Blueberry Compote** *For salsa, chop 1 peach and mix with 2 tablespoons chopped red onion and 1 tablespoon chopped fresh mint or ½ teaspoon dried mint.*	**Baked Greek-Style Fish Fillets*** **Rice with Sliced Scallions** **Spinach and Chick-Pea Salad** **Nectarines** *Top scrod or other white-flesh fish fillets with sliced tomato. Sprinkle with dried oregano and lightly drizzle with olive oil before baking.*
FRIDAY	**Spaghetti Squash with Tomato Sauce** (jarred)***** **Escarole and Chick-Pea Salad with Italian Dressing** **Chocolate Mousse** (mix) *Prick squash all over. Boil for 35 minutes or until tender. Cut in half and discard seeds. Loosen strands with a fork. Toss with the sauce and sprinkle with grated Parmesan cheese.*	**Turkey Tenderloins Tonkatsu*** **Baked Sweet Potatoes** **Steamed Spinach** **Oatmeal Cookies** *Brush turkey tenderloins with bottled tonkatsu sauce, a dark spicy sauce found in the Asian food section of supermarkets, and bake.*	**8-Vegetable Juice Cocktail** **Pan-Fried Calves' Liver and Onions** **Shoestring Potatoes** (frozen) **Corn Salad*** **Italian Ices** *Toss drained canned corn with chopped tomato and scallions and vinaigrette dressing.*	**Spicy Boneless Beef Blade Steaks*** **Buttermilk Biscuits** (refrigerated) **Sautéed Cherry Tomatoes** **Fresh Blueberries** *Rub ground cumin and chili powder on steaks before broiling. Serve with lime wedges.*
SATURDAY	**Braised Lamb Shanks** **Orzo** (rice-shaped pasta)**; make 3 extra cups*** **Green Bean Salad with Mustard Vinaigrette** **Raspberry Yogurt with Sliced Peaches** *Toss 3 cups hot cooked orzo with ⅓ cup olive oil. Cover and refrigerate for Monday.*	**Pita Fajitas*** **Black Bean** (canned) **and Chopped Roasted Peppers** (jarred) **Salad with Italian Dressing** **Raspberry Sherbet in Peach Halves** *Stuff pitas with sliced steak (left over from Thursday), onions, sliced avocado, and lettuce. Top with salsa and sour cream.*	**Broiled Lamb Chops** **Bulgur Pilaf** (mix) **Sliced Tomatoes and Crumbled Feta Cheese with Italian Dressing** **Peaches 'n' Cream Pie** *Prepare two 4-serving packages vanilla pudding. Add ½ teaspoon almond extract. Pour into a 9-inch ready-to-fill graham-cracker pie shell and chill. Top with sliced peaches.*	**Orange-Rosemary Roasted Cornish Hens*** **Oven-Browned Potato Wedges** **Asparagus Spears** **Fresh Mangoes with Raspberry Pourable Fruit** *Before roasting, squeeze fresh orange juice over hens, then put peels in the body cavities and rub the skin with crushed dried rosemary.*

WEEK 33	WEEK 34	WEEK 35	WEEK 36	
Meat Loaf (cook extra for Tuesday) **Golden Mashed Potatoes* Green Peas Watermelon Wedges** *Cook 1 cup finely shredded carrots and 1 teaspoon instant minced onion in water needed to make 4 servings instant mashed potatoes. When carrots are tender, add potatoes as package directs.	**Rice-Stuffed Breast of Veal* Turnip Greens with Diced Turnips** (frozen) **Pistachio Pudding** *Prepare brown and wild rice mix. Stuff into pocket of 3- to 4-pound veal breast. Skewer closed. Roast in 350°F oven for 1½ to 2 hours, basting often with pan juices.	**Roast Breast of Turkey** (shred 2 cups for Tuesday) **Saucepan Stuffing Gingered Brussels Sprouts* Sliced Peaches** (can) with **Pistachio Ice Cream** *Toss cooked Brussels sprouts with 1 table-spoon butter and 1 teaspoon ground ginger.	**Roast Leg of Lamb** (save leftovers for Tuesday) **Roast Potatoes with Rosemary* Steamed Baby Carrots Brownies** *Toss 16 potato wedges with 1 tablespoon oil, 2 teaspoons dried rosemary, and ½ teaspoon salt. Roast on baking sheet 45 minutes, turning twice.	**SUNDAY**
Grilled Chicken Legs, Zucchini Slices, and Onion Wedges* Garlic Bread Ice Cream Sandwiches *Brush chicken and vegetables with Italian dressing and sprinkle the chicken with dried rosemary before cooking.	**Eggplant Parmesan** (frozen) **Sesame Breadsticks Chick-Pea, Chopped Tomato, and Fresh Basil Salad on Lettuce with Italian Dressing Fruit Cocktail Crunch*** *Top canned fruit cocktail with granola.	**Split-Pea Soup** (canned) **Onion and Potato Omelets with Salsa* Tossed Salad with Orange Wedges** *In nonstick skillet, cook 2 cups sliced onions and a one 16-ounce can drained sliced white potatoes in 2 teaspoons oil until browned. Add 6 beaten eggs, cover, and cook until set. Serve with salsa.	**Kid's Choice Mugs of Alphabet Soup Toasted Cheese and Tomato Sandwiches Three-Bean Salad** (jarred) **Peanutty-Caramel Sundaes*** *Mix ⅓ cup bottled caramel sauce with ¼ cup smooth or chunky peanut butter. Spoon over vanilla or chocolate frozen yogurt.	**MONDAY**
Open-Face Meat Loaf Sandwiches with Gravy* Green Beans (canned or frozen) **Grapes, Nuts in Shells** *Heat slices of meat loaf (left over from Sunday) in gravy from a jar, can, or mix.	Broiler Dinner **Ground-Meat Kebabs* Broiled Garlic Toast Mushroom-Zucchini Kebabs Broiled Grapefruit Halves** *Make your favorite meatball recipe, using ground lamb or beef. Press into balls around skewers. Broil for 5 to 6 minutes, turning once. Serve with plain yogurt.	**Beijing Turkey Roll-Ups* Bell Pepper, Cucumber, and White-Bean Salad Melon Slices** *Line flour tortillas with lettuce. Spoon on bottled hoisin sauce. Add shredded cooked turkey (left over from Sunday) and sprinkle with sliced scallions. Roll up.	**Sliced Lamb** (left over from Sunday) **in Whole Wheat Pitas with Sliced Tomatoes, Lettuce, and Cucumber-Yogurt Dressing* Lentil Pilaf** (mix) **Honeydew Wedges** *Purée 1 large peeled seedless cucumber, 1 cup plain yogurt, ½ teaspoon each dried oregano and minced garlic, salt and pepper to taste.	**TUESDAY**
Blender Gazpacho* Bacon-Lettuce-Tomato Sandwiches on Rye Bread Fresh Fruit Cups *Purée two 8-ounce cans tomato juice, 1 cup water, ½ cup each chopped tomato, cucumber, and green bell pepper, and ½ cup chopped onion. Add 2 tablespoons red wine vinegar, and salt and pepper to taste. Serve chilled.	**Crispy Fish Fillets** (frozen) **with Sauce Luis* Corn on the Cob Spinach, Red Onion, and Bell Pepper Salad, Italian Dressing Cantaloupe** *Mix ⅓ cup each mayonnaise or salad dressing and favorite bottled salsa. Serve over fish.	**Fish Cakes** (frozen) **with Cucumber-Dill Sauce* Corn on the Cob Buttered Green Peas Raspberry Sherbet** *Mix ½ cup each finely chopped cucumber and low-fat yogurt with ¼ cup snipped dill and ½ teaspoon ground cumin.	**Grilled Swordfish or Halibut Steaks* Grilled Potato Wedges Grilled Bell Peppers Raspberry-Filled Bar Cookies** *Before grilling, lightly spray fish and vegeta-bles with vegetable oil cooking spray and sprinkle with Italian herb seasoning.	**WEDNESDAY**
Pasta with No-Cook Seafood Sauce* Breadsticks Romaine Lettuce, Italian Dressing Strawberries *Toss 12 ounces hot freshly cooked pasta with 4- to 5-ounce package semisoft garlic-herb cheese. Stir in 12 ounces imitation crabmeat and 2 cups halved cherry tomatoes.	**Macaroni and Cheese Broccoli Spears with Lemon Wedges Cherry Tomatoes Orange Cows*** *Put 2 scoops vanilla frozen yogurt in each tall glass. Fill with orange soda. Serve with long spoons.	**Pan-Fried Pork Chops Hash Brown Potatoes Buttered Carrots Toasted Pound Cake Slices with Hot Plum Sauce*** *Toss 1 pound sliced pitted fresh plums with 2 teaspoons sugar. Heat over low heat until juices are released and plums are hot. Stir in ¼ teaspoon almond extract. Spoon over pound cake slices.	**Chili con Carne on Corn Bread Mixed Green Salad with Italian Dressing Sliced Peaches with Raspberry Cream*** *Mix 1 cup ricotta or cottage cheese and 2 tablespoons raspberry preserves. Spoon over peaches.	**THURSDAY**
Broiled Fish Fillets Olé* Couscous (mix) **Broccoli Spears Vanilla Pudding** *Purée 4-ounce can chopped green chilies with ¼ cup mayonnaise or salad dressing and 2 tablespoons grated Parmesan cheese. Spread over fish before broiling.	**Sweet 'n' Sour Chicken Drumsticks* Mashed Sweet Potatoes Fresh Green Beans Dried Fruit and Nuts** *Brush drumsticks with a mixture of ⅓ cup apricot preserves and 1 tablespoon cider vinegar before and during baking.	**Linguine with No-Cook Fresh Tomato Sauce* Three-Bean Salad on Lettuce Fresh Grapes, Fig Bars** *Chop 4 large tomatoes. Add ¼ cup chopped fresh basil, 1 tablespoon olive oil, and 1 teaspoon minced garlic. Toss with hot pasta.	**Turkey Schnitzel* Mashed Potatoes Mixed Vegetables** (frozen) **Fresh Plums** *Lightly coat turkey cutlets with flour, dip in beaten egg, then in packaged seasoned dry bread crumbs. Pan-fry in a little oil over medium heat 3 minutes per side until golden. Serve with lemon wedges.	**FRIDAY**
Pan-fried Ham Steaks Rice and Vermicelli (mix) **Yellow Squash and Apples* Lemon Yogurt and Gingersnaps** *Melt 1 tablespoon butter in a large skillet. Add 2½ cups sliced squash and 1 cup each sliced apple and onion and ½ teaspoon each dried sage and salt. Sauté for 6 minutes, or until crisp-tender.	**Barbecued Spareribs* Corn on the Cob Tossed Green Salad with Ranch Dressing Hot Caramel Sundaes** *For tender ribs with less fat, boil them in a large pot of water for about 45 minutes before grilling or baking.	**Pan-Broiled Boneless Chuck Steaks with Gravy** (jarred) **Mashed Potatoes with Caramelized Onions* Green Beans Root-Beer Floats with Vanilla Ice Milk** *Pan-fry 2 cups sliced onions in 2 teaspoons oil until well browned. Stir into prepared mashed potatoes.	**Grilled Pork Tenderloin with Applesauce** (jarred) **Grilled Sweet Potatoes Coleslaw Sherbet with Jam*** *Spoon warm melted seedless red raspberry jam over lemon sherbet.	**SATURDAY**

	WEEK 37	WEEK 38	WEEK 39	WEEK 40
SUNDAY	**Boiled Beef Brisket** (slice some for Tuesday) **with Carrots and Potatoes and Lemon-Horseradish Sauce*** **Apple Pie** *Stir 3 tablespoons prepared white horseradish and 1 tablespoon lemon juice into 1 cup white sauce made from a mix.	**Baked Honey-Orange Chicken*** **Potato Pancakes** **Carrots** **Fruit and Nut Platter** *Mix ¼ cup each honey and orange marmalade. Brush on cut-up chicken during the last 20 minutes of baking.	**Roast Beef** (dice 2 ½ cups for Tuesday) **with Pan Gravy** **Roasted Potatoes and Carrots** **Baked Apples*** *Core apples and pare a strip of skin around the middle of each. Fill each with 2 teaspoons sugar, 1 teaspoon butter, and ⅛ teaspoon cinnamon. Pour ¼ inch water into the dish. Bake for 30 to 40 minutes, or until tender.	**Roast Chicken** (roast an extra for Tuesday) **with Pan Gravy** **Saucepan Stuffing** (mix) **Green Beans** **Pears with Blue Cheese*** *Mash equal amounts of cream cheese with blue cheese. Serve on fresh or canned pear halves.
MONDAY	**Broiled Chicken Breasts** **Corn and Black Bean Salad*** **Angel Food Cake with Strawberry Pourable Fruit** *Toss drained canned corn and drained and rinsed canned black beans with chopped zucchini, red onions, and low-fat Italian dressing.	**Split-Pea Soup** (canned) **with Pumpernickel Bread** **Spinach, Mushroom, and Red Bell Pepper Salad with Italian Dressing** **Citrus Ambrosia*** *Combine grapefruit segments (jarred) with mandarin oranges (canned). Top with toasted shredded coconut.	**Turkey Potpies** (frozen) **Romaine, Watercress,* and Tomato Salad with Ranch Dressing** **Banana Cake** (bought) *Not only does watercress add crunch and peppery zest to salad, but it's a great source of vitamins A and C.	**Broiled Lamb Chops** **Broiled Potato Wedges** **Sautéed Swiss Chard*** **Lemon Sherbet with Black-Cherry Pourable Fruit** *In a large skillet heat 1 teaspoon minced garlic in 1 tablespoon oil for about 30 seconds. Add 1 ½ pounds chopped fresh chard. Stir over medium heat until the stems are crisp-tender. Season to taste.
TUESDAY	**Tomato-Rice Soup** **Beef Brisket Sandwiches** (left over from Sunday) **with Lettuce, Red Onion Slices, Coleslaw, & Russian Dressing on Rye Bread** **Pickled Beets** (jar) **Orange-Banana Smoothies*** *Purée 4 ripe bananas, cut into chunks, with 1 ½ cups water and ½ cup frozen orange juice concentrate in a blender or food processor.	**Cranberry Juice Cocktail** **Tuna-Noodle and Broccoli Casserole*** **Tossed Green Salad with French Dressing** **Lime Sherbet with Vanilla Wafer Cookies** *Add one 10-ounce package thawed, drained frozen chopped broccoli to your favorite tuna casserole before baking.	**Corn-and-Beef Chili*** **Tossed Salad with French Dressing** **Doughnuts and Hot Cocoa** *Add 2 ½ cups diced roast beef (left over from Sunday) and 1 drained 12-ounce can Mexican-style corn to canned bean chili. Heat through. Serve with dollops of sour cream.	**Chicken Salad Platter*** **Toasted English Muffins** **Fudge Brownies** *Skin and bone leftover roast chicken from Sunday. Cut meat into chunks. Put on lettuce-lined platter with sliced cucumber, tomato, and avocado. Drizzle with Italian dressing.
WEDNESDAY	**Spaghetti Squash with Tuna-Marinara Sauce*** **Warm Flour Tortillas** **Spinach and Red Onion Salad** **Frozen Fruit Juice Bars** *Prick squash. Boil for 35 minutes. Cut in half, discard the seeds, and loosen strands with a fork. Toss with heated marinara sauce and drained canned tuna.	**Herb-Cheese Burgers* on Kaiser Rolls** **Tossed Green Salad with Mustard Vinaigrette** **Chocolate Chip Cookies** *Top hot cooked burgers with a bell pepper ring. Fill center with semisoft garlic-herb cheese.	**Mugs of Bouillon** **Cheese, Spinach, and Mushroom Pizza*** **Romaine and Chick-Pea Salad with Italian Dressing** **Rice Pudding** *Top frozen or take-out cheese pizza with fresh spinach leaves and thin-sliced mushrooms. Bake until spinach wilts.	**Broiled Catfish Fillets*** **Bulgur Pilaf** (mix) **Broccoli Spears** **Chocolate Chip Cookies** *Spread each fillet with 1 tablespoon ranch dressing and sprinkle with 2 teaspoons grated Parmesan cheese before broiling.
THURSDAY	**Chicken Livers in Spanish Rice** (mix)* **Green Peas** **Flan or Caramel Custard** *When rice is half-cooked, stir in 12 ounces chicken livers, cut into thirds. Cover and cook, stirring twice, until the rice is cooked and the livers are barely pink near centers. Serve with hot pepper sauce.	**Turkey BLTs* on Toast** **Three Bean Salad** **Fresh Strawberries** *For a leaner BLT, make sandwiches with sliced turkey breast, turkey bacon, and reduced-calorie mayonnaise.	**Scrambled Eggs with Tomato and Corn*** **Cheese Grits** **Bell Pepper Rings** **Frozen Fruit Juice Bars** *Stir ½ cup each thawed frozen corn kernels and chopped tomato and scallion into 8 beaten eggs before scrambling.	**Broiled Veal Chops** **Parsleyed Potatoes** **Hungarian Cabbage*** **Dried Fruit Compote** *Steam 4 cups shredded cabbage in a little water for 12 minutes, or until tender. Drain. Stir in ½ cup sour cream, ½ teaspoon caraway seeds, and paprika, salt, and pepper to taste.
FRIDAY	**Broiled Fish Fillets with Almond-Lemon Butter*** **Parsleyed Potatoes** **Green Beans** **Chocolate Sandwich Cookies** *Toast ¼ cup chopped almonds in a small skillet over medium heat. Add 2 tablespoons each butter and lemon juice, swirl the pan to melt and mix. Pour over broiled fish.	**Broiled Codfish Fillets*** **Tomato Risotto** (mix) **Romaine, Bell Pepper, and Watercress Salad with Ranch Dressing** **Frozen Peach Yogurt** *Brush fillets with olive oil. Sprinkle with seasoned bread crumbs and fennel or anise seeds before broiling.	**Fish 'n Chips** (frozen fish sticks and French fries), **with Tartar Sauce** (jarred) **Sweet and Nutty Slaw*** **Pear Wedges with Chocolate Syrup for Dipping** *Add 1 chopped unpeeled apple, ¼ cup chopped nuts, and a handful of raisins to deli coleslaw.	**Antipasto Platter*** **Lasagne** (frozen) **Coffee Frozen Yogurt and Anisette Toasts** *On a platter, arrange (from jars) roasted red peppers, olives, eggplant appetizer, and pickled green beans.
SATURDAY	**Sesame Pork Cutlets*** **Herbed Rice** (mix) **Kale or Turnip Greens** (frozen) **Strawberry Frozen Yogurt** *Brush pork with mixture of 2 tablespoons soy sauce, 1 teaspoon dark Asian sesame oil, ½ teaspoon ground ginger, and ¼ teaspoon ground black pepper. Let stand for 30 minutes. Pan-broil.	**Broiled Ham Steaks with Applesauce** **Spiced Bow-Tie Noodles*** **Brussels Sprouts** **Chocolate Pound Cake** *Toss freshly cooked and drained noodles with butter, chopped parsley, salt, pepper, and mustard seeds to taste.	**Beef Kielbasa with Cabbage and Apples*** **Rye Bread** **Vanilla Frozen Yogurt** *Heat kielbasa sausage in a small amount of water in a covered skillet for 5 minutes. Add shredded cabbage and sliced apples. Sprinkle with caraway seeds. Steam until tender.	**Peppery Beef Shoulder Steak*** **Steamed New Potatoes** **Sautéed Zucchini and Onions** **Pineapple Chunks** *Lightly spread steak with mustard and coarse ground pepper before broiling.

WEEK 41	WEEK 42	WEEK 43	WEEK 44	
Braised Turkey Thighs* **Brown Rice** **Brussels Sprouts** **Seedless Grapes** *Mix 1 packet onion-soup mix, 2 ½ cups water, and 1 teaspoon each dried thyme and marjoram in a Dutch oven. Add skinned thighs. Cover and simmer for 1 ½ hours or until tender.	(cook extra meatballs for Tuesday) **and Tomato Sauce** **Garlic Bread** **Mixed Green Salad with Red Onion Rings & Italian Dressing** **Berries with Ricotta Cream*** *Mix 1 cup ricotta cheese and 2 to 3 tablespoons confectioners' sugar until blended. Spoon on fresh berries.	**Citrus-Stuffed Roast Cornish Hens*** **Long-Grain and Wild Rice** (mix) **Creamed Cauliflower** **Raspberry Sherbet** *Cut 1 orange, 1 lemon, and 1 lime into chunks. Rub the hen cavities with dried thyme, salt, and pepper. Stuff with the fruits. Roast as usual.	**Boiled Corned Beef with Potatoes,** **Cabbage, and Carrots** (save some for Tuesday) **Soda Bread** **Gingered Pineapple*** *Mix two 8-ounce cans pineapple chunks with 1 ½ teaspoons grated orange peel, 3 tablespoons fresh orange juice, and ½ teaspoon minced peeled fresh gingerroot. Chill.	SUNDAY
Tomato Soup (canned) **Cheddar Cheese Omelets** **Toasted Bagels** **Fresh Corn, Red Pepper, and Lettuce Salad*** **Fig Bars** *Mix 1 ½ cups raw corn kernels, ½ cup chopped red bell pepper, ¼ cup sliced green onions, and ⅓ cup bottled light slaw dressing. Toss with 8 cups torn lettuce.	**Chicken Legs with Vegetables*** **Baked Apples** *Brown 2 pounds chicken legs in oil in a Dutch oven. Add cut-up potatoes, carrots, and onions, one 10 ¾-ounce can cream of celery soup, and one 14 ½-ounce can stewed tomatoes. Cover and bake in 350°F oven for 1 hour.	**Mugs of Bouillon** **Spanish Rice** (mix) **with Pork*** **Sliced Cucumbers with Ranch Dressing** **Pear Wedges with Honey** *Cook Spanish rice according to package directions, adding shredded pork (left over from Saturday), ¼ cup pimiento strips, and 1 cup frozen green peas 5 minutes before rice is done.	**Pan-fried Chicken Cutlets** **Garlicky Bow-Tie Noodles*** **Peas and Carrots** **Oranges, Chocolate Cookies** *Cook 8 ounces bow-tie noodles. Drain in a colander. In the same pot, cook 2 slivered cloves garlic in ¼ cup olive oil until golden. Add the pasta, chopped parsley, salt, and pepper. Toss to mix.	MONDAY
Spaghetti Squash with Chick-Pea Sauce* **Garlic Bread** **Spinach Salad** **Lemon Gelatin** *Prick squash. Boil for 35 minutes, or until tender. Cut in half, discard seeds, loosen strands with a fork. Toss with heated marinara sauce and canned chick-peas.	**Lentil Soup** (canned) **Meatball Frittata*** **Prune Plums** *Heat 2 tablespoons oil in a large nonstick skillet. Add 1 cup each diced zucchini and onion. Cook until tender. Add crumbled meatballs (left over from Sunday), 6 beaten eggs, and ¼ cup grated Parmesan cheese. Cook until eggs are set.	**Falafel** (vegetable burger mix) **in Pita Pockets with Cucumber Raita,*** **Shredded Lettuce, and Hot Pepper Sauce** **Chocolate Ice-Milk Sodas** *Peel, halve, and remove seeds from 1 cucumber. Slice thin. Mix with ¼ cup yogurt, 2 tablespoons chopped scallions, salt, and pepper.	**Corned Beef Hash*** **Steamed Spinach** **Pickled Beets** **Applesauce and Gingersnaps** *Mix 2 cups each chopped corned beef (left over from Sunday) and potatoes and ½ cup chopped onion. Pan-fry in 1 tablespoon butter, pressing down with a spatula and turning the mixture once, until browned on both sides.	TUESDAY
Scallop and Potato Stew* **Saltine Crackers** **Sliced Tomatoes on Lettuce** **Raspberry Sherbet** *Cook ½ cup chopped onion in 1 tablespoon oil until tender. Add 2 cans cream of potato soup, 3 soup cans milk, and 12 ounces bay scallops. Heat gently until scallops are opaque.	**Tomato-Juice Cocktails** **Broiled Halibut Steaks with Herb Butter** **Rice Pilaf** (mix) **Green Beans** **Gingerbread with Chunky Pineapple Sauce** (canned)* *Heat chunky pineapple sauce. Serve over warm gingerbread squares.	**Hamburgers Piperade*** **Mashed Potatoes** **Green Beans** **Melon Slices** *Heat 2 tablespoons olive oil in a large skillet. Add 1 cup sliced onion; 1 sliced green bell pepper; 1 large tomato, cut in chunks; and 1 teaspoon minced garlic. Cook until tender. Spoon over burgers.	**Sea Slaw in Whole-Wheat Pitas*** **Cucumber Spears** **Vanilla Pudding** *Mix 4 cups finely shredded cabbage, 12 ounces shredded imitation crabmeat, ⅔ cup bottled ranch dressing, 2 tablespoons each lemon juice and chopped dill. Spoon into pita pockets.	WEDNESDAY
Greek-Style Pork Chops* **Bulgur Wheat Pilaf** (mix) **Sliced Tomatoes with Basil** **Anisette Toasts** *Sprinkle thin-cut pork chops with dried mint, vinegar, and olive oil. Marinate ½ hour before broiling.	**Macaroni and Cheese** **Lemon Broccoli*** **Pickled Beets** (jarred) **Graham Crackers with Peanut Butter and Jam** *Squeeze some lemon juice on the broccoli just before serving.	**Frankfurter Casserole*** **Tossed Green Salad with Italian Dressing** **Grapes and Graham Crackers** *Stir 1 tablespoon each prepared mustard, ketchup, and molasses or pancake syrup into a 16-ounce can vegetarian baked beans. Add sliced chicken or turkey frankfurters. Bake at 350°F until hot.	**Pan-Fried Cubed Steaks with au Jus Gravy** (jarred) **Rice and Vermicelli** (mix) **Sautéed Tomatoes and Squash*** **Chocolate Pudding** *Sauté cherry tomatoes and sliced yellow squash, seasoned with garlic, thyme, salt, and pepper, in a little oil until squash is tender and tomatoes start to split.	THURSDAY
Broiled Scrod Fillets with Lemon Wedges **Scallion Couscous*** **Broccoli Spears** **Apple Bars** *Add sliced scallions and dried basil to couscous. Prepare according to package directions.	**Tomato-Rice Soup** (canned) **Tuna-Cheese Melt on Rolls** **Romaine Salad with Bell Pepper and Onion Rings, French Dressing** **Quick Cherry Crisp*** *Spread canned cherry-pie filling in a 9-inch pie plate. Top with crumbled pecan shortbread cookies. Bake until hot and bubbling.	**Pan-Fried Bay Scallops with Tartar Sauce** (jarred) **Lemon-Herb Orzo*** **Chopped Kale** (frozen) **Cheese and Fruit Platter** *Toss 8 ounces freshly cooked orzo (rice-shaped pasta) with 2 tablespoons butter, 1 tablespoon lemon juice, and ¼ cup chopped parsley. Add salt and pepper to taste.	**Nacho Cheese-Pumpkin Soup*** **Bean Burritos** (frozen) **Orange, Watercress, and Scallion Salad, Lime-and-Oil Dressing** **Strawberry Gelatin** *In a saucepan, blend 1 can nacho-cheese soup, 2 soup cans milk, and 1 can canned pumpkin (freeze remainder for another use). Simmer until hot.	FRIDAY
Beef Stew with Carrots, Celery, and Green Peas **Orzo** (rice-shaped pasta) **Baked Pears and Cranberries*** *Mix 4 sliced, peeled, and cored pears with 1 cup cranberries, ½ cup granulated sugar, 2 tablespoons lemon juice, and ¼ teaspoon pumpkin-pie spice. Bake at 375°F for 30 minutes, or until tender. **Rigatoni Pasta with Meatballs**	**Roast Fresh Pork Shoulder** (dice 1 ½ cups cooked pork for Monday) **Pineapple Acorn Squash*** **Buttered Brussels Sprouts** **Apple Pie** (frozen) *Halve and seed squash. Season with butter and nutmeg. Bake with pork until tender. Fill cavities with canned pineapple sauce.	**Eggplant Parmesan*** **Breadsticks** **Spinach and Mushroom Salad with Italian Dressing** **Carrot Cake** (bought) *To cut calories, lightly brush eggplant slices with oil and broil until tender instead of coating with bread crumbs and frying.	**Skillet Pork Chops with Okra** (canned)* **Hash-Brown Patties** **Cauliflower in Cheese Sauce** **Butterscotch Pudding** *Brown pork chops in oil in skillet. Add jar of gravy, one 16-ounce can cut okra, and ¼ cup sliced scallions. Cover and simmer for 20 minutes, or until tender.	SATURDAY

	WEEK 45	**WEEK 46**	**WEEK 47**	**WEEK 48**
SUNDAY	**Roast Turkey Breast** (save some for Tuesday) **Oven-Roasted Turnips*** **Braised Escarole or Kale** **Pear Wedges with Chocolate** `Halve and lightly oil 2 pounds small turnips. Season with salt and pepper. Put in pan with turkey and roast until tender, about 1 ½ hours.	**Breaded Chicken Cutlets*** **Buttered New Potatoes** **Cauliflower** **Raspberry Sherbet** `Brush cutlets with salad dressing before coating with packaged seasoned bread crumbs and pan-frying.	**Lamb Shoulder Steaks*** **Couscous** (mix) **Stewed Tomatoes** (canned) and **Zucchini†** **Bread Pudding** `Marinate lamb in French dressing 20 minutes before broiling. †Add diced fresh zucchini and a pinch of thyme to tomatoes. Cook until tender.	**Roast Fresh Pork Shoulder** (save some for Tuesday) **Baked Sweet Potatoes** **Steamed Cabbage Wedges** (cook extra for Tuesday) **Chocolate Pie*** `Cook two 4-serving packages chocolate pudding. Pour into a 9-inch ready-to-fill graham cracker crust and chill. Add whipped topping.
MONDAY	**Sweet and Pungent** **Ham Steaks*** **Sweet Potatoes** (canned) **Mixed Vegetables** (frozen) **Oatmeal Raisin Cookies** `Stir some spicy mustard into bottled duck sauce. Brush on ham steaks during broiling.	**Roast Beef Hash*** **Carrot and Beet Salad†** **Sherbet with Fruit Compote** `Cook ½ cup chopped onion in 1 tablespoon oil in a large skillet until soft. Dice reserved potatoes. Add with reserved roast beef and gravy. Heat through. †Toss reserved carrots with drained pickled beets.	**Italian Sausage and Tomato** **Sauce Heros** **Green Salad with Marinated** **Artichoke Hearts** (jarred) **and Oil-Vinegar Dressing** **Tapioca Parfaits*** `Alternate layers of tapioca pudding (mix) with apricot pourable fruit or fruit preserves.	**Spicy Oven-Fried Chicken** **Thighs*** **Buttermilk Biscuits** (refrigerated) **Carrot Slaw with Ranch** **Dressing†** **Raspberry Gelatin** `Coat skinned thighs with spicy coating mix before baking. †Stir sliced scallions and ground cumin into slaw.
TUESDAY	**Chef's Salad: Lettuce, Turkey** (left over from Sunday), **Cherry Tomatoes, Low-Fat Cheese, Red Bell Pepper Strips & Fat-Free Blue Cheese Dressing** **Applesauce Slush*** **Fat-Free Caramel** **Popped-Corn Cakes** `Purée frozen applesauce in a blender. Serve with spoons.	**Hearty Escarole Soup*** **Crusty Italian Bread** **Dried Fruits and Nuts** `Cut 12 ounces hot Italian sausage into ½-inch pieces. Brown in large pot in 1 tablespoon oil. Drain fat. Add 4 cups chicken broth, 2 cups water, one 16-ounce can white beans, and 10 cups chopped escarole. Simmer until escarole is tender.	**Saucy Chicken on Brown Rice*** **Marinated Green Beans** **Sliced Kiwis and Bananas** `Add one 16-ounce package frozen mixed vegetables and 2 cups cooked, cubed chicken (left over from Saturday) to one 15 ½-ounce jar marinara sauce. Cook, stirring often, until hot. Serve over heated rice.	**Oriental Pork and Noodles*** **Oriental-Style Vegetables** (frozen) **Pineapple Wedges** `Bring 4 cups water to a boil. Add two 3-ounce packages Oriental-style noodles and 2 cups shredded pork and cabbage (left over from Sunday). Simmer for 5 minutes. Stir in seasoning packets and 2 sliced scallions.
WEDNESDAY	**Soft Bean Tacos*** **Orange-Radish Salad** **Chocolate Nonfat** **Pudding Cups** `Spread warm tortillas with heated nonfat refried beans. Top with shredded lettuce and low-fat cheese, chopped onion, and chunky salsa.	**8-Vegetable Juice** **Herbed Chicken Livers*** **Mushroom Risotto** (mix) **Green Peas** **Devil's Food Cupcakes** `Cut livers into thirds. Coat with a mixture of flour, sage, and salt. Pan-fry in a little oil over high heat until still slightly pink in centers.	**Fish Cakes** (frozen) **with Tartar** **Sauce** (jarred) **French Fries** (frozen) **Pearl Onions and Peas** (frozen) **Spiced Apples*** **and** **Oatmeal Cookies** `Mix ¼ cup packed brown sugar with 2 teaspoons pumpkin pie spice. Serve as dip for apple wedges.	**Creamy Herb Fish Fillets*** **Cooked Brown Rice** **Sautéed Zucchini** **Red Seedless Grapes and** **Nuts in Shells** `Top each fish fillet with 1 tablespoon creamy herb cheese before baking.
THURSDAY	**Cheese Ravioli or Tortellini** (frozen) **with Pesto Sauce** (jarred) **Italian Bread** **Romaine and Red Onion Salad,** **Oil-Vinegar Dressing** **Strawberry Parfaits*** `Beat one (15-ounce) container ricotta cheese with 2 tablespoons each milk and granulated sugar until smooth. Layer with thawed frozen sliced strawberries.	**Salmon Patties with** **Horseradish-Dill Sauce*** **Bulgur Pilaf** (mix) **Sliced Cucumber with Dijon** **Vinaigrette** **Banana Pudding** `Mix ½ cup plain yogurt, 1 tablespoon each prepared horseradish and chopped fresh dill, 1 teaspoon sugar, and ½ teaspoon each salt and pepper.	**Turkey Burgers* with Gravy** (can, jar, or mix) **Saucepan Stuffing** **Green Peas** **Fruited Gelatin** `Mix 1 pound ground turkey with ½ cup sliced scallions and ½ teaspoon poultry seasoning. Form into patties and pan-fry.	**Hearty Split Pea Soup*** **Pumpernickel Bread** **Lemon Yogurt and Gingersnaps** `In a large pot in 3 quarts water, simmer 1 pound dried split peas, 2 cups each chopped carrots, potatoes, and onions, and 1 teaspoon each dried thyme and salt for 1 hour until tender. Serve sprinkled with shredded low-fat Swiss cheese.
FRIDAY	**Baked Fish Cakes** (frozen) **with Dill Sauce*** **Shoestring Potatoes** (frozen) **Coleslaw** (deli) **Lemon Yogurt** `Mix ½ cup each mayonnaise or salad dressing and plain low-fat yogurt, ¼ cup chopped fresh dill, and 1 teaspoon sugar until blended.	**Pasta with Italian Sausage in** **Tomato Sauce** (cook extra sausage and sauce for Monday) **Rosemary Flatbread*** **Braised Escarole** **Fruit Cocktail** `Unroll one 10-ounce can refrigerated pizza dough on a baking sheet. Brush with olive oil; sprinkle with rosemary and salt and bake.	**Ham and Eggs** **Hash-Brown Potato Patties** (frozen) **Sautéed Zucchini*** **Pumpkin Pie** (frozen) `Heat 1 tablespoon oil in large skillet. Add 2 cups thinly sliced zucchini and ½ cup sliced scallions. Cook for 3 minutes, or until crisp-tender.	**Mexican Turkey Burgers in** **Flour Tortillas*** **Black Bean Salad with Low-Fat** **Italian Dressing** **Grapefruit Sections** `Shape burgers like frankfurters. Broil or pan-fry. Wrap in warm flour tortillas. Serve with canned chopped green chilies, salsa, and nonfat sour cream.
SATURDAY	**Roast Beef with Gravy*** **Baked Potatoes** **Sliced Carrots** **Fresh Fruit Compote** `For Monday's dinner: Shred and reserve 2 ½ cups roast beef, make an extra cup of gravy, bake 2 extra potatoes, cook additional carrots, and make extra compote.	**Roast Chicken** (cook extra for Tuesday) **Bread Stuffing** (mix) **Turnip Greens** **Vanilla Pears*** `Stir a few drops vanilla extract into juice or syrup from canned pears. Spoon over pears.	**Linguine with Pesto, Tuna,** **and Almonds*** **Romaine and Red Onion Salad** **with Italian Dressing** **Cantaloupe and Pineapple** **Chunks** `Save ¼ cup pasta cooking water. Toss hot pasta with reserved water, pesto sauce from a jar, drained canned tuna, and toasted almonds.	**Lasagne** **Garlic Bread** **Chick-Pea Salad on Spinach*** (buy extra spinach for Monday) **Lemon Pudding** `Mix one drained 16-ounce can chick-peas, one 2-ounce jar chopped pimientos, ½ cup chopped celery, and 2 tablespoons chopped onion. Moisten with bottled Italian dressing.

WEEK 49	WEEK 50	WEEK 51	WEEK 52	
Pot Roast* with Carrots, Onions, Potatoes, Turnips, and Gravy (make enough for Tuesday) **Tossed Green Salad with Oil and Vinegar Dressing Baked Apples** ˙Use cuts such as chuck for pot roasting. They're moister and more flavorful than costlier cuts.	**Stuffed Breast of Veal* Baked Butternut Squash Spinach Salad with Dijon Vinaigrette Brownies** ˙Stuff pocket of 3-pound veal breast with prepared herb stuffing mix. Close with picks. Roast in a 350°F oven for 1½ to 2 hours, basting often with melted butter.	**Lasagne Sesame Breadsticks Braised Escarole* Lemon Pound Cake** ˙Heat 1 teaspoon minced garlic in 2 tablespoons olive oil over low heat until garlic releases its aroma. Add 1¾ pounds (12 cups) chopped escarole leaves. Cover and cook until crisp-tender.	**Pork Chop-Sauerkraut Casserole* Noodles with Caraway Seeds Carrots Fresh Fruit Bowl** ˙Brown pork chops in skillet. Fit into baking dish. Top with drained sauerkraut, sliced apples and onions. Cover and bake at 350°F for 24 minutes, or until tender.	SUNDAY
Quick Chicken Paella* Romaine-Cherry Tomato Salad Flan or Custard ˙Stir halved skinned and boned chicken thighs and 2 cups frozen green peas into Spanish rice mix at beginning of cooking. Before serving, sprinkle with chopped cilantro or parsley.	**Mexican Chicken Breasts* 10-Minute Brown Rice Steamed Fresh Spinach Frozen Fruit Juice Bars** ˙Coat chicken in seasoned bread crumbs and pan-fry. Top each piece with 2 tablespoons reduced-fat shredded Cheddar cheese. Cover and heat until the cheese melts. Serve with salsa and lime wedges. **Pasta with Meat Sauce***	**Deviled Chicken Drumsticks* Baked Potatoes Creamed Peas and Onions** (frozen) **Gelatin with Seedless Grapes** ˙Hold chicken skin with paper towel, pull it from drumsticks. Brush chicken with mustard, roll in seasoned bread crumbs. Bake as usual.	**Vegetable and Egg Platter with Cheese Sauce* Whole-Grain Muffins Purple Plums** (canned) ˙Prepare white sauce from a mix. Stir in 1 cup shredded Cheddar or Swiss cheese until melted. Pour over hot cooked cabbage, carrots, broccoli, potatoes, and egg wedges.	MONDAY
Pot Roast Potpie* Tossed Green Salad Frozen Yogurt ˙Put cubes of leftover pot roast into a 2-quart casserole. Stir in leftover vegetables and gravy. Prepare one 8½-ounce package corn muffin mix. Spread over the top. Bake at 400°F for 15 minutes, or until the corn muffin topping is cooked through.	**Tossed Salad with Italian Dressing Fruited Gelatin** ˙Brown 12 ounces lean ground beef and 1 teaspoon minced garlic in 2 tablespoons oil. Add one 15-ounce jar spaghetti sauce. Simmer for 15 minutes for the flavors to develop. Serve over hot pasta. **Glazed Ham Steaks* Mashed Sweet Potatoes**	**Ham and Corn Chowder* Whole Wheat Bread Sticks Carrot and Celery Sticks Orange Wedges and Oatmeal Cookies** ˙Heat 2 cans golden corn soup with 2 soup cans milk. Stir in 1½ cups each diced ham and cooked rice, 1 cup chopped tomato, and ⅓ cup sliced scallions. Simmer for 10 minutes to blend flavors.	**Turkey Tostadas* Sliced Avocado, Red Onion, and Watercress Salad with Ranch Dressing Peach Frozen Yogurt** ˙Top tostada shells with shredded lettuce, shredded cooked turkey, sliced black olives, and salsa.	TUESDAY
Fettuccine with Tuna Alfredo* Broccoli, Bell Pepper, and Onion Salad with Oil-Vinegar Dressing Grapes and Nuts in Shells ˙Prepare 2 cups white sauce (from mix). Stir in one 6½-ounce can tuna, drained and flaked, and ½ cup grated Parmesan cheese. Toss with hot pasta.	**Hot Broccoli Salad with Dijon Vinaigrette† Grapes** ˙Stir prepared mustard into apricot marmalade. Brush on ham during broiling. †Toss freshly cooked broccoli with bottled dressing.	**Bean Tacos with Shredded Lettuce and Cheese Orange-Radish Salad Hot Banana Boats à la Mode*** ˙Broil 4 unpeeled bananas for 3 to 5 minutes until hot. Cool briefly. Cut slit in skin, press ends to open, spoon on vanilla ice milk, eat from "boat."	**Salmon Loaf with Green Chili Sauce* Herbed Rice** (mix) **Green Peas Pineapple Chunks** (canned) **and Gingersnaps** ˙Purée one drained 4-ounce can whole green chilies, 2 tablespoons mayonnaise or salad dressing and 1 tablespoon lemon juice. Spoon onto servings of salmon loaf.	WEDNESDAY
Eggs in Marinara Sauce* Italian Bread Tossed Salad with Chick-Peas Coffee Low-Fat Yogurt Anisette Toasts ˙Heat bottled marinara sauce in a large skillet. Carefully break in 8 eggs. Cover and simmer until egg yolks are semisoft.	**Cream of Broccoli Soup** (canned) **Grilled Sliced Turkey and Cheese Sandwiches on Whole-Grain Bread Raspberry Swirl Ice Milk*** ˙Stir 1 tablespoon raspberry pourable fruit into slightly softened vanilla ice milk.	**Quick-Bake Meat Loaf*** (save leftovers for Saturday) **Mashed Potatoes Peas and Carrots** (frozen) **Canned Plums** ˙Mix 1 package onion-mushroom soup mix, 2 pounds ground beef, 1 cup bread crumbs, 1 egg, and ¼ cup water. Pat evenly into 11 x 7-inch baking pan. Bake at 375°F for 25 minutes, or until done.	**Easy Shepherd's Pie* Watercress and Red Bell Pepper Salad Brownies** ˙Reheat stew (frozen from week 49) in broiler-proof baking dish in oven. Make 4 servings instant mashed potatoes. Spoon dollops on hot stew. Brown under broiler.	THURSDAY
Pork Chops with Applesauce Curried Couscous* Brussels Sprouts Fresh Pineapple ˙Bring 1½ cups chicken broth, ¼ cup raisins, 1 tablespoon oil, and ½ teaspoon curry powder to a boil. Remove the pan from the heat, add 1 cup couscous and ¼ cup sliced scallions. Cover and let stand for 5 minutes, or until tender.	**Pan-Fried Flounder Fillets with Tartar Sauce** (jarred) **Parsleyed Potatoes Shredded Carrots with Orange Butter* Canned Apricots with Vanilla Wafer Cookies** ˙Simmer carrots in orange juice just until tender. Stir in butter and salt and pepper to taste.	**Baked Garlic-Herb Codfish Fillets* Cottage Fries** (frozen) **Broccoli Spears Cherry Gelatin** ˙Top cooked fillets with semi-soft garlic-herb cheese. (Cheese will melt to form a creamy sauce.) Serve immediately.	**Broiled Parmesan Fish Fillets* Scalloped Potatoes** (mix) **Stewed Tomatoes** (canned) **Spinach and Red Onion Salad with Italian Dressing Christmas Cookies** ˙Spread fillets with mayonnaise and sprinkle with Parmesan cheese before broiling.	FRIDAY
Manhattan Scallop Chowder* Oyster Crackers Romaine Radish Salad Tangelos ˙Heat 2 cans condensed vegetable soup and 2 soup cans water. Stir in 12 ounces bay scallops and ½ teaspoon dried thyme. Heat just until scallops are opaque in center.	**Lamb Stew with Carrots, Onions, and Turnips** (make enough for 2 meals; freeze half for week 52) **Baked Potatoes Baked Apples*** ˙Bake apples along with lamb stew.	**Meat Loaf Sandwiches on Kaiser Rolls with Sliced Tomato, Lettuce, and Mustard Pickled Beets** (jarred) **Sweet and Crunchy Apple Wedges*** ˙Dip apple wedges in honey, then granola cereal.	**Roast Chicken Potato Pancakes** (mix) **Glazed Carrots Honeyed Broiled Banana Boats*** ˙Broil unpeeled ripe bananas 3 minutes or until hot. Cool slightly. Cut a lengthwise slit in skin, press ends toward middle to open. Drizzle with honey. Sprinkle with cinnamon.	SATURDAY

APPENDIX

HERBS & SPICES

As a general rule of thumb, herbs come from grassy plants (*Herba* is the Latin for grass) and spices from barks or seeds. Another distinction is that herbs tend to grow in temperate climates, while most spices come primarily from tropical regions. Many home cooks grow and cultivate their own herbs; few grow their own spices. Herbs include familiar specimens such as oregano, thyme, and tarragon. Spices include ingredients such as cinnamon, mustard, black pepper, and nutmeg.

Fresh herbs are increasingly accessible all year long in large supermarkets, greengrocers, and specialty stores. Look for moist, fresh-looking herbs without drooping leaves or black spots. The packaging of herbs has improved in recent years, making it possible to use them even several days after purchase. Follow instructions on the package. Add fresh herbs to a dish close to the end of cooking, unless otherwise instructed by the recipe. If the herb has thick stems, discard the stems and use only the leaves.

Many herbs grow year round in flowerpots set on sunny kitchen windowsills. During warm months, they are easy to grow in containers on decks or planted in gardens. Nothing compares to the flavor and aroma of an herb snipped moments before use.

Dried herbs add excellent flavor to dishes, too, and are more potent than fresh herbs. In most instances, a teaspoon of a dried herb can be used in place of a tablespoon of a chopped fresh herb—which translates to one-third the amount. It's a good idea to rub the dried herb between your fingertips before adding it to the dish; the warmth of your fingers helps release the herb's essential oils and flavor. Store dried herbs in their containers, placed in a cool, dark cupboard (not in a rack above the stove!).

Like dried herbs, spices should be stored in a cool, dark cupboard. Whole spices (such as cloves, nutmeg, peppercorns, coriander, and anise) will keep indefinitely. Date the jars when you open them and be ruthless: toss those that are older than a year after opening. If you won't be using a spice often, buy it in small quantities. For example, depending on your cooking habits, you may prefer large containers of cinnamon and pepper but small canisters of poppy seeds and cardamom.

PRESERVING FRESH HERBS

Most fresh herbs can be dried or frozen and used later, with little loss of flavor or aroma.

TO DRY HERBS:
Tie them in a bunch at the stem end and hang them, stem ends up, in a warm, dry, well-ventilated section of the kitchen or pantry. Or you can dry them by laying them on a screen and leaving them in a dry, well-ventilated place, indoors or out (avoid morning dew and evening moisture). Depending on the size and type of herb, it will dry in one to two weeks. Herbs can also be dried in a microwave oven.

Spread 1/4 to 1/3 cup of fresh herbs on a paper towel and microwave on High for 1 to 3 minutes, rotating about every 30 seconds, until dry and crisp.

TO FREEZE HERBS:
Basil, dill parsely, chervil, and fennel are excellent to freeze. Wash and dry them thoroughly. Discard large stems. Put the herbs in an airtight, rigid plastic container and freeze them. Date the container and consume the herbs within a year, using them as you would fresh herbs (no need to defrost).

COMMON HERBS

BASIL: Sweet and aromatic with a faint licorice flavor, basil is found most often in Italian and Mediterranean cooking. Its marriage with tomatoes is legendary, and its presence in pesto imperative. Basil may have large or small leaves and may be green or purplish-red. Both sizes and colors are equally aromatic. Basil is easy to find fresh all year long, but is also available dried. Dried basil is added mainly to cooked preparations such as soups and stews, rather than to fresh salads and tomatoes.

BAY LEAVES: Bay leaves are also called bay laurel and sweet bay. They are slightly spicy, very aromatic, and one of the three herbs used in a classic bouquet garni. Bay leaves, which are fairly large, grayish-green specimens, are nearly always sold dried, and are added to stews, soups, and other savory dishes. They should be discarded before serving. Turkish bay leaves are greatly preferable to the Californian variety.

CHERVIL: Chervil is sold both dried and fresh and adds a light anise flavor to dishes such as cream soups, dressings, and sauces. Chervil leaves are lacy and pale green.

CHIVES: Long, green, and grassy-looking, chives are a member of the onion family and are available fresh all year long. Freeze-dried chives are not as flavorful as fresh. Chives' mild oniony flavor is welcome in soups, salads, dips, and spreads. They also are used for garnish.

CILANTRO/CORIANDER: Fresh cilantro resembles flat-leaf parsley and for this reason is sometimes labeled Chinese parsley. It is also called fresh coriander. Cilantro finds its way into Mexican, Southwestern, and Asian cooking, as well as many other dishes. Its distinctive, pungent flavor is easy to discern in salsas and other uncooked preparations, although it is less powerful when cooked. Cilantro is rarely sold dried and should not be confused with coriander seeds (see page 677), which impart a very different flavor.

DILL WEED: Fragrant, fresh dill has a sharp, lemony flavor; dried dill weed imparts a similar flavor. Fresh dill is bright green with feathery, delicate leaves. It's used in soups, salads, dips, and spreads. See also dill seed (page 677).

LEMON GRASS: Lemon grass is a pale green stalk with a bulbous base. Only this base is used to infuse dishes with a lovely lemon flavor and scent. Lemon grass is gaining in popularity in the United States, as Thai and Vietnamese cooking become more commonplace.

LEMON THYME: A member of the thyme family, this herb has tiny green leaves and a subtle but recognizable lemony scent and flavor. It is used with meat and fish, as well as salads. Lemon thyme is only available fresh.

MARJORAM: Marjoram, sometimes called sweet marjoram, is sold both fresh and dried. Its flavor somewhat resembles oregano and it may be used in place of it in many dishes. Fresh marjoram leaves are small and grayish-green.

MINT: Mint is one of the most common and recognizable herbs; it is also the easiest to grow. Its cool, fresh flavor adds zip to cold drinks, teas, desserts, and lamb dishes. It is also used very often for garnish. Mint is easy to buy fresh, but is also sold dried.

OREGANO: Oregano is most readily associated with Italian cooking, notably in tomato-based preparations. It also blends well with vegetables and legumes. It has a pungent flavor and aroma and is available both fresh and dried. Fresh oregano has medium-sized dark green leaves.

PARSLEY: Whether curly- or flat-leafed, parsley is our most common herb. It lends mild, grassy flavor to stews, soups, sauces, salads, and dressings and also is a familiar garnish. Parsley, with bay leaves and thyme, is part of a traditional *bouquet garni*. Bright green curly-leaf parsley is most often used as a garnish, while Italian flat-leaf parsley has stronger flavor and is used more often in cooking. Parsley is nearly always used fresh, although it is sold dried.

ROSEMARY: Rosemary is characteristically found in Mediterranean cooking, where its spicy flavor and fragrant scent lend themselves to meat, chicken, and fish dishes as well as soups, breads, vegetables, and legumes. Rosemary is sold both fresh and dried.

SAGE: Sage's fuzzy gray-green leaves are easy to spot among the fresh herbs; its strong, slightly musty flavor is easy to recognize in pork sausage and other meat, poultry, and cheese dishes. When dried, sage is usually ground and powdery. Ground sage loses its flavor much more quickly than do the leaves.

SAVORY: The small pointed green leaves of the savory plant add pleasantly sharp flavor to soups, breads, eggs, fish dishes, and meats. Winter savory is similar in flavor, appearance, and use to summer savory, but is harvested later in the season. The two are interchangeable in recipes. Savory is available fresh and dried.

TARRAGON: Pleasantly aromatic and tasting of licorice, tarragon's slender and somewhat spiky dark green leaves make it easily recognizable. Tarragon is used extensively in French cooking and is a common flavoring added to vinegar. Tarragon is available both fresh and dried.

THYME: Thyme is one of the three herbs found in a classic *bouquet garni* (with bay leaves and parsley), a bundle of herbs used to flavor soups, stews, and stocks. Its slightly strong pungent taste and spicy aroma are also frequently used to flavor chicken and other poultry dishes, including traditional bread stuffing. Thyme, readily available both fresh and dried, has tiny, dark green leaves.

COMMON SPICES

ALLSPICE: Allspice is sold as whole berries or ground. It comes from the seed of a tree indigenous to the Western Hemisphere, which makes it unusual in the world of spices, most of which originated in Asia. It earned the name "allspice" because its flavor resembles a combination of cinnamon, cloves, and nutmeg. Allspice is used in fruit desserts, chutneys, and pickles (it often is an ingredient in pickling spices), as well as for gravies, sauces, stews, and soups.

ANISE SEEDS: Anise tastes very like licorice, although the two are unrelated botanically. Anise is used to flavor cookies, cakes, fruit desserts, breads, stews, and meat dishes. It is sold whole or ground.

ANNATTO SEEDS: Also called achiote, annatto are rusty red seeds with musky flavor. They are used mainly in Mexican and Southwestern cooking and impart a red-to-yellow color to foods. Annatto seeds are available whole or ground.

CARAWAY SEEDS: Caraway seeds taste sweet and nutty and are used to flavor breads, cheeses, coleslaw, sauerkraut, sausages, and vegetable dishes. They are one of the oldest known spices and as such are integral to European and Asian cooking. Caraway seeds are available either whole and ground.

CARDAMOM: Cardamom is widely used in Scandinavian, Indian, and Arab cuisines. It is an essential ingredient in dishes as diverse as Indian curry and Swedish meatballs and breads. The Arabs make coffee from cardamom, a drink they consider a symbol of hospitality. The tiny seeds are sold whole or ground. Cardamom pods are also available, dried or green. They are quite small, containing only a dozen or fewer seeds. Cardamom is the third most costly spice—after saffron and vanilla.

CAYENNE: Cayenne is ground red chilies and is also called ground red pepper. It adds noticeably spicy heat to dishes such as soups, stews, chilies, curries, and vegetables. Use it sparingly. Cayenne is only available ground.

CELERY SEED: Celery seeds are tiny, light brown seeds that provide celery flavor to soups, breads, sauces, stuffings, eggs, and vegetables. However, they do not taste identical to celery; hints of nutmeg and parsley are detected in dishes seasoned with celery seeds. Celery seeds are usually sold whole, although they are available ground. Celery salt is a mixture of finely ground celery seeds and salt.

CHILI POWDER: Chili powder is a deep red, ground seasoning mix that combines chilies, spices, herbs, garlic, and salt. It may be mild, somewhat hot, or fiery hot. Chili powder is used to flavor chilies and other Mexican and Southwestern dishes. It is sold ground.

CINNAMON: Cinnamon, native to Sri Lanka, is a treasured spice used around the world to flavor desserts, baked goods, and some meat dishes. Its warm, sweet flavor is recognizable to nearly everyone. Cinnamon is sold in rolled sticks in various lengths (part of the actual bark of the plant) or ground.

CLOVES: Cloves are the buds of the furled flowers of an evergreen tree and as such are the most important flower spice. They have a sweet, pungent flavor and are used whole to stud ham and pork, and also added to pickles, chutneys, sauces, and vegetable dishes. Ground cloves are used in baked goods.

CORIANDER SEEDS: Coriander seeds are pungent and sweet and are used extensively in North African and South American cooking. Ground coriander is an ingredient in curry powder; whole coriander is used as a pickling spice. Coriander seeds are sold whole or ground.

CUMIN: Cumin imparts a strong, aromatic, somewhat bitter flavor to foods. It is an essential ingredient in most chili powder, and can also be found in curries, vegetable dishes, breads, soups, and pickles. Cumin is available whole or ground.

CURRY POWDER: Curry powder is a blend of numerous spices and is used to flavor many dishes, particularly those referred to as curries and which are inspired by the cooking of India. Not all curry powder blends are identical, but most commercially available in the United States include ginger, cumin, turmeric, black pepper, cayenne, and coriander.

DILL SEED: Dill seed is used most often as a pickling spice, although it is also popular in breads, potato, and vegetable dishes. Dill seeds are sold whole or ground.

FENNEL SEED: Fennel seeds taste of licorice and are used to flavor breads, fish dishes, soups, and sweet pickles. They are available whole or ground. Fennel is the dominant flavor in Italian sausage.

GINGER: Ginger is sold fresh or ground. When fresh, it comes as gingerroot, a knobby, woody root (actually a rhizome) that must be peeled and grated, sliced, or chopped before being used. Ginger is used to flavor both savory and sweet dishes, such as soups, stews, curries, squash, sweet potatoes, carrots, seafood, fruit, preserves, syrups, and sauces. Ginger is essential in many Asian, Indian, and African dishes. Crystallized ginger is sweetened ginger and is used mainly to garnish desserts.

JUNIPER BERRIES: Juniper berries are available both dried and fresh, although most recipes call for dried berries as the fresh berries are exceptionally pungent. Dried berries must be crushed before they are added to preparations. As the berries of an evergreen shrub, they taste somewhat of pine. Their strong flavor blends well with game and game birds, and they are used in the production of gin. Juniper berries are available whole.

MACE: Mace is the reddish-orange, lacy covering (called an aril) of a nutmeg seed and is usually ground into a powder, although it is sometimes available whole. Mace imparts a nutmeg-cinnamon flavor to poultry and fish dishes, pickles, cakes, custard, and puddings.

MUSTARD SEED: The seeds of the mustard plant are sold whole or ground into powder and are used to flavor coleslaws, curries, dressings, and pickles. The most common mustard seeds are brown, although black mustard seeds are more pungent. White mustard seeds are used to make commercially prepared American mustards and some English mustards. Brown mustard seeds are used for Dijon mustards.

NUTMEG: Nutmeg is a favorite among spices and finds its way into any number of baked goods, sauces, fruit desserts, and puddings. Eggnog is not official until it is topped with a sprinkling of nutmeg. Nutmeg is sold ground and whole, although for the best flavor it is advisable to buy the whole seed and grate it as needed.

PAPRIKA: Paprika is made by grinding dried spicy red peppers to powder. Hungarian rose paprika ranges from mild and full-bodied to hot and spicy; Spanish paprika, ground from dried pimientos, is always mild. The spice is essential to the cuisines of both countries and adds red color and mild flavor to many other dishes, particularly those with eggs, vegetables, and cheeses.

PEPPER: Pepper is our most popular spice and accounts for 25 percent of the world's spice trade. The most common pepper is ground from black peppercorns, although white, red, and dried green peppercorns are also available—and often are sold as a mixture. Some recipes specify white pepper because it does not add dark color to the food. Although pepper is sold already ground, it tastes best when ground in a peppermill just before using. Pink peppercorns are the dried berries of a rose plant and not true peppercorns.

POPPY SEEDS: Tiny slate-blue poppy seeds have a crunchy texture and provide sweet, nutty flavor to desserts and baked goods. They frequently are used to top breads and rolls. Poppy seeds are available whole.

SAFFRON: Saffron, the threadlike stigmas from a variety of Spanish crocus, is the world's most expensive spice. The stigmas must be plucked from the flowers by hand—and it requires more than an acre of flowers to produce eight to ten pounds of saffron. Saffron imparts a distinctive yellow color and mild flavor to chicken, seafood, and rice dishes (most notably to paella) and to some breads. Saffron is sold whole and ground, although whole threads are much preferred.

SESAME SEEDS: Also known as benne seeds, sesame seeds were introduced to the Americas by African slaves. Sesame seeds are integral to African, Asian, and Indian cooking and are used in the United States in baked goods, favored for their nutty flavor. The white variety is the most common.

TURMERIC: A member of the ginger family, turmeric is sold ground into a bright yellow-orange powder and is used to flavor curries as well as vegetable, egg, and fish dishes. Turmeric is a significant ingredient in curry powder and prepared mustard, and is also used in pickling. It gives food a pleasantly bitter, mild flavor.

VANILLA: Vanilla is a familiar and popular flavor, used in many desserts, confections, baked goods, beverages, and some savory preparations. Vanilla beans are richer tasting than vanilla extract, although extract can nearly always be substituted in recipes calling for the beans. Pure vanilla extract is far more flavorful than imitation vanilla extract. Vanilla is the second most expensive spice after saffron.

GLOSSARY OF COOKING TERMS

À LA CARTE: Term indicating that every item on a menu is priced separately.

AL DENTE: Term used to describe pasta or vegetables that are cooked just to the point where they still offer resistance when bitten. In Italian, the term means "to the tooth."

AU GRATIN: French term referring to cooking food under a broiler or in a hot oven to form a lightly browned crust. The food can be left plain or topped with the bread crumbs and/or grated cheese to make the crust.

BAIN MARIE: Term referring to the method of gently cooking food in a water bath. A bain marie is made by placing a pan or dish of food in a larger, shallow pan and then adding enough water to the larger pan to come about halfway up the sides of the smaller dish. The bain marie is baked in the oven.

BAKING STONE: A heavy, thick round or rectangular stone designed to be placed on the oven floor. The stone absorbs and retains the oven's heat and promotes even baking. It is used most frequently for baking pizzas.

BASTE: To spoon or coat food with fat or pan drippings as the food cooks. Basting adds flavor and moisture.

BLANCH: To cook food (usually fruits and vegetables) in rapidly boiling water for a minute or less in order to set color, seal juices, loosen skins, or remove odors.

BLIND BAKED: Term used to describe a prebaked, unfilled pie shell. The blind-baked pie shell may be baked further after filling, or not, depending on the recipe.

BRAISE: To cook food slowly in a little liquid, fat, or both in a tightly covered pan on the range top or in the oven. This is a favored cooking method for tenderizing tougher cuts of meat.

BROCHETTE: The French term for a skewer; also refers to foods cooked on a skewer, or *en brochette*.

BROWN: To cook food quickly over high heat—usually in a little fat—to give the food color and seal in juices. Many foods, such as meats, can be browned under the broiler or in the oven.

BUNDT PAN: A style of tube pan with fluted sides.

CARAMELIZE: To heat foods (most often sugar) until they brown and release their natural juices. Sugar liquifies and browns during the process.

CLARIFY: To separate and remove solids and sediment from a liquid to make it clear. Butter is clarified by heating it and pouring off the clear yellow fat, leaving behind the milk solids.

CHOP: To cut solid food into small pieces about the size of peas. Some recipes call for coarsely or finely chopped ingredients, which are pieces either slightly larger or smaller than peas.

CREAM: To beat a fat such as butter or margarine either alone or with sugar until soft, smooth, and fluffy. This method aerates the fat and will give baked goods a lighter texture. An electric mixer makes creaming ingredients easy.

CRIMP: To seal two pastry edges by pinching them together to form a decorative edge.

CURDLE: To separate into lumpy curds and liquid. Foods tend to curdle when they are exposed to prolonged or too high heat, or in the case of milk, combined with acids.

CURE: To preserve meats and fish by smoking, salting, drying, or a combination of two or three.

CUT IN: To incorporate cold, solid fat into a dry ingredient, such as flour, until the mixture resembles coarse crumbs. Most cooks use either two kitchen knives, ta pastry blender, or their fingertips to cut fat into flour.

DEGLAZE: To scrape the browned bits of food from the bottom of the pan after adding liquid and heating it.

DICE: To cut solid food into small, uniformly sized squares or cubes.

DREDGE: To coat food with a powdery dry ingredient such as flour, sugar, or cornmeal.

DRIPPINGS: The fat and juices left in the roasting pan or skillet after meat has cooked.

FLUTE: To make a decorative edge on a pie shell or another pastry, usually in a scalloped pattern.

FOLD: To incorporate a light, aerated mixture, such as beaten egg whites or whipped cream, into a heavier one without deflating the lighter mixture. This is accomplished by gently but decisively cutting through both mixtures with a rubber spatula from the top to the bottom of the bowl, lifting and folding the heavier mixture over the lighter one, rotating the bowl and repeating the process until both mixtures are incorporated.

FRICASSEE: To cook meat (usually chicken) first in fat and then gently in liquid along with aromatic vegetables.

FRITTER: A small amount of thick batter, usually containing a food such as a sliced fruit (apple, banana, pineapple), that is deep-fried.

GARNISH: To decorate a dish with a complementary and attractive food, such as parsley, lemon wedges, sliced radishes, and fresh herbs.

GLAZE: To apply a sweet or savory liquid to food that, after setting or cooking, will provide the food with a smooth, shiny surface.

GRATE: To turn solid food into particles by rubbing it against a serrated utensil, such as a common kitchen grater. Foods may also be grated in rotating graters, food mills, and food processors.

JELLY ROLL PAN: A shallow baking pan used most often to bake sheet cakes. Once cooled, these cakes often are rolled around fillings. Most jelly roll pans are 15½ x 10½ x 1 inch, although some are slightly smaller and others slightly larger. Jelly roll pans are also referred to as half-sheet pans.

JULIENNE: Solid food (usually vegetables) cut into slender, uniformly sized strips, also called matchsticks.

KNEAD: To mix dough with the hands, a mixer fitted with a bread hook, or in a bread machine so that the dough forms a cohesive mass and, at the same time, the gluten in the flour begins to develop.

LUKEWARM: A temperature between hot and cool, usually between body temperature (98°F) and 105°F.

MARINATE: To soak foods, such as meat and fish, in a seasoned liquid. The liquid nearly always contains an acidic ingredient such as vinegar or lemon juice and flavors as well as tenderizes the food. A dry mixture or paste of herbs which is rubbed onto food before it is cooked is also used as a marinade.

MINCE: To cut solid food into tiny pieces.

PAN-BROIL: To cook food (usually meat) in a hot skillet that may or may not contain fat.

PARBOIL: To partially cook food in boiling water. The cooking is usually completed by another method.

PARE: To remove the thin skin of fruit or a vegetable.

PASTRY BLENDER: A tool fitted with rigid, curved wires that is used to cut fat into flour.

PASTRY SCRAPER: A tool fitted with a flat, rigid metal plate and used to scrape dough from countertops and boards. Also made of more flexible plastic.

PINCH: A very small amount, usually less than ⅛ teaspoon.

PIPE: To squeeze a soft mixture (such as frosting) through a pastry bag or tube to make decorative shapes or borders.

POACH: To cook by partially or completely submerging food in a gently boiling liquid.

PROOF: In baking, this term refers to testing yeast to make sure it is alive and capable of leavening bread dough.

PURÉE: To blend in a blender, process in a food processor, or food mill until food is smooth and lump-free. The term also refers to the food that has been puréed.

RAMEKIN: A small ovenproof dish used for individual portions of baked or chilled foods. Ramekins resemble soufflé dishes and are usually ceramic or porcelain.

REDUCE: To cook slowly so that liquid evaporates, volume decreases, and, usually, flavors intensify.

RENDER: To cook food until it releases its fat as liquid.

ROUX: A cooked mixture of flour and fat.

SAUTÉ: To cook gently in a little fat, stirring and shaking the ingredients for much of the cooking time. In French, the term translates as "to jump."

SCALD: To heat liquid until it almost boils and just begins to form tiny bubbles around the rim of the pan. Solid foods are scalded by being dropped in boiling water for a few moments.

SCALLOPED: A term that refers to baking food in a cream sauce (for example, scalloped potatoes). It also refers to making a decorative edge around a pie crust by crimping.

SCALOPPINE: This refers to thin boneless slices of meat, usually veal. These cuts of meat can also be called scallops, for example veal scallops.

SCORE: To make elongated shallow cuts in meat or fish or on loaves of bread.

SEAR: To cook briefly over very high heat to seal the juices in meat.

SIFT: To remove lumps and aerate dry ingredients by passing them through a mesh sifter or strainer.

SIMMER: To boil very gently so that the liquid produces small, occasional bubbles around the edges of the pan and across the surface of the liquid.

SKIM: To use a spoon to remove the surface foam or fat from cooking liquid.

SPRINGFORM PAN: A round baking pan with a high straight side that can be released with a clamp.

STEAM: To cook a food with the steam produced by boiling water. The food is placed on a rack or in a basket so that it does not touch the water and the pot is covered to retain the steam.

STEEP: To soak an ingredient in hot water so that its flavors are released into the water, or in order to soften it.

STIR-FRY: To cook small, uniformly shaped pieces of food over high heat in only a small amount of fat, turning and stirring them continuously, until tender yet still crisp. The term also refers to the prepared dish.

TEMPER: To heat or warm food carefully and gently so that it may be incorporated into preparations requiring longer cooking. Eggs are often tempered by being mixed with a little hot liquid before they are stirred into a sauce or a soup.

TRUSS: To tie poultry or another meat with kitchen twine or to secure it with skewers so that it holds its shape during cooking.

WOK: A round-bottomed pan used in Asian cooking for stir-frying, boiling, and frying.

CHEESE ·PRIMER

Every cuisine that includes dairy products includes cheese. There are so many cheeses, it would be nearly impossible to list them all. To make sense of this enormous variety, it's helpful to think of them in categories. In general, cheeses are classified by texture, either soft, semi-soft, semi-firm, and firm or hard. They can also be classified by the source of the milk: cow, sheep, or goat. And other cheeses are grouped together because they are made by a common process such as blue-veined. Some of the more traditional classifications are outlined below. Keep in mind that these categories are broad and that many cheeses can overlap.

Treat cheeses gently when cooking with them to avoid burning. No cheese actually "cooks"; it simply melts when heated. A cheese's melting properties usually determine its culinary uses. And although many recipes call for cheese, one of the best ways to enjoy many cheeses is to eat them plain (bring the cheese to room temperature) with some good bread and fresh fruit.

SOFT CHEESES:

Rich and creamy with a wide range of flavors describes these spreadable cheeses. They can be broken down into two subcategories:

Fresh cheeses: These are cheeses that have not been permitted to ripen (age). They have a mild flavor and a relatively short shelf life—check their freshness dates. These cheeses may be eaten plain (and are an exception to the rule that cheeses should be served at room temperature), mixed into dips, or used in cooking.

- Boursin
- Cottage cheese
- Cream cheese
- Farmer cheese
- Fresh goat cheese (chabis or tub)
- Fromage blanc
- Mascarpone
- Fresh mozzarella
- Neufchâtel
- Ricotta

Soft ripened cheeses: These cheeses are ripened so that they develop fuller flavor than fresh cheeses. They do not keep for more than two weeks. These cheeses are generally eaten plain or simply with bread. They are rarely used in cooking.

- Boursault
- Brie
- Brillat-Savarin
- Camembert
- Goat cheese boucherons
- Limburger

SEMISOFT CHEESES:

These cheeses are more ripened than soft cheeses. They are springy to the touch, and although soft textured, can be sliced. Semisoft cheeses will keep for up to three weeks in the refrigerator. They are often used in cooking, as many of these cheeses melt extremely well, with the exception of blue-veined cheese (such as blue, gorgonzola, and Stilton) and feta cheese.

- Blue
- Feta
- Fontina
- Gorgonzola
- Gouda
- Havarti
- Monterey Jack
- Mozzarella (packaged)
- Muenster (American)
- Port Salut
- Roquefort
- Stilton
- Taleggio
- Tilsit

SEMIFIRM CHEESES:

These cheeses are ripened to the extent that they develop a full, robust flavor. They have a firm but smooth texture and can be sliced. Ranging from mild to sharp, they are excellent eating cheeses, and are also often used in cooking.

- Asiago
- Beamont
- Cheddar
- Cheshire
- Colby
- Double Gloucester
- Edam
- Gjetost
- Gruyère
- Jarlsberg
- Leyden
- Provolone
- Swiss

FIRM CHEESES:

These cheeses are also called grating cheeses. They are aged until they are very dry and hard and will keep for months in the refrigerator. They range in flavor from mild to sharp and are almost always grated before being used in cooking or passed at the table for sprinkling over cooked dishes.

- Aged Asiago
- Parmesan
- Pecorino Romano
- Sapsago
- Sbrinz

ABOUT GOAT CHEESE

Making cheese from goat's milk is a time-honored tradition in France and other parts of Europe, and it has become increasingly popular in the United States during the past decade. Although much of the goat cheese (chèvre) sold here is imported from France, a growing

percentage is produced in this country.

When very fresh (generally less than a week old), goat cheese may be sold in a tub, sometimes mixed with herbs, or as a round, soft chabis. When it aged a little longer, it is very often sold shaped into a log called a bûcheron. This is the most popular shape for goat cheese. Cheese sold as bûcheron is a little older than fresh cheese and has the distinctive yet mild sharp, salty flavor favored by goat cheese aficionados. Aged goat cheese is dry and very sharp tasting and often is sold in a round, flattened disk called a crottin. Goat cheese is sometimes coated in ash or herbs and is sold in other shapes, too—the most common being a pyramid, which designates cheeses aged to about the same degree as bûcheron.

- Banon
- California Chèvre
- Chabichou
- Montrachet
- Saint-Christophe
- Sainte-Maure

ABOUT BLUE-VEINED CHEESE

We tend to classify all cheeses with blue streaks as "blue cheese." In fact, they differ from one another in how and where they are made. The blue-green mold can occur naturally or from a strain of penicillin that is added during the curing process. The cheese is perforated with wire needles to allow the spread of the mold veins. Roquefort, perhaps the most famous of the blues, is made from sheep's milk and is aged in cool, damp caves in a particular region of France. Stilton, England's revered cheese, requires long aging to acquire its strong, enticing flavor.

Blue-veined cheeses are excellent with bread and wine, crumbled over salads, and accompanying fresh fruit. Bring the cheese to room temperature before serving. They should be well wrapped for storage as their potent aromas can mingle with other foods.

- Bleu de Bresse
- Bleu de Castello
- Danish Blue
- Fourme d'Ambert
- Gorgonzola
- Maytag Blue
- Oregan Blue
- Pipo Crem'
- Roquefort
- Saga Blue
- Stilton

LOW-FAT CHEESES

Cheese's biggest problem has always been its high fat content. But there are many truly delicious lower-fat choices. Some, such as mozzarella and string cheese (especially part-skim), feta, and some goat cheese are naturally lower in calories (about 75 calories per ounce) than Cheddar (at about 115 calories) or a triple crème (which tips the scale at 140 calories).

Other low fat selections include part-skim ricotta and reduced-fat cottage cheese.

HOW TO STORE CHEESE

As a general rule, the harder the cheese, the longer it will remain fresh. Soft cheeses should be eaten within 1 to 2 weeks of purchase. Firmer, drier cheese such as Cheddar may be fine for a month or so, longer if sealed in its original wrapper. Hard grating cheeses may last indefinitely.

All cheese should be covered tightly in plastic wrap to prevent drying, then refrigerated. It's advisable to change the wrapping every few days to prolong the life of the cheese.

Strong-smelling ones such as Limburger should be wrapped and put into a tightly sealed container to prevent their odors from permeating other foods.

Even if cheeses are stored properly, they may develop surface molds. Make sure you slice off ¼ inch of the surface before serving.

If cheese has become dried out you may shred or grate it to use it in cooking.

COFFEE & TEA

HOW TO MAKE A GOOD CUP OF COFFEE

Whether you choose to grind your own beans or buy them already ground, making a good cup of coffee depends on knowing the proportion of coffee to water. The standard ratio is one level tablespoon of ground coffee for every three fluid ounces of water. Standard coffee measuring spoons hold two tablespoonfuls, enough for eight fluid ounces, which is the amount of a cup of coffee. When grinding your own beans, grind only as much as you will need. Once ground, the flavor components in the coffee will begin to evaporate.

Always begin with a clean coffeepot and fresh cold water. If the tap water is artificially softened or tastes of chemicals or minerals, use bottled water. Hot water that has been standing in heating tanks is not as well aerated as cold tap water.

When the water comes into contact with the coffee it should be about 200°F—or just below boiling. This is the temperature to which boiling water drops seconds after it is removed from the heat. Coffee machines and electric percolators maintain water at this temperature during brewing. Never let the coffee boil. Its flavor will change.

Serve coffee as soon after brewing as possible. When allowed to sit for a period of time, it turns bitter. If it is kept hot (at about 190°F), it will hold for an hour or so without any loss of flavor.

WHAT THE ROASTS MEAN

Coffee is grown in many parts of the world, including South and Central America, Africa, the Caribbean, Hawaii, and Indonesia. Blending beans from different trees and regions produces various flavors. How long the beans are roasted also determines the flavor and color of the brewed coffee. Today there are so many blends and roasts you may want to experiment with several. Some blends are flavored with ingredients such as almonds, hazelnuts, and vanilla. There are a few basic roasts:

American roast: This is also often called regular roast and produces coffee that is neither very dark nor especially full bodied.

French roast: This is made from long-roasted beans and results in a strong, rich, deep brown coffee.

Italian roast: Used mainly for espresso, the beans are roasted until they are glossy and dark. They produce very strong-tasting coffee.

Viennese roast: This is a mixture of two-thirds regular roasted beans and one-third dark, long-roasted beans. The coffee is dark and full-bodied.

THE DIFFERENT GRINDS

Drip: Most electric coffee makers employ the drip method and therefore require a "drip" grind. Many commercial coffees are labeled "all method," which means they work well in this type of machine, where the water passes through the coffee and a filter and drips into a waiting carafe.

Fine: Espresso calls for this very fine grind of coffee.

Regular: Percolators and plunger coffee makers call for regular-grind coffee. However, all-method grinds work well for these coffee makers, too.

STORING COFFEE

Store coffee beans in an airtight containers in a cool, dry place for up to two weeks. Store ground coffee in an airtight container for several days at room temperature but refrigerate for longer storage. Coffee beans requiring long storage should be well wrapped and kept in the freezer for up to three months.

A GLOSSARY OF CAFÉ COFFEES

Coffee bars and restaurants serving specialty coffees are extremely popular. Following is a list of terms often used at these emporiums.

Café au lait: This is the French term for coffee with milk and most often refers to equal portions of scalded milk and coffee.

Café brûlot: Famous in New Orleans, this is spiced coffee flavored with citrus peel and brandy. The mixture is ignited (flambéed) before serving.

Café latte: Similar to cappuccino, this calls for a higher proportion of milk to coffee. In many coffee bars, you can request café latte made with skim milk.

Cappuccino: Cappuccino is made by topping espresso with steamed milk, which is pressurized to create a thick creamy foam. Some of the milk mixes with the coffee. Cappuccino is traditionally topped with cinnamon or cocoa.

Espresso: This dark, strong coffee is made from finely ground dark-roast coffee beans (often called Italian roast). During brewing, steam or hot water is forced through the grind, resulting in the characteristic thin layer of foam topping true espresso. In Southern Italy and the U.S., espresso is served in small cups with a piece of lemon peel.

Irish coffee: Usually served in restaurants and bars, this is a potent blending of strong coffee and Irish whisky, sweetened with sugar and topped with a generous spoonful of whipped cream.

Turkish coffee: Defying the common wisdom about never boiling coffee, Turkish coffee is made by repeatedly boiling finely ground coffee beans, water, and sugar for a very brief time in a special pot called an ibrik. After the third boil, the coffee is immediately poured into tiny cups.

CAFFEINATED AND DECAFFEINATED

Caffeine is present in all coffee beans. The average cup of coffee has enough caffeine (about 115 milligrams in a five-ounce cup) to stimulate the heartbeat, increase mental activity, and cause sleeplessness in some coffee drinkers. Those who are sensitive to caffeine can choose to drink decaffeinated coffee. Not long ago, coffee lovers had little selection when it came to decaffeinated coffee, but today there is a wide variety of roasted decaffeinated beans and grinds so that no one who enjoys the flavor of coffee needs to feel deprived.

There are two methods of removing the caffeine from coffee beans. It can be removed by water or by solvents. Using water is more time consuming and therefore more costly than relying on solvents—even so, some coffee drinkers feel that water-decaffeinated beans are inferior. Regardless of the method, 97 percent of the caffeine is removed from the beans, rendering them essentially caffeine-free. The beans are then blended, roasted, and ground.

Surprisingly, a cup of inexpensive American coffee (the sort sold at diners and fast-food outlets) may have as much as 25 percent more caffeine than a cup brewed from gourmet coffee beans. Espresso has slightly less caffeine than percolated coffee.

HOW TO MAKE A PERFECT POT OF TEA

Tea may be brewed to be enjoyed either hot or cold. The preferred method for making a pot of tea is to use loose tea, although tea bags work nearly as well and are easier to use. Begin by filling a metal tea kettle with cold tap water. While the water comes to a boil, fill a ceramic or porcelain teapot with hot tap water to warm it. Just before the kettle boils, pour the hot water from the teapot and add the tea. Use one heaping teaspoon of loose tea or one tea bag for each cup. Add an extra teaspoon or an extra tea bag "for the pot." Pour the boiling water over the tea and let it steep for three to five minutes, stirring once to distribute the flavor. While the length of steeping determines the strength of the tea, if you steep the tea for much longer than five minutes, it will be bitter. Pour the tea directly into the teacups or another warm pot for serving, straining it if necessary.

HOW TO MAKE A PERFECT CUP OF TEA

Just as with a pot of tea, it's important to begin with good, cold tap water. Bring it to a rapid boil and then pour it quickly over a tea bag or over a heaping teaspoon of loose tea that is inside a warmed cup or mug. Let the tea steep for three or four minutes—no need to dunk the tea bag.

TEA VARIETIES:

Teas are made from the leaves of the tea plant, called *Camellia sinensis* and are named according to their region of origin (Assam, Ceylon, Darjeeling) or according to a special blending (Earl Grey, English Breakfast, Irish Breakfast). Tea is grown mainly in India, Sri Lanka (formerly Ceylon), and China. There are numerous teas, each with its distinct flavor, aroma, and origin. We list some of the best known.

Other teas are made from fruit, herbs, spices or flowers. These are called tisanes, or herbal teas.

Assam: This tea, from the Assam district of India, is a strong black tea.

Ceylon: Sri Lanka is known for its superlative teas, which often are referred to as Ceylon teas. Ceylon teas are black teas.

Darjeeling: Another black tea, Darjeeling is named after a region of India in the foothills of the Himalayas and is among the world's most prized teas.

Earl Grey: Named for Charles, the second Earl Grey of Great Britain, this tea is a favorite blending of black teas usually scented with bergamot.

English Breakfast: This brisk tea is a blending of black teas from India and Sri Lanka.

Formosa Oolong: An oolong tea from Taiwan, this is considered the best oolong by connoisseurs. Oolong teas are made from a partially fermented tea that is a cross between a green and black tea.

Lapsang Souchong: This black tea comes from China and has a distinctive smoky flavor.

Orange Pekoe: Although this term usually refers to a popular blending of Ceylon tea leaves, it is also a grade of tea leaf.

A GUIDE TO WINE

With many regions of the United States producing good wine, wine lovers have an ever broadening choice of vintages. Most experts agree that the best wines are produced in France, with those made in Italy and Germany and the northwestern regions of the United States (most notably northern California) following close behind. Admirable wines are also produced in Australia, Chile, and Argentina—as well as many other places. A particular wine's quality depends on several factors, the most important being the skill of the wine maker and the quality of the grape in a given year, which depends as much on the weather as farming practices. This explains why some vintages (years) are better than others—even those coming from the same winery.

The best way to choose a wine is to try it. Barring that, talk with the wine merchant in the local liquor store. There are also numerous guides and reference books available about wine. Knowing a little about the character of the grapes that produce the wine helps in the selection, too.

Wines are named after their grape or the region that produces them. Some of the world's finest wines are made in the Burgundy region of France, which produces both red and white wines, and in the Bordeaux region of France, which also produces both red and white wines. Champagne is produced in the Champagne region of France. Sparkling wines produced elsewhere cannot be called Champagne and so are labeled "sparkling wine."

Following is a list of some of the most popular types of wine:

WHITE WINES

Blanc Fumé: A light wine with herbal, grassy overtones; slightly acidic. Many California vintners reverse the name, calling this type of wine Fumé Blanc.

Chardonnay: A full, rounded wine with toasty, buttery, vanilla and green apple flavors. Made from white burgundy grapes and produced in all major wine-making regions of the world.

Gewürztraminer: A fruity, medium- to full-bodied wine with the flavors of coconut, papaya, and lychee, as well as allspice. Made from grapes of the same name, the pungent wine is popular in Alsace, Germany, and Eastern Europe. California makes good Gewürztraminer wine.

Pinot Blanc and Pinot Bianco: Citrus-tasting, medium-bodied wine with slightly nutty, spicy flavors. The grape used to make this wine is related to the famous Pinot Noir grape. California wine makers use the pinot blanc grape to make muscadet.

Riesling: Light- to medium-bodied wine with overtones of green apples, lime, honey, and sometimes mint. Made mostly in Germany from Riesling grapes, but also made in Alsace, France, Austria, Eastern Europe, Australia, and California, as well as elsewhere.

Sauvignon Blanc: Light-bodied, herbal-tasting, acidic wine with overtones of green peppers and limes. The sauvignon blanc grape is mixed with others to make wines such as Graves and Pouilly-Fumés.

RED WINES

Beaujolais: A light-bodied wine with fruity flavors, reminiscent of summer berries, plums, cherries, and spices. Made mostly in the Burgundy region of France, Beaujolais is one of the best-known wines in the world. Beaujolais Noveau is a new wine bottled without aging and should be consumed within a few months of bottling.

Cabernet Sauvignon: A medium-bodied, woodsy wine with the flavors of blackberries, vanilla, herbs, and Cassis—sometimes with hints of chocolate. Some of the best California wines are made from the cabernet grape. Also made in Australia, South America, and Eastern Europe.

Chianti: A light- to medium-bodied, earthy wine, tasting of oak, cedar, black cherries, and spices. It is made with a blend of grapes and named for the Chianti region of Tuscany in Italy. It is made also in California and Argentina.

Médoc: A medium-bodied wine with earthy, cherry flavors and smoky overtones of herbs and spices. This wine is often from the Bordeaux region of France.

Merlot: A medium- to full-bodied wine, tasting of plums, cherries, and herbs, as well as vanilla and smoke. Wines made with merlot grapes come from France, California, Washington State, and Australia. The wine is often used for blending.

Pinot Noir: Medium- to full-bodied earthy wine with the flavors of cherries, plums, leather, and spices. Wines made with the pinot noir grape are among the most lauded wines of Burgundy. This wine is also made very well in California, the Pacific Northwest, and Australia.

Zinfandel: A medium- to full-bodied wine with flowery overtones, also tasting of spices, berries, and prunes. Nearly all zinfandels are made with zinfandel grapes from California.

SERVING WINE

Rules about which wine to serve with certain foods are far more relaxed than they used to be. If you like the way a red wine tastes with grilled tuna or prefer a chilled fumé blanc with pot roast, serve them. But if you are unsure, following the old adage will never mislead you: red wines generally are best served with red meats and firm cheese; white wines are best served with fish, poultry, and light vegetable dishes. Sweet white wines are served with dessert.

Red wines should be served at room temperature. Open the wine 30 to 60 minutes before pouring and let it breathe. This is not a myth; it works. White wines should be chilled for an hour or so before serving. Champagne, which goes well with nearly everything from the main course to dessert, should be chilled.

Serve wine in stemmed glasses. Not only does it look more festive, the wine actually tastes better when it is drunk from a glass with a bowl large enough for swirling the wine (to develop the bouquet). Also, you are less apt to heat the wine with the heat of your hands if you hold the glass by the stem.

STORING WINE

Store all wine at cool room temperature. Try to find a cool cupboard or area of the cellar, pantry, or utility room. Distance the wine from the oven and stove, where temperature fluctuations are most likely. It's equally important not to store it near the furnace or hot water heater.

EQUIVALENTS & CONVERSION CHARTS

EQUIVALENTS (ALL AMOUNTS ARE APPROXIMATE)

Bread crumbs: 1 slice fresh bread = ½ cup fresh crumbs
1 slice toasted bread = ¼ cup dried crumbs

Butter: ⅛ pound = 2 ounces = 4 tablespoons = ¼ cup = ½ stick
¼ pound = 4 ounces = 8 tablespoons = ½ cup = 1 stick
½ pound = 8 ounces = 16 tablespoons = 1 cup = 2 sticks

Carrots: 1 medium carrot = ½ cup chopped or sliced

Celery: 1 medium rib celery = ½ cup chopped or sliced

Chicken broth: 1 (13¾-ounce) can = 1¾ cups

Chocolate: 1 ounce = 1 square = 2 tablespoons grated

Cocoa: ¼ pound = 4 ounces = 1 cup

Corn: 2 to 3 ears = 1 cup kernels

Cream cheese: 1 (3-ounce) package = 6 tablespoons
1 (8-ounce) package = 1 cup

Eggs: 1 large egg yolk = 1 tablespoon
1 large egg white = 2 tablespoons
4 to 5 large eggs = 1 cup
7 to 8 large egg whites = 1 cup
14 to 15 large egg yolks = 1 cup

Flour: ¼ ounce unsifted flour = 1 tablespoon
2½ ounces unsifted flour = ½ cup
5 ounces unsifted flour = 1 cup
3¾ ounces cake flour = 1 cup

Garlic: 2 cloves garlic = 1 teaspoon minced

Gelatin: 1 (¼-ounce) envelope = 1 scant tablespoon

Lemons: 1 medium lemon = 3 tablespoons juice
1 medium lemon = 2 teaspoons grated peel

Limes: 1 medium lime = 2 tablespoons juice
1 medium lime = 1 teaspoon grated peel

Milk: 1 (14-ounce) can condensed milk = 1¼ cups
1 (5 ⅓-ounce) can evaporated milk = ⅔ cup

Onions: 1 medium onion = ¾ to 1 cup chopped

Oranges: 1 medium orange = ⅓ cup juice
1 medium orange = 3 tablespoons grated peel

Parmesan cheese: ¼ pound = 1 cup grated

Peppers: 1 medium bell pepper = 1 cup chopped

Scallions: 2 medium scallions (white part only) = 1 tablespoon chopped

Sugar: ½ ounce granulated sugar = 1 tablespoon
1¾ ounces granulated sugar = 4 tablespoons (¼ cup)
3½ ounces granulated sugar = ½ cup
5 ounces granulated sugar = ¾ cup
7 ounces granulated sugar = 1 cup
7 ounces brown sugar = 1 cup packed
4 ounces unsifted confectioners' sugar = 1 cup
3½ ounces sifted confectioners' sugar = 1 cup

Tomatoes: 1 medium tomato = ½ cup chopped
1 (35-ounce) can tomatoes, drained = 2 cups chopped

Yeast: 1 (¼-ounce) envelope active dry yeast = 1 tablespoon
1 (2-ounce) cake compressed yeast = 3 envelopes dry
1 (⅗=ounce) cake compressed yeast = 1 envelope dry

CONVERSION CHART FOR WEIGHTS AND MEASURES

Metric amounts are the nearest equivalents.

Liquid measures:

1 teaspoon = 5 milliliters

1 tablespoon = 3 teaspoons = 15 milliliters

⅛ cup = 2 tablespoons = 1 fluid ounce = 30 milliliters

¼ cup = 4 tablespoons = 2 fluid ounces = 60 milliliters

½ cup = 8 tablespoons = 4 fluid ounces = 120 milliliters

1 cup = 16 tablespoons = 8 fluid ounces = 240 milliliters

1 pint = 2 cups = 16 fluid ounces = 480 milliliters

1 quart = 4 cups = 32 fluid ounces = 960 milliliters (.96 liter)

1 gallon = 4 quarts = 16 cups = 128 fluid ounces = 3.84 liters

Weights:

1 ounce = 28 grams

¼ pound = 4 ounces = 114 grams

1 pound = 16 ounces = 454 grams

2.2 pounds = 1,000 grams = 1 kilogram

INDEX

Page numbers in **boldface** indicate photographs.

CREDITS

Abbreviations: T—Top; M—Middle; B—Bottom; L—Left; R—Right

Photographs

Mary Ellen Bartley: 234, 271

Peter Bosch: 409

Ben Calvo: 162

Dennis Galante: 33, 34, 36

Edmund Goldspink: Front cover ML, 162–3, 236, 446, 612

Lisa Koenig: Front cover TR, 89, 128T, 374–5, 483, 520T

Patrick J. La Croix/Image Bank: 243

Steven Mark Needham: 35, 70–1, 71, 90, 272, 410, 410–1, 412

Rick Osentoski: 609, 610–1, 614–5, 616

Judd Pilossof: Front cover TL, 69, 92, 164B, 200, 270, 376, 553

Michael Skott/Image Bank: 393

Marcus Tullis: 554, 555

Tim Turner: 126–7, 164T, 233, 235, 373

John Uher: Front cover BL, front cover BR, 72, 91, 125, 128B, 161, 197, 198–9, 269, 337, 338, 338–9, 340, 375, 445, 447, 448, 481, 482, 484, 517, 518–9, 520B, 556, 589, 590, 591, 592T, 592B, 612–3, 649, 650, 651, 652, 653, 654, 655, 656

Recipes

California Pizza Kitchen: BBQ Chicken Pizza (295), Vegetable-Pesto Pizza (295), BLT Pizza (295), California Pizza (295)

Jean Kressey: Mediterranean Chick-pea Salad (378), Cherries Supreme (485), Blueberry Nectarine Cups (486), Lemon Coconut Bars (492)

Miriam Rubin: Indian-style Seafood Kebabs (178), Spicy Dry-Rubbed Pork Loin (208), Grilled Butterflied Leg of Lamb (229)

Elizabeth Sahatjian: Cashew-Honey Gingerbread (450)

Shirley Sarvis: Spicy Salmon (160), Gremolata Swordfish (168), Orange-Basil Halibut (170)